PROTECTING HUMAN SECURITY IN AFRICA

Protecting Human Security in Africa

Edited by
ADEMOLA ABASS

*Professor of International Law & Organization, Brunel University,
West London and Research Fellow in Peace and Security,
United Nations University Comparative Regional
Integration Studies (UNU-CRIS), Bruges, Belgium*

OXFORD
UNIVERSITY PRESS

OXFORD

UNIVERSITY PRESS

Great Clarendon Street, Oxford OX2 6DP

Oxford University Press is a department of the University of Oxford.
It furthers the University's objective of excellence in research, scholarship,
and education by publishing worldwide in

Oxford New York

Auckland Cape Town Dar es Salaam Hong Kong Karachi
Kuala Lumpur Madrid Melbourne Mexico City Nairobi
New Delhi Shanghai Taipei Toronto

With offices in

Argentina Austria Brazil Chile Czech Republic France Greece
Guatemala Hungary Italy Japan Poland Portugal Singapore
South Korea Switzerland Thailand Turkey Ukraine Vietnam

Oxford is a registered trade mark of Oxford University Press
in the UK and in certain other countries

Published in the United States
by Oxford University Press Inc., New York

British Library Cataloguing in Publication Data

Data available

Library of Congress Cataloging-in-Publication Data

Data available

Typeset by Newgen Imaging Systems (P) Ltd., Chennai, India
Printed in Great Britain
on acid-free paper by
CPI Antony Rowe, Chippenham, Wiltshire

ISBN 978–0–19–957898–6

1 3 5 7 9 10 8 6 4 2

To Nuru Ribadu and John Githongo, Chairmen of the Economic and Financial Crimes (EFCC) in Nigeria and the Kenya Anti Corruption Commission (KACC) respectively for their courageous fight against corruption in Africa

Preface

The last Millennium was a wasted one for Africa, as it was, indeed, for a large chunk of the human race. However, while the last two centuries of that millennium saw the redemption of humanity largely in Europe, North America and, to a reasonable extent, Asia, Africa wallowed in the vicious cycle of slavery, colonialism, self-destructive governance, the looting of collective resources by governments, military adventurism in politics, authoritarianism and general retrogression.

The new Millennium revived the hope for Africa, just as the attainment of political independence from European powers between the late 1950s and 1960s, once did. Across the African continent, momentous developments are currently unfolding which make Africans dare hope again: the wanton plundering of Africa's natural resources by rulers and warlords alike is today being vigorously challenged by an increasingly vocal civil society; the culture of graft and corruption is being confronted by daredevilry across many African countries, as best typified by the vigorous campaigns led by Nuru Ribadu and John Githongo, the former heads of the Economic and Financial Crimes Commission (EFCC) in Nigeria and the Kenyan Anti-Corruption Commission (KACC) respectively. The international law principle of non-intervention in internal affairs of States, which many member States of the Organization of African Unity (OAU) hijacked to shield their reigns of terror from international scrutiny, has now been replaced by a policy of 'no indifference' by the African Union. As a principle, the African Union is now able to intervene in a member State once a situation therein crosses certain thresholds. The International Criminal Court's issuance of an arrest warrant against President Bashir in Sudan in relation to crimes committed in Darfur, if nothing else, serves as a serious symbolic gesture that the era of impunity is fast coming to an end.

Of course, that is not to say that corruption, violent conflicts, theft and mismanagement of natural resources and extensive looting of national wealth will all suddenly cease in Africa. Quite the contrary, the ongoing situations in Darfur, Somalia and the Democratic Republic of Congo (DRC) clearly show that today's violent conflicts in Africa are as nasty as those of yesteryears. Grand embezzlement of public funds still occurs daily across the continent, while the 2007/8 post-election crises in Kenya and Zimbabwe demonstrate the gory determination of political leaders to steal their peoples' democratic victories at all costs. The greater the resolve of the African people to fight HIV/AIDS, the less, it seems, the enthusiasm of multinational pharmaceutical corporations to make antiretroviral drugs available at affordable prices.

This book investigates the various ongoing efforts to address the threats to human security in Africa. Threats, such as environmental insecurity, food insecurity, the proliferation of small arms and light weapons, endemic corruption, labour exploitation, repression of women's rights, refugees, piracy, natural resource-fuelled conflicts, are commonplace in Africa. The contributors to the book are, in their own right, leading academics and practitioners in the various themes of their commentary. In the first part, each chapter analyses the legal and policy frameworks available for dealing with specific human security threats. The second part focuses on the African institutions and mechanisms for advocating, protecting, and vindicating human security in Africa. The African Union, the African Commission of Human and Peoples' Rights, the African Court of Human Rights and Justice, Non-Governmental Organizations and the civil society all play crucial and significant roles in this respect, and as such, receive great attention in this book.

For the various assistance received from the start to the finish of this book, I thank the Oxford University Press team of John Louth, Merel Alstein and Fiona Stables for their support and cooperation. For their assistance with proofreading the manuscripts, I thank especially Edefe Ojomo and Ife Ogbona, and Dominique Mystris. For tolerating my frequent escapes from home and punching away at my laptop at ungodly hours, Eche and Kobi, my wife and kid.

Ademola Abass
Uxbridge
June 2010

Contents

I. OF CERTAIN THREATS TO HUMAN SECURITY IN AFRICA

II. REGIONAL INSTITUTIONS AND MECHANISMS

III. CONCLUSION

List of Contributors

Ademola Abass (Editor) is currently professor of international law and international organizations at Brunel University, West London, Research Fellow in Peace and Security, United Nations University Comparative Regional Integration Studies, Bruges, Belgium, and Associate, Conflict, Security and Development Group (CSDG), King's College London. He was Reader in Law at the University of Reading and previously taught at the Universities of the West of England (Bristol) and Nottingham. Professor Abass was the African Union's First Expert on Regional Mechanisms and drafted the Memorandum of Understanding between the African Union and Regional Economic Communities in the field of peace and security. He also served as the European Commission's Expert on Capacity Building for African regional organizations. He teaches and researches widely in public international law, particularly collective security law, international criminal law, and peace and security. His publications include *Regional Organisations and the Development of Collective Security Law: Beyond Chapter VIII of the UN Charter* (Hart Publishing, 2004), *Complete Equity and Trusts: Text, Cases, and Materials* (Oxford University Press, 2008), *Complete International Law: Texts, Cases, and Materials* (Oxford University Press, forthcoming 2011), as well as several chapters of books and articles in refereed journals. He is a Fellow of Cambridge University Commonwealth Society.

Abiodun Alao is currently Senior Research fellow of the Conflict Security and Development Group, King's College, London. He holds a Doctorate degree in War Studies from King's College, University of London, where he was a Ford Foundation scholar between 1987 and 1991. He was a recipient of other grants including the SSRC/ MacAurthur Post-Doctoral Fellowship. Dr Alao has held teaching and research positions at universities in Nigeria and Zimbabwe and has served as Consultant to many international organizations, including the Bureau for Crisis Prevention and Recovery (BCPR) of the United Nations Development Programme (UNDP), Office of the UN Secretary-General's Special Commission for African Affairs on the Special meeting on the Illegal Exploitation of Mineral Resources in Africa (2006). He was a member of the Four-Person team that undertook a Comprehensive Evaluation of the activities of the first five years of the Bureau for Crisis Prevention and Recovery (BCPR) of the UNDP (2005), and was a member of the Two-Person Team that wrote the Concept Paper for the formulation of the Common Defence and Security Policy for the African Union (2003). Dr Alao's many publications include *The Politics and Diplomacy of Security in Zimbabwe* (I. B. Tauris Press, 2007), *The Tragedy of Endowment: Natural Resources and Conflict in Africa* (University of Rochester Press, 2007), *Peacekeepers, Politicians and Warlords: The Liberian Peace Process* (co-authored with John Mackinlay and Funmi Olonisakin; United Nations University Press, 1999), and *Africa After the Cold War: The Changing Perspective on Security* (African World Press, 1998).

Kwesi Aning currently serves as Head, Conflict Prevention Management and Resolution Department (CPMRD) of the Kofi Annan International Peacekeeping Training Centre (KAIPTC) in Accra, Ghana. Prior to taking up his new position in January 2007, he served as the African Union's first Expert on counter-terrorism, defence and security with responsibility for implementing the continental counter-terrorism strategy and oversight of the African Centre for the Study and Research on Terrorism (ACSRT) in Algiers, Algeria. Kwesi Aning holds a doctorate from the University of Copenhagen, Denmark. His primary research interests deal with broad African security issues, comparative politics, terrorism, and conflicts. He has taught in several universities in Europe and Africa and has several publications to his name. In 2007, he served as a senior consultant to the UN Department for Political Affairs, New York and completed a UN Secretary-General's report on the relationship between the UN and regional organizations, particularly the African Union in maintaining peace and security. He reviews for several scholarly journals and serves on diverse Boards.

Opeoluwa Badaru is currently a PhD Candidate at Osgoode Hall Law School, York University, Canada. Her research areas include economic and social rights, with special emphasis on the realization of the right to food in third world states. She is also interested in and has published in the area of Third World Approaches to International Law (TWAIL). Prior to her current studies, Opeoluwa obtained an LLM in Human Rights and Democratisation in Africa at the Centre for Human Rights, University of Pretoria, South Africa. She graduated as the overall best student in 'Human Rights in Africa' and 'Democratisation in Africa'. As part of her studies, she undertook field trips to Rwanda and Kosovo and also spent some time studying and undertaking an internship in Mozambique. Opeoluwa is a member of the Nigerian Bar where she practised law in several capacities. She has also been involved as a Case Commentator for the Oxford Reports on International Law in Domestic Courts.

Ilias Bantekas LLB (Athens), LLM (Liverpool), PhD (Liverpool), Dip Theology (Cambridge), Professor of International Law at Brunel University School of Law. From 1998 to 2006 Professor Bantekas was an Associate Professor and Director of the International Law Unit at Westminster Law School and during 2003–04 he was a Fellow at Harvard Law School. He is Head of International Law & Arbitration at Mourgelas and Associates Law Firm (Athens), where he specializes also in renewable energy and implementation of the Kyoto Protocol. His publications include *International Criminal Law* (Hart Publishing, 2010), *Oil and Gas Law in Kazakhstan: National and International Perspectives* (Kluwer, 2004), and *Trust Funds in International Law: Trustee Obligations of the United Nations and the World Bank* (Asser/Cambridge University Press, 2009).

Ben Chigara joined Brunel University from Warwick University in 2003 as a Research Professor of Law. He is the founding Director of the Centre for International and Public Law (CIPL). Previously, Professor Chigara taught at the Universities of Warwick, Leeds, Nottingham, and Oxford Brookes University. His research and teaching interests focus on the theory and practice of international organization and the development and protection of standards for the recognition, promotion, and protection of the dignity inherent in all individuals as human beings. Professor Chigara's publications include *Land Reform Policy: The Challenge of International Human Rights Law* (Ashgate, 2002), *Amnesty in International Law: Legality under International Law of National Amnesty Laws* (Longman, 2001), *Legitimacy Deficit in Customary International Law: A Deconstructionist Critique* (Ashgate, 2001). Professor Chigara has consulted for the International Labour Organization (ILO) and the Organisation for Security and Cooperation in Europe's

(OSCE) Office for Democratic Institutions and Human Rights (ODIHR), and several articles and chapters of books.

Ebenezer Durojaye is a doctoral candidate and researcher at the Department of Constitutional Law and Philosophy of Law, Faculty of Law, University of the Free State in South Africa. He also teaches on the LLM Programme on Sexual and Reproductive Rights organized by the same department. His area of research interests includes focusing on human rights issues raised by access to HIV/AIDS treatment and the intersection between gender inequality and HIV/AIDS response in Africa, women's rights, and adolescent sexual and reproductive rights in Africa. Some of his articles have been published in reputable international law journals such as the *Netherlands International Law Review*, *Netherland Quarterly of Human Rights*, *Journal of African Law*, and the *African Journal of Comparative and International Law*. He is currently researching on socio-cultural factors (including religious) issues affecting the sexual rights of adolescents in Africa.

Rachel Murray is currently a Professor of International Human Rights Law at the University of Bristol. She has taught previously at Birkbeck College, the University of the West of England, and Queens University Belfast where she was also the Assistant Director of the Human Rights Centre. She specializes in the human rights mechanisms in Africa including the work of the Organization of African Unity/African Union and its African Commission on Human and Peoples' Rights. Professor Murray advises institutions, non-governmental organizations, and others working in the human rights field. She completed a Nuffield-funded project with the late Professor Stephen Livingstone of Queens University Belfast to evaluate the Northern Ireland Human Rights Commission with comparisons from South Africa. Her publications include *Human Rights in Africa: From OAU to AU* (Cambridge University Press, 2004), *The African Commission on Human and Peoples' Rights and International Law* (with Professor Malcolm Evans; Hart Publishing, 2000), and *The African Charter on Human and Peoples' Rights: The System at Work* (Cambridge University Press, 2002). She is currently working on a book (Hart Publishing) examining the role of national human rights commissions at the international level, and has funding from the Arts and Humanities Research Council with Professor Malcolm Evans, to evaluate the effectiveness of national mechanisms under the UN Optional Protocol to the Convention Against Torture.

Gino J Naldi is Senior Lecturer in Law in the University of East Anglia where he teaches Public International Law, Human Rights, and EC Law. Dr Naldi is a leading commentator on African Regional Organizations. His principal publications include *The Organisation of African Unity: An Analysis of Its Role* (Mansell, 1999). He is a member of the African Society of International and Comparative Law and the British Institute of International and Comparative Law.

Obiora Chinedu Okafor is currently Associate professor of International Law at the Osgoode Hall Law School, Canada. He was recently a Visiting Scholar at Harvard Law School's Human Rights Program. His teaching and research interests are in Public International Law, International Human Rights Law, Refugee Law, Immigration Law, International Institutions and Regimes, The Third World and International Law (TWAIL), Human Rights in Africa, Post-Colonial Theory, Non-Governmental Organizations, International Legal History, International Legal Theory, Social

Anthropology and International Law, Comparative Constitutional Law, and Socio-Legal Studies, and Nigerian Constitutional Law and Policy. Professor Okafor has authored one book, *Re-Defining Legitimate Statehood* and co-edited two books, *Legitimate Governance in Africa* (with Edward Kofi Quashigah) and *Humanizing our Global Order: Essays in Honour of Ivan L. Head* (with O. Aginam; forthcoming). He is currently working on two funded studies relating to the African Human Rights System, and the role of human rights Non-Governmental Organizations in Nigeria. Professor Okafor currently serves as Managing Co-editor of a new international journal, *The Third World and International Law* and sits on the board of the Canadian Law and Society Association.

Maria O'Sullivan is a Lecturer in the Law Faculty at Monash University, Melbourne, Australia. She holds a BA/LLB (Hons) degree from the Australian National University and a LLM in International Human Rights Law from the University of Essex (UK). She has worked in various legal positions, including as a researcher with Matrix Chambers, London, and a legal adviser with the Australian Refugee Review Tribunal. Her primary research interests are administrative and refugee law. She is currently completing a doctorate on Article 1C(5) of the Refugees Convention, dealing with cessation of refugee status.

Efthymios Papastavridis, LLB (Athens), LLM (ULC), PhD (UCL), is an expert and consultant on the international law of the sea and general international law. He has taught part time at UCL and Westminster Law School and has published in numerous leading journals, including the *ICLQ*, the *Syracuse Journal of International Law* and others.

Manisuli Ssenyonjo is a Senior Lecturer in Law, Brunel University and has previously taught law at the University of Nottingham, Makerere University Uganda, and at the Faculty of Law, University of the West of England (Bristol). He has been awarded various grants from funding agencies for research and teaching projects and has acted as a consultant to governments, Inter-Governmental Organizations, and Non-Governmental Organizations. He was an Assistant Editor, *Human Rights Law Review* (2002–04) and *Journal of Conflict and Security Law* (2003–04); and has acted as an external reviewer for a number of academic journals including the *Journal of International Relations and Development*. He is a barrister of the High Court of Uganda. Dr Ssenyonjo's publications include 'Women's Rights to Equality and Non-Discrimination' (2007) 21(4) *International Journal of Law, Policy and the Family* 341–72, 'Economic, Social and Cultural Rights and Non-State Actors' in M. Baderin and R. McCorquodale (eds), *Economic, Social and Cultural Rights in Action* (Oxford University Press, 2007), ch 6, pp 109–38, 'Culture and the Human Rights of Women in Africa: Between Light and Shadow' (2007) 51(1) *Journal of African Law* 39–67.10.

Table of Cases

Table of Legislation

NATIONAL

List of Abbreviations

ABHS	Advisory Board on Human Security
ACDEG	African Charter on Democracy, Elections and Governance
ACHPR	African Charter on Human and Peoples' Rights
ACHPR	African Commission on Human and Peoples' Rights
AFDL	Alliance of Democratic Forces for the Liberation of Congo-Zaire
AIDS	Acquired Immune Deficiency Syndrome
AMIS	African Union Mission in Sudan
APSA	African Peace and Security Architecture
APSOG	Association of Private Security Operators in Ghana
ARBA	Ashanti Region Blacksmiths Association
ARVS	Anti-retroviral Drugs
ASF	African Stand by Force
AU	African Union
CAADP	Comprehensive Africa Agriculture Development Programme
CASDP	Common African Security and Defence Policy
CCEM	Committee against Modern Slavery
CCPCI	Chad-Cameroon Pipeline Consortium Initiative
CDF	Comprehensive Development Framework
CDM	Clean Development Mechanism
CEDAW	Convention on the Elimination of All Forms of Discrimination against Women
CEN-SAD	Community of Sahel-Saharan States
CERD	Committee on the Elimination of Racial Discrimination
CESCR	Committee on Economic, Social and Cultural Rights
CEWARN	Conflict and Early Warning Response Mechanism
CEWS	Continental Early Warning System
CHS	Commission for Human Security
COMESA	Common Market for Eastern and Southern Africa
CPR	Civil and Political Rights
CSO	Civil Society Organizations
CSSDCA	Conference on Security, Stability, Development and Cooperation in Africa
CTF	Combined Task Force
DDI	Diamond and Development Initiative
DDR	Disarmament, Demobilization and Reintegration
DFID	Department for International Development (UK)
DPKO	Department for Peacekeeping Operations (UN)
DRC	Democratic Republic of the Congo
ECHR	European Convention on Human Rights
ECOMOG	ECOWAS Monitoring Group
ECOWAS	Economic Community of West African States

ECOSOCC	Economic Social and Cultural Council
EITI	Extractive Industries Transparency Initiative
ENVSEC	Environmental Security
ESCR	Economic, Social and Cultural Rights
ESF	ECOWAS Standby Force
EU	European Union
EUNAVFOR	European Union Naval Force
FAO	Food and Agricultural Organization
FGM	Female Genital Mutilation
FLC	Forced Labour Convention
FOSDA	Foundation for Security and Development in Africa
GDP	Gross Domestic Product
GEMAP	Governance and Economic Management Assistance Program
GHG	Greenhouse Gases
GPS	Ghana Police Service
HDR	Human Development Report
HIPC	Highly Indebted Poor Countries
HIV	Human Immunodeficiency Virus
HRC	Human Rights Committee
HSTF	High Seas Task Force
ICC	International Criminal Court
ICCPR	International Covenant on Civil and Political Rights
ICERD	International Convention on the Elimination of All Forms of Racial Discrimination
ICESCR	International Covenant on Economic, Social and Cultural Rights
ICISS	International Commission on Intervention and State Sovereignty
ICJ	International Court of Justice
ICRC	International Convention on the Rights of the Child
IDP	Internally Displaced Person
IFAD	International Fund for Agricultural Development
IGAD	InterGovernmental Authority on Development
IHI	International Human Rights Institutions
ILC	International Labour Code
ILC	International Law Commission
ILO	International Labour Organization
IMF	International Monetary Fund
IMO	International Maritime Organization
IRTC	Internationally Recognised Transit Corridor
ITCZ	Intertropical Convergence Zone
IUU	Illegal Unreported and Unregulated Fishing
JDA	Joint Development Authority
JDZ	Joint Development Zone
KACA	Kenya Anti-corruption Authority
KACC	Kenya Anti-corruption Commission
LOSC	Law of the Sea Convention
LPA	Lagos Plan of Action

LRA	Lord's Resistance Army
LURD	Liberia United for Reconciliation and Democracy
MDC	Movement for Democratic Change
MDG	Millennium Development Goals
MODEL	Movement for Democracy in Liberia
MoU	Memorandum of Understanding
MPLA	Popular Movement for the Liberation of Angola
MSC	Maritime Safety Committee
MSC	Military Staff Committee
MSPA	Maritime Security Patrol Area
NATO	North Atlantic Treaty Organization
NEPAD	New Partnership for Africa's Development
NGO	Non-governmental Organization
NHRI	National Human Rights Institution
NJC	National Judicial Council
NLC	Native Labour Code
NPFL	National Patriotic Front of Liberia
NPP	New Patriotic Party
NRCD	National Redemption Council Decree
NSA	Non-state Actor
NTLG	National Transitional Government of Liberia
OAS	Organization of American States
OAU	Organization of African Unity
ODM	Orange Democratic Movement
OECD	Organisation for Economic Co-Operation and Development
OSCE	Organisation for Security and Cooperation for Europe
PLWHA	People Living with HIV and AIDS
PMAD	Protocol on Mutual Assistance and Defence
PNDC	Provisional National Defence Council
PRSP	Poverty Reduction Strategy Papers
PSC	Peace and Security Council
PSC	Private Security Companies
REC	Regional Economic Communities
RENAMO	Resistência Nacional Moçambicana
RoE	Rules of Engagement
RPG	Rocket Propelled Grenades
RRF	Rapid Reaction Force (EU)
SADC	Southern African Development Community
SALW	Small Arms and Light Weapons
SAP	Structural Adjustment Program
SARS	Severe Acute Respiratory Syndrome
SEWS	Sub-regional Early Warning System
SPLA	Sudan People's Liberation Army
SSR	Security Sector Reform
SUA	Suppression of Unlawful Acts

TCN	Troops Contributing Nations
TFG	Transitional Federal Government of Somalia
UDHEM	Universal Declaration on the Eradication of Hunger
UDHR	Universal Declaration of Human Rights and Malnutrition
UNAIDS	United Nations Programme on HIV/AIDS
UNDP	United Nations Development Programme
UNDPKO	UN Department for Peacekeeping Operations
UNEP	United Nations Environment Programme
UNFCC	UN Framework Convention on Climate Change
UNGASS	United Nations General Assembly Special Session on HIV and AIDS
UNHCR	United Nations High Commission for Refugees
UNITA	Union for the Total Independence of Angola
WHO	World Health Organization
WTO	World Trade Organization
ZANU-PF	Zimbabwe African National Union—Patriotic Front

1

An Introduction to Protecting
Human Security in Africa

Ademola Abass

1. Introduction

The phrase 'human security' was thrust upon the international plane in 1994 when, in its Human Development Report (HDR), the United Nations Development Programme (UNDP) broached an entirely new way of thinking about security.[1] In the report, the UNDP proposed a people-centred notion of security. This was a remarkable, if not a path-breaking departure altogether from the traditional conception of security as a state-centric notion.

In the HDR the UNDP restated the essence of the conventional notion of security as 'security of territory from external aggression, or as protection of national interests in foreign policy or as global security from the threat of a nuclear holocaust'. This Westphalian orthodoxy, which was embraced by the international legal order in the 17th century, envisioned that 'the state would monopolize the rights and means to protect its citizens. State power and state security would be established and expanded to sustain order and peace.'[2]

That is not to say, however, that the substantive *idea* which embodies the notion of human security only emerged as recently as 1994. Several decades earlier, to be precise from the 1960s through to the 1980s, scholars had adumbrated broadening the definition of security. But the raison d'être for this early expansionist quest owes mainly to the need felt at that time, that the conception of security should incorporate non-military aspects and the promotion of economic development in poorer countries; it was not a campaign inspired by a particular desire to upscale humans as prime referents of security.[3]

---

[1] UNDP HDR, <http://hdr.undp.org/en/reports/global/hdr1994/chapters/>.
[2] See in particular Chapter 2, p 22 <http://hdr.undp.org/en/reports/global/hdr1994/>.
[3] See in particular R McNamara, *The Essence of Security: Reflections in Office* (New York: Harper & Row, 1968).

The relentless academic strive to wean the notion of security from state centrism triumphed in 1998, when during a bilateral talk at Lysøen, Norway (hence, the term Lysøen process), the Canadian and Norwegian governments hoisted human security as a new *leitmotif* of foreign policy.[4] At the much enlarged talk in Lysøen in May 1999,[5] Canada posited that 'in essence, human security means safety for people both from violent and non-violent threats. It is a condition of state of being characterized by freedom from pervasive threats to people's rights, their safety or even their lives.'[6] The Canadian and Norwegian Foreign Ministers Llyod Axworthy and Knut Vollebæk described human security 'as an umbrella concept to cover a humanitarian agenda that includes support for the International Criminal Court, the ban on landmines, regulation of light arms trade, and prohibition of child soldiers'.[7] From a foreign policy perspective, Canada, in particular, construed human security:

as a shift in perspective or orientation. It is an alternative way of seeing the world, taking people as its point of reference, rather than focusing exclusively on security of territory or governments.[8]

Upon becoming a Security Council member in 1999 and its president in February of that year, Canada placed human security on the Council agenda as a broad category for discussing violations suffered by civilians during conflicts. Thus, the human security notion, broached by Canada and Norway, had an essential humanitarian character, underpinned by a policy aim of civilizing the conduct of wars.[9]

Academics have not been any more successful in seeking a universally accepted definition and conception of human security than states. Scholastic attempts to define the term have been largely circumscribed by the widely divergent meanings that human security has been able to generate, and the various contexts to which it applies.[10] As Suhrke has observed, 'as a social construct, the term [human security] permits many interpretations and those who promote it are still struggling to formulate authoritative and consensual definition. But the idea clearly has roots in the central principles of international humanitarian law—to civilize warfare and to aid its victims.'[11] Thomas and Tow have equally noted that human security 'is a promising but still underdeveloped paradigmatic approach to understanding

---

[4] For a good analysis of the interest of Canada and Norway in promoting human security, see A Suhrke, 'Human Security and the Interest of States' (1999) 30(3) Security Dialogue 265.

[5] Nine states attended this talk. These states were Austria, Chile, Ireland, Jordan, the Netherlands, Slovenia, South Africa, Switzerland, and Thailand.

[6] '"Human Security": Safety for People in a Changing World', Department of Foreign Affairs and International Trade, Ottawa, April 1999, also cited in Suhrke (see n 4 above) 266.

[7] See n 4 above, 266.   [8] Ibid.   [9] Ibid, 268.

[10] See B Ramcharan, 'Human Rights and Human Security' (2004) 1 Disarmament Forum 40; E Newman and J van Selm, *Refugees and Forced Displacement: International Security, Human Vulnerability, and the State* (Tokyo: United Nations University, 2003).

[11] Suhrke (see n 4 above) 269.

contemporary security politics'.[12] The notoriously intractable nature of human security was also reflected in the definition ascribed to it by the Harvard Program on Human Security, which basically regards human security as 'the expected number of years of life spent outside the state of generalized poverty'.[13]

The UNDP did not offer a calibrated definition of human security either. Nonetheless, it articulated, in the HDR, its exact vision of the concept by setting out two broad aspects and four distinct characteristics that, it believes, crystallize the concept of human security it advocated. Accordingly, human security is conceived as 'safety from such chronic threats as hunger, diseases and repression', on the one hand, and 'protection from sudden and hurtful disruptions in the pattern of daily life—whether in homes, in jobs or communities',[14] on the other.

Characteristically, human security is universal (it is relevant to all nations and people, rich or poor); its components are interdependent (threats to human security break down the barrier of territorial immunity so that the misfortunes of one people at one end of the world could trigger a chain of events with devastating consequences for people at the other end); it is much easier to prevent threats to human security than resort (mostly belatedly) to expensive humanitarian actions; and finally, human security is people-centred (it is concerned with how people live and breathe in a society, how freely they exercise their many choices).

Although the identification of people as prime referents of security is common to policy and academic understanding of human security, the characterization of the concept by the UNDP contrasts to that proposed by scholars in two principal respects. First, at its earliest and most rustic stage, the pedagogical elucidation of human security had subsumed, *albeit* not implausibly at the relevant period, the concept under human development, a methodological approach that the UNDP cautioned against despite acknowledging a symbiotic relationship between the two concepts.[15] Secondly, in its more advanced form the academic exposition of human security had conflated the aspirations of normative theorizing—which are the end goal of making humans prime referents of security—with the reality of policy practices. Tadjbakhsh and Chenoy argue that 'with human security [the individual "qua person" rather than "qua citizen"] becomes the ultimate actor taken into account [and] his or her security is the ultimate goal to which all instruments and political actors are subordinated'.[16] There is no doubt that the reference by these commentators to 'humans' as prime referents of security accords with policy thinking on human security; however, subordinating political institutions

---

[12] N Thomas and WT Tow, 'The Utility of Human Security: Sovereignty and Humanitarian Intervention' (2002) 33(2) Security Dialogue 177.

[13] G King and C Murray, 'Rethinking Human Security' Program on Human Security (Center for Basic Research in the Social Sciences, Harvard University, 4 May 2000) (2001–2) 116(4) Political Science Quarterly 585.

[14] UNDP Human Development Report (1994) <http://hdr.undp.org/en/reports/global/hdr1994/>, Chapter 2, p 2 of 25.　　　　[15] Much on this distinction below.

[16] S Tadjbakhsh and AM Chenoy, *Human Security: Concepts and Implications* (London/New York: Routledge, 2007), 13.

to such goals is over-ambitious. As David Chandler observes, 'the assertion that individuals qua persons'—that is, outside a political process—'can suborn power makes little sense in theory, let alone practice'.[17] Amartya Sen also argues that the human-centred approach advocated by human security pundits still involves political processes of collective decision making, choices, and policy trade-offs.[18]

In 2003, the Commission on Human Security (CHS)—a body inspired by Japan and launched during the 2000 UN Millennium Summit—elucidated the new concept of human security and demarcated its province from those of human development and human rights. The CHS defines human security as efforts to 'protect the vital core of all human lives in ways that enhance human freedoms and human fulfilments'.[19] It conceived of human security as a dynamic concept embracing themes ranging from protecting fundamental freedoms—freedoms that are the essence of life such as freedom from critical and pervasive threats and situations to using processes to build on people's strengths and aspirations.

As with the UNDP, the CHS affirmed that human security, in its broadest sense, embraces far more than the absence of violent conflicts, and that it encompasses human rights, good governance, access to education and health care, and ensuring that each individual has opportunities and choices to fulfil his or her own potential.[20] As such, the goal of human security resides in the twin notions of protection and empowerment. Whereas protection connotes the norms, processes, and institutions required to shield people from critical and pervasive threats, hence implying a 'top-down' approach which includes, but is not limited to, establishing the rule of law, institutional accountability and transparency, empowerment, as a strategy, engenders a 'bottom-up' approach that emphasizes people as actors and participants in defining and implementing their vital freedoms.[21]

2. Human security, human rights, and human development

The question may be asked: What distinguishes human security from human rights and human development, the two conceptual frameworks under which the protection of humans from various forms of insecurity was organized and pursued for generations before the advent of the human security paradigm? Put differently, does the human security paradigm engender a distinct set of values,

---

[17] D Chandler, 'Review Essay: Human Security: The Dog That Didn't Bark' (2008) 39 Security Dialogue 427, 429.

[18] A Sen, *Development as Freedom* (Oxford: Oxford University Press, 1999), 33–4, restated in Chandler (see n 17 above) 429.

[19] CHS, *Human Security Now* (New York: United Nations Publications, 2003), 4 (hereafter 'Human Security Now').   [20] Ibid, 4.

[21] S Ogata, 'Human Security as Framework for Post-conflict Nation-building: Lessons from Iraq and Afghanistan' in KM Cahill (ed), *Human Security For All: A Tribute to Sergio Viera De Mello* (New York: Fordham University Press, 2004), 3, 10.

compared to those of human rights and human development, as to justify its adoption as a conceptual framework either in academic scholarship or as policy instrument for human protection?

2.1 Human security and human development

It is mainly in regard to the broadness of approach and the specificity of attention that human security and human development irrevocably diverge. Doubtless that both concepts are concerned with the pursuit of shared goals for human beings—such as longevity, education, and opportunities—they each look at the field from different perspectives.[22]

Human development is about expanding people's choices to live the lives they value, but as a strategy, it is unavoidably fraught with targeting aggregative goals. Human security, on the other hand, keeps the individual at the centre of attention by accounting for the unforeseen downfalls or reversals of development.[23] Thus, whereas human development is the ultimate stage in people's aspiration for decent existence, human security provides them with the tools for attaining that goal. As Bertrand Ramcharan writes, 'the lack of freedom saps the creative capacity of the people and impoverishes them. Where people are free, they are inspired to create and produce.'[24] Ellen Seidensticker notes that sustainability and self-reliance, not just ameliorating a temporary situation, are central to promoting human security.[25] Human security therefore targets securing those fringes of individual lives that are either overlooked or marginalized in the pursuit of the *general* goodness of a society.

The difference between human security and human development is therefore the functional distinction between the general and the particular. In any aggregative concepts, such that human development invariably is, the assumption is tragically that whole units of targets, such as ethnic or tribal groups, rise and fall together. The reality, however, is that even members of an ethnic group can repress others just as much as partners in personal relationships can use violence on each other even when their ethnic or tribal group fares well in the overall equation. Thus while a developmental scheme such as tax relief for married couples in order to encourage marriage may prove useful aggregately in monitoring a society's development indices, it does not, in any useful way, address the daily reality of people involved in domestic violence. Nor would merely providing food for people in famine suffice since, as Ellen Seidensticker notes, if the

[22] See n 19 above, 10.
[23] Ibid. See also M Weissberg, 'Conceptualising Human Security' (2003) 37(3) Swords & Ploughshares: A Journal of International Affairs 4.
[24] B Ramcharan, 'Human Rights and Human Security' (2004) Disarmament Forum 39, 40.
[25] E Seidensticker, Seminar on Human Security, Human Rights, and Human Development, Kennedy School, Harvard University (5 February 2002).

food were withdrawn, deaths would occur.[26] Human security therefore helps not only to identify gaps in the infrastructure of protection, but it also finds ways to strengthen and improve it.

2.2 Human security and human rights

Human security and human rights are mutually reinforcing and, as with human development and human security, are complementary. Certainly, respecting human rights is at the core of human security, the protection and empowering of people. In 2001 the CHS described the relationship between human security and human rights thus:

> We reaffirm the conviction that Human Rights and the attributes stemming from human dignity constitute a normative framework and a conceptual reference point which must necessarily be applied to the construction and implementation of the notion of human security. In the same manner, while acknowledging that norms and principles of International Humanitarian Law are essential components for the construction of human security, we emphasize that the latter cannot be restricted to situations of current or past armed conflict but constitute a generally applicable concept.[27]

The view on the CHS of the relationship between human rights and human security, Boyle and Simonsen observe,[28] is very similar to that advanced by the International Commission on Intervention and State Sovereignty (ICISS), which places an emphasis, just as the CHS has done, on the protection of fundamental freedoms of peoples:

> The traditional, narrow perception of security leaves out the most elementary and legitimate concerns of ordinary people regarding security in their daily lives. It also diverts enormous amount of national wealth and human resources into armament and armed forces, while countries fail to protect their citizens from chronic insecurities of hunger, disease, inadequate shelter, crime, unemployment, social conflict and environmental hazard. When rape is used as an instrument of war and ethnic cleansing, when thousands are killed by floods resulting in a ravaged countryside and when citizens are killed by their own security forces, then it is just insufficient to think of national territorial security alone. The concept of human security can and does embrace such diverse circumstances.[29]

Boyle and Simonsen traced the relationship between human rights and human security to the early stages of the former's development. In his State of the Union address on 6 January 1941, the US President, Franklin D Roosevelt, proclaimed a vision of 'the world founded upon four essential freedoms—freedom of speech,

---

[26] Ibid.

[27] San Jose Declaration (2 December 2001), restated in Boyle and Simonsen (see n 28 below) 6.

[28] K Boyle and S Simonsen, 'Human Security, Human Rights and Disarmament' (2004) Disarmament Forum 5, 6.

[29] ICISS, *The Responsibility to Protect*, Ottawa (2001), p 15, restated in Boyle and Simonsen (see n 28 above) 6.

freedom of religion, freedom from want and freedom from fear'.[30] This vision was to become the foundation for the United Nations. In his report to the US Congress after the San Francisco Conference on the United Nations Organization, the US Secretary of State Edward Stettinus, Jr stated that:

The battle of peace has to be fought on two fronts. The first is the security front where victory spells freedom from fear. The second is the economic and social front where victory means freedom from want. Only victory on both fronts can assure the world of an enduring peace ... No provision that can be written into the Charter will enable the Security Council to make the world secure from war if men and women have no sense of security in their homes and jobs.[31]

Human security helps to identify the rights at stake in particular situations with human rights helping to answer how human security issues can be promoted. While human development is unmistakably a broader concept connoting the process of widening the range of people's choices, it is *these very choices* that constitute the essence of human security and the laudable standards that human rights seek to attain.

Despite the synergy between human security, human rights, and human development, human security has a unique and distinctive streak which makes its particularized treatment highly desirable. The scope of human security is enormous and the ramifications of what threatens it are so pervasive that, as a paradigm, it encompasses the whole of the human existence. A breakdown or malfunctioning of human security has disastrous consequences for human development and human rights: if individuals' security is not guaranteed or protected, the cohesive order of the aggregative society is either unrealizable or invariably destroyed, and the promotion and protection of human rights is permanently ousted or perpetually held in abeyance.

Furthermore, unlike human rights—which are regarded as inherent in human beings and, to a reasonable extent have been so accepted by states, and human development, which can be realized through the efforts of multiple actors such as states, international partners, and donors—human security was, at least until very recently, considered to be the sole responsibility of the state. Hence, dealing with human security issues engenders a much higher level of sensitivity (and volatility) than that associated with either human rights or human development.

3. The essence of a human security approach

Aside from querying whether there are added values *in* human security as a social construct, another question that can be raised is whether such values, if they

---

[30] See Franklin Delano Roosevelt, *State of the Union Address*, 6 January 1941, restated in Boyle and Simonsen (see n 28 above) 6. See also T Hoopes and D Brinkley, *FDR and the Creation of the UN* (New Haven, CT: Yale University Press, 1997).
[31] See UNDP 1994, Human Development Report, and restated in Boyle and Simonsen (see n 28 above) 6.

exist, justify an entirely new approach for addressing human security concerns. This query is different from the one considered above, which principally concerned whether, as a categorical imperative, human security is conceptually different from human rights and human development.

There are at least four compelling arguments in favour of advocating a human security approach, despite the concern that its 'integration into the mainstream of policy making has reinforced, rather than challenged, existing policy frameworks'.[32]

It is undeniable that since the Universal Declaration of Human Rights in 1948 human rights have come a long way and in most parts of the world have become an acceptable standard by which states' protection of their people's fundamental freedoms is measured. Even societies that do not prioritize human rights protection as such still recognize the significance of human rights at least by voluntarily assuming international obligations towards respecting them. Nevertheless, as a body of ideals, human rights regularly fall prey to states' predatory machinations, and are susceptible to being hijacked by and subjugated to states' whims and caprices. The whole essence of the doctrine of 'margin of appreciation' in the human rights jurisprudence, for instance, is to allow states a measure of laxity for derogating otherwise non-derogable rights of their people during periods that states regard as emergencies. Apart from the fact that the process through which states characterize certain periods as emergency is often shrouded in mystery and subjectivity, automatically subduing fundamental human rights in such moments somewhat attests to the levity with which states often treat human rights.

To be sure, there is a need for states to protect themselves from threats or attacks, imminent or anticipated, and to act decisively in real emergencies. The problem is that the state is often the ultimate judge of what constitutes an emergency, its sources and its possible impacts. It is the absence of an objective means of evaluating states' 'emergency' claims, especially by those worst affected by the derogation needed to preserve its life (the people) that makes a human rights approach a tricky business. An emergency is what a state declares as an emergency, and in situations such as those which might serve the selfish interests of government, protecting the human rights of the people is often regarded as nothing more than a minor irritation to be perfunctorily overlooked. States often foist 'emergencies' on their peoples in order to suppress political opposition. Yet, in most genuine emergencies, states have often turned a blind eye towards the protection of people's rights. By adopting a human security approach in which human safety is prioritized, a case can be made for a more transparent and effective scrutiny of states' emergency declarations so that human security will not become a handmaid of state security, as human rights have unfortunately become especially in authoritarian and undemocratic societies.

---

[32] See n 17 above, 428. On various criticisms of human security, see in particular JP Burgess and T Owen, 'Special Section: What is "Human Security"?' (2004) 35(3) Security Dialogue 345.

Secondly, the human rights approach relies heavily on the state as the primary guarantor of its citizens' rights, as well as serving as the ultimate vindicating authority whenever those rights are infringed. Hence, it is only when a state fails to avail wronged citizens with credible redress mechanisms that those citizens may have recourse to regional institutions where such exist. This is the doctrine known in international human rights jurisprudence as the 'exhaustion of local remedies'. The doctrine enjoins those who seek redress for human rights violations before international tribunals first to satisfy the criterion that they have exhausted remedies provided by their states.

Unfortunately, the state, especially in the developing world, is often the worst violator of human rights. Thus, expecting the state to guarantee such rights, let alone provide effective mechanisms to redress infringements, is nothing more than shadow chasing. As will be seen later in this book, the consequences of not protecting human security from threats are often much wider and far more devastating than violations of human rights. Therefore, while human rights violations and threats to human security may both originate from *within* a state, their geographical impacts differ. Protecting human security is guaranteed a more objective regime if violations are brought before regional institutions. This approach also finds support in the monist doctrine in international law, which entrusts international law, in contrast with domestic law, with safeguarding human rights.[33]

Thirdly, the argument has been made that under a human rights approach, economic, cultural, and social rights are often subjected to 'progressive realization' of duties and obligations. Since the only restraint on states is to avoid discriminating among those who can realize these rights, states have tremendous discretion on the pace at which to address social and economic rights. Human security may reduce the discretion given to nation-states in this domain by eliminating the 'way out' that progressive realization has left open.

Fourthly, a human security approach can help to remove the 'generational' distinction between various rights which often erroneously creates the impression that some rights are more equal than others. A generational approach to human rights considerably undermines human security as it gives a rather false impression that, when it comes to protection from threats, human beings can be compartmentalized.

Despite the foregoing arguments, one must caution against exaggerating the utility of a human security approach. While a human security approach undoubtedly implies focusing on people as the prime referents of security, that ideal should not imply the relegation, let alone obliteration, of the state's role in the protection of human security. Rather than advocating the subjugation of the collective decision-making process in a society to individuals, the emphasis of a

---

[33] See J Nijman and A Nollkaemper (eds), *New Perspectives on the Divide between National and International Law* (Oxford: Oxford University Press, 2007).

human security approach should be on prioritizing human security as a necessary imperative for the survival of states. It is only when human security is given a new status that a proper relationship between it and state security can lead to a more effective security regime for both the state and its people.

4. Human security and the special case of Africa

The reality of today's world confutes the traditional thesis that the state is the sole purveyor of human security and that it is *only* when the state's security is threatened that the shield of protection is inevitably removed from its citizens. Contemporary threats to human security are far more diverse and innocuous than previously understood and originate mostly from *within* concerned states. Furthermore, in many parts of the world, the state has today transformed from being the sole purveyor of human security into probably its most potent threat.

It is probably fair to say that in no other continent are threats to human security more dire and the absence of protection infrastructure more conspicuous, than in Africa. Threats to human security vary widely. A cursory look at the catalogue of the CHS, reveals, for instance, that different parts of the world experience different forms of threats to their security. In most Western societies, for example, issues such as financial market fluctuations, developing global patent rights systems, or a sudden decline in share value constitute serious threats to human security. However, when we speak of threats to human security in Africa, we refer to a different class of threats; we imply those conditions of inhumanity, long expelled from many parts of the world, that daily make even the most basic form of human existence in the twenty-first century such a rarity among millions of Africans. By threats to human security in Africa we are concerned with such dehumanizing conditions as violent conflicts, the pandemic HIV/AIDS, proliferation of arms and small weapons, endless streams of refugees and internally displaced peoples, forced labour, exponential violence against women, the 'curse' of natural resources, environmental degradation, abject poverty, corruption, the lack of basic health care, terrorism, and the rape of constitutionalism and the rule of law.

More than half the world's most brutal conflicts are currently located in Africa. The conflicts in Darfur, in the Sudan, Burundi, the Democratic Republic of Congo (DRC), Uganda, and Ivory Coast, to mention but a few, are constant reminders of the internecine conflicts that daily nullify the lives of millions in Africa. But whereas the reoccurring patterns of some of these conflicts have become somewhat familiar, almost to the point of banality, the violent disruption to Kenyans' lives, following controversial democratic elections in January 2008, adds a new urgency to the threat posed to human security by armed conflicts in Africa. Kenya was, until those events, one of the peaceful and stable states in Africa and one that was perhaps generally thought to be beyond violent conflicts.

The heinous post-election violence in Kenya demonstrates that at present no African state is immune to violent conflicts and other man-made disasters.

What is more truly worrying in the Kenyan episode, however, is not just that the country's political class allowed itself to climb the barricades, so to speak, against all precedential permutations: it is the long-term implications of those dastardly acts for Kenyans' security long after those elites responsible have reconciled their political differences through pacificatory power sharing and economic realignments. For it is in the certainty of perilous futurism that the Kenyan debacle sharply contrasts with, and rather ominously surpasses, the situation in Zimbabwe where a petulant dictatorship holds its people in utmost contempt and its country hostage to humanity.

The signature cause of Africa's internecine conflicts, 'ethnicity'—undoubtedly Africans' single biggest killer as the 1994 Rwandan genocide demonstrates—has arguably passed Zimbabwe by. Yet, while it is certain Zimbabwe will rid itself of autocracy in the future, the different nations of Kenya, having crossed the ethnic line, can only hope that they ever truly know peace and security outside the conclaves of their tribal existence.

One of the brutal realities of armed conflicts is the uprooting of peoples from their homes and communities and scattering them across faraway lands.[34] Africa is the world's largest depot for internally displaced persons (IDPs). The ignominious existence of IDPs in refugee camps is too well known to merit reiteration here. The considerable dangers that characterize refugees' daily lives are constantly brought to mind by the attrocious attacks unleashed on Darfur refugee camps by armed militias.

By far, women suffer the worst forms of threats to human security in Africa. The tragedy of women's insecurity is compounded by the fact that apart from bearing the society's worst brunt of diseases, such as HIV/AIDS and economic hardships, they also are exposed to the worst forms of domestic and cultural violence on record. From female genital mutilation (FGM) to predatory sexual victimization, from home to the street, women are daily exposed to brutal physical violence and exploitation across Africa. More perplexing, however, is that, apart from being exposed to severe tribulations by patriarchal traditions, women are mostly left unprotected by the law and institutions of many African states.

The cavalier attitude of African states towards protecting women from all types of violence is comparable to the states' colossal failure to protect the children and youth of Africa from various forms of exploitation and destruction.

It stands to reason, and even confounds commonsense, that a continent blessed with unarguably the world's largest reserves of natural resources accounts for less than 1 per cent of the global Gross Domestic Product (GDP). From the plenitude of diamonds in Sierra Leone, abundance of gold in the DRC, and the rich oil wells

---

[34] JC Hathaway, *The Rights of Refugees under International Law* (Cambridge: Cambridge University Press, 2005).

of Nigeria and Angola, Africans should have among the best living standards in today's world. Quite the contrary, corruption, nepotism, and extensive looting of national treasuries by kleptomaniac governments have turned Africans into the world's most pauperized people. The phrase 'African economy' has become as scarce today as the notion of 'incorrupt African leaders'. Africa has the lowest education integers in the entire human race and it remains the only continent where diseases long forgotten in other continents still kill adults and babies by the million year in and year out.

The overarching research theme of this book is *protecting human security in Africa*. The prime question is how does one tell which threat is more potent than another, and how does one select one over the other? Furthermore, what are the best means of protecting the human security of Africans and who has the responsibility for this?

As mentioned above, human security is a notoriously wide and open-ended paradigm, as are the threats to it. The approach adopted in this book is not to rank one threat above another, but to prioritize those threats that have either proved the most intractable or those that are regularly sidetracked, ignored, or overlooked in both academic and policy analyses.

It is one thing to be able to identify threats to human security in any given society, but it is another thing to be able to protect human security from such threats effectively. It is therefore pertinent that any useful and resourceful work on human security in Africa not only focuses on identifying some of the most potent threats to the security of Africans, but more importantly must discuss the legal and institutional mechanisms for protecting human security of Africans from such threats. The principal purpose of this book is to identify some of the most vicious threats to human security in Africa and to analyse the legal and institutional mechanisms for protecting Africans from such threats.

Most current existing works—although terse and limited—suffer two major methodological setbacks that make the focus and approach of this book distinct. First, most existing literature concentrates on the threats posed to Africans' security by issues arising from the traditional notion of security or simply the lack of adequate human rights protection. Secondly, most analysts assume that human security is not a distinct category from human rights or human development and, as such, does not require a separate recognition or protection regime. Of course, as argued above, there is some overlap between human rights, human development, and human security especially regarding their end goals. However, such convergence does not extend to the *modalities* for realizing the goals of each category. International conventions establish legal regimes for natural resource governance, but this will not necessarily tackle the link between natural resources and deadly conflicts, and the impact of such on the peoples' security.

Thus, by identifying some of the most potent threats to human security in Africa and analysing the regulatory frameworks and institutional mechanisms for protecting Africans from these threats, this book thematically and substantively departs from all existing works on the subject matter in Africa.

5. An overview of the structure and contributions

In addition to this chapter, the book contains 14 other chapters that carefully balance academic and policy perspectives on protecting human security in Africa. Structurally, the chapters are divided into two main parts and a concluding chapter.

5.1 Part I

This part offers analyses of certain threats to human security in Africa and looks at the legal and policy frameworks for tackling such threats.

In Chapter 2, Opeoluwa Badaru takes a critical look at food security and the serious threat posed by food shortage to the security of Africans. The author inquires into why, despite abundant rains in Africa, the continent perennially suffers food shortages. Badaru's analysis is not confined to appreciating the roles and impact of such legal instruments as the African Charter on Human and Peoples' Rights, and a wide array of soft laws, such as the 2000 Millennium Declaration, the 1996 Rome Declaration, or even the 1974 Universal Declaration on the Eradication of Hunger and Malnutrition of protecting Africans from food insecurity, it also deals with several policy instruments and institutional initiatives for dealing with food insecurity in Africa.

Closely linked to the threat of food insecurity in Africa is the threat posed by environmental insecurity covered in Chapter 3. Ilias Bantekas' contribution provides a fresh perspective on this most salient subject. Focusing on the situation in the Great Lake region, Bantekas demonstrates how environmental tensions often lead to armed conflicts as the situation in Darfur reveals. More important is Bantekas' combined analysis of old and nascent environmental regimes, covering a tantalizing spread of issues such as environmental conflicts, threats of deforestation, illegal depletion and exploitation of Africa's mineral wealth, to mention but a few. A major strength of this chapter is its highlighting of the interaction between various international actors, such as the United Nations Environment Programme, the UNDP, the North Atlantic Treaty Organization (NATO), and the Organisation for Security and Cooperation in Europe (OSCE), for the purpose of identifying environmental threats to global security, a prelude to designing appropriate mechanisms, such as Environmental Security (ENVSEC) as well as Swisspeace's Conflict and Early Warning Response Mechanism (CEWARN), applied in Africa.

One consequence of food insecurity, which often results from environmental degradation among others, is the enormous strain on resources available to a populace. Unavoidably, the gap between the rich and the poor widens and this often leads to an upsurge in violent crimes such as armed robbery and assassination. In Chapter 4, Kwesi Aning discusses the particularly dangerous threat posed by the proliferation of small arms and light weapons (SALW) to the security of Africans. He brings to bear his considerable experience researching this issue in Ghana. Although this chapter focuses on Ghana, the problem of SALW is common to most of Africa. Of particular interest in this chapter is the author's identification of the political motivations and dimensions of SALW, making it one of the most difficult threats to tackle. Dealing with this threat is further complicated by the fact that, despite SALW's prominence in security sector reform (SSR) literature, it rarely forms part of the human rights/human development discourse which makes this chapter a unique addition to the book.

When Africans are not killing themselves on the battlefield, they are, especially women and children, being brutally exploited by the stealthy hand of forced and exploitative labour, both in urban centres and in the darkest hinterlands of the continent. The gruesome incidence of forced labour meted out to children, especially in the vast cocoa plantations of Ivory Coast, or women and youths elsewhere across Africa is as troubling as the decimation of these segments of the African population by HIV/AIDS. In Chapter 5, Ben Chigara interrogates how, on the one hand, the various International Labour Organization (ILO) legal regimes that emerged in post-colonial Africa sought to contribute to the protection and enhancement of the human security agenda, while, on the other hand, various colonial powers pursued policies that were arguably antithetical to this goal. He argues that colonial powers' explicit refusal to extend the International Labour Code to their colonies meant that colonial powers not only rejected the futuristic aspirations of the Labour Code, but also presaged the subjugation of human security in Africa. Although subsequent attempts were made to upgrade the labour standards of colonial peoples, the introduction of the Native Labour Code actually gelatinized welfare. A unique strength of Chigara's chapter is the ability to demonstrate that despite the European colonial powers' preferences for such regimes as the Native Labour Code, and its undermining effect on the human security agenda, the ILO was able deftly to re-orientate this acrimonious policy towards supporting its human security objective. Although Chigara underscores the problems associated with the national laws of many African states vis-à-vis issues of forced labour (in particular, the lack of definitional clarity about what 'forced labour' means), this chapter shows some real instances of good practice in the evolution of the regulatory regimes for protecting human security through effective labour regulation. Thus, cases such as *Iversen v Norway* and *Siliadin v France* that upheld human dignity are due to the effective strategy adopted by the ILO to evolve a human security agenda for the world's labour force.

If the exploitation of the African labour force is a major cause for concern, then the threat posed by the mismanagement of natural resources in Africa is, to say the least, a ticking bomb. The tragedy of blood diamonds has been exposed in the literature and, more recently, in films. International responses have started to address how to limit illicit trade in these resources. Apart from noting that these efforts are piecemeal and inadequate, Abiodun Alao's contribution in Chapter 6 also reveals that these initiatives do not go to the root of the problem. Alao not only focuses on natural resources, as many other writers do, but also on the role that land ownership in Africa plays in the governance and management of those resources. This holistic construction of the theme of 'natural resource' is a remarkable feature of this chapter which distinguishes it from any similar previous endeavour. Focusing on at least five case studies, Alao discusses some major international initiatives including the Kimberly Process, Extractive Industries Initiatives, and the Diamond Development Initiatives, as well as some relevant African initiatives concerning the governance and management of natural resources. This is a very important contribution considering that until recently natural resources were rarely perceived as a threat to human security, a fact explaining the virtual non-existence of such views as offered here by Alao.

The threat posed by unconscionable exploitation of natural resources in Africa has worsened with the incidence of those who carry out such exploitation offshore. Piracy both of natural resources such as oil (as in Nigeria) and maritime commodities (as is typical in Somalia and much of East Africa) has become a major threat to human security in Africa. Efthymios Papastavridis's contribution in Chapter 7 tackles the problem of piracy in Africa. Using the case of East Africa, he provides a solid legal analysis of the issue. This chapter considers the many initiatives aimed at dealing with piracy in Africa and highlights the serious shortcomings of those efforts. Papastavridis argues that the threat to food security is one of the prime reasons why many Somalis engage in piracy and why locals ironically see pirates as guarantors of their security. Consequently, the author takes the view that the problem of piracy cannot be solved on the basis of maritime interdiction alone, but by considering the level of protection afforded human security in the region as a whole.

One major consequence of food shortage, environmental insecurity, SALW, etc is the eventual resort to armed conflicts. And once these erupt, they create a situation in which many flee from their homes into refugee camps mostly provided by international humanitarian agencies. Ideally people fleeing their homes and seeking refuge in international camps should enjoy a decent level of security to their person and lives. In Chapter 8, Maria O'Sullivan shows clearly that this is not always the case. Apart from refugees suffering ignominy in temporary camps, their plight is worsened by the inadequate international legal and policy frameworks to address their situation. The problem of refugees stands out as one of the most vicious threats to human security in Africa. While there are several threats to refugees' security, and the existence of refugees also constitutes a threat to state security, one common underlying issue remains, whether the strategies adopted by the various organs responsible for implementing the relevant frameworks relating to refugee problems are effective. O'Sullivan demonstrates the failures of the various legal frameworks and international strategies to address the problems. In addition to recognizing the ubiquity of refugee problems, the chapter also identifies the particularities (and peculiarities) of the African refugee problem and its human security challenges. To the question 'what are the implications of recent UNHCR-led initiatives for human security of refugees within Africa', O'Sullivan offers no easy or simplistic answers.

In Chapter 9, Manisuli Ssenyonjo undertakes a critical and comprehensive survey of the various challenges to women's security. Arguing that the threat to women's security is universal, Ssenyonjo states that although human rights might grant similar rights to women as to men, such as the right to education, this does not necessarily translate to addressing their insecurity of equal wages and professional opportunities. Also, the chapter discusses certain culturally harmful practices against women which undermine the efficacy of human rights regimes in this aspect. The richness of this chapter lies mostly in the breadth of its coverage and the depth of its analysis.

The final chapter in this part deals with an issue which is, by far, the most difficult threat to human security in Africa to tackle. In Chapter 10, Ebenezer Durojaye discusses corruption as a threat to human security in Africa. Such is the viciousness of this threat, and the seeming potency of its immunity to solutions, that it is now almost regarded as a culture in Africa. Durojaye's analyses remarkably demonstrate why corruption is perhaps the worst threat to human security in Africa, as well as why, despite several international and national legal instruments, all efforts to eradicate corruption have borne little fruit. He offers practical and pragmatic suggestions about dealing with the issue.

5.2 Part II

Legal and policy instruments mean nothing without strong and viable institutions to articulate, implement, and apply them. Regional organizations, institutions, and actors, such as the African Union and sub-regional organizations, the African Commission on Human and Peoples' Rights, the African Court of Human and Peoples' Rights, as well as the Civil Society Organizations, play crucial roles in the promotion of human security, as well as in protecting and giving redress to people when their security is threatened or violated. In Part II, the roles of different institutions and organizations vis-à-vis human security in Africa come under scrutiny.

Ademola Abass discusses the role of African regional organizations in protecting African people's security in Chapter 11. He engages this theme from the premise of the nascent African Peace and Security Architecture (APSA). In particular, Abass discusses whether APSA presents a more effective framework for African regional organizations to protect the security of Africans in conflict situations. Using the examples of the African Union, South African Development Community (SADC), and the InterGovernmental Authority for Development

(IGAD), and focusing on the conflicts in Zimbabwe and Kenya (regions where SADC and IGAD are active, respectively) Abass considers whether a greater cooperation regime between the African Union and sub-regional organizations now exists, or will exist in Africa, as anticipated by APSA. He also considers the implications of the African Union's implementation of its declaration against unconstitutional changes of government—under which it suspended Mauritania, Guinea, and Niger from its membership between 2009 and 2010—on the organization's human security agenda.

In the three following chapters—12, 13, and 14—Gino Naldi, Obiora Chinedu Okafor, and Rachel Murray examine the roles of the African Court of Human and Peoples' Rights, the African Commission of Human and Peoples' Rights, and non-governmental organizations (NGOs) and civil society organizations (CSOs), vis-à-vis the human security agenda in Africa.

Gino Naldi's chapter on the African Court of Human and Peoples' Rights considers the efforts to make the African court champion the protection of human rights and human security. The history of the establishment of this court is long and chequered. Naldi's analysis of the various provisions of the protocol establishing the court and the merging of the court with the African Court of Justice makes a compelling case for the use of regional judicial mechanisms to protect human security. This chapter is critical considering that it was only in July 2008 that African states adopted the protocol that merged the two distinct courts that were proposed by two different protocols to deal with the issue of human rights and justice in Africa. The uncertainty generated by the potential merger led to concerns that both courts might be abolished or that only the court without human rights jurisdiction might be allowed to remain. This concern was not unfounded if one considers the general reluctance of most African leaders to have their human rights records scrutinized by courts of any kind. The merging of the two courts in 2008 was therefore a rare victory (at least for now) for human rights/human security in Africa. Naldi's chapter will be one of the first comprehensive accounts of the role to be played by this august court in protecting human security in Africa.

Before the emergence of the African Court of Human and Peoples' Rights, there was (and there still is) the African Commission on Human and Peoples' Rights. This is the premier institution for advancing human rights in Africa. Although much has been written about how dismally this institution has performed since its inception, Obiora Chinedu Okafor's chapter takes the matter further in some important respects. He develops the argument that contrary to the way in which it has generally been imagined in the dominant collective human security literature, the African Commission is, by design and in terms of its institutional practice, an important collective human security resource in Africa. He argues that adherence to the human security approach (as the central basis of collective human security thinking and action) is one way of reversing this historical deficiency in the relevant academic and institutional literature. The human security embrace of, and focus on, the enjoyment of a broad range of human rights renders most palpable the relevance—and indeed centrality—of multilateral institutions such as the African Commission to our contemporary collective human security praxis.

Rachel Murray's chapter, in logical sequence to Okafor's, inquires into the role of NGOs in the African human rights mechanisms and their contribution to the development of standards on human security issues. She examines how NGOs influence the work of the African Human Rights Commission. Hence, whereas Okafor is concerned with how the Commission serves as a collective human security resource, Murray demonstrates how CSOs help the Commission in shaping its objectives and goals. Both chapters, however, show clearly the link between the African Human Rights Commission and the African Court of Human Rights, a link that is all the more important considering the ongoing debate about whether the emergence of the African Court has put paid to the life of the African Human Rights Commission.

6. Part III

In Chapter 15, Abass draws together all the major themes and questions raised in the previous chapters and captures the relevance of these themes to the overarching purpose of the book. In particular, Abass selects certain issues which may adversely affect international efforts to combat some of the threats to human security discussed in the book—for instance, underscoring the irony of certain Western states whose forces are currently fighting pirates off the Somali coast while some of those states are engaged in illegal fishing inside Somali waters. Abass also takes issue with the African Union which always remains silent in the face of tyranny by some of its members but then is quick to declare as unconstitutional military coups that overthrow such dictatorial governments. He advocates a more balanced and transparent approach to protecting human security in Africa.

I

OF CERTAIN THREATS TO HUMAN SECURITY IN AFRICA

2

Food Security in Africa

Opeoluwa Badaru*

1. Human security and food security

The evolution of human security as a new security paradigm has been sufficiently analysed in the first chapter of this book and therefore does not merit repeating here. It suffices to note, however, that one of the components of the emerging concept of security is food security[1] which forms the focus of this chapter. The idea and emerging norm of food security will be examined in the context of Africa and, to this end, the chapter is organized into six sections. It begins with an elaboration of the concept of food security. This will be followed by an evaluation of the state of food insecurity in Africa. Thereafter, an analysis of some of the legal, policy and institutional frameworks addressing food insecurity in Africa will be undertaken.

2. An understanding of food security

The notion of food security has evolved considerably over time. It is estimated that there are approximately 200 definitions and 450 indicators of food security.[2] The reason for the diversity of meanings attached to food security is not far-fetched. It is primarily because the concept lends itself as an object of study in diverse subject fields and also coincides with different sectors of national policy.[3] Nonetheless, one understanding of food security that is generally agreed upon in the literature is that proffered by the Food and Agricultural Organization

* PhD Candidate, Osgoode Hall Law School, York University, Toronto, Canada. LLM (University of Pretoria, South Africa); LLB (Hons) (University of Ibadan, Nigeria). I would like to thank Professor Ademola Abass for inviting me to write this chapter, and Professor Obiora Okafor for his helpful comments and suggestions.
[1] *United Nations Development Programme (UNDP), Human Development Report 1994* (New York: Oxford University Press, 1994) (hereinafter 'HDR 1994'), 24. See also JF Jones, 'Human Security and Social Development' (2004) 33 Denv J Int'l L & Pol'y 92, 100–1.
[2] C Sage, 'Food Security' in EA Page and M Redclift (eds), *Human Security and the Environment: International Comparisons* (Cheltenham: Edward Elgar, 2002), 129.   [3] Ibid.

(FAO)[4] in the Rome Declaration on World Food Security and World Food Summit Plan of Action. Therein, it was stated that:

Food security exists when all people, at all times, have physical and economic access to sufficient, safe and nutritious food to meet their dietary needs and food preferences for an active and healthy life.[5]

Thus, food security implies that all people, from the level of individual households to the level of the world as a whole, should be able to *access* food (in physical and economic terms) at *all times*. Not only should food be accessible, but it should be *sufficient*, *safe*, and *nutritious*, and must also cater to the *dietary needs* and *preferences* of the individual household. Consequently, food security implies that it is not sufficient that there is enough food to go round the whole world. People must have ready access to food as qualified above, either by growing it themselves, by buying it, or through a public food distribution system.[6] It is now an accepted fact that although the availability of food is a necessary condition for food security, it is undoubtedly not sufficient as people can still starve during famines, even when sufficient food is available, if they cannot access the available food.[7] This means that people may be *food insecure* in the midst of available food. Food insecurity may thus not be caused by the failure to produce food, but rather by the failure of livelihood systems to guarantee sufficient access to it.[8]

The above elucidation of the FAO-preferred meaning of 'food security' points to one of several important components within the concept of food security. First, food security is primarily concerned with access to food. To be food secure, households should have the resources necessary to access the food they need for consumption and this access may be in the form of income, land, livestock, tools, or labour, depending on whether the household is rural or urban.[9] Secondly, food security has a temporal component. This denotes the fact that for households to be food secure they must not only have access to food but such access must be consistent or reliable.[10] With this temporal component of food secu-

---

[4] The Food and Agricultural Organization of the UN is a specialized agency of the UN founded in 1945 to lead international efforts to defeat hunger. See HM Haugen, *The Right to Food and the TRIPS Agreement* (Leiden: Martinus Nijhoff, 2007), 116.

[5] FAO, Rome Declaration on World Food Security and World Food Summit Plan of Action, para 1 (hereinafter 'Rome Declaration').

[6] HDR 1994 (see n 1 above) 27. See also K Mechlem, 'Food Security and the Right to Food in the Discourse of the United Nations' in Francis Snyder (dir), *International Food Security and Global Legal Pluralism* (*sécurité alimentaire international et pluralisme juridique mondial*) (Brussels: Bruylant, 2004), 51–2.

[7] A Sen, *Poverty and Famines—An Essay on Entitlement and Deprivation* (Oxford: Oxford University Press, 1983), 1, 45.

[8] M Baro and TF Deubel, 'Persistent Hunger: Perspectives on Vulnerability, Famine, and Food Security in Sub-Saharan Africa' (2006) 35 Annual Review of Anthropology 521, 526.

[9] T Benson, 'Africa's Food and Nutrition Security Situation: Where Are We and How Did We Get Here?', 2020 Discussion Paper 37 (Washington, DC: International Food Policy Research Institute, 2004,) 8 <http://www.ifpri.org/sites/default/files/publications/2020dp37.pdf>.

[10] Ibid.

rity in mind, some authors have classified the various types of food insecurity as including *temporary food insecurity, cyclical food insecurity,* and *chronic food insecurity.*[11] Temporary food insecurity is said to exist when a household is deprived of an adequate diet during some time of the year due to a variety of unanticipated and random factors.[12] Cyclical food insecurity, on the other hand, exists when a household is consistently deprived of an adequate diet at specific times of the year because of reoccurring factors.[13] Lastly, chronic food insecurity is said to exist when a household is deprived of an adequate diet for substantial parts of the year.[14]

A third component of food security that can be gleaned from the definition above is its nutritional aspect. Hence, people should have access not only to any type of food, but one that is safe, sufficient, and nutritious according to their specific dietary needs and preferences. Some authors actually classify this as 'nutrition security',[15] but the discussion of the dichotomy between food security and nutrition security is not within the purview of this chapter. It suffices to acknowledge that food security does have a nutritional aspect, which specifies the type of food necessary for a person to have for an active and healthy life. This understanding of what food insecurity entails and what situations can amount to food insecurity serves as a background for assessing the current situation of food security or insecurity in Africa.

3. Food security in Africa—the facts

According to the FAO, worldwide, a total number of 848 million people suffered from chronic hunger in 2003–05, the period for which the FAO has the most recent complete estimates of undernourishment at the country level.[16] Of this number, sub-Saharan Africa accounted for 25 per cent (212 million) whilst the Near East and North Africa accounted for about 3.9 per cent (33 million).[17] It is estimated that the proportion of people who suffer from hunger in the total population of the world remains highest in sub-Saharan Africa, where one in three persons is chronically hungry.[18] These are grim facts and the only viable conclusion that one can draw from a situation where one in three people is chronically hungry is that such a place is food insecure. Having acknowledged that most countries in Africa are food insecure (of course with some notable exceptions

[11] TP Phillips and DS Taylor, 'Food Insecurity: Dynamics and Alleviation' in JI Hans Bakker (ed), *The World Food Crisis: Food Security in Comparative Perspective* (Toronto: Canadian Scholars' Press, 1990), 64–5. [12] Ibid.

[13] Ibid. [14] Ibid. [15] Benson (see n 9 above) 9.

[16] *The State of Food Insecurity in the World 2008* (Rome: FAO, 2008), 12 (hereinafter 'SOFI 2008').

[17] Ibid. According to the same 2003–05 estimates, the total population of sub-Saharan Africa at the time was 698.3 million while that of the Near East and North Africa was 420 million. See SOFI 2008, 49. [18] Ibid, 12.

such as Nigeria and Ghana),[19] a pertinent question which arises is what historical or current factors converge to place Africa in this precarious position? The answer to this question forms the thrust of the next section of this chapter.

4. The historical and current context of food insecurity in Africa

The current state of food insecurity in Africa did not arise in a vacuum. Food insecurity in Africa has a long and complex history.[20] There are a number of historical and current factors which could explain why many households in Africa are particularly caught in the throes of chronic food insecurity. Some of these factors are discussed below.

4.1 The African environment

Though the African continent is large and its terrain and climate widely variable, one of the challenges it faces is the fact that most of the continent is geologically inactive and hot year-round.[21] As a consequence of this, the soils are highly leached with little plant nutrients and organic material, all leading to low agricultural productivity.[22] Apart from the nature of the African soil, another challenge to the African environment is the pattern of rainfall in many parts of the continent. In many parts of Africa, due to the phenomenon of Intertropical Convergence Zone (ITCZ), rainfall is cyclical or seasonal and is not evenly distributed over the course of the year.[23] These natural resource constraints indeed hinder agricultural productivity in many parts of Africa and could be said to account for some of the food insecurity in Africa. However, a closer analysis of the situation discloses other reasons for food insecurity in Africa, apart from those offered above. For, have such obstacles as identified above not been overcome in some parts of the world with improved skills, techniques, and tools?

4.2 Underdeveloped agricultural sector

In every part of the world, there are likely to be some environmental obstacles that impede agricultural production. What sets regions apart from each other is how their agricultural sectors have innovated techniques to combat the challenges posed by the physical environment. In Africa, one reason why the challenges with

[19] Ibid, 13.

[20] DE Sahn, 'Economic Liberalization and Food Security in Sub-Saharan Africa', in U Kracht and M Schulz (eds), *Food Security and Nutrition: The Global Challenge* (New York: St Martin's Press, 1999), 137.

[21] E Gilbert and JT Reynolds, *Africa in World History: From Prehistory to the Present*, (2nd edn, Upper Saddle River, NJ: Pearson Education, 2008), 16, 19.   [22] Ibid, 19.

[23] DA Livingstone, 'Late Quaternary Climatic Change in Africa' (1975) 6 *Annual Review of Ecology and Systematics* 249, 250–1.

the environment are so pronounced as to have serious adverse effects on food security is the fact that the agricultural sector is, to a large extent, underdeveloped.[24] Technical innovations, such as irrigation and agricultural water management, are not intensively employed in many African countries. And since most crops in Africa are rainfed, the availability of food—and hence, of food security—follows a strongly seasonal pattern.[25] Ironically, the African agricultural sector does have remarkable potential if much more of the available arable land can be utilized.[26] It is actually estimated that only about 10 per cent of the surface area of Africa is used for cultivation when it is actually possible to use up to 13 to 16 per cent.[27] According to the study, Rwanda is the only country in sub-Saharan Africa which may not be able to achieve food self-sufficiency even if all the agricultural and technical possibilities available are used.[28] What these statistics demonstrate is that even with the natural resource limitations that Africa contends with, a developed agricultural sector could at least ensure food availability, which is a crucial but not necessarily sole component of food security.

4.3 The colonial legacy

Food security in Africa suffered a downturn during the colonial era due to several reasons. First, many of the colonial governments emphasized the production of cash crops for export rather than food crops for domestic consumption.[29] This led to food scarcity and by implication, food insecurity. Furthermore, as part of the larger effort to exploit human and natural resources, colonialism often destroyed the indigenous institutions and practices that helped promote food security.[30] Thus, in discussing food insecurity in Africa, the legacy of the colonial period cannot be ignored as one of the factors which explain the current spate of food insecurity. This said, a further question which arises would be why, since the attainment of independence, have countries in Africa not been able to overcome their colonial-era food security challenges? One of the answers to this is the stability or otherwise of such countries; a factor which could impede food security and is discussed in the next section.

4.4 Wars, civil conflict, and political instability

The prevalence of war, civil conflict as well as social and political instability in many parts of Africa is not without its attendant costs to food security in the

---

[24] C Christensen and C Hanrahan, 'African Food Crises: Short-, Medium-, and Long-Term Responses' (1985) 70 Iowa L Rev 1293, 1294. [25] Ibid.
[26] See ML Gakou, *The Crisis in African Agriculture—Studies in African Political Economy* (London: Zed Books, 1987).
[27] T Rauch, 'Food Security in the Context of Global Markets, Agricultural Policy and Survival Strategies of Rural People in Sub-Saharan Africa' in Kracht and Schulz (see n 20 above) 114.
[28] Ibid.
[29] K Abraham, *The Missing Millions: Why and How Africa is Underdeveloped* (Trenton, NJ: Africa World Press, 1995), 4. [30] Sahn (see n 20 above).

region. In fact, one could assert that it is under these situations that food security is most at threat.[31] This is because wars, civil strife, or political instability worsen poverty.[32] This ultimately precludes economic growth and in turn exacerbates food insecurity. For example, the FAO estimates that most of the increase in the number of hungry people in sub-Saharan Africa occurred in the Democratic Republic of Congo (DRC), a single (albeit large) country.[33] There, because of prevalent and persistent conflict, the number of chronically hungry people shot up from 11 million in 1990–92 to 43 million in 2003–05 and the number of undernourished rose from 29 per cent to 76 per cent.[34] In addition, food insufficiency may not only be the result of conflict alone; it may actually itself be an instrument employed in conflict-ridden areas.[35] Thus, situations of wars, civil conflict, and political instability account for some of the reasons for perennial food insecurity in Africa.

4.5 Poverty and economic crises

It is almost trite to assert that economic powerlessness is a crucial cause of food insecurity (especially of a lack of access to food), particularly in the context of Africa.[36] As with everywhere in the world, poverty is one of the major causes of hunger and malnutrition.[37] It is estimated that approximately half the people in sub-Saharan Africa live below the international poverty line, a percentage higher than any other region in the world.[38] Poor people have tremendous difficulty accessing adequate food. Poverty and economic crises thus constitute a major causative factor for the state of food insecurity in Africa.

4.6 Rising food prices

Another plausible explanation for the state of food insecurity in Africa is the current trend of rising food prices. In recent times, every region of the globe has had to deal with an inordinate rise in the cost of food, sometimes leading to protests and riots.[39] The causes of the rise in food prices have been identified to include, among others, stock levels and market volatility, production shortfalls, increase

---

[31] Sage (see n 2 above) 141.   [32] Benson (see n 9 above) 41.   [33] SOFI 2008, 13.
[34] Ibid.
[35] J Clover, 'Food Security in Sub-Saharan Africa' (2003) 12(1) African Security Review 9.
[36] Baro and Deubel, n 8 above.
[37] G Kent, *The Political Economy of Hunger: The Silent Holocaust* (New York: Praeger, 1984), 77.
[38] Clover (see n 35 above). See also D Moyo, 'The Future of Food: Elements of Integrated Food Security Strategy for South Africa and Food Security Status in Africa' (2007) 101 ASIL PROC 103, 106.
[39] E Malkin, 'Thousands in Mexico City Protest Rising Food Prices', *New York Times*, 1 February 2007 <http://www.nytimes.com/2007/02/01/world/americas/01mexico.html?scp= 1&sq=Thousands%20in%20Mexico%20City%20Protest%20Rising%20Food%20 Prices&st=cse>; Reuters, 'Protests Over Food Prices Paralyze Haitian Capital', *The Epoch Times*, 8 April 2008 <http://www.theepochtimes.com/news/8-4-8/68855.html>; L Peabody, 'Rising Food Prices, Rising Food Protests' (Food First/Institute for Food and Development Policy, 11 April 2008) <http://www.foodfirst.org/en/node/2086>.

in petroleum prices, the emerging demand for biofuel, as well as increased consumption in places such as China and India.[40] As a result of these factors, food prices—which have been on the rise since 2000—peaked in early 2008.[41] It is estimated that the prices of food commodities worldwide increased by 130 per cent from January 2002 to June 2008.[42] There are also indications that these prices may remain for another ten years.[43] Though a worldwide cause for concern, the effects of the rising food prices have been particularly acute in Africa because they obviously exacerbate an already dire food security situation.[44]

4.7 Land grabs

Another recent factor which could exacerbate food insecurity in Africa (and which, to some extent, is a consequence of the recent global food crisis) is the new wave of *land grabs*. Land grabs refer to the current phenomenon whereby rich countries and companies from around the world outsource food production by the acquisition of farmland abroad through purchases or leases.[45] Though the idea of land grab is not entirely new (in that it is reminiscent of the kind of land exploitation carried out during the colonial period),[46] what is more worrisome is the blatant nature and the massive scale of these recent grabs.[47] With particular reference to Africa, the land grabbers have included the governments and private sector companies of some rich countries (a few in Africa but mostly from other continents) such as Saudi Arabia, Bahrain, China, South Korea, United Arab Emirates, India, Jordan, Libya, and Egypt.[48] The target countries in Africa have included Ethiopia, Sudan, Eritrea, Liberia, Senegal, Uganda, Mozambique, Tanzania, Cameroon, and Zimbabwe.[49] Recently, a South Korean company failed in its attempt to lease

---

[40] SOFI 2008, 9–11.

[41] Overseas Development Institute, 'Rising Food Prices: A Global Crisis', ODI Briefing Paper 37, April 2008 <http://www.odi.org.uk/resources/download/1009.pdf>.

[42] N Lustig, 'Coping with Rising Food Prices: Policy Dilemmas in the Developing World' (2009) Center for Global Development Working Paper No 164 < http://ssrn.com/abstract=1392424>.

[43] Overseas Development Institute, 'Rising Food Prices: A Global Crisis', ODI Briefing Paper 37, April 2008 <http://www.odi.org.uk/resources/download/1009.pdf>.

[44] See P Moszynski, 'East Africa Faces Starvation as Rising Food Prices Worsen Effect of War and Drought' (2008) 336 BMJ 1211. See also X Diao et al, 'Accelerating Africa's Food Production in Response to Rising Food Prices: Impacts and Requisite Actions' (2008) International Food Policy Research Institute (IFPRI) Discussion Paper 00825 <http://www.ifpri.org/sites/default/files/publications/ifpridp00825.pdf>, 1–3. In addition, see AA Adesina, 'Africa's Food Crisis: Conditioning Trends and Global Development Policy', Paper presented at the International Association of Agricultural Economists Conference, Beijing, 2009. <http://ageconsearch.umn.edu/bitstream/53199/2/Adesina%20final.pdf>, 1–3.

[45] 'Seized! The 2008 Land Grab for Food and Financial Security', GRAIN Briefing October 2008 <http://www.ifpri.org/sites/default/files/publications/ifpridp00825.pdf>.

[46] Refer to the 'Colonial legacy' discussion above in Section 4.3 of this chapter.

[47] 'Buying Farmland Abroad: Outsourcing's Third Wave' *The Economist*, 21 May 2009 <http://www.economist.com/world/international/displayStory.cfm?story_id=13692889>.

[48] A comprehensive list is provided by GRAIN in the annex to its Briefing. See 'Seized! GRAIN Briefing Annex The 2008 Land Grabbers for Food and Financial Security' <http://www.grain.org/briefings_files/landgrab-2008-en-annex.pdf>.   [49] Ibid.

1.3 million hectares of land in Madagascar but not before the potential deal had caused a major political turmoil in that country.[50] The problem with these land grabs is that they have the potential of undermining small-scale farming and rural livelihoods, especially where the target governments arbitrarily acquire customary lands for the purpose of leasing them to investors.[51] To imagine that land in African countries such as Ethiopia and Sudan—which are themselves in constant need of international food aid—could be resorted to for the production of food for export consumption would seem paradoxical.

The factors discussed above are, however, not the only issues affecting food security in Africa. There are, in fact, quite a number of other major factors that can only be mentioned but not discussed in depth in this chapter. These factors include the following: the high population growth rates in Africa relative to available land for growing food (which factor is discussed by Professor Ilias Bantekas in linking population density and conflict in Chapter 3 below);[52] the unfair and inequitable nature of globalization and international trade which act as market access barriers to products from Africa, thereby limiting the accrual of revenue to farmers;[53] prevalent gender inequality and low literacy levels (which are quite important because of the important role empowered and educated women can play in accessing resources to ensure the adequate nutrition of children under their care);[54] the prevalence of diseases such as malaria and HIV/AIDS, which limit the productivity of people affected,[55] and also the negative effects of food aid to Africa (which can enhance food crisis situations by undermining the capacity of people to search independent coping strategies to deal with the crisis and instead increasing their dependency on food aid).[56]

Having identified some of the factors responsible for food insecurity in Africa, the next task is to discuss some of the legal, policy, and institutional frameworks that are applicable within Africa in the area of food insecurity.

5. Legal frameworks for addressing food insecurity in Africa

There are a series of legal frameworks applicable to the issue of food security in Africa. Some of these frameworks exist in the form of provisions enshrined in

---

[50] 'Madagascar leader axes land deal', BBC News, 19 March 2009 <http://news.bbc.co.uk/2/hi/africa/7952628.stm>.   [51] See GRAIN Briefing (n 45 above).
[52] Chapter 3, 'Environmental Security in Africa'. See also KM Leisinger, 'Biotechnology in Third World Agriculture: Some Socio-economic Considerations' in Kracht and Schulz (see n 20 above) 483. In addition, see M Rukuni, 'Africa: Addressing Growing Threats to Food Security' (2002) Journal of Nutrition 3443S, 3443S–3444S.
[53] C Breining-Kaufmann, 'The Right to Food and Trade in Agriculture' in T Cottier, J Pauwelyn, and EB Bonanomi, *Human Rights and International Trade* (Oxford: Oxford University Press, 2005), 341–81.   [54] Benson (see n 9 above) 54–6.
[55] Moyo (see n 38 above) 107. See also A de Waal and J Tumushabe, *HIV/AIDS and Food Security in Africa: A Report for DFID*, 1 February 2003.   [56] Rauch (see n 27 above) 116.

legal instruments, originating at both the international and regional levels. Some of these pertinent legal instruments are discussed below.

5.1 Universal Declaration of Human Rights 1948

One of the foremost international legal instruments addressing food security is the Universal Declaration of Human Rights (UDHR), which was adopted by the General Assembly of the UN as a non-binding resolution on 10 December 1948.[57] Though only a few African countries were members of the UN at the time of the adoption of the UDHR, all 53 African countries are currently members of the UN.[58] The UDHR does not directly mention food security in its provisions but it addresses the basic need for access to food as a right in Article 25(1). This article provides that:

Everyone has the right to a standard of living adequate for the health and well-being of himself and of his family, including food, clothing, housing and medical care and necessary social services, and the right to security in the event of unemployment, sickness, disability, widowhood, old age or other lack of livelihood in circumstances beyond his control.

To this extent, the UDHR expresses the right to food in the context of the right to an adequate standard of living. Bearing in mind that this provision is applicable to all African countries, a pertinent query is the extent to which it has succeeded in addressing food insecurity in Africa. In order to answer this question, an examination of the nature of the UDHR is necessary.

At its adoption, the UDHR was meant to pave the way for more detailed treaties that would be submitted to states for ratification.[59] By itself, the UDHR is a declaration which is not binding on parties to it and therefore lacks the formal authority of a treaty.[60] A treaty would ordinarily be understood as a source of legal obligation,[61] but a declaration is defined by the UN to be an instrument 'suitable for rare occasions when principles of great and lasting significance are being enunciated'.[62] As a declaration, the UDHR has no doubt been a success considering its widespread popularity as the foundation of human rights. Not only does it exert a moral, political, and legal influence worldwide,[63] it has also birthed a number of human rights and influenced the inclusion of human

---

[57] Universal Declaration of Human Rights (adopted 10 December 1948) UNGA Res 217A (III) (UDHR).

[58] The list of members of the UN is available at <http://www.un.org/members/list.shtml>.

[59] HJ Steiner, P Alston, and R Goodman, *International Human Rights in Context: Law, Politics, Morals: Text and Materials* (3rd edn, Oxford: Oxford University Press, 2008), 136.   [60] Ibid.

[61] H Thirlway, 'The Sources of International Law' in MD Evans (ed), *International Law* (2nd edn, Oxford: Oxford University Press, 2006), 119.

[62] 'Memorandum by the Office of Legal Affairs on the use of term "declaration" and "recommendation"', 34 UN ESCOR, Supp (No 8) 15, UN Doc E/CN.4/L.610 (1962).

[63] H Hannum, 'The Status of the Universal Declaration of Human Rights in National and International Law' (1995–1996) 25 Ga J Int'l & Comp L 287, 289.

rights in many constitutions that have been drafted since the end of the Second World War.[64]

However, it was not intended that the UDHR should have legal force, but to possess moral and political force.[65] To this extent, it remains soft law—only of persuasive authority—and this fact is especially obvious from its Preamble where states proclaimed the declaration mainly as a 'common standard of achievement for all peoples and all nations'.[66] The UDHR therefore has no interpretative or enforcement mechanism. While it is now accepted that some of the provisions of the UDHR have attained the status of customary international law,[67] it is instructive to note that as concerning the right to adequate standard of living, including the right to food, this is yet to be the case.[68] Based on the apparent limitations of the UDHR specifically as it concerns the right to food, it cannot constitute an adequate legal framework for ensuring the right to food, or indeed food security in Africa. It is, however, one useful tool in the repertoire of resources available to those who may wish to struggle for the protection of food security on the continent.

5.2 International Covenant on Economic, Social and Cultural Rights 1966

Another international legal instrument which touches upon food security is the International Covenant on Economic, Social and Cultural Rights (ICESCR), which was adopted by the General Assembly on 16 December 1966 and entered into force on 3 January 1976.[69] Though, as with the UDHR, it does not directly mention food security, it specifically expatiates upon the right to food in its provision. Article 11 provides that:

1. The States Parties to the present Covenant recognize the right of everyone to an adequate standard of living for himself and his family, including adequate food, clothing and housing, and to the continuous improvement of living conditions. The States Parties will take appropriate steps to ensure the realization of this right, recognizing to this effect the essential importance of international co-operation based on free consent.

---

[64] EF Defeis, 'Universal Declaration of Human Rights: A Standard for States' (2004) 28 Seton Hall Legis J 259, 267.

[65] A Cassese, *International Law* (2nd edn, Oxford: Oxford University Press, 2005), 381.

[66] See Preamble to the UDHR.

[67] See, eg, *Filartiga v Pena-Irala* 630 F 2d 876, 882 (2d Cir, 1980). See also International Council on Human Rights Policy, *Duties sans Frontières: Human Rights and Global Social Justice* (Geneva: ICHRP, 2003), 30–1 (hereinafter 'ICHRP').

[68] See S Skogly, *The Human Rights Obligations of the World Bank and the International Monetary Fund* (London: Routledge-Cavendish, 2001), 123. See also P Overby, 'The Right to Food' (1990) 54 Saskatchewan L Rev 19, 27.

[69] ICESCR (adopted 16 December 1966, entered into force 3 January 1976) 993 UNTS 3.

2. The States Parties to the present Covenant, recognizing the fundamental right of everyone to be free from hunger, shall take, individually and through international co-operation, the measures, including specific programmes, which are needed:

    (a) To improve methods of production, conservation and distribution of food by making full use of technical and scientific knowledge, by disseminating knowledge of the principles of nutrition and by developing or reforming agrarian systems in such a way as to achieve the most efficient development and utilization of natural resources;

    (b) Taking into account the problems of both food-importing and food-exporting countries, to ensure an equitable distribution of world food supplies in relation to need.

This detailed provision not only recognizes the right to food but also encompasses specific recommendations on what can be done to combat food insecurity. Of itself, the ICESCR is a success when compared to the hortatory aspirations of the UDHR. By incorporating the basic elements of food security in a binding legal framework, the ICESCR provides another useful tool. Not only is the treaty binding, it also has a monitoring mechanism in the Committee on Economic, Social and Cultural Rights (CESCR), which is empowered to examine state reports and interpret the provisions of the Covenant through its General Comments.[70] Hence, at face value, this duty-bearing instrument seems to hold a lot of potential for food security in the world, including Africa.

However, there are several issues with the ICESCR which have limited its utility in practical terms. First, there is no immediacy to the realization of the rights, and the obligations of states are limited to the constraints of their resources.[71] In its General Comment 12 the CESCR underscored this fact by stating that states have a margin of discretion on how best to realize the right to food in their countries.[72] Nonetheless, it attempted to minimize the negative implication of this entitlement by emphasizing that states have a minimum core obligation to mitigate and alleviate hunger as provided for in Article 11(2).[73]

Other critiques of the ICESCR framework are that its normative and institutional aspects were totally neglected in practice.[74] This critique implies that the normative standards on the right to food were vague and needed further clarification. In order to remedy this shortfall, and specifically to link the right to food to national food security, the Council of the FAO of the UN adopted the *Voluntary*

---

[70] The CESCR was established under ECOSOC Resolution 1985/17 of 28 May 1985 to carry out the monitoring functions assigned to the UN Economic and Social Council (ECOSOC) in Part IV of the ICESCR.

[71] See Article 2(1). See also D Marcus, 'Famine Crimes in International Law' (2003) 97 AJIL 245, 249.

[72] UN Committee on Economic, Social and Cultural Rights, General Comment No 12 (1999), UN Doc E/C/12/1999/5, para 21.   [73] Ibid, 6.

[74] P Alston, 'International Law and the Human Right to Food' in P Alston and K Tomasevski (eds), *The Right to Food* (Utrecht: Netherlands Institute of Human Rights (SIM), 1984), 9.

Guidelines in November 2004.[75] The objective of the Guidelines is to provide practical guidance to states in their implementation of the progressive realization of the right to adequate food in the context of national food security. However, considering the fact that they are voluntary guidelines, their utilization and effectiveness for ensuring food security is highly contingent.

Apart from the critique of the normative vagueness of the ICESCR, the institutional aspect was criticized because until very recently it had no individual complaints mechanism like its counterpart treaty, the International Covenant on Civil and Political Rights (ICCPR).[76] This institutional neglect is being remedied: on 10 December 2008, the General Assembly unanimously adopted an Optional Protocol to the International Covenant on Economic, Social and Cultural Rights.[77] Upon the entry into force of the Protocol,[78] the Committee will have the competence to receive and consider individual and group communications.[79] This is instrumental because it means that people may be able to hold their governments accountable for persistent food insecurity. Furthermore, subject to a state recognizing the competence of the CESCR to that effect, the CESCR will be able to entertain inter-state communications,[80] as well as to investigate grave and systematic violations of the ICESCR.[81] Additionally, and quite important regarding the achievement of food security in Africa, the CESCR will be able to foster international assistance and cooperation in order to assist states parties achieve progress in implementing the rights recognized in the Covenant.[82] This is such that the Optional Protocol even establishes a Trust Fund to help build national capacities in the area of economic, social, and cultural rights.[83] These are very good signs that despite its weaknesses,[84] the right to food as provided for in the ICESCR could emerge as a veritable tool for ensuring food security in Africa. This is, however, subject to the enforcement limitation which besets many aspects of international law.

5.3 Universal Declaration on the Eradication of Hunger and Malnutrition 1974

In 1974, the General Assembly of the UN convened a World Food Conference in Rome which adopted the Universal Declaration on the Eradication of Hunger

---

[75] Food and Agricultural Organization of the UN, 'Voluntary Guidelines to support the progressive realization of the right to adequate food in the context of national food security' (Rome, 2005).

[76] MJ Dennis and DP Stewart, 'Justiciability of Economic, Social, and Cultural Rights: Should there be an International Complaints Mechanism to Adjudicate the Rights to Food, Water, Housing, and Health?' (2004) 98 AJIL 462, 462–3.

[77] Optional Protocol to the International Covenant on Economic, Social and Cultural Rights (adopted 10 December 2008), UNGA Res A/RES/63/117.

[78] In line with Art 18, the Optional Protocol requires ten ratifications to enter into force.

[79] Art 2.   [80] Art 10.   [81] Art 11.   [82] Art 14.   [83] Ibid.

[84] K Tomasevski, 'Human Rights Indicators: The Right to Food as a Test Case' in Alston and Tomasevski (see n 74 above). See also S Narula, 'The Right to Food: Holding Global Actors Accountable under International Law (2006) 44 Colum J Transnat'l L 691, 774–5.

and Malnutrition (UDEHM).[85] This Conference was convened following the food scarcities and famines that had overwhelmed a number of developing countries, including many countries in Africa.[86] In terms of the weight to be attached to this Declaration (as with any other declaration in international law), it is instructive to note that it did not include legal obligatory statements per se but it proclaimed the right of every person 'to be free from hunger and malnutrition'.[87] This restatement of the right to food was particularly helpful at the time because the ICESCR had not entered into force. What is however the most successful proclamation of the UDEHM was the repeated calls to developed countries to avail developing countries the financial and material resources needed to improve food security.[88] In 1977, this call led to the establishment of the International Fund for Agricultural Development (IFAD), as a specialized agency of the UN addressing agriculture and rural poverty.[89] The IFAD seems to be fulfilling the purpose of the UDEHM and making progress towards its mandate. By 1980, it had provided 60 loans to the tune of US$870.2 million to 48 developing countries, 22 of which are in Africa.[90] As recently as April 2009, the IFAD approved a total of US$85.93 million to fund several projects related to food security in Africa. Thus, to the extent that it led to the establishment of IFAD which has to some degree helped to improve agriculture and rural development in Africa, the UDEHM has proven to be a practical legal framework.

5.4 World Food Summit 1996—Rome Declaration on World Food Security and World Food Summit Plan of Action

Another important soft law framework which addresses the issue of food security emerged as a result of the World Food Summit. The FAO, with the unanimous endorsement of the UN General Assembly, convened the World Food Summit in Rome from 13–17 November 1996.[91] This was in response to pervasive undernutrition and growing concern about the capacity of agriculture to meet future food needs.[92] The objective of the Summit was 'to renew global commitment at the highest political level to the task of eliminating hunger and malnutrition and to the achievement of sustainable food security for all people'.[93] At the end of

---

[85] EDEMH (adopted 16 November 1974) UN Doc E/CONF. 65/20, para 1.

[86] S Theriault et al, 'The Legal Protection of Subsistence: A Prerequisite of Food Security for the Inuit of Alaska' (2005) 22 Alaska L Rev 35, 36.   [87] Art 1.

[88] Para h and Arts 7 and 10.

[89] P Spitz, 'Investing in the Right to Food' in *The Right to Food in Theory and Practice* (Rome: FAO, 1998).

[90] M Nawaz, 'Legal Aspects of Development Financing in the 1980s: Legal Aspects of Co-financing: The Experience of the International Fund for Agricultural Development' (1982–1983) 32 Am UL Rev 121, 131.

[91] ECOSOC 'Outcome of the World Food Summit, including action to be taken to follow up the outcome at all appropriate levels', UN Doc E/1997/57, A/52/132 (5 May 1997), paras 3 and 5 (hereinafter 'Outcome of WFS').   [92] Ibid, 4.

[93] Ibid, 3.

the Summit, the Heads of Delegation to the Summit—including representatives of some 50 African countries—adopted a composite document titled the Rome Declaration on World Food Security and World Food Summit Plan of Action.[94] One of the most important targets set in this document was to reduce the total number of undernourished people in the world by half by the year 2015.[95] Considering there were between 830 to 840 million undernourished people in the world in 1990–92 (the period to which the estimates cited at the Summit refers), this implies a target of achieving a reduction in the number of undernourished people by at least 20 million every year between 2000 and 2015.[96]

In spite of the limitations inherent in legal effectiveness of declarations in general and their status under international law, the ability of the FAO and UN to convene the World Food Summit and to produce a document adopted by almost 186 countries (though some countries submitted reservations) is quite commendable.[97] To this extent, one can assert that on a general conceptual level, it was a successful meeting. However, the more important assessment is whether this goal is being attained, especially as it concerns Africa. This is where the problem with the Rome Declaration on World Food Security and World Food Summit Plan of Action lies. According to the FAO, because of the current high food prices, the number of chronically hungry people globally rose by 75 million in 2007 to reach 923 million.[98] At 923 million, there are 80 million more undernourished people than in 1990–92, and this makes the task of reducing the number of the undernourished to 420 million by 2015 more difficult.[99] In sub-Saharan Africa, the overall number of undernourished people increased by 43 million.[100] This is not, however, to say that the high food prices were the beginning of the problems of meeting the Summit's targets. Even before the current food price situation, as at 2003–05, well before this crisis, there were 6 million more chronically hungry people in the world than during the Summit baseline period of 1990–92.[101]

It would thus seem that beyond the current high food price crisis, there is a more pertinent problem with the outcome of the Summit, which—it is submitted—is reflective of the long-standing problem with global commitments of this nature. The issue with these types of commitments is that because their implementation is not of an obligatory nature, their success is largely dependent on the political will mustered within individual countries. With respect to African countries, this kind of political will implies that African governments must have the capacity and willingness to translate such policy commitments into specific programmes and actions. Thus, before attempting to foist duties onto governments in Africa, perhaps international organizations should assess whether these countries actually have the physical and human resources needed to carry out these undertakings. It is not enough to convene meetings; it is essential to investigate what

---

[94] FAO (see n 5 above). See also FAO 'Report of the World Food Summit, 13–17 November 1996', WFS 96/REP, Part One.   [95] FAO (see n 5 above).
[96] Clover (see n 35 above) 6.   [97] *Outcome of WFS*, para 21.   [98] SOFI 2008, 4.
[99] Ibid, 6.   [100] Ibid, 12–13.   [101] Ibid, 4.

actions must be taken to ensure that African governments improve the capabilities they require to comply with these commitments.[102]

5.5 United Nations Millennium Declaration 2000

A further international framework initiative which has direct bearing on food security is the UN Millennium Declaration. At the Millennium Summit in September 2000, world leaders adopted the UN Millennium Declaration, committing their nations to a new global partnership to reduce extreme poverty and setting out a series of time-bound targets, with a deadline of 2015.[103] These targets have become known as the Millennium Development Goals (MDGs).[104] The international community, recognizing the links between poverty and hunger, made it a priority issue in the MDGs. Thus, the first MDG (MDG1) is to eradicate extreme poverty and hunger. Under this goal, one of two targets as to what should be halved between 1990 and 2015 is the proportion of people who suffer from hunger.[105] In order to ensure a broad action plan to achieve these goals, the UN Secretary-General and the UNDP launched the Millennium Project to formulate strategies.[106] Within the project are ten task forces that are to devise implementation plans which would allow all developing countries to meet the MDGs. One of these is the Hunger Task Force.[107]

Again, as with the Rome Declaration on World Food Security and World Food Summit Plan of Action, though the Millennium Declaration and the MDGs are not binding under international law, the initiative to gather world leaders to set a crucial target to combat food security is laudable.[108] However, has it been effective in practice in Africa? Having discussed earlier in this chapter the figures from the assessment of the effectiveness of the Rome Declaration on World Food Security and World Food Summit Plan of Action (which is couched virtually the same way as MDG1), it is not necessary to repeat them here. Suffice it to say that in its 2005 Report, the Hunger Task Force itself stated explicitly that Africa is losing the fight against hunger.[109] Once more, the major reasons for the dismal performance of most African states with regard to the implementation of this Declaration are a lack of capacity and political will. As such, there are recent calls for more donor support to enable MDG1 to be realized in

---

[102] Benson (see n 9 above) 5.
[103] UN Millennium Declaration, GA Res 55/2, UN Doc A/RES/55/2 (18 September 2000) (hereinafter '*Millennium Declaration*').
[104] See UN Millennium Project, *About the MDGs,* available at: <http://www.unmillenniumproject.org/goals/index.htm> accessed 5 August 2009.
[105] See UN Millennium Project, *Goals, targets and indicators,* available online <http://www.unmillenniumproject.org/goals/gti.htm#goal1>.   [106] Benson (see n 9 above) 59–60.
[107] Ibid.   [108] Narula (see n 84 above) 789.
[109] UN Millennium Project 2005, 'Halving Hunger: It Can Be Done', Summary version of the report of the Task Force on Hunger, The Earth Institute at Columbia University, New York, 2005, 2 (hereinafter 'Halving Hunger').

Africa.[110] In addition, MDG1 is, at best, soft law. It is not binding, and it is up to African countries to ensure its implementation.[111] As recommended by the Hunger Task Force, countries—especially those in Africa—would have to move from political commitment to action.[112]

5.6 The African Charter on Human and Peoples' Rights 1981

Apart from the international hard and soft law frameworks which address the issue of food security, there are specific legal frameworks and political initiatives at the regional African level. One of these frameworks is the African Charter on Human and Peoples' Rights (Banjul Charter), which is the main regional mechanism for the protection of human rights in Africa.[113] The Banjul Charter was adopted in 1981 by the Assembly of Heads of State and Government of the Organization of Africa Unity (OAU).[114] Unlike the foregoing international human rights instruments, the Banjul Charter is quite progressive in that it incorporates rights and duties. In addition, the fact that all African states, with the exception of Morocco, have either ratified or acceded to this instrument, thereby affirming their obligations to its provisions, also gives added value to its significance as a human rights instrument in Africa. Its shortcoming though is that it makes no explicit mention of the right to food.[115] To make up for this lacuna, the African Commission on Human and Peoples' Rights—which is the monitoring body set up by the Banjul Charter and which is competent to receive individual and group complaints—took a radical measure in its decision in *Social and Economic Rights Action Center and the Center for Economic and Social Rights v Nigeria*.[116] Upon deliberating this Communication, the Commission asserted that the right to food is inseparably linked to the dignity of human beings and is therefore essential for the enjoyment and fulfilment of such other rights as health, education, work, and political participation.

The decision is a noteworthy pronouncement. By reading the right to food into the Banjul Charter, the Commission made a significant contribution to human

---

[110] MDG Africa Steering Group, Achieving the Millennium Development Goals in Africa—Recommendations of the MDG Africa Steering Group June 2008 (New York: UN Department of Public Information, 2008), 7–9.

[111] NJ Udombana, 'Social Rights are Human Rights: Actualizing the Rights to Work and Social Security in Africa' (2006) 39 Cornell Int'l LJ 181, 210–11.   [112] *Halving Hunger*, vi.

[113] African Charter on Human and Peoples' Rights (adopted 27 June 1981, entered into force 21 October 1986) (1982) 21 ILM 58.

[114] GJ Naldi, 'Future Trends in Human Rights in Africa: The Increased Role of the OAU?' in MD Evans and R Murray (eds), *The African Charter on Human and Peoples' Rights: The System in Practice, 1986–2000* (Cambridge: Cambridge University Press, 2002), 5.

[115] D Brand, 'The Right to Food' in D Brand and Christof Heyns (eds), *Socio-Economic Rights in South Africa* (Pretoria: Pretoria University Law Press, 2005), 155.

[116] *The Social and Economic Rights Action Center and the Center for Economic and Social Rights v Nigeria*, Communication No 155/96, Fifteenth Annual Activity Report of the African Commission on Human and Peoples' Rights 2001–2002.

rights jurisprudence.[117] It made the treaty a living law and further advanced the African regional human rights system well ahead of other regional systems, especially in the interpretation and application of social and economic rights.[118] The problem with the Commission lies with the authoritativeness of its decisions. The OAU which adopted the Banjul Charter was based strongly on the principle of non-interference in the affairs of member states.[119] However, the Constitutive Act of the African Union (AU), which succeeded the OAU, permits the AU to intervene in member states in respect of grave circumstances.[120] Thus, even though the Banjul Charter is weakly worded because it does not explicitly mention the right to food, the progressive jurisprudence of the Commission is commendable. What is required is the political will to ensure its effective enforcement.[121] With this in place, the Banjul Charter could emerge as a more potent legal framework to ensure food security in Africa.[122]

6. Policy and institutional initiatives to address food insecurity in Africa

Apart from the legal frameworks discussed above, there are some other policies and institutional initiatives which directly and indirectly address the issue of food insecurity in Africa.

6.1 Structural adjustment programs

The World Bank and the International Monetary Fund (IMF) introduced some of the most important policy frameworks that have to a great extent influenced strategies and programmes for food security in Africa. Foremost among these are the Structural Adjustment Programs (SAPs) and similar neoliberal policies (often referred to as the Washington Consensus).[123] These policies which were mainly in effect during the period ranging from 1980 to 1999 were introduced in a bid to ensure macroeconomic development on the basis that such development would

---

[117] C Downes, 'Must the Losers of Free Trade Go Hungry? Reconciling WTO Obligations and the Right to Food' (2007) 47 Va J Int'l L 619, 673.

[118] D Shelton, 'Decision Regarding Communication 155/96 (Social and Economic Rights Action Center/Center for Economic and Social Rights v Nigeria)' (2002) 96 AJIL 937, 942.

[119] E Bondzie-Simpson, 'A Critique of the African Charter on Human and Peoples' Rights' (1988) 31 How LJ 643, 644.

[120] Art 4(h), Constitutive Act of the African Union (adopted 11 July 2000, entered into force 26 May 2001) OAU Doc CAB/LEG/23.15.

[121] CE Welch, Jr, 'The African Charter and Freedom of Expression in Africa' (1998) 4 Buff Hum Rts L Rev 103, 113.

[122] NJ Udombana, 'Between Promise and Performance: Revisiting States' Obligations under the African Human Rights Charter' (2004) 40 Stan J Int'l L 105, 142.

[123] AI Samatar, 'Structural Adjustment as Development Strategy? Bananas, Boom, and Poverty in Somalia' (1993) 69(1) Economic Geography 25.

trickle down to households and therefore empower people economically, knowing that poverty is a major reason for food insecurity.[124] As a means to improving the balance of payments of a country and to controlling its foreign indebtedness, SAPs encouraged currency devaluation, trade liberalization, reduction in budget deficits, and the size of the public sectors, as well a reduction in government support for social services.[125] Food security was thus nominally addressed by these programs.[126] The question therefore arises whether SAPs and the Washington Consensus effectively addressed food insecurity in Africa.

It was predicted that the implementation of SAPs would have an impact on poverty by fostering economic growth and shifting relative prices in favour of agricultural and rural areas, where most of the poor live.[127] Even if SAPs did promote economic growth (and this is arguable),[128] it has been asserted that what SAPs ultimately did was to exacerbate poverty levels and deepen inequality because they caused increased unemployment, wage restriction, increased food prices, and a reduction in social service programmes by governments.[129] By increasing the vulnerability of the poor, one cannot conclude that SAPs and the Washington Consensus, as policies, were successful as strategies to combat food insecurity in Africa. If anything, one would come to an opposite conclusion.

6.2 Comprehensive Development Framework

In 1999, with growing disaffection against the SAP/Washington Consensus policies, the World Bank embarked on a new policy framework in the guise of the Comprehensive Development Framework (CDF).[130] The objective of the CDF was to have a holistic approach to development—one that will integrate the social, political, environmental, and cultural aspects of a society into its development.[131] With the introduction of the CDF, the World Bank and IMF simultaneously launched a new programme for Highly Indebted Poor Countries (HIPC).[132] The

---

[124] World Bank, *Accelerated Development in Sub-Saharan Africa: An Agenda for Action* (Washington, DC: World Bank, 1981).

[125] NJ Udombana, 'The Summer has Ended and We are Not Saved! Towards a Transformative Agenda for Africa's Development' (2005–2006) 7 San Diego International Law Journal 5, 43.

[126] F Heidhues et al, 'Development Strategies and Food and Nutrition Security in Africa: An Assessment', 2020 Discussion Paper 37 (Washington, DC: International Food Policy Research Institute, 2004), 11.   [127] World Bank (see n 124 above).

[128] CRP Pouncy, 'Stock Markets in Sub-Saharan Africa: Western Legal Institutions as a Component of the Neo-Colonial Project' (2002) 23 U Pa J Int'l Econ L 85, 102.

[129] Samatar (see n 123 above) 41.

[130] The CDF was initiated following several meetings and speeches involving World Bank officials. The need for a new development framework was specifically mentioned in a speech given by the then President of the World Bank. See JD Wolfensohn, 'The Other Crisis: Address to the Board of Governors', 6 October 1998.

[131] J Pender, 'From "Structural Adjustment" to "Comprehensive Development Framework": Conditionality Transformed?' (2001) 22 TWQ 397, 407–8.

[132] L Whitfield, 'Trustees of Development from Conditionality to Governance: Poverty Reduction Strategy Papers in Ghana' (2005) 43 J Mod Afr Stud 641–2.

thrust of this programme is debt relief for some of the poorest countries as long as they formulate their own development strategies through a participatory process and integrate them into their expenditure plan under the guidance of Poverty Reduction Strategy Papers (PRSPs).[133]

The pro-poor thrust of the combination of the CDF, HIPC initiative, and the PRSP policies all seem, at first appearance, to augur well for food security in Africa. It is especially laudable that the World Bank and the IMF responded to the criticisms levelled against SAPs and decided to introduce policies which do not seem top-down but which encouraged the initiatives of the African countries involved. The CDF is especially commendable because the policy envisaged broad stakeholder contributions into the formulation of the PRSPs. However, whether the policies have in fact alleviated food insecurity in practice in most of Africa remains to be seen. Although economic growth for the poor is supposed to underlie the PRSPs, there are criticisms that this is not the case.[134] Furthermore, in writing PRSPs, many countries fail to link food insecurity with poverty; hence, hunger and malnutrition measures are typically absent in the poverty reduction indicators specified for monitoring the progress of the PRSP.[135] Also, while the CDF, PRSP, and HIPC initiatives seem to be a welcome improvement to SAPs, there are assertions that the macroeconomic prescriptions mandated by the World Bank are not only largely similar to earlier stabilization policies but that they are the primary causes of food insecurity in several African countries.[136] With critiques of this nature against the policies under the CDF, it suffices to conclude that there is still room for improvement in order for them to be effective strategies to combat food insecurity in Africa.

6.3 The Lagos Plan of Action

The OAU introduced one of the foremost regional policy initiatives to address food insecurity in Africa. This was done under the Lagos Plan of Action (LPA).[137] The overall objective of the LPA was to foster the economic development of the African continent,[138] but included in the LPA was a chapter on 'Food and Agriculture'.[139] The LPA focused on achieving immediate and long-term food self-sufficiency and advocated the elimination of food imports.[140] At the national level, African

[133] Ibid. See also IMF, Poverty Reduction Strategy Papers (PRSP): A Factsheet, April 2008.
[134] Whitfield (see n 132 above) 657–8.   [135] Benson (see n 9 above) 61.
[136] S Narula (see n 84 above) 716–18.
[137] OAU, Lagos Plan of Action for the Economic Development of Africa, 1980–2000 (OAU, 1981).
[138] J Oloka-Onyango, 'Beyond the Rhetoric: Reinvigorating the Struggle for Economic and Social Rights in Africa' (1995–1996) 26 Cal W Int'l LJ 1, 46–7.
[139] RM D'Sa, 'The Lagos Plan of Action—Legal Mechanisms for Co-operation between the Organisation of African Unity and the United Nations Economic Commission for Africa' (1983) 27 African J Int L 4.
[140] Editorial, 'Africa's Hunger' (1984) 6 TWQ vii, viii. Prior to the LPA, the more technical policy of AFPLAN (Food Plan for Africa) had been approved in 1978 by the OAU Ministers of Agriculture and provided a framework for understanding and improving Africa's agricultural

governments were persuaded to design and implement policies and programmes that would ensure food self-sufficiency while at the intergovernmental level African countries were encouraged to work together to increase food production as well as intraregional and regional trade.[141] What is important to note about the LPA is the fact that unlike the succeeding World Bank and IMF neoliberal policies (SAP and CDF), it placed much emphasis on state control and initiative. This is not surprising considering the fact that it emerged at a point when many newly independent countries in Africa blamed their colonial rulers for the state of the continent and sought to improve the welfare of their people via direct state action.

In evaluating the LPA as a policy designed to alleviate food insecurity in Africa, it would seem that it was quite an excellent proposal at the point of formulation.[142] For the OAU and Africans, the LPA marked an important ideological victory because it was based on a theory of autocentred development that presupposes national control of the economy as opposed to ultra-liberalism.[143] However, whether the policy made for successful implementation at the national level is questionable given the dismal performance of the agricultural sector in many African states during the period for which it was implemented.[144] Some of the provisions of the LPA were largely idealistic and governments could not implement them.[145] The LPA presupposed that African countries had the social and technical capacities to carry through the policy of food self-sufficiency but in practice, this was often not the case.[146] Further, a review of the LPA policy by the World Bank blamed a lack of political will for the limited impact of the implementation of that framework.[147] The poor results of the policy were also attributed to the erstwhile disregard of food production by many African governments, and the slowness or inability of some countries to implement the plans and resolutions under the policy.[148] Overall, the LPA could not sufficiently address the problem of food insecurity in Africa.

6.4 The New Partnership for Africa's Development and Comprehensive Africa Agriculture Development Programme

Moving on from the agenda of the LPA, African leaders sought to address the challenges facing the continent by developing an integrated socio-economic

sector. See FAO, *Report of the Council of FAO*, 87th Session, Rome, 17–28 June 1985, CL 87/REP (FAO, Rome 1985), para 29.

[141] Heidhues et al (see n 126 above) 9.

[142] F Heidhues, 'Africa's Food and Nutrition Security: Where Do We Stand? Successes, Failures, Lessons Learned', CTA Seminar 2004 on the Role of Information Tools in Food and Nutrition Security, Maputo, Mozambique, 8–12 November 2004.

[143] B Founou-Tchuigoua, 'Food Self-Sufficiency: Crisis of the Collective Ideology' in HA Amara and B Founou-Tchuigoua, *African Agriculture: The Critical Choices* (Tokyo: United Nations University Press, 1990).   [144] Heidhues (see n 142 above).

[145] AY Yansané (ed), *Development Strategies in Africa: Current Economic, Socio-Political, and Institutional Trends and Issues* (Westport, CT: Greenwood Press, 1996), 35.   [146] Ibid.

[147] Heidhues (see n 142 above).   [148] Ibid.

framework for Africa. Thus, in July 2001, the 37th Summit of the OAU formally adopted the strategic framework document called the New Partnership for Africa's Development (NEPAD).[149] As concerning food security in Africa, NEPAD, with the assistance of the FAO, developed a detailed Comprehensive Africa Agriculture Development Programme (CAADP).[150]

The CAADP was accepted by African heads of states at the African Union summit in Maputo, Mozambique in July 2003.[151] The main objective of the CAADP initiative is to boost agricultural productivity as a means towards assuring food security.[152] In the CAADP framework, African governments agreed to increase public investment in agriculture to a minimum of 10 per cent of their national budgets, and also to raise agricultural productivity by at least 6 per cent by 2015.[153]

Though implementation of the CAADP is still at its early stages, one question that arises is how much the CAADP has helped to improve food security in Africa in its first six years. On a positive note, the adoption of the CAADP deserves some praise for bringing back agriculture into the African development agenda.[154] The fact that the CAADP is an *African-owned* and *African-led* initiative is also commendable.[155] However, the reliance on donor funding under the auspices of the CAADP Multi-Donor Trust Fund may not ensure that it remains an autonomous policy.[156] Further, on a conceptual level, a criticism of the CAADP is that it would be difficult for its overall objectives to be attained if they are not incorporated into a broader rural development policy.[157]

The CAADP has also encountered some challenges in practice. In a 2006 Progress Report, it was stated that even though 18 countries had already undertaken or were currently actively undertaking major land reforms, the institutional resources for the implementation of reform were often stretched, and maintaining the political momentum necessary to introduce reform was also a challenge.[158] In addition, the Report stated that even though more than one-quarter of arable land in North Africa is irrigated, the overall rate of growth of irrigated land since 1995 in Africa was less than 1 per cent.[159] Thus, there was still much reliance on rainfed agriculture in Africa, a crucial reason for food insecurity in Africa. Most importantly, as regarding one of the ultimate goals of the CAADP—the commitment to allocate at least 10 per cent of national budgets to agriculture—the Report stated that a 2004 survey indicates that the average

---

[149] See NEPAD, *About NEPAD*, available at: <http://www.nepad.org/AboutNepad/sector_id/7/lang/en>. [150] See the CAADP website at: <http://www.caadp.net/>.
[151] Benson (see n 9 above) 60. [152] CAADP (see n 150 above). [153] Ibid.
[154] C Ackello-Ogutu, *CAADP Review*, Fourth CAADP Partnership Platform Meeting, Pretoria, South Africa 26–27 March 2009. [155] Ibid.
[156] CAADP (see n 150 above).
[157] BJ Gemandze, 'The African Union and the Challenge of Rural Development', paper presented at CODESRIA/DPMF Joint Conference, Addis Ababa, Ethiopia, 26–28 January 2004.
[158] Africa Partnership Forum, *Progress Report: Agriculture*, 7th Meeting of the Africa Partnership Forum, Moscow, Russia, 26–27 October 2006, 8. [159] Ibid.

expenditure was at around 3.5 to 4 per cent, indicating only a slight early progress towards this target.[160] It would, therefore, seem that CAADP still requires more effective political will to translate its targets into actualities.[161] An early assessment of the CAADP initiative therefore reveals some of the constant issues that Africa faces with regards to implementing commitments to improve food security in the region. These include a lack of political will to carry through on the commitments, as well as a lack of resources and much reliance on external partners. Again, the capability and willingness of African governments is usually called into question.

7. Improving food security in Africa: the way forward

From the analysis of the factors that cause food insecurity in Africa, several potential answers on what needs to be done emerge. The majority of these answers point to the fact that people need to have *access* to food. The access they need includes physical access (which can be guaranteed through improved agricultural and market systems); economic access (which can be guaranteed through expansion of employment, economic stability, and free and open trade); social access (which can be guaranteed through education, democratic decision making, gender relations improvement, and legal frameworks), as well as physiological access (which can be guaranteed through improved health care and sanitation).[162] Though there have been and there still are legal frameworks, policies and institutions in place to make this access possible, it would seem that by themselves, they may not be able to sufficiently address the issue of food insecurity in Africa. One golden thread, however, binds all that is needed to be done together and this is the need for effective political leadership capable of carrying through the several policies and programmes that could help alleviate food insecurity. Responsibility for ensuring food security lies primarily with the leaders of African countries, who must 'foster the political will, make the decisions, and facilitate the action necessary to remove or mitigate the obstacles to good nutritional status that so many Africans face'.[163] Until there is the political will and wherewithal to carry out these initiatives, they may end up being futile. It would seem that this is actually the starting point of a sustainable solution to the situation of food insecurity in Africa.

---

[160] Ibid.
[161] M Bwalya, *NEPAD-Agriculture 2008–09 Report*, Fourth CAADP Partnership Platform Meeting, Pretoria, South Africa 26–27 March 2009.   [162] Benson (see n 9 above) 44.
[163] Ibid, 46.

3

Environmental Security in Africa

*Ilias Bantekas**

1. Introduction

The term 'environmental security' has been defined as encompassing the availability of environmental services for man and nature.[1] When human societies can feed and stay warm from the resources that nature can provide, any conflicts between such societies will certainly not be rooted in environmental causes, broadly defined. On the contrary, the depletion of a region's natural resources, as well as the destruction of its natural environment through deforestation or soil degradation inevitably brings about resource scarcity. Resource scarcity in turn leads to conflict between contesting groups because the fundamental tenet in the definition of environmental security will have been removed. Equally, the conflict itself leads to further environmental destruction that makes the availability of environmental services scarcer to even more people. This latter result is usually achieved through large-scale forced migration or internal displacement that puts demographic and environmental stress on local resources. Once a conflict erupts, this may subsequently feed into the use of environmental modification techniques as a means of warfare,[2] as well as trigger the looting of mineral resources by warring factions in order to finance the conflict, and the list goes on. Such conflicts are by no means a phenomenon of our era, but have occurred throughout human history.[3]

Although the concept of environmental security has been around for some time, albeit generally employed to describe the impact of conflicts on the

* Professor of International Law, Brunel University School of Law and Head of International Law and Arbitration at Mourgelas & Associates Law Firm.
[1] See NP Gleditsch, 'Environmental Change, Security and Conflict' in CA Crocker et al (eds), *Turbulent Peace: The Challenge of Managing International Conflict* (Washington, DC: US Institute for Peace, 2001), 53ff.
[2] See, eg, 1977 UN Convention on the Prohibition of Military or Any Other Hostile Use of Environment Modification Techniques (adopted 18 May 1977, entered into force 5 October 1978) 1108 UNTS 151.
[3] United National Environment Programme (UNEP), 'Understanding Environment, Conflict and Cooperation' UNEP Doc DEW/0571/NA (2004), 6–7. The authors of the report start as far back as the Peloponnesian war between Athens and Sparta.

environment,[4] until recently, governments had not officially proclaimed the connection between resource scarcity and conflict.[5]

As to be expected, the attitude of states towards addressing threats to environmental security has varied considerably. While some countries are proactive and, it may be argued, more radical in their efforts, some have been less enthusiastic. Resource scarcity as a result of environmental degradation is not only a potential cause of conflict in the traditional sense encompassing armed violence, it is moreover the direct catalyst for all the evils of underdevelopment; including, among others, malnourishment, high child death rates, population movements, and illiteracy. This situation is further compounded by the fact that many African countries can validly be classified as either failed or weak states.[6] Thus, unlike the developed world where the average citizen can generally rely on the state in times of hardship as a matter of social welfare, the average African citizen would not think in those terms.[7] Successive generations of Africans have died of famine, had their mineral resources plundered by authoritarian regimes, and moreover faced brutal repression and harsh dictatorships. Thus, relevant policies must provide an alternative livelihood acceptable to the many hungry and exasperated peoples who have resorted to practices that lead to deforestation with its catastrophic consequences. It is also imperative that this alternative livelihood be sustainable in the long term.

The protection of Africa's fragile environment, however, is not important only in respect of the human security of that continent and the spillover of environmental refugees into other parts of the world. Beyond this obvious calamity, the dense tropical forests of central Africa act as one of the largest natural filters to the carbon dioxide (CO_2) emissions of the world's industrialized nations.[8] If these forests were to disappear this would have an impact not only on the global environment as a whole (since CO_2 would have to be absorbed among others by the

---

[4] See J Lind and K Sturman (eds), *Scarcity and Surfeit: The Ecology of Africa's Conflicts* (RSA Institute for Security Studies 2002); J Barnett, *The Meaning of Environmental Security: Ecological Politics and Policy in the New Security Era* (London: Zed Books, 2001).

[5] See UK Prime Minister's Strategy Unit, 'Countries at Risk of Instability: Future Risks of Instability', PMSU Background Paper No 3 (February 2005), in which environmental security was explicitly mentioned as a future source of serious conflict.

[6] There is no official definition pertaining to weak states, although the Organisation for Economic Co-Operation and Development (OECD) in 2005 launched a 'Fragile States' Initiative in partnership with the World Bank's Low Income Countries under Stress Program. The US Commission on Weak States and National Security has classified as such 50–60 countries on the basis of the following indicators: willingness and ability to provide physical security; legitimate political institutions; economic management; and social welfare. See S Patrick, 'Weak States and Global Threats: Fact or Fiction?' (2002) 29 The Washington Quarterly 27, 28–30.

[7] J Clover, 'Human Centred Environmental Security in Africa' (2005) 14 African Security Review 103.

[8] In a recently published study it was demonstrated that undisturbed forests are absorbing one-fifth of man-made greenhouse gases. The rest is trapped by other forests or stays in the earth's atmosphere. The contribution of Africa is significant if one considers that its rain forests cover 30% of the globe. SL Lewis, 'Increasing Carbon Storage in Intact African Tropical Forests' (2009) 457 Nature 1003.

seas which would turn them acidy and kill remaining fish stocks), but also on the global economy and public health. This fact was recently stressed by African leaders in the context of the 2009 Copenhagen Summit on climate change. They made it clear that if the central African green belt was to remain intact significant funding was required from industrialized nations.

The aim of this chapter is to examine all those elements that bring about environmental insecurity, such as deforestation and land degradation, the role of population densities and pollution of the natural environment that leads to food and resource scarcity. Although these factors are not endemic to Africa, they have been particularly exacerbated in that continent. The chapter will address how the Security Council has dealt with the potential for conflict stemming from Africa's increasing resource scarcity and natural disasters, particularly as a result of desertification[9] and deforestation. This analysis will inform the subsequent discussion as to the more substantive environmental concerns and will provide the reader with some clues as to whether any international action is indeed necessary. The chapter will examine the Darfur crisis as a case study of an environmental conflict, as well as the threats to security and resource scarcity stemming from Africa's illegal exploitation of mineral resources. Given the relevance of climate change to international affairs and the security concerns raised as a result, the chapter will conclude with an assessment of how African nations have dealt with climate change and what use they have made of the Clean Development Mechanism (CDM) in order to rid themselves of carbon-based industries, although Africa is by far the least carbon-polluting continent on the planet. In place of a typical conclusion, the chapter will provide some recommendations to policy makers.

2. UN Security Council concerns over Africa's environmental security

The international community does not fully appreciate the extent of Africa's environmental woes. The EU and the Security Council view their African policies from the viewpoint of 'development' and 'failed local governance' and as a result pay little attention to other less amorphous, but certainly real and rising, issues that have a direct bearing on African security. Environmental degradation and resource scarcity are obvious candidates, particularly given the fact that the Security Council has never before determined that these factors can constitute a threat to international peace and security. On a more practical level, were the

---

[9] The term desertification concerns the deterioration of land through human intervention to such a degree that it leads to loss of vegetation and soil moisture, which are necessary to sustain plant and animal life, not to mention human life. Although climatic variations and changes occurring in the natural environment are contributory factors to this process, desertification comes about principally through excessive river and underwater diversions (or depletions), overgrazing and other evils related to over-population.

Council to identify the link between environment and human security it would also have to undertake concrete actions and allocate resources at a time when these are generally unavailable. This reality probably explains why, although the scientific community has specifically demonstrated the direct links between environmental stresses and the potential for conflict, the UN Security Council has so far chosen, unlike the Secretary-General,[10] to ignore these links in its deliberations regarding peace and security.

The furthest the Council has gone is to concede the links between illegal exploitation of natural resources as a factor exacerbating conflict in the Great Lakes region of central Africa, a theme explored by Abiodun Alao in Chapter 6 below.[11] Nonetheless, the Council did not determine the process of illegal mineral exploitation from the point of view of resource scarcity, being concerned instead with the ramifications of Rwandan and other foreign army incursions into the territory of the Democratic Republic of the Congo (DRC), at a time when it was not capable of controlling and defending the entirety of its territory. Equally, the Council was naturally concerned that the DRC was becoming a haven for paramilitaries and foreign corporations eager to get their hands on the country's mineral wealth, and in the process fuelling violent conflict on its territory.[12]

The Council's 'irritatingly' elaborate references solely to the criminal implications and the narrowly defined security considerations in respect of the Great Lakes and the Darfur conflicts[13] is not likely to change in the very near future. It is not hard to see why the Council has thus far refused to acknowledge the potential for conflict with regard to environmental security, particularly in Africa where it is most acute. For one thing, were the Council to officially acknowledge this link it would have to bring the situation under Chapter VII of the UN Charter. This would then require specifically addressing the situation through concrete means. It is one thing to identify the perpetration of war crimes and the breakdown of security within a state and authorize the dispatch of peacekeepers under a broad mandate to use force, and it is a different thing altogether to

---

[10] Interim report of the Secretary General on the prevention of armed conflict (Report of the Secretary General on the Work of the Organization) UN Doc A/58/365-S/2003/888 (12 September 2003). This was subsequently filtered into the agenda of the Secretary-General's High Level Panel to Study Global Security Threats and Recommend Necessary Changes.

[11] UNSC Res 1698 (31 July 2006) UN Doc S/RES/1698.

[12] This position of the Council was also voiced in previous resolutions, particularly 1291 (24 February 2000) UN Doc S/RES/1291 and 1304 (16 June 2000) UN Doc S/RES/1304, in which it held that illegal mineral exploitation threatened the country's security condition. It therefore moved to act under Chapter VII of the UN Charter.

[13] See UNSC 1861 (14 January 2009) UN Doc S/RES/1861, on Darfur; UNSC Res 1858 (22 November 2008) UN Doc S/RES/1858, on Burundi; UNSC Res 1856 (22 December 2008) UN Doc S/RES/1856, on the DRC; UNSC Res 1828 (31 July 2008) UN Doc S/RES/1828; UNSC Res 1804 (13 March 2008) UN Doc S/RES/1804; UNSC Res 1769 (31 July 2007) UN Doc S/RES/1769. It is instructive that the Council has declined to acknowledge this link even in respect of its annual discussion of the security situation in Africa. See, eg, SC Res 1809 (16 April 2008) UN Doc S/RES/1809.

identify the potential for conflict through an impending environmental disaster. In the latter case, the Council cannot simply authorize the dispatch of a military contingent, but must instead seek to put in place measures that can reverse the effects of deforestation and land degradation. The other obvious reason for the Council's consistent pattern in addressing only particular security issues relates to the actual volatile security considerations on the ground. The Council is only too aware that if it were to link human security with environmental degradation it may be providing an excuse to future plunderers, war lords, and other criminal elements to justify their actions on unavoidable environmental grounds. By way of example, some war lords may claim that the right of their communities to life, or their right to immediate food, requires particular measures of deforestation or environmental modification. While there is some merit in certain of these claims, particularly in respect of their human rights qualities, they cannot be sustained to offer impunity or to deny the environmental degradation of Africa and the planet. These claims by no means set out long-lasting solutions. Nonetheless, these are by no means matters upon which one may find and apply an easy solution, not even the Council.

While acknowledging the practical difficulties inherent in the Council's approach to environmental security, it could at the very least set up an efficient early warning system for environmental issues. At the moment, the UNEP operates such a system, the so-called Initiative on Environment and Conflict Prevention,[14] which does not, however, directly inform the decision-making process of the Security Council. In addition, a collaborative initiative between UNEP, the United Nations Development Programme (UNDP), the North Atlantic Treaty Organisation (NATO), and the Organization for Security and Cooperation for Europe (OSCE) has emerged, with the aim of identifying environmental threats to global security and thereafter dealing with such threats through diplomatic and similar avenues, although at present it does not monitor Africa. This initiative is known as Environmental Security (ENVSEC).[15] Apart from these efforts, a unique project from Swisspeace, the Conflict and Early Warning Response Mechanism (CEWARN), uses a variety of relevant data to forecast conflicts of all types in the Horn of Africa. It is certainly worthwhile for global and regional organizations to take these methodologies into consideration and integrate them in their own security agendas. According to claims, CEWARN has accurately forecasted and prevented pastoral conflicts in Somalia and Uganda.[16] From a regional point of view some more definite steps have been taken, but, it is submitted, the weak governance structures in

[14] See UNEP's Division of Early Warning and Assessment <http://www.unep.org/dewa/index.asp>.

[15] At present, ENVSEC monitors Central Asia and Eastern Europe. See ENVSEC 'The Environment and Security Initiative: An International Partnership for Managing Conflict and Risk' (2006) <http://www.envsec.org/docs/ENVSEC%20Progress%20Report%202006.pdf>.

[16] UNEP 2004 Report (see n 3 above) 44–5.

these countries remain insufficient to carry through the pledges of members.[17] Equally, it is unlikely that most African states possess the resources or the vision to implement programmes of this nature.[18]

3. The links between population density and conflict in Africa and the Darfur crisis as an environmental conflict

High levels of urbanization do not necessarily lead to violent conflict, as is well demonstrated by the experiences of Europe in its post-WW II era. Nonetheless, riots and violent demonstrations have been prevalent in those cities in the developed world suffering from mass unemployment. There are factors, however, that differentiate the European experience from that of Africa. For one thing, European city dwellers do not rely on an agrarian economy for their livelihood and thus are unlikely to turn to mass farming in order to feed their families. Secondly, the apparatus of the State will provide some sort of financial support. Thirdly, the energy needs of such persons will be duly covered by gas, nuclear energy, renewable sources of energy and others, all of which do not place a significant strain on the natural environment. In the African context, demographic stresses are always worrying, because none of the above factors can outweigh reliance on scarce natural resources.

A poignant example of the dangers inherent in imbalanced population densities may be gleaned from the Great Lakes region. The fertile soil of the lands

---

[17] See particularly the 2004 Dar-es-Salaam Declaration on Peace, Security, Democracy and Development in the Great Lakes Region, which recognized the poignancy of environmental security explicitly. Equally, the Nile Basin Initiative is aimed at replacing the Nile Waters Agreement (adopted on 7 May 1929, entered into force on 7 May 1929) 93 LNTS 43, which was far too favourable for Egypt because the agreement was of a bilateral nature (UK–Egypt) and which provided Egypt with exclusive property rights over the Nile's waters, save only for the Sudan among all other riparian states. Sudan is bound by the 1929 Agreement on the basis of a subsequent 1959 Agreement with Egypt on Full Utilization of the Nile's Waters (adopted on 8 November 1959, entered into force on 8 November 1959) 453 UNTS 6519. As a result, it is currently unworkable for the nine current riparian countries. The Nile Basin Initiative aims to diffuse tension between the riparian countries through sustainable socio-economic development and equitable utilization. UNEP 'Africa Assessment: Environmental Conflict and Cooperation in the African Great Lakes Region' (December 2007), 9–11.

[18] This is not mere pessimism. At the African Union (AU) Assembly in July 2003, African heads of state endorsed the Maputo Declaration on Agriculture and Food Security in Africa, which among other things requested African countries to commit themselves to the allocation of at least 10% of national budgetary resources to agriculture and rural development policy implementation within five years. This pledge was further iterated a year later by means of the Sirte Declaration on the 'Challenges of Implementing Integrated and Sustainable Development in Agriculture and Water in Africa'. A high-ranking delegate of the AU recently reported that the implementation of the Maputo Declaration remains modest and only 19 countries have provided compliance data. Three countries are allocating above 10%, (Niger 20.15%, Ethiopia 13.6%, and Chad 11.9%). Four countries are allocating between 5–10% (Tunisia 8.2%, Zimbabwe 6.2%, Swaziland 5.5%, and Sudan 5.4%), with 12 countries allocating below 5%. See RO Olaniyan, 'Statement: An Overview of AU Agricultural and Food Security Program' (2–4 May 2007), 3.

around the Great Lakes have witnessed large influxes of poor internal migrants, some of whom are on the run from neighbouring armed conflicts. Reliable statistics clearly demonstrate that with the exception of Uganda, population density in Rwanda and Burundi is very high. In the Albertine Rift region this amounts to 94.6 people per square kilometre, which is significantly higher than the population density in other parts of sub-Saharan Africa. More worryingly, the population density in lands surrounding protected areas is even higher; 300 per square kilometres in Uganda, as compared to 600 people in certain Rwandan districts.[19] With the exception of Uganda, and, to a lesser degree, the DRC, the statistics reveal a consistently troublesome pattern in respect of deforestation,[20] land degradation,[21] and access to fresh water resources. It is also interesting to note that in the countries that perform better environmentally their Gross Domestic Product (GDP) is significantly higher than that of their struggling counterparts; US$1,206 and US$1,454 in Rwanda and Uganda respectively, as compared with US$699 in Burundi.[22] The World Bank has taken into consideration both environmental stress indicators and demographic stress indicators, with a view to ascertaining the degree of risk of conflict engendered by these factors. With the exception of Rwanda, which was found to face a very high risk, all other nations are deemed to face a high risk.[23]

The high concentration in the Great Lakes of people with no other skills and sources of income than farming and artisanal mining has necessarily put a huge strain on the natural environment. Significant deforestation has taken place and all available tracts of land have been made arable, even slopey hills. The farmers receive no education on sustainable agriculture, nor is there any sensible control on the degree of deforestation.[24] The potential for conflict is twofold. On the one hand, the influx of farm dwellers increases the problem of land scarcity. On the other hand, strong dependence on natural resources has an impact not only on deforestation, but also on the quality of fresh water resources, and the mineral wealth of these nations.[25] There will certainly come a time when the lack of arable land or its scarcity among farmers will give way to violent confrontation, at least at the communal level. These are not problems without solutions, however. Land scarcity can be tackled by adopting an equitable and well-managed land reform programme. Farmers provided with equal land sizes and tenures and who are moreover trained on sustainable agriculture will be incentivized to care for their

---

[19] Institute for Environmental Security (IES), 'Charcoal in the Mist: An Overview of Environmental Security Issues and Initiatives in the Central Albertine Rift' (IES, May 2008), 12ff. [20] This term is explained more fully later in the chapter.
[21] Land degradation encompasses all erosions to the soil that contribute to the reduction of the land's productive capacity. This process is mostly attributed to human activities, such as overgrazing, deforestation, over-cultivation, depletion of the soil's nutrients through the use of pesticides, and others. [22] IES Study (see n 19 above) 13.
[23] See Country Indicators for Foreign Policy (CIFP) 'Conflict Risk Assessment Report: African Great Lakes' (September 2002), 7–9, 25ff, and 36ff. [24] IES Report (see n 19 above) 12–13.
[25] Ibid, 13–15.

land and the surrounding environment. The post-colonial practice of recognizing customary land rights proved to be a major hurdle in this direction, although many countries in sub-Saharan Africa still retain it. In 2005 the Parliament of Rwanda adopted the country's new Land Law that abolished customary tenure, replacing it instead with long leases.[26] This certainly has the potential to bring about social equity and cohesion, but in the present context the application of the Law has been attacked for focusing on privatization and being subject to inequalities in land access based on historical revisionism.[27]

3.1 The Darfur crisis as an environmental conflict

Let us now turn to a case study in order to illustrate the ways in which population density and environmental degradation—not necessarily man-made—have exacerbated local rivalries and have led to the escalation of violence.

The international community prefers to view the Darfur crisis in the Sudan's southwest territory as an armed conflict between government-backed forces and local populations that was instigated by political and ethnic rivalries. The exacerbation of these rivalries has largely been attributed to the despotic authoritarian rule of President Al-Bashir, who as a result was recently indicted by the Prosecutor of the International Criminal Court (ICC).[28]

Yet, few commentators, particularly international law scholars, have paid any attention to the environmental causes behind this tragic conflict. UNEP, for instance, views Sudan's environmental issues as contributing causes of conflict, as opposed to root causes.[29] It lists specifically, competition over oil and gas reserves, water and timber, confrontations over the use of agricultural land, with particular emphasis on rangeland and rainfed land in the drier parts of the country, such as Darfur.[30] These are evidently not environmental factors per se, but conflicts over the use of the natural environment, or as a result of its depletion or degradation. Under normal circumstances pastoralist groups need not compete for agricultural or grazing land, or for natural resources, such as water, which would either exist in abundance or their enjoyment would otherwise be regulated equitably between contesting groups. In the case of Sudan, the largest country in Africa, two environmental factors have contributed to the scarcity of arable land and, hence, to a scramble between competing pastoralists; deforestation and

---

[26] J Pottier, 'Land Reform for Peace? Rwanda's 2005 Land Law in Context' (2004) 6 Journal of Agrarian Change 509.   [27] IES Report (see n 19 above) 32.

[28] *ICC Prosecutor v Al-Bashir* (Warrant of Arrest Re Situation in Darfur) ICC Doc ICC-02/05-01/09 (4 March 2009). Note that there is nothing in the indictment regarding Al-Bashir's intentional or reckless environmental policy. This should not deter the ICC Prosecutor, however, when formulating more detailed charges to lay some stress on this matter, even if only to underline the seriousness of the situation.

[29] See generally DH Johnson, *The Root Causes of Sudan's Civil Wars* (Bloomington, IN: Indiana University Press, 2003).

[30] UNEP, 'Post-Conflict Environmental Assessment', UNEP Doc DEP/0816/GE (2007), 8.

desertification, both of which have led to land degradation.[31] While insufficient and highly variable annual precipitation (that is, rainfalls) brings about climate-based conversion of land types from semi-desert to desert, the degradation of general natural habitats is certainly man-made.[32]

Precipitation records in Darfur have been kept since 1917 and the data clearly show that a dramatic decrease in rainfall in the region has turned millions of hectares of semi-desert land to desert plains. Instructively, between 1946 and 1975, whereas the average annual rainfall was 272.36 mm in Northern Darfur, between 1976 and 2005 it had fallen to 178.90 mm, which represents a decrease of 34 per cent. Within the same time, Southern Darfur experienced a decrease of 16 per cent, while the decline in Western Darfur was approximately 24 per cent.[33] Unfortunately, the climatic forecast for the near future does not paint an optimistic picture. Lack of sufficient rainfall has rendered 24 per cent of Sudanese territory into real deserts. This, in turn, has necessarily forced pastoralists to move to greener belts, albeit with the consequence that there is now less land for more people.

The absence of proper agricultural management brought about the last cycle in this environmental catastrophe. Farmers cut down millions of hectares of woodlands in order to make way for grazing grounds for their cattle and to otherwise free up land for cultivation. Deforestation in Sudan is currently occurring at a rate of 0.84 per cent per annum and it is estimated that between 1990 and 2005 the country lost 11.6 per cent of its forest cover. In Darfur alone, one-third of forest cover was lost between 1973 and 2006.[34] The uncontrolled and wholly unsustainable agricultural policy of the Sudan is aptly reflected in the manner of its livestock breeding. Numbers of livestock have risen from 28.6 million in 1961 to 134.6 million in 2004. It does not take much to realize that this manifold increase in livestock, under particularly arid conditions due to lack of rainfall, resulted in widespread degradation of rangelands that could not subsequently be restored.[35]

Much of this could certainly have been prevented. For example, a large part of the deforestation took place as a result of petroleum production activities and in respect of brick-making, the latter being a major source of income in Darfur. Moreover, Darfur's vulnerability to drought was exacerbated by the tendency to maximize livestock numbers, rather than augment quality, and by the lack of secure water sources, other than rivers and lakes, which led to the depletion of scarce water sources. The poor conditions in Sudan's dry and arid areas are further compounded by occasional flooding and river erosion. Human intervention could have provided alternative energy sources, as well as alternative cattle production, such that would prevent deforestation.

---

[31] Sudan's desertification has in fact been documented as early back as 1953. See EP Stebbing, *The Creeping Desert in the Sudan and Elsewhere in Africa* (Khartoum: McCorquordale & Co, 1953).   [32] UNEP Report (see n 30 above), 8–10.
[33] Ibid, 60.   [34] Ibid, 10–11.   [35] Ibid, 10.

Localized conflicts are not a recent phenomenon in Sudan. Indeed, between 1930 and 2000, competition for pastoral land among Sudan's pastoralists has been a constant cause of conflict.[36] The new twist in the contemporary Darfur crisis, however, lies in the following factors: (a) desertification has persisted at an alarming rate, thus shrinking available arable lands; (b) dramatic increase in livestock; (c) depletion of natural resources, particularly water; and (d) sharp increase in population growth.[37] The combination of all these combustive elements into a single period of human history was more than enough to ignite a bitter conflict between pastoralist and farmer groups competing for space in Darfur. This is not to say that ethnic rivalries or the intervention of the Sudanese government has not played a role in the ensuing humanitarian catastrophe; in fact, other causes are more significant than the effect of environmental scarcity and it has by now become evident that the Al-Bashir government has flamed the conflict through its support of Arab Darfurians.

The Darfur situation is further exacerbated by the fact that internally displaced persons in Darfur are depleting the forests at the edges of the semi-desert areas and are contributing directly to subsequent desertification that will no doubt intensify the conflict if concrete steps are not taken to control the situation. Moreover, lack of arable land means food shortage, as is also the case with fresh water resources. Darfur is, nonetheless, only one of many potential areas in the Sudan facing similar issues. Therein, other issues are also at stake, including the environmental impact of the oil industry,[38] the charcoal industry in central Sudan, the potential for ivory poaching, and the emergence of a timber mafia in South Sudan.[39] These problems are endemic to Africa, and Darfur perhaps represents a microcosm of these African exigencies and realities.

Environmental flashpoints for conflict would be diminished severely if the government instituted countrywide sustainable agriculture and introduced natural resource assessment and management, particularly in the conflict regions, and also elsewhere in the country.[40] The Darfur crisis is not attributable solely to population density or natural environmental disasters; these are just two of its causes that have not been well managed by the Sudanese government. Poor management of scarce resources led to deforestation and sizeable flocks, which culminated in even greater scarcity. The ensuing conflict was only a natural consequence of these successive failures. The role for the international community is discussed briefly in other sections of this chapter, particularly with regard to the role of the Security Council. A brief discussion of possible interventionist

---

[36] Ibid, 83.　　　[37] Ibid, 87.

[38] See Report of the UN Human Rights Commission Special Rapporteur on Sudan, UN Doc E/CN.4/2002/46 (23 January 2002), who stated that oil exacerbated the conflict, while oil exploration continued to cause widespread displacement.　　　[39] UNEP Report (see n 30 above) 95.

[40] See AA Fadul, 'Natural Resources Management for Sustainable Peace in Darfur' in *Conference Proceedings: Environmental Degradation as a Cause of Conflict in Darfur* (Addis Ababa: University for Peace Press, 2004).

and investment measures is included in the recommendations at the close of the chapter.

4. The threat of deforestation

Deforestation is the clearance of forests through the intervention of man with a view to: (a) using the land for grazing; (b) or as a plantation or for housing; (c) using the wood as a commodity; or (d) as charcoal. There is no doubt that some deforestation is necessary as the above purposes, within measure and reason, are beneficial. Nevertheless, the rate of re-forestation should be greater than its deforestation counterpart.

There are two points of view on the state and causes of Africa's deforestation. The first posits that the scale of deforestation in Africa, particularly in respect of West Africa is vastly exaggerated. Studies supporting this position argue that the relevant data on deforestation concentrate on the degree of woodland cultivated by African farmers, but generally fail to consider the beneficial nature of traditional farming practices that are overall more sustainable than any contemporary methods.[41] Some proponents of this view even claim that the collection of wood fuel in certain parts of Africa for household consumption is not destructive at all. It is explained that the misconception as to Southern Africa's deforestation on account of wood fuel demand is derived from the assumption that all the wood and charcoal used in urban areas come from areas cleared primarily to harvest wood.[42] Although it is probably true that traditional African farming practices were sustainable and eco-friendly, the contemporary situation is much different, principally because of increasing population densities, natural-based desertification, and other modern developments/changes.

The more popular school of thought contends that Africa's deforestation is increasing at an alarming rate, and certainly far above that of all the other continents. There is a general trend in the relevant literature to associate the level of deforestation with financial plight. Thus, Africa's current deforestation rate is explained, according to one author, by the fact that 48 per cent of its population lives on less than one dollar a day.[43] It is evident that this assumption is based on a never-ending cycle. If a population lives in dire poverty, it does away with environmental concerns and does not concern itself with

[41] See J Fairhead and M Leach, *Reframing Deforestation Global Analyses and Local Realities: Studies in West Africa* (Aldershot: Ashgate, 1998).

[42] EN Chidumayo, 'Woodfuel and Deforestation in Southern Africa: A Misconceived Association' (1997) 10 Renewable Energy for Development 1.

[43] E Asiedu, 'The Determinants of Employment of Affiliates of US Multinational Enterprises in Africa' (2004) 22 Development Policy Review 371; see also C Brian, 'Tropical Forest and Trade Policy: The Legality of Unilateral Attempts to Promote Sustainable Development under the GATT' (1993) 14 Third World Quarterly 749, who argued as far back as 1993 that poverty is the most serious cause for African deforestation.

sustainable use of limited resources until they are depleted. Poverty is further exacerbated by population density, which places a great deal of stress on already scarce resources. The most interesting observation, however, on the relationship between deforestation and finance, which is particularly worrying for Africa, relates to the so-called environmental Kuznets curve. This essentially stipulates that deforestation is inextricably linked to the degree of a country's economic and industrial development. Up to the point where development is rising, as does the level of income, but is still considered rudimentary, the amount of natural resources needed tends to increase the levels of deforestation. Once a threshold point of development has been attained and people become wealthier, the strain on natural resources decreases as both the people and the market rely less on the exploitation of natural resources and become far more environmentally friendly.[44] It should be noted, however, that some commentators have dismissed the reliability of the Kuznets curve not because it is wrong per se, but on account of the fact that relevant data are believed to be sparse and of dubious quality.[45]

As far as Africa is concerned, and if the Kuznets curve theory is assumed to be valid, this is hardly encouraging news. African nations generally struggle to achieve any real degree of development and by so doing raise the standard of living for their citizens. Much of the population of the continent lives under subsistence conditions and as such is destined to decimate its forest lands because these remain their only means of survival. Moreover, the shrinking of the forests necessarily entails the sprawling of regional conflicts over control of land. If the forests are to survive, it is obvious that what is necessary is raising the standard of living to such a level that no one would need to go to the forest in order to gather wood for cooking, or to fell trees so as to make way for new farm or grazing land.[46] To achieve these objectives, however, local governments and the international community must create sustainable and real working opportunities for the poor of Africa and entrench the farmers with viable property rights.

The alarming rates of deforestation[47] will also cause other types of harm, primary among which is the unfortunate welcoming of desertification, the causes and effects of which have been explained above. Equally, it has now been amply established that tropical deforestation can cause fundamental regional-scale shifts in vegetation structure and diversity on account of the interdependence of tropical habitats. Thus, in studies carried out in Gabon and the DRC researchers found that in some undisturbed national parks adjacent to logging forests, rainfall decreased by as much as 15 per cent, while in others there was a slight

---

[44] See K Martinez, E Crenshaw, and C Jenkins, 'Deforestation and the Environmental Kuznets Curve: A Cross-national Investigation of Intervening Mechanisms' (2002) 83 Social Sciences Quarterly 226.   [45] See UNEP 2004 Report (see n 3 above) 43.

[46] This is not to say that deforestation is not caused for purely logging purposes; this activity is in fact quite prevalent in Africa.

[47] See A Doyle, 'Africa's Deforestation Twice World Rate Says Atlas', *Reuters* (10 June 2008).

increase.[48] Another harmful effect is produced by forcing the wildlife to evacuate its natural reserves. As a result, wildlife is forced to migrate elsewhere in search of food. This not only has serious ramifications for Africa's fledgling tourist industry, which can help it overcome many of its economic woes, but it also contributes to the change of local habitats whose existence relies on particular animal species. To the extent that deforestation is a direct result of local or international conflicts in sub-Saharan Africa, there is little, or nothing, that can be done to prevent it, apart from various strategies for refugee camps devised by the United Nations High Commission for Refugees. As regards those situations that do not involve armed conflict, more succinct measures will be discussed in the final section of this chapter.

5. Illegal depletion and exploitation of Africa's mineral wealth

The UN Security Council's concern over the depletion of Africa's mineral resources since 2000 during armed conflicts in the continent, but particularly in the DRC, has already been highlighted.[49] The Security Council followed its concern by appointing a Panel of Experts, which issued a comprehensive report on the Illegal Exploitation of Natural Resources and other Forms of Wealth of the Democratic Republic of the Congo.[50] The Report underlined the direct or indirect implication of 157 corporations, the operations of which fuelled the purchase of arms, the perpetration of war crimes and crimes against humanity, and the exploitation of Congo's natural resources to the detriment of its people.[51] Moreover, the Prosecutor of the ICC, in his Report to the Assembly of States Parties on 8 September 2003, emphasized that:

those who direct mining operations, sell diamonds or gold extracted [as a result of resource exploitation and general violence taking place in the Congo], launder the dirty money or provide weapons could also be the authors of the crimes, even if they are based in other countries.[52]

The same result was reached by the Council in respect of the illegal trade in diamonds in Sierra Leone,[53] which helped finance the war and thus perpetuate the

[48] SB Roy, PD Walsh, and JW Lichstein, 'Can Logging in Equatorial Africa Affect Adjacent Parks?' (2005) 10 Ecology & Society 6.   [49] See nn 12 and 13 above.

[50] Letter dated 23 October 2003 from the Secretary-General addressed to the President of the Security Council, UN Doc S/2003/1027 (2003) <http://www.un.org/Docs/sc/unsc_presandsg_letters03.html>.   [51] See ibid, paras 10–13.

[52] L Moreno-Ocampo, 'Second Assembly of States Parties to the Rome Statute of the International Criminal Court: Report of the Prosecutor of the ICC' (2003) <http://www.icc-cpi.int/library/organs/otp/030909_prosecutor_speech.pdf>.

[53] UNSC Res 1306 (5 July 2000) UN Doc S/RES/1306, particularly section A, where the Council notes its concern as to the role diamonds play in fuelling the conflict there and in neighbouring countries. See also UN Doc A/62/L.16 (21 November 2007), entitled 'The Role of Diamonds in Fuelling Conflict'.

ensuing conflict and the resulting humanitarian disaster in the country. In both cases, the Council took Chapter VII action and instituted sanctions and monitoring committees, as subsidiary organs, in order to avert the sale and distribution of illegal minerals throughout the world.[54]

The plunder of Africa's mineral wealth is not solely perpetrated by armed groups, as is the case with the DRC; this is simply one of its facets. Resource scarcity has led impoverished people to become artisanal miners in search of minerals that lie close to the surface. In Tanzania, for example, it was well documented that many thousands of artisanal workers and their families depended on small-scale mining from the Bulyanhulu gold mine, until this was purchased by a Canadian mining company. Two potential calamities, as experience has shown, can culminate from artisanal mining and otherwise legal exploitation. Artisanal mining is unsustainable because it is essentially uncontrollable, and it is also destructive for adjacent freshwater resources (both submerged and overground) as a result of toxic residues that are naturally funneled directly into the water or indirectly through the soil.[55] This not only depletes and pollutes fresh water for potable purposes, but it also decreases the potential for agriculture, ultimately leading to resource scarcity.

While mineral extraction is generally beneficial to the economy of producing nations, this is only so where extraction is sustainable and premised on strict environmental assessment criteria, the commission is corruption-free and, moreover, the country under consideration diversifies its economy. In Africa, few, if any, of these preconditions are ever met. In the Bulyanhulu example, mentioned above, a group representing local artisanal miners accused the government of a sell-out to the Canadian company and argued that not only was environmental regulation very lax, but that the company was also implicated in the murder of at least 50 artisanal miners.[56] Such practices are predominant throughout sub-Saharan Africa and they include the pollution of Nigeria's Niger Delta region[57]

---

[54] Panel of Experts on Sierra Leone established pursuant to Paragraph 19 of UNSC Res 1306 (5 July 2000), UN Doc S/RES/1306. The same resolution imposed a blanket prohibition on import of all rough diamonds from Sierra Leone and moreover mandated a Certificate of Origin, paras 2–3. On 1 December 2000 the UN General Assembly duly adopted Res 55/56, through which it developed an international certification scheme for rough diamonds. This developed into a partnership with relevant private actors that led to the institution of the Kimberley Process Certification Scheme.

[55] This is particularly mercury-related pollution. See N Pironne and KR Mahaffey, 'Mercury Pollution from Artisanal Mining in Block B, El Callao, Bolivar State, Bolivia' in MM Veiga et al, *Dynamics of Mercury Pollution on Regional and Global Scales* (Boston, MA: Springer, 2005), 421–50; JA Shandro, MM Veiga, and R Chouinard, 'Reducing Mercury Pollution from Artisanal Gold Mining in Munhena, Mozambique' (2009) 17 Journal of Cleaner Production 525.

[56] CAO, 'Assessment Report Summary: Complaint Regarding MIGA's Guarantee of the Bulyanhulu Gold Mine, Tanzania' (2002) <http://www.cao-ombudsman.org/pdfs/buly%20final.doc>. See I Bantekas, 'Corporate Social Responsibility in International Law' (2004) 22 Boston University International Law Journal 309, 347–8.

[57] See J Brown, 'Niger Delta Bears Brunt After 50 Years of Oil Spills', *The Independent*, 26 October 2006 < http://www.independent.co.uk/news/world/africa/niger-delta-bears-brunt-after-50-years-of-oil-spills-421634.html>.

by hydrocarbon-extracting corporations and others. These cases show that illegal extraction is only one form of evil, which one should not focus on exclusively, and risk losing sight of the problem in its entirety. Corrupt African governments and weak administrations and states fail to apply the full gamut of their environmental and other laws to foreign mining corporations, and as a result they destroy their natural environment for existing and future generations in the same manner as illegal mining. *In fact, it has been suggested that in some cases war may be less destructive to the environment than peace.*[58]

Countries that are currently amenable to natural resource depletion, particularly mineral resources, on account of over-exploitation, without reaping the requisite social and financial benefits, will eventually find themselves in socioeconomic peril. On the other hand, as fate may have it, Africa's richness in mineral resources has only made her poorer. There is perhaps reason to believe, based on the experiences of other nations, that following the depletion of natural resources, concerned African governments will rely on other factors (such as effective fiscal and investment organization, universal education, infrastructures, etc) to boost their economies.

6. The application of the clean development mechanism in Africa

The new generation of environmental treaties focuses on the environmental effects of human activities, particularly carbon-based activities that typically emit greenhouse gases (GHG), on the global climate. The 1992 UN Framework Convention on Climate Change (UNFCCC)[59] represents the cornerstone to relevant efforts. Given that the challenge to remedy the adverse effects of climate change by limiting GHG emissions concerns all states, it was agreed that a significant degree of equity would guide the contribution of each participant on the basis of burden-sharing and in accordance with the principle of common but differentiated responsibilities.[60] This involves a duty on developed states to adopt national policies with a view to limiting their emissions and protecting GHG sinks and reservoirs.[61] Furthermore, developed states undertook an obligation to cover the relevant costs of developing states, incurred as a result of communicating the required information on the implementation of the UNFCCC, as well as other costs related to the transfer of technology and, moreover, agreed to help developing states overcome existing adverse effects of climate change.[62]

---

[58] See J McNeely, 'War and Biodiversity: An Assessment of Impacts' in J Austin and CE Bruch (eds), *The Environmental Consequences of War* (Cambridge: Cambridge University Press, 2000).
[59] (1992) 31 ILM 849.   [60] Ibid, Art 4(2)(a).
[61] Ibid, Art 4(2). These developed states are identified in Annex I to the UNFCCC.
[62] Ibid, Art 4(3)–(4) and (8).

The 1997 Kyoto Protocol,[63] which fulfils the obligations contained in the UNFCCC, sets out two basic duties for developed states: that of protection of sinks and reservoirs and the enhancement of sustainable agriculture and energy efficiency, as well as the duty to limit and/or reduce GHG emissions.[64] The Kyoto package also included a commitment on the part of developed states not to exceed particular levels of GHG emissions with respect to six gases. These are known as 'assigned amounts' and correspond to the maximum of GHG emissions a developed country may emit during the first commitment period. This commitment obliges industrialized countries to gradually reduce overall emissions by 5.2 per cent below 1990 levels between 2008 and 2012.[65] The Kyoto Protocol does not establish uniform emission reduction targets for all participating states, but instead introduces differing rates for individual states and in respect of the sources from which these emissions originate.

Three particular mechanisms are envisaged in the Kyoto Protocol, one of which, however, is of interest to us in this section. This is the so-called Clean Development Mechanism (CDM). This allows industrialized states to establish emission reduction projects in developing countries.[66] The incentive for developed countries lies in the fact that the emissions reductions achieved as a result of the project will be calculated in units (so-called certified emission units) that may be used to calculate compliance with their own target emissions, with a view to gaining emissions credits. These projects no doubt possess the potential for assisting developing states in the fields of both development and environmental protection because they facilitate the abandonment of polluting industries without themselves incurring a financial cost. It is obvious, however, that the CDM requires a supervisory mechanism because of the potential for abuse and corruption. It was agreed, therefore, that proceeds are to be shared between the parties and the host developing state and that the functioning of the mechanism itself be supervised by an executive board. Finally, ceilings on certified emission units were imposed, while the choice of projects and the benefits accrued for the developed state must have a real, measurable, and long-term benefit to the mitigation of climate change.

Although the benefits of a market-based system in order to tackle climate change are not wholly convincing,[67] the potential of the CDM for Africa is significant. In short, African states would only need to identify factories or plants that still employ carbon-based technologies, and arrange for their replacement by non-pollutant alternatives. This would not only reduce GHG emissions overall in Africa, it would moreover render these plants cost-effective as

---

[63] (1997) 37 ILM 22.   [64] Kyoto Protocol, Art 2.   [65] Ibid, Art 3(7).
[66] Ibid, Art 12.
[67] See I Bantekas, *Trust Funds in International Law: Trustee Obligations of the World Bank and the United Nations* (The Hague: Asser Press, 2009), 262–72; see also H Bachram, 'Climate Fraud and Carbon Colonialism: The New Trade in Greenhouse Gases' (2004) 15 Capitalism Nature Socialism 1.

well as energy-efficient; and all this without any charge! At the time of writing (March 2010), out of a total of 1,462 registered projects financed under the CDM in developing countries around the world, Africa had only benefited from 29 projects (1.98 per cent), as opposed to 1,022 in Asia and the South Pacific and 402 in Latin America and the Caribbean.[68] The statistical discrepancy is truly staggering and can only be used to confirm earlier references in this chapter concerning weak states and governance in the African continent.[69]

7. Recommendations

In Darfur, Africa is witnessing its first ever displaced persons as a result of an environmental breakdown. These are agrarian communities driven out of their ancestral lands as a result particularly of desertification, but also increasingly on account of resource scarcity which has subsequently culminated into a conflict between rival communities. The next step may be the emergence of environmental refugees in those extreme cases where people are forced to transcend a national frontier in situations involving critical levels of resource scarcity. The Darfur crisis, and the ensuing conflict, is certainly of this nature, although we have stressed that at the moment the environmental factor is only a contributing element to African conflicts and not their root cause. If this scenario were to escalate, however, it is clear that the international community would confront a situation that it never prepared itself to meet. For one thing, Article 1 of the Refugee Convention does not envisage environmental refugees as falling within the category of people fearing persecution and thus entitled to refugee status.[70] It is also doubtful whether the developed world would be willing to accept environmental refugees even under the most acute circumstances for fear of burdening its own limited resources, among other reasons.[71]

---

[68] See <http://cdm.unfccc.int/Statistics/Registration/RegisteredProjByRegionPieChart.html>.

[69] Among the few countries that have made some good use, compared to others, of the CDM are Gambia, Ghana, and Uganda. See Ugandan Ministry of Waters, 'Lands and Environment, Capacity Building in CDM in Uganda' (June 2001) <http://uneprisoe.org/CDM/CDMCapacityBuildUganda.pdf>. It is true, nonetheless, that in the CDM pipeline lie projects that far outweigh the number of those already registered, with the biggest beneficiary, by far, being South Africa, followed by Kenya. See K Capoor and P Ambrosi, 'State and Trends of the Carbon Market in 2006: A Focus on Africa' (Washington, DC: World Bank, 2006) <http://www.africaclimatesolution.org/features/State_of_the_Carbon_Market_Focus_on_Africa_20090414.pdf>; S Lutzeyer, 'Climate Trading: The Clean Development Mechanism and Africa', Stellenbosch Economic Working Papers No 12/08 (2008) <http://ideas.repec.org/p/sza/wpaper/wpapers60.html>.

[70] Convention Relating to the Status of Refugees (adopted on 28 July 1951, entered into force on 22 April 1954) 189 UNTS 150.

[71] D McDougal, 'The World's First Environmental Refugees', *Ecologist*, 30 January 2009. See also M Conisbee and A Simms, 'Environmental Refugees: The Case for Recognition' (NEF, 2003); for an excellent legal analysis, see particularly D Keane, 'The Environmental Causes and Consequences of Migration: A Search for the Meaning of Environmental Refugees' (2004) 16 Georgetown Int'l Env LR 209.

It is imperative, therefore, that the international community deliberate on the optimal way forward. Without a doubt, the international community cannot stop its peacekeeping missions to Africa, even in those cases where the conflict in question is more of an environmental nature than of any other cause. Security on the ground is of paramount importance. The Security Council must, however, better engage with environment-related conflicts and threats. Two policy suggestions are generally put forward in this chapter. The first recommends the introduction of environmental factors into the conflict prevention debate, while the second contends in favour of introducing conflict prevention into the environmental debate. The chief political protagonists that deal with environmental security (namely the UN through its specialized agencies and subsidiary bodies, as well as the Security Council) seem to back the former, arguing that the latter may lead to 'unnecessary overloading and the securitisation of the environmental discourse'.[72] The UN Security Council, the UN Department for Peacekeeping Operations (DPKO), and all relevant UN agencies (including the Secretariat in its peace-building and conflict mediation role) must place the environmental factor within their conflict-outlook agendas, particularly as this pertains to Africa.[73] The African Union should also take a lead role in this respect, rather than sub-regional organizations such as the Intergovernmental Authority on Development (IGAD), all of which have largely proven to be ineffective.[74] It is also necessary that environmental lobby groups exert the widest possible amount of pressure on UN institutions, and the World Bank, to incorporate environmental factors into their long-term and short-term peace and security plans. The factoring of environmental elements need not be solely in respect of security strategies. For example, where the World Bank is asked to provide a loan to an African nation, the Bank should have in place a mechanism by which to inform the borrowing state of CDM opportunities as well as to advise it, if not expressly make it a conditionality, with regard to granting farmers land rights. While the overall goal of poverty alleviation and development cannot be achieved overnight, some faster steps are certainly feasible. The acquisition of definite and secure land rights will go a long way towards alleviating some of the woes of deforestation and land degradation. This has to be followed

---

[72] Centre for Security Studies (CSS), *Linking Environment and Conflict Prevention: The Role of the United Nations* (Zurich: CSS Publications, 2008), 13.

[73] The CSS Report, ibid 4 and 7, suggests that the topic of environment and conflict prevention should be further integrated within existing UN units by being tagged on as a separate issue (but within the overall context of conflict prevention), rather than improperly mainstreaming it.

[74] In fact, one of the main purposes of IGAD was to contribute to development in the Horn of Africa and reverse the process of desertification in the region. It has failed miserably in this arena, although admittedly it played a significant role in the brokering of the 2002 Machakos Protocol between the governments of Sudan proper and that of South Sudan. In 2002 a Protocol on the Establishment of a Conflict Early Warning and Response Mechanism for IGAD member states was adopted by the parties to IGAD.

with extensive education programmes, given that lack of education has been linked with environmental destruction.[75]

There are two ways of countering and preventing potential conflicts arising out of environmental factors; the first is institutional, whereas the second is of a purely conflict prevention character.[76] The following section will thus focus on the need for institutional reform.

There are numerous countries and regions around the world that lack an abundance of natural resources, are arid, relatively over-populated, and yet their people thrive and resource scarcity is not an issue of concern. Fine examples are Arizona and Nevada in the USA, and Israel in the Middle East. Good governance and environmental management have not prevented people in these regions from enjoying a very high standard of living. It is thus clear that food and water security do not necessarily depend on resource availability, but on access, distribution, institutions, and adequate infrastructure.[77] All these elements are fundamentally lacking in Africa. Obviously, the problem is good governance, since Africa is rich in natural resources and a significant amount of aid is poured into the continent. The international community must, therefore, focus primarily on promoting good governance and institutions. 'Simple' measures such as land reform, or attracting foreign direct investment that will lead to meaningful employment, etc, cannot be performed under the current politico-economic climate.[78] Significant consideration must be given to the idea of building Africa's institutions, and thus catering for its environmental security, through intergovernmental trust funds which operate alongside local governments. The function of these funds will be to embed institutions and manage foreign aid.

Surely, there are other innovative ways for enhancing Africa's ability to generate energy without devastation to the environment. Africa's growing desert lands can be turned to its advantage by investing in huge photovoltaic installations in order to generate energy from the sun. African deserts, both man-made and natural, need not be empty and useless spaces. The Mojave Desert in California is home to the biggest photovoltaic park in the world, generating enough electricity to meet the needs of 500,000 people.[79] Obviously, such a venture requires substantial

---

[75] R Godoy, 'A Comparative Study of Education and Tropical Deforestation among Lowland Bolivian Amerindians: Forest Values, Environmental Externality and School Subsidies' (2001) 49 *Economic Development & Culture Change* 555.

[76] Wealth-sharing schemes may also be encompassed within the broader framework of conflict prevention, either as a means of ending a conflict, or in terms of post-conflict adjustment. The 2004 Agreement on Wealth Sharing in Sudan between the North and the South was a crucial feature of the brokering process. The same is true in respect of Art 112 of the post-Saddam Iraqi Constitution. See Bantekas (n 67 above) 240–5.   [77] CSS Report (see n 72 above) 9.

[78] For some indicative suggestions, see Environment, Development, and Sustainable Peace Initiative (EDSP), 'Contribution of Donor Policies and Programs to Environment, Development, and Sustainable Peace: Lessons Learnt from the EDSP Initiative' (EDSP Working Paper No 6, 2003).

[79] See US Department of Energy, 'Solar through Systems' (1998) < http://www.nrel.gov/docs/legosti/fy98/22589.pdf>.

resources, but it is certainly a worthwhile opportunity for many African nations, as it is not only an investment of colossal dimensions that will generate employment, it has the potential to create energy independence, reverse climatic conditions, and give life to arid deserts. The most significant reason for the relatively modest results from photovoltaic energy in the developed world centres around the fact that it requires intensive land use. In Africa this limitation can be turned into an advantage, given the availability of vast tracts of non-arable land, particularly deserts, that can be employed to serve this purpose. This is not, however, a simple exercise of merely installing photovoltaic reflectors. Potential investors must receive guarantees that such projects will be backed up by sufficient infrastructure (for example, a reliable and accessible grid) and physical security.

As things stand, the international community's role in respect of environmental conflict is of a purely preventive character, but it is hoped that the socio-economic condition of sub-Saharan Africa will improve to such a degree that the very idea of resource scarcity will be a thing of the past.

4

Understanding the Nexus between Human Security and Small Arms in Africa: The Case of Ghana

*Kwesi Aning**

1. Introduction

Small arms and light weapons (SALW) availability in Africa has a long history. However, because of the incidences of both localized and region-wide experiences of SALW-related violence in West Africa, several initiatives have been undertaken that have sought to introduce different types of control measures. Probably, the most widely recognized of these control measures have been the initiatives undertaken by the Economic Community of West African States (ECOWAS) through its initial voluntary Moratorium in 1998 and its eventual transformation into a binding Convention in 2006.

While the political rhetoric around SALW control in ECOWAS has become a mantra in almost all meetings of its political leaders, the challenge has been to translate the political ideas into operational practical initiatives. There seems to be an obvious schism between these two poles: first, there is a political process that perceives SALW availability as a threat to the human security of citizens and stability of states, and, secondly, a totally opposite view taken by citizens of several West African states who identify access to and acquisition of SALW as part of their *identity* and *security*. This raises several questions of which the most important one is whether this apparent chasm between the ideals of ECOWAS' political leaders reflects the non-convergence of these ideals with the realities of their citizens. While such disparities in perception can be observed in all West African states, this chapter focuses on the gapping chasm and contradictions between official political statements and the responses of citizens in Ghana, as a case study.

* Director of Research, Kofi Annan International Peacekeeping Training Centre, Accra, Ghana.

The chapter explores how the concept of human security—basically defined as freedom from want and fear—is expressed within a particular context. This is the challenge of controlling both the demand and supply sides of SALW through official and citizen action in Ghana. Furthermore, weapons availability and misuse also lead to a range of indirect impacts, many with life-threatening potential. These include the displacement of civilians; the militarization of refugee camps; the erosion of sustainable development; the restriction of access to health services, education, and food security; land denial; contributing to obstructions in humanitarian assistance, as well as the use of these weapons to threaten the lives and well-being of communities as a whole. Whilst there is an ongoing discourse about the analytical and operational utility of human security approaches and definitions, work is underway to reconfigure the small arms issue. In Africa, there is a widening body of knowledge highlighting that a purely legalistic approach to linking small arms availability and misuse does not usually respond to the human security challenges posed by such availability. Using a human security framework allows for improved understanding of the challenge of weapons availability and misuse. Human security also offers a much needed bridge between development and security frameworks, overcoming strictly state-centric frameworks which only examine the impacts of arms availability through the prism of the state.

While the issue of SALW is an Africa-wide problem, it is a particular West African challenge. Although there is knowledge about the illicit trade, there is one area where knowledge is limited and that is the artisanal or craft manufacture of SALW. Due to the widespread nature of craft production in Benin, Guinea, Senegal, Nigeria, Togo, and Ghana, it is critical that the multiple dimensions of such manifestation are understood and appreciated. This chapter focuses on Ghana for several reasons. First, there are craft manufacturers throughout all ten regions of the country who produce small arms of increasing sophistication (reportedly including reverse-engineered Kalashnikovs), and do so at a rate of 50,000 to perhaps 200,000 per year.[1]

Armed groups supply themselves with these craft weapons in Ghana and neighbouring states. Secondly, although craft small arms production is present throughout West Africa, Ghana's long-standing and socially embedded gun-making tradition makes it a country of particular concern. Guns 'made in Ghana' are now known regionally for their competitive prices, their effectiveness, and their accessibility. Also, production varies greatly depending on demand, and guns are manufactured in conformity with imported ammunition available on the open market. Thirdly, though gunsmiths are also engaged in the production of a variety of other, mainly agricultural, products which provides opportunities for technological reconversion, gun production, however, clearly constitutes

---

[1] EK Aning, 'The Anatomy of Ghana's Secret Arms Industry' in N Florquin and EG Berman (eds), *Armed and Aimless: Armed Groups, Guns, and Human Security in the ECOWAS Region* (Geneva: Small Arms Survey, 2005).

their most profitable activity. In addition to these, one finds a thriving group of middlemen exporting craft guns to other countries in the region. These include Nigeria, Côte d'Ivoire, and Togo. Therefore, the widespread nature of the SALW industry in Ghana and its extensive marketing network in Africa makes it a significant case study for this chapter.

Ghana has had a turbulent political history with frequent military interventions in domestic politics. While such disruptions have always ended with a return to democratic governance, the militarization of politics has also had an unintended side effect, namely the militarization of sections of Ghanaian society.[2] This chapter discusses how SALW availability potentially threatens human security in Ghana and analyses the different perceptions between the state and the people about the lethality of SALW. The chapter also argues that the extent of the challenges posed by SALW is best understood by evaluating the nature and dimensions of SALW-related crimes. It discusses contemporary crime trends in Ghana and profiles perpetrators by exploring the sources of SALW flows and its impact on the economy. Furthermore, the chapter examines the legal framework governing SALW availability, import controls, and government responses. Finally, due to the sensitivity and politicization of SALW issues in Ghana and the broader West African sub-region, a section of the chapter discusses the challenges of undertaking SALW-related research in Ghana and concludes with avenues and options for policy engagement.

2. Human security and the SALW debate in Africa

Until recently, African governments especially considered security in terms of protecting the state, its institutions and borders, the stability of the regime, and defence of its military. Although this was the usual rhetoric, one can argue that most African states were more concerned with 'regime' survival than state and societal security. Attention has primarily been shifted, therefore, from the security of the state to the security of its people, referred to in general terms as human security, as already dealt with in Chapter 1 above.

In its Non-Aggression and Common Defence Pact, the African Union defines Human security as:

the security of the individual in terms of satisfaction of his/her basic needs. It also includes the creation of social, economic, political, environmental and cultural conditions for the survival and dignity of the individual, the protection of and respect for human rights, good governance and the guarantee for each individual of opportunities and choices for his/her full development.[3]

---

[2] See, eg, AF Musah, 'Small Arms: A Time-bomb under West Africa's Democratization Process' (2002) 9 Brown Journal of World Affairs 1; K Aning, 'Mapping the Threat of Organised Crime to African States: The Case of West Africa' (London: Routledge, 2010).

[3] See ss 6 and 7 of the Common African Defence and Security Policy.

One would easily recognize that the individual is at the centre of the concept of human security. While there is a perception that the ability of a state to fulfil these critical needs of its citizens becomes difficult during periods of instability, this is not always the case. State inability or unwillingness to protect its citizens from violence is widespread in Africa. This is as a result of the fact that the state which is expected to guarantee these provisions becomes engaged with regime protection and survival or the protection of the state. Even in cases where the state, especially in Africa, is not at war, the human security of its citizens is routinely denied or the state is simply incapable of meeting those needs. Often, and especially in both fragile and conflict areas, it is those responsible for the protection of the population who have been known to undermine the security of the civilian population through acts of violence.

In Africa, in particular, the weakness of the state has resulted in its loss of control over sizeable portions of its territory. As a result, the state is unable to exercise its right and responsibility to protect and ensure the security of the citizens. The loss of states' ability to provide societal security implies many interrelated but little understood dynamics. First is that in most West African states there is an increase in firearms-related crimes; secondly is that while crime increases and the states' ability to provide their citizens with protection is weakened, citizens are arming themselves to provide their basic security.

In West Africa the inability of the state to function effectively, leading to weakness and eventually fragility and in worst instances collapse, has resulted in further undermining the human security of the people. To explain the connection between state fragility, collapse, and human security, it is important to analyse some of the most prevalent factors and characteristics of collapsed/failed/collapsing states.

A state which is on the verge of collapse, according to Zartman:

- loses its power to 'demand' loyalty from its citizens and does not serve as a cohesive force;
- as a territorial entity, cannot guarantee its sovereign control over its territory and is peoples; and
- as the authoritative political expression, loses its validity to control and administer its affairs.

In general, the citizens' expectations from such a state are reduced because of its inability to deliver services and control the weapons of violence, thereby leading to increased societal insecurity.[4] Collapse finally ensues when the state is 'in a situation where the structure, authority (legitimate power), law and political order have fallen apart and must be reconstituted in some form, old or new'.[5]

State collapse, therefore, is the breakdown of good governance, law and order. The state as a decision-making, executing and enforcing institution can no longer take and implement

---

[4] W Zartman, 'Introduction: Posing the Problem of State Collapse' in W Zartman (ed), *Collapsed States* (Boulder, CO: Lynne Rienner, 1995).   [5] Ibid.

decisions... [it] is the extended breakdown of social coherence: society, as the generator of institutions of cohesion and maintenance can no longer create, aggregate and articulate the supports and demands that are the foundations of the state.[6]

The primary effect of such adverse developments, as are described above, is that sub-state groups operating largely outside the state purview will begin to exercise authority on such domain reserves of the state, for example control of weapons of violence, primarily to protect their own interests, but also to provide protection for those citizens who may require their services. In the following section, the Ghanaian example is used as an empirical case to illustrate how the dichotomy between the government efforts to control SALW and the citizens' determination to acquire weapons for self-protection is expressed.

3. The origin of the small arms problem in Ghana

Although most foreign and domestic observers see Ghana as a stable and peaceful country, recent events point to the fact that there may be several latent conflicts in which firearms are involved. There are frequent media reports of violent crimes in Ghana and there is an increasing spate of low intensity conflicts, which have the potential to explode at any time; SALW are involved in all these conflicts and are deepening their level of intensity.

Several explanations have been propounded for the escalating utilization of SALW in Ghana. The most critical seems to be the divergent perceptions about firearm possession. For many, possessing a gun is identified with manhood and strength and several traditional festivals are celebrated with musketry and marksmanship. But while in the early 1980s the use of firearms was limited to specific traditional occasions, it has changed dramatically in more recent times. One reason for this is the confused political rhetoric of the early 1980s when former Ghanaian leader, Jerry John Rawlings, returned to political power through his second coup d'état in December 1981.[7]

Having established the Provisional National Defence Council (PNDC), Rawlings initiated a nationwide process of arming his so-called Committees for the Defence of the Revolution and People's Defence Committees in an effort to 'democratise the tools of violence'.[8] These committees were militia-style organizations, usually equipped with AK47s mainly supplied by Libya

---

[6] Ibid.

[7] Jerry John Rawlings first appeared on the Ghanaian political scene on 15 May 1979 when he led an abortive coup d'état against the then Supreme Military Council II headed by General Frederick Akuffo. He was subsequently court marshalled but released from jail to lead the successful takeover of government on 4 June 1979; and established an Armed Forces Revolutionary Council in June 1979 which handed over power to a democratically elected government on 30 September 1979.

[8] See B Ansabah, 'Shocker from Jerry!', *Daily Guide*, 16 September 2003, 1, 8.

and states from the former Eastern bloc, or stolen from armouries.[9] According to Alhassan:

In Ghana during the June 4 [1979] uprising and [the] coup of 31 December 1981, armouries and magazines were broken into and guns were looted. There's never been a public accounting.[10]

There is little or no reliable available information on the quantity of firearms that were distributed nationally. The main rationale for the massive distribution of firearms to purported sympathizers of the regime in the early 1980s was the need to protect the new and revolutionary regime from perceived 'neo-colonialists' and 'imperialist agents'.[11] Thus, the proliferation of SALW in Ghana during this period was politically motivated.[12] Several former PNDC supporters and operatives recall that:

on several occasions, shipments of guns were brought in from outside to be distributed to specific groups. As these shipments moved from Southern Ghana and made its way up North, city mayors and district chiefs picked up as many guns as they thought they needed. There was no register of who took what and for what purpose. No one has any idea as to how many guns were brought in, 'distributed' and where they are now.[13]

However, the government eventually realized the dangerous security implications of its indiscriminate 'distribution' of SALW to its real and imagined supporters. The Christian Council of Ghana also expressed concern about how this SALW proliferation could jeopardize personal security and discourage investors from putting their money into the Ghanaian economy.[14] According to the Council, several measures had to be taken: a review of the number of organizations legally permitted to carry small arms (in order to ensure that such weapons are given only to those directly involved in maintaining national security); a retrieval of small arms from former revolutionaries;[15] and a better monitoring of trans-regional and transnational entry of small arms into Ghana (in particular the activities of armed gangs involved in trans-border crime).[16] This resulted, in 1999, in an inclusive initiative involving the government, churches, the media,

---

[9] AR Alhassan, 'Small Arms', *Accra Daily Mail*, 12 August 2003, 1, 3.   [10] Ibid, 1.

[11] Interview with senior National Security Operative and CID Officer (Accra, 24 August 2008).

[12] Z Yeebo, *Ghana: The Struggle for Power—Rawlings, Saviour or Demagogue* (London: New Beacon Books, 1991).

[13] Diverse interviews with different PNDC operatives (various times between 2001 and 2006).

[14] See 'Ghana–Christians Worried about Small Arms Proliferation' <http://www.nisat.org/west%20africanews%>. Also, the Fellowship of Christian Councils and Churches in West Africa appealed to the government of Ghana 'to equip the security agencies in the country to retrieve arms in illegal hands', see BC Okine and JJ Nkrumah, 'Retrieve Arms in Illegal Hands', *Daily Graphic*, 16 September 2003, 3.

[15] A former revolutionary of the PNDC era, Larry Lawal, has confessed to knowing about stockpiles of weapons hidden in 1996 by the National Democratic Congress administration. Lawal posits that the caches were initially hidden with the 31 December Women's organization. See AR Alhassan, 'Small Arms', *Accra Daily Mail*, 12 August 2003, 3.   [16] Ibid.

and non-governmental organizations (NGOs) that collectively began an infor-mation-gathering, sharing, and exchange process on the acquisition, movement, magnitude, and manifestations of the firearms problem in Ghana.[17]

Due to the political nature of SALW proliferation, the post-1992 re-democratization processes did not focus on the challenges posed to Ghana by SALW. However, in the aftermath of its electoral victory in 2000, the New Patriotic Party (NPP) initiated a collaborative police–military weapons retrieval strategy code-named *etuo mu ye sum*—the gun is dangerous.[18] First, the new administration granted a two-week general amnesty, whereby all Ghanaians could hand in their unregistered guns without fear of punishment; secondly, a weapons buy-back programme was initiated;[19] and thirdly, punitive meas-ures were instituted to collect forcibly any unregistered firearms still in private possession.

There is an ongoing debate about the effectiveness of this three-tiered approach. For example, Alhassan argues that the NPPs efforts at retrieving firearms from society 'met with limited success with intelligence and security sources believing that only the very tip of the hidden pile was touched'.[20] In other words, this well-intentioned but poorly executed strategy can be considered a failure. After almost two years of official self-denial, the government finally accepted that the retrieval process 'has not been successful'[21] with less than 1,000 of the estimated 40,000 illegal guns in circulation in Ghana eventually handed in.

Similarly, a weapons buy-back programme initiated in January 2009 netted only a single gun.[22] This was after post-2008 election-related clashes in Northern Ghana had claimed several lives. In an effort to retrieve weapons from combat-ants, the government once again initiated a weapons buy-back scheme in which GH¢300 (equivalent to US$250) would be paid for every illegal weapon returned to the police. This decision, taken by the Northern Regional Security Council, was presented as part of an innovative weapons' retrieval scheme, after an earlier

---

[17] See 'Ghana Calls for Action Against Small Arms Proliferation' (23 September 1999) <http://www.africanews.org/PANA/news>. A National Commission has been established in accordance with Art 4 of the ECOWAS Moratorium: 'Member states shall establish National Commissions, made up of representatives of the relevant authorities and civil society to ensure the effective implementation of the Moratorium.' Ghana's process started with the setting up of a three-person Task-Force.

[18] This joint operation was led by Lt Colonel Issa Awuni of the 5th Battalion and Commissioner Yaw Adu Gyimah of the GPS. Yaw Adu Gyimah was eventually relieved of his post in late 2001 for allegedly operating armed robbery gangs and supplying them with internal police operational details to evade arrest.

[19] The efficacy of weapons buy-back programmes is contested. For a discussion of such pro-grammes in other parts of West Africa, see UH Abdallah, 'The Menace of the AK 47', *West Africa*, 2–8 April 2001, 8–9.

[20] AR Alhassan, 'Small Arms', *Accra Daily Mail*, 12 August 2003. There have been recent reports of arms caches around the country controlled by both NPP and National Democratic Congress supporters.

[21] See 'Operation Etuo mu esum', *The Statesman*, 17 September 2003, 1, 8.

[22] 'Northern violence update : Only one gun submitted', Citifmonline.

month-long ultimatum for residents to return illegal weapons proved futile.[23] The Northern Regional Police Command had given a moratorium of one more month within which gun owners could voluntarily return their weapons.[24] Furthermore, the Vice President and Northern Regional Minister also issued a separate ultimatum to residents of the region to voluntarily turn in their weapons; which also failed to elicit any response. Consequently, the concerned authorities are now considering other options aimed at addressing the issue.[25]

4. The nature and dimensions of SALW-related crimes

Firearms-related crimes in Ghana comprise armed robberies,[26] land disputes in which land guards are involved to protect the land of individuals or organizations,[27] chieftaincy disputes,[28] identity and citizenship struggles, firearms-related violence during annual festivals,[29] inter-relational disputes, struggles over resource exploitation and distribution, and carjacking.[30]

---

[23] See, eg, C Milmo, '"Craft Guns" Fuel West Africa Crime Epidemic', *The Independent*, 8 July 2008.

[24] 'Tamale Clashes: GH¢300.00 for Every Single Illegal Weapon Returned to the Police'<http://news.myjoyonline.com/news/200903/27892.asp>.

[25] 'No Weapons Surrendered in Tamale' <http://news.myjoyonline.com/news/200903/27884.asp>.

[26] H Selby, 'Ghana: Armed Robbery and a Nation at Ransome', *The Chronicle*, 21 January 2009; K Adjapong, 'Let's Make December 28 be about Stamping-out Armed Robbery' <http://www.ghanaweb.com/GhanaHomePage/NewsArchive/artikel.php?ID=154972>.

[27] See, eg, E Mingle, 'Anyaa Residents Attacked by Thugs', *Ghanaian Times*, 15 May 2003, 3. See also EA Arthur, 'Shooting Scare at Pokuase—Cop Leads Land Guards', *The Independent*, 4 October 2001. In this particular case, 'a group of armed civilians led by police Sergeant Ansah stormed the [building] site and without provocation started firing indiscriminately ostensibly to scare [people] to flee [from] the land'. Also, D Jale and DA Paintsil, 'Land Guards Strike Again, Kill 3, Dump Bodies near Cemetery', *The Chronicle*, 15 September 2003, 1, 3; C Takyi-Boadu and NY Yankson, 'Ghana: Security Agencies Brace Up for Landguards', *The Chronicle*, 31 July 2007; Deputy Commissioner of Police, Jonathan Yakubu, Director General In-Charge of Operations said, 'a comprehensive strategy has been mapped'. He thus noted that in the next couple of days, 'the security agencies will descend heavily and mercilessly on the perpetrators of this nuisance'. To that effect, the police service says no individual or group of persons has the right to form any private security organization, unless as it were, expressly permitted by the law. It has thus declared an unending war on the phenomenon. This position of the police is backed by Legislative Instrument (LI 1571) under the Police Service (Private Security Organization Regulation of 1992) which emphatically states 'no person shall establish an organization to perform services of watching, guarding, patrolling or carriage for the purpose of providing protection against crime, unless that person has been granted a license for that purpose by the Secretary now the Minister of Interior'.

[28] A major source of firearms-related crime is chieftaincy and land disputes in which 'machomen' and 'land guards' are used. See 'Police Arrest 11 Suspected Landguards', *The Ghanaian Times*, 27 November 2004, 3. There are estimated to be over 350 such disputes across Ghana. For a detailed analysis see KE Aning in P Addo and E Sowatey, 'Ghana Conflict Vulnerability Assessment', mimeo (2003), 9.

[29] See C Dompreh, 'Violence at Homowo Festival', *The Ghanaian Times*, 11 August 2003, 1. According to this report, 'people received gunshot wounds and others various degrees of injury…when violence broke out at Kotoku in the Ga District during the celebration of [the] Homowo festival….The violence is believed to be due to an old chieftaincy conflict.' As a matter of fact, 'Closely related to chieftaincy disputes are the celebration of festivals, which is increasingly serving as focal point of mainly chiefly but youth conflicts.' See Aning et al (n 28 above), 'Ghana Conflict Vulnerability Assessment', 19.

[30] A Cobbah-Biney, 'Car Snatcher Arrested, Two on the Run', *The Ghanaian Times*, 15 May 2003, 10.

4.1 Current crime situation in Ghana

Civil insecurity and crime have escalated dramatically in Ghana, especially in urban areas with several armed gangs and some of the larger cities appearing almost ungovernable. The rise in burglary, robbery, and murder affects all classes, although the middle classes are especially vulnerable.[31] Present trends are likely to have negative implications for investment. Official figures from the Ghana Police Service (GPS) show a 15 per cent increase in robbery rates between 1999 and 2000, and the figure for armed robbery doubled between 2000 and 2001.[32]

According to the GPS, another category of firearms-related crime is the land guard phenomenon. The types of arms used by these categories of people to commit crimes are '[l]ocally manufactured pistols or revolvers'.[33] The guns form part of a readily available arsenal of weapons made up of 'single barrel, double barrel, pump action, garden guns and pistols and revolvers [which] are all legally imported into the country'.[34] But the data provided by the Police and the Arms and Ammunition Inventory Committee is not up to date, and most police information on these activities is unreliable.

However, available medical records indicate that the use of firearms is not responsible for any significant number of casualties in the capital. The cases of gunshot wounds found in the country's largest hospital at Korle Bu were quite few. Smaller hospitals in Accra and Madina contacted for this study did not have specific firearms-related injury records.

4.2 Profile of perpetrators

According to the Ghana Prisons Service, the demographic profile of their inmates is evenly distributed among all age groups between 18 and 60 years.[35] A baseline survey undertaken by Raymond Atuguba showed that from 900 convicts interviewed at four prisons (Nsawam Medium Security Prison, James Fort Remand Prison, Tamale Regional, and Navarongo Regional Prison), only 11 per cent of inmates had been convicted of armed robbery.[36] The research also showed that women are usually in more supportive roles than in frontline action (some of the gendered roles involve the general planning of operations, spying on targets, befriending targets, caring for sick and wounded male partners after operations,

---

[31] Interview with Senior Police officers (Akosombo, 21–23 August 2003).

[32] There are two aspects to crime in Ghana. First, is the official ineffective response and, secondly, the meting out of mob justice. See ED Frimpong, 'Mob Lynches Suspected Robber in Kumasi', *Daily Graphic*, 27 November 2004, 1, 3. Almost 24 hours after this incident, the local police at Asokwa, a suburb of Kumasi, claimed that they knew nothing of the case. In Sunyani, a cab was set ablaze after the driver had hit a pedestrian.

[33] Meeting between the Inspector General of Police and UN Conflict Resolution Team (Accra, September 2002), 4.   [34] Ibid, 4–5.

[35] Ghana Prison Service Annual Report (2002), 18.

[36] RA Atuguba et al, 'Projecting, Protecting and Promoting the Rights of Prisoners in Ghana' in Draft Report prepared for the Prison Project of the Legal Resources Centre (Accra: 2003).

etc). Approximately 20 per cent of arrested armed robbers are non-Ghanaians, which seriously dispels the general perception that the increase in firearms-related crime in Ghana is caused by the influx of foreigners.[37]

It should also be noted that belief in the supernatural permeates almost all aspects of Ghanaian life. People tend to seek spiritual protection from churches, traditional priests, and Mallams because of the perceived efficacy of the charms and amulets that they provide. It is common to hear people accuse spiritualists of assisting armed robbers. An example readily comes to mind. In one instance, a notorious armed robber who escaped from a maximum security prison in Ghana was believed to have been spiritually fortified by Mallam Musa Issaka who had made his escape easier. Thus, there is a general perception among some Ghanaians that armed robbers work in league with spiritualists in order to enhance their criminal activities.

4.3 Sources of SALW flow

Although official knowledge about local production is incomplete, there is much detailed information on the legal importation of shotguns into Ghana by registered importers. Since 2001, there have been five major legally authorized gun importers in Ghana (there were previously nine).[38] These are Game Marketing Limited, Yadco Enterprise, Globart Teslria Enterprise, Bradco Trading & Associates,[39] and Ampoma Ahwene Enterprise.[40] These importers, according to the police, 'in the year 2000 alone [imported] 19,468 pieces of shotguns ... authorised by the Ministry of Interior to be imported into the

---

[37] For an earlier work dispelling some of the negative notions of foreigners being involved in crime and robberies, see EK Aning and E Sowatey, 'Coping Mechanisms of Refugees at the Bujumbura Refugee Camp in Ghana', unpublished mimeo (2002), 20ff. Some of the notions that this paper dispels about refugees are that: (a) all foreigners in Ghana are refugees; (b) refugees are a serious economic burden on Ghana; (c) most refugees are rural and thus do not contribute to urban life; and (d) the general criminalization of all refugees.

[38] In all the interviews conducted by this writer, no specific reasons were given for the reduction in the number of arms importers and the criteria for obtaining such a licence.

[39] Cross-border crime and smuggling activities involving firearms are widespread in the West African sub-region. Eg, according to the Interim Report of Arms and Ammunition Inventory Committee, this particular company was involved in a possible transhipment of shotguns and cartridges to two Nigerians involving 14,672 shotguns and 1,313,453 cartridges, see p 5. Similarly, '[t]he Western Marine Command of Nigeria's Customs Service intercepted... in Lagos six Ghanaians in a canoe containing 72,000 rounds of live ammunition and 99 sacks of shotguns from Ghana'. See: <http://www.nisat.org>.

[40] Ibid, 3. This figure is, however, totally undependable as the committee reported that:

> The Police and Customs, Excise and Prevention Service (CEPS) provided the committee with a list each of active and dormant arms dealers. It was observed in the course of the Committee's work that the lists were not up to date. Several of the dealers who were classified as 'Active' were in fact dormant operators who renewed their licenses yearly hoping to re-commence business sometime in the future. On the other hand some dealers whose names appeared on the dormant list turned out to be active operators.

country'.[41] This reflects a steady increase in the number of guns brought into the country[42] between 1994 and 1998 and totalling 182,983 items.[43] In 1999, this led the government of Ghana to initiate efforts to suspend the importation of firearms and to place 'an immediate freeze on sales of existing stocks pending an inventory of all stocks held by private arms dealers and a review of procedures for their acquisition and registration'.[44] There seems to be no government official with any knowledge or information about the outcome of this freeze.[45]

4.4 Economic impact of firearms violence

There is very little information on the impact of firearms-related violence on tourism. An estimated 21,000 tourists refrained from visiting Ghana in 2003.[46] In discussions with hoteliers, car hire company managers, and other individuals involved in the tourism industry, there was a perception that the number of reported firearms-related crimes between 2000 and 2002 did, indeed, contribute to a decrease in the total numbers of tourists.

Another economic consequence of this increase in crime is the fact that most women traders, who normally leave their homes at dawn to go to work, now wait until daylight before leaving, and return home earlier at night. The fear of being attacked is responsible for them losing 4–5 hours of work every day, which results in a loss of income. Although it is difficult to estimate the financial value of such losses, there was consensus among women traders that their fear of firearms-related crimes impacts negatively on their resources and productivity.[47]

---

[41] See Meeting between the Inspector General of Police and UN Conflict Resolution Team, (Accra, September 2002), 5. The Police perspective on SALW smuggling is equally pertinent:

> A few military/police peacekeeping officers returning from UN missions and Ghanaians returning from their sojourn abroad do succeed in smuggling in some weapons, mainly pistols into the country. Also after the war [sic] in neighbouring Liberia and Sierra Leone, some guns are suspected to have been smuggled into or out of Ghana.

'Soldier Busted Over Weapons', *Public Agenda*, 25 June 2008.

[42] See, eg, 'Proliferation of Arms, A Worry to Government'. The former Interior Minister, Alhaji Malik Alhassan Yakubu, confirmed that for the year 2000 alone, the Ministry of Interior authorized 19,468 shotguns to be imported. In the same article, it was estimated that 7,800 guns are manufactured annually, which is a woeful understatement of the extent of illicit firearms proliferation in Ghana.

[43] See Arms and Ammunition Inventory Committee Interim Report (no X), 6.

[44] XINHUA, Chinese News Service (1 August 1999) <http://www.nisat.org>.

[45] Interview with Head of the Criminal Investigation Department Arms Registry, GPS, Accra.

[46] See KW Obeng, 'Emerging Gun Culture Scaring Investors', Interview 15 May 2001, *Weekend Agenda*, 21 May 2009. See also Interview with an official of the US Information Centre, Accra office, 23 August 2003.

[47] Interviews with market women in Madina and Accra between June and August 2003.

5. Legal framework and enforcement

5.1 Domestic regulation

In Ghana, the colonial administration tried to control gun-making, in the same manner that it banned alcohol production, but this indigenous industry nonetheless continues. Blacksmith and locksmith technologies progressed openly with the manufacture of trinkets, gold ornaments, and basic farm implements, while the highly profitable smithing business dealt with gun manufacture. Recent research reveals that gun-making has gained in sophistication and that the products are relatively competitive, both in terms of pricing and quality.[48]

According to research conducted in five of the ten regions of Ghana, there are an estimated 35,000 to 40,000 illegally produced guns, and at least 2,500 blacksmiths with the capacity for production in one region alone. This figure does not include the apprentices who have the capacity to manufacture guns under supervision. These findings have serious implications for the national and sub-regional security of Ghana, although it should be noted that only 30 per cent or less of firearms-related crime involves locally made guns.[49] If gun-making production and culture is so widespread, what is the legal regime governing small arms and ammunition in Ghana?

The major piece of legislation applicable to SALW in Ghana is the Arms and Ammunition Act of 1962 (Act 118). This comprehensive Act regulates arms and ammunition possession and usage in Ghana. Another piece of legislation, the Arms and Ammunition Decree of 1972 (National Redemption Council Decree, or NRCD 9), governs the registration process by establishing a harsh punishment regime (a fine of 10,000 Cedis—approximately US$5,000—or imprisonment of 5 years' maximum, or both).[50] NRCD 9 also abolishes the local manufacture of arms. This licensing regime is substantially more comprehensive than the 1962 Act. Two other key regulations are the Locksmiths Act of 1994 (Act 488) and the Arms and Ammunition (Amendment) Act of 1996 (Act 519). Furthermore, the Security and Intelligence Agencies Act (Act 526) of 1996 is another institutional process designed to tackle a number of security issues—among which are the threats posed by SALW possession to human security.[51]

---

[48] This writer has had several interviews with the leadership of the Blacksmiths Association of Ashanti Region. For more information, see KE Aning, 'Transnational Organised Crime: The Ghana Case Study' (Vienna: UN Office for Drugs and Crime, 2004).

[49] There is some disagreement about this figure. Several senior police officers in the crime departments appeared to have a higher figure, although 30% is more consistent with the cases reported in the newspapers (interview with senior police officers, Akosombo, 21–23 August 2003).

[50] Arms and Ammunition Decree, 1972 (NRCD 9), s11(f)4.

[51] See Government of Ghana, the Five Hundred and Twenty-Sixth Act of the Parliament of the Republic of Ghana entitled the Security and Intelligence Agencies Act, 1996. Especially Part II Sections 5–9 dealing with the establishment of the Regional and District Security Councils.

The Arms and Ammunition Act is currently undergoing revision, and the results will hopefully be laid before Parliament in 2010.[52] However, there seems to be some confusion regarding the legality of guns manufactured by blacksmiths. While one interpretation posits that manufacturing is completely banned, another interpretation states that the Minister of Interior can give exceptional authorization, although the conditions and modalities for issuing such authorization are unclear.

5.2 Import controls

The legislative framework dealing with firearms in Ghana also contributes to the ability of local craft producers to 'flood' the market with their products. Although blacksmiths are not allowed to manufacture guns, they can repair imported firearms which are damaged in Ghana, and have taken advantage of this loophole in the law to experiment with manufacturing techniques. The law allows two categories of arms importers in Ghana: individual first-class arms and ammunition dealers (defined by an annual importation of between 1,000 and 2,000 shotguns and ammunition) and second-class arms and ammunition importers (who import less than 1,000 items a year).[53] The five major arms importers (a figure now reduced to four) import on average 20,000 shotguns per year. It is ironic that the Ghanaian public discourse is that while the government appears quite comfortable with importing foreign weapons without laying down a saturation point for such an exercise, it seems to harbour a quasi-pathological fear of local craft producers and their products.

6. Response mechanisms

6.1 Individual and corporate responses

One of the most visible and direct effects of the increasing prevalence of firearms-related crime in Ghana is the rise of both formal and informal militant community groups that respond to this menace. There are several explanations for communities taking the law into their own hands: first is the serious manpower, financial, and resource constraints faced by the GPS. Successive governments and police administrations have been unable to recruit new officers and even retaining serving officers has been problematic: the GPS is almost 50 per cent understaffed. A second explanation is the public perception of the GPS as

---

[52] The whole process of revising the Arms and Ammunitions Act has been stalled because of delay in establishing the National Commission on Small Arms. Ironically, there are efforts to incorporate the establishment of the National Commission into the revised law.

[53] Government of Ghana, *Arms and Ammunitions Decree*, 1972 (NRCD 9), s 6.

corrupt, inefficient, poorly armed, and under-resourced to respond adequately to the challenges posed by firearms-related crime.[54]

The first visible societal response is the increasing prevalence of mob justice as a response to what is perceived as the impunity of criminals and the lack of efficiency of the criminal justice system. Although the police show concern about mob violence, most people seem not to care about this phenomenon. This confirms the general perception that 'mob action in Ghana is not seen as a crime by most citizens'.[55]

6.2 Private security companies

Another response mechanism to the easy availability of SALW has been an upsurge of private security companies (PSCs) in Ghana, particularly in Accra and its environs. PSCs have become a booming growth industry, with over 110 companies and a turnover running into billions of cedis.[56] This industry is directed at customers who can pay; those who cannot have to resort to vigilantism or other forms of community protection schemes.[57]

One of the fastest growing and most profitable areas for private security firms has been the provision of security services to businesses, individuals, and communities—particularly in urban areas where public security forces alone cannot counter firearms-related crime. Such privatization of police functions means that the guards provide security only for those who pay for it. That deflects criminals to other less wealthy individuals and communities who still depend on the under-manned and under-resourced police. As a result, the rise in private alternatives for security is hardly surprising. Indeed, security appears to be one of the best functioning markets in many West African countries, and Ghana is no exception. What is disturbing, however, is that because of the inability of the regulatory and oversight bodies to work effectively, companies of dramatically varying quality, professionalism, and effectiveness have been established and are flourishing all over Ghana.

Since 2002, the Ghanaian government has sought to streamline the activities of PSCs by establishing an inter-ministerial and inter-sectoral committee to evaluate their activities and re-register those found to be appropriate.[58] The

---

[54] On police corruption, see *The Ghana Governance and Corruption Survey: Evidence from Households, Enterprises and Public Officials*, study commissioned by the World Bank and conducted by the Ghana Centre for Democracy and Development, August 2000.

[55] R Anane, 'Mob Justice—A Threat to True Justice', *Accra Daily Mail*, 24 February 2003, 5.

[56] Several interviews with Peter Awonoor-Renner, CEO, K-9 Security Services and President of the Association of Private Security Organisations in Ghana, Accra.

[57] MA Vinorkor, 'Land Guards Harass North Kwabenya Residents', *The Ghanaian Times*, 18 September, 2003, 16. In this particular instance, residents in this suburb of Accra who felt harassed by land guards were ready to form protection units to 'deal appropriately' with land guards, who were operating as a private army. 'If a private army can be allowed to operate, if thugs can be protected by the police...we must bunch up ourselves to help ourselves.'

[58] The Committee has since released the names of the first 47 PSCs whose licences have been renewed.

first known legislative instrument to govern PSCs in Ghana is the Police Service Act of 1970 (Act 350). But the mechanisms and procedures for controlling these companies are at best ineffective. Until mid-2002, there were over 300 PSCs in Ghana, most of them operating without a state licence. Since June 2002, the government has undertaken strenuous measures to regulate the industry 'properly' and to that extent has reduced the total numbers to simply 105 companies.[59] However, the Ministry of Interior, which oversees these companies, does not seem to have adequate information on them. Of the companies, only 41 per cent are members of the Association of Private Security Operators in Ghana, the professional organization that seeks to organize and set standards for the industry. Considering that this industry employs close to 10,000 workers, it seems critical to put into place tightened legislation and oversight rules.[60]

6.3 Government responses

There is a public perception about a culture of impunity in Ghana, which is related to lack of police performance and even corruption. The phenomenon of 'Pobbers', that is, serving police officers who actively participate in or 'loan' their uniforms or equipment to robbers contributes to such public perception.[61] The police action, or inaction, is perceived as contributing to firearms-related crimes, and the criminal justice system's ability to dispense fair justice has been so undermined that a magistrate once accepted the fact that 'justice [has] been on sale in the country for a long time'.[62] A possible explanation for the difficulties in dealing with firearms-related crime and the culture of impunity is the sheer number of robbery cases involved, a fact which has been acknowledged by a former Chief Justice of Ghana, Justice EK Wiredu.[63]

The culture of impunity is also linked to the incapacity of the criminal justice system to prosecute criminal cases in general and firearms-related crimes in particular. If more than 62 per cent of all reported crimes cannot be dealt with by the official criminal justice agencies, this creates serious problems for public perception concerning the state's capacity to tackle crime effectively.

The government is concerned about the increasing instability in the country, and an official committee was established to examine this problem. Its remit was to 'initiate measures...[to] curb the spate of armed robberies and

---

[59] There is much controversy about the procedures applied by government to select the 105 companies that were cleared. The re-evaluation has subsequently reduced this figure to 47.

[60] Interview with Peter Awoonor-Renner, former Chair of the Association of Private Security Organisations in Ghana, 25 April 2005.

[61] 'Cop Five Others Remanded for Robbery', *The Ghanaian Chronicle*, 12 May 2003, 1. See also 'Policeman Robber Remanded in Prison', *The Ghanaian Times*, 10 May 2003, 1 and 'Cop Nabbed over Robbery', *Daily Graphic*, 13 November 2004, 1.

[62] CN Bamfo, 'Ten Years of the Commission on Human Rights and Administrative Justice— Achievements, Prospects and Challenges', *The Chronicle*, 17 September 2003, 8.

[63] J Mensah, 'Robbery and Offensive Weapons Top Cases', *Daily Guide*, 13 February 2003, 5.

other violent crimes in Ghana'.[64] But by concentrating on *one* particular type of firearms-related crime, namely armed robbery, it ignores other threats posed by firearms to society in general. In this chapter, however, it is posited that by shifting the terminology from 'armed robbery' to 'firearms-related crime' different criminal activities that would hitherto have been ignored would be captured.

Although the general perception in Accra and its environs is that there is an improvement in the fight against crime, the early closure of petrol stations (which used to be open 24 hours a day) is still in force.[65] According to a senior police officer, the waves of violence against petrol stations vary depending on whether particular individuals with specialized skills in robbing and attacking petrol stations are in jail or on bail.[66]

Another indirect aspect of firearms-related crime is the preponderance of roadblocks in and around Accra at night. There is, however, general appreciation among the capital's residents that armed roadblocks are useful and effective and create a sense of security. However, such roadblocks can also lead to instances in which officers take undue advantage of the population, especially traders. According to police sources, such illegal operations are embarked on by police officers to 'get something' for their weekends.[67]

Owing to the transnational nature of certain aspects of firearms-related crime, there are various endeavours for collaboration between the governments of Ghana and Nigeria.[68] Other bilateral initiatives are being undertaken between Ghana and her contiguous neighbours. A first step has been the meeting of security chiefs from Ghana, Togo, and Burkina Faso on information-sharing arrangements on SALW, mercenaries, and rebel movements.[69] Further efforts are being undertaken to bring the Ivory Coast into this process.

7. Challenges of SALW research

While writing about SALW and human security is challenging enough, there is also a dearth of materials on firearms-related crime in Ghana. The first major study on crime was completed in 2001 and analysed small arms proliferation in

[64] See Arms and Ammunition Inventory Committee Interim Report, Accra, November 1999.
[65] *Daily Graphic*, 17 January, 2001.
[66] Interview with Michael Teku, District Police Commander and David Eklu, former Police Public Relations Officer, Accra, 17 June 2008.
[67] Ibid. According to a police source, his colleagues demanded 50 cedis but the driver pleaded and gave them 5 cedis, which they turned down. After some bargaining, the driver gave them 20 cedis and drove away.
[68] See Memorandum of Understanding between Ghana and Nigeria (signed August 1999). Copy in possession of the author.
[69] Interview with senior official of National Security Council, Accra, 21 January 2009.

five of the ten regions in Ghana.[70] That aside, there are virtually no secondary sources on small arms in Ghana other than a few pieces yet to be published.[71] The most readily available resources for research on these issues remain the publicly accessible data from newspapers and from police files, if available.[72] Other accessible materials that go beyond the case of Ghana can be found in *Focus on Small Arms in West Africa* published by the Foundation for Security and Development in Africa (FOSDA).

While information garnered from newspapers can be useful in giving an indication of the extent of the problem, there is a significant level of under-reporting of crime in Ghana. For example, between January and June 2002, the majority of papers reported only 32 cases of armed robberies nationwide. Moreover, there is a need to expand the debate beyond the robberies in which firearms are used.

A methodological difficulty was the deep suspicion in Ghana about 'civilians' dealing with issues normally within the purview of 'securocrats', and the fear that one may be using the cover of 'research' to gather information that will eventually be handed over to the security agencies. Data from emergency wards of hospitals and clinics are virtually non-existent. The main reason for the incomplete official computation of firearms-related crime and injury statistics is the fact that because of the legislation governing arms, most victims are unwilling to disclose information about the type and cause of their injuries.

From the available crime data, it is difficult to differentiate between categories of crime involving firearms. The official crime data gathered by the GPS differentiates between crime types, but seldom endeavours to break down its 29 categories of crime types into those in which a firearm was involved. This lack of precision is evidenced by the category called 'other offences'—from 1992 to 2000, an increasing number of crimes have been put into this category. Equally worrying, is the fact that certain crime categories with as low a frequency figure as five incidences per year have been captured in the data. Unless the types of crime categorized as 'other offences' and their frequency rates are known, the usefulness of the official data as a source for information and analysis will be, at best, tenuous. Some thematic problems related to SALW researches include the following:

- police–public relationship, which deals with issues of trust;
- accessibility to and awareness of police presence;

---

[70] KE Aning, A Yakubu, N Abdulai, and M Dawarula, *Between Indifference and Naiveté: The Need for a National Policy Framework on Small Arms in Ghana* (Delhi: New CHRI and FOSDA, 2001).

[71] KE Aning, 'Local Craft Production and Legislation on Small Arms in Ghana', *West Africa*, 7–13 July, 17–18.

[72] For an analysis dealing specifically with the changing nature of armed robbery in Ghana, see F Agyemfra, 'Combating Armed Robbers in Ghana', paper delivered at African Security Dialogue and Research, November 2002.

- economic status of the victim and capacity to absorb the costs implicit in reporting;
- ancillary factors including perceptions about the police; and
- public access and availability of reporting accessories, such as phones and transportation.

8. Conclusion

The origin of SALW proliferation in Ghana can be traced back to the Rawlings government in the 1980s which, by equipping civilian militias with firearms, militarized entire segments of society. Although the Ghanaian legislation on gun manufacturing is relatively strict, a large number of skilled blacksmiths produce firearms locally, out of sight of the government. There are in Ghana an estimated 35,000 to 40,000 illegally produced guns and the increase in firearms-related crimes has had adverse economic effects, although these are difficult to assess quantitatively. There is a widespread public perception that the police and the justice system are unable to deal with firearms-related crimes, resulting in the creation of militant community groups and sometimes mob justice. The private security business has blossomed in Ghana, but most companies are neither registered nor monitored.

5

The ILO and 'Human Security' of Sub-Saharan African Labour

Ben Chigara*

1. Introduction

The new concept of security, which was popularized by the United Nations Development Programme (UNDP) in 1994, advocates the focusing of attention on individuals and their communities rather than on the protection of the state per se.[1] This development led the UN to create institutions for the promotion and implementation of human security.[2] The Commission on Human Security (CHS) was established in January 2001 for the specific purpose of advancing the twin goals of 'freedom from want' and 'freedom from fear'.[3] The Human Security Unit was created in September 2004 in the UN Secretariat and was tasked with facilitating the integration of particular UN values into the core activities of the Organization.

The CHS defines human security as the protection of:

(a) the vital core of all human lives in ways that enhance human freedoms and human fulfilment;
(b) fundamental freedoms—freedoms that are the essence of life. It means protecting people from critical (severe) and pervasive (widespread) threats and situations and reliance on processes that build on people's strengths and aspirations;

---

* Research Professor of International Law and Director of Enterprise and International Affairs, Brunel Law School, Brunel University, Uxbridge, UK. The writer is grateful to his wife Constance; his sons Ben Jr and Barnabas; and Fred and Barbara for their support.
[1] See Chapter 1 of this volume for a comprehensive discussion of this concept.
[2] Debating the necessity and contribution of international institutions to the furtherance of human rights protection see especially H Steiner, 'International Protection of Human Rights' in MD Evans (ed), *International Law* (2nd edn, Oxford: Oxford University Press, 2006), 755–8; H Steiner et al, *International Human Rights in Context* (3rd edn, Oxford: Oxford University Press, 2008), 671–4.
[3] See CHS website at: <http://www.humansecurity-chs.org/about/Establishment.html>. The Commission concluded its business on 31 May 2003. The Advisory Board on Human Security was established thereafter to carry forward the recommendations of the Commission.

(c) political, social, environmental, economic, military, and cultural systems that together give people the building blocks of survival, livelihood, and dignity.[4]

The goals of the CHS are expressed as:

1. to provide public understanding, engagement and support of human security and its underlying imperatives;
2. to develop the concept of human security as an operational tool for policy formulation and implementation; and
3. to propose a concrete program of action to address critical and pervasive threats to human security.[5]

These goals, which have now become the object of the Advisory Board on Human Security (ABHS),[6] are closely linked to the Millennium Development Goals (MDGs)[7]. Like the latter, they echo a more distant aspiration of states contained in Part XIII of the Treaty of Versailles (1919)[8] that established the International Labour Organization (ILO) as an agency of the League of Nations[9] namely, to ensure the establishment of universal peace and security through the pursuit of social justice. The ILO was established for the specific purpose of preventing conditions of hardship and injustice to labour. These values are reflected in the CHS's description of human security as freedom from want and fear.[10] The ILO is thus one of the earliest international attempts to ensure universal human security.

The ILO's establishment was originally prompted by the need to improve such labour conditions at the end of the First World War, that were perceived to be urgently required

as, for example, by the regulation of the hours of work, including the establishment of a maximum working day and week, the regulation of the labour supply, the prevention of unemployment, the provision of an adequate living wage, the protection of the worker against sickness, disease and injury arising out of his employment, the protection of children, young persons and women, provision for old age and injury, protection of the interests of workers when employed in countries other than their own, recognition of the principle of freedom of association, the organisation of vocational and technical education and other measures. Whereas also the failure of any nation to adopt humane

---

[4] CHS, *Human Security Now* (New York: United Nations Publications, 2003), 4.

[5] See CHS website (n 3 above).

[6] Currently chaired by Sadako Ogata the ABHS is an independent body comprising eight distinguished international figures.

[7] Assessing Africa's progress towards fulfilment of the MDGs by the target date of 2015, see also UN Economic and Social Council Economic Commission for Africa, Twenty-seventh meeting of the Committee of Experts (6 March 2008) E/ECA/COE/27/10; AU/CAMEF/EXP/10(III). In general, see UN, *MDGs Report* (New York: DESA Publications, 2008).

[8] Available at San Diego University website at: <http://history.sandiego.edu/GEN/text/versaillestreaty/vercontents.html>.

[9] Discussing the jurisdiction, competencies, challenges, and achievements of the ILO in relation to the effort to promote the recognition and protection of the dignity of indigenous African workers from empire-building enterprises, see B Chigara, 'Social Justice: The Link Between Trade Liberalisation and Sub-Saharan Africa's Potential to Achieve the United Nations Millennium Development Goals by 2015' (2008) 26 NQHR 9.   [10] CHS website (n 3 above).

conditions of labour is an obstacle in the way of other nations which desire to improve the conditions in their own countries.[11]

Therefore, it is fitting that all preliminary and subsequent efforts to evaluate the work of the CHS and of the MDGs project should take account also of the experience and achievements of the ILO as the beacon of both sets of goals since 1919.[12]

This chapter examines the ILO's contribution to the recognition and promotion of the inherent dignity of sub-Saharan African labour. It argues that in the pursuit of its mandate, the ILO has always focused on individuals' and minority groups' security as a means of ensuring national and world peace. Its long experience in information gathering and processing and development of policy in the prosecution of its mandate could benefit new UN attempts to ensure national and international security by targeting individual and minority group rights rather than the protection of state organs only.

2. ILO competencies and the human security initiative

International law is clear that the purposes for which an entity is created reflect not just its *express* competencies—usually outlined in the constitutive instrument(s)—but also its *implied* competences. In its *Advisory Opinion to the UN General Assembly Concerning Reparations for Injuries Suffered in the Service of the United Nations*,[13] the International Court of Justice (ICJ) stated that the capacity of international organizations to conclude treaties is settled if the specific constituent instrument so authorizes the organization, or if the purpose(s) and objective(s) of the organization make it impossible for it to function without the capacity to conclude treaties. This suggests that constitutive treaties are in a league of their own in that they possess lawmaking capacity. Oppenheim writes that lawmaking treaties 'stipulate new general rules for future international conduct or confirm, define or abolish existing customary or conventional rules of a general character'.[14] Part XIII of the Treaty of Versailles (1919)[15] establishing the ILO is a fitting example of this.

---

[11] Organization of Labour, Treaty of Versailles, Preamble, Part XII, Section I (28 June 1919), available at: <http://www.ilo.org/ilolex/english/constq.htm>.

[12] Discussing the relevance to African states of the current International Labour Code two-thirds of which had been established by the time that they began to join the Organization as politically sovereign entities, see also B Chigara, 'Latecomers to the ILO and the Authorship and Ownership of the International Labour Code' (2007) 28 HRQ 706.

[13] *Reparation for Injuries Suffered in the Service of the United Nations Case* [1949] ICJ Rep 182.

[14] R Jennings and A Watts (eds), *Oppenheim's International Law Vol I* (9th edn, London: Longman, 1996), 26.

[15] See Treaty of Versailles, Pt XIII (28 June 1919) <http://history.sandiego.edu/GEN/text/versaillestreaty/vercontents.html>. See also appendix to the ILO Constitution (1919) available at ILO: <http://www.ilo.org/ilolex/english/constq.htm>.

2.1 The Treaty of Versailles mandate

Although the ILO was first conceived as a response to the ethical considerations about the human cost of the 'Industrial Revolution' of the early nineteenth century, the Peace Treaty of Versailles had mandated the ILO to deal continually with social challenges that threatened 'conditions of hardship, and privation to large numbers of people so as to threaten or, produce unrest so great that the peace and harmony of the world would be imperilled'.[16]

This universal *subject* and *object* jurisdiction of the ILO appeared to favour, more than any other group, the indigenous populations of sub-Saharan Africa, Asia, and South America that were under European colonial domination. Certainly, very few hardships in life compare to the indignities that accompany conquest or occupation by another group or nation,[17] particularly when such occupation is characterized by the practice of apartheid as was more often the case in sub-Saharan Africa.[18] An assessment of the ILO's long-term achievements must therefore be about whether it succeeded in establishing a universal labour code for the promotion of human security, and how successful it is (or would be) at ensuring state compliance. However, the context in which the ILO had been established made this challenge monumental and thus worth considering.

2.2 Context in which the ILO was established

By the time the ILO was established, Europe's colonial powers had already convened a conference for the partitioning of Africa—the Berlin Conference (1884).[19] The main outcome of that conference was the carving out of Africa into spheres of control. This had resulted in France taking control of most of West Africa, and Britain, East and Southern Africa. Belgium had taken control of the vast Congo Basin while Germany had occupied four colonies, one in each of the realm's regions. Portugal had taken a small colony in West Africa, and two large ones in Southern Africa. Europe's colonial powers had ensured the insertion into the Peace Treaty of Versailles, of a colonial phrase that empowered them to deny colonial labour the same protections that it afforded the metropolitan labour.

Therefore, Europe's colonial powers could, and did in fact, reject the application of the emergent international labour code in their colonies. This threatened the

---

[16] Ibid.

[17] More recently the 2003 US-led occupation of Iraq has been characterized also with reports of unbecoming conduct against the civilian population by allied agents and forces. See, eg, Global Policy Forum, 'Atrocities and Criminal Homicides in Iraq' <http://www.globalpolicy.org/security/issues/iraq/atrocitindex.htm>.

[18] See D Judd, *Empire: The British Imperial Experience, From 1765 to the Present* (London: Fontana Press, 1996).

[19] At this conference, colonial powers agreed spheres of control. See Convention Revising the General Act of Berlin, 26 February 1885, and the General Act and Declaration of Brussels, 2 July 1890; 15 AJIL (Supplement: Official Documents Oct, 1921), 314.

development of a universal labour code as envisaged by the Organization's constituent treaty. During negotiations of the Slavery Convention (1926) Europe's colonial powers had vehemently rejected any attempt to curtail coercive labour practices beyond the prohibition of the practice of slavery, even disregarding the fact that the dehumanizing effect of forced labour in the colonies threatened race wars and risked facilitating communist propaganda.[20]

Therefore, the ILO mandate to promote universal human security appeared to be on a collision course with colonial powers' policy of discriminating between native indigenous labour in their colonies on the one hand, and European labour, on the other. This was typified in most Colonial Governing Authorities' support for abusive European agricultural and industrial practices in the name of 'colonial development'. Such support included using institutions of the Administrators to coerce native indigenous populations to provide their labour whenever it was required, contrary to the principle of voluntary and non-coercive labour practice.[21] However, the ILO's legitimacy[22] particularly after the adoption of the Declaration of Philadelphia (1944)[23] depended on the promotion of human security for both metropolitan and native indigenous colonial labours.

Constitutionally, the Philadelphia Declaration concerning the aims and purposes of the ILO (1944) radically transformed the legal competencies of the ILO that had been enumerated in Part XIII, Section 1 of the Peace Treaty of Versailles[24] by extending their scope from workers, to *people everywhere.* This development served to emphasize the urgency in the mission to overcome social injustice and social conditions targeted by the establishment of the ILO.

3. Colonial powers and colonial labour *versus* the legitimacy of the ILO[25]

In sub-Saharan Africa colonial intervention was characterized by social, political, and economic tensions that were often explained in terms of developmental

[20] See also DR Maul, 'The ILO and the Struggle against Forced Labour from 1919 to the present' (2007) 48 Labor History 481. [21] Ibid.
[22] Outlining the tenets of legitimacy which include coherency, consistency, determinacy, transparency, and cultural validation see especially TM Franck, *The Power of Legitimacy Among Nations* (Oxford: Oxford University Press, 1990).
[23] See appendix to the ILO Constitution (n 15 above).
[24] See Primary Documents on The War To End All Wars website at: <http://www.firstworldwar.com/source/versailles.htm>.
[25] Examining barriers to greater recognition of indigenous people's rights, see also C Tennant, 'Indigenous Peoples, International Institutions, and the International Legal literature from 1945–1993' (1994) 16 HRQ 1; J Goudal, 'Agricultural Development and Indigenous Labour in the French Colonies of Tropical Africa' (1939) 40 ILR 209; RL Barsh, 'Indigenous Peoples in the 1990s: From Object to Subject of International Law?' (1994) 7 Harv HRJ 33; SJ Anaya, 'Indigenous Rights Norms in Contemporary International Law' (1991) 8 Ariz JICL 1; DH Getches, 'Indigenous Peoples' Right to Water under International Norms' (2005) 16 Col JIEL & Pol 259; J Debeljak,

necessities. First, the pattern and cycle of expropriation of ancestral lands and domains that the native Africans had held from time immemorial, coupled with their *compulsion* to serve as seasonal, migrant, bonded, or home-based labourers was repeated across the continent.[26]

Secondly, in respect of the development of agricultural production in the colonies[27] the system that emerged regarded European settlers as providers of capital and technical skill, and the native indigenous populations as a mere and incidental source of labour. This approach had engineered a process of social transformation that had disrupted traditional systems of land utilization—themselves products of centuries of adaptation to the environment.[28] It also reduced the native indigenous population to wage labourers that worked directly under the control of settler farm landowners and capital mining organizations. The forms of labour exploitation that had resulted from these developments had triggered both the object and subject jurisdictions of the ILO.[29] Consequently, just two years after its creation, the ILO had begun in 1921 to address the situation of so-called 'native workers' in the overseas colonies of European powers.[30]

3.1 'Indigenousness' as a tool for the protection of native colonial labour

There is no fixity in the idea of indigenousness. Literature on the subject evidences shifting understandings of the term—some more enduring than others. The Masai of Kenya and Tanzania, the Maya of Guatemala, the Roma and the Saami of Europe, the peoples of the Chittagong Hill Tracts of Bangladesh, and the Maoris of New Zealand, Inuits of Canada, and Aborigines of Australia are often cited as examples of indigenous peoples.[31]

Anaya[32] uses social history to problematize the search for a definition of indigenousness and arrives at a liberal characterization of the idea. His approach is inclusive, excluding only 'the most transient or migratory segments of humanity'.[33]

'Barriers to the Recognition of Indigenous People's Human Rights at the United Nations' (2000) 26 Mon ULR 159.

[26] Examining this phenomenon in former German, Portuguese, and British colonies of Southern Africa in the nineteenth century, see B Chigara, *Land Reform Policy: The Challenge of Human Rights Law* (Aldershot: Ashgate, 2004), ch 1. See also CK Meek, *Land Law and Custom in the Colonies* (Oxford: Oxford University Press, 1949).

[27] See also J Goudal (n 25 above) 209.

[28] See also A Tevoedjre, 'A Strategy for Social Progress in Africa and the ILO's Contribution' (1969) 99 ILR 61, 63.

[29] ILO, Background on ILO Work with Indigenous and Tribal Peoples' <http://www.ilo.org/public/english/indigenous/background/index.htm>.

[30] See ILO, *African Labour Survey: Studies and Reports*, New Series No 48 (Lausanne: Imprimeries Réunies, 1958), 295.

[31] See, eg, SJ Anaya, 'International Human Rights and Indigenous Peoples: The Move Toward the Multicultural State' (2004) 21 Ariz JICL 13.   [32] Ibid.

[33] Ibid.

Therefore, although European nationalities that were responsible for colonialism remained indeed indigenous to their homelands, they nevertheless became settled in newer places.

The dominant settler populations that were born of colonial patterns have created societies so that many might now be described as indigenous to the place of settlement. It may even be said that recently migrating populations are in the process of becoming part of the dominant indigenous receiving society or laying down roots that will, over time, establish their own distinctive indigenous connections with the place of migration.[34]

In similar vein others have argued that because of her social history and her participation in both the multilateral and the regional arrangements and regulations on refugee protection, Zimbabwe has become a multicultural state whose indigenous peoples include Zimbabweans of European, American, African, and Asian descents.[35] Therefore, it is arguable that although the term indigenous and terms such as native have for a long time been used to denote:

A particular subset of humanity that represent a common set of experiences that are rooted in historical subjugation by colonisation, or something like colonialism, today, indigenous peoples are identified, and identify themselves as such, by reference to identities that pre-date historical encroachments by other groups and the ensuing histories that have challenged their cultural survival and self-determination as distinct peoples:

their modern liberal meanings are probably more diverse and more inclusive.

3.2 'Indigenousness' as a tool for developing native peoples' labour rights

The International Labour Conference on the Forced Labour Convention (1930) was intended primarily to deal with the continuing direct and indirect dehumanization of native indigenous Africans in colonial territories especially in the effort to construct public utilities such as roads, railways, and harbours for the purpose of facilitating economic penetration.[36] Goudal writes that private undertakings, including plantations and mines required a level of constant labour supply that was simply not to be had on a voluntary basis. This resulted particularly in the inter-war period, in

widespread and systematic imposition of forced labour on the African population, particularly in territories where Europeans did not confine themselves to trading but also engaged in agriculture or mining. Native chiefs were required periodically to supply contingents of able-bodied men, the numbers of which were fixed by the authorities. These men were used primarily for public works, although some of them might have turned

---

[34] Ibid.
[35] See B Chigara, 'From Oral to Recorded Governance: Reconstructing Title to Real Property in 21st Century Zimbabwe' (2001) 30 CLWR 36.   [36] See ILO (n 30 above) 295.

over to private employers. Moreover, even in the case of recruitment by private individuals, coercion played a large part since such operations were carried out with the help and direct participation of the authorities. Taxes imposed on able-bodied men in some territories constituted an indirect form of forced labour, since only through paid employment could many Africans hope to find the necessary money.[37]

Indigenous Africans had been worst affected by coercive labour practice when the institutions of the colonial authority had combined with private economic interests to achieve a system whereby penal sanctions were made an acceptable and appropriate punishment for breaches of employment contracts. Maul[38] reports that worker representatives at the 1939 ILO Conference had condemned this widespread practice as an *unholy alliance* between private profit interests and colonial powers. This collusion between the colonial authority and the European undertakings had disincentivized employers from creating acceptable working and wage conditions. Further, it had exempted them from any legal obligation to create acceptable working and wage conditions.

One consequence of the use of these coercive labour practices was the perpetual pressurization of the natives to cooperate with the colonial administrations by providing labour whenever it was needed, or in the case of Nyasaland, to emigrate 'for the express purpose of earning money to pay taxes'.[39] The British Government Colonial Report of 1934[40] estimated that the native indigenous population of Malawi had reached 1,600,713. It also estimated that approximately 120,000 Nyasaland natives were absent. Approximately 75,000 of that number were reported to have migrated to Southern Rhodesia (present day Zimbabwe); 20,000 to the Union of South Africa (present day Republic of South Africa); and 15,000 to Tanganyika (present day Tanzania).

3.3 The ILO Native Labour Code initiative

The ILO strategy for addressing both the native indigenous emigrant labour problems and the coercion of native indigenous Africans by European undertakings and colonial administrations was constrained by the latter's insistence that the emergent international labour code did not apply in their colonies. The ILO premised its response to this situation upon the construction that membership of a distinctly recognizable group (indigenous blacks) should alone be sufficient to invoke complete legal protection of the inherent dignity of that group as human beings. This was justified by the fact that other distinct groups (settler white Europeans) already enjoyed similar legal protection of their dignity as human beings by virtue of their membership of their group status, or of their access to, or their links with the political establishment. Some 50 years later, the Human

---

[37] Ibid.   [38] DR Maul (see n 20 above) 482.
[39] ILO Reports and Enquiries, 'Recruiting and Native Welfare in Nyasaland' (1936) 33 ILR 850.   [40] Ibid.

Rights Committee relied upon this ratio in the *Lovelace case*[41] and several similar cases that followed.

By this strategy, the ILO had sought to establish standards for the promotion of the human security of indigenous natives by various means, including resort to whatever rights could be secured from one's identity in relation to one's community, one's relationship with one's environment, and one's history. If it worked, then this strategy would consolidate the ILO's place as the vanguard of the protection of the human rights of individuals, especially the human rights of the politically disenfranchised indigenous peoples of Africa.[42] Would it work?

The categorization of colonial labour as a special class of labour enabled the ILO to argue for the development of special labour standards specifically aimed at native indigenous people in colonial territories—a Native Labour Code (NLC),[43] quite separate and distinct from the International Labour Code that comprised the international Conventions and Recommendations. Positive as this might seem, it made the colonies a jurisdiction of separate and 'ultimately less stringent legislation'.[44]

The main weakness in this strategy lay in that it appeared to inadvertently sanction the practice of discrimination between the standards for the protection of the dignity of metropolitan labour on the one hand, and that of colonial territories, on the other. It also appeared to justify the colonial powers' argument that the emergent ILO code did not apply in the colonial territories, contrary to the object and purpose of the ILO Constitution. For instance, the Norwegian government argued before the European Union Commission of Human Rights in *Iversen v Norway* that both Convention 29 and Convention 107 did not apply against Norway because they were a species of regional law, namely, Native Labour Code, adopted 'in the special context of forced labour in colonial or dependent territories'.[45]

On a more positive note, this development emphasizes the importance of one of the ILO's main strategies in the promotion of human security, namely, the gathering and processing of information regarding the welfare and condition of people everywhere in their relations with public and private actors. Without accurate records, situations that threatened conditions of hardship and privation to large numbers of people would fester without much notice and probably develop into social time-bombs.

---

[41] *Lovelace v Canada*, Communication No R 6/24–30 July 1981.

[42] See also A Thomas, 'The International Labour Organisation: Its Origins, Development and Future' (1921) 1 ILR 1. See also ILO, 'The ILO: What It Is and What it Does' <http://www.ilo.org/public/english/bureau/inf/download/brochure/pdf/broch_0904.pdf>.

[43] Discussing the background and procedures to the adoption of the ILO regime against forced labour see also L Swepston, 'A New Step in the International Law on Indigenous and Tribal Peoples: ILO Convention No 169 of 1989' (1990) 15 Ok City ULR 677, 679–82; SJ Anaya (see n 31 above) 13.   [44] DR Maul (see note 20 above) 481.

[45] The Times (London, 13 March 1964).

3.4 Forced labour discourse and the ILO's promotion of human security in the colonies

Due to the fact that negotiations on the Slavery Convention[46] had exposed colonial powers' reluctance to condemn the practice of utilization of man by man beyond slavery, the League of Nations mandated the ILO to conduct a study into the prevention of compulsory labour in order to banish conditions akin to slavery.[47] The ILO utilized this opportunity to push for a normative solution to the problem of forced labour[48] by setting up a Committee of Experts on Native Labour. The committee was then tasked with examining the systems of forced or compulsory labour operating in non-self-governing territories.[49] This resulted in the adoption in 1930 of three ILO NLC instruments, namely: Convention Concerning Forced or Compulsory Labour (C.29); ILO Recommendation No 35 (1930) Concerning Indirect Compulsion to Labour; and the ILO Recommendation No 36 (1930) Concerning the Regulation of Forced or Compulsory Labour.

Both the ILO and the UN have advanced these pioneering anti-coercive labour achievements by adopting further standards. They include the following.

(a) ILO Recommendation No 70 (1944)—Concerning Minimum Standards of Social Policy in dependent Territories, adopted at the Conference meeting in Philadelphia. The Recommendation sets the roadmap for the pursuit of better social conditions for natives of colonized territories by: (i) confirming the application of C.29 to dependent territories; (ii) urging the suppression of forced or compulsory labour in all its forms within the shortest possible period—Article 7; and (iii) reiterating that slave trade and slavery in all its forms has no place in all dependent territories of the colonial powers of Europe.

(b) ILO—Convention Concerning the Abolition of Forced Labour (1957) or C.105 that targeted also the post-war tendencies of using forced labour as a tool of political oppression.[50]

(c) UN—International Convention on the Elimination of All Forms of Racial Discrimination (1966).[51]

(d) UN Declaration on the Elimination of Discrimination against Women (1967).[52]

(e) ILO—Indigenous and Tribal Peoples Convention (1989) or C.169.

(f) ILO—Declaration on Fundamental Principles and Rights at Work (1998). The Declaration obliges all member states parties of the ILO, even if they have

---

[46] See UNHCHR <http://www.unhchr.ch/html/menu3/b/f2sc.htm> accessed 5 May 2009.
[47] DR Maul (see n 20 above) 480.   [48] Ibid.
[49] D Vincent-Daviss, 'Human Rights Law: A Research Guide to the Literature—Part III: The International Labour Organization and Human Rights' [1982–1983] NYUJIL & Pol 241.
[50] Ibid.
[51] 660 UNTS 195 International Convention on the Elimination of All Forms of Racial Discrimination, 7 March 1966, 660 UNTS 195, 5 ILM 352 (entered into force 4 January 1969) (hereinafter 'CERD').   [52] General Assembly Resolution 2263 (XXII) (7 November 1967).

not ratified the ILO Conventions in question, to respect, promote, and realize the principle of the elimination of all forms of forced or compulsory labour and also places a duty on the ILO to assist member states in their efforts to do so.[53]

(g) ILO—Convention on the worst forms of child labour (1999) or C.182.
(h) ILO—Recommendation No 190—Worst forms of child labour (1999).
(i) UN Declaration on the Rights of Indigenous Peoples, 13 September 2007.

ILO Conventions No 105 and No 29 have each been ratified by over 160 states, placing them in the category of the most ratified international conventions. This development demonstrates states' theoretical condemnation of forced or compulsory labour. It privileges also the principle of voluntary labour practice for all and rejects coercive labour practice.

Adopted by the General Conference of the ILO on 10 June 1930, 18 years before the adoption of the Universal Declaration of Human Rights (UDHR, 1948), C.29 inaugurated international legislative concern for the protection of the individual's personal integrity and personal freedom from coercion to work. Prior discourses had examined the issue of forced labour only as a corollary of slave labour. C.29 began the normative process of making labour a voluntary undertaking also in the non-self-governing territories.[54]

As with all groundbreaking pieces of legislation that seek to institute such monumental culture change, C.29 had to be practical by facing up to two realities. One was the dehumanizing effect of forced labour in the colonies, which according to Albert Thomas, could not be sustained without risking race wars and the facilitation of communist propaganda.[55] The other was that colonial powers would not abandon coercive labour practice at the stroke of the pen. Consequently, the ILO had opted for a compromise that was premised on demonstrable tacit acceptance of colonial powers that the widespread use of forced or compulsory labour in the colonies was unsustainable.

The ILO had cited states parties' own pronouncements that coercive labour practices should be abolished incrementally, reservations being allowed for certain purposes deemed transiently necessary for stability and normalcy in the colonies. Had the ILO done anything more radical, such as for instance, producing a treaty proposal that was couched in more stringent terms, the result would have probably been complete failure.[56]

Article 2(1) of C.29 defines the object of the Convention as 'all work or service, which is exacted from any person under the menace of any penalty and for which the said person has not offered himself voluntarily'. The pragmatic provisions of C.29 are contained in Articles 1(1–3) and 2(2)(a)–(e). The latter exempts forced

---

[53] See ILO, *Human Trafficking and Forced Labour Exploitation: Guidance for Legislation and Law Enforcement* (Geneva: ILO, 2005), 17.

[54] ILO (see n 30 above) 296. See also *Iversen v Norway*, The Times, 13 March 1964.

[55] Cited in DR Maul (see n 20 above) 481.

[56] The International Trade Organization (1948) concluded in Havana never came to force because it failed to attract the required minimum number of ratifications.

or compulsory labour in public services, by convicted felons only in cases of public emergency. The former makes the object of abolishing forced or compulsory labour a goal to be achieved within 'the shortest possible period'. In particular, it sets a transitional period of five years within which state parties should draw the curtain on the practice. Recommendation No 35 enumerates the checklist that justifies resort to compulsory or forced labour inside the five-year transition period. It includes:[57]

(a) the population's capacity for labour;
(b) voluntarily available labour;
(c) the negative impact that too sudden a withdrawal/drying up of labour might have on habits of life and the social conditions of the population.

These concerns characterize forced labour as an intolerable evil for both the individual victim and his society at large.[58]

3.5 Defining forced labour

In its guidance on legislation and law enforcement regarding the question of human trafficking and forced labour (2005) the ILO stated that three elements must be established in the case of compulsory or forced labour.[59] The first is that the activity must constitute either work or services that have nothing to do whatsoever with the requirement to undergo education or training.[60] The second is that the work or services must be 'exacted from any person under the menace of a penalty'. Penalty refers in this instance to loss of privileges or loss of rights, constituting duress that impedes the exercise of the individual's will to either accept or reject the offer/request to work. Examples of practices that constitute threat or actual use of a penalty include the use of physical or sexual violence and the threat of denunciation to the authorities, commonly applied against irregular migrant workers.[61]

Thirdly, there must exist the absence of consent in the relationship between the 'worker' and an their 'employer' regardless of: (a) the type of activity performed[62]—whether hazardous or not; or (b) the legality of the activity—whether it is legal, or illegal under domestic law;[63] or (c) the official classification of the activity—whether it is officially recognized as an economic activity or not. Thus, women forced into sex work fall under the regime of C.29 because of the involuntary nature of the work and the menace that sustains their relationship with their employer.[64]

---

[57] See Art 1 of Recommendation No 35 Concerning Indirect Compulsion to Labour.
[58] See also D Vincent-Daviss (n 49 above) 241.
[59] See also J Somavia, *A Global Alliance Against Forced Labour* (International Labour Conference 93rd Session 2005) Report IB, 6.   [60] Ibid, 19.
[61] Listed in ILO Guidance n 59, 20.   [62] Ibid.   [63] Ibid.   [64] Ibid.

The Director General of the ILO has noted that today forced labour is present in some form on all continents, in almost all countries, and in every kind of economy:[65]

At least 12.3 million people are victims of forced labour worldwide. Of these, 9.8 million are exploited by private agents, including more than 2.4 million in forced labour as a result of human trafficking. Another 2.5 million are forced to work by the state or by rebel military groups.[66]

This is troubling because of the contradiction that arises from unrivalled state participation in the two ILO conventions against forced labour—C.29 and C.105. Scholars have advanced several reasons for this conundrum.

The first is that states appear incapable of generating and sustaining the political will to instigate the detailed investigations needed to identify forced labour practices and confront them.[67] Secondly, the victims of forced labour may themselves be reluctant to come forward to provide testimony, fearing not only reprisals from their exploiters but perhaps also action against them by immigration and other law enforcement authorities.[68]

However, the problem is that compulsory or forced labour is an attack not only on the individual victim, but on the society as a whole. Thirdly, the precarious legal status of millions of irregular migrant women and men makes them particularly vulnerable to coercion, because of the additional and ever present threat of denunciation to the authorities.[69] Most worrying of all, Juan Somavia writes, there have been very few prosecutions of forced labour offences anywhere in the world.[70] This is incomprehensible because of the estimated scale of the problem.

If the above summation is correct, then we may infer from this that nation states are presently operating on a combination of socio-economic policies that encourage, facilitate, and support rather than impede and suppress forced labour practices. Juan Somavia writes that with a few notable exceptions, national laws of most countries do not define forced labour in any detail. Consequently, law enforcement agents struggle with identifying and prosecuting forced labour offences.[71]

Secondly, the continued prevalence of compulsory or forced labour probably points to national market regulations and migration policies that are favourable rather than antithetical to forced labour practices.[72] The moral of all of this is that unless states make policy reforms in their migration and labour market regulations in order to deliberately and specifically target suppression of forced labour practices, the practice will be difficult to limit or prevent.

3.6 Impact of C.29 on practice in Europe's African colonies

The Forced Labour Convention (1930) seeks to ensure human security by promoting the policy of free labour and the suppression of coercive labour practices.

[65] Ibid, 1.   [66] Ibid, 10.   [67] Ibid, 1–2.   [68] Ibid, 2.   [69] Ibid.
[70] Ibid.   [71] Ibid.   [72] Ibid.

In effect it envisions a policy of suppression and abolition of coercive labour practices—Articles 1, 4, and 6. In this sense C.29 insists on a paradigmatic cultural change of significant proportions.

In colonial sub-Saharan Africa, European undertakings had protested the applicability of C.29 to no avail. This is because

in most colonies, action in favour of European undertakings was for a long time considered to be not merely the normal practice but even the duty of the administration. European undertakings established in the colonies counted more or less implicitly on the Administration to supply them with labour, and the practice was not explicitly forbidden by labour legislation.[73]

In French West Africa, where for many years, native indigenous labourers were recruited by use of 'work permits' issued by the competent authorities, European undertakings had also protested against the new policy, with a lot of support from France. In practice the work permits served as notices on the native village leaders to supply the required numbers of personnel at appointed intervals. Cooperation of the subjects could not be guaranteed, and this always presented an enormous difficulty for the native indigenous leadership.

In the Ivory Coast, a circular of 18 January 1925 had sought to curtail the practice. A further circular of the Governor-General on 3 November 1936 severely disabled the administrative authorities' involvement in recruitment for European undertakings.[74] On 24 June 1937 France ratified the Forced Labour Convention (1930).

Owing to native indigenous Africans' participation in the agricultural development of their own countries parallel to European undertakings, a serious labour shortage had loomed over the European undertakings that required labour mostly when the native indigenous Africans were busiest on their own farms.[75] By 1937, of the 64,000 hectares under coffee production in the Ivory Coast 12,000 were owned by native indigenous Africans; and of the 80,000 hectares under cocoa production, 69,000 were under native indigenous African cultivation.

In a speech given at a session of the Government Council on 23 November 1937, the Governor-General of French West Africa responded to critics of two policies of his Administration that were linked to labour shortages in the European agricultural sector. He had taken a progressive view of the issue of competition between agricultural output of native indigenous African peasant farmers and European undertakings. In his view, the genie had already escaped from the bottle. Revisionists had had their day and lost it already because developments showed that native indigenous agricultural production and European agricultural production were not only closely connected, but also complimentary. They both deserved applause because they combined to form a harmonious whole.

---

[73] J Goudal (see n 25 above) 229.   [74] Ibid, 218.   [75] Ibid, 219.

Concerning the issue of abolition of forced or compulsory labour, the Governor-General had cited the Forced Labour Convention to the effect that

The recruitment of labour must be free from compulsion. That is one of the principles of our constitutional law, which the Minister for the Colonies has repeatedly affirmed in French West Africa and in France ever since he has been managing the affairs of our Colonial Empire. Forced or compulsory labour for private undertakings is utterly con-demned both by our laws and by the general trend of French thought . . . Will the Africans agree to work for others if they are allowed to choose? Certainly they will, if they feel that it is in their interest to do so. . . . I have made a point to quote that Article (Article 6) because it will, I hope, check useless argument; the officials of this country are faced with imperative legal provisions, which it is their duty to enforce.[76]

Mr Reste, the Governor-General of French Equatorial Africa, dismissed criticisms that strengthening native indigenous farming had created a labour problem that would undermine the colony's development. 'There had never been so much work done in French Equatorial Africa as since the abolition of forced and compulsory labour.'[77] He had argued instead that the challenges created for the European undertakings by compliance to C.29 lay in discovering the right balance between the two forms of cultivation. In the immediate short term, that merely required 'European settlers . . . organise with a view to keeping their (labour) requirements down to a minimum'.[78]

In the Cameroons, the Commissioner of the Republic had argued that com-plaints about shortages of labour resulting from the abolition of compulsory or forced labour was disingenuous. He had adopted a quasi positive discrimina-tion approach to C.29. By an order dated 27 March 1937, he had provisionally suspended throughout the territory further grant of agricultural concessions. Responding to criticisms, he stated that:

The fact must be faced that European settlement in our possessions on the West Coast of Africa has reached its highest point and must now give way to Native settlement.[79]

In similar fashion Governor Boisson celebrated the parallel development of native indigenous farming alongside European concessions aided by the adoption of the voluntary labour policy. He had argued that this showed among other things that France had succeeded in integrating native indigenous Africans into the interna-tional trading system. He also stated that the native indigenous African's aver-sion to the status of wage earner, whether in industry or in agriculture had made reversal of this development unthinkable.[80]

In Madagascar the Chamber of Commerce and other European Undertakings had lobbied the Administration to re-introduce coercion—disguised in one way or another. The Administration had declined, holding fast to the requirement since 24 June 1937 to suppress and abolish forced labour.[81]

[76] Ibid, 220. [77] Ibid, 222. [78] Ibid. [79] Ibid, 223. [80] Ibid.
[81] See ibid.

In spite of the United Kingdom having ratified the Forced Labour Convention in the immediate aftermath of its adoption (3 June 1931), forced labour for private undertakings was authorized in Kenya, Tanganyika, and Nigeria while in Northern Rhodesia, conscript labour under government control was made available to farmers during the war.[82] The British government's resort to compulsory or forced labour had been adopted with great reluctance, and only as a last resort due to the urgent needs dictated by the war effort. This unfortunate episode for a nation that had inspired others in the negotiation of C.29 to support the idea is difficult to understand.

In Tanganyika, in January 1945, the conscript labour force numbered 26,256—representing just over 8 per cent of the total number of African workers in all occupations; in Kenya, in January 1945, conscript labour totalled 21,903. The forced labour used on Nigerian tin mines came to an end in 1944, and in other territories it was decided that no further men should be compulsorily recruited for private employment after 31 December 1945.[83]

Thus, C.29 appeared to have incrementally achieved the cultural turnaround in the colonies of Africa in a relatively short time.

3.7   C.29 and the development of international substantive standards on forced labour[84]

An examination of international treaties reveals that the human rights movement unequivocally abhors forced labour. In theory states do not support it either. Recent recommendations of the Parliamentary Assembly of the Council of Europe, including Recommendations 1523 (2001)[85] on Domestic Slavery and 1663 (2004)[86] on Domestic Slavery, Servitude, au pairs and mail order brides; reports of the Parliamentary Assembly of the Council of Europe; the Report on Equal Opportunities for Women and Men (2001); and a number of cases, including *Iversen v Norway* (1964)[87] and *Siliadin v France* (2005);[88] as well as the work of the French Committee against Modern Slavery, all show that forced labour is a mischief that has become a critical issue in modern Western states.[89] The social perils of globalization, including the mischief of human trafficking now make forced labour a matter of urgent universal concern.

In its Report of 17 May 2001 the Parliamentary Assembly of the Council of Europe observed that:

In France, since its foundation in 1994 the Committee against Modern Slavery (CCEM) has taken up the cases of over 200 domestic slavery victims, mostly originating from

---

[82] ILO, 'Reports and Enquiries: Labour Conditions in East Africa', 54 ILR 38.   [83] Ibid.

[84] See especially D Vincent-Daviss (n 49 above) 240.

[85] See   Council   of   Europe   at: <http://assembly.coe.int/Main.asp?link=/Documents/AdoptedText/ta01/EREC1523.htm>.

[86] See   Council   of   Europe   at: <http://assembly.coe.int/Mainf.asp?link=/Documents/AdoptedText/ta04/EREC1663.htm#_ftn>.   [87] The Times, 13 March 1964.

[88] 73316/01 (Judgment of 26 July 2005).

[89] An idea seemingly perpetuated through to C.107.

West Africa (Ivory Coast, Togo, Benin) but also from Madagascar, Morocco, India, Sri Lanka and the Philippines. The majority of victims were women (95%). One-third arrived in France before they came of age and most of them suffered physical violence or sexual abuse.

The employers mostly came from West Africa or the Middle East. Twenty percent are French nationals. Twenty percent enjoyed immunity from prosecution, among them one diplomat from Italy and five French diplomats in post abroad. Victims working for diplomats mainly come from India, Indonesia, the Philippines and Sri Lanka. It has been estimated that there are several thousand victims of domestic slavery in France.[90]

In *Siliadin v France* the applicant, a Togolese national who was brought to Paris in January 1994, aged 15 by Mrs D, a French national of Togolese origin, had alleged inter alia that France had failed her under Article 4 of the European Convention on Human Rights[91] (ECHR) to ensure her right not to be held in servitude. This is an absolute entitlement from which no derogation is permissible. Consequently, states have a positive obligation to enact criminal law provisions backed up by law enforcement machinery for the prevention, detection and punishment of such provisions.[92]

Siliadin also argued that France had failed her under Article 1 of the ECHR which requires states to set up a system of criminal prosecution and punishment for the purpose of ensuring that victims of servitude had tangible and effective protection of the rights guaranteed under the non-derogable standards—Articles 4 and/or 8.[93] Further, the applicant argued that the exploitation to which she had been subjected while a minor was a consequence of failure by the state to comply with the sum of its positive obligations under Articles 1 and 4 of the Convention which requires states to ensure adequate criminal law provisions to prevent and effectively punish the perpetrators of those acts.[94]

In October 1994 Mrs D 'lent' the applicant to Mr and Mrs B so that the applicant would assist them with housework and look after their young children until Mrs B had given birth. But after the birth of her third child Mrs B decided to keep the applicant, making her work from 7.30 am until 10.30 pm seven days a week, except for when she allowed her special permission to go to mass on Sundays. The applicant had slept on a mattress on the floor of her children's bedroom and had worn old clothes. She had never been paid, but had received two 500-franc notes, from Mrs B's mother.

Following the recovery of her passport which she had entrusted to an acquaintance of Mr and Mrs B, the applicant confided in a neighbour, who had alerted the Committee against Modern Slavery (CCEM), which then reported the matter to the prosecuting authorities.

Mr and Mrs B were prosecuted under Article 225-13 of the Criminal Code for wrongfully obtaining unpaid or insufficiently paid services from a vulnerable or

---

[90] Council of Europe (see n 86 above).   [91] 213 UNTS 221.
[92] ECHR (see n 89 above) para 71.   [93] Ibid, para 67.   [94] Ibid, para 65.

dependent person, and for subjecting that person to working or living conditions incompatible with human dignity under Article 225-14 of the Criminal Code.

The doctrine of 'positive obligations' relied upon by the court to settle this case is traceable to the 1920s arguments of the ILO against what Maul refers to as 'colonial powers'

strong resistance to all the initiatives that went beyond a condemnation of the legal status of slavery and the slave trade and aimed at including wording banning various forms of forced labour.[95]

The ILO had argued that the natives belonged to a *distinct and special class* that required and merited a special Native Labour Code (NLC) binding on both the European economic interests and the colonial Administrations in order to stop compulsory or forced labour. The ILO's objective was then the protection of native indigenous labour from the consequences of a combined onslaught of colonial authority and European economic interest.[96]

In *Siliadin v France* the Court first identified and distinguished Articles 1 and 4 of the ECHR as a class of civil and political rights with inherent positive obligations on the state. This special class of rights requires participating states to adopt measures in their domestic law in order to ensure that protected rights are respected and when they are breached, that victims have adequate legal remedies.[97] The Court stated that, 'the fact that a state refrains from infringing the guaranteed rights does not suffice to conclude that it has complied with its obligations'.[98]

The Court had stated in *Sovtransavato Holding v Ukraine*[99] that the obligation to secure Convention rights establishes for participating states positive obligations. 'In such circumstances, the state cannot simply remain passive, and there is no room to distinguish between acts and omissions.' *X and Y v The Netherlands*[100] is further authority for the proposition that such positive obligations apply also in the sphere of relations between private individuals. It is worth noting that both Articles 1 and 4 are substantive provisions of C.29, itself the cornerstone of the NLC regime.[101] Therefore, there are not only linkages of semantics, purpose, and quality of standards between the provisions of the ECHR and ILO C.29, but also strategic mechanisms employed by the competent judicial authorities to secure those rights.

The Court justified its doctrine of 'positive legal obligations' for the protection of special Convention rights that include Articles 1 and 4 on the principles of inherent, implied tenement and necessity based on the sum of the UN human rights legislative effort starting with the UDHR. The Court realized that:

limiting compliance with Article 4 of the Convention only to direct action by the state authorities would be inconsistent with the international instruments specifically

---

[95] DR Maul (see n 20 above) 480.   [96] Ibid.   [97] ECHR (see n 88 above) para 79.
[98] Ibid, para 77.   [99] (2004) 38 EHRR 1, para 57.
[100] (1986) 8 EHRR 235, para 23.   [101] See Arts 1(1) and 4(1).

concerned with this issue and would amount to rendering it ineffective. Accordingly, it necessarily follows from this provision that Governments have positive obligations, in the same way as under Article 3 for example, to adopt criminal-law provisions, which penalise the practices, referred to in Article 4 and to apply them in practice.

An analysis of the objects and purposes of relevant UN human rights instruments suggests that Article 4 of the ECHR is a special provision which establishes positive legal obligations requiring states to guarantee to every individual on their territory the free will to determine whether or not to work. Such provisions include Article 4 of C.29 (adopted by the ILO on 28 June 1930, and ratified by France on 24 June 1937), Article 1 of the Supplementary Convention on the Abolition of Slavery, the Slave Trade, and Institutions and Practices Similar to Slavery (adopted on 30 April 1956, which entered into force for France on 26 May 1964), Articles 19 and 32 of the International Convention on the Rights of the Child (adopted 20 November 1989 and entered in force for France on 6 September 1990).

The Court also applied constitutional reductionism to argue that Articles 2, 3, and 4 constitute the basic values of the democracies of Europe. Two things are salient and worth noting. The first is that *Siliadin* is authority for the proposition that governments of the democratic societies that constitute the Council of Europe have positive legal obligations to adopt criminal law provisions that penalize breaches of basic provisions of the ECHR, in order to ensure that victims have tangible and effective protection of those rights against the actions of private individuals.

Thus, while the ECHR may initially have been drafted to prevent state institutions from interfering with the civil and political rights of individuals, through a robust application of the Convention the Court has extended the purposes of the Convention to impose positive obligations on the state in order to ensure the recognition, promotion, and protection of the dignity inherent in individuals *qua* human beings.

The second is that the Court's language *is synonymous* with that echoed by the ILO in its effort to tackle the problem of forced labour in the colonies. Thus, the ILO's influence as harbinger in setting up of standards and strategies for the promotion of human security is confirmed. This is arguably the strongest reason for tribunals' increasing resort to the doctrine of positive obligations.[102]

The NLC introduced the principle of states' positive legal obligations in order to protect the indigenous labour force from the excesses of European economic interests and colonial administrations. For instance, Article 25 of C.29 states that:

The illegal exaction of forced or compulsory labour shall be punishable as a penal offence, and it shall be an obligation on any Member ratifying this Convention to ensure that the penalties imposed by law are *really adequate* and are strictly enforced.[103]

---

[102] Problematizing the growth of positive obligations see also H Cullen, '*Siliadin v France*: Positive obligations under Article 4 of the European Convention on Human Rights' (2006) 6 HRLR 4.   [103] Emphasis added.

In *MC v Bulgaria*, the Commission stated that: 'Governments have positive obligations...to adopt criminal-law provisions which penalise the practices referred to in Article 4 and to apply them in practice'.[104]

In its guidance for legislation and law enforcement in aid of the Special Action Programme to Combat Forced Labour (2005), the ILO states that:

the exaction of forced or compulsory labour could be a 'penal offence' under either the criminal or labour law (of the state), although 'adequate' penalties for this basic human rights violation are more likely to be included in the penal or criminal code. Penal sanctions can be imposed in the form of fines or imprisonment. Fines should be high enough to act as an effective deterrent.[105]

While state parties retain discretion regarding the determination of the exact penalty, it is unequivocal that as early as 1930, the ILO had begun to develop positive legal obligations in the effort to protect the dignity of indigenous labour in the colonies. More recently, international tribunals have applied ILO strategies to interpret human rights instruments, which were originally established to prevent 'breaches of the obligation not to interfere with the rights of individuals',[106] in order to promote human security.

4. Concluding remarks

Although the objective of the ILO, namely, to establish and maintain international peace and security through the development and monitoring of standards for the

prevention of the development of conditions of labour involving such injustice, hardship, and privation to large numbers of people as to produce unrest so great that the peace and harmony of the world are imperilled

does not expressly mention 'human security', it is clear from how the Organization has implemented its mandate, particularly in sub-Saharan Africa's colonial days that human security is its implied jurisdiction. This is evident from the immediate clash that ensued between the ILO and Western colonial powers' discriminatory protection of metropolitan and colonial labour. That policy had prioritized the interest of European undertakings over the inherent dignity of native indigenous sub-Saharan labour by, for instance, enforcing penal sanctions against native labour for breach of employment contracts. Colonial administrative agents were empowered to, and did in fact, conduct veritable labour recruitment raids on natives in order to ensure labour supply for European enterprises in the colonies.

---

[104] Application No 39272/98, para 153.   [105] ILO (see n 59 above) 17.
[106] AIL Campbell, 'Positive Obligations under the ECHR: Deprivation of Liberty by Private Actors' (2006) 10 ELR 399.

While the concept of voluntary labour, advocated by the ILO, was promoted in the metropolis, European Administrations had regarded coercion of labour as a *necessary civilizing influence* upon the *primitive* African who needed to learn to appreciate the European work ethic in their colonies.

The fact that the ILO was created after the partition of Africa in 1884, and that its constitutive instrument precluded the application of ILO standards to the colonies was a serious setback for an organization tasked with ensuring social justice for *all* peoples of the world. Thus, the true measure of the ILO's achievements must be whether it has succeeded in establishing a labour code for the protection of the dignity inherent in workers everywhere, including those workers under colonial domination.

The ILO's strategy of distinguishing native indigenous sub-Saharan African workers as a distinct class of people requiring specific labour protection enabled the Organization to establish the NLC for the purpose of protecting native indigenous populations from dehumanizing colonial labour policies. Indeed, one of the positive contributions of the NLC is that it immediately reversed the policy of indigenous labour coercion and substituted it with one of free offer of employment. This, in turn, afforded the native indigenous populations the opportunity to determine their vocational destinies, including the pursuit of political independence. It comes as no surprise, therefore, that international human rights bodies, young and old alike, habitually refer to the substantive standards and operational techniques inaugurated by the ILO through the establishment of the NLC.

The ILO continues relentlessly to advance the recognition, promotion, and protection of the inherent dignity of sub-Saharan African labour. Working in close collaboration with governments, it offers advice and training towards enhancing compliance with the international labour code. However, bad governance often hinders the Organization's aspirations for sub-Saharan Africa. The ILO's gains in human welfare must be insured with the premium of good governance in sub-Saharan Africa lest the Organization risks losing the battle to help sub-Saharan Africans realize their potential to the fullest. The Advisory Board on Human Security that took over from Commission on Human Security is the ILO's latest ally in its campaign to ensure universal human security.

6

Natural Resource Management and Human Security in Africa

Abiodun Alao*

1. Introduction

There are several links between natural resources management and human security in Africa. For example, a number of issues surrounding the management of these resources have been at the centre of many security challenges facing the continent. This apart, the process of resource extraction and the perceived injustices linked to the distribution of opportunities and privileges deriving from these resources have underlined such issues as acrimonious inter-group relations, youth vulnerability, gender insensitivity, and many other issues that are intertwined with human (in)security on the continent. Furthermore, the politics of natural resource management has also resulted in the proliferation of many actors, some of which are also prominent in human security considerations, including environmentalist groups, civil society activists, and international pressure groups.

The objective of this chapter is to tie together the multi-dimensional links between natural resources management and human security in Africa. The central argument advanced in the chapter is that for human security to be well established in the continent, crucial issues linked to the ownership, management, and control of the continent's natural resource endowment have to be taken into consideration and the various conflicts they have caused have to be addressed. The chapter also argues that the success of the various international efforts to address the effective management of Africa's natural resources will only be successful if the structures for managing these resources at the local and national levels are reorganized and made to appreciate the multiplicity of factors underlining various layers of governance in each of the countries.

There are six sections in this chapter, with the first looking at the structure currently in place to manage natural resources on the continent and the extent to which this addresses the needs of the population. The second section discusses

* Abiodun Alao is a Senior Research Fellow at the Conflict, Security and Development Group, Department of War Studies, King's College London.

human security issues that have emerged as a result of the existing governance structures, while the third section focuses on the human security implications of the conflicts that are rooted in natural resource governance. The international initiatives to address human security concerns related to natural resource governance and the extent of their attendant success is discussed in the fourth section, while the fifth section interrogates the initiatives being undertaken by African organizations, including sub-regional organizations, to ensure that the continent's natural resource endowments become blessings rather than a curse. The sixth section concludes the discussions.

2. The inevitability of instability: governance structure for natural resource management

It is not in doubt that Africa is endowed with enormous natural resources. Apart from enormous land suitable for agriculture, there are also mineral resources, ranging from solid minerals such as gold, diamonds, uranium, and others to crude oil. In some of these resources African countries dominate global production,[1] while in many others they compare favourably with other continents.[2] Even though endowments vary from one country to another, each African country has sufficient natural resource endowment to 'feed' and 'clothe' its population and generate enough for development. Consequently, if these resources are not meeting the demands of human security in the continent, there is a need to investigate issues surrounding their management. In Chapter 3, Ilias Bantekas discusses the various environmental factors that militate against the translation of African natural resources into decent livelihoods for most Africans. The thrust of the present chapter is to focus on the role played by the human management of these resources which, even with the most favourable environmental conditions, is most critical if positive results are to be derived from African natural resource endowments.

From the outset of independence, it was inevitable that the management of natural resources would be central to issues surrounding governance, and by logical extension, the security of the African people. First, unlike other parts of the world where revenues accrue to the state from numerous sources, most African countries rely almost exclusively on their natural resources. How to ensure that these resources serve both national and local interests was inevitably going to be a crucial issue for the emerging governments in these countries to address. Secondly, the structures inherited by African governments from colonial powers,

---

[1] Nigeria is the world's largest producer of Columbite, Liberia is the world's largest rubber producer, while Côte d'Ivoire leads the world in the production of cocoa.

[2] Many of Africa's oil-producing nations are among the world's key producers. Eg Nigeria is the world's ninth largest oil-producing nation while the Gulf of Guinea holds a significant percentage of the world's oil deposits.

at the time of independence, were such that they would inevitably create clashes between governments and the people. As would be expected, the management of natural resources during colonial rule was largely under the control of central governments, especially as one of the central aims of colonialism was to maximize opportunities coming from the natural resource endowments of the colonies. Consequently, after independence, new governments in most African states wanted to continue the same practice.

The governance structure that has been in place for managing natural resources in Africa since the time of independence has a number of issues that link it to the issue of human security, of which four are particularly important. The first is the diversity in the sources of laws governing the management of these resources. Broadly, there are four types of law that govern the management of natural resources in Africa, and the contents of these laws are not always easy to synthesize. These are local traditions/customs, religious edicts, national constitutions, and international obligations and agreements. The first problem concerns the relations of these laws to one another. For instance, there are always controversies about which law takes precedence in any given situation. For natural resources such as land, there are local traditions and custom, religious edicts, and national constitutions all governing land tenure. For most mineral resources, the national constitution is the central tool, but because these resources dwell on land, local customs are often in contention with national constitutions, while for resources such as the management of international river basins international obligations have been the dominant determinant of policy options. The implication, as will be shown later in the chapter, is the general confusion that characterizes the management of natural resources and the consequent inability of the structure to meet the demands of human security in the continent.

The second issue that links natural resource governance to human security in Africa is the weakness of the constitution of many of the countries. While it is true that there are many laws governing the management of natural resources as enumerated above, the national constitution takes precedence over all other laws. Among others factors, it is for the constitution to determine who gets what, how, and when. It is also within the prerogative of the constitution to determine key issues, such as revenue allocation, that are central to the well-being of the population. It is, however, the case that despite the enormous burden placed on the constitution, especially in the management of proceeds derived from natural resources, constitutions across Africa are often too weak. In some cases constitutions are not truly representative of the people's aspirations, because the processes leading to their promulgation are often at fault, thus leading to their rejection by sections of the population.[3] Consequently, in many countries the formulae

---

[3] In many cases, these constitutions are handed out by the military after they have been forced to relinquish power (as is often the case with Nigeria's successive constitutions) or are mere documents put together by elites without proper consultation with the population.

for distributing the opportunities and privileges accruing from natural resources have been contentious and, as will be shown later in the chapter, have been at the centre of threats to human security.

Closely related to this is the weakness of the institutions designed to manage natural resources. In virtually all the countries in the continent, there are complaints about the institutions which manage natural resources, and many of the issues linking human security to natural resource management are related to this. In some ways, the antecedents can be traced to the colonial period, where the management of natural resources was largely under the control of the colonial government. After independence, many governments created spurious boards and ad hoc institutions to manage the resources in ways that continued to benefit the government to the detriment of the local population, especially those on whose land the resources were being exploited.

The final factor is the corruption and mismanagement of the proceeds from natural resources by the political elites. Because of the aforementioned irregularities in the governance of natural resources, successive political elites in all the countries have been indicted, mostly in the court of public opinion, for corrupt management of proceeds of the countries' natural resources—African history records the havoc caused by such leaders as Mobutu Sese Seko, Idi Amin, Bokassa, Abacha, and a number of others. Initial efforts to prevent this looting of natural resources by governments created cataclysmic human rights violations, as characterized in Ghana by Jerry Rawlings and in Liberia by Samuel Doe, with the illegal trials and summary executions of their predecessors in office for mismanaging proceeds from natural resources, among other things. As has been noted by this writer elsewhere, regardless of the justification or otherwise of this method of accountability, one clear outcome was that it introduced a dangerous precedent into political leadership in Africa.[4]

From the foregoing discussion, it can be seen that the structures governing natural resources in Africa have serious implications for human security. While in the immediate post-independence period some countries were able to handle some of the emerging issues or were able simply to explain them away as initial challenges of state-building, the picture later began to alter as will be seen below.

3. Human security issues emerging out of the governance structures of managing resources

It should be stressed from the outset that it is impossible to identify all the key human security issues linking natural resource management to governance. Consequently, this section addresses only some of these issues. Broadly, the

---

[4] A Alao, *Natural Resources and Conflict in Africa: The Tragedy of Endowment* (Rochester: University of Rochester Press, 2007).

governance mechanism identified above has brought about at least five main human security issues.

3.1 Acrimonious inter-group relations

The first serious human security issue raised by defective governance structures is the acrimonious inter-group relations (ethnic, racial, and professional) that characterize relations among various affected communities and people and their governments. While the human security dimensions of these wars are discussed in the next section, it should be pointed out here that there have been many conflicts which have occurred as a direct result of the governance mechanisms in place to manage natural resources in the continent and these have human security dimensions.

Acrimonious inter-group relations affecting human security in Africa can generally be grouped under ethnic, racial, and professional categories. Most of the ethnic conflicts over natural resources are rooted in communal clashes over land. Across the continent, there are several hundreds of conflicts involving land and these have wrought disastrous consequences on human security, including the loss of several thousands of lives. There is, indeed, almost no country in Africa where there are no violent communal conflicts over land. In Nigeria, for example, two communities—the Umuleri and Aguleri—were at war between 1995 and 2000 over the control of a parcel of land along their common border,[5] which resulted in the deaths of several hundred people. Also the Kuteb and the Chamba, in the northern part of Nigeria, engaged in conflict in 1995 over the ownership of land along their borders.[6] Many examples of this type of conflict have also been recorded in Kenya, where the Kikuyu, Masai, Kalenjin, Kissi, and Luo, amongst others, are involved in interwoven conflicts: the Kikuyu vs the Masai, the Kikuyu vs Kalenjins, and the Kissi vs Luo, in the coastal region between the Mijikenda and the non-coastal people, and the Kipsigi and Kissi on the Bomet and Nyamira district border in the South West.[7] Neighbouring Tanzania also has a number of ethnic-based conflicts over land ownership, most pronounced in the North, the Kagera region, where the Haya and Sukuma are engaged in internecine conflict. In the South, conflicts exist between African coastal ethnic groups and the Arabs.[8] Other countries that have recorded clashes of this nature, though on a comparatively low scale, include Ghana, where the Gonja and Nawuri were at war in May 1992,[9] and Guinea, where there have been clashes between the Peul and the Soussou.[10]

---

[5] Okechukwu Ibeanu completed a comprehensive study on the Aguleri Umuleri conflict, see 'Aguleri-Umuleri Conflict in Anambra State' in Thomas Imobigbe (ed), *Civil Society and Ethnic Conflict Management in Nigeria* (Ibadan: Spectrum Books, 2003), 164–222.

[6] For more on this, see 'The Tiv Crises', *The News*, 12 November 2001.

[7] *African Research Bulletin*, July 1992, 10658.

[8] This is the *Zaramos* (coastal African groups and Arab Swahili). Although this has taken a religious dimension (Christians vs Muslims) it is, in origin, a resource-based problem.

[9] *African Research Bulletin*, May 1992, 10583.

[10] *African Research Bulletin*, March 1993, 10935.

With regards to acrimonious inter-group relations on the basis of race, Zimbabwe presents the best example. In the last decade, tensions have underlined relations between the blacks and whites in the country over land ownership. There have been cases of forceful farm occupation and suppression of popular protests. However, there have also been problems with the electoral processes which have, in turn, exacerbated the problem of land politics in the country, with consequences affecting Zimbabwe's neighbours in some instances.

The third inter-group crisis affects professional groups, and the best manifestation of this is among the pastoralists and the agriculturalists of many African countries. Countries such as Kenya, Uganda, and Nigeria present some of the worst examples. At the root of most such conflicts is the divergent attitude of these groups to land usage. While the agriculturalists regard land as a 'permanent' endowment, the pastoralists see land as a transient resource which they must use to provide pasture for their herds and generally apply to servicing their nomadic existence. Many of the conflicts arising from this divergent recourse to land are particularly visceral as can be seen, for instance, in the Darfur crisis between African farmers and Arab nomads.

3.2 Corruption

The threat posed by corruption to human security is fully explored in this book. However, the corrupt handling of revenue from natural resources has a particularly negative impact on human security in Africa. The legitimate expectation of the people is that revenues derived from natural resources ought to benefit them, and if this is not happening, it can hardly be denied that the human security of the affected people is being violated in some respects. Across the African continent, the existing structures for managing natural resources allow room for corruption. Writing in Chapter 10 on the issue of corruption, Ebenezer Durojaye notes that even the Nigerian National Assembly—the combined houses of legislature in Nigeria—lamented its inability to secure access to the accounts of the Nigerian National Petroleum Corporation, the body tasked with overseeing oil resources in Nigeria.

Indeed, many of Africa's resource-rich countries have been unable to provide basic amenities to improve the quality of lives of its population simply because revenues coming from these resources have been looted by the ruling elites and their accomplices. For example, despite its enormous wealth, Sierra Leone remains one of the world's poorest countries, unable even to provide drinkable water for its population. Also, the Democratic Republic of Congo (DRC), despite being one of the world's most endowed countries, has been unable to impact positively on the lives of its people due to the corruption of its political class.

3.3 Neglect of resource endowed regions

One prominent feature of the link between human security and natural resource governance is the neglect of the specific regions of individual countries producing these resources. Many communities from whose lands natural resources are being extracted often bear the worst brunt of the mega activities of the multinational corporations. In addition, these communities are often unfairly treated by their own governments. Despite the serious environmental consequences suffered by these communities through exploratory activities, their clamours for development are only too frequently ignored. As will be shown later in this chapter, two examples of this have been particularly prominent; namely, the situations in the diamond-producing regions of Sierra Leone and the oil-producing region in Nigeria, the Niger Delta.

3.4 Youth vulnerability and exclusion

Across Africa, the governance structures for managing natural resources have brought forward activities associated with youth vulnerability and exclusion, with devastating implications for human security. Most countries in the continent have recorded cases of restive youths agitating for better treatment in the management of natural resources in their respective countries. Again, the Niger Delta region of Nigeria presents perhaps the best example. Here, youths forming armed groups have challenged successive governments and fought for a better and more equitable management of natural resources. As would be expected in conflicts of this nature, there has been violence, sometimes resulting in loss of life.

From the above, it is clear that the structures exiting for the management of natural resources in the continent have affected the quality of human security. However, a clearer picture of the link between natural resource management and human security emerges when one considers those civil wars that are linked to natural resource management.

4. Civil wars, natural resource politics, and human security

As background, it is important to note that many of the conflicts that are often categorized as concerning natural resources are, in actual fact, not so. Most such conflicts arise primarily from governance issues and later assume natural resource dimensions as, for example, the cases of Liberia, Sierra Leone, the Sudan, and the DRC demonstrate. Nonetheless, there are some conflicts that are directly linked to natural resources, as in the case, for example, of the Niger Delta. In this section, the chapter looks at some of these civil wars, specifically with the aim of identifying issues linked to human security.

4.1 Liberia

In the last two decades, Liberia has experienced two major civil wars: 1989–97 and 1999–2004.[11] The first saw a rebel force, the National Patriotic Front of Liberia (NPFL), under Charles Taylor, taking up arms against the government of the late President Samuel Doe,[12] while the second saw two armed groups, Liberia United for Reconstruction and Development (LURD), and the Movement for Democracy in Liberia (MODEL), fight against the Taylor administration.[13] The natural resources prominent in the war were iron, rubber, and, to a lesser extent, diamonds. Different armed groups emerged during the course of the war (at one stage up to eight) and financed the war through the control of natural resources. Indeed, it is widely believed that the intensity of the war was due to the desire of these armed groups to ensure continued control of these resources. The Liberian war claimed more than 150,000 lives with up to a million people displaced internally and within the region.

4.2 Sierra Leone

Several aspects of the Sierra Leonean civil war have already received considerable attention from commentators.[14] The war broke out when a rebel force, the Revolutionary United Front (RUF) under the leadership of the late Foday Sankoh,[15] initiated a military campaign and fought four successive governments

---

[11] People in the country often say that the war has come in three phases. The first war was the one against Doe, while the war against Taylor has been divided into three. This is potentially confusing for those without sufficient knowledge about the history of events in the country. Thus, for convenience here, the war has been divided into two: the first against Doe, and the second against Taylor.

[12] Among the factions that emerged in the course of the conflict were: the NPFL under Charles Taylor; the Independent National Patriotic Front of Liberia of Prince Yomie Johnson; Liberian Peace Council of George Boley; ULIMO K of Alhaji Kromah; and ULIMO J of Roosevelt Johnson.

[13] The LURD began its campaigns in September 1999. It later joined with another group, MODEL. In June 2003, their actions degenerated into a bloody civil war, and its attendant cataclysmic three phases are referred to in the local Liberian parlance as World War I, II, and III.

[14] See, eg, P Richards, 'Rebellion in Liberia and Sierra Leone: A Crisis of Youth?' in O Furley (ed), *Conflict in Africa* (London: IB Tauris, 1995) and I Abdullahi, 'The Lumpen Proletariat and the Sierra Leone Conflict' (1998) 36 Journal of Modern African Studies 2. These include D Shearer, *Private Armies and Military Intervention* (London: IISS Adelphi Paper, 1998); W Shawcross, 'In Praise of Sandline', *The Spectator*, August 1998; F Olonisakin, 'Mercenaries Fill the Vacuum', *World Today*, June 1998. Examples of these include F Olonisakin, 'Nigeria and the Peacekeeping Mission in Sierra Leone', *Jane's Intelligence Review*, July 1998; P Conton, 'The Battle for Freetown', *West Africa*, 2–15 March 1998; D Davies, 'Peacekeeping: African Style', *West Africa*, 4–17 May 1998. See, among others, E Garcia, *A Time of Hope and Transformation: Sierra Leone Peace Process Report and Reflection* (London: International Alert, 1997).

[15] Foday Sankoh was a member of the Sierra Leone armed forces. He was arrested and jailed for alleged involvement in a military coup against the government of the late President Siaka Stevens. After his jail term, he went into exile from where he planned his rebellion. He died in July 2003 from a stroke.

between 1994 and 2002, resulting in several thousand deaths and many more displaced persons.[16] Aside from the RUF, several other actors, including the national army, local civil defence units, regional peacekeeping force, ECOMOG, the United Nations military team, mercenaries, and members of the British army, were involved in different stages of the conflict.[17] The mineral resource at the centre of the Sierra Leone conflict was diamond, which is the country's primary mineral resource.

As with Liberia, it is impossible to obtain accurate figures of casualties in the Sierra Leonean civil war, but a figure of approximately 120,000 has often been suggested. However, what distinguished the war in Sierra Leone from any other in the region was the massive human rights abuses committed in the conflict. For example, people (sometimes children) had their hands amputated by rebel groups in an attempt to prevent them from voting and political opponents were publicly executed. Whereas the conflict pitched the national army against the RUF, the involvement of a local militia known as the *kamajoors* made things more complex.[18] This group traded loyalty between the government and rebel forces apparently to their own economic advantage. This category of fighters became known in national sobriquet as *so-bels*, a corruption of the words 'soldier' and 'rebel'.

4.3 Democratic Republic of Congo

The conflict in the DRC is more complex than those in Liberia and Sierra Leone discussed above. Indeed, the incessant instability that has characterized the country's post-independence history seems to have arisen from the efforts of local and international interest groups to control its enormous resources, as well as the inability of its government to manage the resources for the benefit of the people.[19] At one stage in the war, there were up to ten inter-related conflicts simultaneously taking place in the country.[20] In 2003, a peace initiative

---

[16] The number of those who died in the Sierra Leone civil conflict has been quoted as being between 75,000 and 200,000. It is, of course, impossible to obtain an accurate figure, but 100,000 seems to be a sensible approximation.

[17] For a discussion on these actors in the civil war, see L Gberie, *Sierra Leone: Destruction and Resurgence* (London: Hurst, 2005).

[18] The word '*Kamajor*' is the Mende (one of the main ethnic groups in Sierra Leone) word for hunter.

[19] The instability in the country dated back to the period immediately after independence, when conflicts between its leaders resulted in a bloody civil conflict that ultimately resulted in the dispatch of the UN's first international peacekeeping force in Africa in 1963.

[20] These are: the Congolese government vs assorted rebel groups; the Rwandan government vs the Congolese government; the Rwandan government vs Rwandan insurgents; the Ugandan government vs Sudan-supported rebels; the Ugandan government vs the Congolese government; the Ugandan and Rwandan government vs the Zimbabwean and Angolan governments; Rwandan-backed Congolese rebels vs Ugandan-backed Congolese rebels; the Ugandan government vs the Rwandan government; the Burundian government vs the Burundian rebel factions; the Angolan government vs UNITA and any group supporting UNITA; Mai Mai elements vs the

championed by South Africa's President Thabo Mbeki resulted in the signing of yet another peace agreement between Joseph Kabila's government and the main rebel factions. Under this agreement, Kabila maintains his position as president, and there are four vice presidents.[21] However, this arrangement has not brought lasting peace to the country.

4.4 Angola

The Angolan civil war, which began as a result of a flawed decolonization process by Portugal, was one of the world's most brutal civil wars. The National Union for the Total Independence of Angola, better known by its Portuguese appellation *União Nacional para a Independência Total de Angola* (UNITA), waged a long-running war against the Popular Movement for the Liberation of Angola or Movimento Popular de Libertação de Angola (MPLA) government with military assistance, at different times, from apartheid South Africa and the USA. The history of the Angolan civil war has been well recorded.[22] However, while there might have been ideological connotations to the war, the conflict also had profound natural resource undercurrents. Both the MPLA government and UNITA rebels exploited oil and diamonds to prosecute the war and to serve the greed of their leaders. Indeed, it is widely believed that despite their open declarations of peace, both the MPLA governments and UNITA rebels deliberately prolonged the war in order to advance their selfish motives. Key individuals in the government allegedly benefited from oil,[23] while UNITA with its elaborate illegal trade in diamonds was able to develop extensive contacts, going as far as West and North Africa, and allegedly involving presidents of many African countries. The implications of this for human security of Angolans are enormous. By the time the war ended, Angola had lost up to half a million people, with many more displaced. The country also has the highest number of amputees in the world.

4.5 Sudan

The civil war in the Sudan has many ramifications. Apart from conflict between the north and south of the country, there is also conflict in the Darfur region,

Rwandan government and RCD (Rally for Congolese Democracy); the Sudanese government vs the Ugandan government.

[21] Two of the vice presidents are from the rebel factions, one is from the political opposition, while the fourth is allied with President Kabila. All the cabinet ministries were also divided among the factions.

[22] FA Guimaraes, 'The Origins of the Angolan Civil War: Foreign Intervention and Domestic Political Conflict' (Basingstoke: Palgrave Macmillan, 2001).

[23] The international non-governmental organization (NGO), *Global Witness*, has come up with a number of official publications on the role of the government in the politics of natural resource (mis)management in Angola.

which has now become one of the world's most publicized. The link between oil and the conflict in the Sudan has a complex history which is also tied to ethno-racial and religious division in the country. Historically, the largely Moslem, Arab north controlled the central government in Khartoum, while the oil deposit is in the southern parts of the country, occupied by the predominantly Christian black population. After several years of bitter fighting resulting in the death of up to a million people, some form of agreement was reached between both sides. Under the umbrella of the Machakos Protocol signed in 2002 between the Sudanese government and the Sudan People's Liberation Army (SPLA), a rebel group,[24] a highly contentious issue has been the management of oil revenue. In January 2004, an agreement was reached between the government and the SPLA over wealth sharing.[25] Under the agreement, there will be a roughly equal division of revenue from oil. The country's central bank will have two laws: in the north, there would be Islamic banking laws, while in the south there would be secular banking regulations. There will also be two currencies for the north and the south, respectively.[26]

5. Global initiatives to address natural resources and the link with human security

There has been increased global attention focused on the management of natural resources partly due to the human tragedies now associated with the handling of natural resources by many countries and partly because of corruption that impedes development of many resource-rich countries, especially in Africa.

A discussion of the global initiatives towards enhancing natural resource management is important for three reasons. First, the two reasons underlining the establishment of these initiatives—human tragedies arising from conflicts and corruption—are key to any discussion on human security in Africa; secondly, some of these initiatives have components that specifically address several aspects of human security that are not necessarily linked to natural resource management; and thirdly, the relative success of at least one of these initiatives has raised hopes about the relevance of the human security approach towards the governance of natural resources in Africa. It is therefore necessary to investigate the extent to which these international mechanisms can assist in addressing Africa's incessant conflicts over natural resources.

[24] Available at: <http://www.c-r.org/our-work/accord/sudan/key-texts-machakos.php>.
[25] See International Crisis Group, 'Power and Wealth Sharing: Make or Break Time in Sudan's Peace Process', 18 December 2002, available at: <http://www.crisisgroup.org/home/index.cfm?l=1&id=1866>.
[26] P Morton, 'Sudan Lurches towards Peace' (March 2004) 14 Federations 1, p 15.

There are five main initiatives that have been instituted to address the management of natural resources. These are the Kimberley Process;[27] the Extractive Industries Transparency Initiative (EITI);[28] the Governance and Economic Management Assistance Programme (GEMAP);[29] the Chad-Cameroon Pipeline Consortium;[30] and the Diamond and Development Initiative (DDI).[31]

5.1 Kimberley Process

As a result of the various natural resource-instigated conflicts in Africa, the image of the diamond altered from being a gem to 'blood diamond'. This adverse publicity necessitated the emergence of the Kimberley Process in 2003 as a global instrument aimed at preventing warlords and terrorists from obtaining illegal mining and trade in diamonds for, among other things, arms purchase and money laundering activities. All states participating in the Kimberley Process undertake to issue every rough diamond with a government-backed certificate of origin. Countries outside the agreement are not allowed to sell or trade in rough diamonds.

The most important achievement of the Kimberley Process is that it brought together the key actors in diamond production, including diamond companies, NGOs, and diamond-producing countries. Since its introduction, it has become more difficult to trade in conflict diamonds and many of the diamond-producing countries have recorded significant increases in profit.

However, from the outset, critics have noted gaps in the Kimberley Process, as it relies on the goodwill of participating countries and thus does not possess strong enforceable regulation. As William Wallis has noted, nothing shows the flaw in this scheme as much as the relationship between the DRC and Congo Brazzaville.[32] While the DRC has one of the world's largest reserves of industrial diamonds, Congo Brazzaville has no diamonds. With the admission of the latter into the Kimberley Process, both have been licensed to trade in diamond. In 2001, Congo Brazzaville traded $223 million worth of diamonds,[33] most of which are believed to have come from the DRC and Angola—two countries at war. However, in July 2004, the Kimberley Process published a new list of participants from which Congo Brazzaville was removed.[34] The Kimberley Process team

---

[27] Available at: <http://www.kimberleyprocess.com/>. See also Chair's report to the Plenary on the activities of KPCS during 2008, ibid.   [28] Available at: <http://eitransparency.org/>.

[29] Available at: <http://www.gemapliberia.org/>.

[30] Available at: <http://www.hydrocarbons-technology.com/projects/chadcameroon/>.

[31] Available at <http://www.globalwitness.org/media_library_detail.php/393/en/diamond_ development_initiative_begins>.

[32] W Wallis, 'Kimberley Process: Africa's Conflict Diamonds: Is the UN-backed Certification Scheme Failing to Bring Transparency to the Trade?' *Financial Times*, 29 October 2003.

[33] Ibid.

[34] The Kimberley Process Review Mission visited the country between 31 May and 4 June 2004 to conduct a review process. The Mission was headed by Abbey Chikane of South Africa, and was

sent to the country concluded that the Republic of Congo 'cannot account for the origin of the large quantity of rough diamonds that it is officially exporting'.[35] The country was also prohibited from importing or exporting diamonds to or from countries that are members of the Kimberley Process. Another country that is believed to have violated the terms of the Kimberley Process is Liberia, under Taylor. According to the UN Security Council Expert Panel, as late as 6 August 2002, less than a week before Charles Taylor was forced out of office, Liberia was still swapping diamonds for weapons.[36] A third country, Togo, is also believed in many quarters to be in violation of the Kimberley Process, although attention at present seems to be on Congo Brazzaville.

Although the Kimberley Process has significantly changed the nature of trade in rough diamonds, there are now growing concerns that its scope has to be expanded if the process is to stand the future pressures. For example, there are concerns about the objectives of the process as it aims only at preventing rebel groups from dealing in diamond trade, without looking at how governments manage the resource. In short, its definition of 'conflict' is very narrow, and it seems to have been adopted to satisfy the many disparate groups which came together to initiate the process. In a recent report on Angola, there were calls for the Kimberley Process to expand its definition of conflict diamonds to include cases of diamond mining based on the systematic violation of human rights.[37]

Secondly, the Kimberley Process does not adequately address the issue of artisanal actors, who are often the actual purveyors of illegal exploitation and major actors in armed insurrections in West Africa. In short, the Kimberley Process needs also to focus on, or integrate with, other initiatives designed to promote accountability and transparency in formal natural resource exploitation (the extractive industry transparency initiative for example), not the least because legal exploitation neither precludes the misuse and misappropriation of rents from natural resources nor prevents the use of small arms and light weapons to redress perceived and real grievances and greed. Moreover, the Kimberley Process needs to address the often heavy criticism that it is an externally driven initiative, lacking local ownership and legitimacy. This can be addressed by domesticating the process through greater involvement and capacity building by local civil society

accompanied by experts representing Canada and Israel, the World Diamond Council, and the Ottawa-based Partnership Africa-Canada.

[35] *World Bank/IMF Annual General Meeting Daily*, 2 October 2004, 25.

[36] *Other Facets: News and Views on the International Efforts to end Conflict Diamonds, Number 12* (December 2003).

[37] For a brief discussion of the ills of the Kimberley Process, see Andrew Bone, 'Address to Kimberley Process Intersessional', 23 June 2009, available at: <http://www.debeersgroup.com/en/Media-centre/Speeches/2009/Address-to-Kimberley-Process-Intersessional/>. For a comprehensive account of the Kimberley Process, see 'Fatal Transaction: The Kimberly Process and the United Nations, Lessons Learned and Recommendation', Briefing Paper in preparation for Seminar on Natural Resources and Conflicts, 19–20 February 2008, available at: <http://www.ipisresearch.be/download.php?id=202>.

groups to monitor legal and illegal exploitation of natural resources, especially against the backdrop of claims that government officials often collude with, and are complicit in, both legal and illegal exploitation.

5.2 The Extractive Industries Transparency Initiative

Another major initiative is the EITI advanced by the British government, with the sole purpose of ensuring transparency through full publication and verification of company payment and government revenues from oil, gas, and mining.[38] The initiative was formed under the assumption that transparent management of resources, backed by strong government, can prevent the situation where resource-rich countries face serious security challenges as a result of their natural resource endowment.

At the centre of the EITI is the effort to ensure that multinational corporations involved in extractive business are transparent in their activities, and in the process, prevent graft culture that is prevalent in many resource-producing countries. On paper, this initiative will enhance natural resource governance through the promotion of transparency and accountability, greater oversight function for civil society, and it will undercut the tendency of civil servants and politicians to defraud the state.

Although the EITI appears to be making good progress, and has proved to be popular among states, the initiative nonetheless faces a number of challenges. First, it is limited in its focus, as it deals mostly with 'extractive' natural resources and has no consideration for non-extractive natural resources, especially land and international waters. Secondly, the success depends, to a large extent, on the willingness of multinational corporations and even political leaders to open their records for public scrutiny. Thirdly, it aspires only to put extractive industries under close monitoring, without establishing any means of holding governments accountable for management of natural resources in their countries.

Moreover, the question of accountability and transparency is not always about the 'political will', sometimes it is connected to institutional capacity, especially on the part of national governments in Africa. As such, the EITI process will be greatly enhanced if it is interlocked with initiatives such as the Kimberley Process to prevent 'grey areas' and loopholes that could be exploited by different actors. As it stands, the EITI is only focused on 'legal' exploitation. In addition, the EITI and related initiatives need to broaden their scope and begin to address issues related to fair and equitable use of natural resources and their proceeds in African countries in order to draw attention to the relative poverty in natural resource-bearing communities. The EITI will equally

---

[38] For detailed information about this initiative, see: <http://eitransparency.org/>. For a legal analysis of EITI and its implications for companies, see Arnold and Porter LLP, 'Firms Can Avoid EITI, FCPA Pitfalls' (2008) Oil & Gas. For a response, see Matthew Genasci, ibid.

achieve greater successes if it includes making multinational corporations involved in natural resource exploitation in Africa accountable for their overseas business conduct and ethics in host African countries, as is often the case in the defence industry. Finally, EITI is likely to yield only marginal results unless it is connected to regional arrangements and initiatives such as the Economic Community of West African States (ECOWAS), the New Partnership for Africa's Development (NEPAD), and the Southern African Development Community (SADC) amongst others, in contradistinction to its current state-by-state basis.

5.3 The Chad-Cameroon Pipeline Consortium Initiative

The CCPCI represents a project-specific, trilateral arrangement involving two African countries (Chad and Cameroon), and the World Bank (and, by extension, the private sector). The CCPCI is an arrangement whereby the World Bank and a consortium involving Petronas of Malaysia and the USA's Exxon and Chevron agreed to construct a 1,070 kilometre pipeline to transport 250,000 barrels of oil a day from Doba basin in Southern Chad (a landlocked country) to the Southern Cameroonian port of Kribi. The project is expected to earn approximately $13 billion over the next 25 years.[39] Of this, Chad was set to earn at least $2 billion, which was calculated to increase its income per capita from $250 to $550 per year year by 2005.[40]

The CCPCI arrangement was complex from the outset. The World Bank provided $300 million towards financing the project, with other sections of the Bank providing concessional loans to the governments of Chad and Cameroon for capacity building before oil production commenced. To prevent the precedence in other countries where oil discovery leads to poverty and misery, the World Bank laid down conditions for undertaking the project. Specifically, the Bank extracted an agreement from the government of Chad to an arrangement whereby the revenue coming from the sale of oil would be placed in a separate account and managed by a consortium, which involved the international community, civil society, and the government of Chad.[41] The agreement also subjected the country to spending the revenue accruing from oil on specific poverty-alleviation projects, with a specific percentage reserved for future generations. The government agreed to this project, but in October 2005, it announced its intention substantially to modify the agreement by abrogating the percentage put aside for future generations. The Chad-Cameroon project has been controversial from the outset, and it is possible to assume that the Chadian government

---

[39] This is on the assumption that the oil price does not fall below $15 per barrel.

[40] *African Research Bulletin*, 16 September–15 October 2003, 15799.

[41] See Tim Carrington, 'World Bank, Govt of Chad Sign Memorandum of Understanding on Poverty Reduction', available at: <http://web.worldbank.org/WBSITE/EXTERNAL/COUNTRIES/AFRICAEXT/>.

agreed to it in order to obtain the World Bank's agreement to undertake the project.[42] Central to the controversy is the crucial question of sovereignty, especially as to the extent to which a country should have control over the management of its natural resources.[43]

5.4 The Governance and Economic Management Assistance Program

A country-specific initiative that has gained prominence in recent times is the GEMAP in Liberia.[44] It is a framework designed to assist in the reformation of economic and natural resource management in post-war Liberia. Unlike the Chadian-Cameroon Pipeline, which was created to prevent fraud, the GEMAP was specifically suggested to address suspected fraud and other unsatisfactory practices of the National Transitional Government of Liberia (NTLG).[45] At the centre of the initiative are key donor countries and agencies including the African Union, European Commission, IMF, ECOWAS, Nigeria, Ghana, the USA, and the World Bank. The objective was to put structures in place to ensure proper management of the economic affairs of the country. In its operation, the GEMAP has six components: financial management and accountability; improving budgeting and expenditure management; improving procurement practices and granting of concessions; establishing effective processes to control corruption; supporting key institutions; and capacity building. Under the arrangement, all state-owned enterprises will be reformed, and financial experts with signatory powers will be recruited from abroad to supervise and assist their local government counterparts. Much more importantly, an external supervisor with binding co-signatory authority will be brought in to key governmental institutions such as the Bureau of Customs and Excise, Ministry of Land, Mines and Energy in order to assist transparency and accountability. The Program was signed into law in September 2005, and was to last for 36 months.

Opinions in Liberia are divergent on the issue of GEMAP as to whether to accept or condemn the Program. Those who support the Program argue that some form of externally monitored initiative was needed to prevent graft-in

---

[42] For current developments on the Chad-Cameroon Agreement, see ST Mforgham 'Chad-Cameroon Pipeline to be rerouted', available at: <http://www.africanews.com/site/ChadCameroon_pipeline_to_be_rerouted/list_messages/27099>.

[43] For an excellent commentary on the Chad-Cameroon project, see Scott Pegg, 'Chronicle of a Death Foretold: The Collapse of the Chad-Cameroon Pipeline Project' (2009) *African Affairs* 1, also available at: <http://afraf.oxfordjournals.org/cgi/pdf_extract/adp003v1>.

[44] See US Institute of Peace, 'GEMAP in Liberia: A Model for Economic Management in Conflict-Affected Countries' available at: <http://www.usip.org/events/gemap-liberia-model-economic-management-conflict-affected-countries>.

[45] Foreign donors were unsatisfied with the reports of two sets of investigations set up to look into the affairs of the countries. The first of the reports was sponsored by the European Commission to audit the Liberian Central Bank as well as five parastatals—Monrovia Freeport, Robertsfield International Airport, the Forestry Development Authority, the Bureau of Maritime Affairs, and the Liberian Petroleum Refinery Company. The second was undertaken by ECOWAS, and investigated the operations of the Transitional Government itself.

governance. But those who oppose GEMAP are concerned about the loss of sovereignty that comes with the external vetting of Liberian financial accounts.

Regardless of where one stands in the controversy, there are some issues that raise concern in the GEMAP initiative. First, the level of civil society involvement, especially local civil society groups, is almost non-existent. As such, its local content and ownership is seriously questioned, hence making it susceptible to criticism that it is nothing but a foreign-imposed initiative by the donor community. Secondly, the GEMAP was signed by an interim government that had less than six months left in office. Consequently, the extent to which the government took into consideration the interests of the in-coming government was questionable. Finally, the GEMAP plan is restricted to Liberia whereas the problem of illegal exploitation of natural resources is a region-wide problem in the Mano River area.[46]

Against this background, it is contended that the initiative was assented to by the interim government primarily to satisfy the donor community and to give the impression that it had turned over a new leaf. Hence, the initiative needs to be broadened to incorporate the key border countries of Sierra Leone, Guinea, and Côte d'Ivoire which have similar natural resources to those found in Liberia.

5.5 The Diamond Development Initiative

Another recent initiative is the DDI, which emerged out of a meeting co-hosted in January 2005 by De Beers, Global Witness, and Partner Africa-Canada.[47] Key individuals who played an important role in the formation include Andrew Bone from De Beers, Alex Yearsley of Global Witness, and Ian Smilie of Partner Africa-Canada. The initiative was to ensure that gaps in the Kimberly Process were addressed, especially those relating to the activities of alluvial artisanal miners and the several associated security dimensions. Among those who supported the initiatives were representatives of the UN, European Commission, the UK, the US and Canadian foreign ministries, the Department for International Development (DFID), and USAID. Specifically, DDI is aimed at establishing a positive business and developmental environment for artisanal diamond miners in producing countries, especially those with weak governance structures such as Sierra Leone, Angola, and the DRC. At its formation, the focus was on West and

---

[46] The Mano River Union was established in 1973 by Liberia and Sierra Leone—and was joined in 1980 by Guinea—for the purpose of fostering economic integration among member states. See CM Conteh, 'The Mano River Union Approach', 1975 10(4) Intereconomics, 102; also available at: <http://www.springerlink.com/content/477m828281520831/>.

[47] See 'De Beers to Help Reduce Poverty Among Alluvial Diamond Miners', Corporate Social Responsibility (CSR) Press Release, 22 September 2006 available at: < http://www.csrwire.com/press/press_release/17359-De-Beers-to-Help-Reduce-Poverty-Among-Alluvial-Diamond-Miners>.

Central Africa, with the intention of widening the scope in future years. At the time of writing, the initiative is just over a year old, and it is too early to undertake any meaningful assessment of its activities. It is, however, commendable that the initiative hopes to work closely with other existing efforts such as the Kimberley Process. Already, it has established two working groups to study the challenges and opportunities for artisanal miners in micro- and macroeconomic terms.

5.6 The Nigeria-Sao Tome Joint Development Zone

The Nigeria-Sao Tome Joint Development Zone (JDZ) represents another bilateral, project-specific initiative involving the government of Nigeria and Sao Tome and Principe.[48] It was established by a bilateral treaty in 2001 with the sole aim of recognizing the dual claims of both countries to the natural resources (oil and gas) found along their common borders. The JDZ lies approximately 200 km offshore from Nigeria. It is to be managed by a Joint Development Authority (JDA), with proceeds from natural resource exploitation to be shared in the ratio 60:40 in favour of Nigeria.

Since inception, the JDA (on behalf of the two countries) has signed production-sharing contracts with oil companies on two deepwater blocks. The JDA signed a production-sharing contract for a 666^2 km block with a consortium—US Independent Anadarko Petroleum Corp, US-based ERHC, and Canada-based Addax—with a signature bonus of US$40 million. The JDZ initiative aims to prevent inter-state conflicts over natural resources and may serve as a model for sharing natural resources deposited in border regions across Africa.

In all, there appear to be many initiatives targeting different aspects of natural resource exploitation in both its legal and illegal forms in Africa. What is missing, however, is the ability to synergistically integrate these initiatives for optimal functioning. Particular concerns include: the failure to anchor the initiatives at sub-regional and regional levels (especially given the regional dimension of the twin problems of illegal exploitation and the flow of small arms and light weapons that combine to cause conflict, and the reality of extant regional socio-economic and political institutions); the inability to domesticate ownership and procedures, indexed by the involvement of civil society groups; and the relatively scant attention paid to building the capacity of national governments and civil society groups in Africa.

More importantly, the above initiatives fail to apply the 'responsibility to protect' principle on issues bordering on the rights and needs of natural resource-bearing regions and their inhabitants, who continue to be short-changed by their governments, as evidenced by the relative poverty of natural resource-bearing regions across Africa. Perhaps there is a need to generate national and international initiatives that will earmark a minimum benchmark of proceeds from

---

[48] For details of this initiative, see: <http://www.nigeriasaotomejda.com/>.

natural resource exploitation accruable to natural resource-bearing regions. More often, it is the perceived and real injustices, unfairness, and unequal distribution and use of proceeds from natural resource exploitation that encourage illegal exploitation, as much as generate the socio-economic and political discontent that fuel armed conflict.

6. African initiatives to manage natural resources and the link with human security

In recent times, there have been steps taken by African countries to introduce some form of governance structure to ensure that the continent's natural resource endowment satisfies the demands of human security. While some of these initiatives are not specifically linked to natural resource management, their contents have addressed issues relating to these resources, and their proper execution is expected to bring about a better quality of life in the continent.

Civil society and regional organizations in the continent have come up with initiatives to address natural resource management. For example, the West African sub-regional organization, ECOWAS, has also taken an interest in the conflict between livestock and crop farmers and in January 2003, the Council of Ministers adopted a regulation and a number of recommendations on the subject.[49] Part of the resolution deals with effective implementation of the rules governing transhumance and the establishment of a regional framework for consultation in the area of pastoral resource management. In April 2004, the ECOWAS delegation on trans-border pastures made visits to three countries—Burkina Faso, Ghana, and Togo.[50]

Another effort at managing African conflicts comes through the activities of the African Union (AU), formed in July 2002 from the former Organization of African Unity. Among other considerations, the AU adopted a Common Defence and Security Policy for Africa, and one of the issues included for consideration in the proposed policy is the management of natural resources.[51] The Union also established a Peace and Security Council to promote peace, security, and stability in Africa and to promote and encourage democratic practices, good governance, respect for human rights, and the rule of law. Also worth noting is the formation of NEPAD, an initiative for economic recovery and sustainable development of Africa.[52] The NEPAD initiative has many segments, and some of these address

---

[49] In October 1998, the ECOWAS heads of state and government took decisions on transhumance in the region. See 'International Conference on the Future of Transhumance Pastoralism in West and Central Africa', 20–24 November 2006, available at: <http://www.landcoalition.org/pdf/ev06NigeriaPastoralism.pdf>.   [50] *This Day*, Lagos, 5 May 2004.

[51] This was formally adopted at the Assembly of Heads of States and Governments meeting in Maputo, Mozambique, July 2003.

[52] This came from the merging of different initiatives designed to equip Africa for the challenges of the future. The two prominent initiatives were Millennium Partnership for African Recovery

aspects of governance and conflict. There are debates as to the extent to which NEPAD can address the challenges of Africa's development, with some people criticizing the initiative because it came mainly from the leaders without much input from civil society and the population and also because it adopts the same neoliberal approach to developmental problems that they believe require a radical policy response.[53] Others, however, are of the opinion that the initiative should be given a fair chance, with the hope that it may, after all, provide the answers that have so far eluded the continent.

7. Conclusion

The effective management of natural resource endowments remains Africa's best chance of ensuring credible human security protection. This can only be realized if there are effective structures governing these resources. As pointed out at the beginning of this chapter, Africa's main challenge is not that there are insufficient resources; on the contrary, the endowments are certainly sufficient. The crucial issue is how to ensure that these resources are well governed to ensure that they benefit African people. Indeed, for Africa, the link between natural resource management and human security is not so much the issue of addressing scarcity but the complexities of managing abundance.

(MAP), initiated by Presidents Mbeki, Obasanjo, and Bouteflika, respectively of South Africa, Nigeria, and Algeria, and the Omega Plan, championed by President Abdulaye Wade of Senegal.

[53] Those in this group derisively describe the initiative as 'Kneel-pad', derogatively coined to reflect Africa's submissive position to the West in the search for economic assistance.

7

Piracy off Somalia: The 'Emperors and the Thieves of the Oceans' in the 21st Century

*Efthymios Papastavridis**

1. Introduction

For elegant and excellent was the pirate's answer to the great Macedonian Alexander, who had taken him: the king asking him how he durst molest the seas so, he replied with a free spirit, 'how darest thou molest the whole world? But because I do with a little ship only, I am called a thief: thou doing it with a great navy, art called an emperor.[1]

St Augustine

It is highly unlikely that a Somali pirate would ever utter such words to the Commanding Officer of a vessel belonging to the European Union Naval Force (EUNAVFOR) or to the Combined Task Force (CTF) in the Gulf of Aden; however, he could—along the same lines—claim that the persons whose security is really threatened are not 'the emperors' but the 'thieves' of the oceans. The edited volume at hand addresses the acute problem of human security in Africa, which is undoubtedly interconnected with the scourge of piracy in the Gulf of Aden, especially as far as the need for food and personal security is concerned.[2]

* Adjunct Professor, University of Thrace, Faculty of Laws, Research Fellow, Academy of Athens, Greece, LLM (Athens), LLM (UCL), PhD (UCL). This chapter was submitted on 15 November 2009 and does not therefore refer to some subsequent developments.

The author would like to express his gratitude to Professor Ademola Abass (Brunel University) and to Professor Ilias Bantekas (Brunel University) for having read and commented on drafts of this work as well as to the anonymous referee for the useful remarks. Needless to say that the responsibility for any error or omission lies exclusively with the author.

[1] St Augustine, *The City of God*, Liv IV, Ch 4, cited in A Pérotin-Dumon, 'The Pirate and the Emperor: Power and the Law on the Seas, 1450–1850' in C Pennel (ed), *Bandits at Sea: A Pirates Reader* (New York: New York University Press, 2001), 25.

[2] On human security in general, see K Krause, 'Human Security' in V Chetail (ed), *Post-Conflict Peace Building: A Lexicon* (Oxford: Oxford University Press, 2009), 47.

The extraordinary growth in piracy in the region in recent months has attracted unprecedented media coverage and has led to a multipronged international response.[3] According to statistics collated by the International Maritime Bureau's Piracy Reporting Centre,

a total of 306 incidents were reported . . . in the first nine months of 2009, while in 2008, the total number of attacks for the year was 293. The total number of pirate attacks in the Gulf of Aden and off east-coast Somalia so far in 2009 has already overtaken the figure for all of 2008.[4]

Moreover, several nations as well as NATO and the European Union have sent naval assets to patrol the Gulf of Aden in an effort to protect international commercial shipping. The UN Security Council has passed a series of Resolutions under Chapter VII of the Charter that give these forces unprecedented legal authority to pursue pirates.[5] In addition, a Contact Group on Piracy off the Coast of Somalia has been created since 14 January 2009 pursuant to Security Council Resolution 1851 (2008). This is a voluntary ad hoc international forum meeting quarterly at the UN with the view to 'coordinating political, military, and other efforts to bring an end to piracy off the coast of Somalia and to ensure that pirates are brought to justice'.[6]

It is beyond the remit of this chapter to canvass every legal aspect of the current situation in the Gulf of Aden and of the maritime interception operations involved therein.[7] Rather, its purpose is to assess the legality of the interception

---

[3] Suffice it to peruse the daily international press to realize the extent of the international concern in respect of the present issue. See, inter alia, CNN, 'Somali Piracy Threatens Trade, Boosts Terrorists, Analysts Say', 1 October 2008, <http://edition.cnn.com/2008/WORLD/africa/10/01/piracy.terror/index.html>, BBC, Somali Piracy: Global Overview', 17 April 2009, <http://news.bbc.co.uk/2/hi/africa/8003124.stm>, BBC, Putland Turns against Somali Pirates and Pirate Global Map Overview, 1 June 2009, <http://news.bbc.co.uk/1/hi/world/africa/8072188.stm#map>, BBC, Q&A: Somali Piracy, 2 November 2009, <http://news.bbc.co.uk/2/hi/africa/7734985.stm>.

[4] IMB, 'Unprecedented Increase in Somali Pirate Activity', 21 October 2009. <http://www.icc-ccs.org/index.php?option=com_content&view=article&id=376:unprecedented-increase-in-somali-pirate-activity&catid=60:news&Itemid=51>. See further information, inter alia, at: <http://www.imo.org/home.asp?topic_id=1178>.

[5] See, inter alia, SC Res 1816 (2008), 1846 (2008), and 1851 (2008).

[6] '45 countries and seven international organizations (the African Union, the League of Arab States, the European Union, INTERPOL, International Maritime Organization, NATO, and UN Secretariat) now participate in the Contact Group, along with two major maritime industry groups, BIMCO and INTERTANKO, who take part as Observers': <http://www.state.gov/t/pm/ppa/piracy/contactgroup/index.htm>.

[7] There is an increasing number of articles devoted to this topical issue; see, inter alia, E Kontorovich, 'International Legal Responses to Piracy off the Coast of Somalia', *ASIL Insights,* 6 February 2009; <http://www.asil.org/insights090206.cfm> (hereinafter 'Kontorovich'); A Trancedi, 'Di Pirati e Stati "Falliti": Il Consiglio di Sicurenza Autorizza il Ricorso alla Forza Nelle Acque Territoriali della Somalia' (2008) 4 Rivista di Diritto Internazionale 937; Voelckel, 'La piraterie entre Charte et Convention: à propos de la resolution 1816 du Conseil de Sécurité' (2008) 12 Annuaire du droit de la mer 479; J Kraska and T Wilson, 'Repressing Piracy in the 21st Century: An International Maritime Threat Response Plan' (2009) 40 Journal of Maritime Law and Commerce 43; T Treves, 'Piracy, Law of the Sea, and Use of Force: Developments off the Coast of Somalia' (2009) 20 EJIL 399. In addition see the Report of the International Expert Group on

of suspect vessels and of the subsequent exercise of enforcement jurisdiction over the pirates against the background of general international law, in particular law of the sea as well as international human rights law. Accordingly, after a succinct reference to the factual background of piracy in the region and to the relevant international legal regime, the chapter will first consider the possible legal justifications for the current counter-piracy operations and, secondly, will scrutinize the relevant measures taken *a posteriori*, such as the detainment and arrest of the pirates as well as their transfer to Kenya. The ensuing analysis will demonstrate that the present situation gives rise to a host of international legal questions, including the problem of human security. It is a truism that pirates are treated as *hostes humani generis* and this has inescapable ramifications with regard to the protection of their human rights. Furthermore, it is posited that the international community and the states involved in the relevant counter-piracy operations, far from aiming at eliminating the veritable sources of this activity, such as the political situation in Somalia, the extreme poverty, the depletion of fishing resources, and waste dumping in the latter's shores, are engaged in short-term and ambivalent measures which only temporarily alleviate the problem.[8]

It is asserted that the causes of the phenomenon of piracy in the region as well as its potential resolution are inextricably linked with the question of human security. It is not the purpose of the present chapter to discuss extensively the factual and legal parameters of the latter question in respect of Africa and in particular in respect of Somalia. However, it is significant to comprehend that the problem of piracy will hardly be resolved solely with maritime interdiction measures; on the contrary, its resolution is partly contingent upon the level of the protection of human security in the region. The latter encompasses

the full gamut of human well-being: not merely safety from harm and injury to territory, but access to basic necessities that are should ordinarily be due to every person, like water, food, shelter, health, and employment.[9]

It goes without saying that these basic necessities are manifestly lacking in Somalia especially due to the civil strife in the country since the early 1990s.[10]

Piracy off the Somali Coast commissioned by the Special Representative of the S-G of the UN to Somalia <http://www.imcsnet.org/imcs/docs/somalia_piracy_intl_experts_report_consolidated.pdf> (hereinafter 'UN Working Group Report').

   [8] UN Secretary-General Ban Ki-Moon told delegates at a donors' conference sponsored by the UN that 'piracy is a symptom of anarchy and insecurity on the ground' and that 'more security on the ground will make less piracy on the seas'; see CNN, 'Donors Pledge Over $250 Million for Somalia', 23 April 2009, <http://abcnews.go.com/International/wireStory?id=7407956>.

   [9] N Myers, *Ultimate Security* (New York: WW Norton, 1993), 31, quoting John Hoddinott, *Operationalizing Household Food Security in Development Projects: An Introduction* (Washington, DC: International Food Policy Research Institute, 1999).

   [10] See, eg, W Clarke, *Learning from Somalia: The Lessons of Armed Humanitarian Intervention* (Boulder, CO: Westview Press, 1997).

In more detail, it is evident that the lack of food security has played a paramount role in the involvement of many Somalis in the 'piracy' business as well as in the tacit approbation that this business enjoys in large parts of the Somali population.[11] Especially as far as the involvement of Somali fishermen in this illicit activity is concerned, it is argued that it is mainly due to the fact that

Somali waters have become the site of an international 'free for all' with fishing fleets from around the world illegally plundering Somali stocks and freezing out the country's own rudimentarily-equipped fishermen.[12]

This has led many Somali anglers to engage in piratical activity in order to meet their everyday needs. Of course, this is not the sole ground for the rise of piracy in the region. According to the UN Working Group Report,

Poverty, lack of employment, environmental hardship, pitifully low incomes, reduction of pastoralist and maritime resources due to drought and illegal fishing and a volatile security and political situation all contribute to the rise and continuance of piracy in Somalia.[13]

While the international community has responded to the latter problem in a robust fashion, noticeable by its absence is condemnation of the equally significant matter of Illegal, Unreported and Unregulated (IUU) fishing.[14] According to the High Seas Task Force (HSTF),

there were over 800 IUUs fishing vessels in Somali waters at one time in 2005 taking advantage of Somalia's inability to police and control its own waters and fishing grounds. The IUUs, which are estimated take out more than $450 million in fish value out of Somalia annually [sic]...[15]

This perceived one-sided approach of the developed world to the latter problem is certainly a source of contention for the African communities and it is not contributive to the permanent resolution of the problem of piracy in the region. It is asserted that military effort may divert resources from other more effective action, which unequivocally includes protecting food and human security in general in Somalia.

---

[11] According to a definition provided by the Food and Agricultural Organization (FAO) in the Rome Declaration on World Food Security and World Food Summit Plan of Action, 'food security exists when all people, at all times, have physical and economic access to sufficient, safe and nutritious food to meet their dietary needs and food preferences for an active and healthy life'; FAO, Rome Declaration on World Food Security and World Food Summit Plan of Action, para 1. See further discussion in Chapter 2 above, 'Food Security in Africa'.

[12] See I Tharoor, 'How Somalia's Fishermen Became Pirates', CNN, 18 April 2009, <http://www.time.com/time/world/article/0,8599,1892376,00.html>.

[13] UN Working Group's Report, at 15.

[14] According to the HSTF, IUU does not respect national boundaries or sovereignty. It puts unsustainable pressure on stocks, marine life, habitats, undermines labour standards, and distorts markets; see further <http://www.high-seas.org/>. See also FAO, *International Plan of Action for Reducing Incidental Catch of Seabirds in Longline Fisheries* (Rome: FAO, 1999); *International Plan of Action to Prevent, Deter and Eliminate Illegal, Unreported and Unregulated Fishing* (Rome: FAO, 2001).

[15] See n 12 above.

2. Background

Piracy off the Somali coast has been a threat to international shipping since the early 1990s. However, it was not until 2005 that many international organizations, including the International Maritime Organization and the World Food Programme, started to express serious concerns over the rise in acts of piracy in the region. It appears that the base for most pirates in Somalia has been Puntland, the semi-autonomous region in the northeast of the country. A small number of acts of piracy in the Gulf of Aden have also originated in Yemen.[16] According to a BBC report, the pirates can be divided into three main categories, first

local Somali fishermen considered the brains of the pirates' operations, secondly, ex-militiamen who used to fight for the local clan warlords and finally technical experts who operate equipment such as the GPS devices.[17]

Somali pirates are attacking vessels in the northern Somali coast in the Gulf of Aden and in the eastern Somali coast in the Somalia basin, usually firing automatic weapons and Rocket Propelled Grenades (RPG) in order to board and to hijack vessels. Once the attack is successful and the vessel hijacked, the pirates sail the vessel to the Somali coast and thereafter demand a ransom for the safe release of the vessel and crew.[18] In addition, they are using 'mother vessels' to launch attacks further away from the coast. These 'mother vessels' are able to proceed far out to sea and launch smaller boats to attack and hijack passing ships.[19] The high rate of their success is partly due to the geography of the region and its impact on the routes of maritime commerce: all vessels transiting the Suez Canal must pass through the narrow strait between the Horn of Africa and the Arabian Peninsula, where cargo vessels with unarmed crews become easy prey. In addition, it should be underscored, on the one hand, that pirate leaders evidently

---

[16] R Middleton, *Piracy in Somalia: Threatening Global Trade, Feeding Local Wars*, Chatham House Briefing Paper, October 2008, <http://www.chathamhouse.org.uk/publications/papers/view/-/id/665/>.

[17] BBC News, 'Somali Pirates Living the High Life', 28 October 2008, <http://news.bbc.co.uk/2/hi/africa/7650415.stm>. According to Global Security there are four main groups operating off the Somali coast. The National Volunteer Coast Guard (NVCG) is said to specialize in intercepting small boats and fishing vessels around Kismayu on the southern coast. The Marka group is made up of several scattered and less organized groups operating around the town of Marka. The third significant pirate group is composed of traditional Somali fishermen operating around Puntland and referred to as the Puntland Group. The last set is the Somali Marines, which are reputed to be the most powerful and sophisticated of the pirate groups with a military structure, a fleet admiral, admiral, vice admiral, and a head of financial operation; see <http://www.globalsecurity.org/military/world/para/pirates.htm>.

[18] A single seizure can earn each pirate $150,000. (In Somalia, per capita gross domestic product (GDP) is $600 and male life expectancy is around 47 years.) See CIA World Factbook, Somalia, <https://www.cia.gov/library/publications/the-world-factbook/geos/so.html>.

[19] See ICC Commercial Crimes Services, 'Piracy Prone Areas and Warnings', <http://www.icc-ccs.org/index.php?option=com_content&view=article&id=70&Itemid=58>.

have more power than the government and, on the other hand, that they enjoy a considerable degree of acceptance from the local population, which makes the possibility of their arrest in Somalia, especially in Puntland, highly unlikely.[20] As was mentioned above, this reflects the interconnection of the present problem with the overall problem of human security in the region, which entails that the former problem will not find any permanent solution if human security is not effectively protected.

As a result, piracy has contributed to an increase in shipping costs and has impeded the delivery of food aid shipments; 90 per cent of the World Food Programme's shipments arrive by sea, and ships have required a military escort. In August 2008, Combined Task Force 150, a multinational coalition task force, took on the role of fighting Somali piracy by establishing a Maritime Security Patrol Area (MSPA) within the Gulf of Aden. CTF 150 was replaced by a new multi-national naval force on 8 January 2009 under the command of the US Navy, designated as Combined Task Force 151 (CTF-151). The increasing threat posed by piracy also caused significant concerns in other leading commercial states, such as India, Russia, and China, which responded to these concerns by deploying warships in the region. Furthermore, the European Union has established EUNAVFOR *Operation Atalanta*, to coordinate the European naval response to piracy and to protect international shipping in the region.[21] In addition, since August 2008 the UK Maritime Trade Organization has promulgated an Internationally Recognised Transit Corridor (IRTC), which merchant ships are strongly advised to employ.[22] Finally, many vessels have been instructed to use the alternative, yet far more time-consuming route of the Cape of Good Hope.

In the meantime, in 2008, the UN Security Council passed several Resolutions pursuant to Chapter VII of the UN Charter, dealing with Somali piracy—more Resolutions than on any other subject in that year.[23] These Resolutions have bolstered the powers of the multinational armada in the Gulf of Aden by expanding the authority of the navies beyond acts permitted on the high seas under general international law. The first was Resolution 1816 on 2 June 2008, which authorized nations to take action against pirates in

[20] It is reported that 'many local residents appreciate the rejuvenating effect that the pirates' on-shore spending and re-stocking has had on their impoverished towns, a presence which has oftentimes provided jobs and opportunity when there were none'.

[21] On 15 June 2006, the Council of the European Union decided that the EUNAVFOR *Atalanta* would patrol for another year off the Somali coast from the current end date of 13 December 2009. For further information on this and generally on *Operation Atalanta* see: <http://www.consilium. europa.eu/showPage.aspx?id=1518&lang=en>.

[22] Masters using the IRTC are not relieved of their obligation and should continue to maintain a strict 24-hour lookout using all available means to obtain an early warning of an approaching threat. Ships are encouraged to conduct their passage through the IRTC in groups based on their transit speed. Further information is available at: <http://www.mschoa.org>.

[23] SC Res 1814 (15 May 2008), SC Res 1816 (2 June 2008), SC Res 1838 (7 October 2008), SC Res 1846 (2 December 2008), and SC Res 1851 (16 December 2008).

sovereign Somali waters,[24] while the last was Resolution 1851 (17 December 2008), which allowed for the first time the land pursuit of pirates.

Despite this authorization to interdict and detain pirates at sea, the central legal question of the current anti-piracy campaign is what to do with apprehended pirates and where to prosecute them. As response to these questions, the UK and subsequently the European Union have entered into agreements with Kenya to permit pirates and sea robbers captured by the Royal Navy and by the EUNAVFOR *Operation Atalanta* correspondingly to be tried in Kenyan courts.[25] In addition, the European Union has concluded an agreement with Somalia regarding the status of EU personnel therein[26] as well as another agreement with Djibouti to facilitate the transfer of suspected pirates under national custody to the capturing state.[27] Consequently, pirates captured by various states' navies are mainly standing trial in Kenya, while a few of them are indicted in France, the Netherlands, and the USA.[28] In general, it is observed that 'navies have had some success in their primary aim of disrupting piratical activity and the success rates for pirate attacks has dropped from around 1 in 3 to about 1 in 4'.[29]

In addition, it should be noted that on 26 January 2009, a high-level meeting of 17 states from the Western Indian Ocean, Gulf of Aden, and Red Sea areas was convened by the International Maritime Organization (IMO) in Djibouti to help address the present problem. The meeting has adopted a Code of Conduct concerning the Repression of Piracy and Armed Robbery against Ships in the

---

[24] See D Guilfoyle, 'Piracy off Somalia: UN Security Council Resolution 1816 and IMO Regional Counter-Piracy Efforts' (2008), 57 ICLQ 690 (hereinafter 'Guilfoyle').

[25] 'Republic of Kenya and the United Kingdom Sign A Memorandum Of Understanding On Piracy Along The Coast Of Somalia', <http://www.mfa.go.ke/mfacms/index.php?option=com_content&task=view&id=305&Itemid=62> and also Exchange of Letters between the EU and the Government of Kenya on the conditions and modalities for the transfer of persons suspected of having committed acts of piracy and detained by the European Union-led naval force (EUNAVFOR) from EUNAVFOR to Kenya (6 March, 2009); <http://eur-lex.europa.eu/LexUriServ/LexUriServ.do?uri=OJ:L:2009:079:0049:0059:EN:PDF> (hereinafter 'EU-Kenya Agreement'). There is also a US-Kenya Agreement on transferring pirates for trial (January 2009), see relevant practice at: <http://www.reuters.com/article/worldNews/idUSTRE52480N20090305>.

[26] See Agreement between the European Union and the Somali Republic on the status of the European Union-led naval force in the Somali Republic in the framework of the EU military operation Atalanta, done at Nairobi, 31/12/2008, Official Journal of the European Union (15.1.2009) L10/29.

[27] See Agreement between the European Union and the Republic of Djibouti on the status of the European Union-led forces in the Republic of Djibouti in the framework of the EU military operation Atalanta, done at Djibouti, 5 January 2009, Official Journal of the European Union (3.2.2009) L33/43.

[28] eg, on 18 May 2009, Abduhl Kadir Muse, a Somali pirate who was arrested after the kidnapping of a US captain, pleaded not guilty to ten charges before the federal grand jury in New York, <http://news.bbc.co.uk/2/hi/americas/8062717.stm>. Very recently, on 16 November 2009, two Somalis were indicted for the first time by a Spanish judge on the count of armed robbery at sea; see CNN, 'Somali Pirate Suspects Indicted in Spain', 16 November 2009, <http://edition.cnn.com/2009/WORLD/europe/11/16/spain.pirates/index.html>.

[29] See Chatham House, Briefing Note, 'Pirates and How to Deal with Them', Africa Programme and International Law Discussion Group, 22 April 2009, <http://www.chathamhouse.org.uk/files/13845_220409pirates_law.pdf> (hereinafter 'Chatham House, Piracy').

Western Indian Ocean and the Gulf of Aden).[30] Lastly, it is well worth mentioning that revised guidance on combating piracy and armed robbery against ships was agreed by IMO's Maritime Safety Committee (MSC) in its 86th session from 27 May to 5 June 2009. In more detail, the MSC produced updated Recommendations to Governments for preventing and suppressing piracy and armed robbery against ships and Guidance to ship owners and ship operators, shipmasters and crews on preventing and suppressing acts of piracy and armed robbery against ships. The guidance to shipmasters and crew includes a new annex aimed at seafarers, fishermen, and other mariners who may be kidnapped or held hostage for ransom. An MSC circular on Piracy and armed robbery against ships in waters off the coast of Somalia was also adopted, to include Best Management Practices to Deter Piracy in the Gulf of Aden and off the Coast of Somalia. It was agreed that flag states should strongly discourage the carrying and use of firearms by seafarers for personal protection or for the protection of a ship.[31]

3. Piracy and armed robbery under general international law

Piracy *jure gentum* has traditionally been described as 'every unauthorized act of violence by a private vessel on the open sea with the intent to plunder (*animo furandi*)'.[32] English jurisprudence historically treated the crime of piracy as felony or robbery carried out on the high seas. In 1934 the British Privy Council concluded that piracy has evolved as a crime from one of 'acts of robbery and depredations upon the high seas which, if committed upon land, would have amounted to felony there' to 'any armed violence at sea which is not a lawful act of war'.[33] However, this broad concept[34] was narrowed down by the conventional definitions of the 1958 Geneva Convention on the High Seas[35] and the UN Convention on the Law of the Sea,[36] which should be considered, on

---

[30] See IMO-sponsored Code of Conduct concerning the Repression of Piracy and Armed Robbery Against Ships in the Western Indian Ocean and the Gulf of Aden, adopted in Djibouti on 29 January 2009, <http://www.imo.org/About/mainframe.asp?topic_id=1773&doc_id=10933> (hereinafter: Djibouti Code of Conduct).

[31] See for further information <http://www.imo.org/home.asp?topic_id=1178>.

[32] L Oppenheim, 'Disputes, War and Neutrality' in H Lauterpacht (ed), *International Law: A Treatise* (8th edn, London: Longman, 1955), 608. The qualification *jure gentum* serves as the distinguishing trait between piracy under international law and piracy under national law.

[33] *In Re Piracy Jure Gentium*, 49 Lloyd's List L Repts (1934), 411. Piracy was similarly treated in the USA, see A Van Zwanenberg, 'Interference with Ships on the High Seas' (1961) 10 ICLQ 785, 802.

[34] A very informative perusal of the case law concerning piracy is offered by R Constantinople, 'Towards a New Definition of Piracy: The *Achille Lauro* Incident' (1986) 26 Virginia Journal of International Law 723, 727.

[35] Art 15 of the Geneva Convention on the High Seas (1958) 450 UNTS 52.

[36] UN Convention on the Law of the Sea (1982), 1833 UNTS 397; entered into force 16 November 1994; as at 20 July 2009, LOSC has 159 parties, including the EC (hereinafter 'LOSC').

this point, as declaratory of customary international law.[37] Article 101 of LOSC defines piracy as consisting of any of the following acts:

1) any illegal acts of violence or detention, or any act of depredation, committed for private ends by the crew or passengers of a private ship..., and directed: (a) on the high seas, against another ship...(b) against a ship, aircraft, persons or property in a place outside the jurisdiction of any State...

It reiterates actually the definition furnished by the relevant provision of the Geneva Convention, which, in turn, has heavily relied on the 1932 Harvard Research Draft.[38]

The most salient and controversial limitation on this conception of piracy is the requirement that acts must be committed for 'private ends', as opposed to 'public ends'.[39] The concept of 'private ends' may not necessarily denote the classic element of *animus furandi*, which is no longer considered as *sine qua non*,[40] albeit, arguably, it still excludes purely politically motivated acts.[41] According to the Harvard Research,

[it] excludes from its definition of piracy all cases of wrongful attacks on person or property for political ends, whether they are made on behalf of states or of recognized belligerent organizations or of unrecognized revolutionary bands.[42]

Noteworthy is also the two-ship requirement contemplated in the relevant provisions, which entails that situations in which only one vessel is involved, such as the crew seizure or passenger takeover of their own vessel, are explicitly excluded from the definition of international sea piracy.[43] Finally, it is stipulated that the crime of piracy *jure gentium* should take place on the high seas or in the Exclusive

[37] It is a truism that the relevant provisions of LOSC have attained the status of a customary rule; this is also countenanced by states non-signatories to LOSC, such as the USA; see US Naval Commander Handbook (2007), para 1–2. See also D Momtaz, 'The High Seas' in R-J Dupuy and D Vignes (eds), *A Handbook on the New Law of the Sea* (Dordrecht: Martinus Nijhoff, 1991-I), 417.

[38] Harvard Research in International Law, Draft Convention on Piracy, reprinted in (1932) 26 AJIL Supp 743 (hereinafter 'Harvard Research').

[39] See in this regard S Davidson, 'International Law and the Suppression of Maritime Violence' in R Burchill et al (eds), *International Conflict and Security Law* (Cambridge: Cambridge University Press, 2005), 265, 271.

[40] See the Commentary of the International Law Commission to Draft Article 39, reprinted in II YbILC (1956-II), 282. See also M McDougal and W Burke, *The Public Order of the Oceans: A Contemporary International Law of the Sea* (New Haven, CT: Yale University Press, 1962), 810.

[41] For relevant arguments per and contra this view see, inter alia, B Bornick, 'Bounty Hunters and Pirates: Filling in the Gaps of the 1982 UNCLOS' (2005) 17 Florida Journal of International Law 259; T Garmon, 'International Law of the Sea: Reconciling the Law of Piracy and Terrorism in the Wake of September 11th' (2002) 27 Tulane Maritime Law Journal 257.

[42] Harvard Research, 786. On the historical debate over the belligerent naval rights of insurgencies see L Moir, *The Law of Internal Armed Conflict* (Cambridge: Cambridge University Press, 2002), ch 1.

[43] Cf art 101(a)(ii), which alludes to acts of piracy directed against a ship, aircraft, person, or property in a place outside the jurisdiction of any state, ie a *terra nullius*.

Economic Zone (EEZ), in which the relevant provisions apply subject to the coastal state rights therein.[44]

It follows that acts of violence that occur in the territorial or in the internal waters of the coastal state fall beyond the ambit of the international regulation of piracy *jure gentium*. This raises significant problems, since the majority of the relevant incidents in the twenty-first century has occurred in territorial waters or ports of states, while the ships were at anchor or berthed. Accordingly, acts of piracy committed, for example, in the territorial waters of states littoral to Malacca Straits as well as in the territorial sea of Somalia cannot be designated as piracy *jure gentium*. In view of this, the international community, and in particular IMO, created a separate crime in the Draft Code for the Investigation of the Crimes of Piracy and Armed Robbery against Ships called 'armed robbery against ships', which means any unlawful act of violence or detention or any act of depredation or threat thereof, other than an act of piracy, directed against a ship or against persons or property on board such a ship, within a state's jurisdiction over such offences.[45]

As far as the suppression of the international crime of piracy is concerned, it has customarily been recognized and codified under LOSC that the warships of all states are allowed to visit and board any ship on the high seas, of whatever flag, reasonably suspected of being engaged in piracy (article 110 LOSC), while those on board a pirate vessel may be arrested by the seizing vessel and may be subsequently tried by any state before whose courts they are brought and be subject to penalties imposed by its laws (article 105 LOSC).[46] It is common knowledge that for as long as sovereignty-based jurisdictional principles have existed (that is, at least since the early seventeenth century), any nation could try any pirates it caught, regardless of the pirates' nationality or where on the high seas they were apprehended.[47] The legitimacy of universal jurisdiction over piracy throughout the past several hundred years has been recognized by jurists and scholars of every major maritime nation. Universal jurisdiction over pirates applies to both civil and criminal proceedings. For example, when a pirate ship was captured and brought into port, where the ship and its accoutrements would be sold in a prize proceeding, those robbed by pirates could

---

[44] See arts 56, 58, and 60(4), (6) of LOSC and also M Nordquist (ed), *United Nations Convention on the Law of the Sea, A Commentary*, Vol III (Dordrecht: Martinus Nijhoff, 1985), 537.

[45] IMO, Code of Practice for the Investigation of the Crimes of Piracy and Armed Robbery against Ships, adopted 29 November 2001, Res A.922(22), art 2(2), <http://www.pmaesa.org/Maritime/Res%20A.922(22).doc>. Cf also art 1 of the Regional Cooperation Agreement on Combating Piracy and Armed Robbery against Ships in Asia (28 April 2005) (2005), ILM 829.

[46] On the provisions of LOSC concerning piracy see M Nordquist, n 44 above, 182. On piracy in general see H Dubner *The Law of International Sea Piracy* (2nd edn, The Hague: Martinus Nijhoff, 1988); A Rubin, *The Law of Piracy* (2nd edn, New York: Transnational, 1998).

[47] The law of nations also permitted any nation that caught a pirate to summarily execute him at sea; see J Kent, *Commentaries* in P Kurland and R Lerner (eds) 3 *The Founders' Constitution* (1987), 87 cited by E Kontorovich, 'The Piracy Analogy: Modern Universal Jurisdiction's Hollow Foundation' (2004) 45 Harvard International Law Journal 190.

bring suit in admiralty court requesting compensation from the proceeds of the sale.[48]

Finally, it should be noted that the visit of pirate vessels under article 110 constitutes a right and not an obligation of the flag states under international law.[49] Thus, should states abstain from taking enforcement measures against piracy, it can be argued that they would not incur state responsibility, notwithstanding the provision of LOSC, which requires states to cooperate in the repression of piracy 'to the fullest possible extent' (article 100). The latter sets forth a general obligation of cooperation and not of conduct or of result, which entails that it would be difficult to substantiate a breach of international law.

4. The legality of visit of Somali pirate vessels under international law

With regard to the issue at hand, namely piracy in the Gulf of Aden and the legality of the visit of suspect vessels therein, a fundamental distinction must be made, at the outset, between the acts of piracy *jure gentium* and armed robbery at sea. As far as the former is concerned, it is uncontested that according to article 110 of LOSC, all warships are entitled to board and search vessels suspected of being engaged in such activity. This provision reflects customary law; hence it is not required that the flag states should be parties to LOSC. The only requirement that article 110 sets out is that there are 'reasonable grounds' to suspect that the vessel has been engaged in the proscribed activity as well as that the boarding warship or the other 'duly authorized state vessel' abide by the *modus operandi* laid down in article 110(2)–(3) of LOSC. It goes without saying that the visit itself presupposes that the vessel is suspected of being engaged in piracy *jure gentium*, as it is defined in article 101.

In the case of Somalia, it is submitted that the above requirements of both articles 101 and 110 are in the majority of the cases well satisfied. Indeed, most piratical incidents occur on the high seas and involve two vessels, while the ends pursued by the pirates are predominantly private rather than political. Further, the warships of the international forces present in the region comply in general terms with the relevant modus operandi, that is, they first board the vessel to suppress an ongoing *actum piratum* or to identify the vessel's character and if suspicions remain, they thoroughly search the vessel and collect the necessary evidence.[50] According to the EU Guidance on the Collection of Evidence

---

[48] Ibid, 192.

[49] Cf the hortatory and not mandatory wording used in both arts 105 and 110 of LOSC.

[50] Cf the Flow Chart of the EU NAVFOR, ANNEX C TO OP ATALANTA EU OHQ SOP LEGAL 001, dated 26 March 2009 (on file with the author; hereinafter 'EU Flow Chart').

and Transfer of Suspected Pirates, Armed Robbers and Seized Property from EUNAVFOR to Kenya

the primary objective on boarding a suspect dhow or coming alongside a suspect skiff is to complete a security sweep of the vessel to ensure there is no threat to own person-nel...If following the securing of the vessel suspicions still remain that persons onboard are engaged in piracy or armed robbery at sea, the boarding team should take appropriate steps to preserve the scene until the evidence 'collection' team can be transferred from the warship to the dhow/skiff.[51]

It is also accepted that if no grounds exists to continue with search of the vessel, the latter and its crew are released.

Notwithstanding this prima facie legality of such interdiction operations, the following comments are in order: first, pursuant to the EUNAVFOR Rules of Engagement (RoE), there are certain types of boarding, namely cooperative boarding or unopposed boarding and non-cooperative boarding.[52] It is submit-ted that there is no need for such distinctions in the case of piracy, since the visit of a suspected pirate vessel constitutes a customary right of warships of all states, regardless of the consent of the flag State or of the Master of the suspect vessel.[53] This right, however, presupposes that there exist *a priori* 'reasonable grounds' to suspect the vessel concerned. Such grounds are obviously present in cases of an ongoing piracy as well as in case of an unsuccessful attack on a merchant ship. Nevertheless, in cases in which the attack on the merchant vessel has not yet materialized, it is apt to question the applicable standard of 'reasonableness of the grounds' to board a suspect vessel.

In general, it is asserted that due to the exceptional character of the right to visit to the fundamental principle of the freedom of navigation on the high seas, this phrase must be construed as amounting to more than a mere suspicion. Moreover, this suspicion has to be constructed as objectively as possible and not left to the complete discretion of the commander of the warship or of the officer in command of the boarding party, as they might be prone to abuse of the right to visit.[54] According to another strand of legal doctrine, less than actual evidence is required, while sufficient cause for suspicion is the yardstick for this provision.[55]

---

[51] See ANNEX C TO OP ATALANTA EU OHQ SOP LEGAL 001 dated 26 March 2009, para 6.2 (on file with the author; hereinafter 'Guidance to EUNAVFOR').

[52] See EU Flow Chart.

[53] On consensual boarding see D Wilson, 'Interdiction on the High Seas: The Role and Authority of a Master in the Boarding and Searching of his Ships by Foreign Warships' (2008) 55 Naval Law Review 157.

[54] In contemplation of this, both the 1958 and 1982 Conventions provide that the ship boarded 'shall be compensated for any loss or damage...in all cases the suspicion proves unfounded'; see also LB Sohn, 'International Law of the Sea and Human Rights Issues' in T Clingan (ed), *The Law of the Sea: What Lies Ahead?* (Hawaii: Law of the Sea Institute, 1988), 57.

[55] See X Hinrichs, 'Measures against Smuggling of Migrants at Sea: A Law of the Sea Related Perspective' (2003) 36 Revue Belge de Droit International 434.

Even more flexible criteria apply in the context of EUNAVFOR *Operation Atalanta*: the relevant RoE have set out certain presumptions that may furnish the legal basis not only of the right of visit but also of the detention and the transfer to Kenya of the suspects. For example, in the case of an unaccompanied skiff, the most likely factors, according to the Guidance to EUNAVFOR, to indicate whether there is sufficient evidence are, inter alia, the skiff contains firearms with ammunition. In particular, the number and type of weapons are such that they are in excess of that required for personal self-defence (for example, RPGs); the skiff is located on the high seas in areas known to be used by pirates or in the territorial waters of Somalia; there is no compelling evidence that the skiff is engaged in lawful activity such as fishing (for example, no nets on board, recently caught fish).[56]

It is submitted that such factors or such circumstantial evidence would not suffice to support the prosecution of the persons on board; however, insofar as the right of visit as such, it is suggested that there is room for a different reading of the 'reasonable grounds' *in casu* in comparison to the other law enforcement cases of article 110. In more detail, due to the high number of piratical incidents in the region carried out almost exclusively by such skiffs or dhows, it can be maintained that the flexible criterion of 'reasonableness' has been adjusted to the exigencies of the suppression of piracy in the region. Thus, such evidence or *indicia* of piratical activity may suffice to allow the boarding of the vessels in question. This, of course, does not deprive the boarding vessels of the obligation to abide by the relevant requirements of international law as well as to compensate the suspect vessel in accordance with articles 110(3) and 106 of LOSC.

Lastly, in respect of the 'private ends' requirement of article 101 of LOSC, it is questioned whether there is room for the contention that certain acts of the Somali pirates might have a political character and thus might fall beyond the scope of the relevant provision. This brings to the fore the whole discourse regarding the proper interpretation of the 'private ends' requirement, which has aroused considerable doctrinal controversy.[57] Historically, the requirement that a pirate act had to be committed for 'private ends' had its origin in the distinction between piracy and privateering.[58] The Declaration of Paris abolished privateering in 1856,[59] but

the distinction between private and public ends was maintained because courts and states wanted to differentiate between piracy and acts of maritime depredation carried out by insurgents or rebels.[60]

---

[56] Guidance to EUNAVFOR, 4.1.   [57] See text to n 39 above.

[58] On privateering see D Petrie, *The Prize Game: Lawful Looting on the High Seas in the Days of Fighting Sail* (Naval Institute Press, 1999) and F Stark, *The Abolition of Privateering and the Declaration of Paris* (New York: Columbia University Press, 1897).

[59] See Declaration Respecting Maritime Law, 16 April 1856, published in 1 AJIL (Supp 1907), 89. The Paris Declaration is given an exhaustive treatment in F Piggot, *The Declaration of Paris 1856* (London: University of London Press, 1919).

[60] M Murphy, 'Piracy and UNCLOS' in P Lehr (ed), *Violence at Sea: Piracy in the Age of Global Terrorism* (London: Routledge, 2007), 155, 160.

Consequently,

it is regretted that the League of Nations Committee and its successors chose this formulation and not the one that stems most logically from the pirate-privateer distinction, that is to say piracy is an act undertaken without *due authority*. After all, the insurgents that customary law and in turn the Committee and then the Group sought to protect were bodies that had won some form of recognition or whose acts would have been legal if they had been recognized, and who directed their depredations solely against the vessels of the country whose government they sought to overthrow.[61]

Drawing from this insight, it is submitted that there will be cases of maritime violence, where, despite the political ends involved, the lack of 'a due authority' and 'legitimate targets' will be decisive for the designation of the acts concerned as *acta pirata* under customary law. For example, any such act by a recognized belligerent or rebel group against vessels of third states and not of the state towards which they are in revolt, regardless of its motive, would not fall within the 'political ends' exception and thus if the other requirements of article 101 of LOSC exist, it could be considered as piracy.[62] Accordingly, the words 'for private ends' must be construed broadly and all acts of violence lacking 'due authority' and legitimacy, according to international law, are acts undertaken 'for private ends'.[63] It follows from the foregoing that even if it is conceded that certain acts of Somali pirates have 'political ends', the simple fact that they target third states' vessels suffices to designate these acts as piratical.

Moving now to the possibility of interdiction of pirates in the territorial waters of Somalia, it should be reiterated that acts of violence and depredation committed exclusively in the coastal states' territorial waters do not constitute piracy under international law. They might be legally classified as piracy under the national law of the coastal state, or, according to the IMO, armed robbery at sea. In addition, vessels committing piracy on the high seas and fleeing to the territorial waters, *in casu* of Somalia, cannot be visited therein. Neither is there a right of

---

[61] Ibid, 160 (emphasis added). In accord is Guilfoyle writing that

the words 'for private ends'...were originally included to acknowledge the historic exception for civil-war insurgencies who attacked only the vessels of the government they sought to overthrow (at 693).

See also Harvard Draft, 798 and 857.

[62] Cf also Colombos writing,

If a warship rebels and confines her attentions solely to political acts done for political ends against the State towards she is in revolt, principle and practice require such ships to be left unmolested by the ships of war of other States

Id, *International Law of the Sea* (6th rev edn, London: Longmans, 1967), 450. See also, inter alia, the *Huascar case* (1877) and *Montezuma case* (1887) in Pitt-Cobett, *Leading Cases on International Law* (1931), 299, 301.

[63] Probably, this was the *ratio decidendi* in the case of *Castle John* before the Belgian Cour de Cassation; see *Castle John and Nenderlandse Stichting Sirius v Nv Marjlo and Nv Parfin* (1986), 77 ILR 537 and commentary in SP Menefee, 'The Case of the Castle John, or Green Beard the Pirate?' (1993) 24 California Western International Law Journal 1.

reverse hot pursuit or land pursuit.[64] All these were considered significant obstacles to the effective suppression of piracy off Somalia and they were surpassed by the adoption of a series of Security Council Resolutions under Chapter VII of the UN Charter. The most significant for the present purposes was, first, Security Council Resolution 1816 (2008), which in paragraph 7 *decided* that

For a period of six months from the date of this resolution, States *cooperating with the TFG* [Transitional Federal Government of Somalia] in the fight against piracy and armed robbery at sea off the coast of Somalia, for which advance notification has been provided by the TFG to the Secretary-General, may:

(a) Enter the territorial waters of Somalia for the purpose of repressing acts of piracy and armed robbery at sea, in a manner consistent with such action permitted on the high seas with respect to piracy under relevant international law; and

(b) Use, within the territorial waters of Somalia, in a manner consistent with action permitted on the high seas with respect to piracy under relevant international law, all necessary means to repress acts of piracy and armed robbery.[65]

It is apparent from this paragraph that an ad hoc authorization was given to states to visit vessels engaged in armed robbery and piracy in the territorial waters of Somalia, regardless of the *locus delicti*.[66] The sole requirements posed in this regard were the general obligation to comply with relevant international law as well as the 'cooperation' and the 'advance notification provided by the TFG to the Secretary-General'. This has also been affirmed in paragraph 9, namely that

this authorisation has been provided only following receipt of the letter from the Permanent Representative of the Somalia Republic to the United Nations . . . conveying the consent of that State.

Given the latter stipulation, it is rightly observed that the

Security Council Resolutions were not strictly necessary, since the Transitional Government could have granted permission for foreign States to conduct law enforcement operations within its waters . . . without them.[67]

Notably, the Council underscored that this authorization shall not be considered as establishing customary international law and this authorization applies only with respect to the situation in Somalia.[68]

---

[64] Reverse hot pursuit is considered the hot pursuit of delinquent vessels from the high seas to the territorial waters, while land pursuit refers to the continuation of such pursuit in the land of the coastal state; see on these notions in the context of drug trafficking, J Kramek, 'Bilateral Maritime Counter-Drug and Immigrant Interdiction Agreements: Is this the World of the Future?' (2000) 31 University of Miami Inter-American Law Review 121.

[65] See n 23 above (emphasis added).

[66] This authorization was effectively renewed for a period of 12 months on 2 December 2008 by SC Res 1846 (2008), para 10.

[67] Chatham House, Piracy, at 3. In accord is Treves (see n 7 above) 406.

[68] See SC Res 1816 (2008), para 9. Cf also SC Res (1851), para 10.

Furthermore, as Judge Treves states,

the Security Council has framed the relevant resolutions very cautiously. It has introduced a number of limitations which make the provisions adopted less revolutionary
than they might appear, and seem aimed, in particular, at fending off possible criticism of
the Council acting as a 'legislator'.[69]

For example, the authorization given is limited *ratione temporis*;[70] while, the
Resolutions request that activities undertaken pursuant to the authorizations
they set out 'do not have the practical effect of denying or impairing the right of
innocent passage to the ships of any third State'.[71]

In Resolution 1851 (2008), the Council went even further and authorized
the 'land pursuit' of the pirates in Somalia; more specifically, it decided that the
member states cooperating with the TFG

may undertake all necessary measures that are appropriate *in Somalia*, for the purpose of
suppressing acts of piracy and armed robbery at sea, pursuant to the request of TFG...'[72]

Similar to Resolution 1816 (2008), the Council stresses that 'the measures undertaken shall be undertaken consistent with applicable international humanitarian and human rights law'.[73] The remark made above with respect to the legal
necessity of Resolution 1816 applies equally here, namely the consent of Somalia
would suffice for states to enter the territorial waters as well as the land of Somalia
and pursue the pirates in cooperation with TFG, pursuant to article 20 of the
ILC Articles on State Responsibility.[74] The latter sets forth that

consent by a State to particular conduct by another State precludes the wrongfulness of
that act in relation to the consenting State, provided the consent is valid and to the extent
that the conduct remains within the limits of the consent given.[75]

The consent of Somalia conveyed by the letter of 9 December 2008 to the UN,
prior to the adoption of the Resolution in question, functions not only as a

---

[69] Treves, n 7 above, 404. See also Dalton, Roach, and Daley, 'Introductory Note to United
Nations Security Council: Piracy and Armed Robbery at Sea: Resolutions 1816, 1846 and 1851'
(2009) 48 ILM 129.

[70] eg, the authorization to undertake all necessary measures 'in Somalia' set out in Res 1851 is
limited to the 12 months starting with the adoption of Res 1846.

[71] SC Res 1816, at para 8; SC Res 1846, at para 13 and Treves (see n 7 above) 405.

[72] SC Res 1851 (2008), para 6 (emphasis added). It is reported that concerns raised by other
Council members led the USA to withdraw draft language referring to operations in Somali 'air-
space' though the USA argues that the effect of the Resolution remains the same, and that use of
Somali airspace is permitted; see Kontorovich, 3.   [73] Ibid, para 6 *in fine*.

[74] See Report of the International Law Commission on the Work of its Fifty-third Session
Regarding the Commission's Draft Articles on Responsibility of States for Internationally
Wrongful Acts, UN.GAOR ILC 56th Session, Supp 10 at UN Doc A/56/10, art 20. On the
customary nature of the majority of its provisions, see, inter alia, *Application of the Convention
on the Prevention and Punishment of the Crime of Genocide* (*Bosnia and Herzegovina v Serbia and
Montenegro*), ICJ, Judgment of 26 February 2007, paras 173, 385, and 388, <http://www.icj-cij.
org/docket/files/91/13685.pdf>.   [75] See YbILC (2001-II), 173.

circumstance precluding the wrongfulness of the infringement of the sovereignty which the coastal state enjoys in its territorial waters and in its territory, but also as a circumstance precluding wrongfulness for the exercise of enforcement jurisdiction therein. With respect to the question of jurisdiction over pirates, it is patent from the face of the Resolution that it does not create any new jurisdictional basis aside from Chapter VII powers. Hence, there are sound reasons to conclude that the authorization provided by Resolution 1851 as well as by previous relevant Resolutions was not legally necessary for the exercise of the right to visit and seize vessels engaged in piracy off Somalia.

Finally, the question of use of force in the course of repression of piracy in the present context merits certain discussion. In general, the issue of the permissibility of the use of force in interception operations at sea is not free from perplexity. At the outset, it is readily apparent that the LOSC provides no concrete answer to this question.[76] Nonetheless, resort to coercive measures under enforcement provisions of the LOSC[77] or of other treaties pertaining to illicit traffic of drugs or to maritime terrorism[78] is not a *terra incognita* in state practice; however the permissibility of the use of force in that context should not be lightly presumed. According to the preponderant view,[79] the use of force in law enforcement activities at sea should not be *ipso jure* disallowed. On the contrary, it is submitted that the state concerned may, in principle, use force but in extreme moderation and in strict accordance with the requirements of necessity and proportionality, since it is considered as a *lex specialis* case to the generic issue of the prohibition of the use of force, that is, such force is rather within the normative bounds of law enforcement at sea than within the purview of the prohibition of article 2(4) of the UN Charter.[80] This approach is not without resonance in the jurisprudence

[76] The LOSC itself does not contain any such authorization, but on the contrary it reiterates the prohibition of Art 2(4) of the Charter in art 301, which entails that the use of force remains, in principle, *extra muros* of the Convention.

[77] The sole reference to the degree of force to be used in enforcement measures under LOSC appears in art 225; see also IA Shearer, 'Problems of Jurisdiction and Law Enforcement against Delinquent Vessels' (1986) 35 ICLQ 342.

[78] See, eg, art 12 of the 1995 Council of Europe Agreement on Illicit Traffic by Sea (European Treaty Series No 156), which provides that,

> In the application of this Agreement, the Parties concerned shall take due account of ... d) the need to restrict the use of force to the minimum necessary to ensure compliance with the instructions of the intervening State.

[79] See, inter alia, AV Lowe, 'National Security and the Law of the Sea', 17 Thesaurus Acroasium (1991), *The Law of the Sea with Emphasis on the Mediterranean Issues*, 162.

[80] In particular, it is averred that

> Although the terms 'territorial integrity' and 'political independence' are generally not intended to restrict the scope of the prohibition of the use of force they lend an argument in favour of the widely accepted view that certain cases of the threat or use of force within the law of the sea are not comprised by article 2 (4).

See A Randelzhofer, 'Art 2(4)' in B Simma (ed), *The Charter of the United Nations: A Commentary* (2nd edn, Oxford: Oxford University Press, 2002), 124.

of international courts and tribunals.[81] In addition, it goes without saying that force could lawfully be used as self-defence in case of an attack during the boarding operation.[82]

In respect of the current operations in Somalia concerning piracy and armed robbery at sea, it is true that there have been several cases of use of lethal force against pirates on the high seas.[83] Nevertheless, in the majority of the cases, it is not evident from the relevant reports whether the use of force was in exercise of self-defence or a necessary and proportionate measure to apprehend the pirates. Given the fact that the pirates are always armed with light weapons and do not hesitate to open fire to achieve their purposes, it should generally be accepted that prima facie the use of deadly force, where it is unavoidable, is within the bounds of international law. Reportedly, an exception to this was the case of the Indian warship *Tabar*, which attacked a suspected pirate vessel, sunk the ship, and caused loss of life. However, it was later reported that the ship that was attacked was identified as a recently hijacked fishing vessel with hostages on board; it was not a pirate ship.[84] It goes without saying that India incurred international responsibility in accordance with article 106, 110(3) of LOSC as well as with the relevant general international law.[85]

Besides the general regime of the law of the sea, it is of particular interest to have regard to the *lex specialis*, that is, the relevant Resolutions as well as the Rules of Engagement promulgated by the international organizations and the nations taking part in counter-piracy operations. It is patent from the face of the Resolutions in question that they are silent on the permissible degree of force to be employed as such; Resolution 1816, however, expressly urges states to 'use all necessary means... in a manner consistent with such action permitted on the high seas with respect to piracy under the relevant international law'.[86] Even though this Resolution is adopted under Chapter VII and it employs the

---

[81] See *M/V SAIGA II*, which expressed the view that 'international law requires that the use of force must be avoided as far as possible and, where force is unavoidable, it must not go beyond what is reasonable and necessary in the circumstances' at para 155. This pronouncement was also reiterated in the arbitration between Guyana and Suriname (2007); see Award of the Arbitral Tribunal of 17 September 2007, at 148 <http://www.pca-cpa.org/upload/files/Guyana-Suriname%20 Award.pdf> and comments in P Jimenez-Kwast, 'Maritime Law Enforcement and the Use of Force: Reflections on the Categorization of Forcible Action at Sea in the Light of Guyana/Suriname Award' (2008) 13 JCSL 49, 88–9.

[82] The issue of the use of force in the course of the boarding operations is subject to a different legal framework from the question of the permissible use of force during the detainment of the suspect pirates, which is markedly a matter of the applicable human rights law; see n 138 above and corresponding text.

[83] See, eg, BBC News, French Warship Captures Pirates', 15 April 2009, <http://news.bbc. co.uk/2/hi/africa/8000447.stm>.

[84] See Chatham House, Piracy, 4. Cf, however, the opinion of the Indian navy that it attacked a pirate's mother ship, <http://www.nytimes.com/2008/11/19/world/asia/19iht-20pirate.17953692. html>.

[85] On state responsibility arising from interdiction operation in general see P Wendel, *State Responsibility for Interferences with the Freedom of Navigation in International Law* (Berlin: Springer, 2007).   [86] See n 23 above, para 6.

'magic formula' of the usual authorization, that is, 'to use all necessary means',[87] it is asserted that the explicit allusion to the regime of 'piracy under the relevant international law' entails that the counter-piracy operations in question are not subject to the *jus ad bellum*, but to the peacetime law enforcement at sea. This would be in harmony with the textual interpretation of the relevant Resolution as well as with the 'object and purpose' of the latter, which is the repression of the crime of piracy and armed robbery in the region.[88] Resolution 1851, on the other hand, authorizes the land pursuit of the pirates and thus it is not relevant to the issue of the use of force at sea; it does, however, makes reference to the 'applicable international humanitarian and human rights law', which has consequences concerning the detention of these persons.[89]

As far as the RoEs of the multinational operations involved in Somalia are concerned, it is reported that in the context of the EUNAVOR *Operation Atalanta*, the decision to use deadly force is of the Force Commander according to the applicable RoE and thus the Commanding Officer is obliged to request the relevant authorization prior to the engagement.[90] In addition, the Guidance to EUNAVFOR sets forth that

any incident during a counter-piracy operation in which shots are fired by EUNAVFOR personnel resulting in the death or injury of any person or where death or injury is believed to have occurred, should be reported, recorded, reviewed and investigated in accordance with the TCN's [Troops Contributing Nation's] national Shooting Incident Review procedures.[91]

In conclusion, the interdiction of pirate vessels on the high seas and in the Somali waters seems prima facie to be of clear legal authority; however, there are certain legal issues that merit closer scrutiny, such as the 'reasonable grounds' of article 110(1) of LOSC or the permissibility of use of force and the implementation of the relevant Security Council Resolutions. Equally important is the consideration of the question of the applicability of human rights law to the subsequent phase of the detainment and arrest of the pirates, which will be scrutinized in the following section.

5. The detainment, arrest, and transfer to Kenya of suspect pirates under international law

The starting point of the present discussion is the relevant provision of LOSC (article 105), which sets forth that every state may seize a pirate ship on the

---

[87] Cf SC Res 678 (1990), para 2.
[88] On the interpretation of SC Resolutions see E Papastavridis, 'Interpretation of Security Council Resolutions under Chapter VII in the Aftermath of the Iraqi Crisis' (2007) 56 ICLQ 83.
[89] See relevant remarks in Kontorovich, 4.
[90] See Flow Chart and personal communication with anonymous source (25.5.2009).
[91] Guidance to EUNAVFOR, 5.3.

high seas and prosecute the pirates under its national law. In codifying the customary principle of universal jurisdiction in this regard, this provision entitles any state involved in counter-piracy operations, which visits a pirate vessel, to apprehend the pirates and have them adjudicated upon by its courts. This, of course, presupposes that the state concerned would have enacted the necessary national laws which would criminalize piracy *jure gentium* and hence would have given jurisdiction to its courts pursuant to the principle of universal jurisdiction. However, this should not be taken for granted for many national jurisdictions; it is reported that in the case of Somalia there have been a number of instances where pirates have been apprehended by naval forces which subsequently have had to release them. In some cases this is due to the non-existence of relevant laws and in others due to the peculiarities of the laws of the capturing state.

For example, Denmark and Germany can prosecute pirates only if they have threatened national interests or citizens. Under French law, a captain may apprehend and hold pirates, but only a judicial authority can arrest and detain them.[92]

More importantly, it is generally observed that even the states that have enacted such laws usually prefer to abstain from prosecuting and from trying pirates before their courts.[93] This is also affirmed in the present context, namely there has scarcely been any case in which the capturing warships have brought the alleged pirates before their national authorities.[94] In practice, the nations patrolling the Gulf of Aden have consciously chosen not to prosecute pirates because of the anticipated difficulty and expense.[95] Further, returning pirates to Somalia for trial has not been considered an option because of the lack of a functioning government; only France is consistently sending pirates to Puntland.[96] Therefore, the dominant approach has been to avoid capturing pirates in the first place, or, if captured, releasing the pirates without charging them with a crime or transferring them to Kenya.[97] Accordingly, both the UK and the USA have entered into Memoranda of Understanding with the latter state on the prosecution of pirates, while the EU–Kenya Exchange of Letters is the most recent and notable example of this policy. Finally, it should be noted that the Djibouti Code of Conduct specifically mentioned that

each signatory intends to review its national legislation with a view towards ensuring that there are laws in place to criminalize piracy and armed robbery against ships, and

---

[92] Chatham House, Piracy, 4.

[93] As Professor Rubin has shown in his authoritative history of piracy law, very few criminal prosecutions for piracy can be found that depended on universal jurisdiction. He enumerates fewer than five cases in the past 300 years; see A Rubin (n 46 above) 302, 348.

[94] It is reported that 'some pirates have been brought to France and the Netherlands to stand trial'; see Chatham House, Piracy, 6. Cf also the case of Abduhl Kadir Muse, who has been prosecuted in the USA. However, in this case, the head of jurisdiction could also be the passive nationality principle, since he was charged for the kidnapping of the US captain (see n 28 above).

[95] See Kontorovich, 3.   [96] See Chatham House, Piracy, 6.   [97] Kontorovich, 3.

adequate guidelines for the exercise of jurisdiction, conduct of investigations, and prosecution of alleged offenders.

However, it is not certain whether this provision has started to be fully implemented by the states in the region.

This practice of states raises some perplexing legal questions: first, it must be ascertained whether transferring suspects to Kenya is in compliance with the relevant international law. As far as the law of the sea is concerned, it should be underscored that article 105 of LOSC provides that the prosecution should be by 'the courts of the state *which carried out the seizure*'.[98] The drafting history and more specifically the pertinent Report of the International Law Commission reveals that this provision was intended to preclude transfers to third-party states.[99] It follows that the assertion of enforcement jurisdiction by Kenya, which is not the boarding state, is in dissonance with article 105 and it remains to be seen whether this issue will emerge in any of the ongoing or future trials in Kenya.[100] In any event, it stands to reason to seriously dispute the relevance of article 105 in the contemporary legal order of the oceans.

The next question to address is whether Kenya has the necessary prescriptive jurisdiction to try the alleged offenders.[101] Section 69(1) of the Penal Code of Kenya, which was the law in force at the time of the signature of the EU–Kenya Exchange of Letters, established an offence of piracy, namely: 'Any person who, in territorial waters or upon the high seas, commits any act of piracy *jure gentium* is guilty of the offence of piracy.'[102] While recognizing that piracy is contrary to the Laws of Nations, Section 69 seemed rather problematic: on the one hand, it did not define the elements of the 'piracy', which might give rise to interpretative misgivings and on the other, it assimilated piracy *jure gentium*, that is, piracy on the high seas with piracy in its territorial waters, namely piracy under national law or armed robbery at sea.[103] Section 69 was repealed in September

---

[98] Art 105 of LOSC (emphasis added).

[99] In the words of the ILC Report,

> this article gives any State the right to seize pirate ships . . . and to have them adjudicated upon by its Courts. The right cannot be exercised *at a place under the jurisdiction of another State*.

See Report of the International Law Commission to the UN General Assembly, Commentary to article 43 (1956), reprinted in YbILC (1956–2), 283 (emphasis added).

[100] For a contrary opinion see T Treves, who asserts that

> The rule in Article 105 does not, however, establish the exclusive jurisdiction of the seizing state's courts. Courts of other states are not precluded from exercising jurisdiction under conditions which they establish (n 7 above, 402).

[101] On jurisdiction in general and the distinction between prescriptive and enforcement jurisdiction see AV Lowe, 'Jurisdiction' in M Evans (ed), *International Law* (2nd edn, Oxford: Oxford University Press, 2006), 335. See also M Gavouneli, *Functional Jurisdiction in the Law of the Sea* (The Hague: Martinus Nijhoff, 2007), 5–32.

[102] Penal Code of Kenya at: <http://www.kenyalaw.org/kenyalaw/klr_app/frames.php>.

[103] Kenya has been a party of LOSC since 1989; LOSC table of ratifications at: <http://www.un.org/Depts/los/reference_files/status2009.pdf>. See also the relevant comments in Guidance to EUNAVFOR, 11.

2009 and replaced with new offences under Part XVI of the Merchant Shipping Act 2009. In particular, article 369 reiterates the definition of piracy under article 101 of LOSC as well as disassociating it from other similar offences in Kenyan territorial waters.[104] In addition, this Act includes the offences under SUA Convention (1988) as separate offences under the heading of maritime security.[105] Notwithstanding this amelioration, suffice it to note that the applicable law for the initial trials pursuant to the Exchange of Letters will be Section 69 and not the latter Act.

What about armed robbery against vessels in the Somali territorial waters? It bears repeating that the phenomenon of armed robbery therein has been very common, especially in the first phase of the Somali piracy and this constituted the raison-d'être for the adoption of Security Council Resolution 1816 (2008). This notwithstanding, the Kenyan Law fell short of including such offences in the ambit of article 69, which stands to reason, since the offence of armed robbery at sea in third states is not subject to universal jurisdiction. Hence, Kenya has no jurisdiction to adjudicate upon the relevant cases in its courts according to its national legislation. It is rather unfortunate that the Guidance to EUNAVFOR and the EU–Kenya Exchange of Letters have not addressed this issue.

In contemplation of possible legal solutions to this problem, Resolution 1816

calls upon all States, and in particular flag, port and coastal States, States of the nationality of victims and perpetrators of piracy and armed robbery, and other States with relevant jurisdiction under international law and national legislation, to cooperate in determining jurisdiction, and in the investigation and prosecution of persons responsible for [these] acts.[106]

This provision is not very instrumental to the prosecution of Somali armed robbers in Kenya, since there is no universal jurisdiction enshrined therein. On the contrary, Resolution 1851 seems to acknowledge this problem and offers some possible legal bases for the jurisdiction of Kenyan authorities, such as in paragraph 3, which encourages the use of 'ship-riders', a system allowing law enforcement personnel from regional states to embark on warships and effect the arrest, provided that the advance consent of the TFG is obtained for the exercise of third-state jurisdiction by ship-riders in Somali territorial waters.[107]

Such system was set forth by the Djibouti Code of Conduct, which has been effective since 29 January 2009 and, according to the respective IMO Briefing, 'covers the possibilities of shared operations, such as nominating law enforcement or other authorized officials to embark in the patrol ships or aircraft of

---

[104] See art 369 of Kenyan Merchant Shipping Act 2009 <http://www.kenyalaw.org/Downloads/Acts/The_Merchant_Shipping_Act_2009.pdf>.   [105] Art 373, ibid.

[106] See n 23 above, para 11.

[107] The use of ship-riders in law-enforcement operations is very common in the context of counter-drug trafficking operations; see in this respect Kathy-Ann Brown, 'The Ship-Rider Model: An Analysis of the US proposed Agreement Concerning Maritime Counter Drug Operations in its Wider Legal Context' in A Burgess (ed), *Contemporary Caribbean Legal Issues* (1999), 26.

another signatory'.[108] However, it should be stressed that this Code of Conduct is a non-binding agreement and thus it falls short of setting out concrete legal obligations for the participant states.[109] This is also inferred by the fact that it makes explicit reference to the authorization of the coastal state as requisite for such operations.

It follows that should the institution of ship-riders start to be implemented, Kenyan officials, for example, will be able to arrest the offenders in the territorial waters of Somalia and prosecute them under their jurisdiction; however, this would require the prior establishment of legislative jurisdiction in this regard, which in the case of Kenya is non-existent. In addition, it would require, as it is mentioned in the Resolution, the prior consent of Somalia as well as a form of arrangement between the flag state of the warship and the sending state of the ship-rider, which eventually would assert enforcement jurisdiction. It should be noted that to the knowledge of the author no such agreement exists at present. Absent such an arrangement, there could be other issues raised, besides the legal basis for the interdiction, which still remains Security Council Resolutions 1816 and 1851.[110] For instance questions may arise as to responsibility for any violation of the applicable international law in the course of the operation. Under the rules on state responsibility, this could be a situation in which an organ of a state is effectively put at the disposal of another state so that the organ may temporarily act for its benefit and under its authority.[111] However, this would be contingent upon the degree of control exerted to the third state's vessel by the ship-riders.[112] If the warship of the third state retains a portion of its authority and apparently there is joint police activity, then the logical conclusion would be that there exists joint or concurrent responsibility of both the flag state of the warship and of the ship-rider's sending state.

In addition, Resolution 1851 makes reference to SUA Convention (1988)[113] and the UN Convention against Transnational Organised Crime (2001)[114] as

---

[108] They are also mentioned as 'Embarked Officers' in the present Code of Conduct (Art 7).

[109] See also Treves (n 7 above) 405.

[110] It is true that neither the EU–Kenya Exchange of Letters nor the MoUs between the UK and Kenya contain similar provisions.

[111] See art 6 of the ILC Articles and its Commentary, 46.

[112] This is inferred from the Commentary on ILC Articles, which specifically stipulates that

not only must the organ be appointed to perform functions appertaining to the State at whose disposal it is placed, but in performing the functions entrusted to it by the beneficiary State, the organ must also act in conjunction with the machinery of that State and under its exclusive direction and control, rather than on instructions from the sending State.

See ibid, 44.

[113] Convention for the Suppression of Unlawful Acts against the Safety of Maritime Navigation, IMO Doc SUA/CONF/15, reprinted in 27 ILM (1988) 672 (hereinafter 'SUA Convention'). The SUA Convention was amended by a Protocol adopted in October 2005; IMO Doc LEG/CONF.15/21, 1 November 2005, <http://www.state.gov/t/isn/trty/81727.htm>.

[114] UN Convention against Transnational Organised Crime (2001) annexed to UNGAR 55/25 (8 January 2001) 40 ILM 353.

possible legal foundations of the jurisdiction of neighbouring states.[115] More pertinent is the SUA Convention, the application of which could facilitate states such as Kenya to surmount the obstacles of the lack of universal jurisdiction. This treaty, which was adopted in the aftermath of the celebrated *Achille Lauro* incident,[116] aims at criminalizing certain unlawful acts against maritime navigation committed in waters beyond the outer limit of the territorial waters of the state parties.[117] More importantly, the SUA Convention adopts the key element of the mechanism provided in the terrorist conventions, namely the principle *aut dedere aut judicare*.[118] Consequently, it obliges the state party where the offender is found either to extradite him to another state that has established its jurisdiction or to submit the case without delay to its competent authorities for the purpose of prosecution. Given in the present context that Kenya is a state party to the SUA Convention,[119] it can prosecute the alleged offenders in accordance with the latter Convention. However, it must be stressed that the Convention does not apply with regard to offences committed exclusively within Somali territorial waters[120] as well as that the offences must be directed against a vessel of a state party, since Somalia is not a party to the Convention.

Another matter of importance is the application of international human rights law in the present context; in particular, from the time of the interdiction of pirate vessels off Somalia until the time of the transfer to the capturing state or to Kenya or of the release of suspect pirates. This does not mean that the international human rights law is not relevant to the actual process of the trials, for example, in Kenya; however, this matter is beyond the scope of the present analysis.[121] As a necessary prelude, it is well worth having regard to the practice of the states participating in EUNAVFOR *Operation Atalanta*.

According to the EUNAVFOR Flow Chart, if there is sufficient evidence after the search of the pirate vessel, the Commanding Officer (CO) will decide

---

[115] In its words, it

> Further encourages all States … to implement the SUA Convention, the United Nations Convention against Transnational Organized Crime and other relevant instruments to which States in the region are party, in order to effectively investigate and prosecute piracy and armed robbery at sea offences.

SC Res 1851 (2008) para 5.

[116] See, inter alia, M Halberstam, 'Terrorism on the High Seas: The *Achille Lauro*, Piracy and the IMO Convention on Maritime Security' (1988) 82 AJIL 269.

[117] See art 4 of SUA Convention. See also commentary in C Joyner, 'The 1988 IMO Convention on the Safety of Maritime Navigation: Towards a Legal Remedy for Terrorism at Sea', 31 German Yearbook of International Law (1988) 230.

[118] See art 6(4) of the SUA Convention.

[119] See: <http://www.imo.org/includes/blastDataOnly.asp/data_id%3D25670/status-x.xls>. Cf also n 104 above.

[120] Cf the erroneous statement of Kontorovich that 'SUA is not limited to acts on the high seas'; 3.

[121] It should be mentioned that the relevant procedures will be subject to the relevant provisions of ICCPR and the African Charter of Human Rights. See also relevant discussion in Chatham House, Piracy, 6–7.

to detain the suspected pirates and seize the property. The decision either to transfer or to release has to be made within 48 hours after the CO's decision to detain. The CO informs the national authorities, which either opt for or against a national transfer in view of prosecution. Should the capturing state opt for the former solution, the CO informs the Operational Commander and then EU Headquarters in Brussels. It is a matter for the state whether it prefers to keep the warship under the operational control of *Operation Atalanta*, which means that pirates stay detained by EUNAVFOR until they are transferred to national authorities,[122] or to chop the warship under national control, which means that pirates are automatically transferred to national authorities.

In the case that state authorities cannot or do not wish a national transfer in view of prosecution, the Operational Commander (OC) will evaluate the collected evidence and may seek advice from the EU Legal Division (EU OHQ LEGAD) on whether the evidence is sufficient to support a prosecution against any, or all, of the suspected pirates. If there is not enough evidence, the OC will decide to release the suspects; otherwise, he will request the Kenyan authorities to accept the suspects in accordance with the terms of the EU–Kenya Exchange of Letters. In case Kenya declines to accept the suspects, the CO will have to decide to release them. Lastly, it is underscored that the responsibility to transfer or release lies with the EUNAVFOR.[123]

The first question which comes to the forefront is whether and at what point the suspect pirates come under the jurisdiction of the capturing EU state as well as when the responsibility of this state ceases. Should it be decided that the suspect pirates come under the jurisdiction of the latter, this would mean that they might also enjoy the protection of the European Convention on Human Rights (ECHR).[124] The crux of the matter here is the *ratione loci* scope of the Convention, that is, whether the protection of the Convention extends beyond the European continent, *in casu* off the Somali coast. According to the prevailing view it does, provided that the state exercises effective control through its organs over the persons concerned.[125]

In more detail, this issue has been the source of much controversy, especially as far as the application of the ECHR in the territory of third states, that is, beyond the *'espace juridique'* of the Convention, is concerned.[126] Nevertheless,

---

[122] In this case, EUNAVFOR Detention guidance and national procedures on Detention apply.

[123] See EU Flow Chart and further analysis in Guidance to EUNAVFOR.

[124] Convention for the Protection of Human Rights and Fundamental Freedoms, 4 November 1950, 213 UNTS 221 (hereinafter 'ECHR'). Under art 1, 'The High Contracting Parties shall secure to everyone within their jurisdiction the rights and freedoms defined in Section I of this Convention'.

[125] On this issue see generally M Gondek, 'Extraterritorial Application of the European Convention on Human Rights: Territorial Focus in the Age of Globalisation?' (2005) 52 Netherlands International Law Review 349.

[126] In *Banković v Belgium*, however, the Court noted that the European Convention applies 'in an essentially regional context and notably in the legal space (*espace juridique*) of the Contracting

this apparent geographical limitation on the extraterritorial application of the Convention has not been consistently upheld in a series of post-*Banković* decisions,[127] and more importantly, it is not even necessary in the present context to argue against the *Banković* judgment, since the instance of a state vessel intercepting another vessel on the high seas fits squarely within that judgment's exclusion of 'the activities... on board... vessels registered in, or flying the flag of that State'.[128] Hence, even on the footing of the actual words of this decision, these activities come under the ambit of the Convention. This assertion is further warranted by the *Xhavara* case, involving the sinking of an Albanian vessel by an Italian warship on the high seas[129] and by the *Rigopoulos v Spain* and *Medvedyev v France* cases, which pertained to the interdiction of drug-smuggling vessels on the high seas.[130]

It follows from the foregoing that there is cogent support for the view that the Convention applies on the high seas. Similarly, it should be accepted that it equally applies to the interdiction operations carried out by EU member states in the territorial sea of Somalia pursuant to the authority of Security Council Resolution 1816 (2008). Despite the fact that the interdictions occur in another state's territorial sea, it is submitted that the responsibility lies with the flag state of the warship and not with Somalia, since the latter falls short of exercising exclusive command and control. It is also noted that the pertinent Security Council Resolutions make explicit reference to the need for compliance with international human rights law. The latter is imported either by the provisions of the ECHR as far as EU states are concerned or by the provisions of the International Covenant on Civil and Political Rights (ICCPR).[131]

The only argument that the EU states could plead in the present context would be that, along the lines of the *Behrami* and *Saramati* cases, the ECHR

States' and it was not designed to be applied throughout the world, even in respect of the conduct of the contracting states. See *Banković and Others v Belgium et al*, App No 52207/99, Admissibility Decision of 12 December 2001, 41 ILM (2002), 417; at para 80. For comment see R Wilde, '"The Legal Space" or the "*Espace Juridique*" of the European Convention on Human Rights: Is it Relevant to Extraterritorial State Action?' (2005) 2 European Human Rights Law Review 116.

[127] See, inter alia, *Öcalan v Turkey* (Merits), App No 46221/99, Chamber Judgment of 12 March 2003 and Grand Chamber Decision of 12 May 2005 and *Issa and Others v Turkey*, App No 31821/96, Judgment of 16 November 2004. For a general review of the relevant cases and views see R Lawson, 'Life after *Banković*: Extraterritorial Application of the European Convention on Human Rights' in F Coomans and M Kamminga (eds), *Extraterritorial Application of Human Rights Treaties* (Antwerp: Intersentia, 2004) 83.

[128] In *Banković*, the Court opined that the application of the Convention is limited to cases, amongst others, that involve 'the activities of its diplomatic or consular agents abroad and on board craft and vessels registered in, or flying the flag of that State'; see n 126 above, para 73.

[129] See *Xhavara and Others v Italy and Albania* (App No 39473/98), Admissibility Decision of 11 January 2001, <http://www.echr.coe.int/echr/>. See also E Lagrange, 'L' Application de la Convention de Rome à des Actes Accomplis par les Etats Parties en dehors du Territoire National' (2008) 112 RGDIP.

[130] See *Rigopoulos v Spain*, Decision of 12 January 1999 (37388/97 *Recueil des arrêts et décisions* 1999-II) and *Medvedyev et al v France*, Decision of 10 July 2008 (Fifth Section, App No 3394/03).

[131] See ICCPR (adopted 16 December 1966, entered into force 23 March 1976) 999 UNTS 171.

is not applicable *ratione personae* and thus European states could not incur individual responsibility *in casu*.[132] Nevertheless, it is contended that the situation here is different: first, as far as the interception of pirate vessels on the high seas or in Somali waters is concerned, the legal basis for the relevant action is either article 110 of LOSC or the authority of the relevant Security Council Resolution, which is granted in general to states cooperating with TFG. Therefore, the responsibility for any violation of the relevant provisions as well as the applicable international human rights law in the course of this interception lies with the EU member states rather than with the international organization as such. It is beyond the compass of the present chapter to discuss in detail whether the EU incurs international responsibility separately from the member states in the context of EUNAVFOR. Suffice it to note, however, that such responsibility could potentially arise with regard to the application of the EU–Kenya Exchange of Letters.[133] In any event, the states concerned would be subject to the relevant provisions of the ICCPR and of the customary human rights law.

Given thus that the ECHR or the ICCPR may have application in interdiction operations on the high seas as well as in third states' territorial seas, provided that the states concerned exert sufficient control over the alleged pirates, it is questioned whether there is truly such control in the present realm and when does it start. It is worth repeating here that on the basis of the EU Flow Chart, the responsibility to transfer or to release suspected pirates lies exclusively with the EUNAVFOR and the member states. Hence, it can be argued that from the moment that the CO decides to detain the suspects and until the detainees are either transferred to Kenya or to the national authorities or released, due to the refusal of Kenya to try them, the pirates fall under the jurisdiction of the boarding state and therefore under the jurisdiction of the ECHR. Two issues call for specific comments: first, it is observed that, according to the RoE of EUNAVFOR, a considerable amount of time might pass between the decision of the CO to search the vessels and the suspects, which might also involve the transfer of the latter to the warship, and the decision of the CO to release or detain them. Does the Convention apply also during this period? Neither the Flow Chart nor the Guidance to EUNAVFOR make any reference to the legal status of the suspected pirates in this particular time period; they only set forth a few elementary safeguards for the protection

---

[132] See European Court of Human Rights (Grand Chamber), *Agim Behrami & Bekir Behrami v France; Ruzhdi Saramati v France, Germany & Norway*, Decision of 2 May 2007 (Joined App Nos 71412/01 & 78166/01) and commentary by M Milianovic and T Papic, 'As Bad as It Gets: The European Court of Human Rights's Behrami and Saramati Decision and General International Law' (2009) 58 ICLQ 267.

[133] See relevant discussion of the international responsibility of the EC in S Talmon, 'Responsibility of International Organizations: Does the European Community Require Special Treatment?' in M Ragazzi (ed), *International Responsibility Today: Essays in Memory of Oscar Schachter* (Leiden: Brill, 2005), 405.

of their life and dignity.[134] Nonetheless, it is submitted that it would be in harmony with international law to assert that these persons do come under the jurisdiction of the interdicting states and *ergo* within the purview of the ECHR. The reason for this is merely that there is no need for the formal detainment of the persons concerned to be considered as subject to the protection of the Convention; the cornerstone criterion is the existence of sufficient control of these persons by the organs of a state party to the latter.

Similarly, it is disputed whether the Convention applies in the situation

where the pirates are not taken on board the naval vessel, especially in cases where there are no naval officers aboard the pirate vessel (for example, where it has been surrounded and subdued).[135]

Most EU countries would regard such a degree of control to be covered by the Convention. But some would not.[136]

The problem here lies in the simple fact that the '*Bankovic* criterion', regarding jurisdiction by warships, is not present and the requisite criterion of 'control' must accordingly be substantiated otherwise. It is opined that the latter criterion is contingent upon the relevant facts of each case; mainly upon whether the persons concerned are deprived of their freedom to a significant extent. This is certainly the case here and hence it is asserted that these persons fall under the jurisdiction of the capturing state.

Having determined that the suspect pirates are entitled to the basic protection of the ECHR and of the ICCPR, it is apt to refer to particular provisions that might accordingly apply. Taking as an example the ECHR, it is readily apparent that the most significant human rights in need of protection are the right to life (article 2), the prohibition of torture and of degrading and inhumane treatment (article 3), and the prohibition of arbitrary deprivation of liberty (article 5).[137] It should be noted, from the outset, that the EU Guidance to EUNAVFOR set out a number of general principles for the treatment of detainees, which by and large reflect the above-mentioned provisions.[138]

---

[134] See Guidance to EUNAVFOR, Enclosure 8 to Annex B. It has anonymously been reported to the author that the persons under the present circumstances are not considered to enjoy the full protection of human rights treaties; on the contrary, they are perceived to be *persones extra judicates* (communication with the author, 25 April 2009).

[135] Chatham House, Piracy, 5.   [136] Ibid.

[137] It goes without saying that similar provisions are also included in the ICCPR.

[138] In its words,

[detainees] are to be treated humanely and are entitled [, inter alia,] to respect for their person, honour, convictions and religious practices. In particular they are not to be subject to: a. Violence, b. Punishments c. Humiliating and degrading treatment, d. Reprisals, e. Threats of any of the above. Detainees are entitled to: a. Shelter, food and drinking water; b. Health and hygiene safeguards, c. Practise their religion and, if requested, appropriate and possible, to receive spiritual assistance from chaplains or similar persons....

Annex A to Operation Atalanta EU OHQ SOP Legal OO1, dated 26 March 2009.

With regard to the right of life in particular, it is expressly provided in the above instrument that 'OP ATALANTA RoEs prohibit the use of deadly force to prevent the escape of detainees'.[139] Only when it is necessary and reasonable may force be used to restrain detainees 'in accordance with national law on self-defence and Op ATALANTA ROEs'.[140] To the knowledge of the author, there is no recorded incident of deaths of detainees by EU forces.[141] As far as the prohibition of article 3 of the ECHR is concerned, the relevant Guidance to EUNAVFOR as well as the EU–Kenya Exchange of Letters make explicit provision on this peremptory norm of international law.[142] The reference to the prohibition of torture in the latter instrument is significant for another reason, namely it purports to safeguard that the European states parties to the ECHR will not infringe the relevant provision by transferring a person under their jurisdiction to a third state, where he or she might face torture or degrading and inhumane treatment.[143]

This reflects also the principle of non-refoulement, which is primarily enshrined in article 33(1) of the Refugee Convention (1951),[144] and prescribes, broadly, that no refugee should be returned to any country where he or she is likely to face persecution, other ill-treatment, or torture.[145] It is an unassailable fact that the principle of non-refoulement is a fundamental component of the treaty as well as customary prohibition of torture, cruel, inhuman, and degrading treatment or punishment.[146] Apart from the express prohibition of refoulement in article 3 of the 1984 Convention against Torture,[147] this principle has been construed as implicit in the pertinent prohibition of torture or cruel, inhuman, or degrading treatment enshrined in various human rights treaties, such as the ICCPR (article 7),[148] the ECHR (article 3),[149] and 1969 ACHR (article

---

[139] Ibid, Section 3.   [140] Ibid.

[141] Nevertheless, deaths have occurred in the course of the actual visit of pirate vessels, but not by EUNAVFOR.

[142] See E de Wet, 'The Prohibition of Torture as an International Norm of *Jus Cogens* and its Implications for National and Customary Law' 15 EJIL (2004) 97.

[143] See European Court of Human Rights, *Soering v UK* (1989) 98 ILR 270, para 88.

[144] Art 33(1) reads as follows:

1. No Contracting State shall expel or return ("*refouler*") a refugee in any manner whatsoever to the frontiers of territories where his life or freedom would be threatened on account of his race, religion, nationality, membership of a particular social group or political opinion.

See Convention Relating to the Status of Refugees (adopted 28 July 1951, entered into force 22 April 1954) 189 UNTS 137 (Refugee Convention) art 33.

[145] On this principle see the excellent treatise on the issue by Sir E Lauterpacht and D Bethlehem, 'The Scope and Content of the Principle of *Non-Refoulement*: Opinion' in E Feller et al (eds), *Refugee Protection in International Law: UNHCR's Global Consultations on International Protection* (Cambridge: Cambridge University Press, 2003) 87 and C Wooters, *International Legal Standards for the Protection from Refoulement* (Oxford: Hart Publishing, 2009).

[146] See Lauterpacht and Bethlehem, ibid, 144.

[147] See art 3(1) of the Convention against Torture and Other Cruel and Inhuman or Degrading Treatment or Punishment (1984); 213 UNTS 221.

[148] See art 7 of ICCPR. In addition, the UN Human Rights Committee, in its General Comments No 20 and No 31, has construed the obligation set out in art 7 as including a non-refoulement component.

[149] See, inter alia, *Ahmed v Austria* (1997) 24 EHHR 278, paras 39–40 and *Saadi v Italy* (2008), para 125.

22, para 8).[150] The principle of non-refoulement in the human rights context is absolute and non-derogable, preventing extradition, expulsion, or removal in any manner whatsoever.[151]

Moreover, in contrast to the principle in the refugee context, which is focused on asylum-seekers, non-refoulement in the human rights context is not predicated on any given status of the individuals at risk.[152] Therefore, it applies to all persons compelled to remain or return in a territory where substantial grounds can be shown for believing that they would face a real risk of being subjected to torture or cruel, inhuman, or degrading treatment. This is also important, since, arguably a suspect pirate could not be a refugee where there are 'serious grounds' for considering him to have committed a 'serious crime' pursuant to article 1(f) of the Refugee Convention and thus the protection against refoulement in the ambit of refugee law could be less broad for such persons.

The foregoing analysis attains even more importance in the event of the release of the detainee after the decline of Kenya to initiate judicial proceedings or after the OC decides that the evidence is not sufficient. Both the EU Flow Chart and the Guidance to EUNAVFOR are silent regarding non-refoulement; on the contrary, they stipulate that arrangements should be made for their safe repatriation. It is readily apparent that this practice fails to take into consideration the prohibition under scrutiny and thus it might be in violation of article 3 of the ECHR, should the returned suspect face torture or inhuman and degrading treatment in Somalia or in another state. In addition, it might run counter to the Refugee Convention as such, which arguably applies on the high seas and protects potential refugees from such refoulement practices.[153] Thus, it is submitted that there must always be a screening process of the detainees for the purpose of determining whether there is a substantial fear of persecution or torture in Somalia or in another country, for example in Kenya or Yemen, where they might be sent. In the latter case, the principle of non-refoulement should be fully respected.

For example, this was not respected in the case reported by Judge Treves of the Danish Navy ship *Absalon,* which on 17 September 2008 captured ten pirates in the waters off Somalia. After six days of detention, the Danish government decided to free the pirates by putting them ashore on a Somali beach, for they 'had come to the conclusion that the pirates risked torture and the death penalty if surrendered to (whatever) Somali authorities'.[154] However, the prohibition of non-refoulement not only protects the official repatriation but, in general, the return by any means of the persons concerned.[155]

---

[150] See article 22(8) of the American Convention on Human Rights, 22 November 1969, UNTS 123.   [151] See Lauterpacht and Bethlehem (n 145 above) 162.

[152] See ibid, 158.

[153] On this issue see E Papastavridis, 'Interception of Human Beings on the High Seas: A Contemporary Analysis under International Law' (2009) 37 Syracuse Journal of International Law and Commerce (forthcoming).   [154] See Treves (n 7 above) 408.

[155] See n 144 above.

Finally, the right to personal liberty, enshrined, inter alia, in article 5 of the ECHR, seems of primary significance in the present context. The most pertinent provisions are the following:

Article 5

1. Everyone has the right to liberty and security of person. No one shall be deprived of his liberty save in the following cases and in accordance with a procedure prescribed by law:

    c the lawful arrest or detention of a person effected for the purpose of bringing him before the competent legal authority on reasonable suspicion of having committed an offence or when it is reasonably considered necessary to prevent his committing an offence or fleeing after having done so;

3. Everyone arrested or detained in accordance with the provisions of paragraph 1.c of this article shall be brought promptly before a judge or other officer authorised by law to exercise judicial power and shall be entitled to trial within a reasonable time or to release pending trial. Release may be conditioned by guarantees to appear for trial.[156]

Given that the European nations contributing to EUNAVFOR are parties to the ECHR, they bear responsibility for any acts or omissions that infringe article 5 of the Convention, even if they occur on the high seas or in the territorial sea of Somalia. Accordingly, it is asserted that, on the one hand, any arrest or detention should have a legal basis in domestic law, which 'must be sufficiently accessible and precise, in order to avoid all risk of arbitrariness'.[157] On the other hand, there is the obligation of the state concerned promptly to bring the suspect pirates before a judge or other officer authorized by law to exercise judicial powers. These obligations in the context of interdiction of vessels on the high seas formed the subject matter of a recent case before the European Court of Human Rights, namely the *Medvedyev v France* case, which involved the exercise of enforcement jurisdiction over a drug-smuggling vessel on the high seas.[158]

In this case, the Court concluded that the applicants had not been deprived of their liberty in accordance with a procedure prescribed by law and consequently held, unanimously, that there had been a violation of article 5(1). However, considering that the length of that deprivation of liberty had been justified by the 'wholly exceptional circumstances' of the case, in particular, the inevitable delay entailed by having the drug-smuggling vessel *Winner* tugged to France, the Court concluded, by four votes to three, that there had not been a violation of article 5(3).

---

[156] See also *Amuur v France* (1996) 22 EHHR 533 (1996-III), 826 and *Malone v UK*, Judgment of 2 August 1984, Ser A, No 82, at 32. Cf also article 9 of ICCPR.

[157] See *Amuur*, ibid, para 50.

[158] See n 130 above and European Court of Human Rights, *Rigopoulos v Spain*, Decision of 12 January 1999 (37388/97 *Recueil des arrêts et décisions* 1999-II). See also E Papastavridis, 'Human Rights and Policing of the High Seas: The Recent Decision of the European Court of Human Rights in *Medvedyev v France*' (2010) 59 ICLQ (forthcoming).

Accordingly, it is submitted that the European states that apprehend pirates in the course of *Operation Atalanta* and initiate judicial proceedings before their courts should have in place prior established, precise, and foreseeable national laws concerning the offences in question; otherwise, in view of the *Medvedyev case*, they will be in violation of article 5(1) of the ECHR. It is observed in this regard that not all European states have such precise and non-arbitrary laws and this might be one of the reasons why they prefer to transfer the alleged offenders to Kenya. As far as the 'promptness' of the transfer to the forum state, the *Medvedyev* case is instructive in this regard, that is, the Court considered that even though

a period of sixteen days does not at first sight appear to be compatible with the concept of 'brought promptly' laid down in Article 5 § 3 of the Convention, . . . having regard to the wholly exceptional circumstances of the instant case, the time which elapsed between placing the applicant in detention and bringing him before the investigating judge cannot be said to have breached the requirement of promptness in paragraph 3 of Article 5.[159]

Thus, when there are such objective reasons for the delay to bring the detainees before 'a judge or other officer authorised by law to exercise judicial power', the Court is lenient concerning the application of article 5(3) of the Convention. It is apt to reiterate here that the EU has instructed states participating in EUNAVFOR *Operation Atalanta* to make a decision either to transfer or to release the suspects within 48 hours after the CO's decision to detain. In addition, it has made an agreement with Djibouti to facilitate the air transfer of the suspects either to Kenya or the respective European states.

6. Concluding remarks

It is certain that the problem of piracy off Somalia and the multifaceted response of the international community raise a host of legal questions and have attracted the considerable interest of the academic legal doctrine. To contribute to this discourse, the present chapter attempted to highlight certain points of interest regarding the legality of the seizure of pirate vessels and the subsequent detainment and arrest of the alleged offenders. Accordingly, it assessed the various legal justifications for the interdiction of pirate vessels both on the high seas and in Somali waters against the background of the law of the sea and general international law. It concluded that even if the relevant practice seems to be in keeping with international law, there are some points of ambivalence, such as the 'reasonable grounds' asserted by the EUNAVFOR. Most interesting, however, was the analysis of the practice of states involved in the counter-piracy operations to

---

[159] *Medvedyev case*, para 67. See also *Rigopoulos v Spain*, ibid, 9.

transfer the suspects to Kenya to be tried for their alleged offences. It appears that an 'ad hoc international criminal tribunal for piracy off Somalia' has been established in the latter state and it remains to be seen how effective it will be and whether it will guarantee the right of fair trial of the suspected pirates.

It is true that the international community and in particular the flag states of the warships involved in the suppression of piracy in the region are not very willing to prosecute the pirates. This means that this role has been ascribed to the neighbouring African states, which are called to do justice in this regard. In this vein, it has been suggested that 'for future success in dealing with captured pirates, local capacity-building in Somalia and the region should continue'.[160] The major difficulty, however, in this respect is the absence of relevant legislation.

The IMO and the United Nations Office on Drugs and Crime have been involved with assistance and support for the adoption of local legislation. The Djibouti Code of Conduct has been signed by nine regional states, with undertakings to review local laws.[161]

These measures will enhance the ability of the African community to deal with the problems in the region on their own, such as suppression of piracy. Nevertheless, it can reasonably be questioned whether these measures are sufficient to strike at the heart of the problem and whether the international community is aiming in the right direction. As was noted in the Introduction, the real roots of the Somali piracy can be found, among other things, in the ongoing civil strife, in the depletion of fishing resources, and in extreme poverty. It is highly unlikely that the interest of the international community is directed to the elimination of the above grounds or to the suppression of criminal activity, which is detrimental to international maritime commerce. Rather, it is once again a case of the 'emperors' of the oceans asserting their powers in order to protect their interests and the 'thieves' of the oceans trying to claim a little portion of the world's wealth.

---

[160] Chatham House, Piracy, 7.　　　[161] Ibid.

8

Human Security and the Protection of Refugees in Africa

*Maria O'Sullivan**

1. Introduction

The African continent has been the site of a number of long-standing intra-state and inter-state conflicts of a religious, ethnic, and political nature. This has resulted in, amongst other things, the production of large numbers of refugees,[1] most of whom have sought asylum in fellow African nations. These situations raise a number of security issues—both for refugees themselves, but also, in some instances, for the African region more generally. Of particular concern in this regard is the fact that many asylum host states in Africa are developing countries with fragile economic and political structures.

Refugees in Africa are in some ways similar to refugees in other parts of the world and thus certain aspects of the analysis in this chapter can be applied to refugees more generally. For instance, all refugees face the reality that today's asylum host states (particularly those of the industrialized countries in the 'North' such as certain European nations, the USA, and Australia) have developed increasingly restrictive border controls[2] and refugee policies,[3] which have severely curtailed the ability of today's refugees to seek asylum.

---

* Lecturer, Faculty of Law, Monash University, Melbourne, Australia.
[1] Note that this chapter is focused on the issues pertaining to refugees and does not deal with the complex and very different issues arising from the large numbers of internally displaced persons that currently exist in Africa.

[2] ie, the use of interdiction, carrier sanctions, visa restrictions, and offshore processing of refugee claims. See discussion in A Francis, 'Bringing Protection Home: Healing the Schism Between International Obligations and National Safeguards Created by Extraterritorial Processing' (2008) 20(2) International Journal of Refugee Law 273–313; S Kneebone, 'The Pacific Plan: The Provision of "Effective Protection"' (2006) 18 (3–4) International Journal of Refugee Law 696–721; and SH Legomsky, 'The USA and the Caribbean Interdiction Program' (2006) 18 (3–4) International Journal of Refugee Law 677–95.

[3] ie, detention of asylum seekers and national legislation which dilutes states' obligations under international refugee law; see eg the refugee policies and national legislation of Australia—discussed in S Kneebone, 'The Australian Story: Asylum Seekers outside the Law' in S Kneebone

Despite certain commonalities, there are also certain characteristics of the refugee population in Africa which set them apart from refugees in other parts of the world. First, the nature of the persecution from which refugees tend to flee in Africa (arising from long-standing religious, ethnic, and political conflict, and in some cases, acts of genocide) has tended to produce situations of mass influx. This has made individually based refugee determination difficult to undertake in certain cases. Therefore there has been a tendency in Africa to use group-based determinations for refugee status and the granting of only temporary rather than permanent protection. Secondly, many African host states have dealt with mass influxes by housing these refuges in closed refugee camps, rather than allowing local integration, which has caused a number of security concerns. Thirdly, many of these conflicts have been of a long-standing nature, leading to Africa having a substantial number of what the Office of the United Nations High Commissioner for Refugees (UNHCR)[4] categorizes as 'protracted refugee situations'.[5] This has had flow-on effects in terms of the detriment to both the physical security and psychological well-being of many of these refugees.

Although UN agencies, principally UNHCR, have attempted over many years to address the particular concerns of refugees within Africa, many problems remain unresolved. In recognition of this situation, and also more generally an acknowledgement that the concept of asylum is 'under threat', the UNHCR has in recent years adopted a 'solution-oriented' approach to refugee protection. Thus, the current emphasis in the UNHCR programmes both in Africa and elsewhere is on finding long-term or so-called 'durable solutions' to the problems faced by refugees. These include a commitment to voluntary repatriation as the 'preferred' durable solution, the promotion of 'burden sharing' amongst asylum host states (which is very much focused on encouraging Northern states to provide funding to developing states in the South in order to improve their capacity to host refugees), and in addressing the 'root causes' of refugee flows.[6] This represents a fundamental shift in the UNHCR's role, in that it has historically focused on

---

(ed), *Refugees, Asylum Seekers and the Rule of Law: Comparative Perspectives* (Cambridge: Cambridge University Press, 2009), 171–227.

[4] UNHCR is the UN body mandated to 'lead and co-ordinate international action to protect refugees and resolve refugee problems worldwide'. See UNHCR, 'Basic Facts', <http://www.unhcr.org.uk/about-us/basic-facts.html>. As part of this it is responsible for supervising the application of the 1951 Refugees Convention and its 1967 Protocol (see Art 35 of the 1951 Convention relating to the Status of Refugees, 189 UNTS 150, supplemented by the 1967 Protocol relating to the Status of Refugees, 606 UNTS 267).

[5] As Jeff Crisp, writing as a member of the UNHCR's Evaluation and Policy Analysis Unit, notes 'by far the majority of these [protracted refugee situations] are to be found in Africa'; J Crisp, 'No Solution in Sight: The Problem of Protracted Refugee Situations in Africa', *New Issues in Refugee Research Working Paper No. 75* (January 2003) UNHCR, pp 1–2 <http://www.unhcr.org/research/RESEARCH/3e2d66c34.pdf > . See also Executive Committee of the UNHCR (Ex Com), *Protracted Refugee Situations* (10 June 2004) UN Doc EC/54/SC/CRP.14.

[6] See UNHCR's Agenda for Protection and Convention Plus initiatives, discussed below at Section 3.2 (text at nn 55–9).

supervising adherence by states to the 1951 Convention relating to the Status of Refugees (the '1951 Convention')[7] in relation to the protection of refugees under law, rather than undertaking a broader humanitarian and developmental role.

The premise underlying the above 'solutions' appears to be that they will be able to appeal to states' collective interests in preventing refugee flows and, when they occur, containing those flows. This obviously has important implications for the human security of refugees in Africa. This chapter therefore asks: what are the implications of recent UNHCR-led initiatives for the human security of refugees within Africa?

Due to the highly complex and diverse nature of refugee flows in Africa, the focus of this chapter will be on the so called 'protracted'[8] refugee situations which have proved the most problematic in terms of human security in Africa and the way in which recent UNHCR-led initiatives may address these concerns. In order to discuss this, this chapter will first outline the legal and political environment in which refugee movements occur, the nature of refugee flows in Africa, and the security concerns which have arisen from these. Secondly, it will discuss the meaning of 'human security' as it applies to refugee situations; and thirdly, it will consider the implications that recent UNHCR initiatives and the restrictive refugee policies of many asylum host states may have for the human security of refugees within Africa. Finally, the chapter will question whether the concept of 'human security' is one that should be utilized in the refugee context at all.

2. Background: the legal and political environment

Before examining the nature of the refugee flows within Africa and the problems which have arisen in relation to human security, it is necessary briefly to set out the legal and political environment in which these issues operate.

2.1 Relevant international refugee law

Many states in Africa are a party to the primary international instrument dealing with refugee law, the 1951 Convention relating to the Status of Refugees[9] and also the African regional convention adopted by the Organisation of African Unity (OAU) in 1969 (the '1969 Convention').[10]

---

[7] 1951 Convention (see n 4 above).

[8] This has been defined by UNHCR's Executive Committee as one in which refugees find themselves in a 'long-lasting and intractable state of limbo'. See UNHCR Ex Com (n 5 above) 3.

[9] A total of 44 African states have ratified the 1951 Convention. As of 1 October 2008, neither Libya nor Eritrea had ratified it: see UNHCR, 'States Parties to the 1951 Convention relating to the Status of Refugees and the 1967 Protocol' <http://www.unhcr.org/protect/PROTECTION/3b73b0d63.pdf>.

[10] 1969 Convention governing the Specific Aspects of Refugee Problems in Africa, 1000 United Nations Treaty Series 46, done 10 September 1969, entered into force 20 June 1974. As of 15 April

Both the 1951 and 1969 Conventions apply to persons fleeing persecution for religious, political, racial, or other reasons, that is:

any person who... owing to a well-founded fear of being persecuted for reasons of race, religion, nationality, membership of a particular social group or political opinion is outside the country of his nationality and is unable or, owing to such fear, is unwilling to avail himself of the protection of that country... [11]

Importantly, Article 1(2) of the 1969 Convention also provides a further and wider definition of refugee which encompasses those persons who have fled due to 'external aggression, occupation, foreign domination or events seriously disturbing public order in either part or the whole of his country of origin or nationality',[12] which reflects the type of refugee situation that commonly arises in Africa.

The ultimate provision for protection of refugees in both the 1951 and 1969 Conventions is said to be the non-refoulement principle, which prohibits states parties from returning a refugee to a territory where his or her life or freedom would be threatened for one of the reasons set out in the refugee definitions of the respective Conventions.[13] As discussed later in this chapter, this is said to have been breached a number of times in Africa due to forced repatriation of refugees back to their countries of origin.[14]

There are also important differences between the text of the 1951 and 1969 Conventions which have relevance for the focus of this chapter. Importantly, the 1969 Convention provides that:

- member states shall use their 'best endeavours' to receive refugees and secure the settlement of those refugees who are unable to return to their country of origin or nationality for well-founded reasons;[15]
- where a member state finds difficulty in continuing to grant asylum to refugees, it may appeal to other member states who shall 'in the spirit of African solidarity and international cooperation take appropriate measures to lighten the burden of the Member State granting asylum'.[16] It therefore provides for a form of responsibility-sharing amongst African nations in relation to refugees; and
- that the 'essentially voluntary character of repatriation shall be respected in all cases and no refugee shall be repatriated against his will'.[17]

2002, 45 OAU member states had ratified this Convention. See 'Documents', 25.1 Refugee Survey Quarterly 163–4.

  [11] 1951 Convention (see n 4 above) Art 1A(2).
  [12] 1969 Convention (see n 10 above) Art 1(2).
  [13] 1951 Convention (see n 4 above) Art 33; 1969 Convention (see n 10 above) Art 2(3). Note that the precise wording of these non-refoulement provisions differs somewhat, in that the OAU non-refoulement principle is understood to apply not only to non-return of refugees from countries but also prohibits rejection at a country's frontier.
  [14] See discussion below at Section 2.3 (text at nn 32–9).
  [15] 1969 Convention (see n 10 above) Art 2(1).   [16] Ibid, Art 2(4).   [17] Ibid, Art 5.

This is significant given that the voluntary character of certain repatriations in the African region has been questioned by some commentators and non-governmental organizations (NGOs).[18]

It should be noted that the terms of the 1951 and 1969 Conventions have proved to be problematic for both states parties and refugees given the nature of refugee flows in Africa. First, both Conventions apply to 'any person' and are therefore understood to necessitate an *individualized* assessment process. This has presented problems in Africa due to the fact that the large-scale nature of refugee arrivals make such an individualized refugee determination process difficult to achieve.

Secondly, it is understood that most states' obligations under the Conventions are only enlivened when an asylum seeker enters the *jurisdiction* of that state.[19] Hence, many states parties have in recent years concentrated on erecting strict border controls to prevent the entry of non-citizens into their respective jurisdictions.[20]

Moreover, many academic commentators have noted that international refugee law no longer elicits the level of respect from states parties that was the case when the Convention was agreed upon in 1951. For instance, Professor James Hathaway, a leading refugee law scholar, has stated that:

the reality today is that a significant number of governments in all parts of the world are withdrawing in practice from meeting the legal duty to provide refugees with the protection they require.[21]

2.2 The nature of refugee flows within Africa

The latest available statistics reveal that the number of refugees falling under UNHCR's responsibility is estimated to total 10.5 million, of which 2.1 million are from Africa.[22]

---

[18] See below at Section 2.3 (text at nn 35–9).

[19] See JC Hathaway, *The Rights of Refugees under International Law* (Cambridge: Cambridge University Press, 2005), 160.

[20] ie, see the creation by Australia of the so-called 'Pacific Solution'. This policy (which operated from 2001–08) was aimed at, amongst other things, preventing asylum seekers from entering the Australian 'migration zone': see further discussion in S Kneebone 2006 (n 3 above). See also the use of surveillance and interdiction by Spain and Italy in North Africa, discussed in S Kneebone, C McDowell, and G Morrell, 'A Mediterranean Solution? Chances of Success?' (2006) 18 (3–4) International Journal of Refugee Law 492–508; A Betts, 'Towards a Mediterranean Solution? Implications for the Region of Origin' (2006) 18 (3–4) International Journal of Refugee Law 652–76.

[21] Hathaway (see n 19 above) 998. See also G Goodwin-Gill and J McAdam, *The Refugee in International Law* (3rd edn, Oxford: Oxford University Press, 2007), Preface p v, 555; S Kneebone, 'Introduction: Refugees and Asylum Seekers in the International Context—Rights and Realities' in S Kneebone (ed) (see n 3 above) 3–4, 26–28.

[22] UNHCR, '2008 Global Trends: Refugees, Asylum-seekers, Returnees, Internally Displaced and Stateless Persons', June 2009, 2, 8. <http://www.unhcr.org/4a375c426.pdf>.

As mentioned in the introduction, refugee flows in Africa have certain characteristics, some of which include the following:

- refugee flows in Africa are characterized by situations of mass influx;[23]
- the majority of refugees fleeing persecution in Africa seek asylum in other developing nations in the African region, rather than the wealthier, industrialized nations of the North;[24]
- due to the large-scale nature of many refugee flows within Africa, African host states have moved away from individual refugee assessments (due to resource constraints) and now tend to provide temporary protection on a group determination basis;[25]
- as part of the temporary nature of protection given to such refugees, they are often held in large, closed camps;[26]
- many refugee situations in Africa are protracted in nature;[27]
- some African host states have housed large numbers of refugees in closed refugee camps for extended periods, which has contributed to security concerns both within camps and in the region. These include attacks

The figures for internally displaced persons (IDPs) are higher. According to the Internal Displacement Monitoring Centre, at the end of 2007, Africa hosted almost half the global IDP population (ie, 12.7 million people) and generated nearly half the world's newly displaced (ie, 1.6 million people): see Internal Displacement Monitoring Centre, Global Overview of Trends and Developments in 2007, April 2008, 7 <http://www.internal-displacement.org/8025708F004BE3B1/(httpInfoFiles)/BD8316FAB5984142C125742E0033180B/$file/IDMC_Internal_Displacement_Global_Overview_2007.pdf>. As stated in n 1 above, the focus of this chapter is on refugee flows rather than the different problems arising from IDPs.

[23] As an example of this, UNHCR has estimated that in 2004 approximately 146,900 refugees fled Sudan and sought asylum primarily in the African countries of Chad, Uganda, and Kenya. See UNHCR, *Refugees by Numbers 2005*, 'Major Refugee Arrivals during 2004' (September 2005), 9.

[24] See *Refugees by Numbers*, ibid. Indeed, the UN Security Council has even recognized this in Resolution 1208 in which it noted that the international community needed to 'share the burden borne by African States hosting refugees', SC Res 1208 (19 November 1998), UN Doc S/RES/1208 (1998), para 6.

[25] In cases of mass influx, asylum seekers might be recognized as a group as prima facie refugees (ie, are refugees in the absence of evidence to the contrary). For a discussion of this, see UNHCR, *Protection of Refugees in Mass Influx Situations: Overall Protection Framework, Background Paper prepared for the Global Consultation on International Protection* (19 February 2001), UN Doc EC/GC/01/4, para 6.

[26] The Executive Committee of UNHCR (Ex Com) states: 'in times of crisis, the granting of asylum to large numbers of prima facie refugees is often premised on their being confined to camps'. See UNHCR Ex Com, 'Protracted Refugee Situations' (n 5 above) 9. The Executive Committee of UNHCR is comprised of 69 member states and meets annually in Geneva to approve UNHCR's programmes, protection regime, and other policy guidelines.

[27] ie, the UNHCR Ex Com has stated that the vast majority of the world's protracted refugee situations are to be found in Africa, which has 22 major protracted refugee situations, totalling approximately 2.3 million refugees: see UNHCR Ex Com, ibid, 5.

on camps by militia[28] and the forced recruitment of refugees by armed groups;[29] and

- African refugees face great difficulty in obtaining access to countries outside Africa in order to claim refugee status, resettle, and start a new life due to the strict border controls and restrictive refugee policies of those states (particularly those European nations which are geographically close to Africa).[30]

2.3 To what extent do African states respect refugees' rights under international refugee law?

When one examines the history of refugee protection in Africa, it appears that between the period of the early 1960s and late 1980s (during a time of post-colonial conflicts), many African nations opened their doors to refugees flowing from other African nations.[31] This, however, seems to have changed from the late 1980s onwards, when many African states began to adopt restrictive asylum and border policies. For instance, in the 1990s some African states closed their borders to refugees and deported those who had arrived back to their countries of origin.[32] Significantly (in terms of the concept of burden sharing), it appears that in some instances, border closures were seen as necessary because African host states were unable to obtain relief assistance from the international community to enable them to deal with the large numbers of refugees flowing into the country.[33]

Of the issues arising from this shift towards restrictive refugee policies, two are of central relevance to this chapter: first, the issue of the voluntariness of repatriation and, secondly, the security concerns arising from refugee camps within Africa. These issues will be discussed in turn.

[28] eg, on 13 April 2006, a large armed group entered and briefly took control of one of the UNHCR-run refugee camps in Chad, Goz-Amer, which houses approximately 70,000 Sudanese refugees. See UNHCR, 'UNHCR Alarmed over Consequences for Refugees of Political Upheaval in Chad', UNHCR News Stories 13, April 2006 and UNHCR, 'Chad: Armed Group Enters Goz Amer Camp, UNHCR Concerned by Growing Insecurity', UNHCR Briefing Notes, 11 April 2006 <http://www.unhcr.org>.

[29] eg, UNHCR reports that in March 2006, several hundred Sudanese refugees (mostly men and boys aged between 15 and 36) from two camps in Chad were recruited by armed groups. See UNHCR, 'UNHCR Condemns Forced Recruitment of Sudanese Refugees in Chad Camps', UNHCR News Stories, 31 March 2006 <http://www.unhcr.org>.

[30] See discussion below at Section 3.1 (text at nn 52–3).

[31] The history of African states' attitude to refugee flows is discussed in detail in B Rutinwa, 'The End of Asylum? The Changing Nature of Refugee Policies in Africa' (2002) 21(1/2) Refugee Survey Quarterly 12–41.

[32] See ibid, 20–8. For instance, Rutinwa points out that Tanzania closed its borders with Rwanda after the 1994 genocide in order to prevent further refugee flows (at 23).

[33] ie, both the Tanzanian Minister for Foreign Affairs and a UNHCR representative have acknowledged that the decision by Tanzania to close its borders to Rwandan refugees in 1994 was influenced by the lack of assistance given by the international community to support those refugees. See ibid, 30.

2.3.1 Cases of involuntary repatriation within Africa

There are unfortunately many examples of circumstances in which African states have repatriated refugees to their countries of origin under duress. This is so despite the fact that the 1969 Convention specifically provides that repatriation of refugees to their country of origin should take place on a voluntary basis.[34] Indeed, Crisp points out that information collected by the US Committee for Refugees suggests that in Africa 'at least 12 major repatriation movements took place under duress during 1998, involving seven different countries of asylum …'.[35] One particularly troubling example dates from 1996 when hundreds of thousands of Rwandan refugees residing in refugee camps in Tanzania were directed by the Tanzanian government to return to Rwanda by the end of the year. According to reports from NGOs such as Amnesty International, many of these refugees were forcibly returned to Rwanda in breach of the 1951 Convention.[36]

More recently, cases of refoulement and ill-treatment of refugees appear to be of most concern in the African 'transit' states to Europe, such as Libya and Morocco. For instance, Amnesty International's 2005 Annual Report documented a number of cases in which African persons attempting to seek asylum in Libya were returned to Eritrea, some of whom have reported that they were detained and mistreated by Eritrean authorities.[37] In 2007, Amnesty International also reported that approximately 430 Eritrean nationals who had fled Eritrea to seek asylum were being held in detention in Libya and had testified that they had been ill-treated by guards.[38] Further, in 2009, Human Rights Watch released a detailed report which raises serious concerns about the treatment of asylum seekers in Libya.[39]

The above examples clearly raise significant concerns for the human security of refugees in Africa and for their right to protection under international refugee law.

2.3.2 Security concerns arising from refugee camps

UNHCR Africa specialist, Jeff Crisp, has detailed the significant number of security concerns arising from the large, long-standing refugee camps present

---

[34] 1969 Convention (see n 10 above).

[35] J Crisp, 'Africa's Refugees: Patterns, Problems and Policy Challenges', *New Issues in Refugee Research*, Working Paper No 28 (Geneva: UNHCR Evaluation and Policy Analysis Unit, 2000), 16.

[36] Hathaway (see n 19 above) 933.

[37] Amnesty International, *Annual Report 2005*, ch on Libya, 103. For instance, Amnesty reports that in one instance, authorities in Libya attempted forcibly to return 76 Eritrean nationals, including six children, to Eritrea. They were eventually able to escape to Sudan, where they applied for asylum. Many said they had been ill-treated and denied medical attention while in custody in Libya.

[38] Amnesty International, 'Urgent Action—Libya: Forcible Return/torture and Ill-treatment' (8 February 2007), AI Index: MDE 19/004/2007. See also Amnesty International, 'Document—Libya: Forcible Return/torture and Ill-treatment' (4 September 2007), AI Index MDE 19/014/2007.

[39] Human Rights Watch, 'Pushed Back, Pushed Around: Italy's Forced Return of Boat Migrants and Asylum Seekers, Libya's Mistreatment of Migrants and Asylum Seekers', 21 September 2009 <http://www.hrw.org/en/reports/2009/09/21/pushed-back-pushed-around>.

in a number of African states.[40] The concerns most relevant to the focus of this chapter include the following:

- the camps tend to be populated by a large numbers of children and adolescents, women, and the elderly;[41]
- many of the camps are entirely dependent on international humanitarian assistance;[42]
- such refugees have limited legal rights (refugees in such camps tend not to have residence rights in the country of asylum or any right to work);[43]
- social tension and physical violence has occurred in some camps;[44] and
- there is evidence that the protracted nature of these refugee situations has caused tension between the host state and the inhabitants of the refugee camps (in some cases the local population has come to see the camp as a source of insecurity and environmental problems).[45]

These security concerns have also been acknowledged by the Executive Committee of UNHCR[46] and leaders of a number of African states.[47] In particular, the UNHCR's Executive Committee has raised concerns about the militarization of refugee camps and their potential for causing further insecurity, noting that 'Large, disaffected and alienated populations relying on subsistence-level handouts are prime targets for recruitment into armed groups.'[48] The issue of security in refugee camps has become not only a UNHCR and African state issue, but has also been the subject of a UN Security Council resolution passed in 1998 which emphasized that:

the provision of security to refugees and the maintenance of the civilian and humanitarian character of refugee camps and settlement ... can contribute to the maintenance of international peace and security.[49]

Moreover, in terms of the focus of this chapter on human security, there is evidence that refugees in these protracted refugee situations who are housed in camps experience serious psychological problems, including depression, traumatisation, stress, and other emotional and behavioural problems.[50]

Given the above discussion, it appears that the human security and protection of many refugees in Africa is not being fulfilled. The question that therefore arises

---

[40] Crisp (see n 5 above) 6–7.   [41] Ibid, 8.

[42] In this regard, the emphasis on refugee self-sufficiency in UNHCR's 'Convention Plus' initiative may be a valuable one (see discussion of Convention Plus below at Section 3.2, text at nn 57–8).   [43] Crisp (see n 5 above) 11–12.

[44] Ibid, 17.

[45] Ibid, 18–19. For instance, Crisp points to the attitude of the government of Guinea towards refugees from Sierra Leone and Liberia during 2000–02.

[46] UNHCR Ex Com (see n 5 above) 8.

[47] See, eg, 'Refugees in Africa: The Challenges of Protection and Solutions', Declaration—Preamble, Conference Report, Cotonou, Benin, 1–3 June 2004 <http://www.ipu.org/splz-e/cotonou.htm>.   [48] UNHCR Ex Com (see n 5 above) 13.

[49] SC Res 1208 (19 November 1998), Preamble, UN Doc S/RES/1208 (1998).

[50] Crisp (see n 5 above) 15–16.

is what are the future prospects for recent UNHCR initiatives to improve the human security of these refugees, particularly given the increasing emphasis in non-African host states on restricting border entry?

3. Recent developments at the international level

3.1 Border and refugee policies of the 'Northern' states

Coupled with the inability or unwillingness of many African states to accept refugees into their borders, the so-called 'Northern countries' of the EU, the USA, and Australia have in recent years also adopted increasingly restrictive policies towards refugees. As with African states, many states outside Africa also seem concerned with the security risks that are perceived to arise from the arrival of refugees at states' borders. This has become particularly acute in the post-September 11 world. For instance, it has been reported that the number of refugees resettled to the USA declined from 70,000 in 2001 to only 27,000 in 2002 because of the stringent security checks which were instituted after the events of September 11.[51]

Restrictive border controls have become a particular problem in the Mediterranean region, where there have been a number of highly publicized incidents during which African asylum seekers and migrants have died whilst attempting to cross the sea to enter Spain. Amnesty International has released a report which has been highly critical of the Spanish government in this regard.[52] It has also implicated the EU in the human rights abuses perpetrated by Spanish authorities on the basis that the EU has placed pressure on countries close to Africa (such as Spain) to stem refugee flows as part of the EU's 'Fortress Europe' strategy.[53]

The above factors are central to understanding the pressures placed on those refugees in Africa who wish to seek asylum outside Africa. That is, it raises the very real question: do refugees in Africa have any meaningful choice in terms of the asylum decisions they are able to make? In short, the answer appears to be *very little choice.*[54]

---

[51] *Human Security Now* (New York: Commission on Human Security, 2003), ch 3, 48, citing (2002) 9(12) Migration News 4.

[52] Amnesty International, 'Spain: The Southern Border—The State Turns its back on the Human Rights of Refugees and Immigrants' (20 June 2005)' AI Index: EUR 41/008/2005.

[53] See Amnesty International EU Office, Press Release, 11 October 2005, AI Index: IOR 61/019/2005:

> The present dire situation in North Africa, where people trying to gain entry to EU territory are reportedly being shot dead, or even dumped in the desert without food or water, relates directly to pressure exerted by EU countries to strengthen fortress Europe.

The reference to EU territory in North Africa is a reference to Spain's Northern African enclaves of Melilla and Ceuta.

[54] The implications of this for the human security of refugees in Africa are discussed at Section 4.2 (text at nn 72–85).

Given all the above, that is, that traditional asylum host states both within Africa and outside it are adopting increasingly restrictive refugee policies and border controls, what is currently being done in the international community, primarily via UN agencies, to address this?

3.2 UNHCR initiatives

UNHCR has adopted a number of new initiatives in the past decade in an attempt to encourage states parties to the 1951 Convention to abide by its obligations under international refugee law. The two main initiatives are the 'Agenda for Protection' (released in 2001) and the 'Convention Plus' initiative (launched in mid 2003).

The Agenda for Protection is a UNHCR document designed to 'reinvigorate and improve protection for refugees worldwide'.[55] The Agenda sets out six goals to achieve; one is of particular relevance to this chapter, namely Goal 3, which is directed towards more equitable burden sharing of refugees and the building of host-state capacities to receive and protect refugees. Importantly, states parties who participated in this project declared that of all 'durable solutions', voluntary repatriation is the 'preferred solution'.[56]

'Convention Plus' is intended to build on the obligations set out in the 1951 Convention (hence the term 'plus') by encouraging the countries in the North and South to develop agreements to ensure improved burden sharing and tries to address what the UNHCR has identified as 'three priority challenges'. These are:

- 'The strategic use of resettlement as a tool of protection, a durable solution and a tangible form of burden-sharing';
- 'More effective targeting of development assistance to support durable solutions for refugees, whether in countries of asylum or upon return home'; and
- 'Clarification of the responsibilities of States in the event of irregular secondary movements of refugees and asylum-seekers'.[57]

Since Convention Plus was introduced, the UNHCR has also launched further initiatives designed to build upon the focus on durable solutions to refugee protection via the strengthening of protection capacities in source countries. For instance, the UNHCR in cooperation with the European Commission and a

---

[55] UNHCR Ex Com (see n 5 above) 23.

[56] 'Declaration of States Parties' in *Agenda for Protection* (Geneva: UNHCR, 2003), 28, 13. That approach has also been explicitly stated in several UNHCR Executive Committee Conclusions: see, eg, 'General Conclusion on International Protection' No 95 (LIV) 2003; 'Durable Solutions' No 87 (L) 2001 and 'Resettlement' No 90 (LII) 2001. This has also been acknowledged by the UN General Assembly, which reaffirmed in 2006 that 'voluntary repatriation . . . remains the preferred solution': see UN General Assembly, Resolution on the Office of the UN High Commissioner for Refugees (24 January 2006) 13, UN Doc A/RES/60/129.

[57] See UNHCR, 'Convention Plus at a Glance', 1 June 2005, 1 <http://www.unhcr.org/protect/PROTECTION/403b30684.pdf>.

number of European states launched a 'Strengthening Protection Capacity Project' in 2004 which is designed to strengthen the refugee protection capacities of four African countries: Kenya, Tanzania, Benin, and Burkina Faso.[58] The UNHCR states that this includes 'enhancing refugees' means of self-reliance and expanding opportunities for durable solutions'. The focus appears to be on training and finding employment for refugees within the camps in local areas so that those refugees may be prepared for eventual return to their home countries.[59]

The EU's evolving approach to refugee issues also places emphasis on some of UNHCR's stated priorities, such as 'burden sharing' and 'capacity building'.[60] However, it should be noted that the EU has focused much more on providing funds for capacity building in host states in the developing world[61] rather than on more concrete 'burden sharing', that is, by actually opening up more avenues for asylum seekers from Africa to seek asylum in its member states.

Given this background, what particular problems does the current environment (both regionally and internationally) pose for the human security of refugees in Africa?

4. Implications of the international development for the human security of refugees in Africa

Before examining the implications of the above discussion for the human security of refugees in Africa, one must establish what is meant by the term 'human security' in the context of refugee protection.

4.1 What is 'human security'?

It is difficult categorically to state the meaning of 'human security', as there is no one accepted definition of what the term means. Some scholars, particularly in the international relations discipline, have analysed this concept in depth.[62]

---

[58] UNHCR, 'Strenghtening Protection Capacity Project' <http://www.unhcr.org/pages/4a1673d46.html>. The initiative is co-funded by the European Commission and the governments of Denmark, Germany, the Netherlands, and the United Kingdom.

[59] See, eg, UNHCR, 'ILO-UNHCR Partnership through Technical Cooperation: Multi-bilateral Programme of Technical Cooperation: Final Report—Self-reliance and Sustainable Livelihoods for Refugees in Dadaab and Kakuma camps', September 2005 <http://www.unhcr.org/protect/PROTECTION/4326a7542.pdf>.

[60] 'Communication from the Commission to the Council and the European Parliament: Towards more Accessible, Equitable and Managed Asylum Systems [COM(2003)315 final]', 1 September 2005.

[61] See, eg, Communication on Regional Protection Programmes (September 2005) and the European Commission's Communication on Strengthened Practical Cooperation in the area of asylum (17 February 2006).

[62] See, eg, contributing authors to E Newman and J van Selm, *Refugees and Forced Displacement: International Security, Human Vulnerability, and the State* (Tokyo: United Nations University Press, 2003).

Although Chapter 1 of this book has dealt with the notion of human security substantially, it is important to highlight, for the purpose of this chapter, that a number of international bodies and commentators have emphasized a link between human security and the *empowerment* of people. For instance, the Commission on Human Security notes that the concept of human security 'seeks to protect people against a broad range of threats to individuals and communities and, further, to *empower* them to act on their own behalf'.[63] Sadako Ogata, UN High Commissioner for Refugees from 1991 to 2000, has also pointed out that:

Protection against critical and pervasive threats is at the centre of human security and should be linked to a strategy that *empowers people*. In many respects, the *protection* and *empowerment* of people are mutually reinforcing strategies.[64] (Emphasis added.)

This has important implications for the way in which UNHCR's recent initiatives affect the human security of refugees in the African region.[65]

Whilst there are many different definitions accorded to 'human security', the key to understanding it is its link to *national* security. The traditional conception of 'security' in international relations discourse has been on *state* security and, as part of that, *state* sovereignty. The notion of human security therefore seeks to change the focus from the *state*, to the human beings *within* that state. Thus, it is understood to broaden the security discourse to recognize that human security is not merely about military defence, but also about elements such as economic development, social justice, environmental protection, and respect for human rights.[66] Hence, it tends to have a developmental and human rights, rather than a defence focus.

Naturally, the application of a human security approach to refugees has particular resonance given the fact that refugees are by definition lacking the protection of their home country and are therefore both vulnerable and lacking security. As the (then) United Nations High Commissioner for Refugees Sadako Ogata noted in 1999:

the importance of human security as a concept is clear if you consider that my Office deals on a daily basis with people who are, by definition, 'insecure'. Refugees and internally displaced people are a significant symptom of human insecurity crises.... Refugees are doubly insecure: they flee because they are afraid; and in fleeing they start a precarious existence.[67]

---

[63] Ibid, ch 1, 2.   [64] Ibid, S Ogata, 'Foreword', p x.

[65] See discussion below at Section 4.2 (text at nn 72–85).

[66] See, eg, K Annan, 'Towards a Culture of Peace', UNESCO Letters to Future Generations series, 22 August 2001, excerpt reproduced at: <http://www.gdrc.org/sustdev/husec/Definitions. pdf>.

[67] Keynote speech by Mrs Sadako Ogata, United Nations High Commissioner for Refugees, at the Ministerial Meeting on Human Security Issues of the 'Lysoen Process' Group of Governments, 'Human Security: A Refugee Perspective', Bergen, 19 May 1999, on file with the author.

The significance of the human security approach in the context of this chapter is neatly summarized by the words of UN Secretary-General Kofi Annan:

Human security in its broadest sense, embraces far more than the absence of violent conflict. It encompasses *human rights, good governance, access to education and health care* and ensuring that each individual has opportunities and choices to fulfill his or her own potential. Every step in this direction is also a step towards reducing poverty, achieving economic growth and preventing conflict. Freedom from want, freedom from fear and the freedom of future generations to inherit a healthy natural environment—these are the interrelated building blocks of *human*—and *therefore national*—*security*.[68] (Emphasis added.)

There are a number of things to note about Annan's definition of 'human security'. First, if this term encompasses human rights, good governance, access to education and health care, can it be said that these rights are being fulfilled in the refugee situation in Africa (particularly those who have been detained in closed refugee camps for long periods of time)? Secondly, his notion of human security is said to encompass individuals having *choices* to fulfil their own potential. Given the very limited choices that African refugees face in their desire to seek asylum, can it be said that they have any real choices about their future? Thirdly, Annan makes a link between human security and the prevention of conflict, and thus *national* security. As this chapter demonstrates, it is indeed true that lack of human security for refugees can lead to further refugee flows, and thus the creation of further displacement, thereby contributing to further destabilization of a country or region. However, there is also a problem in linking human security and the prevention of conflict. These matters are addressed in more detail below in the conclusions to this chapter.[69]

4.2 What are the implications of the UNHCR-led initiatives for human security in Africa?

The series of UNHCR initiatives focusing on durable solutions for refugees are a welcome development in that they highlight the need for international refugee law to be supplemented by more practical means of improving compliance with protection obligations. As a complement to international refugee law, the encouragement of schemes such as burden sharing and developmental assistance therefore has the potential to improve the level of protection given to refugees in some circumstances.

However, the success of these UNHCR initiatives is very much premised on a perception by Northern states that there is a sufficient incentive for them

---

[68] K Annan, 'Secretary-General Salutes International Workshop on Human Security in Mongolia', Ulaanbaatar, 8–10 May 2000, UN Press Release, UN Doc SG/SM/7382, 8 May 2000 <http://www.un.org/News/Press/docs/2000/20000508.sgsm7382.doc.html>.

[69] Text at nn 84–92.

to provide the necessary funds and other assistance to support such initiatives. Given the past and current practice of many Northern states, there is reason to be very sceptical about whether such states will indeed be willing to fully engage with these initiatives, and thereby to improve the human security of refugees in regions such as Africa. This scepticism predominantly arises from a fundamental concern about the willingness of Northern states to engage fully in the burden-sharing elements of the UNHCR initiatives, both in relation to resettlement and funding of capacity building. These issues will be discussed in turn.

4.2.1 Northern states' approach to resettlement

One of the three priority areas identified by Convention Plus is that of resettlement (as a form of burden sharing). However, many states have been reluctant to agree to resettle significant numbers of refugees in the past, and there is little or no indication that states intend to change that approach.[70] As Jeff Crisp points out, between 1992 and 2001 only approximately 90,000 African refugees were resettled in other parts of the world, which equates to only a 'tiny proportion' of Africa's refugee population.[71] Furthermore, latest statistics from the UNHCR show that in 2008 the number of refugees given resettlement totalled only 88,000.[72] This is clearly negligible given that there are over 2.1 million refugees in Africa and a worldwide refugee population of 10.5 million.[73] Thus, at present, it appears that the capacity for resettlement to achieve durable solutions and to meet the human security needs of refugees in protracted situations in Africa is, at best, minimal.

That said, it should also be noted that obviously not all refugees may wish to resettle in another country and, indeed, many may wish to return to their home country if conditions are safe. However, it is clear from the demand for resettlement places across the globe that there are a significant number of refugees who are unable or unwilling to return to their country of origin for various reasons. In this regard, the need to prevent further traumatization of refugees (and to therefore respect their human security needs), must be considered by states. In essence, refugees must be given a level of choice as to whether they are able to return to their country of origin, or wish to resettle elsewhere and in the current international environment, these choices are very limited.

---

[70] ie, Amnesty International notes that the EU proposal for Regional Protection Programmes endorsed in 2004 says 'very little' about the commitment of EU member states to host refugees under resettlement schemes, despite the fact that the EU had earlier announced that these programmes *would* include some significant steps to improving solidarity with those countries housing large numbers of refugees. See Amnesty International EU Office, 'EU Regional Protection Programs: Enhancing Protection in the Region or Barring Access to the EU Territory?', September 2005 <http://www.amnesty-eu.org/static/documents/2005/05_09_22_protection_programs_EPC.pdf>.   [71] Crisp (see n 5 above) 4 and n 8.

[72] UNHCR, *Refugees by Numbers* (see n 24 above) 16–17.   [73] Ibid.

4.2.2 *Problems with the concept of 'burden sharing'*

It is questionable whether Northern states will in fact properly fund developing nations to undertake refugee protection in the way in which the UNHCR expects this to occur. States such as the USA and many EU nations already spend vast sums on development aid and debt relief programmes to assist developing nations within Africa in addition to the funding of refugee programmes within their *own* jurisdictions. Given this, how receptive are such states going to be to further requests for the funding of capacity-building projects within Africa? UNHCR has in past years found it increasingly difficult to attract donor funding for its activities.[74] In this light, is it likely that states will also readily agree to further expenditure on refugee programmes? Such an assumption will be particularly questionable if the programmes do not in fact prevent and contain refugee flows within Africa in line with the expectations of the Northern states. Similar concerns have also been raised by a number of academic commentators. For instance, Deborah Anker and others have raised doubts about the willingness of Northern states to provide the necessary funds that burden sharing requires, particularly once refugees are 'contained in the South'.[75]

Accordingly, there are serious questions raised by what Northern states understand to be required by the concept of 'burden sharing'. If it is limited to providing funds to developing countries to enable them to house the large numbers of refugees within their borders then it is in essence part of a *containment* strategy to keep refugees within Africa, rather than a genuine responsibility-sharing arrangement whereby Northern states *also* agree to allow those African refugees who wish to claim asylum outside Africa to do so.[76]

There are inherent dangers in allowing states to interpret 'burden sharing' in this manner and these concerns have been echoed by prominent academic commentators. For instance, Alexander Betts notes that Convention Plus attempts to link the funding of protection capacities in regions of origin with states' interests in the North, by principally appealing to a 'containment agenda'.[77] That is, it attempts to engage the attention of states by holding out a promise that by

---

[74] See A Bookstein, 'UNHCR and Forgotten Emergencies: Can Funds be Found?', Forced Migration Review (10 April 2001) <http://www.fmreview.org/FMRpdfs/FMR10/fmr10.15.pdf>.

[75] D Anker, J Fitzpatrick, and A Shackove, 'Crisis and Cure: A Reply to Hathaway/Neve and Shuck' (1998) 11 Harvard Human Rights Journal 300. The article was written in reply to earlier proposals by Professor James Hathaway and R Alexander Neve for the development of a collective framework of refugee protection which encompassed mechanisms for burden sharing based on the transfer of funds by Northern states to asylum host states in the South (see JC Hathaway and RA Neve, 'Making International Refugee Law Relevant Again: A Proposal for Collectivised and Solution-Oriented Protection' (1997) 10 Harvard Human Rights Journal 115).

[76] This ties in with the discussion of resettlement above at Section 4.2.1 (text at nn 72–5).

[77] A Betts, 'Convention Plus: Continuity of Change in North/South Responsibility-Sharing', Paper prepared for 'New Asylum Paradigm' Workshop, Centre on Migration Policy and Society (COMPAS), Oxford, 14 June 2005, 5 <http://www.compas.ox.ac.uk/fileadmin/files/pdfs/Non_WP_pdfs/Events_2005/C+%20Paper%20(2).pdf>.

assisting regions of origin to provide protection, there will be a reduction in the numbers of asylum seekers and refugees coming to the borders of states outside that region.[78] As Betts argues, there is a risk that by linking funding of protection capacity in countries of origin in this way, the long-term commitment to and funding of such projects by Northern states might be affected if the capacity-building programmes did not result in any decline in spontaneous arrivals.[79]

The analysis by Betts is compelling. It is clear that it is highly unlikely that the Northern states of the EU, the USA, and Australia will continue to fund expensive capacity-building projects in Africa whilst also accepting substantial numbers of refugees through their own domestic systems via what is seen by many states as a high-cost domestic refugee determination process.

More generally, when one examines the history of the African region and particularly given the political instability of many of the developing countries in that region, can it be said that capacity building (even if funded sufficiently) is necessarily going to ensure the human security and protection of refugees seeking asylum in those countries?[80]

Moreover, there are also broader moral and ethical issues raised by Northern states seeking to fund developing states in Africa (and elsewhere) to undertake the obligations that those Northern states would otherwise have under international refugee law to provide protection to refugees. As UN Secretary-General Kofi Annan has stated, the current policies of the industrialized North equate to a containment strategy by which 'this world's more fortunate and powerful countries seek to keep the problems of the poorer at arm's length'.[81] Thus, as international law scholar, JP Fonteyne, once said

International solidarity therefore must go beyond the facile provision of financial assistance by a group of rich nations to countries initially affected by the refugee problem at hand, and, of necessity, must carry over into the second stage of refugee protection. Emergency provision of safe havens for victims of persecution and the organisation of durable solutions for the situation are complementary elements of an integrated international refugee policy, and burden-sharing must operate, where required, at both levels.[82]

The implication of the above discussion is that if the burden-sharing initiatives driven by the UNHCR fail, then refugees in Africa will face a most perilous future. Given the high numbers of refugees in protracted situations in parts of

[78] As Betts notes, the then High Commissioner for Refugees Rudd Lubbers referred to this link at the opening of the First forum on Convention Plus, 27 June 2004; ibid, 11.   [79] Ibid, 11.

[80] As James Hathaway has pointed out, 'the political instability of many developing states may mean that what is a "safe" region today may be dangerous tomorrow', JC Hathaway, *The Law of Refugee Status* (Toronto: Butterworths, 1991), 18–19.

[81] Kofi Annan, UN Secretary-General, Address to the 51st session of the Executive Committee of UNHCR, Palais des Nations, Geneva, UN Press Release SG/SM/7570, 2 October 2000.

[82] JP Fonteyne, 'Burden-Sharing: An Analysis of the Nature and Function of International Solidarity in Cases of Mass Influx of Refugees' (1980) 8 Australian Yearbook of International Law 162, 176.

Africa, and the inability of many host states properly to accommodate such refugees (particularly in situations where refugee camps are seen to be causing insecurity in local communities and regions), then there is a very real danger that further cases of involuntary repatriations of the type discussed above will ensue.[83]

5. Conclusion

In addition to discussing the human security concerns arising from UNHCR-led initiatives for refugees in Africa, it is also necessary in the final section of this chapter to question the validity of the human security approach as it applies to refugees.

A focus on human security in the refugee context recognizes the reality of refugee protection in the twenty-first century. That is, to remain effective, refugee-protection initiatives must appeal to the security interests of states. As James Milner argues, solutions to refugee situations need to be based on an understanding of the importance of the state as well as the importance of refugees and so 'any system dedicated to protecting refugees can, and must, function in a way that is mindful of the needs of states'.[84] A human security approach is therefore beneficial by appealing to the interests of states in ensuring the security of their national borders and encouraging them to perceive refugee protection as a collective, international security concern. It therefore might be a useful tool in seeking the cooperation of Northern states in some of the UNHCR initiatives discussed above.

However, the concept also poses problems in the refugee context in a number of ways. First, there are situations where national security considerations conflict with those of human security. For instance, it is often national security issues which lie at the heart of the restrictive border and refugee policies of certain EU countries.[85] Thus, it is unclear as to how effective a human security approach will be when faced with overwhelming national security concerns. The danger that a human security approach poses in this regard is particularly apparent when both states and international agencies are striving towards the prevention of conflict in a region (conflict prevention being one of the UNHCR's stated 'durable solutions'). What happens when the desire to prevent conflict in a region conflicts

---

[83] See above at Section 2.3.1 (text at nn 34–9).

[84] J Milner, 'Sharing the Security Burden: Towards the Convergence of Refugee Protection and State Security', Refugee Studies Centre Working Paper No 4, Refugee Studies Centre, University of Oxford, May 2000, 28.

[85] eg in many EU countries, governments seem to justify restrictive refugee policies by pointing to national security concerns, often influenced by public and media opposition to refugee intakes. For instance, government policies on asylum in the UK have become a powerful electoral issue and are the subject of widespread, often very critical, reports in the tabloid press: see discussion in T Sifrin, 'Asylum and Immigration: The Issue Explained', *The Guardian*, 27 April 2004 <http://www.guardian.co.uk/society/2004/apr/27/asylum>.

with the obligation to protect refugees pursuant to international refugee law? The answer to this question is illustrated by the repatriation of Rwandan refugees from Zaire and Tanzania in the 1990s in circumstances where there were strong indications that the situation in Rwanda was not safe for return (controversially this repatriation was assisted by the UNHCR itself). The then High Commissioner of Refugees, Sadako Ogata, explained that UNHCR's support for the repatriation was heavily influenced by the threat posed by the Rwandan refugees to the security of the region:

When refugee outflows and prolonged stay in asylum countries risk spreading conflict to neighbouring states, policies aimed at early repatriation can be considered as serving prevention ...[86]

Thus, although one view may be that conflict prevention may assist in enhancing human security, it is also clear that it poses some dangers for the protection of refugees.

A related issue is how does one address conflict between the human security of citizens within a state and the refugees either within a state or attempting to enter a state? That is, when one speaks of 'human security', which group takes precedence—the citizen or the refugee? This is significant in terms of the validity of the human security approach to refugees in that some scholars have interpreted human security as encompassing the basic security needs of the *citizens* residing within a state.[87] Obviously this creates problems for refuges who are not citizens of the asylum host state to which they are seeking asylum. Therein lies the dilemma of human security as applied to refugee situations: what happens when the 'human security' of citizens within a host state is seen as threatened by security concerns raised by the presence of refugees? Anne Hammerstad illustrates the problems in utilizing a human security approach thus:

Whose security counts, that of the refugee fleeing from violence or repression, or that of the host community concerned over job competition, welfare, cultural cohesion and international crime in the face of large refugee influxes or steady streams of asylum seekers?[88]

Thus, when we speak of human security in the refugee context, we also need to bear in mind that generally the overriding interest of states is in their sovereignty and their interests in protecting their citizens, rather than to those perceived as being 'outsiders'. That is, human security as a concept has an inherent weakness in

---

[86] S Ogata, 'Remarks at a Conference of the Carnegie Commission on the Prevention of Deadly Conflict', Geneva, 17 February 1997, cited in BE Whitaker, 'Changing Priorities in Refugee Protection: The Rwandan Repatriation from Tanzania' (2002) 21(1/2) Refugee Survey Quarterly 337.

[87] P Upadhyaya, 'Human Security, Human Intervention, and Third World Concerns' (2004) 33(1) Denver Journal of International Law and Policy 74.

[88] A Hammerstad, 'Whose Security? UNHCR, Refugee Protection and State Security after the Cold War' (2000) 31(4) Security Dialogue 399.

that it will not necessarily protect the rights of refugees in all situations given that states generally give priority to those 'humans' who are part of their sovereignty, ie, citizens. Any application of a human security paradigm to refugee law must therefore take account of these important sovereignty and citizenship issues.

Examining the issue more broadly, it may be argued that there is also an inherent danger in reinforcing the link between refugees and security. In this respect, Alexander Betts points out that 'Convention Plus' has attempted to link protection capacity in regions of origin with the interests of states on the basis of security.[89] As Betts points out this is problematic given that some states have alleged that certain refugee camps provide a source for Islamic terrorism.[90] Thus, he states that although an association with security might be used by UNHCR to attract donor commitment, it 'also poses the dilemma of potentially reinforcing a discourse of securitisation in relation to refugees and asylum seekers'.[91]

It therefore appears from the preceding discussion that we must be cautious about overly relying on the concept of human security in the context of refugee protection.

In summary, the following can be said about the human security of refugees in today's world: it is true that the international community has evinced a declining commitment to international refugee law and has instead focused on policies of confinement and border control. It is also true that the durable solutions posed by the UNHCR have the potential to achieve some improvement in the way in which developing nations such as those in Africa are able to deal with their large, long-standing refugee populations. However, there is also a great danger that a focus on conflict prevention, developmental assistance and burden sharing will leave refugees attempting to flee persecution and conflict with either limited or, in some cases, no meaningful choices in relation to asylum. This is important in terms of human security, given that the existence of meaningful choices about the decision to seek asylum is surely central to the empowerment of refugees and, more broadly, their access to human security.

The above will be of particular concern if the assumptions upon which the UNHCR initiatives are based do not materialize, that is, if Northern states fail to increase resettlement numbers and to fund capacity building sufficiently in host states in the African region. Human security is focused on the need to protect the rights of individuals within a state and, as Sadako Ogata and others have noted, to *empower* refugees to act on their own behalf and therefore to enhance their *protection*.[92] The very real danger posed by current UNHCR initiatives is that in the future, Northern states will continue to adopt restrictive border controls and refugee policies, whilst also declining to engage fully with the priorities required for durable solutions in Africa. Some may view this as an overly pessimistic approach, but it is one that needs to be considered in future programmes aimed at refugee protection. Ultimately, asylum host states in both the North and South

---

[89] See n 79 above, 11.   [90] Ibid, 11.   [91] Ibid, 11.   [92] See text at nn 65–6.

must recognize that refugees are vulnerable persons who not only desire, but *need* protection. Whilst burden-sharing initiatives can go some way in improving the capacity of some Southern states to provide this protection, it should not act as a substitute for Northern states also acknowledging their responsibility to accept these most vulnerable people into their borders and, if required under law, to grant them asylum.

9

Human Rights of Women in Africa: A Prerequisite for Human Security

*Manisuli Ssenyonjo**

1. Introduction

The focus of this chapter is on the protection and promotion of human rights of women in Africa since the protection and promotion of women's human rights (civil, political, economic, social, and cultural rights) is a prerequisite for human security. Although there is no universally accepted definition of the term 'human security', it is used in this chapter to include two key dimensions, 'freedom from fear' and 'freedom from want'.[1] Indeed, one perspective to human security is that it entails 'freedom from pervasive threats to *people's rights*, safety or lives'[2] and the protection of 'the vital core of all human lives in ways that enhance *human freedoms* and human fulfilment'.[3] In this respect, gross human rights violations can amount to threats to human security. Thus the realization of human rights including the rights of women enhances human security.

Despite this most women in Africa have been denied the equal enjoyment of their human rights with men, in particular by virtue of the lesser status ascribed to them by tradition and custom (broadly culture), or as a result of overt or covert discrimination. Many women in Africa experience distinct forms of discrimination due to the intersection of sex with such factors as race, colour, language, religion, political and other opinion, national or social origin, property, birth, or other status, such as age, ethnicity, disability, marital, refugee, or migrant status, resulting in compounded disadvantage. Underlying each of these problems is the fact that individuals and groups suffering the most from human rights

---

* Senior Lecturer in Law, Brunel Law School, Brunel University, London.
[1] United Nations Development Programme (UNDP), *Human Development Report 1994* (Oxford: Oxford University Press, 1994), 24–5.
[2] *Freedom from Fear: Canada's Foreign Policy for Human Security* (Ottawa: Department of Foreign Affairs and International Trade, 2000), 3 (emphasis added).
[3] *Human Security Now: Protecting and Empowering People* (New York: Commission on Human Security, 2003), 4 (emphasis added).

violations—the poor in general and poor women in particular—often lack the political voice needed to claim or assert their rights. Consequently, much remains to be done to realize the human rights of women in Africa.

This chapter examines the relationship between culture and the realization of the human rights of women in Africa and makes some recommendations for the effective realization of these rights. The intention is not to address all cultural issues but to consider some selected cultural obstacles and threats that have caused major difficulties. The chapter adopts the following structure. After this introduction (Section 1), Section 2 provides an overview of human rights of women in Africa. Section 3 examines prejudicial cultural practices as an obstacle to the realization of the human rights of women. Such prejudicial cultural practices affect negatively women's security. Section 4 provides some concluding observations noting that the promotion of women's human rights advances society as a whole and contributes to attaining human security.

2. Human rights of women in Africa: an overview

2.1 Background

In 1995, the United Nations (UN) reported 'in no society today do women enjoy the same opportunities as men'.[4] More than 15 years later, discrimination against women persists not only in the developing African states,[5] but also in the more developed states including Germany[6] and Luxembourg.[7] Every day millions of women and young girls are forced to spend hours collecting and carrying water for their families (restricting their opportunities and their choices), a ritual that reinforces gender inequalities in employment and education.[8] In a

---

[4] UNDP, *Human Development Report 1995: Gender and Human Development* (1995) 29 <http://hdr.undp.org/en/reports/global/hdr1995/>. The term 'women' is used in this chapter to mean persons of female gender, including girls.

[5] S Tamale, 'Gender Trauma in Africa: Enhancing Women's Links to Resources' (2004) 48(1) Journal of African Law 50–61.

[6] See, eg, Committee on Economic, Social and Cultural Rights (CESCR), *Concluding Observations: Germany*, UN Doc E/C.12/1/Add.68 (24 September 2001), 19. See also Human Rights Committee (HRC), *Concluding Observations: Germany*, CCPR/CO/80/DEU (4 May 2004), 13 noting that the 'number of women in senior positions is still very low' and that there are 'wide disparities, in the private sector, of remuneration between men and women'.

[7] CESCR, *Concluding Observations: Luxembourg*, UN Doc E/C.12/1/Add.86 (23 May 2003), 22:

> The Committee notes with concern that women are still underrepresented in the work force. While taking note that the disparities between wages of men and women have been reduced, the Committee also notes with concern that the current level of wage difference (women receiving 15 per cent lower wages than men) remains a matter of concern.

[8] See UNDP, *Human Development Report 2006: Beyond Scarcity: Power, Poverty and the Global Water Crisis*, v <http://hdr.undp.org/en/reports/global/hdr2006/>.

2002 Joint Declaration of Special Rapporteurs on Women's Rights, it was noted that:

Violence against women and girls is perpetrated in every country in the world. This occurs in situations of peace and conflict. However, the State agents and private actors responsible are not held to account. This climate of impunity encourages the persistence of such violations.[9]

As the Parliamentary Assembly of the Council of Europe has pointed out, although slavery was officially abolished more than 150 years ago, 'domestic slavery' persists in Europe and concerns thousands of people, the majority of whom are women.[10] This is also true of other jurisdictions. In Africa, for example, slavery still persists in some states such as Mauritania to the detriment of women.[11] On 27 October 2008, in a judgment handed down by the Community Court of Justice of the Economic Community of West African states (ECOWAS Court), the state of Niger was found in violation of its international obligations to protect a woman (Hadijatou Mani) from slavery.[12]

In every state where data are available, for example, notwithstanding favourable legislation, women's average wages are less than those of men regardless of education,[13] and women experience the onus of the 'double duty'.[14] It is, therefore, less surprising that, worldwide, over 60 per cent of those working in family enterprises without pay are women.[15] Women are often subjected to discriminatory employment practices such as the requirement to present a non-pregnancy certificate to gain employment or to avoid dismissal from employment.[16] Thus,

---

[9] UN, Joint Declaration of Special Rapporteurs on Women's Rights, 8 March 2002 <http://www.un.org/news/Press/docs/2002/wom1330.doc.htm>. The Declaration was made by Ms Marta Altolaguirre, Special Rapporteur on Women's Rights Inter-American Commission on Human Rights; Ms Radhika Coomaraswamy, Special Rapporteur on violence against women, its causes and its consequences, UN Commission on Human Rights; and Ms Angela Melo, Special Rapporteur on the Rights of Women in Africa, African Commission on Human and Peoples' Rights.

[10] European Court of Human Rights, *Siliadin v France*, App No 73316/01, Judgment of 26 July 2005 (2006) 43 EHRR 16, 111.

[11] African Commission on Human and Peoples' Rights (ACHPR), *Bah Ould Rabah v Mauritania*, Communication No 197/97 (2005) 12 IHRR 872, 29.

[12] See ECOWAS Court, *Hadijatou Mani Koraou v The Republic of Niger*, 27 October 2008, ECW/CCJ/JUD/06/08. For a comment on this case see H Duffy, 'Hadijatou Mani Koroua v Niger: Slavery Unveiled by the ECOWAS Court' (2009) 9(1) Human Rights Law Review 151–70.

[13] UN Development Fund for Women, *Progress of the World's Women* (New York: United Nations, 2000), 92.

[14] AM Cotter, *Gender Injustice: An International Comparative Analysis of Equality in Employment* (Aldershot: Ashgate, 2004), 93–215. 'Double duty' refers to the reality that women worldwide who join the paid labour force nevertheless continue to shoulder more than their fair share of household and family responsibilities.

[15] See *The Millennium Development Goals Report 2005* (New York: United Nations Press, 2005), 16 <http://unstats.un.org/unsd/mi/pdf/MDG%20Book.pdf>, noting that: 'In the home, women perform most of the chores. This work is also unpaid, often little valued and not reflected in national production statistics.'

[16] CESCR, *Concluding Observations: Mexico*, UN Doc Future E/C.12/CO/MEX/4 (17 May 2006), 15: 'The Committee reiterates its concern about the practice of employers in the *maquiladora*

notwithstanding comprehensive international and domestic laws proscribing sex discrimination and promoting equality (see Section 2.2 below), human rights of women are 'systematically denied'[17] and 'women [are] poorer than men across class, race, national, economic and ethnic lines'.[18] It is, therefore, not surprising that women are generally 'over-represented in low-paid employment'.[19]

Despite significant achievements in the quest for women's equality, in particular since the entry into force of the Convention on the Elimination of All Forms of Discrimination against Women (CEDAW),[20] which, by April 2009 has been ratified by 186 states representing over 90 per cent of the UN members, ensuring gender equality in all states remains an enormous challenge.[21] To look at Africa in particular, a statement by the chairperson of the African Union merits recalling:

Violence against women and girls has assumed unprecedented levels across Africa...Harmful traditional practices against women and girls such as female genital mutilation, virginity tests, early and forced marriages and widow inheritance continue to bedevil continental efforts towards gender equality and women's empowerment. The situation of women in conflict situations in Africa is deplorable. Gross human rights violations are perpetrated against civilians in general but against women and girls in particular.[22]

Although African states have ratified several human rights instruments protecting women's human rights, generally the severe political, economic, and social difficulties facing African states have had a negative impact on the efforts to respect, protect, and fulfil the human rights of women. The prevalence of prejudicial traditional practices and customs that legitimize women's inequality, prevailing particularly in rural areas of most African states, hamper the effective implementation of human rights generally, and of women as a vulnerable group in particular. Although obstacles to women's realization of civil and political rights (CPR), as well as economic, social, and cultural

---

(textile) industry to require women to present non-pregnancy certificates in order to be hired or to avoid being dismissed.'

[17] Human Rights Watch, 'Women's Rights in the Middle East and North Africa', <http://199.173.149.120/women/overview-mena.html>. See *Human Rights for Human Dignity: A Primer on Economic, Social and Cultural Rights* (London: Amnesty International, 2005), 50–1. See also generally S Kelly and J Breslin (eds), *Women's Rights in the Middle East and North Africa* (New York: Freedom House/ Lanham, MD: Rowman & Littlefield, 2010).

[18] See n 14 above, 273 (fn omitted).

[19] CESCR, *Concluding Observations: Liechtenstein*, Future E/C.12/CO/LIE/1 (19 May 2006), 13.

[20] GA Res 34/180, 34 UN GAOR Supp (No 46) 193, UN Doc A/34/4, entered into force 3 September 1981.

[21] UN Press Release, 'High Commissioner for Human Rights Points to Challenges and Opportunities in Promoting Women's Rights', 8 March 2006, <http://www.unhchr.ch/huricane/huricane.nsf/view01/754BA777E8ACE0A6C125712B004B0387?opendocument>.

[22] Statement by the African Union Chairperson, Professor Alpha Oumar Konare in Celebration of the International Women's Day of 8 March 2007 (on file with the author).

rights (ESCR), traditional practices and customs disproportionately affect ESCR since traditionally this category of rights has been often marginalized rather than prioritized.[23] In turn, this marginalization disproportionately affects women since women's lives are lived out largely in the private sphere and women experience disproportionate levels of poverty and resource inequality.[24] Most violations of ESCR (for example, the right to education which plays 'a vital role in empowering women' to participate fully in their communities)[25] often continue unchallenged since they are regarded as not justiciable and thus 'not-quite-rights'.[26] The overwhelming majority of children deprived of basic education, and adults unable to read, are female mainly in sub-Saharan Africa. It is in such a context that '72 million children worldwide were denied the right to education in 2007. Almost half of these children live[d] in sub-Saharan Africa, followed by Southern Asia, home to 18 million out-of-school children.'[27] Without access to the most basic form of education, those denied primary education live in insecurity, they are less likely to claim their human rights, challenge violations of such rights, and lack the power to make their own informed choices, making it difficult to secure a life of dignity for themselves and their family. In Togo, for example, there is an extremely high rate of illiteracy among women, which in 1998 stood at 60.5 per cent in the rural areas and 27.6 per cent in the urban areas.[28] The denial of women's ESCR in turn undermines women's ability to enjoy their CPR, which then limits women's capacity to influence decision and policy making in public life.[29]

[23] See, eg, J Oloka-Onyango, 'Reinforcing Marginalised Rights in the Age of Globalisation: International Mechanisms, Non-State Actors and the Struggle for Peoples' Rights in Africa' (2003) 18(4) American University International Law Review 851–914; S Skogly, 'Crimes Against Humanity—Revisited: Is There a Role for Economic and Social Rights' (2001) 5(1) International Journal of Human Rights 58.

[24] F Banda, 'Understanding Women's Economic and Social Human Rights' (2007) 12(2) East African Journal of Peace & Human Rights 232–53, 237.

[25] CESCR, *General Comment 13: The Right to Education* (21st Session, 1999) UN Doc E/C.12/1999/10 (8 December 1999), 1.

[26] K Tomasevki, 'Has the Right to Education a Future Within the United Nations? A Behind-the-Scenes Account by the Special Rapporteur on the Right to Education 1998–2004' (2005) 5(2) Human Rights Law Review 205–7, 216 noting that: 'As the Cold War has not ended as yet within the [UN Commission on Human Rights], economic, social and cultural rights are still a casualty.'

[27] UN, *The Millennium Development Goals Report* (2009), available at <http://www.un.org/millenniumgoals/pdf/MDG%20Report%202009%20ENG.pdf>, 15. See also K Watkins, *The Oxfam Education Report* (Oxford: Oxfam, 2000), 3 noted: 'Two-thirds of the children not in school—and a similar proportion of adults who are illiterate—are female.'

[28] CEDAW, *Concluding Observations: Togo*, UN Doc CEDAW/C/TGO/CO/3 (3 February 2006), 24–5. Togo's Ministry of Education circular no 8478/MEN-RS prohibits pregnant schoolgirls or students from attending school. This partly accounts for the high dropout rate of girls owing to pregnancy and early and forced marriage and their low enrolment rates in higher education.

[29] See 'Montreal Principles on Women's Economic, Social and Cultural Rights' (2004) 26 Human Rights Quarterly 760–80, 763 (hereinafter 'Montreal Principles').

2.2 Non-discrimination and equality

Systematic discrimination against women denies women equality with men and threatens women's security. In view of the fact that all human beings are born 'free and equal in dignity and rights',[30] the principles of non-discrimination and equality are fundamental components of international human rights law and relevant to the enjoyment of human rights of women.[31] These two principles are included in various international and regional human rights instruments.[32] The main women's human rights instruments in Africa—most notably the African Charter on Human and Peoples' Rights (ACHPR or the African Charter),[33] and the Protocol to the African Charter on Human and Peoples' Rights on the Rights of Women in Africa (African Women's Rights Protocol or the Protocol)[34]— prohibit discrimination and protect the equal enjoyment of the rights of men and women.[35]

It is widely recognized that international norms of non-discrimination and equality, which demand that particular attention be given to vulnerable groups (such as women) and individuals from such groups, are integral elements of

[30] Universal Declaration of Human Rights (UDHR), GA Res 217A (III), UN Doc A/810 at 71 (1948), Art 1.

[31] See A McColgan, 'Principles of Equality and Protection from Discrimination in International Human Rights Law' (2003) 2 European Human Rights Law Review 157–75; M MacEwen, 'Comparative Non-Discrimination Law: An Overview' in T Loenen and P Rodrigues, *Non-Discrimination Law: Comparative Perspectives* (The Hague: Kluwer, 1999), 427–35; M Ssenyonjo, 'Towards Non-Discrimination against Women and De Jure Equality in Uganda: The Role of Uganda's Constitutional Court' (2008) 16(1) African Journal of International and Comparative Law 1–34.

[32] See, eg, UN Charter, 26 June 1945, 59 Stat 1031, TS 993, 3 Bevans 1153, entered into force 24 October 1945, Art 1(3); UDHR, Art 2; International Covenant on Civil and Political Rights (ICCPR), GA Res 2200A (XXI), 21 UN GAOR Supp (No 16) 52, UN Doc A/6316 (1966), 999 UNTS 171, entered into force 23 March 1976, Arts 2(1) and 26; International Covenant on Economic, Social and Cultural Rights (ICESCR), GA Res 2200A (XXI), 21 UN GAOR Supp (No 16), 49, UN Doc A/6316 (1966), 993 UNTS 3, entered into force 3 January 1976, Arts 2(2) and 3; International Convention on the Elimination of All Forms of Racial Discrimination (ICERD), GA Res 2106 (XX), Annex, 20 UN GAOR Supp (No 14) 47, UN Doc A/6014 (1966), 660 UNTS 195, entered into force 4 January 1969, Art 1(1); CEDAW, n 20, Art. 1; [European] Convention for the Protection of Human Rights and Fundamental Freedoms (ECHR), 213 UNTS 222, entered into force 3 September 1953, Art 14; American Convention on Human Rights, OAS Treaty Ser No 36, 1144 UNTS 123, entered into force 18 July 1978 (hereinafter 'AMCHR'), Art. 1; African Charter on Human and Peoples' Rights (ACHPR), adopted 27 June 1981, OAU Doc CAB/LEG/67/3 rev.5, 21 ILM 58 (1982), entered into force 21 October 1986, Art 2; Commonwealth of Independent States Convention on Human Rights and Fundamental Freedoms ('CIS Convention'), <http://hei.unige.ch/~clapham/hrdoc/docs/CIS%20convention.doc> Art 20(2); League of Arab States, Revised Arab Charter on Human Rights, 22 May 2004, reprinted in (2005) 12 IHRR 893, Art 3.

[33] Adopted 27 June 1981, OAU Doc CAB/LEG/67/3 rev.5, 21 ILM 58 (1982), entered into force 21 October 1986. For the analysis, see C Heyns, 'The African Regional Human Rights System: The African Charter' (2004) 108 Penn State Law Review 679–702.

[34] Adopted by the 2nd Ordinary Session of the Assembly of the African Union, Maputo, CAB/LEG/66.6 (11 July 2003); reprinted in 1 African Human Rights Law Journal 40, entered into force 25 November 2005. The Protocol is available at <http://www.achpr.org/english/_info/women_en.html>.   [35] ACHPR, Arts 2, 3, 18(3).

the international human rights normative framework sometimes categorized as norms of *jus cogens*.[36] In the *Barcelona Traction case* the International Court of Justice (ICJ) referred to the category of *erga omnes* obligations as including specifically 'the basic human rights of the human person, including protection from slavery and racial discrimination'.[37] As the ICJ stated in the *Namibia* case 'to enforce distinctions, exclusions, restrictions and limitations exclusively based on grounds of race, colour, descent or national or ethnic origin . . . [constitutes] a denial of fundamental human rights'.[38] Although discrimination on the ground of sex was not included specifically in the category of *jus cogens* above,[39] it would also be difficult for a state to justify a difference in treatment in the enjoyment of human rights based on the sole ground of sex (even if this is based on traditional, religious, or cultural practice, or domestic laws and policies).[40]

In protecting women against *de jure* and *de facto* discrimination, more attention should be paid to the most vulnerable groups of women. While vulnerability varies depending on the context, vulnerable groups of women include refugee women, women migrant workers, the girl child, women with disabilities, and women belonging to an ethnic or religious minority. It is worth noting that international conventions on the rights of refugees, stateless persons, children, migrant workers and members of their families and persons with disabilities oblige respective state parties not to discriminate against these groups.[41] In line with the global protection of women's human rights, the issue of the legal protection of women's human rights in Africa has been addressed in two main human rights instruments, namely the African Charter on Human and Peoples' Rights and its Protocol on the Rights of Women as shown below.

[36] See L Weiwei, *Equality and Non-Discrimination under International Human Rights Law* (Oslo: Norwegian Centre for Human Rights, University of Oslo, 2004) <http://www. mittendrinundaussenvor.de/fileadmin/bilder/0304.pdf>; W Vandenhole, *Non-Discrimination and Equality in the View of the UN Human Rights Treaty Bodies* (Antwerp: Intersentia, 2005).

[37] [1970] ICJ Rep 3, 32.

[38] See *Legal Consequences for States of the Continued Presence of South Africa in Namibia (South West Africa) Notwithstanding Security Council Resolution 276 (1970)*, Advisory Opinion of 21 June 1971 [1971] ICJ Rep 16, 57.

[39] For a discussion see H Charlesworth and C Chinkin, 'The Gender of Jus Cogens' (1993) 15(1) Human Rights Quarterly 63–76.

[40] A similar approach has been applied by the European Court of Human Rights. The Court requires 'very weighty reasons' before a difference of treatment on sole ground of sex could be regarded as compatible with the ECHR. See, eg, *Burghartz v Switzerland*, App No 16213/1990, Judgment of 22 February 1994, [1994] ECHR 2, 27; *Schuler-Zgraggen v Switzerland*, App No 14518/89, Judgment of 24 June 1993 (1993) 16 EHRR 405, 67.

[41] See Convention relating to the Status of Refugees, 189 UNTS 150, entered into force 22 April 1954, Art 3; Convention relating to the Status of Stateless Persons, 360 UNTS 117, entered into force 6 June 1960, Art 3; Convention on the Rights of the Child, GA Res 44/25, annex, 44 UN GAOR Supp (No 49) at 167, UN Doc A/44/49 (1989), entered into force 2 September 1990, Art 2; International Convention on the Protection of the Rights of All Migrant Workers and Members of Their Families, GA Res 45/158, annex, 45 UN GAOR Supp (No 49A) 262, UN Doc A/45/49 (1990), entered into force 1 July 2003, Arts 1 and 7; International Convention on the Protection and Promotion of the Rights and Dignity of Persons with Disabilities, GA Res 61/106, Annex I, UN GAOR, 61st Sess, Supp No 49, 65, UN Doc A/61/49 (2006), entered into force 3 May 2008, Arts 2, 3 and 4.

2.3 The African Charter and the Rights of Women in Africa

The African Charter on Human and Peoples' Rights contains four main provisions protecting women against discrimination. First is the general non-discrimination clause contained in Article 2 of the Charter, which states: 'Every individual shall be entitled to the enjoyment of the rights and freedoms recognised and guaranteed in the present Charter without distinction of any kind such as . . . sex.' Secondly, Article 3 of the Charter reinforces this provision and deals with equal protection in the following terms: '(1) Every individual shall be equal before the law; (2) Every individual shall be entitled to equal protection of the law.' Thirdly, for the avoidance of doubt, Article 18(3) of the Charter, which generally deals with the protection of the family states:

The State shall ensure the elimination of *every* discrimination against women and also ensure the protection of the rights of the woman and the child as stipulated in international declarations and conventions. (Emphasis added.)

Finally, Article 60 of the Charter states that the African Commission on Human and Peoples' Rights (the African Commission) will draw inspiration from international human rights instruments (such as CEDAW). In view of the above provisions, which clearly prohibit discrimination against women on the basis of sex, why was it considered necessary to adopt an additional protocol to the African Charter on the rights of women?

The answer lies in the fact that the above provisions were considered inadequate to address the human rights of women in Africa. For example, while Article 18 prohibits discrimination against women, it does so only in the context of the family. In addition, explicit provisions guaranteeing the right of consent to marriage and equality of spouses during and after marriage are absent. These omissions are compounded by the fact that the Charter places emphasis on traditional African values and traditions without addressing concerns that many customary practices, such as female genital mutilation, forced marriage, and wife inheritance, can be harmful or life threatening to women. By Article 18(2) of the Charter: 'The State shall have the duty to assist the family which is the custodian of morals and traditional values recognized by the community.' Under Article 29(7) the individual has a duty

to preserve and strengthen positive African cultural values in his relations with other members of the society, in the spirit of tolerance, dialogue and consultation and, in general, to contribute to the promotion of the moral well being of society.

What are the 'positive African cultural values'? Can this provision be interpreted as protecting discriminatory cultural practices against women?

The scope of 'positive African cultural values' is subject to debate. Given that gender inequality in Africa is entrenched in all societal structures, positive African cultural values could possibly reinforce masculine and patriarchal prejudices that are discriminatory against women. However, if this is interpreted in light of the overall object and purpose of the African Charter, Article 29(7) cannot be properly interpreted as trumping the non-discrimination provisions in the Charter.[42] Thus, taken in its totality as a human rights treaty, it is arguable that the 'positive African values' described in the African Charter are those that are consonant with the principles of equality and non-discrimination. In this respect, a progressive and liberal construction of the Charter as a 'living instrument' would clearly leave no room for the discriminatory treatment of women.[43] The adoption by the African Commission, in *Legal Resources Foundation v Zambia*, of the definition of discrimination drawn by the HRC in *General Comment 18*, which itself is based on CEDAW Article 1 and CERD Article 1, suggests that there can be no derogation of the equality principle, not even for culture.[44] Finally, the African Commission guidelines to states on reporting, which are based on CEDAW reporting guidelines, encompass both public and private sphere violations.[45] Interpreting the Charter in light of the present day conditions would thus entail holding a state responsible for human rights violations by non-state actors (including individuals, groups, corporations, and other entities as well as agents acting under their authority) where a state fails to prevent non-state actors from interfering in any way with the enjoyment of human rights of women,[46] or in some contexts holding non-state actors directly responsible for violations of women's human rights.

By and large, however, by ignoring making explicit provisions to critical issues affecting women such as custom and marriage, it was argued that the African Charter inadequately protects women's human rights.[47] It is against this background that during its 23rd Session held in April 1998, the African Commission endorsed the appointment of the first Special Rapporteur on the Rights of Women in Africa with a mandate that included working towards the adoption and ratification of the Protocol to the African Charter on the Rights of Women in Africa and making recommendations geared towards improving the situation

---

[42] See C Beyani, 'Toward a More Effective Guarantee of Women's Rights in the African Human Rights System' in R Cook (ed), *Human Rights of Women: National and International Perspectives* (Philadelphia, PA: University of Pennsylvania Press, 1994), 285.

[43] M Mutua, 'The African Human Rights System: A Critical Evaluation' <http://hdr.undp.org/en/reports/global/hdr2000/papers/mutua.pdf> 9.

[44] See the African Commission on Human and Peoples' Rights, *Legal Resources Foundation v Zambia*, Comm No 211/98, Decisions on Communications Brought before the African Commission, 29th Ordinary Session (Tripoli, May 2001) 63; HRC, *General Comment 18: Non-Discrimination* (37th Session, 1989), UN Doc HRI/GEN/1/Rev.1 (1994), 26.

[45] F Viljoen, 'State Reporting under the African Charter on Human and Peoles' Rights: A Boost from the South' (2000) 44(1) Journal of African Law 110.

[46] See the African Commission on Human and Peoples' Rights in *Zimbabwe Human Rights NGO Forum v Zimbabwe*, Communication No 245/2002, Annex III, Twenty-first Annual Activity Report, 54. For a commentary see C Beyani, 'Recent Developments in the African Human Rights System 2004–2006' (2007) 7(3) Human Rights Law Review 582–608, 604–8.

[47] M Wandia, 'Rights of Women in Africa: Launch of Petition to the African Union' (June 2004) <http://www.choike.org/nuevo_eng/informes/1944.html>.

of Women in Africa.[48] What are the prospects of Africa's Protocol on Women's Rights? Does it provide a strong legal basis for the protection of women's human rights which in turns contributes to women's security?

2.4 Protocol to the African Charter on the Rights of Women in Africa

The Protocol was adopted on 11 July 2003 during the Second Ordinary Heads of States and Governments Summit held in Maputo, Mozambique. It was a long-awaited realization, as it had taken eight years for the draft text of this critical new human rights instrument for African women to be adopted. On 25 November 2005, the Protocol came into force having received the required 15 ratifications. By 26 May 2007, nearly four years after the adoption of the Protocol, only 21 (out of 53) African states had ratified the Protocol.[49] The reluctance to ratify the Protocol is itself indicative of attitudes towards women's human rights in Africa. However, human rights instruments in Africa have historically taken a long time to be ratified and enter into force due to the lack of political will. The African Charter, adopted in 1981, only came into force five years later in 1986; the Protocol establishing the African Court on Human and Peoples' Rights came into force in 2004, six years after its adoption in 1998; and the African Charter on the Rights and Welfare of the Child,[50] which was adopted in 1990, took nine years to enter into force.

The Protocol protects the civil and political rights of women, their economic, social, and cultural rights and also their collective rights.[51] Apart from re-emphasizing and extending UN instruments on human rights of women, the Protocol enshrines the mainstreaming of human rights and gender equality in African affairs,[52] an objective and principle of the African Union (AU).[53] The specific

---

[48] ACHR, Special Rapporteur on Women's Rights: Resolution and Mandate <http://www.achpr.org/english/_info/index_women_en.html#1>; ACHPR, Background Information on the Mandate of the Special Rapporteur on the Rights of Women in Africa, <http://www.chr.up.ac.za/ggp/coursematerial/gen_equality/Background%20S.R.W.R%20ACHPR.doc>; F Banda, 'Blazing a Trail: The African Protocol on Women's Rights Comes into Force' (2006) 50(1) Journal of African Law 72.

[49] These were Benin, Burkina Faso, Cape Verde, Comoros, Djibouti, Gambia, Libya, Lesotho, Mali, Malawi, Mozambique, Mauritania, Namibia, Nigeria, Seychelles, Rwanda, South Africa, Senegal, Tanzania, Togo, and Zambia. See African Commission website at: <http://www.achpr.org/english/ratifications/ratification_women%20protocol.pdf>.

[50] OAU Doc CAB/LEG/24.9/49 (1990), entered into force 29 November 1999.

[51] See M Ssenyonjo, 'Protocol to the African Charter on Human and Peoples' Rights on the Rights of Women in Africa: Introductory Note' (2004) 11 International Human Rights Reports 859; M Baderin, 'Recent Developments in the African Regional Human Rights System' (2005) 5 Human Rights Law Review 117–24; F Banda, 'Protocol to the African Charter on the Rights of Women in Africa' in MD Evans and R Murray (eds), *The African Charter on Human and Peoples' Rights: The System in Practice*, 1986–2006 (2nd edn, Cambridge: Cambridge University Press, 2008), 441–74.

[52] VO Nmehielle, 'Development of the African Human Rights System in the Last Decade' (2004) 11(3) Human Rights Brief 6.

[53] Constitutive Act of the African Union, OAU Doc CAB/LEG/23.15, entered into force 26 May 2001, Art 3(h) states: 'The objectives of the Union shall be to: Promote and protect human

rights protected under the Protocol are, broadly, the rights to: non-discrimination (Article 2); dignity (Article 3); life, integrity, and security of the person (Article 4); equal rights in a marriage separation, divorce, or annulment of marriage (Articles 6 and 7); access to justice and equal protection before the law (Article 8); participation in the political and decision-making process (Article 9); peace (Article 10); protection of women in armed conflicts (Article 11); education and training (Article 12); economic and social welfare rights (Article 13); health and reproductive rights including a woman's right to have 'medical abortion in cases of sexual assault, rape, incest, and where the continued pregnancy endangers the mental and physical health of the mother or the life of the mother or the foetus' (Article 14);[54] food security (Article 15); adequate housing (Article 16); live in a 'positive cultural context' (Article 17); healthy and sustainable environment (Article 18); sustainable development (Article 19); widows' rights (Article 20); and inheritance (Article 21). The Protocol contains special provisions protecting elderly women (Article 22), women with disabilities (Article 23), and women in distress (Article 24). Some human rights (such as the rights of women to vote, own property, and to participate in the cultural life of the community itself) are not specifically mentioned. However, there is no evidence to suggest that this was deliberate.

Article 26 of the Protocol states the obligations of the state parties in the following terms.

1. States Parties shall ensure the implementation of this Protocol at national level, and in their periodic reports submitted in accordance with Article 62 of the African Charter, indicate the legislative and other measures undertaken for the full realisation of the rights herein recognised.
2. States Parties undertake to adopt all necessary measures and in particular shall provide budgetary and other resources for the full and effective implementation of the rights herein recognised.

In particular, states parties are obliged by Article 5 of the Protocol to take all 'necessary legislative' and 'other measures' to eliminate harmful practices which negatively affect the human rights of women and which are contrary to recognized international standards, including:

(a) creation of public awareness in all sectors of society regarding harmful practices through information, formal, and informal education and outreach programmes;
(b) prohibition, through legislative measures backed by sanctions, of all forms of female genital mutilation, scarification, medicalization and paramedicalization of female genital mutilation and all other practices in order to eradicate them;

and peoples' rights …'. Article 4(1)(l) provides: 'The Union shall function in accordance with the following principles: Promotion of gender equality'. See K Stefiszyn, 'The African Union: Challenges and Opportunities for Women' (2005) 5 African Human Rights Law Journal 358.

[54] See also HRC, Karen, *Noelia Llantoy Huamán v Peru*, Communication No 1153/2003, UN Doc CCPR/C/85/D/1153/2003 (2005).

(c) provision of necessary support to victims of harmful practices through basic services such as health services, legal and judicial support, emotional and psychological counselling, as well as vocational training to make them self-supporting;

(d) protection of women who are at risk of being subjected to harmful practices or all other forms of violence, abuse, and intolerance.

Unlike some human rights treaties,[55] the Protocol neither prohibits the formulation of reservations (either expressly or impliedly) nor mentions any permitted type of reservation(s). During the drafting of the Protocol, it was suggested by the Southern African Development Community member states (SADC group) that reservations should be expressly prohibited, but this suggestion was not taken up.[56] While this position was adopted to secure wider ratification of the Protocol by African states which consider that they have difficulties in guaranteeing all the rights in the Protocol but can nonetheless accept the generality of obligations in that instrument, it left some questions unaddressed. First, what reservations are permissible (or not permissible) under the Protocol given that it does not exclude or permit the possibility of reservations? Secondly, who should decide whether a reservation under the Protocol is invalid? Is it a matter exclusively for a reserving state and those states objecting to such reservations or should the African Court pronounce on the compatibility with the object and purpose, when the need arises? And if a reservation under the Protocol is invalid, what legal remedy should follow the determination of a reservation to the Protocol as invalid (unacceptable, irregular, impermissible, or inadmissible)?

In accordance with the rules of customary international law that are reflected in Article 19 of the Vienna Convention on the Law of Treaties,[57] reservations can be made to the Protocol, provided they are compatible with the object and

---

[55] See, eg, Convention for the Protection of Human Rights and Fundamental Freedoms, signed at Rome 4 November 1950, 213 UNTS 222, entered into force 3 September 1953 (ECHR). Article 57 ECHR provides:

> 1. Any State may, when signing this Convention or when depositing its instrument of ratification, make a reservation in respect of any particular provision of the Convention to the extent that any law then in force in its territory is not in conformity with the provision. Reservations of a general character shall not be permitted under this article.
> 2. Any reservation made under this article shall contain a brief statement of the law concerned.

See also the Convention against Discrimination in Education, 429 UNTS 93, entered into force 22 May 1962. Article 9 states: 'Reservations to this Convention shall not be permitted.' See also Supplementary Convention on the abolition of slavery, the slave trade and institutions and practices similar to slavery, 226 UNTS 3, entered into force 30 April 1957, Art 9 stating that 'No reservations may be made to this Convention.'

[56] F Banda, *Women, Law and Human Rights: An African Perspective* (Oxford: Hart Publishing, 2005), 75–9.

[57] Done at Vienna on 23 May 1969, entered into force 27 January 1980, 1155 UNTS 331, 8 ILM 679, Art 19; A Aust, *Modern Treaty Law and Practice* (2nd edn, Cambridge: Cambridge University Press, 2007), 125–61.

purpose of the Protocol. A reservation would be incompatible with the object and purpose of the Protocol if it has a 'serious impact' on the essential rules, rights, or obligations indispensable to the general architecture of the Protocol, thereby depriving it of its raison d'être.[58] This must also include all interpretative declarations whose effect is that of reservations. This is consistent with the practice in other existing international human rights treaties such as CEDAW,[59] the Convention on the Rights of the Child (CRC),[60] and the ICERD,[61] all of which protect some human rights of women and prohibit expressly reservations that are incompatible with the object and purpose of the respective treaties. It is also in line with the conclusions reached by the ICJ in its Advisory Opinion of 28 May 1951 in the case concerning *Reservations to the Convention on the Prevention and Punishment of the Crime of Genocide* (1951 ICJ Advisory Opinion).[62]

It is useful to note that in accordance with state practice, not all reservations to substantive provisions of a human rights treaty are inherently incompatible with the object and purpose of a particular treaty. However, reservations that offend peremptory or higher norms (*jus cogens*)[63] or obligations that concern or bind all states (obligations *erga omnes*) and norms of customary international law would arguably be difficult to reconcile with the object and purpose of the treaty.[64] For

---

[58] See Tenth Report on Reservations to Treaties, UN Doc A/CN.4/558/Add.1 (see n 1 above) 14, Guideline 3.1.5, and UN Doc A/CN.4/572 (21 June 2006), 3, 7–8.

[59] Art 28(2) CEDAW states: 'A reservation incompatible with the object and purpose of the present Convention shall not be permitted'.

[60] GA Res 44/25, annex, 44 UN GAOR Supp (No 49) at 167, UN Doc A/44/49 (1989), entered into force 2 September 1990. For the text of declarations and reservations to the CRC, see UN Treaty Collection at: <http://www2.ohchr.org/english/bodies/crc/index.htm>. For analysis see WA Schabas, 'Reservations to the Convention on the Rights of the Child' (1996) 18(2) Human Rights Quarterly 472–91 and K Hashemi, 'Religious Legal Traditions, Muslim States and the Convention on the Rights of the Child: An Essay on the Relevant UN Documentation' (2007) 29(1) Human Rights Quarterly 194–227. Article 51(2) CRC provides: 'A reservation incompatible with the object and purpose of the present Convention shall not be permitted'.

[61] GA Res 2106 (XX) Annex, 20 UN GAOR Supp (No 14) 47, UN Doc A/6014 (1966) 660 UNTS 195, entered into force 4 January 1969. Article 20(2) CERD provides:

> A reservation incompatible with the object and purpose of this Convention shall not be permitted, nor shall a reservation the effect of which would inhibit the operation of any of the bodies established by this Convention be allowed. A reservation shall be considered incompatible or inhibitive if at least two thirds of the States Parties to this Convention object to it.

[62] [1951] ICJ Rep 62, 15. The ICJ noted that: 'The object and purpose of the Convention thus limit both the freedom of making reservations and that of objecting to them'.

[63] Vienna Convention, Art 53 defines a 'peremptory norm' of general international law (also called *jus cogens*, Latin for 'compelling law') as 'a norm accepted and recognised by the international community of States as a whole as a norm from which no derogation is permitted and which can be modified only by a subsequent norm of general international law having the same character'. On the effect of *jus cogens*, see U Linderfalk, 'The Effect of Jus Cogens Norms: Whoever Opened Pandora's Box, Did You Ever Think About the Consequences?' (2008) 18(5) EJIL 853–71.

[64] See HRC, *General Comment 24(52), General Comment on issues relating to reservations made upon ratification or accession to the Covenant or the Optional Protocols thereto, or in relation to declarations under article 41 of the Covenant* [ICCPR], UN Doc CCPR/C/21/Rev.1/Add.6 (1994), 8. For a discussion see CJ Redgwell, 'Reservations to Treaties and Human Rights Committee General

example, a reservation to the obligation to combat all forms of discrimination against women (Article 2) would not be acceptable. Nor may a state reserve an entitlement not to take the necessary steps at the domestic level to give effect to the rights protected in the Protocol (Article 26). Reservations to CEDAW made by Egypt, Libyan Arab Jamahiriya, Mauritania, and Morocco specifically referred to the traditional male-centred interpretations of Islamic law (*Sharia*) provisions.[65] In particular, Egypt's reservation to Article 16 of CEDAW, concerning the equality of men and women in all matters relating to marriage and family relations during the marriage and upon its dissolution, states:

The provisions of the *Sharia* lay down that the husband shall pay bridal money to the wife and maintain her fully and shall also make a payment to her upon divorce, whereas the wife retains full rights over her property and is not obliged to spend anything on her keep. The *Sharia* therefore restricts the wife's rights to divorce by making it contingent on a judge's ruling, whereas no such restriction is laid down in the case of the husband.[66]

The CEDAW Committee has urged states to expedite the steps necessary for the withdrawal of such reservations incompatible with the object and purpose of the Convention.[67] In particular, the Committee's view is that Articles 2 and 16 of CEDAW are central to the object and purpose of the Convention and that, in accordance with Article 28, paragraph 2, they should be withdrawn.[68] However, states have continued to observe these reservations in practice and thus violate human rights of women.

In recent years, there has been a tendency for some states, and certain commentators, to view the 1951 ICJ Advisory Opinion as stipulating a regime of inter-state laissez-faire in the matter of reservations, in the sense that while the object and purpose of a convention should be borne in mind both by those making reservations and those objecting to them, everything in the final analysis is left to the states themselves.[69] According to this view, no one beyond the

---

Comment No 24(52)' (1997) 46 ICLQ 390–412; EA Baylis, 'General Comment 24: Confronting the Problem of Reservations to Human Rights Treaties' (1999) 17 Berkeley Journal of International Law 277–329; K Korkeli, 'New Challenges to the Regime of Reservations under the International Covenant on Civil and Political Rights' (2002) 13(2) EJIL 437–77; S Joseph et al, *The International Covenant on Civil and Political Rights: Cases, Materials and Commentary* (2nd edn, Oxford: Oxford University Press, 2004), 797–819.

[65] See Declarations, Reservations and Objections to CEDAW, available at: <http://www.un.org/womenwatch/daw/cedaw/reservations-country.htm>. Although Egypt has withdrawn its reservation to Art 9(2) of CEDAW, it has maintained the reservations in respect of Arts 2 and 16.

[66] Ibid.

[67] See the CEDAW Committee's statement on reservations in the report on the 19th Session, *Official Records of the General Assembly, Fifty-third Session, Supplement No 38*, UN Doc A/53/38/Rev.1, part two, ch I.

[68] CEDAW, *Concluding Observations: Egypt*, UN Doc CEDAW A/56/38 (2001) 327.

[69] ICJ Rep, *Judgment of 3 February 2006, Armed activities on the territory of the Congo (New Application: 2002) (Democratic Republic of the Congo v Rwanda), Jurisdiction of the Court and Admissibility of the Application* (hereinafter '*Congo v Rwanda*'), Joint separate opinion of Judges Higgins, Kooijmans, Elaraby, Owada, and Simma, para 4.

states themselves has anything to say on reservations. It should, however, be noted that the 1951 ICJ Advisory Opinion did not foreclose legal developments in respect of the law on reservations and should not be read in such a restrictive way.[70]

The practice of the relevant human rights bodies supports this view. For example, the European Court of Human Rights, the Inter-American Court of Human Rights, and the HRC have not followed the 'laissez faire' approach attributed to the 1951 ICJ Advisory Opinion; they have pronounced on the compatibility of specific reservations to the ECHR, the American Convention on Human Rights, and the ICCPR respectively.[71] They have not thought that it was simply a matter of bilateral sets of obligations, left to individual assessment of the states parties to the Convention concerned. The practice of such bodies is not to be viewed as 'making an exception' to the law as determined in 1951 by the ICJ; but rather a development of the law to meet contemporary realities or to cover what the Court was never asked at that time, and to address new issues that have arisen subsequently.[72] In addition, the practice of the ICJ itself reflects this trend. For example, in 2006 in *Congo v Rwanda*,[73] the ICJ considered the impact of Rwanda's reservation to Article IX of the Genocide Convention. The ICJ made its own assessment of the compatibility of such a reservation[74] and went beyond noting that a reservation had been made by one state, which did not occasion an objection by the other. The Court found that Rwanda's reservation 'does not appear contrary to the object and purpose of the Convention'.[75] The ICJ's opinion supports the view that the compatibility of the reservation with the object and purpose of the treaty is subject to assessment by the competent (judicial and quasi-judicial) bodies.

Accordingly the African Commission, in the course of monitoring the legislative and other measures undertaken for the full realization of the rights recognized in the Protocol (Article 26), and the African Court of Justice and Human Rights (in the course of the interpretation of matters arising from the application or implementation of this Protocol under Article 27), should assess the compatibility of reservations to the Protocol on Women's Rights in Africa with the object

---

[70] Ibid, 13; R Higgins, 'Human Rights in the International Court of Justice' (2007) 20(4) Leiden Journal of International Law 745–51, 746–47.

[71] See in particular, *Belilos v Switzerland*, Judgment of 29 April 1988, ECHR (1988) Ser A, Vol 132 (1988) 10 EHRR 466; *Loizidou v Turkey*, Judgment of 23 March 1995, Ser A No 310; *The Effect of Reservations on the Entry Into Force of the American Convention*, Advisory Opinion OC-2/82, Inter-American Court of Human Rights (ser A) No 2 (1982); *Restrictions to the Death Penalty*; Advisory Opinion OC-3/83, Inter-American Court of Human Rights (ser A) No 3 (1983); *Rawle Kennedy v Trinidad and Tobago*, HRC, Communication No 845, UN Doc CCPR/C/67D/845/1999 (31 December 1999). This trend was observed in a Separate Opinion referred to in n 69 above, para 16.   [72] See *Congo v Rwanda* (n 69 above) 16 and 22.

[73] *Congo v Rwanda* (see n 69 above).   [74] Ibid, 67.

[75] See *Armed Activities on the Territory of the Congo (New Application: 2002) (Democratic Republic of the Congo v Rwanda)*, Provisional Measures, Order of 10 July 2002 [2002] ICJ Rep 246, para 72.

and purpose of the Protocol. To assess the compatibility of a reservation with the object and purpose of the Protocol, account should be taken of the following:[76] (a) the indivisibility and interdependence of the rights set out in the Protocol; (b) the importance that the right (or rights) which is (or are) the subject of the reservation has (or have) within the general architecture of the Protocol, and (c) the seriousness of the impact the reservation has (or is intended to have) upon a particular right, relevant rights or the Protocol as a whole. Impermissible reservations are likely to include any general and broad reservations subjecting the Protocol to domestic law incompatible with the Protocol or those extending to minimum core obligations which are non-derogable and thereby depriving the Protocol of its raison d'être.

The Commission can advance the protection of women's rights in Africa by requiring reserving states through their reports to explain: (a) the nature and scope of reservations or interpretative declarations; (b) the reason(s) why such reservations were considered to be necessary and have been maintained; (c) the precise effect of each reservation in terms of national law and policy; (d) any plans to limit or modify the effect of reservations and ultimately withdraw them within a specific time frame.[77] Where applicable, the Commission in its recommendations to states could highlight the lack of consistency among reservations formulated to certain provisions protected in more than one treaty and encourage the withdrawal, whether total or partial, of a reservation on the basis of the availability of better protection in other international conventions resulting from the absence of a reservation to comparable provisions. On its part, the Court should treat reservations incompatible with the object and purpose of the Protocol as invalid, and therefore of no legal effect. Unless a state party chooses to withdraw from the Protocol (this may not be legally possible because the Protocol does not provide for denunciation or withdrawal and it does not have a temporary character typical of treaties where a right of denunciation is deemed to be admitted, notwithstanding the absence of a specific provision to that effect), such reservations should generally be severable. This means that the Protocol will be operative for the reserving state without benefit of the reservation, however phrased or named.

2.5 The state of women's rights in Africa in practice

Every state in Africa is a party to at least one international treaty prohibiting discrimination on the basis of sex in the enjoyment of human rights or a party to an international treaty providing for the equal rights of men and women to the enjoyment of all human rights. Despite this, it is essential to note:

(1) Women are often denied equal enjoyment of their human rights, in particular by virtue of the lesser status ascribed to them by tradition and

---

[76] See Alain Pellet, Tenth Report on Reservations to Treaties, UN Doc A/CN.4/558/Add.1, 7.

[77] See also Report of the Meeting of the Working Group on Reservations, UN Doc HRI/MC/2007/5, para 16 (9); HRC, *General Comment 24(52)* (see n 64 above) 20.

custom, or as a result of overt or covert discrimination. Many women experience distinct forms of discrimination due to the intersection of sex with such factors as race, colour, language, religion, political and other opinion, national or social origin, property, birth, or other status, such as age, ethnicity, disability, marital, refugee, or migrant status, resulting in compounded disadvantage.[78]

(2) For example, persons with mental disabilities are often subjected to human rights abuses including: rape and sexual abuse by other users or staff; forced sterilizations; being chained to soiled beds for long periods of time, and, in some cases being held inside cages; violence and torture; the administration of treatment without informed consent; grossly inadequate sanitation; and a lack of food.[79] However, women with mental disabilities are especially vulnerable to forced sterilization and sexual violence, a violation of their sexual and reproductive health rights.[80] Moreover, women with disabilities belonging to ethnic and racial minorities often experience compounded disadvantage due to the intersection of sex with ethnicity and race though this has been historically neglected.[81] This is because

Certain forms of racial discrimination may be directed towards women specifically because of their gender, such as sexual violence committed against women members of particular racial or ethnic groups in detention or during armed conflict; the coerced sterilization of indigenous women; abuse of women workers in the informal sector or domestic workers employed abroad by their employers.[82]

In Libya, for example, there are 'numerous reports about the existence of racial prejudices against Black Africans, which on some occasions has led to acts of violence against them'.[83] Women have been the worst victims since the human rights of women are often subordinated to rigid social norms condoned and reinforced by the Libyan government.[84] Consequently, there are circumstances in which

---

[78] CESCR, *General Comment No 16*, E/C.12/2005/4 (11 August 2005), 5.

[79] P Hunt, *Report of the Special Rapporteur on the Right of Everyone to the Enjoyment of the Highest Attainable Standard of Physical and Mental Health*, E/CN.4/2005/51 (11 February 2005), 9.

[80] Ibid, 12; KL Raye, *Women's Rights Advocacy Initiative: Violence, Women, and Mental Disability* (Washington, DC: Mental Disability Rights International, 1999); L Dowse and C Frohmader, *Moving Forward: Sterilisation and Reproductive Health of Women and Girls with Disabilities* (Rosny Park: Women with Disabilities, 2001).

[81] CESCR, *General Comment No 5, Persons with Disabilities* (11th Session, 1994), UN Doc E/1995/22 (1995), 19 stating: 'Persons with disabilities are sometimes treated as genderless human beings. As a result, the double discrimination suffered by women with disabilities is often neglected.'

[82] CERD, *General Recommendation No 25: Gender Related Dimensions of Racial Discrimination*, UN Doc A/55/18 (20 March 2000), Annex V, 2.

[83] CESCR, *Concluding Observations: Libyan Arab Jamahiriya*, E/C.12/LYB/CO/2 (25 January 2006), 12.

[84] Human Rights Watch, *Libya: A Threat to Society? Arbitrary Detention of Women and Girls for 'Social Rehabilitation'*, February 2006, vol 18, no 2(E) <http://hrw.org/reports/2006/libya0206/>.

discrimination (on grounds of disability or race) only or primarily affects women, or affects women in a different way, or to a different degree than men. For example, women often have less access to education and health care than men which compromises their opportunities for employment and advancement.[85] For instance, in 2006 in Botswana women refugees had 'access neither to the Anti Retroviral (ARV) Therapy Programme nor the Prevention of Mother-to-Child Transmission of [the] HIV Programme'.[86] Therefore, despite the ratification of human rights instruments by the majority of African states, women in Africa still continue to be 'victims of discrimination and harmful practices' which violate the human rights of women.[87] In some states critical issues affecting women's human rights are excluded from constitutional provisions of non-discrimination. For example, section 15(4)(c) of the Constitution of Botswana 1966 exempts 'adoption, marriage, divorce, burial, devolution of property on death or other matters of personal law' from the prohibition of discrimination. This provides a legal basis for authorization of violations of women's rights to equality and non-discrimination as this provision impairs gender equality and leads to gender discrimination in the family. In Senegal the husband is still the head of the family and is vested with the authority to make decisions 'in the common interest of the household and children' (see *Code La Famille Senegalaise* 1972, Article 152). One of the key obstacles to the realization of women's human rights in Africa is deeply rooted in culture.

3. Prejudicial cultural practices and customs as an obstacle to the realization of women's human rights in Africa

3.1 African culture in general

Although various definitions of 'culture' have been postulated, culture encompasses, inter alia:

ways of life, language, oral and written literature, music and song, non-verbal communication, religion or belief systems, rites and ceremonies, sport and games, methods of production or technology, natural and man-made environments, food, clothing and shelter and the arts, customs and traditions through which individuals, groups of individuals and communities express their humanity and the meaning they give to their existence, and build their world view representing their encounter with the external forces affecting their lives. Culture shapes and mirrors the values of well-being and the economic, social and political life of individuals, groups of individuals and communities.[88]

---

[85] CESCR, *General Comment No 18: The Right to Work*, E/C.12/GC/18 (6 February 2006), 13.

[86] CERD, *Concluding Observations: Botswana*, CERD/C/BWA/CO/16 (4 April 2006), 19.

[87] African Women's Rights Protocol, preamble, 12.

[88] CESCR, *General Comment 21: Right of Everyone to Take Part in Cultural Life (Art 15, para 1(a), of the International Covenant on Economic, Social and Cultural Rights)*, UN Doc E/C.12/GC/21 (21

In this respect, culture is a macro concept, which subsumes religion as an aspect of culture.[89] It is important to note that cultures have no fixed borders and this is clear given that the phenomena of migration, integration, assimilation, and globalization have brought cultures, groups, and individuals into closer contact than ever before, at a time when each of them is striving to keep their own identity in a diverse and multicultural world.[90]

Although a number of African states have ratified treaties which guarantee the equality of men and women and have incorporated the principles of equality and non-discrimination into national constitutions, the persistence of deep-rooted adverse patriarchal attitudes and firmly entrenched stereotypes with respect to the role of women and men in the family and society limit the full implementation of the human rights of women.[91] The widespread and continuing existence of harmful traditional practices in African states affect the equal right of men and women to the enjoyment of all human rights.[92] While it is acknowledged that culture (as reflected in customary law in Africa) in some cases can protect some of women's human rights, the prevalence in Africa of certain harmful traditions, customs, and cultural practices (often enforced as customary law which is largely patriarchal and systematically oppressive toward women) leads to substantial discrimination against women thereby preventing them from fully exercising their human rights.[93] Although 'everyone' has a right to cultural participation,[94] including cultural rights of

December 2009), para 13. For various definition of culture see R Stavenhagen, 'Cultural Rights: A Social Science Perspective' in H Niec (ed), *Cultural Rights and Wrongs: A Collection of Essays in Commemoration of the 50th Anniversary of the Universal Declaration of Human Rights* (Paris/ Leicester: UNESCO Publishing and Institute of Art and Law, 1998), 1–20. See also F Raday, 'Culture, Religion, and Gender' (2004) 1(4) International Journal of Constitutional Law 663–715, 665–6.

[89] See Raday (n 88 above) 665.　　　[90] CESCR, *General Comment 21* (n 88 above) para 41.

[91] See, eg, CEDAW, *Concluding Observations: Botswana*, UN Doc CEDAW/C/BOT/CO/3 (5 February 2010), para 23; *Mali*, UN Doc CEDAW/C/MLI/CO/5 (3 February 2006), 17; *Egypt*, A/56/38 (2 February 2001), 325; *Cameroon*, A/55/38 (26 June 2000), 53–4; *Democratic Republic of Congo*, A/55/38 (1 February 2000), 230–2; *Guinea*, A/56/38 (31 July 2001), 122, 138; *United Republic of Tanzania*, A/53/38/Rev.1 (6 July 1998), 229–30. See also S Williams, 'Nigeria, Its Women and International Law: Beyond Rhetoric' (2004) 4(2) Human Rights Law Review 229–55.

[92] See, eg, CESCR, *Concluding Observations: Zambia*, UN Doc E/C.12/1/Add.106 (23 June 2005), 10 noting that 'the persistence of customs and traditions harmful to women' is one of the factors impeding the implementation of the ICESCR.

[93] Ibid, 14, 23, 32. In para 23, the CESCR was 'concerned about the harsh living conditions of widows and girl orphans due to, among other things, harmful traditional practices such as "widow-cleansing", early marriages and denial of inheritance'. Similarly, in para 32 the CESCR noted that in Zambia 'traditional attitudes [against girl education] continue and that discrimination against girl children is prevalent in the State party'. See also n 88 above, 663–715.

[94] See ICESCR, Art 5(a); UDHR, Art 27(1) stating: 'Everyone has the right freely to participate in the cultural life of the community…'; CERD, Art 5(e)(vi); the Additional Protocol to the American Convention on Human Rights in the Area of Economic, Social and Cultural Rights (Protocol of San Salvador), Art 14; and ACHPR, Art 17(2).

specific groups,[95] African cultures and traditions as they presently exist are mainly made for and by men![96] In Eritrea, for example, while participation in the National Service creates eligibility for access to land and other economic resources, women are exempt from the National Service on grounds of marriage, thus losing eligibility for access to land and other resources.[97] This serves to perpetuate women's subordination in the family and society and constitutes serious obstacles to women's enjoyment of their human rights.

Some of these cultures are enforced through (criminal) legislation. The Nigerian Penal Code offers an excellent example. It permits husbands to use physical means to chastise their wives as long as it does not result in 'grievous harm', which is defined as loss of sight, hearing, power of speech, facial disfigurement, or life-threatening injuries.[98] In more traditional areas of Nigeria, the courts and police have been reluctant to intervene to protect women who formally accused their husbands of abuse if the level of alleged abuse did not exceed customary norms in the areas.[99] This has denied women in Africa 'the right to live in a positive cultural context and to participate at all levels in the determination of cultural policies' affecting their lives.[100] The right of everyone to cultural participation seeks to encourage the active contribution of all members of society to the progress of society as a whole. As such, it is intrinsically linked to, and is dependent on the enjoyment of, the other human rights such as the right to own property alone as well as in association with others,[101] the freedom of expression

---

[95] See ICCPR, Art 27; CEDAW, Art 13(c); the CRC, UNGA Res 44/25, annex, 44 UN GAOR Supp (No 49) 167, UN Doc A/44/49 (1989), entered into force 2 September 1990, Art 31 and the International Convention on the Rights of All Migrant Workers and Members of their Families, UNGA Res. 45/158 (18 December 1990) entered into force 1 July 2003, Art 31.

[96] J Oloka-Onyango, 'Who's Watching "Big Brother"? Globalization and the Protection of Cultural Rights in Present Day Africa' 2005 (4) Human Rights Quarterly 1245–73, 1268. Courts have upheld some discriminatory cultural practices against women. Eg, in the case of *Mifumi (U) Ltd & 12 others v Attorney General and Kenneth Kakuru*, Constitutional Petition No 12 of 2007 [2010] UGCC 2 (26 March 2010), the Constitutional Court of Uganda by a majority decision of four to one held that:

> the cultural practice of bride price, the payment of a sum of money or property by the prospective son-in-law to the parents of the prospective bride as a condition precedent to a lawful customary marriage, is not barred by the Constitution. It is not *per se* unconstitutional. The Constitution does not prohibit a voluntary, mutual agreement between a bride and a groom to enter into the bride price arrangement. A man and a woman have the constitutional right to so choose the bride price option as the way they wish to get married.

[97] CEDAW, *Concluding Observations: Eritrea*, UN Doc CEDAW/C/ERI/CO/3 (3 February 2006), 14.

[98] US Department of State, *Country Reports on Human Rights Practices—2005*, Nigeria. Released by the Bureau of Democracy, Human Rights, and Labor, 8 March 2006 <http://www.state.gov/g/drl/rls/hrrpt/2005/61586.htm>. According to the 2003 *Nigeria Demographic and Health Survey* (NDHS), 64.5% of women and 61.3% of men agreed that a husband was justified in hitting or beating his wife for at least one of six specified reasons, including 'burning food and not cooking on time'.   [99] Ibid.

[100] African Women's Rights Protocol, Art 17(1).

[101] See UDHR, Art 17; ICERD, Art 5(d)(v); Protocol No 1 to the ECHR, Art 1; the American Convention on Human Rights, Art 21; and ACHPR, Art 4.

including the freedom to seek, receive, and impart information and ideas of all kinds,[102] the right to the full development of the human personality,[103] and freedom of movement.[104]

Women are often denied travel documents just because they are female—they are subjected to legal or de facto requirements which prevent them from travelling, such as the requirement of consent of a third party to the issuance of a passport or other type of travel documents to an adult woman. One case from Libya demonstrates the effect of violations of women's freedom of movement on the women's enjoyment of other human rights. In *Loubna El Ghar v Libyan Arab Jamahiriya*,[105] the author, of Libyan nationality, had lived all her life in Morocco with her divorced mother and held a residence permit for that country. As a student of the French law at the Hassan II University faculty of law in Casablanca, she wished to continue her studies in France and to specialize in international law. To that end, she applied to the Libyan Consulate in Morocco for a passport beginning in 1998. In 2002, the Libyan consul indicated to the author that it was not possible to issue her a passport but that she could be given a laissez-passer (travel document) for Libya, by virtue of a 'regulation' that was explained neither orally nor on the laissez-passer itself. The passport application submitted to the Libyan Consulate was thus rejected without any explanation of the grounds for the decision, the only comment being that since the author 'is a native of Morocco and has not obtained a passport, this travel document [laissez-passer] is issued to enable her to return to national territory'.

The HRC considered that 'this laissez-passer cannot be considered a satisfactory substitute for a valid Libyan passport that would enable the author to travel abroad'.[106] The Committee concluded that

the facts before it disclose a violation of article 12, paragraph 2, of the Covenant (ICCPR) insofar as the author was denied a passport without any valid justification and subjected to an unreasonable delay, and as a result was prevented from travelling abroad to continue her studies.[107]

The Committee urged 'the State party to issue the author with a passport without further delay' and to 'take effective measures to ensure that similar violations do not recur in future'.[108] It is clear that the refusal to issue a passport to a female student on the basis of an 'unwritten regulation' (that is, apparently because the applicant was female and she had no consent from a male third party—father) in this case did not only violate her freedom of movement (a civil and political right) but also prevented her from travelling abroad for fur-

---

[102] See UDHR, Art 19; ICCPR, Art 19(2); ECHR, Art 5; the American Declaration on Human Rights, Art 13, and ACHPR, Art 9.   [103] See UDHR, Art 26(2); ICESCR, Art13(1).
[104] ICCPR, Art 12(2) provides: 'Everyone shall be free to leave any country, including his own'.
[105] HRC, Communication No 1107/2002, UN Doc CCPR/C/82/D/1107/2002 9 (15 November 2004).   [106] Ibid, 7.2.
[107] Ibid, 8.   [108] Ibid, 9.

ther studies (a violation of the right to education—an economic, social, and cultural right).[109]

It is, therefore, not surprising that many features of customary law in Africa effectively operate 'against the dignity, welfare or interests of women (and) undermine their status'.[110] Generally, it has been noted that:

Traditional cultural practices reflect values and beliefs held by members of a community for periods often spanning generations. Every social grouping in the world has specific traditional cultural practices and beliefs, some of which are beneficial to all members, while others are harmful to a specific group, such as women. These harmful traditional practices include female genital mutilation (FGM); forced feeding of women; early marriage; the various taboos or practices which prevent women from controlling their own fertility; nutritional taboos and traditional birth practices; son preference and its implications for the status of the girl child; female infanticide; early pregnancy; and dowry price.[111]

In the African context, the main harmful traditional practices include 'the practice of female genital mutilation [FGM],[112] as well as scarification and ritual killing of children',[113] corporal punishment (in the family, schools, and other institutions),[114] high level of acceptance of domestic violence towards

---

[109] See also LE Chamblee, 'Rhetoric or Rights?: When Culture and Religion Bar Girls' Right to Education' (2004) 44 Virginia Journal of International Law 1073–143.

[110] Oloka-Onyango (see n 96 above) 1268, citing the Constitution. of the Republic of Uganda (1995) arts 33(6), 32(1); and cultural objective no xxiv in the Preamble, which encourages the incorporation into aspects of Ugandan life all cultures and customary values consistent with fundamental rights and freedoms and human dignity.

[111] Fact Sheet No 23, *Harmful Traditional Practices Affecting the Health of Women and Children* < http://www.ohchr.org/Documents/Publications/FactSheet23en.pdf>.

[112] K Bowman, 'Comment: Bridging the Gap in the Hopes of Ending Female Genital Cutting' (2005) Santa Clara Journal of International Law 132; N Mendelsohn, 'At the Crossroads: The Case For and Against a Cultural Defense to Female Genital Mutilaton' (2004) 56 Rutgers Law Review 1011–38; CESCR, *Concluding Observations: Egypt*, E/C.12/1/Add.44 (23 May 2000), 16: 'The Committee further notes with concern that the percentage of women who are victims of FGM remains alarmingly high: WHO statistics for 1995 showed an estimated 97 per cent prevalence of FGM ("Female Genital Mutilation: An Overview", WHO, Geneva, 1998, p. 13)'; CEDAW, *Concluding Observations: Eritrea*, CEDAW/C/ERI/CO/3 (3 February 2006), 18 stating that 'the Committee is concerned at the high incidence of female genital mutilation in the country and the State party's reluctance to expedite the adoption of legislation aimed at eradicating this practice'.

[113] Committee on the Rights of the Child (CRC Committee), *Concluding Observations: Nigeria*, CRC/C/15/Add.257(13 April 2005), 56. In respect of Uganda, the CRC Committee expressed its concern in 2005 that 'FGM is not specifically prohibited by law and is still widely practised in the State party' CRC Committee, *Concluding Observations: Uganda*, CRC/C/UGA/CO/2 (23 November 2005), 55.

[114] In Nigeria, eg, the *Shariah* legal code to children prescribes 'penalties and corporal punishment such as flogging, whipping, stoning and amputation, which are sometimes applied to children'. CRC Committee, *Concluding Observations: Nigeria*, ibid, 38(d). See also CRC Committee, *Concluding Observations: Uganda*, CRC/C/UGA/CO/2 (23 November 2005), 39 noting that: 'While taking note that corporal punishment has been prohibited in schools by a circular of the Ministry of Education, and in the penal system under the Children's Act, the Committee remains concerned that corporal punishment is still traditionally accepted and widely practised in the family and in other settings'; G Muhwezi, 'Teacher's Canes Paralyse Student', *Sunday*

women,[115] forced and/or early marriages,[116] polygamy (more specifically polygyny—a man having more than one wife), and the denial of inheritance rights
to women.[117] Many customary laws discriminate against women mainly in the
areas of inheritance, marriage, and divorce.[118] These areas are, therefore, key to
a deeper understanding of why women in Africa do not enjoy their rights. Yet
some states have only shown limited efforts to directly address such discriminatory cultural practices and stereotypes and maintain that 'women themselves
are primarily responsible for changing their position of disadvantage'.[119] How
can women change such entrenched discriminatory position without the necessary political will to confront holistically discriminatory laws and entrenched
cultural practices? The next section discusses random cases of violations of
women's rights in Africa, focusing especially on (some) traditional customs in
areas of inheritance, polygyny, and divorce.

3.2 Inheritance

In many African states, women cannot inherit under the relevant customary law
which applies the rule of male primogeniture in the African customary law of
succession. In Zambia, for example, customary land, which represents over 80
per cent of all land, is traditionally inherited by the man's family in accordance
with rules of male primogeniture, to the detriment of widows and, especially, girl
children.[120] It is a widely held view that 'a [married] woman is property because
she's been bought, so how can property own property?'[121] Disappointingly, discriminatory provisions are entrenched in Zambia's 1996 Constitution. As noted
by the CEDAW Committee, Zambia's 1996 Constitution contains:

contradictory provisions...whereby article 11 guarantees the equal status of women
and article 23(4) permits discriminatory laws to exist in the area of personal law,

---

Monitor, Uganda, 30 July 2006; and Lawfulness of Corporal Punishment: Uganda: <http://www.
endcorporalpunishment.org/pages/progress/reports/uganda.html>.

[115] CRC Committee, *Concluding Observations: Nigeria* (see n 113 above) 44. See also CG
Bowman, 'Theories of Domestic Violence in the African Context' (2003) 11 American University
Journal of Gender, Social Policy and the Law 847–63.   [116] CRC Committee, ibid, 54.

[117] See, eg, COHRE, *Bringing Equality Home: Promoting and Protecting the Inheritance Rights of
Women—A Survey of Law and Practice in Sub-Saharan Africa* (Geneva: Centre on Housing Rights
and Evictions, 2004); CESCR, *Concluding Observations: Senegal*, E/C.12/1/Add.62 (24/09/2001),
15 noting that discriminatory practices against women and girls in Senegal include 'polygamy,
restricted access to land, property, housing and credit facilities, and the inability to inherit land'.

[118] See, eg, PO Davies, 'Marriage, Divorce, and Inheritance Laws in Sierra Leone and their
Discriminatory Effects on Women' (2005) 12(3) Human Rights Brief 17; B Oppermann, 'The
Impact of Legal Pluralism on Women's Status: An Examination of Marriage Laws in Egypt, South
Africa, and the United States' (2006) 17 Hastings Women's Law Journal 65–92.

[119] CEDAW, *Concluding Observations: Togo*, CEDAW/C/TGO/CO/3 (3 February 2006), 14.

[120] CESCR, *Concluding Observations: Zambia*, E/C.12/1/Add.106 (23 June 2005), 27.

[121] COHRE (see n 117 above) 143.

namely:...devolution of property on death, or other matters of personal law and customary law with respect to any matter.[122]

Undoubtedly, this provision is a serious flaw in the legal protection of women's human rights, and it fosters patriarchy and discrimination. It is, therefore, necessary to repeal Article 23(4) of the Constitution, which permits discrimination in the area of law that affects women most.[123]

Surprisingly, in some cases, where customary law contravenes international human rights or the statutory law, the customary law continues to be upheld and applied.[124] Perhaps the best case to illustrate this point is the decision of the Supreme Court of Zimbabwe in *Venia Magaya v Nakayi Shonhiwa Magaya*.[125] The main issue in this case was whether a woman (a 58-year-old Venia Magaya) could inherit her father's estate if he died without a will. At the community court (which was presided over by a female officer), Venia was indeed appointed as heir to the estate of her father. However, Venia's half-brother from her father's second wife and other male relatives then contested this appointment. They argued before the magistrate's court that customary law does not permit a daughter to inherit from her father's estate. The magistrate agreed with this argument and substituted one of the half-brothers as heir. Venia then appealed to the Supreme Court, which dismissed the appeal. Denying that a woman could indeed inherit on account of the custom of the community from which she came, the learned judge in the case upheld discrimination against women and observed that the 'nature of African society' dictates that women are not equal to men, especially in family relationships. The judge noted that 'the woman's status is therefore basically the same as that of any junior male in the family'.[126] The 5:0 male ruling awarded the father's estate to her half-brother, making reference to African cultural norms, which say that the head of the family is a patriarch, or a senior man, who exercises control over the property

---

[122] CEDAW, *Zambia: Concluding Observations*, A/57/38 (21 June 2002), 230. Article 11, of Zambia's Constitution (1996), on fundamental rights and freedoms, protects various civil and political rights for all Zambians, regardless of, inter alia, sex. This provision also prohibits the taking of property without appropriate compensation. Disappointingly, however, Art 23(4) specifically excludes from the application of the non-discrimination clause to all law:

> (c) with respect to adoption, marriage, divorce, burial, devolution of property on death or other matters of personal law; (d) for the application in the case of members of a particular race or tribe, of customary law with respect to any matter to the exclusion of any law with respect to that matter which is applicable in the case of other persons.

[123] Ibid.
[124] HRC, *Concluding Observations: Zimbabwe*, CCPR/C/79/Add.89 (8 April 1998), 12.
[125] Supreme Court of Zimbabwe, Judgment No SC 210/98/Civil Appeal No 635/92 (1999) (1) ZLR 100. For the analysis of this case, see DM Bigge and A von Briesen, 'Conflict in the Zimbabwean Courts: Women's Rights and Indigenous Self-Determination in *Magaya v Magaya*' (2000) 13 Harvard Human Rights Journal 290–313.   [126] Ibid, 10.

and lives of women and juniors.[127] The Court noted that the woman could not inherit

because of the consideration in the African society which, amongst other factors, was to the effect that women were not able to look after their original family (of birth) because of their commitment to the new family (through marriage).[128]

The Supreme Court found further that, although the practice of preferring males is discriminatory, it did not contravene the Zimbabwean Constitution, as it does not forbid discrimination based on sex in the distribution of a deceased person's estate under customary law. Indeed Section 23 of the Zimbabwean Constitution[129] allows blatant discrimination in several areas including 'the application of African customary law'.[130] Essentially, the Supreme Court elevated discriminatory customary law above human rights obligations. Given the fact that human rights are 'fundamental, inalienable and universal entitlements belonging to individuals and, under certain circumstances, groups of individuals and communities' and 'human rights are timeless expressions of fundamental entitlements of the human person',[131] it is important not to elevate customary norms over human rights of women. In this respect, the *Magaya* decision has been described as 'outrageous' and 'one of the world's most egregious cases of court-condoned discrimination'.[132]

Unfortunately, the *Magaya* decision is not an isolated one since numerous jurisdictions around Africa regularly give more weight to cultural practices that support patriarchy and discrimination than they do to the rights of women.[133] This limits women's access to land (the most valuable economic resource and main source of income in the developing African states) and thereby subordinates women's economic dependence and survival on men, a fact that perpetuates women's vulnerability, insecurity and the attendant human rights violations. Undoubtedly, the continued existence of, and adherence to, customary laws perpetuates discrimination against women, particularly in the context of the family. Such prevailing traditional and socio-cultural attitudes towards

---

[127] COHRE (see n 117 above) 169 observed: 'The *Magaya* case should be seen as a warning to all women—that all the laws in the world will amount to nothing if they continue to be interpreted by discriminatory men.'

[128] *Magaya v Magaya* [1999] (1) ZLR 100.

[129] The Constitution was last reformed in the year 2000. Shortly after the decision, Venia Magaya died in 2000 homeless and destitute. See generally WLSA, *Venia Magaya's Sacrifice: A Case of Custom Gone Awry* (Harare: WLSA, 2001).

[130] Section 23(3) states that:

Nothing contained in any law shall be held to be in contravention of subsection (1)(a) [which provides that 'no law shall make any provision that is discriminatory either of itself or in its effect'] to the extent that the law in question relates to any of the following matters:
a) adoption, marriage, divorce and inheritance ...
b) the application of African customary law ...

[131] CESCR, *General Comment 17*, E/C.12/GC/17 (12 January 2006), 1 and 2.

[132] COHRE (see n 117 above) 162 and 169.   [133] See n 96 above.

women contribute to the perpetuation of negative images of women, which limits women's participation at the decision-making level and impedes their emancipation.[134] As the UN Human Rights Committee (HRC) observed:

Inequality in the enjoyment of rights by women throughout the world is deeply embedded in tradition, history and culture, including religious attitudes...States parties should ensure that traditional, historical, religious or cultural attitudes are not used to justify violations of women's right to equality before the law and to equal enjoyment of all Covenant [ICCPR] rights...[135]

One way of ensuring that the implementation of customary laws does not violate women's right to equality is to interpret customary laws in the light of present day conditions. Under this approach, customary laws must be interpreted in a way that promotes the equal enjoyment of human rights—civil, political, economic, social, and cultural rights—by men and women. It follows that the courts would be able to strike down, for example, the rule of male primogeniture in the African customary law of succession. This would ensure that the meaning and application of customary law can vary so as to adapt to new and enhanced ideals of human rights protection. An example from South Africa will adequately illustrate this point.

In the *Bhe* case in South Africa, there was a constitutional challenge to the rule of male primogeniture as it applies in the African customary law of succession.[136] In this case the deceased's partner (Ms Nontupheko Bhe) had two minor children, both extra-marital daughters, by the deceased (Mgolombane), who died intestate. The daughters had failed to qualify as heirs in the intestate estate of their deceased father. The court appointed the deceased's father as sole heir of the deceased's estate, in accordance with the relevant domestic law.[137] The general rule (custom) was that only a male related to the deceased qualified as intestate heir. Women did not participate in the intestate succession of deceaseds' estates. In a monogamous family, the eldest son of the family head was his heir. If the deceased was not survived by any male descendants, his father succeeded him. If his father also did not survive him, an heir was sought among the father's male descendants related to him through the male line.[138]

The application in the *Bhe* case was made on behalf of the two minor daughters of Ms Nontupheko Bhe and her deceased partner. It was contended that the

[134] CEDAW, *Concluding Observations: Zimbabwe A/53/38* (14 May 1998), 139.

[135] HRC, *General Comment 28: Equality of Rights Between Men and Women (Article 3)*, UN Doc CCPR/C/21/Rev.1/Add.10 (2000), para 5.

[136] Constitutional Court of South Africa, *Nonkululeko Letta Bhe and Others v The Magistrate, Khayelitsha and Others*, Case CCT 49/03, 2004 (2) SA 544 (C) (2004 (1) BCLR 27) (hereinafter 'Bhe' case); *Shibi v Sithole and Others*, Case CCT 69/03 (hereinafeter 'Shibi' case); *South African Human Rights Commission and Another v President of the Republic of South Africa and Another*, Case CCT 50/03 (15 October 2004) <http://www.saflii.org/za/cases/ZACC/2004/17.pdf>.

[137] *Black Administration Act*, 38 of 1927, S 23, read with the regulations published thereunder, as well as s 1(4)(b) of the Intestate Succession Act 81 of 1987, purported to give effect to customary law. Extra-marital children were not entitled to succeed to their father's estate in customary law.

[138] *Bhe and Others v The Magistrate, Khayelitsha and Others*, Case CCT 49/03, 77.

impugned provisions and the customary law rule of male primogeniture unfairly discriminated against the two children in that they prevented the children from inheriting the estate of their late father. In the *Shibi* case for similar reasons, Ms Shibi was prevented from inheriting the estate of her deceased brother. The South African Human Rights Commission and the Women's Legal Trust were permitted direct access to the Court in the third case which was brought in the public interest, and as a class action on behalf of all women and children prevented from inheriting by reason of the impugned provisions and the rule of male primogeniture.

The South African Constitutional Court held that the exclusion of women from heirship, and consequently from being able to inherit property, was in keeping with a patriarchal system which reserved for women a position of subservience and subordination in which they were regarded as perpetual minors under the tutelage of fathers, husbands, or heads of the extended family. Basing its decision on Sections 9 (equal protection) and 10 (right to dignity) of the South African Constitution,[139] the Constitutional Court found, rightly, that excluding women from inheriting on the ground of gender is,

a form of discrimination that entrenches past patterns of disadvantage among a vulnerable group, exacerbated by old notions of patriarchy and male domination incompatible with the guarantee of equality under this constitutional order.[140]

The Court noted that customary laws 'have over time become increasingly out of step with the real values and circumstances of the societies they are meant to serve and particularly the people who live in urban areas'.[141] Langa DCJ, writing for the majority of the Court, held, inter alia, that:

The principle of primogeniture also violates the right of women to human dignity as guaranteed in s 10 of the Constitution as, in one sense, it implies that women are not fit or competent to own and administer property. Its effect is also to subject these women to a status of perpetual minority, placing them automatically under the control of male heirs, simply by virtue of their sex and gender. Their dignity is further affronted by the fact that as women, they are also excluded from intestate succession and denied the right, which other members of the population have, to be holders of, and to control property...In

---

[139] The Constitution of the Republic of South Africa Act 108 of 1996. Section 9 provides:

(1) Everyone is equal before the law and has the right to equal protection and benefit of the law.
(2) Equality includes the full and equal enjoyment of all rights and freedoms...
(3) The State may not unfairly discriminate directly or indirectly against anyone on one or more grounds, including race, gender, sex, pregnancy, marital status, ethnic or social origin, colour, sexual orientation, age, disability, religion, conscience, belief, culture, language and birth...

Section 10 provides:

Everyone has inherent dignity and the right to have their dignity respected and protected.

[140] *Bhe and Others v The Magistrate, Khayelitsha and Others*, Case CCT 49/03, 91.
[141] Ibid, 82.

denying female and extra-marital children the ability and the opportunity to inherit from their deceased fathers, the application of the principle of primogeniture is also in violation of s 9(3) of the Constitution.[142]

It was concluded that

the primogeniture rule as applied to the customary law of succession cannot be reconciled with the current notions of equality and human dignity as contained in the Bill of Rights. As the centrepiece of the customary-law system of succession, the rule violates the equality rights of women and is an affront to their dignity. In denying extra-marital children the right to inherit from their deceased fathers, it also unfairly discriminates against them and infringes their right to dignity as well. The result is that the limitation it imposes on the rights of those subject to it is not reasonable and justifiable in an open and democratic society founded on the values of equality, human dignity and freedom.[143]

The above decision shows that courts can play a positive role in developing women's human rights jurisprudence. Judicial oversight is crucial in ensuring that women are protected against discriminatory laws.[144] However, the impact of progressive judicial decisions is limited if court decisions are not enforced adequately. It can be noted that the court in South Africa took a progressive view of culture—by taking into account human rights principles of equality and non-discrimination—while the court in Zimbabwe placed emphasis on the domestic constitutional provisions and avoided interpreting these in light of the well-established human rights principles of equality and non-discrimination. The cases considered above also lead to some interesting questions, for example, why did the South African Constitutional Court give such a progressive view of customary laws as opposed to the Supreme Court in Zimbabwe? Is it because of the differences in the socio-political dynamics at play in these two jurisdictions?

Undoubtedly, however, African governments need to take a more proactive role at a national level by introducing concrete measures to abolish all discriminatory customs and practices including extending gender-sensitive training to the judiciary. In the context of inheritance, it is essential to note that Article 21 of the Protocol to the African Charter on the Rights of Women in Africa protects the right to inheritance problem in the following terms:

1. A widow shall have the right to an equitable share in the inheritance of the property of her husband. A widow shall have the right to continue to live in the matrimonial house. In case of remarriage, she shall retain this right if the house belongs to her or she has inherited it.
2. Women and men shall have the right to inherit, in equitable shares, their parents' properties.

---

[142] Ibid, 92–3.   [143] Ibid, 95.

[144] Recent examples from Uganda support this position. See M Ssenyonjo, 'Towards Non-Discrimination Against Women and De Jure Equality in Uganda: The Role of Uganda's Constitutional Court' (2008) 16(1) African Journal of International and Comparative Law 1–34.

This can be used as a minimum standard to which all inheritance customary laws must be subjected. In addition, the codification of family and customary laws, incorporating only those customary laws and practices which promote gender equality and the empowerment of women has the potential to enhance the realization of women's human rights in Africa.

3.3 Polygamous marriages

Some traditional practices in Africa are so firmly established that while they are generally considered as contrary to women's equality with men, they are recognized even in the African Women's Rights Protocol. One of the clearest examples is polygamy,[145] which according to the HRC discriminates against women and violates their dignity:

It should also be noted that equality of treatment with regard to the right to marry implies that polygamy is incompatible with this principle. Polygamy violates the dignity of women. It is an inadmissible discrimination against women. Consequently, it should be definitely abolished wherever it continues to exist.[146]

Although the African Women's Rights Protocol prohibits discrimination against women and guarantee women's right to dignity,[147] it recognizes polygamy. Article 2(1) of the Protocol recognizes that: 'States Parties shall combat all forms of discrimination against women through appropriate legislative, institutional and other measures', and under Article 2(2):

States Parties shall commit themselves to modify the social and cultural patterns of conduct of women and men through public education, information, education and communication strategies, with a view to achieving the elimination of harmful cultural and traditional practices and all other practices which are based on the idea of the inferiority or the superiority of either of the sexes, or on stereotyped roles for women and men.

More specifically, under Article 5: 'States Parties shall prohibit and condemn all forms of harmful practices which negatively affect the human rights of women and which are contrary to recognised international standards.' One would have expected such prohibited harmful cultural and traditional practices which are contrary to international human rights standards to include

---

[145] The term polygamy in social anthropology can be defined as any form of marriage in which a person has more than one spouse. It covers both *polygyny* (one man having more than one wife simultaneously), or *polyandry* (one woman having more than one husband simultaneously), or, less commonly as 'polygamy' (one person having many wives and many husbands at the same time). In this chapter, polygamy has been used to mean *polygyny*. For a discussion of polygamy see S Chapman, *Polygamy, Bigamy and Human Rights Law* (Philadelphia, PA: Xlibris Corporation, 2001).   [146] HRC, *General Comment 28* (n 135 above) 24.
[147] African Women's Rights Protocol, Art 3(1): 'Every woman shall have the right to dignity inherent in a human being and to the recognition and protection of her human and legal rights.'

polygamy. Nevertheless, with respect to polygamy, the Protocol simply states in Article 6(c):

States Parties shall ensure that women and men enjoy equal rights and are regarded as equal partners in marriage. They shall enact appropriate national legislative measures to guarantee that: monogamy is encouraged as the preferred form of marriage and that the rights of women in marriage and family, including in polygamous marital relationships are promoted and protected.

This might be seen as being consistent with the ACHPR which makes it a 'duty' of the state and the individual to promote and protect the morals and 'traditional/cultural values' recognized by the community.[148] Clearly then, African states parties to the Protocol are only obliged to 'encourage' monogamy. This is a weaker obligation since, in its ordinary and natural meaning, the obligation to 'encourage' only extends to 'inspire with the courage or confidence'.[149] The obligation is not to eliminate polygamy immediately. During the drafting of the African Women's Rights Protocol, there was a vigorous debate on whether polygyny should be abolished. While non-governmental organizations demanded its abolition, government experts actively resisted its abolition because 'Shari'a and many customary personal law systems recognised the rights of men to marry more than one wife' and that its abolition would result in 'hardship being suffered by women already in polygynous unions'.[150] It is recognized under the Protocol that it is possible to 'promote' and 'respect' women's rights in polygamous marital relationships, although it is less clear as to how this can be achieved in practice. By implication, therefore, polygamy under the Protocol is not seen as one of those practices which violate the dignity of women or inadmissible discrimination against women (at least in the short run).

Given the fact that polygyny in Africa is deeply entrenched, it is considered to be very difficult to ban it outright, and if it was banned it might cause harm to many women living in these relationships, whose only protection at the moment might be provisions of the impugned customary law. Therefore, it was seen as a necessary flexibility device, reflecting the realities of the situation in Africa and the difficulties involved in agreeing to a regional human rights treaty on women's human rights. This is especially the case given the fact that some states in Africa (for example Egypt, Sudan, and Uganda) apply some aspects of Islamic law (*Sharia*) interpreted by some

---

[148] ACHPR, Art 17(2): 'The State shall have the duty to assist the family which is the custodian of morals and traditional values recognised by the community'. Article 29(7): 'The individual shall also have the duty: to preserve and strengthen positive African cultural values in his relations with other members of the society, in the spirit of tolerance, dialogue and consultation and, in general, to contribute to the promotion of the moral well being of society.'

[149] See *Collins English Dictionary* (London: HarperCollins, 1999), 510.

[150] F Banda, 'Blazing a Trail: The African Protocol on Women's Rights Comes into Force' (2006) 50(1) Journal of African Law 72, 77.

scholars as not providing for equality between men and women,[151] and permitting a man to marry up to four women.[152] Such interpretation of the Quran has been contested on the basis that the Quran 'never discriminates on the basis of gender. It is the interpretation of the Quran, reflecting masculine and patriarchal prejudices of the interpreters, that is discriminatory.'[153] Indeed depending on the way Islamic injunctions in the Quran are interpreted and applied, they may contribute towards the realization of women's human rights. This view has been supported by the CRC Committee noting that 'the universal values of equality and tolerance [are] inherent in Islam'.[154] It is also interesting to note that representatives of Islamic states such as the Saudi Arabian delegation before the CEDAW Committee have also recently assured that 'there is no contradiction in substance between the Convention [on the Elimination of Discrimination against Women] and Islamic *Sharia*'.[155] It has to be noted, however, that the recognition of polygyny is difficult to reconcile with the above view of the HRC and the view of the UN Committee on the Elimination of Discrimination against Women (CEDAW). According to the CEDAW Committee:

Polygamous marriage contravenes a woman's right to equality with men, and can have such serious emotional and financial consequences for her and her dependants that such marriages ought to be discouraged and prohibited. The Committee notes with concern that some States parties, whose constitutions guarantee equal rights, permit polygamous marriage in accordance with personal or customary law. This violates

---

[151] eg, a renowned Islamic scholar Sheikh Muhammed Salih Al-Munajjid, asserted that:

Those who say that Islam is the religion of equality are lying against Islam...Rather Islam is the religion of justice which means treating equally those who are equal and differentiating between those who are different. No one who knows the religion of Islam would say that it is the religion of equality...Not one single letter in the Qur'an enjoins equality, rather it enjoins justice.

See Islam Question and Answer, 'Does Islam Regard Men and Women as Equal?' <http://www.islam-qa.com/index.php?ref=1105&ln=eng&txt=equality>. For the interpretation of the Quranic provisions regarding women, see generally M Bin Abdul-Aziz Al-Musnad, *Islamic Fatawa Regarding Women* (Riyadh: Darussalam, 1996).

[152] A Mashhour, 'Islamic Law and Gender Equality—Could There Be a Common Ground?: A Study of Divorce and Polygamy in Sharia Law and Contemporary Legislation in Tunisia and Egypt' (2005) 27 Human Rights Quarterly 562–96; J Allain and A O'Shea, 'African Disunity: Comparing Human Rights Law and Practice of North and South African States' (2002) 24 Human Rights Quarterly 86–125; W Amien, 'Overcoming the Conflict between the Right to Freedom of Religion and Women's Rights to Equality: A South African Case Study of Muslim Marriages' (2006) 28 Human Rights Quarterly 729.

[153] See, eg, NA Shah, 'Women's Human Rights in the Koran: An Interpretive Approach' (2006) 28(4) Human Rights Quarterly 868–903, 903. See also J Rehman, 'The Sharia, Islamic Family Laws and International Human Rights Law: Examining the Theory and Practice of Polygamy and Talaq' (2007) 21 International Journal of Law, Policy and the Family 108–27, 123 claiming that in the development of the classical schools of Islamic law, 'the Islamic jurists frequently adopted male-centric approaches towards women's rights and family laws'.

[154] See CRC Committee, *Concluding Observations*, Egypt, UN Doc CRC/C/15/Add.145 (21 February 2001), 6; Qatar, UN Doc CRC/C/15/Add.163 (6 November 2001), 9; Saudi Arabia, UN Doc CRC/C/15/Add.148 (22 February 2001), 6.

[155] See CEDAW Committee, *Concluding Observations: Saudi Arabia*, CEDAW/C/SAU/CO/2 (1 February 2008), 10.

the constitutional rights of women, and breaches the provisions of article 5 (a) of the Convention.[156]

Article 5(a) of the Convention on the CEDAW, ratified as of 5 May 2009 by all African states except only two states (Sudan and Somalia), which is substantially similar to Article 2(2) of the African Women's Rights Protocol, provides:

States Parties shall take all appropriate measures: To modify the social and cultural patterns of conduct of men and women, with a view to achieving the elimination of prejudices and customary and all other practices which are based on the idea of the inferiority or the superiority of either of the sexes or on stereotyped roles for men and women.

Since polygamy violates CEDAW Article 5(a), it is submitted that the African Court on Human and Peoples Rights/African Court of Justice and Human Rights, which under Article 27 of the African Women's Rights Protocol is 'seized with matters of interpretation arising from the application or implementation of this [Women's Rights] Protocol',[157] should similarly interpret polygamy as violating Article 2(2) of the Protocol. This would generally be consistent with the view that the 'Court shall apply the provision of the Charter and any other relevant human rights instruments ratified by the States concerned'[158] without prejudice to 'more favourable provisions for the realisation of the rights of women contained in the national legislation of States Parties or in any other regional, continental or international conventions'.[159] Under Article 60 of the African Charter, the African Commission on Human and Peoples' Rights (African Commission) and arguably the Court, since it complements the protective mandate of the African Commission,[160] are required to 'draw inspiration from international law on human and peoples' rights, . . . the Universal Declaration of Human Rights, other instruments adopted by the United Nations . . . of which

---

[156] CEDAW, General Recommendation 21, Equality in marriage and family relations (13th Session, 1992), UN Doc A/49/38, 1 (1994), 14.

[157] The first Judges of the African Court on Human and Peoples' Rights were elected on 22 January 2006 at the 8th Ordinary Session of the Executive Council of the African Union, held in Khartoum. These were: Dr Fatsah Ouguergouz (Algeria); Jean Emile Somda (Burkina Faso); Dr Gerard Niyungeko (Burundi); Sophia A.B. Akuffo (Ghana); Kellelo Justina Masafo-Guni (Lesotho); Hamdi Faraj Fanoush (Libya); Modibo Tounty Guindo (Mali); Jean Mutsinzi (Rwanda); El Hadji Guissé (Senegal); Bernard Ngoepe (South Africa); and George W Kanyeihamba (Uganda). For a discussion of the Court see AP Van Der Mei, 'The New African Court on Human and Peoples' Rights: Towards an Effective Human Rights Protection Mechanism for Africa?' (2005) 18 Leiden Journal of International Law 113–29. The African Court on Human and Peoples' Rights merged with the African Court of Justice in 2008 to form the African Court of Justice and Human Rights. See Protocol on the Statute of the African Court of Justice and Human Rights, adopted 1 July 2008 <http://www.africa-union.org/root/au/Documents/Treaties/treaties.htm>.

[158] Protocol to the African Charter on Human and Peoples' Rights on the Establishment of an African Court on Human and Peoples' Rights, 9 June 1998, OAU Doc OAU/LEG/EXP/AFCHPR/PROT (III), Art 6.

[159] African Women's Rights Protocol, Art 31.

[160] Protocol to the African Charter on Human and Peoples' Rights on the Establishment of an African Court on Human and Peoples' Rights, Art 2.

the parties to the present Charter are members'. Such instruments, undoubtedly, include CEDAW.

It follows, therefore, that under this approach, the obligation to 'encourage' must be read in the light of the overall objective, indeed the raison d'être, of the Protocol which is to establish clear human rights obligations for states parties in respect of the full realization of the human rights of women. The increasingly high standard being required in the area of the protection of human rights correspondingly and inevitably requires greater firmness in assessing breaches of equality and non-discrimination as the fundamental values of democratic societies. Therefore, the Court should have regard to the fact that the Protocol is a 'living instrument which must be interpreted in the light of present-day conditions'.[161] As stated in the preamble to the Protocol, this is 'to ensure that the rights of women are *promoted, realised* and *protected* in order to enable them to enjoy fully all their human rights'.[162] Three specific obligations arise here—protect, promote, and realize.

The obligation to *protect* requires states parties to take steps aimed directly towards the elimination of prejudices, customary and all other practices that perpetuate the notion of inferiority or superiority of either of the sexes, and stereotyped roles for men and women.[163] States parties' obligation to protect under the Protocol includes, inter alia, the respect and adoption of constitutional and legislative provisions on the equal right of men and women to enjoy all human rights and the prohibition of discrimination of any kind; the adoption of legislation to eliminate discrimination and to prevent third parties or private actors (individuals, groups, corporations, and other entities as well as agents acting under their authority) from interfering directly or indirectly with the enjoyment of women's human rights;[164] the adoption of administrative measures and programmes, as well as the establishment of public institutions, agencies, and programmes to protect women against discrimination.[165]

States parties have an obligation to monitor and regulate the conduct of non-state actors (NSAs) to ensure that they do not violate the equal right of men and women to enjoy civil, political, economic, social, and cultural

---

[161] A similar approach has been used by the European Court of Human Rights in interpreting the ECHR. See, eg, *Selmouni v France*, App No 25803/94, Judgment of 28 July 1999 (2000) 29 EHRR 403, 101; *Tyrer v United Kingdom*, App No 5856/72, Judgment of 25 April 1978 (1979–80) 2 EHRR 1, 31.   [162] African Women's Rights Protocol, preamble, para 14 (emphasis added).

[163] CESCR, *General Comment No 16*, 19.

[164] See *The Social and Economic Rights Action Center & the Center for Economic and Social Rights/ Nigeria*, Communication No 155/96, 44; *Union des Jeunes Avocats v Chad*, Communication No 74/92 (ACmHPR); *X and Y v Netherlands*, 91 ECHR (1985) (Ser A) 32 (European Court of Human Rights); *Velasquez Rodriguez v Honduras*, Judgment of 19 July 1988 (ser C) No 4 (Inter-American Court of Human Rights) holding that a state has a positive duty to prevent human rights violations occurring in the territory subject to its effective control, even if such violations are carried out by third parties.

[165] CESCR, *General Comment No 16*, 19; African Women's Rights Protocol, Art 2.

rights.[166] This obligation applies, for example, in cases where public services have been partially or fully privatized,[167] or where armed rebels—such as the notorious Lord's Resistance Army in Uganda—violate human rights including subjecting women to torture (for example rape) or sexual slavery.[168]

The obligation equally applies where NSAs formulate policies that discriminate against women. A 1992 case from Zambia illustrates this point.[169] This case involved challenging the NSA—the Intercontinental Hotel—which had a policy of refusing women entry, unless they were accompanied by a male escort. The hotel justified the policy as a necessary measure against prostitution. A security guard stopped a woman (Longwe) when she tried to retrieve her children from a party at the hotel. On another occasion, the same hotel refused Longwe admittance when she had arranged to meet a group of women's activists in the hotel's bar. Longwe made a claim at the Zambian High Court, arguing that the hotel's actions violated her right to freedom from discrimination under both Zambia's Constitution and under Articles 1, 2, and 3 of CEDAW. The High Court of Zambia noted that Zambia, being a party to international treaties such as the ACHPR and the CEDAW, must respect and conform to the notion of gender equality. Reading international instruments and the Zambian Constitution in conjunction, the Court held that discriminating acts on the basis of gender carried out by NSAs violated the plaintiff's fundamental equality rights and women's rights. This case is notable because it applied human rights obligations to NSAs. The implication is that states must put an end to discriminatory actions 'both in the public and the private sector'.[170] In particular, states should implement laws and policies to ensure that 'pregnancies must not constitute an obstacle to employment and should not constitute justification for loss of employment'.[171]

The obligation to *promote* and *realize* requires states parties to take steps to ensure that, in practice, men and women enjoy their civil, political, economic, social, and cultural rights on the basis of equality. Such steps should include, but not be limited to, the following.[172]

First, the availability and accessibility of appropriate remedies, such as compensation, reparation, restitution, rehabilitation, guarantees of non-repetition,

---

[166] CESCR, *General Comment No 16*, 20; M Ssenyonjo, 'Non-state Actors and Economic, Social and Cultural Rights' in M Baderin and R McCorquodale (eds), *Economic, Social and Cultural Rights in Action* (Oxford: Oxford University Press, 2007), ch 6.

[167] Ibid. See also, generally, K de Feyter and F Gomez (eds), *Privatisation and Human Rights in the Age of Globalisation* (Antwerp: Intersentia, 2005).

[168] M Ssenyonjo, 'Accountability of Non-state Actors in Uganda for War Crimes and Human Rights Violations' (2005) 10(3) Journal of Conflict and Security Law 405–34; and ICC-02/04–01/05, *The Prosecutor v Joseph Kony, Vincent Otti, Okot Odhiambo and Domic Ongwen*.

[169] *Sara H Longwe v Intercontinental Hotels*, 1992/HP/765 (1993) 4 LRC 221 (High Court of Zambia). For the discussion, see T Kankasa-Mabula, 'The Enforcement of Human Rights of Zambian Women: Sara Longwe *v* Intercontinental Hotel revisited' (1989–1992) 21–24 Zambia Law Journal 30–47.   [170] HRC, *General Comment No 28*, 4.

[171] CESCR, *General Comment No 18: The Right to Work*, E/C.12/GC/18 (6 February 2006), 13.

[172] CESCR, *General Comment No 16*, 21.

declarations, public apologies, educational programmes, prevention programmes, revised policies, benchmarks, and implementation programmes.[173] Domestic courts must not shy away from confronting discriminatory customary practices against women. A decision of the Nigerian Court of Appeal, affirmed by the Supreme Court, shows how domestic courts can enforce human rights of women.[174] This case involved a challenge of a local custom in Nigeria known as *Nrachi* or *Idegbe*.[175] This custom involves the performance of a ceremony whereby a man could keep one of his daughters perpetually in his home unmarried in order to care for the children, especially males, to succeed him (and thereby perform 'women's traditional role'). Relying upon the CEDAW, Article 2, the Nigerian Court of Appeal found the custom to be discriminatory on the basis of sex and in violation of the right to marry and women's equality rights. The Court stressed the importance of eliminating discriminatory customary practices in order to give international human rights practical effect. In holding that a female child can inherit from her deceased father's estate without the *nrachi* ceremony being performed, the Court observed:

In view of the fact that Nigeria is a party to the Convention [CEDAW], courts of law should give or provide teeth to its provisions. That is one major way of ameliorating the unfortunate situation Virginia found herself in, a situation where she was forced to rely on an uncouth custom not only against the laws of Nigeria but also against nature...[176]

Secondly, the establishment and maintenance by states parties of appropriate effective venues for redress against human rights violations, including violations against ESCR. Such venues include independent courts and tribunals, administrative mechanisms, and national human rights and women's commissions that are accessible to all on the basis of equality, including the poorest and most disadvantaged and marginalized women.

Thirdly, the design and implementation of policies and programmes to give long-term effect to the civil, political, economic, social, and cultural rights of both men and women on the basis of equality. These may include the adoption of temporary special measures to accelerate women's equal enjoyment of their rights, gender audits, and gender-specific allocation of resources.[177]

---

[173] Montreal Principles (see n 29 above) 36; African Women's Rights Protocol, Art 25. See also generally D Shelton, *Remedies in International Human Rights Law* (2nd edn, Oxford: Oxford University Press, 2005).

[174] *Muojekwu v Ejikeme* [2000] 5 Nigerian Weekly Law Reports (NWLR) 657, 402.

[175] This situation usually arises when a deceased man leaves an estate, but no surviving male issue to inherit it. The idea underlying this practice is to save the lineage 'from extinction'. The daughter, now considered an *idegbe* or *nrachi*, is entitled to inherit both movable and immovable property from her deceased father's estate. The legal interest vests in her until she gives birth to her own children. However, if she bears sons and daughters, the sons rather than the daughters succeed her in accordance with the rule of primogeniture.

[176] See n 174 above, 410.

[177] See CEDAW Committee, *General Recommendation No 25: Temporary Special Measures*, A/59/38 Part I; CEDAW/C/2004/I/WP 1/Rev.1 (2004); I Boerefijn et al (eds), *Temporary*

Finally, the promotion of equal representation of men and women in public office and decision-making bodies, and the promotion of participation of men and women in development planning, decision making, and in the benefits of development and all programmes related to the realization of all human rights.

As noted above, the custom of polygyny discriminates against women, for example:

This custom can place women at a severe disadvantage by treating wives as commodities to be bought and sold. Even in cases where women's rights to inheritance and child support are recognised, polygamy leaves less to split among the wives. Polygamy is also one of the major reasons African men have difficulty supporting their families placing heavier burdens on women to produce and support their children.... A major problem exists since women bear a risk of getting infected [with HIV/AIDS] by men who have multiple partners/wives.[178]

Viewed in this context, Article 6(c) of the African Women's Rights Protocol may be interpreted as imposing an obligation on the African states parties to move as expeditiously and effectively as possible towards that goal of monogamy (and thus an implied obligation progressively to eliminate polygamy). If the Protocol was to be read in such a way as not to establish such an obligation to move towards monogamy, it would be largely deprived of its raison d'être since polygyny discriminates against women and thus goes to the root of equality and non-discrimination. However, attempts to outlaw polygyny in Africa on the above basis are likely to be opposed by those who argue that polygyny protects women[179] and is recognized in Shari'a and African culture.[180] For example, some of Uganda's marriage laws—in particular the Customary Marriage (Registration) Act, Chapter 248 and the Marriage and Divorce of Mohammedans Act, Chapter 252—recognize potentially polygynous marriage. Yet, at the same time Article 31 of Uganda's Constitution 1995 (as amended in 2005) protects

---

Special Measures: Accelerating de facto Equality of Women under article 4(1) UN Convention on the Elimination of All Forms of Discrimination Against Women (Oxford: Hart Publishing, 2003).

[178] AK Wing and TM Smith, 'The New African Union and Women's Rights' (2003) 13 Transnational Law & Contemporary Problems 33–81, 40, 45 (fns omitted). See also EN Mayambala, 'Changing the Terms of the Debate: Polygamy and the Rights of Women in Kenya and Uganda' (1997) 3(2) East African Journal of Peace and Human Rights 200–39.

[179] See, eg, MC Ali, *Who Practices Polygamy?* (Institute of Islamic Information and Education, nd) <http://www.iiie.net/index.php?q=node/28>, who argues that:

The truth of the matter is that monogamy protects men, allowing them to 'play around' without responsibility ... Men are the ones protected by monogamy while women continue to be victims of men's desires. Polygamy is very much opposed by the male dominated society because it would force men to face up to responsibility and fidelity. It would force them to take responsibility for their polygamous inclinations and would protect and provide for women and children.

[180] See, eg, M Salih Al-Munajjid, 'The Ruling on Plural Marriage and the Wisdom Behind It' (Islam Question and Answer) <http://www.islam-qa.com/index.php?ref=14022&ln=eng&txt=polygamy>.

'equal rights at and in marriage' in the following terms:

A man and a woman are entitled to marry only if they are each of the age of eighteen years and above and are entitled at that age—

(a) to found a family; and
(b) to equal rights at and in marriage, during marriage, and at its dissolution.

The Constitution further provides in Article 33 that 'Women shall be accorded full and equal dignity of the person with men' and requires that: 'Laws, cultures, customs or traditions which are against the dignity, welfare or interest of women or which undermine their status, are prohibited by this Constitution'. Does the practice of polygyny contravene the above constitutional provisions?

The practice of polygyny was challenged before Uganda's Constitutional Court on 8 February 2010 by a local human rights group, Mifumi Uganda Ltd, claiming that the practice violated the dignity, welfare, and interest of women and undermined their status. It asked Uganda's Constitutional Court to declare that the practice violated the right to equality between men and women (since a woman was not allowed to marry more than one husband) and therefore it was unconstitutional. The state through the Attorney General defended the practice of polygyny by stating that the law does not stop two consenting adults from choosing the marriage of their choice and that polygyny was protected under Article 37 of Uganda's 1995 Constitution which protects the right of everyone 'to belong, practise, enjoy, profess and promote any culture, tradition and religion of his or her own choice'. It is hoped that the Constitutional Court will find that the practice of polygyny violates the principle of equality and is thus unconstitutional since cultural practices protected under the constitution must be compatible with the principles of equality and non-discrimination.

3.4 Divorce

Traditional divorce law in many states in Africa discriminates against women. For example, in Egypt, Shari'a is the primary source of legislation and practices that conflict with the government's interpretation of Shari'a are prohibited.[181] Women seeking divorce through unilateral repudiation by virtue of Act No 1 of 2000 (*khul*) must in all cases forego their rights to financial support and, in particular, to their dowries.[182] This leads to financial discrimination against women and may bar women from seeking divorce through unilateral repudiation. In some states, women have to meet stricter evidentiary standards than men to prove grounds for divorce. In Uganda, for example, before 15 October 2004, males were able to divorce their wives solely on the ground of adultery, whereas for a wife to petition for divorce, she had to prove adultery plus an additional

---

[181] See entry on 'Egypt' in Bureau of Democracy, Human Rights, and Labor, International Religious Freedom Report 2007 <http://www.state.gov/g/drl/rls/irf/2007/90209.htm>.
[182] HRC, *Concluding Observations: Egypt*, CCPR/CO/76/EGY(28/11/2002), 8; CEDAW, *Concluding Observations: Egypt*, A/56/38 (2 February 2001), 328.

ground.[183] Uganda's Constitutional Court, on 11 March 2004, held that these provisions were inconsistent with Articles 21 (equal protection), 31 (equal rights in marriage), and 33 (right to dignity) of the 1995 Ugandan Constitution.[184] In a leading judgment, Twinomujuni JA stated that:

It is, in my view, glaringly impossible to reconcile the impugned provisions of the Divorce Act with our modern concepts of equality and non-discrimination between the sexes enshrined in our 1995 Constitution.[185]

This was a landmark case in the history of women's rights to equality and non-discrimination in Uganda for three reasons. First, the Court was unanimous in declaring the impugned provisions of the Divorce Act null and void. The state did not appeal against this judgment to the Supreme Court implying that it was in total agreement with the Constitutional Court's judgment. Secondly, the effect of declaring the impugned provisions of the Divorce Act was understood in later cases to mean that 'the grounds of divorce stated in section 4(1) and (2) are now available to both sexes and therefore, provide for equal justice'.[186] As one High Court Judge noted, 'after constitutional petition No. 2 of 2003, each of the grounds for divorce specified in Section 4 of the Divorce Act, Cap. 249, is available equally to both the husband and the wife'.[187] Understood in this context, the decision of the Constitutional Court is in accordance with Uganda's international human rights obligations under the ICCPR and CEDAW. The HRC interpreted the ICCPR as requiring that the 'grounds for divorce and annulment should be the same for men and women'.[188] Thirdly, the Constitutional Court signalled that it would in the future declare similar discriminatory laws null and void if challenged before the court. Indeed the court appears to have directly invited future petitions challenging discriminatory laws.[189] In her judgment, Lady Justice Mpagi-Bahigeine stated:

There is urgent need for Parliament to enact the operational laws and scrape all the inconsistent laws so that the right to equality ceases to be an illusion but translates into real substantive equality based on the reality of a woman's life, but where Parliament procrastinates, the courts of law being the bulwark of equity would not hesitate to fill the void when called upon to do so or whenever the occasion arises.[190]

---

[183] These included: incest, bigamy, polygamy, rape, sodomy, bestiality, cruelty or desertion. See the Divorce Act (cap 249) Laws of Uganda, 1964, section 4(2)(b).

[184] Constitutional Court of Uganda at Kampala, *Uganda Association of Women Lawyers v The Attorney General*, Constitutional Petition No 2 of 2003 (10 March 2004). Article 21 states: 'All persons are equal before and under the law in all spheres of political, economic, social and cultural life and in every other respect and shall enjoy equal protection of the law.'

[185] Ibid, Judgment of Twinomujuni JA.

[186] See Judgment of Hon Justice LEM Mukasa-Kikonyogo, DCJ (18 November 2005) in *Pamela Sabina Mbabazi v Henry Mugisha Bazira*, Civil Appeal No 44 of 2004. Kitumba JA and Steven BK Kavuma JA agreed with Mukasa-Kikonyogo, DCJ.

[187] *Dr Speciosa Wandira Naigaga Kazibwe v Eng. Charles Nsubuga Kazibwe*—High Court Divorce Cause No 3 of 2003, Judgment of VF Musoke-Kibuuka of 9 October 2004.

[188] HRC, *General Comment 28*, 26.

[189] *Uganda Association of Women Lawyers v The Attorney General*, Constitutional Petition No 2 of 2003 (10 March 2004). [190] Ibid, Judgment of Mpagi-Bahigeine.

This is a welcome development consistent with the right for 'women and men [to] enjoy the same rights in case of separation, divorce or annulment of marriage'.[191] As noted above, law-making organs should be sensitive to issues affecting women.

However, it is important to note that even if adultery as a ground for divorce is available to both men and women, some aspects of the domestic law set out different standards of adultery for husbands and wives.[192] In the case of Uganda, adultery is currently classified as one of the 'Offences Against Morality', meaning it is one of the mechanisms that sets sexual moral standards for married couples.[193] Under Section 154(1) of Uganda's Penal Code, a husband is guilty of adultery if he has sexual intercourse with a 'married woman' not being his wife. But a wife, under Section 154(2), commits adultery when she has sexual intercourse with 'any man' other than her husband (married or not married)! Here, the law clearly imposes double standards on sexual norms. It endorses male sexual promiscuity (as long as a married man is not trespassing on another man's 'property'), but imposes stricter control over women's sexuality. Thus, the law ensures that women remain monogamous and stick to one partner, while it sanctions the polygynous sexuality of men. In addition, the husband in the case of an adulterous wife is said to be an 'aggrieved party' whereas the wife of an adulterous husband is not.[194] Accordingly, a convicted adulterer must pay compensation (for the damaged goods?) to the husband of the adulteress.[195] The fact that only an aggrieved husband can obtain compensation reduces a married woman to the position of her husband's property who should be compensated for the damage occasioned to it.[196] It also ensures that husbands exercise almost rights of legal ownership over wives, thus reducing married women to the status of 'objects' or being held in 'slavery'.[197] Clearly, this means of determining human relations is undoubtedly archaic, and discriminatory against women.[198] It is interesting to note that on 4 April 2007, Uganda's Constitution Court found that the provision of section 154 of the Penal Code Act was inconsistent with Uganda's Constitution (Articles 20(1), (2), (3), 24, 31(1), and 33(6) of the Constitution) and declared it was null and void.[199]

---

[191] African Women's Rights Protocol, Art 7.
[192] See, eg, Penal Code Act (Chapter 120, Laws of Uganda).   [193] Ibid.
[194] CEDAW, *Third Periodic Reports of States Parties: Uganda*, CEDAW/C/UGA/3 (3 July 2000), 67.
[195] Ibid.   [196] Ibid.
[197] According to Art 1 of the Slavery Convention, 60 LNTS 253, entered into force 9 March 1927, which corresponds to the 'classic' meaning of slavery as it was practised for centuries, 'slavery is the status or condition of a person over whom any or all of the powers attaching to the right of ownership are exercised'.
[198] See S Tamale, 'Adultery Law Violates Our Constitution', *The New Vision*, Kampala, 11 April 2006; O Oloya, 'Uganda: Adultery Law is Archaic, Oppressive to Women', *The New Vision*, Kampala, 12 April 2006.
[199] See *Law and Advocacy for Women in Uganda v Attorney General of Uganda*, Constitutional Petition Nos 13 of 2005 and 05 of 2006, Judgment of 5 April 2007 (SG Egwau, A Twinomujuni, CNB Kitumba, CK Byamugisha, and SBK Kavuma).

4. Conclusion: the duty to uproot prejudicial cultural practices enhances human security

This chapter has focused on only a handful of the many cultural issues that arise in the debate over the protection and promotion of women's human rights in Africa. It cannot be disputed that 'human rights of women and of the girl-child are an inalienable, integral and indivisible part of universal human rights'[200] and that these rights are essential for human security in general and women's security in particular. Women cannot be free from fear and from want without enjoying equality in rights with men.

However, it is clear from the foregoing that despite a wide range of human rights instruments protecting the human rights of women in Africa, these rights are yet to be realized by all women in Africa. African states still face several obstacles in protecting human rights generally and women's rights in particular, including persistent armed conflicts especially between rebel groups and government armed forces (in Sudan, Chad, Central African Republic, Somalia, Eritrea, and in the Democratic Republic of Congo), lack of human and food security due to poverty and underdevelopment, corruption, and lack of good governance[201] as well as the long-term effects of 'the historic injustices imposed on Africa such as slavery, colonization, [and] depletion of natural resources'.[202] Such obstacles to the realization of human rights must be addressed before legal guarantees of women's human rights are realized in practice.

While the Protocol to the African Charter on the Rights of Women in Africa sets a strong legal basis for the protection of human rights of women at a regional level, its application is replete with difficulties. As noted above, nearly four years after the adoption of the Women's Rights Protocol, only 21 (out of 53) African states have ratified the Protocol. Why are other states not ratifying (even if with some reservations) if they are committed to human rights of women in their respective states and Africa in general? As yet, the reluctance to ratify the Protocol raises some questions as to the commitment of states to the regional protection of women's human rights in Africa. In addition, the prevailing harmful traditional practices and theological premises (broadly speaking 'culture') have had a disproportionately negative effect on the realization of women's human rights in Africa. As noted above, states should ensure that traditional, historical, religious,

---

[200] UN World Conference on Human Rights, Vienna Declaration and Programme of Action, 25 June 1993, UN Doc A/Conf.157/23 (1993), 1, 18; Fourth World Conference on Women, Declaration and Platform for Action, Beijing, UN Doc A/Conf.177/20 (1995), 213.

[201] See Resolution on the Impact of the Ongoing Global Financial Crisis on the Enjoyment of Social and Economic Rights in Africa, ACHPR/Res 159(XLVI)09, adopted in Banjul by the African Commission on Human and Peoples' Rights, 25 November 2009, preamble para 6.

[202] See the African Youth Charter, adopted by the African Union Assembly in July 2006, preamble para 5, available at <http://www.africa-union.org/root/UA/Conferences/Mai/HRST/Charter%20english.pdf>.

or cultural attitudes are not used to justify violations of women's right to equality before the law and to equal enjoyment of all human rights.[203]

The key question which arises here is what are the underlying dynamics that make culture as an obstacle to women's human rights in Africa so entrenched and difficult to change? The simple answer is that cultural obstacles in Africa have been so deeply entrenched for centuries and most states have not adopted immediate and effective measures, particularly in the fields of teaching, education, culture, and information, to combat discrimination against women. As required by both CEDAW (Article 5(a)) and the Protocol to the African Charter on the Rights of Women in Africa (Articles 2 and 12), it is now time for states to take 'appropriate measures'—both legislative and non-legislative—to modify 'social and cultural patterns of conduct' to achieve elimination of prejudices and of practices based on the idea of the inferiority of women or on stereotyped roles of either sex. It is, therefore, necessary for African states to give urgent attention to the general duty of states to modify the social and cultural patterns of conduct of women and men through public education.[204] It is useful to view culture as a dynamic aspect of every state's social fabric and life and therefore subject to change. As Steiner writes,

Culture is plastic, made and remade through the course of history, not unshakable and essentialist in character but in many respects contingent, open to evolution and to more radical change through purposeful human agency informed by human rights ideals.[205]

States should realize that cultural practices which deny women the right to equality and freedom from discrimination, as well as the opportunity to access economic resources and assets necessary for their economic, political, and social empowerment, violate women's human rights including the rights to development and self-determination. These violations and denials of women's human rights continue to bolster the marginalization of women, feminization of poverty, HIV/AIDS, and insecurity in Africa which are not in the best interest of any single African state. It is not too late to recognize that promoting and defending women's human rights advances society as a whole and contributes to attaining human security.

---

[203] HRC, *General Comment 28* (n 135 above) para 5. See also the High Court of Kenya in *Jesse Kamau & 25 others v Attorney General* [2010] eKLR at www.kenyalaw.org/CaseSearch/case_download.php?go...link=-Kenya.

[204] Protocol to the ACHPR on the Rights of Women in Africa, Art 2(2). See also CEDAW, Art 10(c); CERD, Art 7; CRC, Art 12(1).

[205] HJ Steiner, 'International Protection of Human Rights' in MD Evans (ed), *International Law* (2nd edn, Oxford: Oxford University Press, 2006), 753–82, 777.

10

Corruption as a Threat to Human Security in Africa

*Ebenezer Durojaye**

When you fight corruption, corruption fights back[1]

1. Introduction

One of the greatest challenges facing African countries today is the issue of corruption. Although no society is insulated from the problem of corruption, Africa has remained the region that is worst affected by this social malaise. It is an antithesis that the region that is grappling with problems such as poverty, conflict, and disease, is the same that has exhibited perhaps the greatest tolerance for corrupt practices.

Various reasons such as poor wages, weak political institutions, and poorly developed checks-and-balances mechanisms among the institutions of governments have been attributed to the prevalence of corruption in Africa.[2] It is estimated that approximately US$20 billion is lost to corruption in Africa each year.[3] Corruption breeds poverty and underdevelopment. Indeed, it has been argued

* Researcher and doctoral candidate at the Department of Constitutional Law and Philosophy of Law, Faculty of Law, University of the Free State in South Africa where he also teaches on the LLM Programme on Sexual and Reproductive Rights organized.
[1] See: <http://thefastertimes.com/world/2010/02/23/an-interview-with-nuhu-ribadu-nigeria%e2%80%99s-corruption-fighter/>; see also *Washington Post* interview with Nuhu Ribadu Nigeria's former anti-corruption chief, <http://www.washingtonpost.com/wp-dyn/content/article/2009/05/22/AR2009052202025.html>, for more on Ribadu's views on corruption in Nigeria.
[2] W Laurence, 'The Perils of Payoff: Corruption as a threat to Global Biodiversity' (2004) 19(8) Trends in Ecology and Evolution 399, 400.
[3] G Acquaah-Gaisie, 'Grand Corruption: A Crime against Humanity' (2003) <http://www.personal.buseco.monash.edu.au/~geraldg/Temp/grand_corruption.pdf>.
The author notes that due to the grave consequences of corruption on the lives of people in poor regions such as Africa, perpetrators of corrupt practices should be tried for committing crimes against humanity.

that 'deep-rooted corruption in Africa is one of the most serious developmental challenges facing the continent'.[4] It also undermines democratic governance in any society.

Corruption may be described as the interface of political and economic elites at global, regional, and national scale.[5] More importantly, corruption is a threat to human security as millions of lives, particularly in Africa, have been lost to lack of social amenities such as good roads and health care services, mainly due to corrupt practices. Corruption is believed to be prevalent in Africa due to the absence of strong institutional and legal frameworks to combat it.

Due to its serious impact on the socio-economic development of any country, the problem of corruption has increasingly received the attention of the international community in recent times. Thus, there has been a steady rise in the number of international instruments to combat corruption at the international and regional levels. These include the Convention on Combating Bribery of Foreign Public Officials in International Business Transactions (agreed by member states of the Organisation for Economic Co-Operation and Development (OECD) in 1997)[6] and the UN Convention against Corruption, which was adopted in 2003.[7]

At the regional level, the African Union has adopted a treaty known as the Convention on Preventing and Combating Corruption (AU Corruption Convention) in 2003.[8] Although in recent times several African countries have enacted specific legislation to address the problem of corruption, due to lack of political will and weak judicial system these laws have remained 'paper tigers'. Against this backdrop, this chapter examines the prevalence of corruption in Africa and its impact on human security, drawing on experiences of countries such as Kenya, Zimbabwe, and Nigeria as case studies. Moreover, the chapter considers strategies (particularly legislative frameworks) employed to combat corruption in Africa and the weaknesses of such strategies. The chapter then provides some important suggestions that African governments should consider in combating corruption in their countries.

---

[4] See T Snider and W Kidane, 'Combating Corruption through International Law in Africa: A Comparative Analysis' (2007) Cornell International Law Journal 692 where the authors quoted the World Bank estimation that corrupt governments along with their business partners take in excess of US$1 trillion in bribes each year and more subtle forms of corruption vitiate another US$1.5 trillion in procurement decisions.

[5] G Frase-Moleketi, 'Towards a Common Understanding of Corruption in Africa' (2009) 24(3) Public Policy and Administration 331, 332.

[6] OECD Convention on Combating Bribery of Foreign Public Officials in International Business Transactions (18 December 1997) 37 ILM 1.

[7] UN Convention against Corruption (7 October 2003), UN Doc A/58/422.

[8] See African Union Convention on Preventing and Combating Corruption (11 July 2003) 43 ILM. The Convention came into force on 6 August 2006 upon ratification by the 50th African country.

2. The meaning of corruption

Corruption, like many other concepts, is incapable of a precise or generally accepted definition. This is because what amounts to corruption may differ from one society to another.[9] Nonetheless, different attempts have been made to describe what may constitute corruption. For instance, corruption has been generally described as the abuse of public office for personal gain. This definition will include unilateral abuses by government officials such as embezzlement and nepotism as well as extortion, influence peddling, and fraud.

Beyond this narrow definition, corruption has also been described as not only limited to the public sector but also prevalent in the private sector. In Bayley's view, corruption means the 'misuse of authority as a result of consideration of personal gain, which need not be monetary'.[10] According to Werlin, political corruption (which is very common in Africa) is the diversion of public resources to non-public use.[11] Nye has attempted to describe corruption broadly as involving

behaviour which deviates from the normal duty of a public role because of private-regarding (family or close clique), pecuniary or status gain, or violates rules against the exercise of certain types of private-regarding influence.[12]

Corruption also arises where an individual, who is granted power by society to perform certain public functions, undertakes, as a result of personal gain or reward, actions that may affect negatively the welfare of the society or even injure the public interest.[13]

While there is no agreed definition of corruption, it is important to note that there are different forms of corruption. Often a distinction is made between 'petty corruption' and 'grand corruption'. The former refers to minor corrupt practices such as corruption involving small amounts of money, granting of minor favours by those seeking preferential treatment, or the employment of friends or relatives into minor positions, whereas the latter refers to corrupt practices on a large scale which often pervade the highest levels of a national government, leading to a broad erosion of confidence in good governance, the rule of law, and economic stability.[14] Also, Smith et al have made a major distinction between what

---

[9] See A Adeniran, 'Anti Corruption Measures in Nigeria' (2008) Kings Law Journal 57, 59.

[10] DH Bayley, 'The Effect of Corruption in Developing a Nation' (1966) 19 The Western Political Science Quarterly 719–32.

[11] H Werlin, 'The Consequences of Corruption: The Ghanaian Experience' (1973) 88 Political Science Quarterly 71–85.

[12] J Nye, 'Corruption and Political Development: A Cost-Benefit Analysis' (1967) 61 American Political Science Review 417–21.

[13] C Fredrich, 'Corruption Concept in Historical Perspective' in Hiedenheimer et al (eds), *In Political Corruption: A Handbook* (New Brunswick, NJ: Transaction, 1990), 15–24.

[14] S Rose-Ackerman, 'Democracy and Grand Corruption' in R Williams (ed), *Explaining Corruption* (Cheltenham: Elgar Reference Collection, 2000), 321–36.

is known as collusive and non-collusive corruption.[15] According to their definition, collusive corruption occurs when the briber and a government official con-
spire or agree to rob the government of revenue. On the other hand, non-collusive
corruption implies a situation whereby a government official demands a bribe
in order to perform a legally obligated function. From this distinction it would
appear that collusive corruption is far more threatening to the resources (including natural resources) of a state than non-collusive corruption. This form of corruption is also difficult to detect or eradicate as it is highly decentralized.

Similarly, a distinction has been made between political and bureaucratic corruption.[16] According to Mbaku, political corruption usually refers to activities by
political coalitions to capture the apparatus of government or maintain a monop-
oly of power.[17] Examples of political corruption include vote rigging, manipulation of the voters' register, and the falsification of election results. On the other
hand, bureaucratic corruption involves efforts by civil servants to enrich themselves usually through illegal means.[18] From this discussion it is clear that there
are different forms of corruption even if there is no universally agreed meaning of
what constitutes corruption.

3. Some common forms of corruption in Africa

In this section an attempt will be made to describe some important examples of
corruption that are rampant in African countries.

3.1 Bribery

Bribery is perhaps the most common type of corruption among political and
public office holders in Africa. It refers to the act of offering money or benefit in
anticipation of a reward or favour or to influence a decision. Bribery can be initiated by someone who seeks or solicits a bribe or by a person who offers and then
pays a bribe.[19]

Several international instruments have attempted to define or describe
what constitutes bribery.[20] The use of the word 'benefit' in the above-rendered

---

[15] J Smith et al, 'Illegal Logging, Collusive Corruption and Fragmented Government in
Kalimantan, Indonesia' (2003) International Foreign Review 293–302.

[16] J Mbaku, 'Bureaucratic Corruption in Africa: The Futility of Cleanups' (1996) 16 Cato Law
Journal 99, 102.   [17] Ibid, 102.

[18] Ibid.

[19] UN Office on Drugs and Crime, *The Global Programme against Corruption: UN Anti-
corruption Toolkit* (The Ministries of Foreign Affairs, Netherlands and Norway, 2004).

[20] See eg Art VI of the Inter-American Convention against Corruption of 29 March 2006, 35
ILM 724. This Convention enjoins states parties to criminalize the offering of or the acceptance by
a public official of an undue advantage in exchange for any act or omission in the performance of
the official's public function. Similarly, Art 1 of the Convention on Combating Bribery of Foreign

definition should be construed broadly to cover several acts such as company shares, insider information, sexual or other favours, entertainment or employment, or a mere promise of incentives.[21] Such a benefit may directly or indirectly be in favour of the person bribed or a third party (a family member, relative, associate, favourite charity, private business, or a political party). The conduct for which the bribe is paid may be active or passive. It is the former if the conduct involves the exertion of political power or influence. On the other hand it is passive if it involves turning a blind eye to an offence or obligation.[22] Usually a bribe is paid to an individual on a case-by-case basis, or it may be a continuous process whereby a public official receives regular benefits in exchange for regular favours. Bribery may be carried out between individuals or even corporate entities. The recent Halliburton bribery scandal in Nigeria provides a good example of a highly organized corporate bribery scheme, which involves foreign firms.[23]

As will be seen below, bribery constitutes a criminal offence under international and national laws. However, according to some of these laws, the criminalization of bribery is limited to cases where the recipient is a public official or where the interests of the public are likely to be affected. The implication of this is that instances of bribery which do not fall into those categories are left to be resolved by non-judicial means.[24]

3.2 Embezzlement, theft, and fraud

Embezzlement and theft, on the one hand, involve the taking or conversion of money, property, or other valuable items by an individual who is not ordinarily entitled to them but who, by virtue of his or her position or employment, has access to them.[25] On the other hand, fraud consists of the use of false or misleading information to induce the owner of the property to relinquish it voluntarily. For example, the diversion or selling by a public official of a consignment of building materials intended for construction of low-cost housing for the population can be said to amount to theft or fraud. Also, a public official who induces an aid agency to over-supply aid or who inflates the price of items will be said to have committed fraud.

As with the case of bribery, many international and national instruments have attempted to address the challenges posed by embezzlement, fraud, and theft

Public Officials in International Business Transactions provides that states should criminalize the offering of bribes by a national of one state to a government official of another state. In conjunction with a business transaction, the UN Convention on Corruption (7 October 2003, UN Doc A/58/422) enjoins states to criminalize the bribery of foreign public officials.

[21] Corruption Toolkit (see n 19 above).   [22] Ibid.

[23] This was a case where it was established that the officials of Halliburton paid a total of approximately US$180 million as bribes to Nigerian government officials in order to secure oil contracts. See 'Halliburton pays USD560m for Bribing Nigerian Officials', *Sahara Reporter* <http://www.saharareporters.com/index.php?>.   [24] See n 19 above.

[25] Ibid.

as criminal offences.[26] This approach has often targeted public officials where the interests of the public are affected. It should be noted that the word 'theft' is distinguishable from 'bribery' in the sense that the former is broader than the latter since it also includes the taking of any property by a person who does not have the right to take it. Thus, if a public official is involved in the act of taking something which does not belong to him or her, or that he or she does not have permission to take, then he or she would be said to have committed theft. On the other hand, where a public official is involved in taking public property entrusted to him or her for personal use then this will amount to embezzlement. Although 'theft' is often defined in relation to tangible materials such as money, furniture, or electronic items, it may also apply to non-tangible materials such as revealing vital information to unauthorized persons. An unauthorized withdrawal by a public official who has access to the account of a government establishment or parastatal, or making available information to that effect, will amount to theft.

3.3 Abuse of discretion

Corruption can arise where an individual vested with public powers or authority to purchase goods or award contracts on behalf of a government establishment decides to use such powers for personal gain. For instance, an abuse of discretion may arise where such a person exercises his or her discretion to purchase goods or services in a company in which he or she has a personal interest. Also, it will amount to an abuse of discretion if such a person decides to propose a real estate development that may increase the value of his or her personal property. This form of abuse is usually common among government officials who often wield broad powers without proper checks or accountability mechanisms to curtail the abuse of such powers.[27]

3.4 Favouritism and nepotism

Acts of favouritism and nepotism are generally abuses of discretion. These forms of abuse, however, are not motivated by gains directly accruing to a public official who engages in them. Rather, the gains accruing are often for the benefit of someone directly or indirectly linked with the public official through family ties, political party allegiance, tribe, or affiliation to religious or other groups. If recruitment to a position is considered solely on the basis of the above situations without recourse to the qualifications of the person employed, this will amount to an abuse of office tantamount to corruption. In many parts of Africa, particularly in the public sector, acts of favouritism and nepotism are very common especially in societies where there are strong alliances to political, religious, or ethnic groups. These forms of abuse tend to breed incompetence and poor performance in the public sector.

---

[26] See, eg, Arts 15–20 of the UN Convention against Corruption.
[27] See, eg, n 16 above.

4. The reasons for the rampancy of corruption in Africa

Several reasons have been adduced for the rampancy of corruption in many African countries. Mbaku argues that the African extended family practice tends to put pressures on civil servants or government officials to engage in corrupt practices in order to meet the needs of the extended family members.[28] He notes further that bureaucrats are believed to exploit their public positions to generate benefits for themselves, their families, and their ethnic or social cleavage.

Inefficiency and incompetence on the part of civil servants or public officials have also been cited as reasons for gross acts of corruption in many African countries. It is generally believed that the backbone for the sustenance of any economy is the level of competence and professionalism of its civil service. However, in many African countries, the civil service is technically deficient and lacks professionalism. This is because employment procedures are frequently marred by malpractices such as nepotism and favouritism and are therefore not based on merit. The civil service is unable to carry out proper plans for development projects in many African countries and politicians often use the civil service as an avenue for repaying their supporters regardless of their competence or qualifications.

Pervasive poverty, high levels of material deprivation and inequalities in the distribution of resources in many parts of the region have also been given as excuses for corrupt practices in many African states. Africa is undeniably one of the poorest regions of the world.[29] Many Africans are said to live on US$1 per day. Unemployment rates are generally high across the continent; therefore many Africans find it difficult to make ends meet. Those who are fortunate enough to be employed are often grossly underpaid. While these factors should not provide justification for the thriving of corruption in Africa, they no doubt reflect reality on the ground in many African countries, as well as underscoring the need for African governments to tackle corruption. Other causes of corruption include cultural practices,[30] greed and obsession for materialism, and extensive involvement of government in economic activities.[31]

---

[28] Ibid.

[29] See United Nations Development Programme (UNDP), *Human Development Report: Human Index Ranking* (New York: UNDP, 2009), in which approximately 182 countries were ranked, with African countries accounting for 20 of the 22 lowest rated countries on the table.

[30] There is the argument that the act of giving gifts which is common in many African traditions has provided an easy avenue for bribery in the post-colonial era. However, some commentators have disputed this position claiming that it is untrue and mischievous, see eg GT Ware and GP Noone, 'The Culture of Corruption in the Post-conflict and Developing World' in A Chayes and M Minow (eds), *Imagine Coexistence: Restoring Humanity after Violent Ethnic Conflict* (San Francisco, CA: PON Books/Jossey-Bass, 2003), 191, 192 .

[31] See n 9 above, 61.

5. Effects of corruption

It is no longer in contention that corruption poses serious political and economic challenges to countries in Africa. Some of the negative impacts of corruption on the lives of the African people will be examined in this section and while it considers the general impact of corruption in Africa, it emphasizes the impact of corruption on human security in Africa.

5.1 Impact on political development

Corruption is a potential threat to democracy, since it undermines good governance by subverting the formal process. Whenever there is widespread corruption in the electoral process, there is a tendency for the beneficiaries of corruption to be less accountable to the public or electorate. This is particularly true of many African countries where most elections are rigged—electoral malpractice seems to be the norm rather than the exception. With the exception of a few countries, such as South Africa and Ghana, which have been able to conduct relatively fair elections in recent times, elections in most African countries such as Nigeria, Kenya, and Zimbabwe have been characterized by rigging, violence, incompetence, and manipulation. In countries where electoral malpractices are rife, the so-called elected representatives of the people in both the legislative and executive arms of government often show little regard to the needs and welfare of the populace. A good example is the case of Nigeria where the election that saw the current government assume power in 2007 was believed to have been rigged to a massive extent. The situation in Nigeria today is such that elected representatives work at cross-purposes with the wishes and needs of the people they claim to serve. It is a matter of fact that these 'elected' representatives are accountable to their 'Godfathers' or the political parties sponsoring them. This situation often leads to a disconnection between the electorate and their representatives at various levels of government which, in turn, leads to the erosion of good governance with 'elected' representatives accounting to no one but themselves.

Also, corruption in the judiciary can lead to the abuse of rule of law and the total breakdown of law and order. Since the judicial arm of government provides checks on both the legislative and executive arms, any attempt to compromise the integrity of the judiciary can spell doom for any society. This is because the poor and underprivileged in society will be unable to seek redress for violations of their fundamental rights; a situation that not only contradicts the well-known maxim *ubis jus ibi remedium* (where there is a right there must be a remedy), but also negatively impacts on society.

The impact of corruption on the economy can be devastating as economic growth is undermined and a loss of revenue may be experienced. Generally, corruption may lead to inefficiency and ineptitude in handling of economic decisions thereby leading to high costs for transacting business in the country. In most cases where corruption is rampant awards of contracts are often inflated leading to unnecessary expenditure and increased risk in conducting business. Corruption allows inefficient producers to remain in business, encourages governments to pursue perverse economic policies, and provides opportunities to bureaucrats and politicians to enrich themselves through extortion of bribes from those seeking government favour.[32] Thus, corruption distorts economic incentives, discourages entrepreneurship, and slows economic growth.[33] Commenting on the effects of corruption in society Sanchez, a Nobel laureate, has noted that

When the public at large demonstrate for more accountability and decent government in so many countries of the world they are motivated, to no small extent, by anger over corruption: corruption that humiliates the poor who must bribe officials for minimal services; corruption that bankrupts the honest trader; corruption that empowers unscrupulous captains of commerce and their partners, dishonest politicians; corruption which spreads like a cancer to kill all that is decent in society.[34]

Interestingly, however, some commentators have argued that corruption can lead to lower costs of conducting business and may even speed up the process.[35]

6. Corruption as a threat to human security

By far the gravest consequence of corruption in Africa is the threat it poses to human security. Political and bureaucratic corruption have serious implications for the enjoyment of individuals' rights to life, health, and dignity all guaranteed under international and regional human rights instruments. For example, corruption in electoral processes in some Africa countries has sparked unrest and led to loss of life. Two recent examples are the situations in Kenya and Zimbabwe.

The 2007 presidential election in Kenya was hotly contested between the incumbent President Mwai Kibaki and the opposition leader Raila Odinga. There were confirmed reports from international observers that the electoral process was characterized by rigging and malpractice.[36] The European Union's head observer during the election, Alexander Graf Lambsdorff, declared it to be flawed.[37] He

---

[32] See n 16 above.

[33] J Mbaku, 'Bureaucratic Corruption as Rent-Seeking Behavior' (1992) Konjunkturpolitik 38 247–65; see also, DJ Gould, *Bureaucratic Corruption Underdevelopment in the Third World: The Case of Zaire* (New York: Pergamon Press, 1980).

[34] A Sanchez, a statement made at the opening of the Transparency International office in Berlin in November 1993.

[35] D Osterfiled, *Prosperity versus Planning: How Government Stifles Economic Growth* (New York: Oxford University Press, 1992).

[36] See 'Kenya's Election seen as Badly Flawed', Reuters, 18 September 2008 <http://africa.reuters.com/world/news/usnLI387861.html>.

[37] J Gettleman, 'Disputed Vote Plunges Kenya Into Bloodshed', *New York Times*, 31 December 2007.

further claimed that the Electoral Commission was unable to establish 'the cred-ibility of the tallying process to the satisfaction of all parties and candidates'.[38] In the early stages of vote counting Odinga was in the lead, and it appeared that a new president would emerge. However, towards the latter stages, the huge gap recorded earlier in favour of Odinga began to shrink in a manner that aroused justified suspicions of malpractice. On 30 December 2007, the same day that Odinga formally alleged fraud in the electoral process, Kibaki was declared the winner by the electoral body. The final result showed that Kibaki had overtaken Odinga by as many as 300,000 votes. It was strongly believed that the final result of the election was doctored to ensure that the ruling party did not lose.

The Chairman of the Electoral Commission, Samuel Kivuiti, admitted that there were irregularities in the election but absolved the Commission of any blame.[39] He was later reported to have claimed that pressures were mounted on him by the ruling party to release the result at all costs without verifying the authenticity of the result.[40] As expected, this disclosure did not go down well with many of the electorate, particularly those from the opposition party and this resulted in massive protests and violent reaction. After the unrest it was estimated that 1,000 persons had lost their lives and 250,000 persons were displaced.[41] The situation was so grave that many people became refugees in their own country. It was further aggravated by the issue of ethnicity as violent protests were targeted at the Kikuyus, the ethnic group of President Kibaki.

Moreover, the unprofessional manner with which the police handled the unrest was far from satisfactory. In short, what had been a peaceful and serene country was thrown into pandemonium with a total breakdown of law and order. It took the intervention of the international community, ably represented by the former UN Secretary-General Kofi Annan, to broker a truce between President Kibaki and the opposition leader Odinga.

Another country which experienced massive corruption, as a result of which its people have suffered various forms of insecurity, is Zimbabwe. The case of Zimbabwe is a wretched one and provides a good example of how political and economic corruption can become threats to human security.

In the late 1980s and early part of the 1990s, the Zimbabwean economy was buoyant and the country was often regarded as the food basket of southern Africa. However, the situation began to worsen towards the end of the 1990s when the Mugabe government resorted to Machiavellian tactics to maintain its hold on power and silence the opposition. The controversial land reform programme,

---

[38] 'Kibaki Re-elected as President of Kenya', *Financial Times*, 30 December 2008.

[39] J Gettleman, 'Tribal Violence Breaks out in Kenya over Disputed Election Result', *International Herald Tribune*, 30 December 2007.

[40] I Ongiri, 'I acted under a pressure, says Kivuitu', *Standard Newspaper* (online edn), 2 January 2008.

[41] See Open Democracy 'Kenya: Root of Crisis' <http://www.opendemocracy.net/article/democracy_power/kenya_roots_crisis>.

which divested the white minority of land ownership, was poorly implemented thereby leading to low food production and food insecurity. The land reform pro- gramme was fraught with malpractice as senior government officials struggled to attain lands otherwise meant for farming. This led to a situation whereby the hitherto productive lands were shared among government loyalists and cronies.

A report by the Physicians for Human Rights has linked Mugabe's misman- aged economy and pervasive corruption to food insecurity, malnutrition, and the collapse of the health system in Zimbabwe.[42] The report states that the contro- versial land reform policy destroyed Zimbabwe's agricultural sector which had hitherto provided approximately 45 per cent of the country's foreign exchange revenue and contributed to the livelihoods of more than 70 per cent of the popu- lation. According to the report, as at December 2008 there were no functioning critical beds in the public health sector in the country. Access to essential medi- cines remains a serious concern; essential items such as drugs, medical supplies (including soaps, syringes, surgical gloves, and bandages) are in critically short supply. Moreover, high transportation costs boths for heath-care providers and patients have remained a barrier to accessibility of health-care services for the majority of the population.

In addition to all these problems, there is a lack of health determinants, such as potable water, clean sewage and sanitation systems, and nutritious food. Thus, in August 2008 there was an outbreak of cholera and the government was unable to respond adequately to curtail its spread which led to the death of approximately 3,000 people. The UN report on this incident discloses that cholera had spread to all Zimbabwe's ten provinces and to 55 of the country's 62 districts. It states further that the cumulative fatality rate is approximately 5.4 per cent, almost five times gre~ .er than usual in outbreaks of cholera.[43] HIV/AIDS continues to pose a serious threat to life for millions of Zimbabweans (with about 400 deaths per day), tuberculosis is on the increase, and maternal mortality has continued to rise (from 160 per 100,000 in 1990 to 1,100 per 100,000 in 2005). As a result of these health challenges, life expectancy at birth has fallen dramatically from 62 years for both sexes in 1990 to approximately 36 years in 2006 (37 for males, 34 for females) making it the lowest life expectancy in the world.[44]

The nexus between corruption and human security can be explained further using the Nigerian example. This is a country that gained independence from British rule in 1960 with great hopes of becoming a major power among devel- oping countries. However, these hopes and aspirations were not to be realized due to, among other things, the problem of pervasive corruption. Nigeria is still regarded as one of the most corrupt nations in the world.[45]

---

[42] *Health in Ruins: A Man-made Disaster in Zimbabwe* (Boston, MA: Physicians for Human Rights, 2009).   [43] Ibid.
[44] Ibid.
[45] ie, Transparency International ranked Nigeria 142nd out of 163 countries in its 2006 Corruption Perceptions Index: <http://www.transparency.org/policy_research/surveys_indices/cpi/2006>.

It is estimated that Nigeria has lost nearly 380 billion Naira to corruption since independence.[46] The corollary of this is the emergence of weak infrastructures in every facet of human endeavour, lack of a useable road infrastructure, lack of health-care services, and poor electricity supply. At 1,100 deaths per 100,000 live births, the maternal mortality ratio in Nigeria is also said to be one of the highest in the world;[47] a recent report has shown the link between pervasive corruption and the high maternal mortality ratio in the country.[48] The recent uprising in the Niger Delta area—which has led to loss of lives, incessant cases of kidnapping, and attacks on oil facilities—is a result of mismanagement and corruption among the ruling class.

Despite its abundant natural and human resources, Nigeria is still classified as a poor country. Unemployment rates have risen, life expectancy has fallen dramatically, and the crime rates are rising by the day, all due to egregious corruption among the ruling class. Moreover, the fact that there are often excessive displays of ill-gotten wealth by public officials and politicians has led to increases in crime rates in the country. Desperate unemployed youths have resorted to armed robbery or kidnapping. In virtually every part of the country there have been reported cases of kidnapping, a crime hitherto confined to the restive Niger Delta area alone. The near absence of social amenities and facilities, such as good roads and functional health-care centres, has further led to avoidable loss of life. Indeed, it is generally believed that the wanton loss of life due to non-existent or appalling social infrastructures, particularly in the health sector, is traceable to corruption among the ruling class.

7. Legal frameworks for combating corruption

In recent years different strategies have been adopted to combat the menace of corruption in Africa. This section of the chapter will only focus on the various legal frameworks aimed at combating corruption in Africa. It is not the intention here to examine the legal frameworks in all African countries, but rather to focus

Transparency reports that although Nigeria's ranking has subsequently improved over the years, it is still generally believed that corruption is pervasive. See A Aderonmu at: <http://aderinola.wordpress.com/2007/12/05/nigeria-is-still-the-most-corrupt-country-in-the-world/> where the author notes that Nigeria is still the most corrupt country in the world. The only solution to eradicating or minimizing corruption in Nigeria is to punish all living and serving offenders but for over 47 years it has been difficult to prosecute effectively any of the key players who have aided the demeaning of Nigeria.

[46] Nigerian leaders are estimated to have stolen or wasted between US$380–480 billion through corruption since 1960: 'Nigerian Leaders "Stole" $380bn', BBC News, 20 October 2006 <http://news.bbc.co.uk/2/hi/ africa/6069230.stm>.

[47] The World Health Organization (WHO), UNICEF, the United Nations Population Fund, and the World Bank, *Maternal Mortality in 2005 Estimates* (Geneva: WHO, 2007), 33.

[48] See, eg, Center for Reproductive Rights (CRR), *Broken Promises: Human Rights, Accountability and Maternal Death in Nigeria* (New York: CRR, 2008).

on Nigeria and Kenya as case studies. The selection of these countries is on the basis that they are two of Africa's most corrupt countries, but which have made considerable attempts in recent times to deal with corruption. However, where necessary, references will be made to other countries in the region for comparative analysis.

As earlier mentioned, there exist conventions at the international and regional levels dealing specifically with corruption. In addition to these efforts, many African countries have enacted legislation directly or indirectly to deal with the issue. However, despite these efforts, corruption has not abated and in some countries the situation has actually worsened.

As stated above, Nigeria has attained international notoriety for corruption. Attempts to combat corruption in the country predate modern times. For instance, under the Yoruba customary law bribery was forbidden and the imposition of heavy fines or imprisonment, or both, awaited anyone found guilty of bribery.[49] Corruption has been described as one of the most debilitating economic and social problems affecting the country.[50] Shortly after independence in 1960 the political leaders who took over at the helm of affairs were alleged to have mismanaged the economy and engaged in grand corrupt practices. This led to military intervention through coups d'état. Unfortunately, rather than bringing succour to the people, military rule exacerbated their suffering. Military rule in Nigeria took corruption to new heights and perpetuated it as a way of life.[51] In particular, the Babangida and Abacha regimes (1985–93 and 1993–97, respectively) were noted for brazenly and recklessly looting the country's treasury. Due to the pervasiveness of corruption, Transparency International has often rated Nigeria as one of the most corrupt countries in the world.[52] While the criteria used in arriving at its rating have been criticized,[53] it is not in doubt that corruption is rife in Nigeria.

Although corruption, particularly in the public sector, has always been criminalized under the Nigerian Criminal[54] and Penal[55] Codes, little effort has been made to bring the culprits to book and this lack of enforcement inevitably brought about a culture of impunity for corrupt practices.

---

[49] The Yorubas constitute one of Nigeria's three large ethnic groups and are to be found in the Western part of Nigeria. See, eg, AT Oyeowo and OB Olaoba, *A Survey of African Law and Custom—With Particular Reference to the Yoruba Speaking People of South-Western Nigeria* (Ibadan: Jator Publishing, 1999), 108; see also AK Ajisafe, *The Laws and Custom of Yoruba People* (London: George Routledge and Sons, 1924), 32.

[50] N Okogbue, 'An Appraisal of the Legal and Institutional Framework for Comanting Corruption in Nigeria' (2006) 13(1) Journal of Financial Crime 92, 93.

[51] S Tolofari, *Exploitation and Instability in Nigeria: The Orka Coup in Perspective* (Lagos: Press Alliance, 2004), 27.   [52] See Transparency (n 45 above).

[53] See W De Maria, 'Measurement and Market: Deconstructing the Corruption Perception Index' (2008) 21 International Journal of Public Sector Management 777–97.

[54] See the Schedule to the Criminal Code Act cap 77 Laws of the Federation 1990 applicable to the southern part of Nigeria.

[55] Cap 89 Laws of Northern Nigeria 1963, applicable to the northern part of Nigeria.

When Olusegun Obasanjo assumed the presidency of Nigeria in 1999 one of the major tasks for his Administration was to address decisively the challenges posed by corruption. To this effect, the government enacted two important pieces of legislation, in addition to the existing legislation mentioned above. The first piece of legislation is the Independent Corrupt Practices Act of 2000 (ICPA) which aims specifically at addressing corruption in the public services, and which established the Independent Corrupt Practices Commission (ICPC). The second is the Economic and Financial Crime Commission Act of 2004 (EFCC), which aims at dealing broadly with financial crimes including corruption in both public and private sectors in the country. These pieces of legislation are without prejudice to the provisions of the Constitution Public Conduct Code.[56]

The provisions of the ICPA are worthy of further consideration. The most relevant are sections 10 and 12 of the Act.

By virtue of section 10 of the Act, the Commission is empowered to

- where reasonable grounds exist for suspecting that any person has conspired to commit or has attempted to commit or has committed an offence under this Act or any other law prohibiting corruption, to receive and investigate any report of the conspiracy to commit, attempt to commit or the commission of such offence and in appropriate cases make its recommendation for prosecution or otherwise to the office of the Attorney-General of the Federation or of the State;
- examine the practices, systems and procedures of public bodies and where, in the opinion of the Commission such practices, systems or procedures aid or facilitate fraud or corruption, to direct and supervise a review of them;
- instruct, advise and assist any officer, agency or parastatals on ways by which fraud or corruption may be eliminated or minimized by such officer, agency or parastatal;
- advise heads of public bodies of any changes in practices, systems or procedures compatible with the effective discharge of the duties of the public bodies as the Commission thinks fit to reduce the likelihood or incidence of bribery, corruption and related offences;
- educate the public on and against bribery, corruption and related offences; and
- enlist and foster public support in combating corruption.

Additionally, the Act, in several provisions, deals with various forms of corrupt practices in the country.[57] From this provision it is clear that in addition

---

[56] See the fifth Schedule to the Constitution of the Federal Republic of Nigeria 1999.

[57] These include offences such as abuse of office, among which are: accepting gratification (section 8); fraudulent acquisition of property (section 12); fraudulent receipt of property (section 13); making a false statement or return (section 16); bribing a public officer (section 18); use of office or position for gratification (section 19); bribery in relation to auctions (section 21); bribery in relation to contracts (section 22); and failure to report bribery transactions (section 23).

to punishing the offence of corruption the Act also aims to supplement punitive measures with education. This is highly commendable. Experience has shown that the adoption of punitive measures to combat corruption is merely reactionary and does not necessarily address the root causes. Indeed, some commentators have cautioned against the use of the 'one-size-fits-all' approach to combating corruption.[58] It has been suggested that for any effort at anti-corruption reform to succeed, such must include a clear understanding and diagnosis of the problem rather than merely treating the symptoms. Education and awareness programmes on corruption can change orientation and thoughts about corruption. As important as criminalization of corruption is, this in itself may not necessarily deter corrupt practices. In fact, the Nigeria situation has shown that there is more that needs to be done besides merely criminalizing corrupt practices. It should be noted that the ICPC has devoted much time and attention to prosecuting corruption but little success has been recorded so far.

Under section 12 of the Act it is provided that any person who corruptly

- asks for, receives, or obtains any property or benefit of any kind for himself or for any other person; or
- agrees or attempts to receive or obtain any property or benefit of any kind for himself or for any other person, on account of:
  - anything already done or omitted to be done, or for any favour or disfavour already shown to any person by himself in the discharge of his official duties,
  - or in relation to any matter connected with the functions, affairs or business of a government department, or corporate body or other organization or institution in which he is serving as an official, or
  - anything to be afterwards done or omitted to be done or favour or disfavour to be afterwards shown to any person, by himself in the discharge of his official duties or in relation to any such is guilty of an offence of official corruption and is liable to imprisonment for seven years.

Other forms of corrupt practices criminalized under the Act include inflation of contract costs, prices, or goods,[59] and services and offering and acceptance of advantage or inducement by anyone.[60]

As earlier above the provisions of the EFCC do not specifically address corruption in public sector, nonetheless, some provisions of the Act are relevant in combating corruption in that sector. Indeed, some of these provisions have been invoked to charge public officials with corrupt practice. For instance, under

---

[58] See for instance, A Abdullai, 'Political Will in Combating Corruption in Developing and Transition Economies: A Comparative Study of Singapore, Hong Kong and Ghana' (2009) 16 (4) Journal of Financial Crime 387, 388.   [59] See section 25(3) of the Act.

[60] Ibid, section 24(1).

section 6 of the EFCC the Commission is given wide powers to address all forms of financial and economic crimes including those perpetrated by an individual corporate body or groups in either the private or public sector. More importantly, section 47 of the Act defines economic and financial crime to include any form of fraud, narcotic drug trafficking, money laundering, embezzlement, bribery, looting and any form of corrupt malpractice, illegal arms deal, smuggling, human trafficking and child labour, illegal oil bunkering and illegal mining, tax evasion, and foreign exchange malpractice. It is important to mention here that both the ICPC[61] and the EFCC[62] contain provisions on the forfeiture or seizure of property or goods which are believed to be by-products of corruption. These provisions are important in the sense that they reinforce the weight given by the government to discouraging and stamping out corrupt practices in Nigeria.

In addition to the ICPC and EFCC, the Money Laundering Decree[63] is also of indirect importance in combating corruption. This legislation criminalizes all forms of activities relating to money laundering by any individual in Nigeria. It is noted that most of the public officials accused of corrupt practices are said to be involved in laundering of public money to offshore accounts.

Moreover, Nigeria has ratified two important treaties—the UN Convention on Corruption[64] and the AU Corruption Convention.[65] Although by virtue of section 12 of the Nigerian Constitution these treaties are not directly enforceable in Nigeria, nonetheless, they provide good reference points for combating the menace of corruption. For instance, the UN Convention against Corruption contains a detailed and elaborate provision on bribery which can be invoked to supplement the provisions existing under local laws.[66] Also, the Convention addresses both the supply and demand ends of corruption. It equally addresses the need to strengthen the judicial arms of government in this respect;[67] a very important provision, given the crucial role the judiciary plays in combating corruption in any society. As will be demonstrated below, one of the problems associated with fighting corruption in Africa is the tendency for the judiciary to become enmeshed in corrupt practice which frequently makes the fight against corruption particularly difficult in any country. The UN Convention criminalizes offences indirectly linked to corruption, such as concealment of illegal proceeds and obstruction of justice.[68]

---

[61] See, eg, section 45 which empowers the Commission to seize movable property in the custody of a bank or any other institution where such property is the subject of investigation under the Act.

[62] See sections 22 and 23 of the Act.

[63] Money Laundering Act Cap M18, Vol 9 Laws of the Federation of Nigeria 2004.

[64] See n 7 above.   [65] See n 8 above.

[66] See Arts 15–20. These provisions dealing with corrupt practices apply to a wide range of individuals and officials including officials of governments and public international organizations.

[67] See Art 11(1) which requires states parties to take measures to strengthen integrity and to prevent opportunities for corruption among members of the judiciary. Such measures may include rules with respect to the conduct of members of the judiciary.   [68] See Arts 24–25.

In its own right, the AU Corruption Convention calls for the involvement of civil society groups and the media in the fight against corruption.[69] The Convention also targets two different levels of enforcement mechanisms— national and international—with regard to the offences contained therein. Under the national mechanism, the AU Convention mandates states parties to establish appropriate enforcement mechanisms including the enactment of laws to effectuate the Convention at the national level.[70] It also recognizes the importance of access to information in the fight against corruption[71] and the role of civil society groups in monitoring, implementing, and enforcing the principles contained in the Convention at the national level.[72]

More importantly, the Convention lays emphasis on the need to observe the need for a fair trial and respect for fundamental human rights in all cases relating to corruption.[73] As regards enforcement at the international level, the AU Convention covers situations such as extradition and collaboration with non-states parties to the Convention, to prevent culprits from benefiting from the proceeds of their corrupt practices in countries that are not parties to it.[74]

In Kenya, considerable attempts have been made to address corruption.[75] In 1987 the government amended the 1956 Prevention of Corruption Act and created a body known as the Kenya Anti-corruption Authority (KACA). This body was formally inaugurated in 1997 with a director appointed to head it. However, the Authority did not function as expected due to lack of funds and it was some time before it could commence serious work after support was eventually forthcoming from the government and international donors.

Unfortunately, just as KACA was beginning to gain momentum, a high court declared it unconstitutional due to reasons beyond the scope of this chapter. However, a new law known as the Anti-corruption and Economic Crimes Act no 3 of 2003 was enacted and KACA was consequently re-established. The Act contains a number of interesting provisions concerning corruption.

For the purpose of determining the culpability of a person accused of corruption, the 2003 Act distinguishes between an agent and a principal. Accordingly, an agent is 'a person who, in any capacity, and whether in the public or private sector, is employed by or acts for or on behalf of another person'. On the other hand, a principal is defined as 'a person whether in the public or private sector, who employs an agent or for whom or on whose behalf an agent acts'.[76] A noticeable trend in this regard is that the drafters appear to be more concerned with addressing corruption generally rather than addressing

---

[69] See Art 12 of the AU Convention.   [70] See generally Arts 5–6, 10–11.   [71] Art 9.
[72] Art 12.   [73] Art 14.   [74] Art 19(3).
[75] In 2003, a Transparency International survey of perceived corruption rated Kenya 122nd out of 133 countries.   [76] Section 38(1) of the Act.

the subject matter of corruption. In other words, the Act punishes corrupt practices generally including exchange of gifts or benefits or even information and is not restricted only to exchange of money. The important thing is to determine if the benefit, favour, or information is given for the purpose of an inducement or for a reward, as the case may be. Thus, section 39 provides as follows:

(1) This section applies with respect to a benefit that is an inducement or reward for, or otherwise on account of, an agent
   (a) doing or not doing something in relation to the affairs or business of the agent's principal; or
   (b) showing or not showing favour or disfavour to anything, including to any person or proposal, in relation to the affairs or business of the agent's principal.
(2) For the purposes of subsection (1)(b), a benefit, the receipt or expectation of which would tend to influence an agent to show favour or disfavour, shall be deemed to be an inducement or reward for showing such favour or disfavour.
(3) A person is guilty of an offence if the person—
   (a) corruptly receives or solicits, or corruptly agrees to receive or solicit, a benefit to which this section applies; or
   (b) corruptly gives or offers, or corruptly agrees to give or offer, a benefit to which this section applies.

From this provision it is clear that the Act intends to discourage the offering and receiving (that is, both the demand and supply) of bribes. It is also important to note that the Act not only punishes the actual commission of an offence but also punishes the mere agreement to give or receive benefits in a corrupt manner. In other words, in the same manner as the UN Convention on Corruption, KACA deals with both the demand and supply aspects of bribery. The Act also punishes self-inducement under section 41. This interesting section provides as follows:

(1) This section applies with respect to a benefit that is an inducement or reward for, or otherwise on account of, the giving of advice to a person.
(2) A person is guilty of an offence if the person—
   (a) receives or solicits, or agrees to receive or solicit, a benefit to which this section applies if the person intends the benefit to be a secret from the person being advised; or
   (b) gives or offers, or agrees to give or offer, a benefit to which this section applies if the person intends the benefit to be a secret from the person being advised.
(3) In this section, 'giving advice' includes giving information.

It would appear from this provision that deliberate withholding of information from a person being advised will amount to a crime. The inclusion of this provision in the Act is surely to prevent a situation where access to crucial information is used to the detriment of the society. It is also a criminal offence if an agent has a direct or indirect interest in a matter but fails to disclose it to the principal, while knowing that the principal is expected to make a decision on that matter.[77]

The Kenya Anti-corruption Commission (KACC) established by the Act is empowered to investigate and punish culprits of corruption in the country. Indeed, after its establishment the KACC commenced investigations into high-profile corruption cases; some of which include the Goldenberg scandal in which an estimated US$600 million was alleged to have been paid by the treasury between 1991 and 1994 in export credits for non-existent gold exports.[78] However, by the time the investigation was concluded in 2006 no major prosecutions had been brought. Although the former education minister, George Satoti, was temporarily forced to resign his appointment due to the scandal, his counterpart in the justice ministry, Amos Wako, who was also implicated in the scandal, remained in office without suffering any consequence.[79] In 2004 the KACC was also involved in the investigation of another major scandal known as the 'Anglo Leasing' scam, which involved the payment of large sums of money to a fake company for a contract to supply passports. The then head of KACC, John Githongo, was determined to get to the root of the scandal and gathered a series of evidence, including detailed payments made to fictional companies, but suffered repeated attempts by top government officials and ministers to dissuade him from continuing the investigation. Githongo eventually had to resign as the head of KACC due to persistent interference with his investigation.[80] He subsequently relocated to the United Kingdom for fear of persecution and threat to his life.[81] This situation further confirms that little success will be recorded in the fight against corruption if African governments are not truly committed to the fight.

7.1 An assessment of the effectiveness of legal frameworks for combating corruption

As seen above, there is no doubt that neither Nigeria nor Kenya lacks appropriate legislation to address the menace of corruption. That notwithstanding, corruption has remained the bane of these countries. One of the major shortcomings of the provisions of the existing laws in these countries is that they lay too much emphasis on enforcement agencies and prosecution without focusing on educating the populace about the disastrous impacts of corruption on their society.

---

[77] See section 41 of the Act.
[78] R Simons, 'The Impact of Anti-corruption Institutions on Corruption in East Africa' (2008) African Policy Journal 5. [79] Ibid.
[80] 'Kenya Safe for Anti-graft Czar' BBC News <http://news.bbc.co.uk/2/hi/africa/4649566. stm>. Githongo specifically mentioned that the Vice-President Moody Awori, Energy Minister Kiraitu Murungi, Finance Minister David Mwiraria, and sacked Transport Minister Chris Murungaru attempted to block his investigation into the scandal. [81] Ibid.

In addition, there are other reasons for the inability of legislation to effectively combat corruption and these are discussed below.

7.1.1 Lack of political will

It is not sufficient for any government to claim that it has enacted the requisite laws to combat corruption, it is equally important for that government to show that it is genuinely taking steps to combat corruption. This means that no one must be treated as a 'sacred cow' and any form of double standard must be eschewed. Johson and Kpundeh have noted that without demonstrated political will, measures taken to curb corruption will amount to empty gestures or camouflage for continue abuse.[82]

Political will, in the context of combating corruption, has been described as

the demonstrated credible intents of political actors (elected or appointed, leaders, civil society watchdogs, stakeholders groups etc) to attack perceived causes or effects of corruption at a systemic level.[83]

In other words, it refers to the sincerity of the government's pledge to combat corruption both by words and by deeds.[84] If the public are expected to take the government seriously then it is important that the government does not interfere in the prosecution of any culprit of corrupt practices no matter the status or affinity of such a person. Moreover, government should not be seen to shield or be reluctant to prosecute anyone involved in corruption. In recent times, Nigerian citizens have remained sceptical about their government's commitment to tackle corruption due to various incidents. While it true that a number of high-profile corruption cases have been successfully prosecuted in Nigeria, the fact that some well-known 'looters' of the public treasuries still walk free has cast deep suspicion in the minds of the public about the sincerity and fairness of the government's efforts. For instance, a number of former state governors, who were indicted on offences of money laundering and looting of their states' treasuries, are still very much involved in the day-to-day running of the government. Some of these persons are members of the federal legislature, ministers, special advisers, or consultants to the present government. This situation tends to give an impression that the government lacks the moral and political will to address corruption in the country.

One of the criticisms of the efforts of the Obasanjo government (1999–2007) at combating corruption in Nigeria was their perceived selective approach. It has been alleged that the anti-corruption fight during that regime was mainly targeted at opponents of the administration or those who were not in the president's 'good books'. While this allegation may not present the full picture, the fact that

---

[82] M Johnson and S Kpundeh, 'Building a Clean Machine: Anti-Corruption Coalitions and Sustainable Reform', World Bank Policy Research Working Paper (2004), 4.

[83] <https://owal.brunel.ac.uk/exchange/Ademola.Abass/Drafts/RE:%20index.EML/1_text.htm#_ftn1>.

[84] <https://owal.brunel.ac.uk/exchange/Ademola.Abass/Drafts/RE:%20index.EML/1_text.htm#_ftn2>.

the regime levelled allegations of corruption against the Vice President after he fell out with the President and decided to run for the office of the President in the impending elections, did little to douse allegations that the government used its anti-corruption fight against its political opposition. A situation such as this weakens rather than strengthens government efforts to combat corruption, not least because civil society groups, and the entire public, may not give much-needed support.

Equally, the failure on the part of the Kenyan government to prosecute those indicted in the Goldenberg scandal tends to reveal the government's unwillingness or reluctance to deal decisively with corruption at the national level. Such acts of reluctance send negative signals to the international community that a government is not serious about combating the problem.

The fight against corruption should never be used as a tool for vendetta or for gaining cheap political popularity; nor should it be used as an instrument of political manipulation. Experience has shown that in some situations efforts to combat corruption may arise out of a government's bid to divert public attention away from the inadequacies of its economic and political policies. Commenting on this, Mbaku notes that

An incumbent leader faced with deteriorating economic and social conditions and a challenge from opposition parties or groups may initiate a campaign to clean up corruption with his administration in an effort to direct attention away from existing problems and the government's inability or unwillingness to provide effective solutions to those problems... In many African countries politicians regularly use clean up campaigns to help them stay in power. Clean up programs can be used to discredit members of a previous regime, to destroy the reputations of leaders of opposition, and to improve support among the population for the incumbent regime.[85]

Any attempt to combat corruption must be holistic, impartial, and all-encompassing regardless of whose ox is gored. The removal from office of the former head of the EFCC, Nuhu Ribadu, and his subsequent 'persecution' including his dismissal from the Nigerian police force, was not perceived in a good light by many Nigerian citizens and some international observers.[86] Although the government justified Ribadu's removal from office as a routine exercise and a bid to build a stronger institution, there were concerns that the fall of Nigeria's former

---

[85] See n 16 above, 109.

[86] In December 2007, Inspector-General of Police, Mike Okiro, ordered that Ribadu be temporarily removed from his position as EFCC chairman and ordered him to attend the National Institute of Policy and Strategic Studies in Kuru, Jos, Plateau State for a mandatory one-year course. This decision was criticized by notable Nigerians such as the Nobel laureate Prof Wole Soyinka, members of the House of Representatives, and opposition political parties. In addition, the head of the UN crime office said that Ribadu's removal could hobble the crackdown on graft in Africa's most populous country, and send the wrong signal to EU donors who poured US$35 million into the project. See 'Group Worried over Nigeria's New Anti-graft Chief', Reuters <http://uk.reuters.com/article/idUKL3072154320080530>. He was subsequently dismissed from the Nigerian police force on 22 December 2008 by the Nigerian Police Service Commission.

anti-corruption chief might be due to his dogged determination to prosecute highly placed corrupt politicians who are believed to be close allies of the present administration.[87] Ribadu has recently alleged that he fled Nigeria because his life was under threat. He once said that when one fights corruption in Nigeria, corruption will fight back.[88]

Where a government is seen, either by words or actions, to be meddling in the investigation or prosecution of corruption charges, this can easily undermine the effectiveness of the government's measures to combat corruption. It can also erode the confidence of the public in the sincerity of the government. The government must not be seen or perceived to be paying lip service to combating corruption, particularly when top government officials or personalities are implicated. The recent attitude and statements by the Attorney General of Nigeria have been a major concern to civil society groups and the public as a whole. On taking office, the Attorney General attempted to stop the EFCC from prosecuting corruption cases. Also, the Attorney General's reluctance to cooperate with the British government with regard to the money laundering case pending against a former governor of Delta state, coupled with his controversial role in other cases and transactions, has portrayed Nigeria's current administration as playing at politics.[89] Obviously the attitude of the Attorney General does not tally with the government's avowed commitment to fight corruption in the country.

It should be noted that despite the report of a panel set up by the Nigerian government indicting the former military leader General Babangida of mismanagement of US$12 billion during the oil windfalls in the early 1990s, no charges of corruption have been brought against him to date.[90] The failure or unwillingness of the government to investigate or prosecute Babangida has merely reinforced scepticism about the government's commitment to fight corruption in the country. This gives the impression that when it comes to corruption matters, some people are 'untouchable'.

It has been suggested that one way of combating political corruption is to decentralize the public sector. Since it is believed that corruption often

---

[87] See J Phee, 'Outrage over Ouster of Nigeria's "Eliot Ness"' <http://abcnews.go.com/Blotter/story?id=4542906&page=1>. Osita Ogbu, the secretary of Transparency International in Nigeria, was quoted to have said that the President never wanted to retain Ribadu, and the move to replace Ribadu calls into question President Yar'Adua's pledge to fight corruption. He said further 'We know that he has said that he intends to do that, but he is not showing that he is committed to doing that.'   [88] See n 1 above.

[89] See, eg, 'Aondoakaa Indispensable', Saharareporters <http://www.ocnus.net/artman2/publish/Africa_8/Aondoakaa_Indispensable.shtml>. This article details some of the activities of Mr Aondoakaa, tending to portray him as a corrupt public official who would do anything to hinder the fight against corruption in Nigeria. Writing on his roles with regard to corruption cases against former governors pending before English courts, the article notes 'A source at the Metropolitan told Saharareporters that the department found Aondoakaa too connected to corrupt Nigerians to be a credible collaborator in corruption investigations concerning Nigerian politicians.'

[90] See '$12.4 Billion Gulf Oil Money: IBB Knows Fate June 17', Point Blank News <http://www.pointblanknews.com/os911.html>.

arises from the over-concentration of powers in the hands of a few powerful politicians and public officials, a process which allows greater access to public institutions will significantly reduce opportunities for corruption within the country. In essence, emphasis should be placed on political deregulation and opportunities should be created for greater participation of citizens in government.[91]

7.1.2 Weak judiciary

Another important challenge to combating corruption in Africa is the inability of the judiciary to play its role of monitoring the legislative and executive arms effectively. The success or otherwise of enforcing legislation to combat corruption depends largely on a reliable, impartial, independent, and competent judiciary. Where the judiciary is perceived to be weak, partial, or corrupt it will be unable to punish corrupt officers effectively. Sadly, however, the judiciary in Nigeria has not displayed the necessary qualities to assure the public that it can deal with corruption. In recent times, allegations of corruption and partiality have been levelled against the judiciary which has tended to impugn the credibility of the judicial arm of government in serving effectively as a check on other arms of government. In some cases the court has been used as an avenue to scuttle or frustrate prosecution of corruption cases. More disturbingly, some judges have perfected the art of granting spurious and ridiculous injunctions shielding some indicted politicians or individuals from investigation or prosecution.[92] This worrisome development has attracted the attention of the judiciary regulatory body—the National Judicial Council (NJC)—which has had to suspend or remove some judges on the ground of compromising their position.[93] Bastler has rightly observed that 'Nigeria's international reputation as a leader in the fight against corruption hinges on the independence and impartiality of its anti-corruption institutions'.[94]

---

[91] See n 16 above, 108.

[92] See, eg, *Attorney-General for Rivers State v the Economic and Financial Crimes Commission & 3 Others Unreported Suit No* FHC/PHC/CSI78/2007, a case involving the former governor of Rivers State. Dr Odidli, a Port-Harcourt Federal High Court judge, curiously granted an injunction forbidding the EFFC from investigating, arresting, or prosecuting the former governor for any acts of corruption. This raised concern among civil society groups and in response to one of the petitions against this decision, the NJC has commenced an investigation into the judges' attitudes in this case. A similar injunction was granted by the Abia State High Court to the former governor of the State, Dr Orji Kalu.

[93] eg L Okenwa, 'NJC to Obasanjo: Retire Justice Ego Egbo', *This Day Newspaper*, 16 November 2004 < http://www.thisdayonline.com/archive/2003/10/12/20031012> last accessed 30 December 2009. See also 'CJN Suspends Four Judges for Akwa-Ibom Election Petition Bribery and Corruption', Nigeria Muse <http://www.nigerianmuse.com/essays/?u=CJNSuspends4.htm>. The names of the suspended judges include Justice MM Adamu of Plateau State High Court; Justice BT Ahura of Benue State High Court; Justice AM Elelegwu of the Customary Court of Appeal, Delta State; and Justice Chris Senlong of the Federal High Court, Lagos.

[94] 'Group Worried over Nigeria's New Anti-graft Chief', Reuters <http://in.reuters.com/article/oilRpt/idINL3072154320080530>.

It is generally believed that placing hope in a 'corrupt' judiciary to try corruption cases effectively is akin to asking an unqualified doctor to diagnose a patient. Although in a few cases, the judiciary has been able to live up to expectations by convicting highly placed personalities or politicians on charges of corruption,[95] the overall public impression is that when it comes to fighting corruption in Nigeria the judiciary leaves much to be desired. A recent decision by an Asaba Federal High Court, in which all 170 charges against James Ibori—the former governor of Delta State, currently standing trial for money laundering before a British court—were quashed for not disclosing a prima facie case against the accused, has sparked intense public debate.[96] Some commentators have argued that the judgment was premeditated by events preceding the ruling;[97] others hold that the judgment was well-reasoned as the prosecution had not shown sufficient evidence to proceed.[98] While it appears that the judge was able to come to a relatively balanced conclusion with regard to the weight of evidence against the accused, the recent negative perception of the public about the judiciary, particularly in election matters, may have robbed the judgment of public acceptability.

[95] A former serving Inspector General of Police, Tafa Balogun, was convicted of corruption-related matters in 2005 and sentenced to six months in prison in addition to forfeiting stolen assets worth 150 million Naira. See 'Nigerian Ex-police Chief Jailed Six Months', BBC News <http://news.bbc.co.uk/2/hi/africa/4460740.stm>. Also, a former governor of Edo State pleaded guilty to corrupt practices and was fined approximately 12 million Naira. More recently, a former Vice-Chairman of the ruling political party (PDP), Chief Bode George, with five others was sentenced to a two-year prison term for corruption-related matters during his tenure as the board chairman of the Nigerian Port Authority; see *Federal Republic of Nigeria v Olabode George and others*, unreported Suit No ID/71C/2008 delivered on 26 October 2009. Justice Olubunmi Oyewole in his judgment said:

> When public office is abused, the entire populace is assaulted. This must not be condoned or treated with kid gloves. If the quality of service in our public life is to be altered to the appreciable standard of the civilised world, the right deterrent should be given. For the right deterrent to be served, therefore, sufficient firmness must be demonstrated.

[96] See *Federal Republic of Nigeria v Ibori and others*, unreported Suit No FHC/ASB/IC/09 delivered on 17 December 2009. Justice Marcel Awokulehin held as follows:

> In summary, the prosecution framed a total of 170 counts against the accused persons and correctly identified the essential ingredients of the offences for which the accused persons are charged. However, the proof of evidence supplied by the prosecution has failed to disclose only prima facie case against any of the Accused/Applicants. The Prosecution failed to produce the evidence to show the essential ingredients of the offences charged.

[97] O Indibe, 'Money no Loss?', *The Sun Newspaper*, Nigeria, 21 December 2009. Indibe observed:

> I predict that history will take a harsh view of this judgment. Ibori's wholesale clearance has struck many Nigerians as a case of the Nigerian state displaying its propensity for protecting highly connected suspects from rigorous prosecution. Truth be told, this was a case where, it appeared, the state summoned every available instrument to ensure the exoneration of a man widely perceived as embodying scant regard for the sacredness of the public trust.

[98] See, eg, I Izeze, 'Ibori Case: How EFCC Deliberately Boggled the Prosecution' <http://www.thetimesofnigeria.com/Article.aspx?id=2354>. The author argues that it would have been difficult for the judge to reach a different judgment based on the several errors on the part of the EFCC prosecuting team.

The citizens are disillusioned and sceptical about the ability of the judiciary to remain impartial and forthright in the midst of a series of allegations of corruption. There are also fears that the closeness of Ibori to the presidency may have worked in his favour. Ibori remains today one of the biggest financiers of the President Yar'Adua's election campaign. It is therefore necessary for the NJC to be more decisive in dealing with malpractice and allegations of corruption against judges in order to redeem the battered integrity of the judiciary. In particular, the NJC should revisit the frivolous and incessant granting of injunctions barring anti-corruption agencies from investigating or prosecuting anyone indicted of corrupt practice. And any judge found to have compromised his or her position should be dealt with appropriately. More training programmes should be organized for judges to build their capacity to deal with corruption cases more effectively. Essentially, the independence of the judiciary must be guaranteed. Under no circumstances should judges be pressurized, threatened, or induced by anyone, particularly members of the legislature or executive. An independent judiciary is not only a bulwark against tyranny and injustice but is also one of the sacrosanct principles of the rule of law, which is necessary to enable the judiciary to carry out checks on other arms of government.

In addition to a lack of confidence in the judiciary, there is also a problem of delay in the administration of justice in Nigeria. Often cases take an unduly long time before they are disposed of. This sometimes makes it difficult for the public to trust the judicial system. Experience has shown that lawyers acting on behalf of the accused often deliberately employ all manner of tactics to frustrate the prosecution of the case. The fact that some judges still write in long-hand tends also to prolong the duration of cases unnecessarily. In other situations, due to incompetence or lack of expertise on the part of investigating officers, the collection and collation of evidence is painstaking. This may lead to a situation where it becomes difficult to gather sufficient evidence for the successful prosecution of a corruption case.

7.1.3 Limitation of the legislative approach

One of the weaknesses of the criminal law approach to corruption is that it often overlooks the fact that legislation alone does not change human behaviour. The act of corruption is often conceived and executed by the individual; therefore to address its root cause, remedial efforts must be targeted towards changing human behaviour. Corruption thrives where there is a collapse of the moral values of a society. There is therefore a need for renewal of the moral values of that society and such efforts must begin with targeting the early stages of an individual's life. Breman and Buchanan have observed that in order to understand how individuals or organizations behave in any society, it is imperative to understand the rules that regulate their activities.[99] In other words, the behav-

---

[99] G Brennan and J Buchanan, *The Reason of Rules: Constitutional Political Economy* (New York: Cambridge University Press, 1985).

iour of public officials and private entrepreneurs who engage in corrupt practices can only be properly understood in the context of existing rules in a society. Accordingly, rules define how individuals interact with each other, provide a means for conflict resolution, and generally curtail behaviour of individuals and groups. Where effective rules exist, individuals or groups are able to pursue their private ends in a manner that will not interfere with others' ability to do the same. Adeniran has also observed that one of the problems with legislation on corruption is that state-enacted laws are not usually self-enforcing; therefore, compliance with such laws depends not so much on state enforcement machinery but rather on social rules or norms.[100]

Generally, rules that regulate socio-political interaction may be contained in written documents (such as a constitution) or based on custom and tradition.[101] Based on the assumption of an existing rule, corrupt practices or behaviour may be viewed as opportunistic arising from a problem with effective implementation of laws relating to corruption. Thus, it is suggested that an effective means of combating corruption should necessarily involve reform of existing rules and the subsequent adoption of new rules which will lead to the outcome desired by society.[102]

This is where the need to intensify education programmes on corruption becomes imperative. Embarking on education and awareness programmes has the advantage of changing people's views about and attitude towards corruption. Already there exist provisions in some anti-corruption laws to this effect. What is required is for the anti-corruption agencies to place more emphasis on this mode of combating corruption. Public officials at all levels need to undergo training and awareness programmes through which they will learn to understand the linkage between corruption and good governance. Moreover, as a long-term approach to combating corruption, it may be desirable to adopt the teaching of civic studies as a subject in primary schools. This will help in inculcating into pupils at an early stage values such as service, selflessness, contentedness, honesty, trustworthiness, truth, gratitude, and other important virtues and values of a society. The overall aim of such teaching is to build a future generation who will show an aversion to corruption.

Also, there is need for transparency and access to key information about government activities. In a situation where a government's activities are shrouded in secrecy and no one knows what goes on behind the scenes, this provides fertile ground for corruption to thrive. Transparency of accounting systems and official payments made in awarding contracts to firms and companies, including monthly payments to state and local government areas, will ensure easy monitoring of how money is spent and will enable the public to demand accountability. Therefore, the delay in enactment of the Freedom of Information Bill in Nigeria is a hindrance to the fight against corruption. Recently the National Assembly

---

[100] See n 9 above, 67.   [101] See n 16 above, 110.   [102] Ibid.

lamented the difficulty it was having in accessing the accounts of the Nigerian National Petroleum Corporation (NNPC).[103] This is highly regrettable, and will serve to fan the embers of corrupt practice in government's establishments. There is no reason why a government establishment funded with tax payers' money should not disclose relevant information to the public, particularly when this will ensure accountability on the part of the establishment.

Adeniran has also argued that the state-centric approach by the Nigerian government to combating corruption has been the Achilles heel of the country's fight against corruption.[104] He opines that the provisions of the ICPC and EFCC both fail to assign any role to civil society groups in combating corruption. He therefore concludes that this was a serious omission which has weakened the participation of civil society groups in the fight. But the truth of the matter is that civil society groups have always been part and parcel of the fight against corruption in Nigeria. And, despite not being assigned an official role, it has not particulary prevented them from monitoring the steps and measures taken by the Nigerian government to combat corruption. Indeed, as mentioned above, civil society groups at one time or another have criticized government's double standards and insincerity in combating corruption.

8. Conclusion

The fight against corruption remains a big challenge in Africa and is threatening the lives and existence of millions of Africans. Pervasive corruption has continued to stand in the way of economic and political developments in many parts of the continent. Indeed, corruption is reversing several years of gains in the economic and political development of many African countries. Moreover, corruption has remained a big threat to human security in the region and millions of people have died due to corrupt practices. Recent efforts to combat corruption have not yielded the desired results due to a number of reasons including weak and corrupt judiciary, insincerity on the part of governments, and lack of transparency. It is therefore important that African governments revisit their strategies towards combating corruption. This will require a deeper involvement of civil groups, strengthening of the judiciary, and providing education and awareness programmes on corruption which target various members of the community and different stakeholders in society.

---

[103] See A Babalola et al, 'Nigerians Back NASS for NNPC Probe', *The Punch Newspapers*, 6 December 2009 <http://www.punchng.com/Articl.aspx?theartic=Art200912061231895>.

[104] See n 9 above, 63.

II

REGIONAL INSTITUTIONS AND MECHANISMS

11

African Peace and Security Architecture and the Protection of Human Security

*Ademola Abass**

1. Introduction

That the notion of human security, as a social construct, is not explicitly enshrined in the constituent treaty of any regional organization in Africa owes partly to the historical *casus fœderis* of these organizations and partly due to the nascence of human security as a *leitmotif* of foreign policy. However, that is not to imply a fatal disconnection between the aspirations of African organizations and the pursuit of human security goals.

Indeed, virtually every African organization, which is today active in the peace and security sphere, was, at inception, either inspired by the anti-colonial struggle of the late 1950s and 1960s or motivated by the ideals of regional economic integration of the 1970s and 1980s. Doubtless these struggles were, in themselves, underlined either by a quest for the realization of certain fundamental freedoms, such as collective self-determination *inter alia*, or improved socio-cultural standards of the African people. Either way, those ideals mirror the objectives of human security, even if tenuously.

That is not to say that African regional organizations have generally pursued the specific goals of human security from inception, or have prioritized, in any remarkable shade or form, the protection of human security of the African people in their development. To be sure, the Organization of African Unity (OAU),[1] the premier, umbrella organization under the auspices of which much of the

* Professor of International Law & Organizations Brunel University, West London, and former African Union Expert on Regional Mechanisms. Although the present author negotiated and drafted the MoU between the AU and RECs in the field of peace and security, which is commented on in this chapter, the views presented here are those of the author and do not, in any way, represent those of the AU or any of its organs. Thanks to Obiora Okafor and Jean Allain for their comments on the draft of this chapter.
[1] Adopted in Addis Ababa, 25 May 1963, 479 *UN Treaty Series* 70; 3 ILM 1116.

anti-colonial struggle in Africa was organized and executed, was not as concerned with the general welfare of the African people, as a core objective of its existence, as it was with its overarching desire to reclaim the governance of Africa for Africans. It is a matter of historical relevance that when the establishment of the OAU was initially considered, African states rejected the inclusion of provisions which would guarantee the human rights of Africans in the Charter of the new organization.[2] When the final draft of the OAU Charter was eventually adopted, no references to the protection of Africans from insecurity featured in the instrument.[3] The only reference to 'human rights' in the OAU Charter exists in Article II(e) which enjoins the organization 'to promote international cooperation, having due regard to the Charter of the United Nations and the Universal Declaration of Human Rights'.[4]

The OAU's distinct lack of appetite for human rights and civil liberties is further manifested in the fact that it took almost 20 years, that is to say, nearly half the organization's life span, before its members adopted the Charter on Human and Peoples' Rights (ACHPR) in Banjul, the Gambia.[5] It was not until five years later that the Charter entered into force.

One possible explanation for the OAU's lacklustre attitude towards human rights was perhaps that the organization was born at a critical time when most African countries were emerging from colonization by European powers. Upon attaining independence, the priority of the new African elites was to replace colonial administrations immediately to consolidate political power. All other issues could wait. The pervasive political mood of the time was succinctly captured by Kwame Nkrumah, the first president of Ghana, who famously proclaimed that African leaders should seek first the political kingdom and all other things would be added unto it.

Though the attainment of independence by most African states before the end of the 1960s undoubtedly afforded the OAU the space to begin focusing more robustly on such issues as human rights, which it arguably could ill afford at the time of its birth, the brutal repression of black Africans by racist regimes in both Southern Rhodesia (now Zimbabwe) and South Africa meant that the OAU was mainly condemned to pursuing the main political goal to which it had originally committed—ridding Africa of colonialism and all vagaries of its manifestations.

---

[2] For good background reading on the emergence of the OAU, see NJ Padelford, 'The OAU' (1964) 18 International Organization 521.

[3] Charter of the Organization of African Unity (1964) 3 ILM 1116 (adopted on 26 May 1963).

[4] Art II lists five purposes (objectives) for the OAU viz: (a) to promote the unity and solidarity of the African states; (b) to coordinate and intensify their cooperation and efforts to achieve a better life for the peoples of Africa; (c) to defend their sovereignty, their territorial integrity, and independence; (d) to eradicate all forms of colonialism from Africa; and (e) to promote international cooperation, having due regard to the Charter of the United Nations and the Universal Declaration of Human Rights.

[5] African Charter on Human and Peoples' Rights (adopted 27 June 1981) OAU Doc CAB/LEG/67/3 rev.5, 21 ILM 58 (1982) entered into force 21 October 1986.

Certainly, achieving total independence for Africa was crucial to the OAU's credibility, yet, its unifocal commitment to that goal inexorably masked the growing culture of repression and violations of Africans' human rights in most independent African countries.

The rather deleterious approach of the OAU towards human rights and the general security of the African people, even if politically expedient at the time of the organization's birth, presaged two maleficent traits that would characterize most African regional organizations' attitudes towards protecting African people from insecurity. At the institutional level, there was a total lack of effective policy strategies and structures to address the problems of chronic violent conflicts and endemic vices, such as corruption, blighting much of Africa. When individual sub-regional organizations eventually began to engage with peace and security matters, there were no effective continental frameworks and mechanisms to coordinate and harmonize the various efforts of these organizations inter se, and between them and the OAU.

The attempt by the African Union (AU), the organization which replaced the OAU in 2002,[6] to establish an African peace and security architecture (APSA) was the first time an African-wide organization had sought seriously to address the mammoth crises bedevilling Africa as a whole. The APSA aims primarily to coordinate the efforts of African regional organizations in peace and security matters, as well as to serve as the structure within which the security of Africans, among other things, will be protected.

So far, both the AU and its sub-regional counterparts have shown great resolve towards operationalizing APSA. But, as is to be expected, while certain organizations have shown commitment to the ideals of APSA, others have lagged behind. In addition, while it has proved relatively easy to develop certain elements of APSA, other aspects have proved to be far more complex and sensitive to deal with.

The aim of this chapter is to inquire into how and whether African regional organizations, acting within the framework of APSA, can ensure an effective regime of human security in Africa. The chapter studies the APSA and considers whether it is capable of re-orientating African regional organizations towards protecting the security of Africans. Given that the implementation of APSA—hence, the effective protection of human security in Africa—depends to a large extent on the relationship between the AU and sub-regional organizations, this chapter critically examines the various legal instruments that establish and regulate this relationship. Additionally the chapter considers the role (if any) played by the AU and the concerned Regional Economic Communities

---

[6] See the Constitutive Act of the African Union, available at <http://www.africa-union.org/root/au/AboutAu/Constitutive_Act_en.htm>. See generally PW Schroth, 'The African Union and the New Pan-Africanism: Rushing to Organize or Timely Shift: National and International Constitutional Law Aspects of African Treaties and Laws Against Corruption' (2003) 13 Transnational Law and Contemporary Problems 83.

(RECs, the alternative name by which African sub-regional organizations are called) in the post-2007 election crisis in Kenya and the 2008 political violence in Zimbabwe. This is in order to study whether within the formal structure of APSA, the AU and the two RECs concerned in those crises—the South African Development Community[7] and the InterGovernmental Authority for Development (SADC and IGAD)—were able to cooperate more effectively to protect the lives of Kenyans and Zimbabweans than they would have done individually.[8]

As has been highlighted by some of the chapters in this volume, the absence of good governance is central to the tumorous state of human security in Africa. In a continent where the theft of electoral victories and military adventurism frequently underline political ascendancy, seeking effective human security protection before building virile democratic institutions is putting the cart before the horse. Consequently, this chapter will examine the role of the AU in ensuring democratic governance in its member states. In particular, the chapter discusses the response by the AU to the unconstitutional takeover of governments in Madagascar, Guinea, and Niger between 2009 and 2010. Overall, the chapter seeks to establish whether there are early signs that APSA has a good chance of succeeding or whether the concept is nothing more than another instalment in the African organizations' rich repertoire of vacuous dreams.

Structurally, in addition to this introduction, the chapter is divided into four parts and a conclusion. The first part briefly recounts the nature of the relationship between the OAU and RECs as a prelude to understanding the relationship that has evolved between the AU and the RECs. The second part discusses how the AU has conceptualized human security. The third part examines the operation of APSA and attention here is focused on cooperation between the AU and the RECs within the framework of APSA to determine how this might augur for the protection of human security of Africans. Thus, whether the AU notion of human security (which as expected will be adopted in its operations individually or with the RECs) is one that the AU and RECs are capable of advancing and protecting will be determined largely by the issues concerning the operation of APSA.

The fourth part discusses the roles played by AU/RECs in the Zimbabwe and Kenyan crises, as well as the AU's response to the unconstitutional takeover of governments in Africa.

---

[7] (1993) 32 ILM 116.

[8] Established 17 August 1992. See treaty establishing SADC (1993) 32 International Legal Materials 116. SADC comprises Angola, Botswana, Democratic Republic of Congo, Lesotho, Malawi, Mauritius, Mozambique, Namibia, Seychelles, South Africa, Swaziland, Tanzania, Zambia, and Zimbabwe. For interesting background reading on SADC, see J Cilliers, 'The Evolving Security Architecture in Southern Africa' [1995] African Security Review 40.

2. The OAU/AU, the RECs, and peace and security in Africa: a historical context

2.1 The OAU and the RECs

Much ink has been spilled on the inability of the OAU to address the problems of conflict and insecurity in Africa effectively—especially from approximately 1989 until its demise—with the urgency and temerity that were required. But so far little, if anything, has been said about the relationship between RECs contemporary to the OAU and the OAU itself. Interestingly, at the peak of the OAU's failure to respond effectively to the exponential conflicts amongst its member states in the 1990s, there was some significant development, especially in West Africa, where the Economic Community of the West African States (ECOWAS)[9] had intervened in the Liberian and Sierra Leone conflicts in 1990 and 1997 respectively.

Two observations are particularly remarkable about these earlier sub-regional initiatives. First, ECOWAS had steadily pursued a constitutional transformation of its objectives from merely an economic grouping into a collective security system. The adoption of the Protocol on Mutual Assistance and Defence (PMAD) in 1981[10] was ECOWAS' first constitutional step towards its re-orientation, although the adoption of the Non-Aggression Protocol in 1978 somewhat foreshadowed ECOWAS' future role in peace and security, even if ambiguously.[11] In 1999, ECOWAS adopted a ground-breaking protocol on collective security, which I have previously described as the most radical treaty on intervention by any regional organization at the time.[12]

Of particular note in these ECOWAS 'constitutional moments', is that while the organization was swiftly (even if sometimes tawdrily) responding to situations of desperate conflict unravelling in West Africa, both through a pivotal constitutional re-orientation of its original remits and a reconfiguration of its military assets, the OAU had, to all intents and purposes, remained ineffectual. As a matter of fact, save its unsuccessful intervention in the Chadian conflict in 1981, Burundi (1993–96), Comoros (1997–99), and the Democratic Republic of

---

[9] ECOWAS was established in 1975. See revised Treaty of the Economic Community of West African States, 24 July 1993 (1996) 25 ILM. 660. ECOWAS members are Benin, Burkina Faso, Ivory Coast, The Gambia, Guinea, Guinea-Bissau, Ghana, Liberia, Mali, Mauritania (now suspended from ECOWAS), Niger, Nigeria, Senegal, Sierra Leone, Cape Verde, and Togo.

[10] Signed 28 May 1981, UN Doc A/SP3/5/81 (1990); 4 *Nigeria's Treaties in Force*, 1988.

[11] Adopted November 1999. See text in A Abass, 'The New Collective Security Mechanism of ECOWAS: Innovations and Problems' (2000) 5(2) Journal of Conflict and Security Law 211 (hereinafter, Abass, 'ECOWAS Innovations and Problems').

[12] See A Abass, *Regional Organizations and the Development of Collective Security: Beyond Chapter VIII of the UN Charter* (Oxford: Hart Publishing, 2004); A Abass, 'The New Collective Security Mechanism of ECOWAS: Innovations and Problems' (2000) 5(2) Journal of Conflict and Security Law 211.

Congo (DRC) from 1999, the OAU might as well not have existed in the 1980s and the following decade insofar as maintaining peace and security in Africa was concerned.[13]

It was not until 1993 that the OAU adopted its first legal framework for peaceful settlement of disputes.[14] Although the Cairo Mechanism was intended to resolve intra- and inter-state disputes of OAU member states, judging from the amount of civil and inter-state conflicts that erupted across Africa from 1990 onwards, it is fair to state that the mechanism was not a success in any significant way.

The second remarkable observation is that the OAU missed a rare opportunity to utilize the RECs to shore up its seeming inadequacies in maintaining peace in Africa by entering into the type of relationship the AU broached with the RECs immediately after its inauguration in 2002. Whether the OAU's inaction is a reflection of its inceptional lack of vision in the field of peace and security or was motivated by its unwillingness to be perceived as ceding its 'responsibility' to (then) less important and little recognized sub-regional organizations, or both, must remain conjectural. What is certain is that save the occasional rhetorical and hortatory solidarity speeches, with which the OAU mainly became associated in its day, the organization did not stamp its authority on or endeavour to reach out to the burgeoning class of sub-regional actors such as ECOWAS. The major consequence of this lackadaisical attitude was the gradual but definite sub-regionalization of peace operations in Africa which, in turn, rendered the OAU ultimately irrelevant in the socio-political development of Africa.

2.2 The AU and the RECs

In the contemporary setting, three legal instruments govern the relationship between the AU and RECs and their role in maintaining peace and security in Africa. These are viz: the Constitutive Act of the African Union (AU Act), the Protocol Establishing the Peace and Security of the African Union (PSC Protocol), and the Memorandum of Understanding between the AU and RECs in peace and security (AU/RECs MoU). The AU Act and the PSC Protocol will be treated together while the MoU, which contains the most extensive provisions on AU/RECs relations, as well as their role in implementing APSA, will be given separate attention.

---

[13] *Keesings's Contemporary Archives* (1982) 31677–80. See K Graham and T Felício, *Regional Security and Global Governance, A Study of Interaction between Regional Agencies and the UN Security Council with a Proposal for a Regional-Global Security Mechanism* (Brussels: VUB University Press, 2006); EG Berman and KE Sams, 'The Peacekeeping Potential of African Regional Organizations' in J Boulden (ed), *Dealing with Conflict in Africa: The United Nations and Regional Organizations* (New York: Palgrave, 2003), 35–77.

[14] The Mechanism for Conflict Prevention, Management and Resolution, adopted by the 29th Ordinary Session of the Assembly of Heads of State and Government of the OAU, held in Cairo, 28–30 June 1993.

2.2.1 *The AU Act and the PSC Protocol*[15]

The Constitutive Act of the African Union contains terse provisions on the AU/RECs relationship. Article 3(l) of the Act states that the AU shall 'coordinate and harmonize policies between existing and future Regional Economic Communities for the gradual attainment of the objectives of the Union'. Aside from this rather inchoate provision, one could point only to the reference in Article 4(d) to the 'establishment of a common defence policy for the African Continent' to infer an intention, on the part of the AU, to develop a synergetic relationship with other actors in defence policy.

Clearly, the text of Article 3(l) says little: only that the AU and RECs will coordinate and harmonize their policies. But that *harmonization* is not explicitly stated to be for the purpose of peace and security, and could as well have referred to harmonization of socio-economic related issues such as initially inspired the evolution of RECs. Indeed, it is only by reference to Article 3(f), prescribing the promotion of peace and security as an objective of the AU, that a link can be made between 'harmonization' and 'peace and security'.

The first comprehensive indication as to the nature of the AU/RECs relationship emerged with the rather belated inauguration of the Peace and Security Council of the African Union. Although the PSC Protocol entered into force much earlier than was predicted,[16] it must be remembered that the PSC itself did not form part of the original organs of the AU listed under Article 5 of its Act. While this curious omission raises questions about AU's inceptive strategy towards its peace and security goals, the proposal by Nigeria in 2003, for the establishment of the PSC, pursuant to Article 9(1)(d) of the AU Act undoubtedly saved the AU from early embarrassment.[17]

Be that as it may, Article 16 of the PSC Protocol enshrines the organic ideas of how the AU foresees its relationship with the RECs. This article, appropriately titled 'Relationship with Regional Mechanisms for Conflict Prevention, Management and Resolution' contains nine salient provisions. In paragraph 1, Article 16 states that 'the Regional Mechanisms are part of the overall security architecture of the Union, which has the primary responsibility

---

[15] Protocol on the Establishment of the Peace and Security Council, available at: < http://www.africa-union.org/root/au/index/index.htm>; see also PSC/AHG/Comm (X). See Communiqué, Solemn Launching of the Peace and Security Council, 10th Meeting, Addis Ababa, 25 May 2004. See also Assembly/AU/Dec.13 (II), AU Doc Assembly/AU/6/ (II), Decision on the African Defence and Security Policy; AHG/Dec.160 (XXXVII), adopted by the 37th Ordinary Session of the Assembly of Heads of State and Government of the OAU, Lusaka, 9–11 July, 2001; AHG/Dec.142 (XXXV) on Unconstitutional Changes of Government, adopted by the 35th Ordinary Session of the Assembly of Heads of State and Government of the OAU, Algiers, 12–14 July 1999.

[16] The Protocol entered into force on 26 December 2003, at least one year earlier than predicted.

[17] See Art 5 of the AU Constitutive Act (as amended).

for *promoting peace, security and stability* in Africa'. 'In this respect', the provision continues:

the Peace and Security Council and the Chairperson of the Commission shall:

(a) harmonize and coordinate the activities of Regional Mechanisms in the field of peace, security and stability to ensure that these activities are consistent with the objectives and principles of the Union;

(b) work closely with Regional Mechanisms, to ensure effective partnership between them and the Peace and Security Council in the promotion and maintenance of peace, security and stability. The modalities of such partnership shall be determined by the *comparative advantage* of each and the prevailing circumstances.

Paragraphs 2 to 9 merely elaborate on the specifics of the AU's relationship with RECs. Thus, the Peace and Security Council shall consult with regional mechanisms for the promotion of initiatives aimed at anticipating and preventing conflicts and, in circumstances where conflicts have occurred, peacemaking and peace-building functions.[18] The obligation on regional mechanisms, according to Article 16(3), is through the AU Chairperson, to keep the Peace and Security Council fully and continuously informed of their activities and to ensure that these activities are closely harmonized and coordinated with the activities of the Peace and Security Council. In a reciprocal gesture, the article equally requires the Peace and Security Council, through the Chairperson of the Commission, to keep the Regional Mechanisms fully and continuously informed of its activities.

The notion of harmonization, which features both in Article 3(l) of the Constitutive Act and Article 16(a) of the PSC Protocol is concretized by Article 16(4) of the PSC Protocol. This article provides that 'in order to ensure close harmonization and coordination and facilitate regular exchange of information, the Chairperson of the Commission shall convene periodic meetings, but at least once a year, with the Chief Executives and/or the officials in charge of peace and security within the Regional Mechanisms'.

The rest of Article 16 concern the responsibilities of the AU Chairperson 'to ensure full involvement of Regional Mechanisms in the establishment and effective functioning of the Early Warning System and the African Standby Force',[19] inviting regional mechanisms 'to participate in the discussion of any question brought before the Peace and Security Council whenever that question is being addressed by a regional mechanism is [sic] of special interest to that Organization',[20] and the invitation of the AU Chairperson to RECs' meetings.[21] Article 16(8) provides for the establishment by the AU of liaison offices to the RECs in order to strengthen cooperation and coordination, while Article 16(9) provides for the conclusion of a Memorandum of Understanding on Cooperation between the Commission and the Regional Mechanisms.

---

[18] Art 16(2) PSC Protocol.   [19] Ibid, Art 16(5).   [20] Ibid, Art 16(6).
[21] Ibid, Art 16(7).

Thus far, it is in Article 16(1) of the PSC Protocol that the idea of an African peace and security architecture is first mentioned: what became APSA was therein cast as an 'overall security architecture'.

Interestingly, the provisions of Article 16(1)(b) recognize the importance of the AU and RECs operating on the basis of comparative advantages. This principle is in recognition of the fact that some RECs were far more advanced than the AU in certain areas of competence as far as peace operations were concerned.

Yet, if by guaranteeing a cordial relationship with RECs the AU, through the PSC Protocol, attempted to stave off potential distrust between it and its subregional counterparts, the exegesis of other provisions is not so reassuring. In Article 16(6) for instance, the PSC limits the participation by RECs in AU meetings to instances where matters before the PSC are being addressed by a regional mechanism. The implication of this is that RECs are not generally invited to discussions on peace and security which are initiated by the AU itself. It is also doubtful whether a REC can attend a 'peace and security' meeting convened at the AU by another REC since Article 16(6) permits a REC to attend such a meeting *only* if the attending organization has a special interest in the subject matter.

The exclusion of RECs from general discussions of peace and security matters at the AU proved to be one of the most contentious issues during the negotiation of the AU/RECs MoU in 2005.[22] Many RECs lamented what they perceived as an arrogant posturing by the AU, in which the Union regarded RECs as subordinates rather than partners. This allegation was not particularly helped by the fact that Article 16(7), which extends an invitation to the AU Chairperson to attend RECs, contains no such caveats as are present in Article 16(6). Indeed, by virtue of Article 16(7), the AU Chairperson is entitled to attend *all* meetings and deliberations (note, not only discussions as in Article 16(6)) of regional mechanisms. Thus, to many RECs the evolving peace and security architecture, the foundations of which were being laid in the PSC Protocol, is fraught with many Orwellian traps.

That aside, the AU has actually gone one step further, in the practice of international organizations, in certain aspects of its relationship with the RECs. For instance, Article 16(3) obligates RECs to keep the PSC informed of their activities, but that article also provides that the PSC shall keep RECs informed of its own activities. This reciprocal reporting obligation is an advancement, so to speak, of the scheme of Article 54 of the UN Charter. Whereas Chapter VIII of the UN Charter deals with such matters as Article 16 of the PSC speaks to, the provision of Article 54 has been one-sided: it obligates states to keep the Security Council fully informed of actions taken or contemplated with no reciprocal responsibility flowing from the Security Council to regional organizations. Of

---

[22] The documents relating to the negotiation and drafting of the MoU between the AU and RECs on peace and security are on file with the author. As they are not public documents, they remain classified.

course, it might be argued that the Security Council is a *primus inter pares* and that the UN Charter's collective security schema does not afford such prolixity as contained in Article 16(7) of the PSC Protocol. Additionally, Article 53(1) does not envisage a symbiotic relationship between the Security Council and regional organizations, but rather a situation in which the former delegates its powers to the latter and not vice versa. Thus, it is logical that it is only upon *delegatees* (regional organizations) that the obligation to keep the delegator (the Security Council) informed is imposed.

So far, the AU has faithfully implemented Article 16(4) by convening regular meetings between it and the RECs. Considering that such meetings are extremely important to understanding the nature of activities being pursued by each side, the fact that this practice has continued gives some hope.

2.2.2 *The AU/RECs MoU on peace and security*[23]

Article III(1) of the AU/RECs MoU establishes the headline goals of the AU/RECs relationship in terms distinguishable from all previous efforts both by their specificity and clarity. The article states that:

the parties shall institutionalize and strengthen their cooperation and closely coordinate their activities towards their shared goal of ridding the *continent of the scourge of conflicts* and laying the foundation for sustainable peace, security and stability.

The inclusion of the phrases 'institutionalize' and 'ridding the continent of the scourge of conflicts' in the MoU was informed by the AU's desire to move Africa's search for peace and security from being moral abjurations to concrete, realizable goals.[24] It will be recalled that both the drafters of the AU Act and the PSC Protocol had been rather ambivalent in crafting the tasks of the AU and RECs in relation to peace and security. Instead of such specific wording as now contained in Article III of the MoU, those instruments have merely provided for promotion of peace, security, and stability without specifying the means of achieving them.

The other objectives of the MoU, stated in Article III(2)(iii)–(viii) are, at most, a mere reiteration of the objectives enunciated in the PSC Protocol. The only major difference, perhaps, remains Article III(2)(iv) which provides that the AU and RECs shall 'develop and implement joint programmes and activities in the area of peace, security and stability in Africa'.

The exactitude and poignancy of Articles III(1) and III(2)(iv) are greatly enhanced by the provision of Article IV of the MoU which embodies the principles underlining the relationship between the AU and the RECs. While Article IV(i) firmly establishes that the MoU shall be implemented in accordance with

---

[23] The Memorandum of Understanding on Cooperation in the Area of Peace and Security between the AU, the RECs and the Coordinating Mechanisms of the Regional Standby Brigades of Eastern Africa and Northern Africa, available at: <http://www.africa-union.org/root/AU/AUC/Departments/PSC/ps/PSC%20Publications/MOU_AU_RECs_E.pdf>.

[24] Records of negotiation of the MoU on file with the author.

the principles and provisions of the AU Act and the PSC Protocol, Article IV(ii) codifies the primary responsibility of the AU in the maintenance of peace and security in Africa. Although this article defers to Article 16 of the PSC as the legal authority for AU primacy, it is doubtful whether the AU intends the provision of Article IV(ii) to override Article 24(1) of the UN Charter which invests the Security Council with primary responsibility for the maintenance of peace and security.

In legal analysis it matters less the effect the AU intends these two provisions to have. By virtue of Article 103 of the UN Charter, if obligations entered into by UN member states are in conflict with their obligations under the UN Charter, the latter, without any doubt, prevail. Thus, in purporting to confer the AU with primary responsibility for peace and security in Africa, the provisions of Article 16 of the PSC Protocol and Article IV(2) of the AU/REC MoU conflict with Article 103 of the UN Charter. Consequently, to the extent of their inconsistency with the Charter obligation, the obligation of AU member states under those provisions is void. The only permissible ground for the AU's assertion of primary responsibility for peace and security in Africa, it must be emphasized, is if its claim relates to the distribution of roles between it and the RECs, and not between it and the UN Security Council.

Thus far, the provisions of the MoU relating to the maintenance of peace and security can be said to capture effectively the overarching raison d'être of the AU/RECs relationship which is to maintain peace and security and rid the continent of the scourge of conflicts. In this regard, the AU/RECs MoU is a remarkable improvement on both the AU Act and the PSC, and a world away from the legacy of the OAU.

However, the ability of the AU and the RECs to maintain peace and security in Africa hinges greatly on the ability of these organizations to operationalize the African peace and security architecture (APSA) effectively. The relationship between the AU and RECs, as mentioned earlier, is the core element of APSA. This is particularly important with respect to, namely, how the AU and RECs intend to share responsibilities for making political decisions for deploying troops and dealing with other serious matters concerning peace and security. While these themes will be fully explored later in this chapter, it is important now to consider briefly the approach of the AU to human security.

3. The AU and the notion of human security

As observed above, there is no provision in the AU Act that makes mention of human security in direct terms. What is commonly found in the constitutive treaties of African organizations is the duty to maintain peace and security in general. However, there is a conceptual difference between the type of security that African regional organizations generally commit to maintain and the notion of human security advanced in Chapter 1 above. Security, as used by the various instruments of the AU discussed above, largely implies the absence of war whether civil or among states. It is an idea of security that forms part of, but is not coterminous with, the evolving concept of 'human security' and is far narrower than the latter notion embraces.

Only ten years after the United Nations Development Programme (UNDP) popularized the concept of 'human security', the AU laid down its understanding of the term in a definition encrypted in the African Non-Aggression and Common Defence Pact:

Human security means the security of the individual with respect to the satisfaction of the basic needs of life; it also encompasses the creation of the social, political, economic, military, environmental and cultural conditions necessary for the survival, livelihood, and dignity of the individual, including the protection of fundamental freedoms, the respect for human rights, good governance, access to education, healthcare, and ensuring that each individual has opportunities and choices to fulfil his/her own potential.[25]

This definition of human security by the AU is much more expansive than that offered by the UNDP and the Human Security Commission (see Chapter 1), or the notion of security originally embraced by the AU. None of the definitions offered by those entities included the creation of military conditions, which is reminiscent of the state-centric notion of security which held sway before the advent of human security as a global concept. An important dimension in the AU's definition is also the direct incorporation of human rights as adjuncts of human security. This strengthens the view put forward in Chapter 1 that human security and human rights have much more to do with each other than is presently realized.

As will be recalled from Chapter 1, the paradigmatic shift from state to human security entails a corresponding transformation in the nature of responsibility shouldered by states, and, in the present case, by the AU towards the African people. To protect human security of Africans effectively, means that the military, the creation of which is envisaged by the APSA to deal with armed conflicts (expressed as 'military conditions' in the AU definition of 'human security'), is not one that will be utilized mainly to protect states from their own insecurity but, more importantly, one that will be utilized to protect Africans from the scourge of conflicts. As will be seen in the section dealing with the operation of the APSA, the idea of using the military for human security purposes will have to contend with issues of political sovereignty and/or territorial integrity of member states. Crossing this barrier will be crucial for the AU military force—the African Standby Force—which will be established for the purpose of human security.

---

[25] See Draft Text adopted at the first meeting of African Ministers of Defence and Security on the Establishment of the African Standby Force and the Common African Defence and Security Policy (Addis Ababa, 20–21 January 2004), Art 4(1).

The role of African regional organizations in protecting human security of Africans is particularly crucial. It was argued in the introductory chapter that using regional institutions, as opposed to national structures, presents the best chance of securing a more effective regime of human security for several reasons. Consequently, it is important that African regional organizations have the legal and practical capabilities to implement the objectives contained in the aforementioned instruments and the numerous goals of human security that the AU set out in its definition in order effectively to protect the human security of its people.

4. Operationalizing APSA: the AU, the RECs, and the potential paralysis

The main components of the APSA are listed under Article VI of the MoU. They are: the African Standby Force (ASF) and the Military Staff Committee (MSC),[26] the Continental Early Warning System,[27] and the Panel of the Wise.[28] The Common African Security and Defence Policy (CASDP) and the Non-Aggression Declaration, which are often stated to fall within the ambit of APSA, are, strictly speaking, not legitimate components of APSA as such.[29] Rather these are appurtenants primarily derivable through national, not regional, authorities, and as such, can only be incorporated into APSA by reference and necessary implication.

4.1 Early warning system: the tension between the regional and sub-regional systems

The Continental Early Warning System (CEWS) is intended to be the nerve-centre of APSA. According to Article 12 of the PSC Protocol, CEWS is intended to facilitate the 'anticipation and prevention of conflicts'. The CEWS is to be located in the 'Situation Room' of the Conflict Management Directorate, a division of the Peace and Security Department of the AU. Staffed by analysts, the Situation Room collates and processes information and data coming to the AU from RECs and other sources across the continent. The end product is used by the AU Chairperson to advise the PSC on the state of security in the continent.

The establishment of CEWS proved to be one of the most daunting tasks during the negotiation of the AU/RECs MoU. Certain RECs were already advanced in their own Sub-regional Early Warning Systems (SEWS). Two RECs in particular, the InterGovernmental Authority for Development (IGAD) and ECOWAS

---

[26] Art VI (3) MoU, Art 13 PSC Protocol.   [27] Art VI (2) MoU, Art 12 PSC Protocol.
[28] Art VI(4) MoU, Art 11 PSC Protocol.
[29] On CASDP, see OA Touray, 'The Common African Defence and Security Policy' (2005) 104(417) African Affairs 635.

(with their early warning headquarters in Addis Ababa and Abuja respectively) were reluctant to dovetail their systems into a supposed continental system being developed in the AU headquarters in Addis Ababa.[30] Reasons for the reluctance by ECOWAS/IGAD are wide ranging. But the most commonly asserted justification was that the AU system was far from developed and would amount to nothing but a retardation of the SEWS if they were to be guided by the AU. In addition, most of the RECs recognized by the AU within the prism of APSA do not have functional early warning systems as such. This is either a reflection of the fact that such RECs, for instance the Common Market for East and Southern Africa (COMESA), are still more economic rather than security-integration processes, or was an indictment of the AU's deepening policy of minimal communication with RECs, leaving the latter utterly clueless about what Addis Ababa expected from them.

The passage of time and the activation of a regular rapport between the AU and RECs have considerably eased information flow between the two sides. More importantly, each REC is now fully aware of its performance targets in regard to developing components of APSA. In turn, the AU and RECs are now able to coordinate their early warning systems much better than previously.

That said, there remains, as yet, one particularly resilient concern expressed by the majority of RECs during the negotiation of the MoU, which, regardless of how much communication is exchanged between RECs and the AU, will likely hinder the implementation of the CEWS within a fully functional APSA. There is lack of clarity as to where the boundary between intelligence gathering, for the sake of early warning, and potential espionage activities is to be drawn. Quite naturally, several states are unwilling to provide their sub-regional organizations with unhindered access to information and data concerning domestic issues. This has ensured that many RECs are not able to provide or feed useful and timely information to the CEWS, even if they genuinely are disposed to doing so. How this problem will be resolved remains to be seen but if the rather cavalier attitude adopted by the AU towards this formidable problem during the negotiation of the MoU is anything to go by, then it does not appear that a solution is to be expected soon.

It might be that in an effective APSA system there will be less need for the CEWS to be fully fed by or need to rely on SEWS. For in that hypothetical situation, it would be the case that fully capacitated RECs, each relying on their own early warning systems, would be in a position to deal with matters arising, be these mere civil uprisings or full-scale conflicts. The obligation on the concerned REC would be, in addition to furnishing the AU with information prior to taking any action, to also provide the premier organization with the information it

---

[30] On IGAD, see C Mwaûra, G Baechler, and B Kiplagat, 'Background to Conflicts in the IGAD Region' in C Mwaûra and S Schmeidl (eds), *Early Warning and Conflict Management in the Horn of Africa* (Lawrenceville, NJ: Red Sea Press, 2002), 40.

was unable to provide before its intervention. But since this proposition assumes, first and foremost, a logical distribution of responsibility between the AU and RECs, a full discussion of this issue is deferred until later.

4.2 The Standby Force and APSA

The role of a standby force—in context, a force dedicated to the pursuit of collective security—is best illustrated by the UN system. Article 43 of the UN Charter envisages the establishment of such a force for the exclusive use of the Security Council. The rationale for this is simple, or so it was thought when the UN Charter was negotiated. In order for the Security Council to be able to discharge its primary responsibility for maintaining international peace and security 'promptly and effectively', as Article 24(1) of the Charter endows, it is crucial that the Council possess the military capacity to do so.

In 1945, the issue was not whether the Security Council should have the capacity to deploy collective security with its own force, but *how* to obtain those forces. If the availability of such military capacities were to be decided in the face of a full-blown war, and worse still one in which some of the Security Council's permanent members might be involved or might otherwise be interested in, then such an effort might become hostage to the vagaries of Security Council politics. Certainly, the effort might be either too little or too late, if it ever came. If, on the other hand, desirous to avoid this potential immobilization of collective security the Council were to obligate UN members, at the outset of the UN, to set aside permanently certain numbers of troops from within their national contingents, such an option would be unbearably expensive for many UN member states to maintain. That option might also be difficult to justify considering the infrequent use of such forces in practice. Consequently, the UN adopted the decentralized option whereby whenever the Security Council requires troops from UN members, it calls on 'able and willing' states to provide them.[31]

The drafters of the MoU between the AU and the RECs understood these antecedents well, as they did the sensitivity, dynamics, and intricacies of assembling an effective continental force.[32] Political discussions around the ASF show the divergent ideas of AU leaders about the nature and composition of the ASF. The Libyan leader, Colonel Mohammar Ghadaffi, had proposed a force similar to Ghana's Kwame Nkrumah's African Command. In Ghadaffi's radical proposal, the African Standby Force would be a single army, headquartered in a single country, operating under a single commander.[33] Ghadaffi's proposal should be understood within his overall ambition for a supranational African Union which,

---

[31] See ND White and Ö Ülgen, 'The Security Council and the Decentralised Military Option: Constitutionality and Functionality' (1997) 44(3) NILR 378.

[32] Records on negotiation on file with author.

[33] See 'Speech by the Leader of the revolution at the Evening Session of the African Summit' (Closed Session) on 10 July 2001, p 6, on file with the author.

had he had his way, would be conceptually different from, and arguably more powerful than, that which eventually emerged.[34]

4.2.1   Composition of the ASF: confusion and perplexity

The ASF supported by the majority of African leaders is one which, according to Article 13(1) of the PSC Protocol, 'shall be composed by multidisciplinary contingents, with civilian and military components in their countries of origin and ready for rapid deployment at appropriate notice'. It seems obvious, from the provision of Article 13(2) of the PSC Protocol, that the ASF is intended to be assembled from national contingents of AU member states. This article states that:

for that purpose, the Member States shall take steps to establish standby contingents for participation in peace support missions decided on by the Peace and Security Council or intervention authorized by the Assembly.

Thus, according to this provision, the AU member states shall set up (earmark) troops from their national contingent for the ASF, along much the sames lines as Article 43 of the UN Charter.

Article VI(3) of the MoU is at variance with Article 13(2) of the PSC Protocol. The former article refers to the Policy Framework of the African Standby Force and Military Staff Committee, 'which, among other things, provides for the establishment of five regional brigades to constitute the African Standby Force'. Deconstructed, this provision implies that the ASF will be composed of five regional brigades. This, however, does not defer to Article 13(2) of the PSC Protocol, stated above, that the ASF itself shall be composed from national contingents, despite a contradiction apparently existing between the two provisions. Therefore, the prime question is: of what impact is the constitution of the ASF by regional brigades, if the ASF is to be composed, at the same time, by national contingents?

The practical implications of the evident conflicting provisions of Article 13(2) of the PSC and Article VI(3) of the MoU are quite telling. It thus means, on the one hand, that should there be a competing need for a REC to deploy to a sub-regional conflict, it is uncertain whether that REC will deploy its regional brigade as such or deploy components of its member states operating as such. If the former applies, then a further question arises as to whether the REC can deploy a regional brigade to its member states' conflicts since Article VI(3) MoU deems such a regional brigade to constitute the ASF. In a legal analysis, such a

---

[34] According to Ghadaffi,

once the Union is established, States will still have their Parliaments and Governments will still be free to run their own affairs as long as that does not conflict with the Rules of the Union or the Pan African Parliament or the Assembly or the Executive Council or the Court or the African Central Bank. *These institutions are the high authority*; and their decisions and policies will be binding on Member States.

Emphasis added; see ibid, 6.

deployment by the REC of a regional brigade will be subject to a decision by the AU itself for the reason stated. If, on the other hand, a REC deploys only troops acting as national contingents of its member states, it remains to be seen how RECs intend to maintain separate troops for the purpose of regional brigades constituting the ASF, and those for the exclusive use of RECs. These situations beg the question how exactly the AU intends the ASF to be composed by national contingents of its member states (Article 13(2) PSC Protocol) and regional brigades (Article VI(3) AU/RECs MoU and the ASF Policy Framework).

In December 2009, the ECOWAS Chiefs of Defence Staff approved the establishment of the ECOWAS Standby Force (ESF), a regional brigade of the ASF.[35] The ESF, which is a multidimensional force comprising the Main Brigade and a Task Force, will have a capacity of 6,500 personnel ready to deploy within 14 days of notice.[36] While the much needed clarity about the relationship between the ESF and the ASF is expected to emerge later, it stands to reason whether it is logical for the constitution of the ASF to be based on regional brigades, as against national contingents per se. To begin with, not all states in any given sub-region are members of the sub-regional REC. One consequence of composing the ASF from regional brigades is therefore that it risks alienating potentially powerful players which may not subscribe to the concerned REC.

That point stands apart from the question of the efficacy of the plan. For instance, the East Brigade (hereinafter EASTBRIG) is headquartered in Kenya, but its planning element (PLANELM) is located in Addis Ababa, Ethiopia. While the separation of the two headquarters is politically expedient, especially in light of tension between certain members of the EASTBRIG, it portends nothing short of operational disaster to keep the two arms apart. This problem also manifests, to some extent, in the tension between Egypt and Libya, two important members of the Northern Brigade (NORTHBRIG).

The fact also that there is extensive cross-pollination and overlap of membership among RECs makes it extremely difficult to predict how states holding multiple REC memberships will contribute their troops for the purpose of composing the ASF. For instance, all members of ECOWAS are members of CEN-SARD,[37] a Libya-led REC in North Africa, which is in direct contest with the Arab Maghreb Union.[38]

The above reasoning shows the various issues that will most likely undermine the implementation of APSA. The AU, as a matter of urgency, needs to revisit the

[35] 'Regional Defence Chiefs Approve Structure for ECOWAS Standby Force', available at: <http://allafrica.com/stories/200912141618.html>.

[36] Ibid.

[37] Established on 4 February 1998 in Tripoli, during a Heads of State meeting attended by leaders of Libya, Chad, Mali, and Niger, the Community of Sahel-Saharan States was recognized by the OAU as a REC at the 36th Ordinary Session of the Heads of State and Government of the Organization of African Unity in Lomé, Togo, on 6–8 July 2000. See: <http://www.cen-sad.org/new/index.php?option=com_content&task=view&id=33&Itemid=76>.

[38] Cape Verde is the only ECOWAS member which is not a CEN-SARD member.

provisions governing the composition of the ASF lest the APSA is doomed from the start. If there is a serious lesson to be learned from the deployment of the AU Mission in Sudan (AMIS), it is that operationalizing the ASF has a greater chance of success if its composition is based on national contingents rather than regional brigades. It was Nigeria, and a few other states, that provided the majority of the AMIS troops, not the regional brigades. It is extremely doubtful if ECOWAS would have been able to deploy its Monitoring Group (ECOMOG) to Darfur, considering that such deployment would have required the consent of all member states, and not only Nigeria which dominates it, and which was able to take its own decision to go to Darfur on its own.

Certainly ECOWAS has now composed its regional brigade, the ESF, in fulfilment of the specific requirement of the ASF to that effect. However, considering that the same troops who compose the ESF (for the purpose of the ASF), will be used in a typical ECOWAS mission (for the purpose of ECOMOG), and both forces will most likely be provided by the same group of countries—Nigeria, Ghana, and a few others—the possibility of conflict of interest between ECOWAS (ESF) and AU (ASF) missions is very high. Resolving such conflicts will depend, inter alia, on the interplay between regional and sub-regional needs/interests, but more importantly on the jurisdictional competence of the AU and RECs over deployment matters. This is particularly so with regard to the ultimate political authority for taking decisions to utilize either the ASF or ECOMOG where regional/sub-regional interests clash, or decisions to use a sub-regional brigade in conflicts occurring outside the region. But since this jurisdictional issue is much wider than issues relating to the ASF per se, it is proposed to deal quickly with the ASF mandate being the only outstanding issue concerning the force worthy of examination before returning to the issue of jurisdiction.

4.2.2 *The ASF mandate and political responsibility for deployment*

The general mandates of the ASF derive mainly from the combination of remits established both by the Constitutive Act of the AU and the PSC Protocol. According to Article 13(3) of the PSC Protocol, the ASF mandates include both preventative and reactive deployment of troops. In its reactive role, the ASF will:

(a) observe and monitor missions,
(b) undertake other types of peace support missions, and
(c) intervene in a member state in respect of grave circumstances or at the request of a member state in order to restore peace and security, in accordance with Article 4(h) and (j) of the Constitutive Act respectively.

In its preventative role, the ASF will:

(d) deploy in order to prevent:
    (i) a dispute or a conflict from escalating;

(ii) an ongoing violent conflict from spreading to neighbouring areas or states, and;

(iii) the resurgence of violence after parties to a conflict have reached an agreement.

Article 13(3)(g) invests the PSC with an omnibus power to prescribe any other functions for the ASF as it may deem necessary. In addition, it is for the PSC, acting upon the recommendation of the AU Commission, to decide the details of the tasks of the ASF and its modus operandi.[39]

The above provisions are concise and clear about the situations that will trigger an ASF preventative or reactive intervention. However, the position is far from clear concerning who decides *when* and *what form* of intervention is to be taken. The matter is less complicated where a troubled member state of the AU invites the organization's intervention pursuant to Article 4(j) of the Act. In that case, the intervention will be more or less a peacekeeping operation, having been enabled by host state consent.

However, it is a different issue where the AU decides, on its own initiative, to intervene under Article 4(h) of the Act on the basis that one of the trigger situations listed under that article has been activated.[40] Yet, that article does not prescribe the modality for determining when the trigger thresholds are crossed. As I have argued elsewhere, whether an act of aggression, war crime, crime against humanity, or genocide has been committed is not a political or populist decision. These are heinous international crimes the determination of which is reserved for the competent international judicial organs and Inquiry Commissions.[41]

As the Darfur debacle has clearly shown, whether the crime of genocide in particular has been committed is not one often capable of easily ascertaining, not only because of the daunting legal ambiguities surrounding genocide as an international crime, but also due to the constant and frustrating interference of political considerations into this most charged of all legal minefields. A determination that the crime of genocide has been committed in a given situation imposes an obligation on concerned political orders to take action towards its cessation. This is the recommendation of the 1948 Genocide Convention. But in a world where actions seldom match rhetoric, political leaders often prefer to play politics with words rather than shoulder such considerable responsibility as imposed on them by the Genocide Convention. US President Bill Clinton's administration obstinately refused to use the word 'genocide' to characterize the events in Rwanda in 1994 at the appropriate time, only for the president to use the word 11 times

[39] Art 13(5) PSC Protocol.

[40] Art 4(h) provides for 'the right of the Union to intervene in a Member State pursuant to a decision of the Assembly in respect of grave circumstances, namely: war crimes, genocide and crimes against humanity'.

[41] See A Abass, 'The United Nations, the African Union and the Darfur Crisis: Of Apology and Utopia' (2007) 54 NILR 415; A Abass, 'Proving State Responsibility for Genocide: The ICJ in Bosnia v Serbia and International Commission of Inquiry for Darfur' 31 Fordham Int'l LJ 871.

within minutes of his arrival in Kigali during his visit to Rwanda after the extermination had ceased.

The question, therefore, is whether it is for the AU to determine that one of the crimes listed in Article 4(h) of the Act as a trigger situation for its intervention has been committed, thus necessitating its intervention. What if the AU determines that a crime has been committed under Article 4(h), but a concerned REC in the affected sub-region thinks otherwise? Will the AU's decision in that instance overreach the REC, and if that is the case, is the REC bound to supply the regional brigade to intervene in a situation it does not think merits intervention?

The legal intricacies surrounding the trigger situations enshrined in Article 4(h) of the AU Act are by no means a domain reserve of the AU system. It is precisely because of such difficulties that neither the UN Charter nor the Statute of the International Criminal Court (the Rome Statute) defines the crime of aggression. And for those crimes that are defined—such as genocide, war crimes, and crimes against humanity—the ability of the UN to authorize an intervention on these grounds depends on whether the Security Council determines, in accordance with Article 39 of the UN Charter, that the situation threatens international peace and security. Yet, while the International Criminal Court can prosecute anyone within its jurisdictional competence, who commits any of the crimes listed under Articles 5 to 8 of the Rome Statute, the Security Council is empowered to suspend an investigation of a situation or trial of such a crime for 12 renewable months;[42] this is clearly to preserve international peace and security.[43] In addition to the fact that a regional organization requires the authorization of the Security Council if it intends to undertake enforcement action under Chapter VIII of the UN Charter, the Security Council can also terminate a regional intervention not involving the use of force either under Chapter VI of the UN Charter or Article 52(1) of the Charter if international peace and security is endangered.

The relevance of the above analysis to the issue at hand is that the AU Act and the PSC Protocol do not contain any of the balancing provisions that regulate decision processes between the UN and regional organizations. Thus, a REC may decide to intervene without the authorization of the AU and the AU may decide to intervene in spite of a REC's position on the matter. An example of this scenario occurred shortly after the death of President Gnassingbé Eyadéma of Togo and the attempted unconstitutional succession to the throne by his son, Faure Eyadéma in 2005. The AU and ECOWAS had initially adopted different approaches and measures. While the AU was rather mellowed in pressurizing

---

[42] Art 16, Rome Statute.

[43] See A Abass, 'The Competence of the Security Council to Terminate the Jurisdiction of the International Criminal Court' (2005) 40 Tex Int'l LJ 263; C Stahn, 'The Ambiguities of Security Council Resolution 1422 (2002)' (2003) 14 EJIL 85.

Faure Eyadéma, ECOWAS had swiftly imposed sanctions against Togo and threatened the use of force.[44] These measures were constitutional and legitimate under Articles 10 and 22 of the 1999 ECOWAS Protocol which not only disaggregated consent of ECOWAS member states to its collective security measures, but which, in fact, entitles ECOWAS to act against erring member states without their consent.[45]

4.3 APSA: the jurisdiction of the AU and the RECs over regional conflicts

4.3.1 *Who may intervene in conflict situations?*

The issue of jurisdiction of the AU and RECs over conflicts is different from the question of political competence to authorize deployment of the regional brigades constituting the ASF as per the mandate discussed above. The jurisdictional issue concerns such questions as, between the AU and a REC, which organization is competent to react to a situation occurring in a particular sub-region? Hypothetically, if there is a conflict in Southern Africa, is the AU or SADC the competent body to respond to such a crisis?

This question is not a mere academic exercise. For as the UN practice vis-à-vis regional organizations demonstrates, different organizations do hold divergent views over what measures to take in a particular situation. A good example of this situation was when the UN decided to deploy a peacekeeping mission in Sierra Leone, a country where, at the relevant time, there was no peace to keep. ECOWAS, being the concerned REC whose members obviously bore the brunt of the crisis, decided to deploy an enforcement action. The UN was acting under its Charter and the general law of peacekeeping; ECOWAS was acting under its 1999 Protocol which permitted the use of force against its member states under certain circumstances.[46] The consequence of this divergence in approach was an unavoidable collision of the UN and ECOWAS operations forcing Nigeria, the largest troop contributor to ECOMOG, to withdraw its forces from Sierra Leone in 2000. Although Nigeria was persuaded to return to Sierra Leone, it insisted that ECOWAS must, among other things, retain command and control of the mission and implement its own mandate, which was, as to be expected, enforcement action.[47]

---

[44] See 'African Group Imposes Sanctions on Togo' available at: <http://www1.voanews.com/english/news/a-13-2005-02-20-voa12-67522552.html>.

[45] See Abass, n 11 above.

[46] For analysis of this Protocol, see Abass, n 11 above.

[47] A Abass, 'The Implementation of ECOWAS New Protocol and Security Council Resolution 1270 in Sierra Leone: New Development in Regional Intervention' (2002) 10 University of Miami International and Comparative Law Review 177.

The authors of the AU/RECs MoU on peace and security ensure that provisions governing the jurisdictional competencies of the AU and REC are enshrined in the MoU with clarity and exactitude. Article XX(1) of the MoU states that

Without prejudice to the primary role of the Union in the promotion and maintenance of peace, security and stability in Africa, the RECs and, where appropriate, the Coordinating Mechanisms shall be encouraged to anticipate and prevent conflicts within and among their Member States and, where conflicts do occur, to undertake peace-making and peace-building efforts to resolve them, including through the deployment of peace support missions.

This provision attempts to cast the jurisdictional relationship between the AU and the RECs in the mould of Chapter VIII of the UN Charter. To cement that arrangement, Article XX(2) obligates RECs and the Coordinating Mechanisms to keep the Chairperson of the AU Commission 'fully and continuously informed and ensure that their activities are in conformity with the objectives of the PSC Protocol'. Clearly this provision is a thinly disguised Article 54 UN Charter which obligates regional arrangements and agencies to keep the Security Council informed of the actions they take or contemplate.

In a sense, Article XX(1) appears to be a tepid version of Article 33(1) of the UN Charter by which the Security Council encourages regional arrangements and agencies to resolve their members' disputes through diplomatic means. The reference to 'anticipate and prevent conflicts among their Member States' is a clearly veiled restatement of the diplomatic settlement mechanisms enumerated in Article 33(1) of the UN Charter. But Article XX(1) of the MoU goes one step further. Whereas Article 33(1) stops short of excluding peacekeeping as one of the pacific means regional organizations can take to settle their members' disputes, Article XX(1) seems to do exactly that. In so doing, the article firmly establishes the legal basis for the AU/REC peacekeeping operation in the MoU.

However, the preclusion of the RECs from deploying peacekeeping missions under Article XX(1) is fraught with certain problems. First, as a matter of general international law, states and regional organizations do not require the approval of any other authority in order to undertake peacekeeping actions. What is important is that the state or organization seeking to intervene should obtain the consent of the state in which the conflict exists. Therefore, it does not make any legal sense for the AU to attempt to preclude RECs from peacekeeping.

Secondly, there is nothing contained in Article XX(1) that explicitly forbids RECs from taking enforcement actions without the authorization of the AU. Such a provision is absolutely essential in cementing the legal distribution of political powers and responsibility for deciding intervention between the AU and RECs. The whole structure of Chapter VIII of the UN Charter is premised on the fact that it is unlawful for regional arrangements or agencies to take enforcement action without the authorization of the Security Council. Certainly, in the practice of international organizations, the provision contained in Article 53 of the UN Charter has been interpreted very liberally to suppose that it permits regional organizations to act first and later seek approval from the Security Council. Even if political expediency has so far prevented the Security Council from refusing such retroactive approvals, the fact that a formal requirement is explicitly stated in the Charter for its authorization before regional enforcement actions are taken means that the possibility of jurisdictional conflict between the Security Council and regional organizations is far less likely than between the AU and the RECs in the absence of an Article 53-type provision in the AU Act, the PSC Protocol, or the AU/RECs MoU.

In addition to the absence of legal restraints on the ability of RECs to take enforcement actions, it is highly unlikely that most RECs will concede to the AU the authority to decide on intervention in conflicts occurring in their regions. It is true that the leaders of these RECs are also those who compose the Assembly of the AU, yet the geopolitical dynamics at the sub-regional level rabidly differ from those at the continental level; this is likely to impact decision processes of the AU to the advantage of RECs. To begin with, the RECs are much more likely to react more quickly to their regional conflicts than the AU and may thus present the latter with a *fait accompli*. In such circumstances the AU will have little choice than to toe the line drawn by the REC.

4.3.2 *Extra-jurisdictional deployment of assets and regional brigades*

One of the most important contributions of the AU/RECs MoU to the law of international organizations and the jurisprudence of international law is the salubrious provision in Article XX(3). This article states that

The RECs managing regional brigades within the framework of the African Standby Force and the Coordinating Mechanism shall, upon decision by Council, make available their assets and capabilities, including planning, to other RECs and Coordinating Mechanisms or the Union, in order to facilitate the deployment of peace support operations outside their areas of jurisdiction.

Article XX(4) strengthens this provision:

The RECs and Coordinating Mechanisms shall, upon decision by Council, make their regional brigades available for deployment as part of a peace support operation undertaken outside of jurisdiction.

The effect of these two provisions is to empower the AU to authorize RECs not only to deploy their assets outside their jurisdiction, but also to make available to *other* RECs their own brigades in furtherance of peace operations. The beneficiaries of such assistance can be RECs, the Coordinating Mechanisms, or, indeed, the AU itself.

As a legal rule, the provisions contained in Article XX(3) and (4) are a rarity in international law and state practice. There is no other known treaty, general or regional, that categorically authorizes regional organizations to deploy their troops or assets outside their own regions. Not even the UN Charter does so. The power of the Security Council to deploy regional organizations outside their own regions is one of the most controversial issues in the law of international organizations. It is generally believed that the Security Council acts ultra vires its powers if it authorizes a regional organization to intervene outside its region, although contrary views hold that nothing in the UN Charter fetters the power of the Security Council to so act. *Operation Artemis,* deployed by the EU to the DRC in 2003, was effectively a Chapter VII action, therefore it avoided being caught up in the 'vires debate'. It is also relevant that the Security Council originally delegated *Operation Artemis* to France, which then decided to lay it upon the European Union, while choosing to remain the Framework Nation.[48]

Article XX(3) and (4) confer certain benefits on APSA. First, it means that in the absence of an effective REC in a region experiencing a conflict, other RECs are legally entitled, and obligated, to intervene. Furthermore, the fact that there is a capable REC within the affected region will not, *ipso facto*, prevent other RECs from intervening. The possibility, therefore, of external RECs intervening in a conflict in another region could help to dilute the interest and stranglehold the region's REC may have over that conflict. It may also mean that the warring parties may find those external RECs more acceptable to deal with and a quicker solution to the conflict is found. Lastly, effective implementation of those provisions could do much to enhance the collective security system developed for APSA.

Be that as it may, the legal principles enunciated in Article XX(3) and (4) are fraught with problems. It is one thing for the law to prescribe that RECs shall yield their assets to others, it is quite another to expect a smooth implementation of this obligation in practice. Lessons from a similar, but unidentical, situation concerning the relations between the EU and NATO, in light of emerging independent European security, are instructive.[49] The EU, in a bid to establish its own collective security system, proposed the Rapid Reaction Force (RRF), following the adoption of the Treaty of the European Union at Nice, France (Nice Treaty). The Helsinki (EU Presidency) Frameworks[50] that set out the headline goals of the RRF had provided that NATO should make its assets available to the RRF. The problem, however, arises with European states in NATO which are not EU members, in particular Turkey.

Prior to the Franco-British St Malo Summit of December 1998, which proposed an autonomous EU collective security system—that is, autonomous from

---

[48] See A Abass, 'Extraterritorial Collective Security: The European Union and Operation Artemis' in M Trybus and N White (eds), *European Security Law* (Oxford: Oxford University Press, 2007), 134.

[49] For a general discussion of the relationship between the EU and NATO, see M Reichard, *The EU-NATO Relationship: A Legal and Political Perspective* (Aldershot: Ashgate, 2006).

[50] European Council, Helsinki, Presidency Conclusions, 10–11 December 1999, II Annex IV, CP 47.

NATO—the issue was much simpler. The North Atlantic Council, NATO's highest decision-making organ, would usually decide the question concerning deployment of NATO assets to either the EU or the Western European Union operations by consensus. The requirement of consensus ensured that non-EU NATO members such as Turkey were not prejudiced or,[51] as it is often blatantly expressed, not discriminated against by EU NATO members in that process.[52]

However, after St Malo, things changed and it became possible, in theory, for EU NATO members to discriminate against non-EU NATO members, such as Turkey, in deciding whether NATO should make its assets available. This possibility—coupled with the explicit reference in the Helsinki Framework that non-EU European NATO allies would be excluded from deliberations on the deployment of NATO assets—provoked sharp reactions from those states, especially Turkey. NATO, however, quickly defused the situation by categorically stating, during its strategic meeting in 1999, that decisions about asset deployment would be taken by consensus.[53]

The difference between the NATO example and the system proposed by the AU is that the latter seeks to impose asset-sharing obligations on RECs by fiat. Although it was the 'nothing-to-worry-about-for-now' attitude of many parties to the AU/RECs MoU that helped the AU to steamroller in those provisions, serious problems await their implementation. It is inconceivable, to say the least, that RECs would want to give up their assets—including the brigades they maintain—for the use of other RECs. While such an agreement is not in principle impossible, it is one that should have been left to the RECs themselves and not subject to the whim of the AU.

Experience from the fate of the UN Military Staff Committee, envisaged by Article 47 of the UN Charter for the purpose of the proposed UN Standby Force, foretells what should be expected of Article XX(3) and (4) of the MoU in practice. It is widely known that the reluctance of the USA and Russia to share their military intelligence hampered the development of the MSC. Thus, the obligation laid on the RECs in Article XX(3) of the MoU to share even their 'planning' is at best naïve.

The implications of the above analysis on the role of African organizations in protecting human security are several. The lack of a clear demarcation of responsibilities, as well as confused implementation strategies, will have a devastating impact on the mission deployment, in particular, when a situation arises. It is to be expected also that most RECs will not defer to the AU in matters of asset sharing, nor will they allow themselves to be dictated to by the AU with regard to

[51] TH Oğuzlu, 'Turkey and the European Union: The Security Dimension' (2002) 3 Contemporary Security Policy 78.

[52] See S Rynning, 'Why Not NATO? Military Planning in the European Union' (2003) 26(1) Journal of Strategic Studies 64.

[53] See JS Ignarski, *North Atlantic Treaty Organization*, Bernhardt (ed) (1997) Encyclopaedia of Public International Law III (J–P) 648.

where or when to deploy their troops. Short of a clear enunciation of these roles and powers in a binding instrument, and an *ex ante* agreement by all sides, it is most unlikely that the provisions of the MoU concerning jurisdictional competencies, asset sharing, and responsibility sharing will ever be implemented as envisaged.

5. AU and RECs and the Zimbabwean/Kenyan conflicts

5.1 A short overview

The circumstances leading to the crises in Zimbabwe and Kenya between 2007 and 2008 are too well known to recount here. Suffice to say that both conflicts, although they had different root causes, were catalysed by disputed results of elections.

The claims and counterclaims that were traded by parties to the conflicts were essentially similar: they concerned allegations of electoral fraud by incumbent governments (and, of course, similar counter-allegations by those governments against the contenders to powers); deliberate acts of the ruling governments to prevent their contenders from gaining political control; and, in the case of Zimbabwe, there was an added allegation by Robert Mugabe's ruling party, the ZANU-PF, that the leader of the Movement for Democratic Change (MDC), Morgan Tsvangirai, was a puppet of the West, especially the United Kingdom.

With regard to Kenya, a more sinister trait of African political culture—ethnicity—fuelled the rift between two bitterly opposed political camps leading to heinous violence such as had never previously been witnessed in the country. There was a popular claim that the Raila Odinga-led Orange Democratic Movement (ODM) won the elections conducted in December 2007 in Kenya, and that the incumbent president, Kibaki, applied political gimmickry, not uncommon in Africa, to swing the election results in favour of his Party for National Unity.

In ethnic terms, Raila Odinga hails from the Luo ethnic group while Kibaki hails from the Gikuyu tribe. Although relations between these two major Kenyan tribes have always been tense, it is widely believed that the December 2007 elections transcended tribal divides. If this belief holds true, one would be right to conclude that the conflict in the aftermath of the Kenyan elections had less to do with entrenched tribal differences than with using the facade of ethnicity to disguise an outright theft of a popular mandate given to the ODM.

Regardless of the merits or otherwise of each party's claim, however, the situations in Zimbabwe and Kenya escalated and led to mob violence where several thousands of lives were lost in both countries. In Zimbabwe, the crisis was worsened by the outbreak of cholera which resulted from a total breakdown of the water and sewage infrastructures.

5.2 The roles of SADC and IGAD

Following a massive international condemnation of violence adopted by ZANU-PF against MDC members, SADC mandated former President Thabo Mbeki of South Africa, to broker peace between Mugabe and Tsvangirai.[54] Robert Mugabe's government effectively prevented international or regional actors (save SADC) from intervening. SADC eventually succeeded in bringing the contending parties to accept a power-sharing government in which Robert Mugabe remains the president and Tsvangirai became the prime minister of Zimbabwe. Similarly, following the efforts of the Kenya National Dialogue and Reconciliation and the Panel of Eminent African Personalities, led by former UN Secretary-General Kofi Annan, a hastily concocted constitutional arrangement ensured that Kibaki remains the president with Odinga becoming the prime minister of Kenya.

Of particular interest here is how the AU and the concerned RECs (SADC and IGAD) responded to the crises. As said, SADC was active in resolving the conflict although it did not condemn the actions of either party. Clearly the decision of SADC not to take a formal stance on the wide allegations of electoral fraud, and political violence allegedly committed by Mugabe's ZANU-PF against the MDC, ensured that the sub-regional organization had a role to play in resolution of the conflict. With respect to Kenya, although IGAD made attempts to hold talks with both sides in the conflict, its advances were rebuffed by the ODM leadership on the basis that Kibaki's government was not legitimate.[55]

The reactions by both SADC and IGAD to the Kenyan and Zimbabwean crises follow much the same pattern as most African regional organizations' responses to political and constitutional disorders in their member states, perhaps with the exception of ECOWAS. The latter has proved, on many occasions, that it is not only capable of taking a principled stance against unconstitutional changes of governments in its member states, but that it is also capable of applying decisive sanctions, both military and economic, to deal with those situations.[56]

---

[54] For commentary on the role of SADC in the Zimbabwe crisis, see especially C Peter-Berries, 'The Zimbabwe Crisis and SADC: Dealing with a Deviant Member State' (2002) 2 SAY 197, also available at: <http://www.kas.de/db_files/dokumente/7_dokument_dok_pdf_2759_1.pdf#page=197>; LM Sachikonye, 'Wither Zimbabwe: Crisis & Democratisation' (2002) 9 Review of African Political Economy 13; B Raftopolous, 'Briefing: Zimbabwe's 2002 Presidential Election' (2002), 101, 413.

[55] See D Kilner, 'Diplomatic Initiatives Multiply in Attempt to Resolve Kenya Crisis' (Nairobi, News VOA.com, 8 February 2008) <http://www1.voanews.com/english/news/a-13-2008-02-08-voa31-66630392.html>.

[56] A prominent example was when Faure Essozimna Gnassingbé ascended the leadership of Togo after the death of his father, President Gnassingbé Eyadéma, in 2005. The application of sanctions by ECOWAS, coupled with threats of military invasion against the unconstitutional government, compelled the new government to hold a democratic election which it eventually won.

There is no doubt that one of the factors that limited the role SADC and IGAD could have played in the Kenyan and Zimbabwean crises is the fact that neither organization has any legal regime that explicitly illegalizes an unconstitutional takeover of government in their member states. If such legal instruments were available then, potentially, either organization might have suspended and/or imposed sanctions on the concerned states, although whether tampering with election results constitutes an unconstitutional takeover of government is a separate question to be dealt with below. It suffices to say here that under a similar legal regime, ECOWAS suspended Togo in 2005.

5.3 The AU's response to the Kenyan and Zimbabwean crises

It was the former Chairperson of the AU, Alpha Konare, who made one of the earliest calls on the AU not to remain silent in the face of the tragedy unfolding in Kenya.[57] This was significant in itself, even if ironic. It will be recalled that Alpha Konare was the AU Chairman when, in 2005, the current Ethiopian government was accused of using political violence to silence opposition following wide allegations of electoral fraud allegedly committed by the government. Whether the opposition's claim in Ethiopia was right or wrong is beside the point. What was surprising was that the AU not only remained silent during this time but actually went ahead and endorsed the ruling party which won the widely discredited election.

On record, the AU debated the crisis in Zimbabwe, especially during its 11th Summit in Egypt. But despite calls by Kenya and several Western nations, the organization did not condemn Mugabe's tampering with the election results and his party's use of political violence against members of the opposition.[58] Rather, the AU called on both parties to the conflict to resolve the crisis. The AU did not attempt to redeem its weak reaction to Zimbabwe when it came to dealing with the Kenyan situation. Not even the self-confession by the Kenyan Electoral Commission Chairman, Samuel Kivuitu, that he acted under pressure to declare Kibaki the winner of the election was sufficient to elicit a more than parsimonious reaction from the AU to the crisis.[59]

Yet, since 2000, the AU has taken the stance that none of its members should recognize governments which come to power through dubious means. This is aside from the several declarations of principles obligating the Union to act against

---

[57] See 4th Extraordinary Session of the African Commission on Human and Peoples' Rights, restated in the International Federation for Human Rights (FIDH). After a too long silence, the ACHPR has to take a position on human rights situations in Kenya, *Position Paper*, on file with the author.

[58] 'Kenya PM Calls for "Suspension" of Mugabe from AU', Reuters UK, 30 June 2008, available at: <http://uk.reuters.com/article/idUKCAW92070720080630>.

[59] See S Ongiri, 'Kivuitu Confesses: "I Acted under Pressure"' <http://kenyastockholm.com/2008/01/01/kivuitu-confesses-i-acted-under-pressure/>.

unconstitutional changes of governments in Africa. In order to understand the implications of the AU's docile response to both the Kenyan and Zimbabwean crises, and its impact on the role of the AU as a protector of human security in Africa, it is pertinent to consider the nature of the obligations imposed on the AU by numerous instruments against unconstitutional governments.

5.4 The AU and unconstitutional governments in Africa

Article 4(m) of the AU Act provides that 'Governments which shall come to power through unconstitutional means shall not be allowed to participate in the activities of the Union'. Since Article 4 of the AU Act embodies the principles of the AU, it follows that the prohibition of unconstitutional governments in Africa is a fundamental principle of the Union and implies derogation from the principle of non-interference and territorial sovereignty of AU member states.[60]

The essence of Article 4(m) is to promote democratic governance in Africa, a concept that is essential for an effective human security regime. Some commentators have even gone so far as to argue that 'democratic governance has emerged as a human right under general and particular international law...dictatorship in every...manifestation, has become a taboo in Africa',[61] and that governments that do not predicate their rule by democratic means will violate international law.[62]

Africa's trouble with unconstitutional governments dates back to the era of the OAU when African states regarded the manner in which a government came to power as a matter squarely within the domestic jurisdiction of every state, a constitutional stance that was secured by the international law principle of non-interference. While this view prevailed from the 1960s to the early 1990s, the annulment of a democratic election in Nigeria in 1993 by a military regime brought two crucial norms of the OAU into collusion with unconstitutional changes of government. On the one hand, Article 13(1) of the African Charter of Human and Peoples' Rights (Banjul Charter) provides that

every citizen shall have the right to participate freely in the government of his country, either directly or through freely chosen representatives in accordance with the provisions of the law.

On the other hand, Article 20(1) of the Charter states that

all peoples shall have the right to existence. They shall have the unquestionable and inalienable right to self-determination. They shall freely determine their political status and

---

[60] See CA Odinkalu, 'Concerning Kenya: The Current AU Position on Unconstitutional Changes of Governments', available at: <http://www.afrimap.org/english/images/paper/AU&Un constitutionalChangesinGovt_Odinkalu_Jan08.pdf>.

[61] N Udombana, *Human Rights and Contemporary Issues in Africa* (Lagos: Malthouse Press, 2003), particularly ch 2, pp 35–106.

[62] BR Roth, *Governmental Illegitimacy in International Law* (Oxford: Oxford University Press, 2000), 37–8.

shall pursue their economic and social development according to the policy they have freely chosen.

The combined effect of these provisions is to guarantee democratic governance.

In a communication brought before the African Commission on Human and Peoples' Rights challenging the annulment of the Nigerian elections, the Commission decided that the annulment violated Articles 13 and 20 of the African Charter.[63] A few years later, the former President of the Gambia, Dawda Jawara, brought an action before the Commission concerning the overthrowing of his government by a military junta. The Commission had declared that

military *coup d'état* was … a grave violation of the right of Gambian people to freely choose their government as enshrined in Article 20(1) of the [African] Charter.[64]

Previous efforts by the OAU to address the problem of unconstitutional changes of government include the setting up of a Committee of Ambassadors in 1995 to consider how to deal with unconstitutional governments;[65] the 1997 OAU endorsement of the right of participation as the basis of governmental legitimacy;[66] and the stipulation of time frames within which unconstitutional governments must restore democracy in their countries.[67]

In 2000, the OAU adopted the Declaration on the Framework for an OAU Response to Unconstitutional Changes of Government.[68] The declaration defines situations that constitute an unconstitutional change of government as follows:

i.   military coup d'état against a democratically elected government;
ii. intervention by mercenaries to replace a democratically elected government;
iii. replacement of democratically elected governments by armed dissident groups and rebel movements; and
iv. the refusal by an incumbent government to relinquish power to the winning party after free, fair and regular elections.

Aside from supplying a list of offending acts, the 2000 Declaration also provides for measures to be taken by the OAU if a member state violates any of these conditions. These include the suspension of the culprit regime from the OAU, a stipulation of a maximum six months within which the regime must

---

[63] Communication No 102/93, *Constitutional Rights Project and Civil Liberties Organisation v Nigeria* (2000) AHRLR 191, 198, paras 50–3. See also Odinkalu, n 60 above.

[64] Communications Nos 147/95 and 149/95, *Sir Dawda K Jawara v The Gambia* (2000) AHRLR 107, 118, para 73.

[65] OAU, Report of the OAU Central Organ Sub-Committee on the Preparation of a Blue Print for Dealing with Unconstitutional Changes of Government in Africa, Sub-Cttee/Central Organ/Rpt (III) (1996).

[66] Decision on the Rights of Political Participation, AHG/Dec.141 (XXXV) 1999, restated by Odinkalu (n 60 above) n 15.

[67] Decision on Unconstitutional Changes in Government, AHG/Dec.142 (XXXV), 1999.

[68] AHG/Decl.5 (XXXVI).

organize a democratic election, and, finally, the application of pressure by the Eminent Persons Contact Group as may be instigated by the Chairperson of the OAU.[69]

In 2002, the OAU adopted the Declaration on the Principles Governing Democratic Elections in Africa.[70] However, this declaration makes no reference to unconstitutional changes to governments. Rather, it focuses on identifying the requisite elements of democratic elections and the role to be played by the OAU in realizing these.[71]

It is noteworthy that all the foregoing efforts by the OAU towards dealing with the scourge of unconstitutional governments in Africa did not impose hard legal obligations on its member states. Most of these efforts, as has been seen, were merely either diplomatic measures or declarations which constituted soft law. This approach was to change, however, with the adoption by the AU of a treaty on unconstitutional change of governments in Africa.

5.5 African Charter on Democracy, Elections and Governance in Africa[72]

On 30 January 2007, at the 8th Ordinary Session of its Assembly of Heads of State and Government, the AU adopted the Charter on Democracy, Elections and Governance in Africa (ACDEG), which consolidated all the principles enunciated in the Declarations and Decisions adopted by the OAU on the same subject. In many respects, ACDEG is a significant and decisive legal regime on regulating unconstitutional governments in Africa. Therefore, in order fully to appreciate its import, it is necessary to consider the various provisions of the Charter especially those dealing with the meaning of unconstitutional governments and sanctions against perpetrators.

5.5.1 ACDEG and a new definition of unconstitutional change of government

Chapter 8 (Articles 23 to 26) of ACDEG contains the AU definition of 'unconstitutional governments' and the sanction regime to deal with any such situation. Under Article 23, there are five situations in which an unconstitutional change of a government can occur. These are viz:

(1) Any putsch or coup d'état against a democratically elected government.
(2) Any intervention by mercenaries to replace a democratically elected government.
(3) Any replacement of a democratically elected government by armed dissidents or rebels.

---

[69] See also Odinkalu, n 60 above.   [70] OAU AHG/Decl.1 (XXXVIII), 2002.
[71] Ibid, see Part IV(a)–(h).
[72] Adopted at the 8th Ordinary Session of the African Union Assembly, Addis Ababa, 30 January 2007. See: <http://www.ipu.org/idd-E/afr_charter.pdf>.

(4) Any refusal by an incumbent government to relinquish power to the winning party or candidate after free, fair and regular elections; or

(5) Any amendment or revision of the constitution or legal instruments, which is an infringement on the principles of democratic change of government.

The classification of any 'amendment or revision of constitution or legal instruments' as an unconstitutional means is telling. The obvious gap in the OAU definition of unconstitutional government, which, as seen above, had not included amendments to constitutions, had been capitalized on by several African leaders either to prolong their stay in power or simply to perpetuate their government ad infinitum. While an attempt by Nigeria's Olusegun Obasanjo constitutionally to extend his term for another four years in 2007, having already served the two four-year terms allowed by the Nigerian Constitution, was successfully resisted by Nigerians, Ugandans were not so fortunate. In 2005, the Ugandan President, Yoweri Museveni, successfully lifted a 19-year constitutional ban which restricted presidential terms to two of five years. Under the new order, there is no limit to the presidential tenure.

Interestingly, as early as 1995, the Sub-Committee of the Central Organ of the OAU Conflict Resolution Mechanism had proposed a much broader definition of unconstitutional government than the one incorporated in the OAU Declarations and Decisions.[73] In addition to the manipulation of the constitution in order to prevent a democratic change of government, the Sub-Committee had suggested as unconstitutional changes of government namely: refusal by a government to call for general elections at the end of its term of office (which condition is far wider than refusal to recognize election results); any form of election rigging and electoral malpractice, duly established by the OAU or ascertained by an independent and credible body established for that purpose; systematic and persistent violation of the common values and principles of democratic governance referred to above; and any other form of unconstitutional change as may be defined by the OAU policy organs, as constituting unconstitutional changes of government. Curiously, none of the OAU Declarations incorporated any of these suggestions.

5.5.2 ACDEG and the new sanction regime

The occurrence of an unconstitutional change of government in any AU member state triggers the sanction regime provided for by Article 25 of the ACDEG. This article empowers the AU Peace and Security Council (PSC) to take a number of steps. The PSC shall first explore diplomatic means to reverse the situation, failing which it

shall suspend the said State Party from the exercise of its right to participate in the activities of the Union in accordance with the provisions of articles 30 of the Constitutive Act and 7(g) of the Protocol [and] the suspension shall take effect immediately.[74]

---

[73] Report of the OAU Central Organ Sub-Committee on the Preparation of a Blue Print for Dealing with Unconstitutional Changes of Government in Africa, Sub-Cttee/Central Organ/Rpt (III) (1996).   [74] Art 25(1).

Contrary to the practice whereby governments which come to power unconstitutionally conduct democratic elections—which they invariably win—Article 25(4) disqualifies such governments from participating in elections or holding any positions of responsibility in the state. This aspect of Article 25(4) is capable of reversing the trend in Africa whereby rebel forces prosecute brutal wars and oust democratic governments in the hope that even if they do not succeed in establishing a new government they will retain strategic ministerial and other positions in the evolving governments of 'national unity'. Examples include Sierra Leone where Fodah Sankoh, the leader of the Revolutionary United Front, a rebel group which prosecuted one of the most brutal wars in Africa against a democratic government, not only became a vice-president in the government but also ensured that he obtained lucrative positions for his lieutenants. Article 25(6) provides for the imposition of sanctions by the AU against any of its members that instigate or support an unconstitutional change of government.

The highlight of the ACDEG sanction regime is found in Article 25(5) under which the PSC 'may prosecute perpetrators of unconstitutional changes in an African Union court',[75] and 'shall impose sanctions on a member State which instigated or supported the unconstitutional change'.[76] Clearly this is a groundbreaking sanction in a continent where, less than two decades ago, it was impossible to persuade the OAU to speak out against unconstitutional governments in its member states even in the mildest of terms. To cement this new sanction, Article 25(8) forbids AU member states to 'harbour or give sanctuary to perpetrators of unconstitutional governments', obligates them to prosecute or extradite such perpetrators apparently found on their territory (*aut dedere aut judicare* principle) (Article 25(9)), and encourages states parties to conclude bilateral agreements on extradition and mutual agreements to that effect.

5.5.3 AU application of the anti-unconstitutional government principle in Africa: 2008–2010

Despite the fact that the ACDEG was adopted in 2007, no single state in Africa has ratified the Charter. The implication of this is that the treaty, as yet, has not attained the status of a legally binding instrument.

However, the non-ratification of the ACDEG does not necessarily mean that the AU cannot apply its anti-unconstitutional governments principle. The ACDEG is but only *one* of the many legal instruments which enunciate this principle. The 2000 OAU Declaration (see above) was adopted by a consensus of all the organization's states parties. Although the declaration constitutes soft law, it is nonetheless 'law' and having being adopted and accepted by the OAU's highest decision-making body (the Assembly), it could arguably be applied to erring member states. In fact, when the AU suspended Mauritania from its membership in August 2008 following a military coup, the AU invoked as the basis of its

---

[75] Art 25(5).   [76] Art 25(6).

decision the ACDEG and *other* AU conventions which Mauritania had signed up to. Clearly, the invocation of the ACDEG is problematic given that the treaty is not yet in force. However, no AU state had challenged the invocation of the ACDEG or other OAU/AU conventions as the basis for the Union's action against Mauritania. Could this be interpreted as acceptance of the ACDEG by conduct?

Yet, the AU did not suspend either Zimbabwe or Kenya despite refusal by the governments of both countries to recognize electoral victories by the opposition which constituted a flagrant violation of the OAU/AU anti-unconstitutional government norms. In particular, the refusal by Kibaki's government to relinquish power to Raila Odinga's party, especially following the Electoral Commission Chairman's admission of declaring Kibaki the victor under pressure, constituted a violation of the fourth clause of Article 23 ACDEG. Also, the AU members did not refrain from recognizing governments which come to power through dubious means. Uganda's Museveni, for instance, recognized Kibaki's government claiming that he was legally required to do so by international law and conventions on diplomatic relations.[77]

It is feasible that the possibility of resolving the Kenyan and Zimbabwean crises through diplomatic means prevented the AU from suspending either state. After all, Article 25 of the ACDEG predicates any robust sanction by the AU against unconstitutional governments after the failure of diplomatic measures. However, what is also revealed by the Kenyan and Zimbabwean situations, on the one hand, and the cases of Mauritania, Madagascar, Guinea, and Niger (see below), on the other hand, is that the AU responds differently to unconstitutional changes brought about by military coups d'état and those installed by other means, such as refusal to recognize electoral victories. There seem to be no sound reasons, however, to treat one form of unconstitutionality differently from another. All unconstitutional means of assuming powers must rank pari passu.

It may be that such measures as suspending delinquent states from membership of organizations risks alienating those states and shutting the window on diplomatic resolutions against them. Persuasive as this view may seem, it does not answer certain questions. First, what is the point of establishing robust sanction regimes if a people's right to choose their leaders democratically can be truncated, and their resistance violently crushed, if perpetrators are forever to be entreated to diplomatic solutions? What purpose does diplomatic settlement serve, if not to protect authoritarianism, if it is pursued at all costs and without regard to the rule of law?

It is noteworthy that the same ACDEG, which obligates the AU to act whenever unconstitutional changes of government occur in any of its member states, enjoins the Union to work towards a sustainable human security. Articles 9 and

---

[77] For a short critique of President Museveni's stance, see J Oloka-Onyango, 'Diplomatic Recognition not a Legal Act', obtained by this author from the Archive of the Kenyan Peace, Truth and Justice (KPTJ).

39 of the ACDEG are clear on this.[78] Thus, by not applying the ACDEG in either Kenya or Zimbabwe notwithstanding the prospect of diplomatic solutions, the AU violated its own Charter and greatly undermined its own norms against anti-unconstitutional changes of government.

By contrast, the Organization of American States (OAS)[79] suspended the membership of Honduras from the organization following the overthrowing of President José Manuel Zelaya's government on 28 June 2009. But this constitutionally robust reaction did not stop the organization from mandating its Secretary General, José Miguel Insulza,

to reinforce all diplomatic initiatives and to promote other initiatives for the restoration of democracy and the rule of law in the Republic of Honduras and the reinstatement of President José Manuel Zelaya Rosales.[80]

Acting under Article 21 of its Charter, the OAS impressed that such diplomatic initiatives will not 'imply recognition of the regime that emerged from this interruption of the constitutional order'.[81]

In December 2008, the AU suspended Guinea from its membership following a military takeover of the government of that country. At its 165th meeting, the AU PSC said that it took the decision 'in accordance with the relevant provisions of the AU Constitutive Act and the Lome Declaration of July 2000 on unconstitutional changes of government'.[82] Also, following a military coup against the government of President Mamadou Tandja in the Niger Republic in February 2010, the AU swiftly suspended the country. Although this time the AU did not explicitly invoke the 2000 Declaration, its Chairperson had proclaimed a new 'zero tolerance' policy on those who take power by force.[83]

The AU continued this streak when it suspended Madagascar in March 2009 following a rather unusual takeover of the government by a coup staged through a mass demonstration of the citizens against the ruling government. This facilitated the coupists taking over from President Marc Ravalomanana.[84] Despite claims by the perpetrators that there was no coup and that the mass protests

---

[78] Art 9 states that 'State Parties undertake to design and implement social and economic policies and programmes that promote sustainable development and human security'. According to Art 39, states parties shall promote a culture of respect, compromise, consensus, and tolerance as a means to mitigate conflicts, promote political stability and security, and to harness the creative energies of the African peoples.

[79] The Charter of the Organization of American States (30 April 1948) UNTS, vol 119, 3 (48); (1994) 33 ILM 981.

[80] Press Release: 'OAS Suspends Membership of Honduras' (5 July 2009) <http://www.oas.org/OASpage/press_releases/press_release.asp?sCodigo=E-219/09>.

[81] Ibid.

[82] 'AU Suspends Guinea's Membership Due to Coup', available at: <http://en.ce.cn/World/Africa/200812/30/t20081230_17833775.shtml>.

[83] 'African Union Suspends Niger after Military Coup', available at: <http://news.bbc.co.uk/1/hi/8525665.stm>.

[84] See Aaron Maasho, 'AU Suspends Madagascar over Coup', 20 March 2009, available at: <http://www.mg.co.za/article/2009–03-20-au-suspends-madagascar-threatens-sanctions>.

against the overthrown government were an expression of democracy by the people, the AU, backed by the international community, still suspended the country from membership.

Clearly, the coup in Madagascar did not fall squarely within the usual typologies in Africa. Nevertheless, the AU's decision that the events constituted a coup was a correct and commendable interpretation. Had it chosen, instead, to accept the coupists' rather restrictive understanding of the term 'coup', then the AU would have undoubtedly opened a loophole for circumvention in its definition of 'unconstitutional changes'.

The non-ratification of the ACDEG continues to undermine the legal authority of the treaty and the AU's striving towards total eradication of unconstitutional changes of government in Africa. African states and organizations are particularly notorious for their eagerness to adopt legal instruments and their resilience in ignoring the obligations assumed under them. To that extent, it is commendable that the AU has started applying the anti-unconstitutional changes principles on the basis of its Declarations and Decisions and even the ACDEG by necessary implication.

6. Concluding remarks

Protecting human security is a full-time responsibility and one that cannot be discharged by half-measures. African regional organizations active in peace and security have endeared themselves to the ideals of human security. But whether the AU and the RECs will rise to this responsibility is as much a function of strict adherence to constitutionality and the rule of law by these organizations and their member states, as it is of the enthronement of effective institutional frameworks and mechanisms dedicated to implementing the goals of human security in Africa.

APSA is admittedly in its embryonic state, but care must be taken not to attempt to do too much at the same time. Careful consideration must go into fashioning out of APSA a sound and well-thought-out strategy for the continent to deal with errant states, to repel unconstitutional practices, to meet badly behaving states, and, more importantly, to protect Africans' security in conflict and other situations.

Unfortunately, the record of African regional organizations in peace and security issues reveals a serious deficiency in the core vision of these organizations at inception. It was a vision that did not primarily include the protection of Africans from threats to their security but one which hoisted up states as the prime referents of security thereby subsuming all else under that objective. The OAU attempted, rather belatedly, to redress this original problem but met with no significant success. The AU seems to have started out well, but considering its performance so far, one must temper hope with caution.

When African regional organizations conclude treaties either among themselves or with other organizations, it is extremely important that they pay serious attention to implementing the obligations assumed under these instruments. To continue to expect that the hijacking of free and fair democratic processes by roguish means must invariably be cured by diplomatic settlement—notwithstanding clear constitutional guidelines for dealing with such situations robustly—is the best panacea for self-abnegation.

At this critical moment, the AU in particular has an historical role to play in protecting human security in Africa. If any lesson has been learned from the Darfur crisis, it is that when all the chips are down Africans must take responsibility for their own actions. African leaders cannot always create disorder and expect foreigners to resolve it. A continental organization of the magnitude of the AU, with the huge international support and goodwill that it currently enjoys, must take its responsibilities seriously and show accountability in its functioning. Rushing to conclude treaties as though there is a medal for quantity is as futile as using continental frameworks to sustain authoritarianism and perfidious governments.

12

The Role of the Human and Peoples' Rights Section of the African Court of Justice and Human Rights

*Gino J Naldi**

1. Introduction

That an environment that, at best, is unconcerned about human rights or, at worst, presides over flagrant and systematic violations of human rights, undermines and poses a threat to human security is well accepted. It does not seem to be an exaggeration to claim that acceptance of this article of faith is one of the keystones of modern civilization. It informs the very nature of the human rights movement. Peace and human security are essential conditions for the effective guarantee and enjoyment of human rights, and vice versa. The two situations are inextricably linked and are mutually reinforcing. If one is subverted so is the other. The causal link between the lack of security and human rights violations has long been accepted by the United Nations (UN)[1] and the international community generally.[2] The then UN Secretary-General, Kofi Annan, drew attention to this unhappy relationship with reference to Africa in his Report on the Causes of Conflict and the Promotion of Durable Peace and Sustainable Development in Africa in 1998.[3] The Organization of African Unity (OAU) also reached the same conclusion and acknowledged the need

* Senior Lecturer, Norwich Law School, University of East Anglia.

[1] See, in particular, the Vienna Declaration and Programme of Action, adopted by the World Conference on Human Rights 1993 (1993) 32 ILM 1661. In Resolution 60/1 on the 2005 World Summit Outcome, the General Assembly stated , inter alia, 'We recognize that development, peace and security and human rights are interlinked and mutually reinforcing', A/RES/60/1, para 9. See further generally, Progress report on the prevention of armed conflict, Report of the Secretary-General, A/60/891. UN documents may be accessed at: <http://www.un.org>.

[2] See, eg, Section VII, Helsinki Final Act, adopted at the Conference on Security and Co-operation in Europe (1975) 14 ILM 1292.

[3] A/52/871-S/1998/318. See further, UNSC Res 1318 (2000) UN Doc S/RES/1318 and UNSC Res 1625 (2005) UN Doc S/RES/1625.

to address this problem.[4] In its Declaration on the Conference on Security, Stability, Development and Cooperation in Africa (CSSDCA) 2000 the OAU accepted that security is 'an indispensable condition for peace, stability, development and cooperation'.[5] African leaders unequivocally committed themselves in the New Partnership for Africa's Development (NEPAD) Declaration in 2001, inter alia, to promoting and ensuring peace and security.[6] One of the fundamental objectives of the African Union (AU), the organization that succeeded the OAU in 2002, is to 'promote peace, security, and stability on the continent'[7] and it explicitly recognizes that this cannot be achieved without creating a peaceful and secure environment that respects, inter alia, human rights, the rule of law, and good governance.[8] One way of trying to achieve this objective has been to build upon and reinforce the legislative and institutional measures put in place by its predecessor, the OAU, to promote security[9]

---

[4] Grand Bay (Mauritius) Declaration 1999, *Compendium of Key Human Rights Documents of the African Union* (Cape Town: Pretoria University Law Press, 2005), 69. Regional African organizations, such as the Economic Community of West African States (ECOWAS), have also taken measures to strengthen peace and security, see, eg, the ECOWAS Protocol Relating to the Mechanism for Conflict Prevention, Management, Resolution, Peace-Keeping and Security 1999, <http://www.ecowas.int>. According to Art 163(1) Treaty Establishing the Common Market for Eastern and Southern Africa (COMESA) 1993, <http://www.comesa.int>, 'The Member States agree that regional peace and security are pre-requisites to social and economic development and vital to the achievement of regional economic integration objectives of the Common Market.'

[5] Para 10(a), *Compendium of Key Human Rights Documents of the African Union*, 77. The Conference further established, para 9(h), that, 'Democracy, good governance, respect for human and peoples' rights and the rule of law are prerequisites for the security, stability and development of the continent.'

[6] See: <http://www.chr.up.ac.za>. See E Baimu, 'Human Rights in NEPAD and its Implications for the African Human Rights System' (2002) 2 African Human Rights Law Journal 301.

[7] Art 3(f) Constitutive Act of the African Union 2000, <http://www.africa-union.org>.

[8] Arts 3 and 4 Constitutive Act. See also, the Kigali Declaration 2003, *Compendium of Key Human Rights Documents of the African Union*, 80. A concrete step towards consolidating these values is the unratified African Charter on Democracy, Elections and Governance 2007, see: <http://www.africa-union.org>. See further, A Abass and MA Baderin, 'Towards Effective Collective Security and Human Rights Protection in Africa: An Assessment of the Constitutive Act of the African Union' (2002) 49 Netherlands International Law Review 1.

[9] In 1993 the OAU set up the Mechanism for Conflict Prevention, Management and Resolution (1994) 6 African Journal of International and Comparative Law 158. Its primary task was the anticipation and prevention of conflicts, with emphasis on anticipatory and preventive measures. See GJ Naldi, *The Organization of African Unity: An Analysis of its Role* (2nd edn, London: Mansell, 1999), 32–4. One of the first acts of the AU was to create the Peace and Security Council with the mandate, inter alia, to promote peace, security, and stability in Africa, to anticipate and prevent conflicts, to assist in peace-building, and to promote and encourage democratic practices, including the protection of human rights and fundamental freedoms, see Protocol relating to the Establishment of the Peace and Security Council of the African Union 2002, <http://www.africa-union.org>. The Peace and Security Council is listed as an organ of the AU under Art 5 of the, as yet unratified, Protocol on Amendments to the Constitutive Act of the African Union 2003, <http://www.africa-union.org>. See further, F Viljoen, *International Human Rights Law in Africa* (Oxford: Oxford University Press, 2007), 205–11; KD Magliveras and GJ Naldi, *The African Union* (The Hague: Kluwer Law International, 2009), 130–41.

and to protect human rights.[10] This chapter is concerned with the latter purpose, specifically the overdue creation of an African court dealing with human rights. It will examine whether the court's mandate is sufficiently robust to meet the significant challenges to the enjoyment of human rights that exist in Africa, particularly in light of the latest reforms.

2. The African human rights system—a brief overview

The principal regional instrument for the protection of human rights in Africa is the African Charter on Human and Peoples' Rights (Banjul Charter), adopted by the OAU in 1981.[11] The Banjul Charter has the distinction of enshrining all three categories of human rights, civil and political, economic, social, and cultural rights, and peoples' rights.[12] The task of promoting and protecting the rights enshrined in the Banjul Charter was entrusted to the African Commission on Human and Peoples' Rights (African Commission),[13] a quasi-judicial organ with powers akin to those of the UN Human Rights Committee or the, now defunct, European Commission on Human Rights.[14] There was insufficient support at the time for the proposition that the protective role be assigned to a court on the basis that such a mechanism was alien to the African concept of justice.[15] In truth, however, it seems that many African states, committed to the primacy of the state or adherents of the so-called 'diplomatic school' of international law that prefer flexible and amorphous princi-

---

[10] The Preamble to the Protocol on the Statute of the African Court of Justice and Human Rights 2008 explicitly makes the link between peace, security, and stability, and the protection of human and peoples' rights, <http://www.africa-union.org>.

[11] See: <http://www.africa-union.org> (1982) 21 ILM 58. In force 21 October 1986. All the member states of the AU have ratified the Banjul Charter. Other important human rights treaties are the African Charter on the Rights and Welfare of the Child 1990, ratified by 45 member states, and the Protocol to the African Charter on Human and Peoples' Rights on the Rights of Women in Africa 2003, ratified by 27 member states, <http://www.africa-union.org>. See Magliveras and Naldi (n 9 above) 155–233; Viljoen (n 9 above) 260–75; F Banda, 'Blazing a Trail: The African Protocol on Women's Rights Comes into Force' (2006) 50 Journal of African Law 72.

[12] Magliveras and Naldi (see n 9 above) 166–99; Viljoen (see n 9 above) 235–53; UO Umozurike, *The African Charter on Human and Peoples' Rights* (The Hague: Martinus Nijhoff, 1997), 29–61. The Banjul Charter has nevertheless been described as 'modest in its objectives and flexible in its means', BO Okere, 'The Protection of Human Rights in Africa and the African Charter on Human and Peoples' Rights: A Comparative Analysis with the European and American Systems' (1984) 6 Human Rights Quarterly 141, 158.   [13] Arts 30 and 45 Banjul Charter.

[14] On the African Commission's mandate, see Magliveras and Naldi (n 9 above) 199–217; Viljoen (n 9 above) 216–19, 310–417; A Ankumah, *The African Commission on Human and Peoples' Rights: Practice and Procedure* (The Hague: Martinus Nijhoff, 1996), 20–110. On the European Commission on Human Rights, see JG Merrills and AH Robertson, *Human Rights in Europe* (4th edn, Manchester: Manchester University Press, 2001), 271–87.

[15] P Amoah, 'The African Charter on Human and Peoples' Rights—An Effective Weapon for Human Rights?' (1992) 4 African Journal of International and Comparative Law 226, 237–8.

ples that provide them with considerable latitude, were simply loath to subject themselves to such scrutiny.[16]

A school of thought has argued that the failure to establish a judicial body with the mandate to apply and enforce its provisions rendered the Banjul Charter fatally flawed. The claim was advanced that without such an organ human rights in Africa could never be adequately protected.[17] The African Commission was, for various reasons, perceived as too weak to undertake this role effectively.[18] Much of the criticism focused on its lack of enforcement powers, in particular on the fact that the African Commission's decisions were not formally binding.[19] The egregious violations of human rights in Africa, often on a large scale, appeared to lend support to this view and rendered the opposition to a court untenable. Consequently, in 1994 the OAU decided to examine the possibility of setting up a human rights court[20] and after various drafts, the Protocol on the Establishment of an African Court on Human and Peoples' Rights was finally adopted by the OAU in 1998.[21]

3. Truncated existence of the African Court on Human and Peoples' Rights

The Protocol on the Establishment of an African Court on Human and Peoples' Rights, adopted as has been stated in 1998, came into force on 25 January

[16] UO Umozurike, 'The Protection of Human Rights Under the Banjul (African) Charter on Human and Peoples' Rights' (1988) 1 African Journal of International Law 65, 78, who writes that it 'was an attempt to avoid exposing a government or the Head of State closely identified with the government for its wrong doings'.

[17] RM D'Sa, 'The African Charter on Human and Peoples' Rights: Problems and Prospects for Regional Action' (1981–83) 10 Australian Yearbook of International Law 101; R Gittleman, 'The African Charter on Human and Peoples' Rights: A Legal Analysis' (1982) 22 Virginia Journal of International Law 667.

[18] G Robertson, *Crimes Against Humanity: The Struggle for Global Justice* (London: Penguin, 1999), 58–9; KO Kufuor, 'Safeguarding Human Rights: A Critique of the African Commission on Human and Peoples' Rights' (1993) 18 Africa Development 65, 74; Z Motala, 'Human Rights in Africa: A Cultural, Ideological, and Legal Examination' (1989) 12 Hastings International and Comparative Law Review 373, 405; M wa Mutua, 'The African Human Rights System in Comparative Perspective' (1993) 3 Review of the African Commission on Human and Peoples' Rights 5, 11.

[19] Ankumah (see n 14 above) 24, 74–5; D'Sa (see n 17 above), 'The African Charter on Human and Peoples' Rights', 126. However, it must be acknowledged that the African Commission has grown into its protective roles in recent years and has become a much more forceful defender of human and peoples' rights, see Magliveras and Naldi (n 9 above) 156–60.

[20] AHG/Res 230 (XXX).

[21] Protocol to the African Charter on Human and Peoples' Rights on the Establishment of an African Court on Human and Peoples' Rights, adopted by the Assembly of Heads of State and Government, 34th Ordinary Session, Ouagadougou, Burkina Faso, 8–10 June 1998, <http://www.africa-union.org>. Note that mention in the Protocol to the OAU should now be taken to refer to the African Union. In some respects the final version of the protocol may be considered regressive compared to the initial Cape Town draft, see OAU/LEG/EXP/AFCHPR (I), reproduced in (1996) 8 African Journal of International and Comparative Law 493. See further, GJ Naldi and KD Magliveras, 'The Proposed African Court on Human and Peoples' Rights' (1996) 8 African Journal of International and Comparative Law 944.

2004.[22] At the time of writing it has been ratified by 25 states.[23] Its future in its current form, however, may be somewhat limited. In July 2004 the AU decided that the African Court on Human and Peoples' Rights should be merged with the African Court of Justice,[24] the principal judicial organ of the AU.[25] A draft protocol on the merger of the two courts was submitted for consideration in 2006.[26] While practical reasons may have been at the core of this development,[27] including a desire for rationalization,[28] and the potential problem of overlapping jurisdiction between the two courts,[29] the decision was initially greeted

[22] Upon ratification by 15 states, see Art 34(3) Protocol on the Establishment of an African Court on Human and Peoples' Rights. For analysis, see Viljoen (n 9 above) 418–75; GW Mugwanya, *Human Rights in Africa: Enhancing Human Rights Through the African Regional Human Rights System* (Ardsley, NY: Transnational Publishers, 2003), 315–36; VO Nmehielle, *The African Human Rights System: Its Laws, Practice and Institutions* (The Hague: Martinus Nijhoff, 2001), 259–308; J Harrington, 'The African Court on Human and Peoples' Rights' in MD Evans and R Murray (eds), *The African Charter on Human and Peoples' Rights: The System in Practice, 1986–2000* (Cambridge: Cambridge University Press, 2002), 305–34; N Krisch, 'The Establishment of an African Court on Human and Peoples' Rights' (1998) 58 Zeitschrift für ausländisches öffentliches Recht und Völkerrecht 713; GJ Naldi and KD Magliveras, 'Reinforcing the African System of Human Rights: The Protocol on the Establishment of a Regional Court on Human and Peoples' Rights' (1998) 16 Netherlands Quarterly on Human Rights 431; NJ Udombana, 'Toward the African Court on Human and Peoples' Rights: Better Late than Never' (2000) 3 Yale Human Rights and Development Law Journal 45. Basic facts on the African Court on Human and Peoples' Rights can be found at: <http://www.aict-ctia.org/courts_conti/achpr/achpr_home.hmtl>.

[23] Algeria, Burkina Faso, Burundi, Côte d'Ivoire, Comoros, Gabon, Gambia, Ghana, Kenya, Libya, Lesotho, Malawi, Mali, Mauritania, Mauritius, Mozambique, Niger, Nigeria, Rwanda, Senegal, South Africa, Tanzania, Togo, Tunisia, and Uganda.

[24] Decision on the Seats of the African Union, Assembly/AU/Dec.45 (III), para 4 (2004); Decision on the Merger of the African Court on Human and Peoples' Rights and the Court of Justice of the African Union, Assembly/AU/Dec.83 (V). Viljoen (see n 9 above) 457–8; I Kane and AC Motala, 'The Creation of a New African Court of Justice and Human Rights' in MD Evans and R Murray (eds), *The African Charter on Human and Peoples' Rights: The System in Practice, 1986–2006* (2nd edn, Cambridge: Cambridge University Press, 2008), 406, 409–13.

[25] Art 18 Constitutive Act, Art 2(2) Protocol of the Court of Justice of the African Union 2003, <http://www.africa-union.org>. For analysis of the African Court of Justice, see KD Magliveras and GJ Naldi, 'The African Court of Justice' (2006) 66 Zeitschrift für ausländisches öffentliches Recht und Völkerrecht 187.

[26] Draft Protocol on the Statute of the African Court of Justice and Human Rights, EX.CL/211 (VIII) Rev.1. Viljoen (see n 9 above) 458; Kane and Motala, 'The Creation of a New African Court of Justice and Human Rights', 406–40.

[27] According to the AU, the 'institutional merging of the two courts is aimed at integrating justice more concretely into the institutional mechanism of the African Union. It will also make it possible to bring together the competences of these two statutory organs of the AU', Press Release No 66/2008.

[28] Kane and Motala (see n 24 above) 416; NJ Udombana, 'An African Human Rights Court and an African Union Court: A Needful Duality or a Needless Duplication?' (2003) 28 Brooklyn Journal of International Law 811. According to Interights, the merger was motivated by the desire to ensure adequate funding for an effective court <http://www.interights.org/AfricanSingleProtocolAdopted/index.htm>.

[29] The African Court on Human and Peoples' Rights appears to have the capacity to pronounce on the Constitutive Act, given that the promotion and protection of human rights are stated as core principles and objectives, under Art 3(1) Protocol on an African Court on Human and Peoples' Rights, a conclusion supported by the recent jurisprudence of the ECOWAS Court of Justice and the SADC Tribunal, see n 98 below, whereas the African Court of Justice seems to have jurisdiction

with dismay.[30] The African Commission itself expressed concern at the 'negative impact' that the decision could have on the establishment of an effective African Court on Human and Peoples' Rights, drawing attention to the different mandates and litigants of the two courts.[31] However, the draft statute seemed to be cognizant of these criticisms and therefore proposed the creation of a single court composed of two sections,[32] one of which was a Human Rights Section with jurisdiction over alleged violations of human rights.[33] Given that the autonomy of the Human Rights Section appeared to be preserved a leading commentator expressed his support for the proposed merger.[34] Pending further development on the draft statute the AU nevertheless decided to allow the African Court on Human and Peoples' Rights to become operational.[35] Steps were therefore taken to make the African Court on Human and Peoples' Rights functional, judges have been elected for instance.[36] However, progress towards the merger was by now gaining impetus and at its summit in Sharm el-Sheikh, Egypt, the AU Assembly took the momentous decision on 1 July 2008 to adopt the Protocol on the Statute of the African Court of Justice and Human Rights (hereinafter 'Protocol').[37] The Protocol replaces the Protocol on the Establishment of an African Court on Human and Peoples' Rights and the Protocol on the Court of Justice,[38] and merges the African Court on Human and Peoples' Rights and the Court of Justice into a single court, the African Court of Justice and Human Rights.[39] The African Court of Justice and Human Rights is now stated to be 'the main judicial organ of the African Union'.[40] The Protocol makes a number of transitional arrangements. The term of office of the judges on the African Court on Human and Peoples' Rights ends once

over the African Charter on Human and Peoples' Rights under Art 18(1)(b) Protocol of the Court of Justice.

[30] Thus Amnesty International criticized the decision on the ground that it undermines the effective functioning of the African Court on Human and Peoples' Rights, 'African Union: Assembly's Decision should not Undermine the African Court' <http://www.commondreams.org/news2004/1021–05.htm>. Kane and Motala have questioned the legality of the whole process stating that the proper procedures for amendments were not followed (see n 24 above), 414–15.

[31] Resolution on the Establishment of an Effective African Court on Human and Peoples' Rights, ACHPR/Res.76 (XXXVII) 05 (2005), <http://www1.umn.edu/humanrts/africa/resolutions/rec81.html>. See also, F Viljoen and E Baimu, 'Courts for Africa: Considering the Co-existence of the African Court on Human and Peoples' Rights and the African Court of Justice (2004) 22 Netherlands Quarterly on Human Rights 241.

[32] Art 16 Draft Statute of the African Court of Justice and Human Rights.

[33] Arts 17(2) and 35 Draft Statute of the African Court of Justice and Human Rights.

[34] Viljoen (see n 9 above) 458–9.   [35] Assembly/AU/Dec.83 (V), para 3.

[36] See: <http://www.aict-ctia.org/courts_conti/achpr/achpr_bios.hmtl>. See also, Assembly/AU/Dec.202 (XI).

[37] Decision on the Single Legal Instrument on the Merger of the African Court on Human and Peoples' Rights and the African Court of Justice, Assembly/AU/Dec.196 (XI).

[38] Art 1 Protocol. The Protocol on the Court of Justice has become a dead letter; it never entered into force notwithstanding the fact that in 2007 the 15th instrument of ratification necessary to do so under Art 60 thereof was deposited.   [39] Art 2 Protocol.

[40] Art 2(1) Statute of the African Court of Justice and Human Rights.

the judges of the African Court of Justice and Human Rights are elected.[41] However, they will remain in office until the latter judges are sworn in.[42] Cases pending before the African Court on Human and Peoples' Rights that have not been concluded before the Protocol enters into force will be transferred to the Human Rights Section of the African Court of Justice and Human Rights to be considered on the basis of the Protocol on the Establishment of an African Court on Human and Peoples' Rights.[43] Following the Protocol's entry into force, the Protocol on the Establishment of an African Court on Human and Peoples' Rights is to remain in force for a transitional period no longer than one year or any other period as determined by the Assembly in order for the assets, prerogatives, rights, and liabilities of the African Court on Human and Peoples' Rights to be transferred to the African Court of Justice and Human Rights.[44] While predicting the entry into force of treaties is never an exact science the AU's enthusiasm for the merged court suggests that its ratification sooner rather than later is likely. The African Court on Human and Peoples' Rights may be living on borrowed time.

4. The Human Rights Section of the African Court of Justice and Human Rights

Since the African Court on Human and Peoples' Rights has already been subjected to considerable critical analysis[45] it seems apposite to examine the Human Rights Section of the African Court of Justice and Human Rights (hereinafter 'Court') which is where the future ultimately lies. As has been stated, the Protocol on the Statute of the African Court of Justice and Human Rights was adopted by the AU in 2008. The Statute of the African Court of Justice and Human Rights (hereinafter 'Statute') is annexed to the Protocol and constitutes an integral part thereof.[46] It requires 15 ratifications to enter into force.[47] The Protocol in effect amends the Constitutive Act in that references to the Court of Justice in the Constitutive Act must henceforth read as references to the African Court of Justice and Human Rights.[48] The roles of the African Court on Human and Peoples' Rights and the Court of Justice are fundamentally retained in that the former is replaced by a Human Rights Section and the latter by a General Affairs Section.[49] The Human Rights Section is competent to hear all cases on human and peoples' rights.[50] The essential mission of the Human Rights Section as described in the Preamble to the Protocol is to secure the objectives of the

---

[41] Art 4 Protocol.   [42] Ibid.
[43] Art 5 Protocol. There are no such cases at the time of writing.   [44] Art 7 Protocol.
[45] For literature on the African Court on Human and Peoples' Rights see above n 22.
[46] Art 1 Protocol.   [47] Art 9(1) Protocol. No ratifications at the time of writing.
[48] Art 3 Protocol.   [49] Art 16 Statute.
[50] Art 17(2) Statute. Cases on human and peoples' rights are specifically excluded from the jurisdiction of the General Affairs Section, Art 17(1) Statute.

Banjul Charter. Its purpose is to supplement and strengthen the mission of the African Commission and the African Committee of Experts on the Rights and Welfare of the Child.[51] While this could simply be considered a statement of intent on strengthening the protective system it could also be seen as a reference to the fact that these human rights bodies have an enhanced role to play as they have access to the Human Rights Section. Nonetheless, one of the effects of the single instrument is that the distinctive identities of the two African courts is diminished because both sections share features in common, and this observation seems truer of the African Court on Human and Peoples' Rights. Viewed overall, it would appear that the Statute has drawn inspiration from, and has more in common with, the Statute of the International Court of Justice (ICJ) than with universal or regional human rights systems. It may be that the Rules of the Court will augment the human rights dimension of the court.[52]

An important item that is omitted from the Protocol and Statute is the matter of reservations.[53] It appears that agreement on this issue could not be reached at the drafting stage.[54] In accordance with the rules of general international law silence on this issue allows states to enter reservations on condition that the reservations are not incompatible with the object and purpose of the treaty in conformity with Article 19(c) Vienna Convention on the Law of Treaties 1969. However, it may well be that in relation to human rights treaties the scope that states have for entering reservations is much narrower.[55] Answers will be forthcoming only if states enter reservations when ratifying the Protocol, and only if the Court is called upon to address this question.

4.1 Structure, organization, and composition

The Court is the main judicial organ of the AU[56] and is composed of 16 judges.[57] This is under one-third of the actual membership of the AU (53) and should

---

[51] The African Committee of Experts on the Rights and Welfare of the Child is set up under Art 32 African Charter on the Rights and Welfare of the Child. Its mandate to promote and protect the rights and welfare of children is detailed in Art 42 thereof.

[52] Art 27 Statute. Art 27(2) Statute reminds the Court to 'bear in mind the complementarity it maintains with the African Commission and the African Committee of Experts'.

[53] Cf Art 75 American Convention on Human Rights (ACHR), <www.oas.org/juridico/english/treaties> and Art 57 European Convention on Human Rights (ECHR), <http://conventions.coe.int>.   [54] Kane and Motala (see n 24 above) 423–4.

[55] UN Human Rights Committee, General Comment 24 on Reservations to the International Covenant on Civil and Political Rights (1995) 2 International Human Rights Reports 10.

[56] Art 2(1) Statute. Art 18 Constitutive Act describes the Court as 'the principal judicial organ' of the AU. Art 25(1) Statute states that the Seat of the Court is the same as that of the African Court on Human and Peoples' Rights, that is, Arusha, Tanzania, Press Release No 66/2008. However, the Court may sit in another member state if necessary with its consent. Cf Art 3 ACHR, and Rule 19(1) European Court of Human Rights, <www.echr.coe.int>. The official and working languages of the Court are those of the AU, Art 32 Statute. See further, Art 25 Constitutive Act. Cf Art 20 Rules of Procedure of the Inter-American Court of Human Rights, <http://www.corteidh.or.cr> and Rule 34 European Court of Human Rights.

[57] Art 3(1) Statute. However, upon the recommendation of the Court the Assembly may review the number of judges, ibid.

ensure that the Full Court does not become unwieldy.[58] As has already been mentioned, the Court is actually made up of two sections, a Human Rights Section and a General Affairs Section, each composed of eight judges.[59] To be quorate the Human Rights Section must consist of six judges.[60] Provision is made for the constitution of one or several chambers by the sections.[61] The judges must be nationals of states parties, that is, nationals of a state that has ratified the Protocol.[62] Since no two judges may be nationals of the same state an immediate difficulty arises.[63] It will be recalled that the Protocol requires 15 ratifications to enter into force; yet the Court is composed of 16 judges all of different nationalities drawn from states parties only. The arithmetic does not add up. It may be that this problem remains a theoretical one if a sufficiently large number of states are prompt in ratifying the Protocol. Each state party may nominate up to two candidates[64] and, in a progressive move, consideration must be given to adequate gender representation.[65] Article 4 of the Statute, which is virtually identical to Article 2 of the Statute of the ICJ, requires the judges to possess the appropriate qualifications but with the added proviso, in an implied reference to the Human Rights Section, that expertise in human rights law may also be required.[66] This stipulation should put to rest the fears expressed by some critics when the proposed merger was first aired that the AU's commitment to human rights was being undermined because there was no requirement that the judges had to have proficiency in the field of human rights.[67]

The judges are elected by the Executive Council in a secret ballot, and appointed by the Assembly.[68] A two-thirds majority of the AU member states is required, a not insignificant hurdle.[69] This fact may result in non-states parties being able to

[58] The European Court of Human Rights consists of the same number of judges as there are states parties, currently 47, Art 20 ECHR. Given that such a bench would be unmanageable, the European Court usually sits in Committees of three judges, Chambers of seven judges or a Grand Chamber of 17 judges, Art 27(1) ECHR. The Inter-American Court of Human Rights is composed of seven judges, Art 4(1) Statute of the Inter-American Court of Human Rights, <http://www.corteidh.or.cr>.   [59] Art 16 Statute.

[60] Art 21(3) Statute.   [61] Art 19(1) Statute. Cf Art 26 ICJ Statute.

[62] Art 3(1) Statute. Cf Art 34 Banjul Charter which requires that members of the Commission 'must have the nationality of one of the States Parties to the present Charter'. By way of contrast, the Inter-American Court of Human Rights specifies that judges must be nationals of OAS member states, Art 52(1) ACHR and Art 4(1) Statute of the Inter-American Court of Human Rights. Curiously, the ECHR is silent on this issue.

[63] Art 3(2) Statute. Cf Art 52(2) ACHR and Art 4(2) Statute of the Inter-American Court of Human Rights.

[64] Art 5(2) Statute. There are two lists of candidates, one for each of the sections, and states can choose the list on which their candidates are placed, Art 6 Statute. Cf Art 53(1) ACHR, Art 7(2) Statute of the Inter-American Court of Human Rights, and Art 22(1) ECHR, both systems permitting the nomination of up to three candidates.

[65] Note Rule 14 European Court of Human Rights which seeks to secure a 'balanced representation of the sexes'.

[66] Cf Art 52(1) ACHR and Art 4(1) Statute of the Inter-American Court of Human Rights. Curiously the ECHR makes no explicit reference to expertise in human rights, Art 21(1) ECHR.

[67] Viljoen and Baimu (see n 31) 241.   [68] Art 7(1)–(2) Statute.

[69] Art 7(2) Statute. See also para 3 thereof. By way of contrast, the ACHR specifies an absolute majority, Art 53(1) ACHR and Art 9 Statute of the Inter-American Court of Human Rights, and the ECHR simply requires a majority, Art 22(1) ECHR.

exercise a vote, which does not seem a desirable scenario.[70] The same procedure applies where vacancies result from death, resignation, or removal from office.[71] Adequate gender representation in the election of the judges must be secured,[72] which demands that the candidatures of a certain number of women must survive the nomination process.[73] Africa's regions and its principal legal traditions, which must be interpreted to include the civil, Roman-Dutch, common, and Islamic legal systems, must be represented on the Court.[74]

The judges are elected in an individual capacity, that is, they do not represent states or other agencies nor must they be under their control or direction.[75] They must therefore abstain from any pursuit that is incompatible with their independence or impartiality or the demands of their office.[76] This obligation accompanies the commitment to the independence of the bench which seeks to ensure that the judges are not subjected to inducements, pressure, influence, threats, or other interference.[77] Judges are, of course, under a general duty to consider all cases impartially.[78] The corresponding obligation on the Court is expressly spelt out in Article 12(2) of the Statute. The Statute seeks to avoid conflicts of interest by requiring a judge who has had previous involvement with a case to recuse himself or herself.[79] In fact, in order to avoid any semblance of partiality, a judge who is a national of a state that is a party to a case is not permitted to hear the case.[80] Not only is this a departure from accepted international practice but it does not appear to be reconcilable with the assertion of the judges' independence.[81] No provision is made for replacing a judge in such circumstances with an interim or substitute judge.[82]

---

[70] The US system restricts voting to states parties to the ACHR, Art 53(1) ACHR and Arts 7(1) and 9(1) Statute of the Inter-American Court of Human Rights. The same is true of the European system, Art 22(1) ECHR.   [71] Art 10(3) Statute.

[72] Art 7(5) Statute. Cf Rule 25(2) European Court of Human Rights.

[73] Provided the policy is proportionate and based on objective and reasonable criteria, neutral, specific to individual candidates, *Guido Jacobs v Belgium*, Case No 943/2000, UN GAOR A/59/40, Vol II, annex IX, sect S (Human Rights Committee, 7 July 2004).

[74] Art 7(4) Statute. Art 3(3) Statute states that where possible each geographical region of Africa is to represented by three judges except for the Western Region which will have four judges. Cf Rule 25(2) European Court of Human Rights.

[75] Art 12(3) Statute. Cf Art 21(2) ECHR which expressly states that judges serve in their individual capacity.

[76] Art 13 Statute. Cf Art 18(1) Statute of the Inter-American Court of Human Rights which is more detailed. See also Art 21(3) ECHR and Rule 4 European Court of Human Rights.

[77] Art 12(1) Statute. See also Art 4 Statute. Cf Art 26 Banjul Charter.

[78] See Art 11(1) Statute on the oath of office.

[79] Art 14(1) Statute. Additionally, if the President is of the view that a judge should not participate in a case that judge, with the agreement of the Court, will be excluded from the case, Art 14(2) Statute. Cf Art 19(1) Statute of the Inter-American Court of Human Rights and Rule 28(2) European Court of Human Rights.   [80] Art 14(3) Statute.

[81] Cf Art 31(1) ICJ Statute and Art 55(1) ACHR. By way of contrast, the ECHR prevents judges from presiding in cases involving a contracting party of which they are nationals, Rule 13 European Court of Human Rights.

[82] Cf Art 19(4) Statute Inter-American Court of Human Rights and Rule 29(1)(a)–(b) European Court of Human Rights.

Conspicuous by its omission from the Statute is any reference to the appointment of ad hoc judges. This is a manifest difference with the ICJ and other regional human rights systems which make provision for ad hoc judges.[83] However, as has just been mentioned, the fact that a judge who is a national of a state party to a case cannot hear that case would appear to obviate the need for ad hoc judges and consequently the omission may be justified on this basis.

The judges are elected for a term of office of six years with the possibility of one further renewable period.[84] In order to ensure that the elections are held on a staggered basis, at the end of two years following the first election, the terms of office of eight judges, four from each section, shall expire after four years.[85] All judges, except for the President,[86] are part time.[87] Vacancies may result from death, resignation, or removal from office.[88] In such circumstances, another judge is elected to complete the predecessor's term of office.[89] A judge may be suspended or removed from office when two-thirds of the other members of the Court are of the view that he or she no longer fulfils the requirements of office.[90] However, the Court's recommendation must be accepted by the Assembly which has the final say.[91]

4.2 Competence of the Court

By virtue of Article 28 of the Statute the Court has jurisdiction over all cases and legal disputes submitted to it concerning: (a) the interpretation and application of the Constitutive Act; (b) the interpretation, application, or validity of other AU treaties and all subsidiary legal instruments adopted by the AU and/or OAU; (c) the interpretation and application of the Banjul Charter, the African Charter on the Rights and Welfare of the Child, the Protocol on the Rights of Women, and any other legal instrument relating to human rights that a state party has ratified; (d) any question of international law; (e) all acts, decisions, regulations, and directives of the AU organs; (f) all matters specifically provided for in other agreement/s that state parties may conclude among themselves or with the AU conferring jurisdiction on the Court; (g) the existence of any fact which, if established, would constitute a breach of an obligation owed to a state party or to the

---

[83] Cf Art 31(2)–(3) ICJ Statute, Art 55(2)–(4) ACHR, Art 10 Statute Inter-American Court of Human Rights, and Rule 29 European Court of Human Rights.

[84] Art 8(1) Statute. This is identical to the ACHR, see Art 54(1) ACHR. Judges to the European Court of Human Rights are also elected for an initial period of six years and may be re-elected, Art 23(1) ECHR. However, they must retire at the age of 70, Art 23(6) ECHR.

[85] Art 8(1) Statute.

[86] Art 22(1) Statute. The President serves a term of office of three years and may be re-elected once.   [87] Art 8(4) Statute.

[88] Art 10(1) Statute.   [89] Art 8(3) Statute.   [90] Art 9(2) Statute.

[91] Art 9(4) Statute. Cf Art 21(2) Statute Inter-American Court of Human Rights. In Europe the decision rests with the European Court of Human Rights only, Rule 7 European Court of Human Rights.

AU; and (h) the nature or extent of the reparation to be made for the breach of an obligation. The Human Rights Section is competent to hear all cases relating to human and/or peoples' rights[92] and cases brought before it must indicate the rights alleged to have been violated and, if possible, the treaty provisions on which they are based.[93] However, any case may be referred to the Full Court.[94] Although no guidance is provided as to when a referral may be considered appropriate this could happen when a particularly salient matter is at stake, for example the interpretation of the human rights provisions of the Constitutive Act are at issue, or when a case happens to be politically sensitive.[95] It is important to note that the Statute does not confer on states the right to appeal a section's refusal to refer the case to the Full Court. The inclusion of 'any other legal instrument relating to human rights' that a state party has ratified within the Court's reach is especially worthy of note because of its innovative character which sets the Court apart from its OAS and European counterparts which have a relatively limited competence.[96] It is sweeping in its scope[97] and the Court has potentially been granted jurisdiction to pronounce on UN treaties such as the International Covenants on Human Rights, the Convention on the Elimination of Discrimination Against Women, and the Convention on the Rights of the Child, but also the treaties of African regional organizations such as ECOWAS, COMESA, and the Southern African Development Community (SADC) which contain commitments to human rights.[98] Motivated it would seem by the desire to enhance the protection of human rights in Africa,[99] a laudable aim in itself, and to avoid a descent into

---

[92] Art 17(2) Statute.   [93] Art 34(1) Statute.   [94] Art 18 Statute.

[95] Under the European system, a referral to the Grand Chamber may be made where a case raises serious questions affecting the interpretation or application of the ECHR and Protocols, or a serious issue of general importance, or where a Chamber's decision may prove inconsistent with a judgment of the Court, Art 43(2) ECHR and Rule 72(1) European Court of Human Rights.

[96] Cf Art 32(1) ECHR. Under Art 64(1) ACHR and Art 60 of its Rules the Inter-American Court of Human Rights can give advisory, or interpretative, rulings on 'other treaties concerning the protection of human rights in the American states'. See *'Other Treaties' Subject to the Consultative Jurisdiction of the Court (Art 64 of the American Convention on Human Rights) (Advisory Opinion)* [1982] (ser A) No 1. See further, JM Pasqualucci, *The Practice and Procedure of the Inter-American Court of Human Rights* (Cambridge: Cambridge University Press, 2003), 55–7.

[97] The corresponding provision in the Protocol on the African Court on Human and Peoples' Rights, Art 3(1), which uses very similar language, has been described as bestowing upon the Court an 'almost unlimited substantive jurisdiction', Harrington, (see n 22 above) 318.

[98] See, eg, Art 4(g) Revised ECOWAS Treaty 1993 <http://www.ecowas.int> Art 6(e) COMESA Treaty 1993, and Art 4(c) amended SADC Treaty 2001 <http://www.sadc.int>. It is interesting to note that in judgments handed down in 2008 both the ECOWAS Tribunal and the SADC Tribunal held that human rights issues were justiciable under their respective treaties, see *Hadijatou Mani Koraou v Republic of Niger*, unreported, 27 October 2008, Judgment No ECW/CCJ/JUD/06/08, and *Mike Campbell (Pvt) Ltd et al v The Republic of Zimbabwe* SADC (T) Case No 2/2007, at: <http://www.saflii.org/sa/cases/SADCT/2008/2.pdf>. Such a development has occurred in the US context, see *'Other Treaties' Subject to the Consultative Jurisdiction of the Court (Art 64 of the American Convention on Human Rights) (Advisory Opinion)* [1982] (ser A) No 1; *Right to Information on Consular Assistance Within the Framework of the Guarantees of Legal Due Process (Advisory Opinion)* [1999] (ser A) No 16. See further, Pasqualucci (n 96 above) 56–7.

[99] Nmehielle, *The African Human Rights System* (Leiden: Brill, 2002), 264.

cultural relativism,[100] the possibility does arise of inconsistent interpretations of international human rights law.[101] The direction that the judges have expertise in human rights assumes a greater importance therefore.

The power to determine the nature or extent of reparations, or compensation, to be made for breach of an obligation is a significant one. It is reinforced by Article 45 of the Statute which authorizes the Court to order any appropriate measures for a violation of human rights.

While Article 28 of the Statute reflects Article 36(2) of the ICJ Statute it will be observed that the former is broader in scope than the latter; it does not simply replicate the ICJ model but has been drafted with a specifically African perspective.

Curiously, the Statute does not address explicitly the possibility of challenges to the jurisdiction of the Court given that such disputes are bound to arise. Both the ICJ and the Inter-American Court of Human Rights make provision for preliminary objections in their Rules and it may be that the Court will follow suit.[102] The power of the court to determine its own jurisdiction is one exercised by other comparable international tribunals[103] but a provision to this effect was dropped from the final version of the Statute.[104] It may be that such a scenario would be covered by the binding force of the Court's judgments expressed in Article 46(1) of the Statute.

The fundamental question of *locus standi* is governed by Articles 29 and 30 of the Statute. The applicants entitled under Article 29(1) of the Statute to submit cases include: (a) state parties to the Protocol; and (b) the Assembly, the Parliament, and other AU organs authorized by the Assembly, for example, the Executive Council.[105] This category could be described as privileged applicants since they can approach the Court on any dispute listed in Article 28 of the Statute, including human rights violations.

A couple of observations need to be made about this provision. First, while Article 28 of the Statute states that, 'The Court shall have jurisdiction over ... all legal disputes submitted to it', Article 29(1) of the Statute says that entities can

---

[100] Mugwanya (see n 22 above) 323.

[101] See generally, B Kingbury, 'Is the Proliferation of International Courts and Tribunals a Systemic Problem?' (1999) 31 New York University Journal of International Law and Politics 679; T Buergenthal, 'Proliferation of International Courts and Tribunals: Is it Good or Bad?' (2001) 14 Leiden Journal of International Law 267.

[102] Art 79 ICJ's Rules of Procedure and Rule 36 Inter-American Court of Human Rights.

[103] Cf Art 3(2) Protocol on the African Court on Human and Peoples' Rights which declares that the matter shall be settled by the decision of the Court. This corresponds to a fundamental principle of international law, namely, 'the inherent power of a tribunal to interpret the text establishing its jurisdiction', see Judge Lauterpacht's Separate Opinion in the *Norwegian Loans Case (France v Norway) (Judgment)* [1957] ICJ Rep 9, 34. Cf Art 36(6) ICJ Statute, Art 32(2) ECHR. On the approach of the Inter-American Court of Human Rights see, eg, *Constitutional Court v Peru (Competence)* [1999] (ser A) No 55, and further, Pasqualucci (n 96 above) 33–6.

[104] Kane and Motala (see n 24 above) 428.

[105] The third category is AU employees on appeal, in the context of a labour dispute in accordance with the relevant stipulations in the Staff Rules and Regulations.

submit cases to the Court 'on any *issue or* dispute provided for in Article 28' (emphasis added). While the word 'dispute' has a technical meaning in international law[106] it is not clear whether the different form of words used in Article 29(1) of the Statute is intended to make a substantive difference by allowing the 'privileged applicants' the capacity to submit to the Court questions of law other than disputes and without invoking the Court's Advisory Jurisdiction or whether there has simply been a 'slip of the pen'. The ICJ has definitely expressed the view that a dispute is a prerequisite for exercising its judicial function[107] and it will not entertain cases where the dispute is no longer extant.[108] Secondly, neither the African Commission nor the African Committee of Experts on the Rights and Welfare of the Child have standing under Article 29 of the Statute since they are not AU organs.[109] Thirdly, it is not immediately apparent whether the phrase 'the Parliament and other AU organs' should be read conjunctively or disjunctively, that is, whether the Parliament as well as the other AU organs must obtain the Assembly's permission to submit a case, or rather has Parliament the independent will to submit cases whereas all other AU organs require the Assembly's permission. It is submitted that the latter interpretation is preferable in view of Parliament's status.

The second category of applicants listed in Article 30 of the Statute entitled to submit cases to the Court relating to violations of human rights as set out in Article 28(c) of the Statute are: (a) state parties to the Protocol; (b) the African Commission; (c) the African Committee of Experts on the Rights and Welfare of the Child; (d) African Intergovernmental Organizations; (e) African National Human Rights Institutions; and (f) individuals and NGOs accredited to the AU or its organs.[110] This list invites some comment. First, with one exception, access to the Court is automatic upon ratification of the Protocol and is not dependent on further declarations by state parties.[111] It is evident that inter-state cases are envisaged. This is apparent from the language of subparagraph (a) but also if viewed in the context of the complaints procedure available under the Banjul Charter. Under Articles 47 to 49 Banjul Charter the African Commission is empowered to entertain inter-state complaints, allowing states to institute proceedings claiming that another state is in breach of its obligations under the Banjul Charter.[112]

---

[106] An international dispute has been defined as 'a disagreement on a point of law or fact, a conflict of legal views or of interests', *Mavrommatis Palestine Concessions (Greece v United Kingdom) (Jurisdiction)* [1924] PCIJ (ser A) No 2, 11.

[107] *Nuclear Tests (Australia v France; New Zealand v France) (Judgments)* [1974] ICJ Rep 253, 270–1.　　　　　　　　　　　　　　　　　　　　　　　[108] Ibid, 271.

[109] See Art 5 Constitutive Act.

[110] Cf Art 61(1) ACHR and Art 33 ECHR. Art 5(1) Protocol on the African Court on Human and Peoples' Rights is considerably more complex.

[111] Art 8(3) Protocol and Art 30(f) Statute. Cf Art 62 ACHR.

[112] See further, Magliveras and Naldi, *The African Union* (n 9 above) 205–6. In *Interights (on behalf of Pan African Movement and Citizens for Peace in Eritrea) and Interights (on behalf of Pan African Movement and Inter Africa Group) v Eritrea*, Communication Nos 233/99, 234/99, Sixteenth Annual Activity Report 2002–2003, 44, the African Commission stated that the 'ini-

There is no requirement for the complainant to prove any special interest but, as with the other regional systems, all states parties are deemed to have a collective interest in upholding the provisions of the Banjul Charter. Whether states will be granted the opportunity of appealing adverse rulings by the African Commission remains to be seen.[113]

Secondly, that standing has been granted to such a broad category of applicants, including African National Human Rights Institutions, is particularly welcome.[114] Indeed, it is possible that the Court will become an 'appeals body' for the African Commission[115] and the African Committee of Experts on the Rights and Welfare of the Child. It is encouraging that the African system recognizes in principle the *locus standi* of duly accredited individuals and NGOs before the Court,[116] although the point has been made that the requirement of accreditation may have a restrictive effect.[117] However, this standing is made subject to the critical condition set out in Article 8(3) of the Protocol, the substantive section of which states that,

Any Member State may...make a declaration accepting the competence of the Court to receive cases under Article 30(f) [of the Statute] *involving a State which has not made such a declaration* (emphasis added).

Despite the tortuous language used, and the French version is no clearer,[118] it seems that this provision is designed to make the Court's jurisdiction to receive petitions from these complainants contingent upon states making a separate declaration,[119] which begs the question why not simply repeat

tiation of an inter-state complaint is dependent on the voluntary exercise of the sovereign will of a State party to the Charter, which decision can only be made by States in accordance with the Charter'. To date only one such complaint has been submitted, *Democratic Republic of Congo v Burundi, Rwanda and Uganda*, Communication No 227/99, Twentieth Annual Activity Report 2005–2006. The African Commission's decisions on communications can be accessed at: <http://www.achpr.org>.

[113] Viljoen, 'Admissibility under the African Charter' in MD Evans and R Murray (eds), *The African Charter on Human and Peoples' Rights: The System in Practice, 1986–2000* (Cambridge: Cambridge University Press, 2002), 97; Harrington (see n 22 above) 330–1.

[114] Kane and Motala especially approve of the conferral of standing on African National Human Rights Institutions (see n 24 above) 430.

[115] Harrington (see n 22 above) 331.

[116] Traditionally individuals have not had standing before a court in international human rights law, see, eg, Art 61(1) ACHR. The ECHR was the first regional human rights treaty to accept the standing of individuals with the entry of Protocol No 11 in 1998, see now Art 34 ECHR.

[117] Kane and Motala (see n 24 above) 431–2.

[118] The French version reads as follows, 'Tout Etat partie...peut faire une déclaration acceptant la compétence de la Cour pour recevoir les requêtes énoncées à l'article 30(f) et concernant un Etat partie qui n'a pas fait cette déclaration.'

[119] This is the interpretation of Art 8(3) Protocol given by Interights, <http://www.interights.org/AfricanSingleProtocolAdopted/index.htm>. See also O Elias, 'Introductory Note to the Protocol on the Statute of the African Court of Justice and Human Rights' (2009) 48 ILM 334, 335.

verbatim Article 34(6) of the Protocol of the African Court of Human and Peoples' Rights which makes it plain that that Court 'shall not receive any petition under article 5(3) involving a State Party which has not made such a declaration'. Such a situation is highly regrettable given the import of standing for individuals and NGOs since it is likely that some of the worst perpetrators of serious human rights abuses will not be brought to account given that it is improbable that they will accept the Court's exceptional jurisdiction relating to these applicants. It is ironic that whereas the Statute could be said to provide for what may amount to public interest litigation, at the same time complaints from certain applicants can only be instituted in extremely restrictive circumstances.[120] Those applicants who find their route to the Court blocked by a state's refusal to accept this head of jurisdiction will need to rely on the African Commission, African National Human Rights Institutions, African Intergovernmental Organizations, and willing states to air their complaints before the Court.

Thirdly, unlike the more restrictive European system, the applicant need not be the victim of the alleged violation.[121] The African system has understandably preferred the OAS approach which 'basically allows anyone to file a human rights petition with the Inter-American Commission'.[122] The justification for such extensive standing, which applies equally in the African context,[123] is to be found in 'poverty, lack of education and lack of legal assistance', in addition to the possible intimidation of lawyers, which 'might otherwise hinder access to the enforcement organs of the regional system'.[124] In its interpretation of admissibility requirements under the Banjul Charter the African Commission has held that applications in the form of an *actio popularis* are allowed.[125]

Fourthly, the Statute is silent on the issue of hurdles of admissibility. It may be that detailed conditions governing admissibility shall be dealt with by the Rules of Procedure.

---

[120] According to Interights this limitation 'renders access to justice illusory for human rights victims', ibid.

[121] Cf Art 34 ECHR. See further, Merrills and Robertson (n 14 above) 307–10.

[122] Pasqualucci (see n 96 above) 100. See Art 44 ACHR.

[123] Viljoen (see n 113 above) 75.   [124] Pasqualucci (see n 96 above) 101–2.

[125] *Article 19 v Eritrea*, Communication No 275/2003, Twenty-second Annual Activity Report 2006–2007, 65; 'wisely allowed', *The Social and Economic Rights Action Center and the Center for Economic and Social Rights v Nigeria*, Communication No 155/96, Fifteenth Annual Activity Report 2001–2002, 49. In *The Law Office of Ghazi Suleiman v Sudan*, Communication Nos 222/98 and 229/99, Sixteenth Annual Activity Report 2002–2003, 39, the African Commission stated that states' obligations were of an *erga omnes* nature not dependent on individuals. See also Viljoen (n 113 above) 76.

4.3 Sources of law

Article 31(1) of the Statute sets out in descending order the applicable law which the Court must have regard to in determining the cases before it:

(a) The Constitutive Act;
(b) International treaties, general or particular, ratified by the contesting States;
(c) International custom, as evidence of a general practice accepted as law;
(d) General principles of law recognized either universally or by African states;
(e) As subsidiary means for the determination of the rules of law, judicial deci-sions[126] and the writings of the most highly qualified publicists of various nations as well as the regulations, directives and decisions of the AU; and
(f) Any other law relevant to the case.

In addition, the Court has the power to decide a case *ex aequo et bono* should the parties agree.[127]

This clause is based on Article 38(1)–(2) of the ICJ Statute but it will be observed that there are some differences reflecting the Statute's regional setting in light of Article 28 of the Statute.[128] Worthy of note is the prescription to the Court to have regard to the Constitutive Act. This is perfectly rational in view of the fact that the Constitutive Act is the constitutional document of the AU. However, this instruction must be read in the light of the primacy of the UN Charter.[129] The reference to international treaties in subparagraph (b) must necessarily encompass all OAU/AU treaties, for example, the Convention on Refugees, the African Charter, and the Protocol on the Rights of Women,[130] and should include regional treaties such as the SADC Treaty. It should also extend to duly ratified UN treaties such as the Convention on the Elimination of All Forms of Racial Discrimination 1965, the International Covenants on Human Rights, the Convention Against Torture and Other Cruel, Inhuman or Degrading Treatment or Punishment 1984, and the Protocol to the Convention on Rights of the Child on Involvement in Armed Conflict 2000.[131] However, it must be noted that the language of this provision differs from its analogous

---

[126] It is clearly stated that judicial decisions have no binding force except as between the parties to a particular case in accordance with Art 46(1) Statute.　　　　　[127] Art 31(2) Statute.

[128] Under Arts 60 and 61 Banjul Charter the African Commission is authorized to draw inspi-ration from various sources of law, see *Civil Liberties Organisation, Legal Defence Centre, Legal Defence and Assistance Project v Nigeria*, Communication No 218/98, Fourteenth Annual Activity Report 2000–2001, para 24; *African Institute for Human Rights and Development (on behalf of Sierra Leonean refugees in Guinea) v Republic of Guinea*, Communication No 249/2002, Twentieth Annual Activity Report 2005–2006, 37–8.

[129] See Art 103 UN Charter, and *R (on the application of Al-Jedda) v Secretary of State for Defence* [2007] UKHL 58.

[130] The texts of these treaties are available at: <http://www.africa.union.org>.

[131] See, eg, *Civil Liberties Organisation, Legal Defence Centre, Legal Defence and Assistance Project v Nigeria*, Communication No 218/98, Fourteenth Annual Activity Report 2000–2001; *Purohit and Moore v The Gambia*, Communication No 241/2001, Sixteenth Annual Activity Report

provision in the ICJ Statute by containing the qualification 'treaties...ratified by the contesting States'. Hence regional treaties such as the ECHR cannot be directly applied under this provision but there seems to be no good reason why the Court, if it were so minded, should not be able to take account of such treaties, and pay heed of the rich jurisprudence of the Inter-American Court of Human Rights and the European Court of Human Rights, in accordance with the references in the other subparagraphs to international custom,[132] which should include relevant norms of *jus cogens*,[133] to general principles of law,[134] to judicial decisions,[135] and any other law relevant to the case, which gives the Court an unfettered discretion. Potentially significant is the fact that the Court is directed to take account of general principles of law accepted in Africa, and there is no reason to believe that regional customary law would be excluded, so that included in such principles could be a right to development[136] and second and third generation human rights,[137] albeit inspired to a significant degree by the provisions of the Banjul Charter.

4.4 Provisional measures

Under Article 35(1) of the Statute the Court can, *proprio motu*, or at the request of a party to the case, indicate such provisional measures to preserve

2002–2003, 76; *Garreth Anver Prince v South Africa*, Communication No 255/2002, Eighteenth Annual Activity Report 2002–2003, 42.

[132] As expressed in the Universal Declaration of Human Rights for instance, see *Zimbabwe Human Rights NGO Forum v Zimbabwe*, Communication No 245/2002, Twenty-first Annual Activity Report 2005–2006, 180. [133] *Prosecutor v Furundzija* (1999) 38 ILM 317, 153.

[134] In *Democratic Republic of Congo v Burundi, Rwanda and Uganda*, Communication No 227/99, Twentieth Annual Activity Report 2005–2006, 70, 78, the African Commission invoked the Geneva Conventions 1949 and the Additional Protocols 1977 as general principles of law recognized by African states. In *Purohit and Moore v The Gambia*, Communication No 241/2001, Sixteenth Annual Activity Report 2002–2003, and *Lawyers for Human Rights v Swaziland*, Communication No 251/2002, Eighteenth Annual Activity Report 2002–2003, the African Commission relied on UN soft law in the form of the UN Principles for the Protection of Persons with Mental Illness and the Improvement of Mental Illnesses and the Improvement of Mental Health Care, and the UN Basic Principles on the Independence of the Judiciary respectively. Human rights first emerged in EC law as a general principle of law developed by the European Court of Justice, Wyatt and Dashwood's *European Union Law* (5th edn, London: Sweet & Maxwell, 2006), 258–61.

[135] *Zimbabwe Human Rights NGO Forum v Zimbabwe*, Communication No 245/2002, Twenty-first Annual Activity Report 2005–2006.

[136] Such a right has been asserted by the African Commission, see, eg, *The Social and Economic Rights Action Center and the Center for Economic and Social Rights v Nigeria*, Communication No 155/96, Fifteenth Annual Activity Report 2001–2002; *Bissangou v Republic of Congo*, Communication No 253/2002, Twenty-first Annual Activity Report 2005–2006. See further, Magliveras and Naldi (n 9 above) 196–7; R Murray, *Human Rights in Africa: From the OAU to the African Union* (Cambridge: Cambridge University Press, 2004), 240–1.

[137] *The Social and Economic Rights Action Center and the Center for Economic and Social Rights v Nigeria*, Communication No 155/96, Fifteenth Annual Activity Report 2001–2002; Magliveras and Naldi (see n 9 above) 191–9; Murray, *Human Rights in Africa* (Cambridge: Cambridge University Press, 2004), 245–59.

the respective rights of the parties. This provision corresponds in every material respect to Article 41(1) of the ICJ Statute[138] and replaces the more stringent wording of the Protocol on the African Court on Human and Peoples' Rights.[139] A number of questions remain to be answered. Can a request for provisional measures be submitted to the Court at the same time as the main proceedings are instituted?[140] Will the Court want to satisfy itself that it has jurisdiction, prima facie or otherwise, before adopting provisional measures?[141] Furthermore, what will the Court's approach be towards interim measures adopted by the African Commission?[142] These issues should be addressed by the Rules.

An important consideration is whether such interim measures will be deemed legally binding. The language of the relevant provision of the Statute provides no clues on this point[143] and the practice of the African Commission is inconclusive, refraining from a decisive answer.[144] However, the fact that the ICJ,[145] the Inter-American Court of Human Rights,[146] the UN Human Rights Committee,[147] and the European Court of Human Rights[148] have established that interim measures issued by them have binding effect gives the Court the perfect opportunity to follow this approach. Of course, the Court could do worse than adopt the African Commission's approach which is to

[138] And additionally Arts 73–78 ICJ's Rules of Procedure.

[139] Art 27(2) Protocol on the African Court on Human and Peoples' Rights requires the existence of 'extreme gravity and urgency', and the need 'to avoid irreparable harm to persons'.

[140] Cf Art 73(1) ICJ's Rules of Procedure.

[141] The ICJ's established practice is that as long as prima facie jurisdiction is apparent it will entertain the request for interim measures, even if it later turns out that it lacks jurisdiction, see *Military and Paramilitary Activities in and against Nicaragua, Provisional Measures* [1984] ICJ Rep 169; *Application of the Convention on the Prevention and Punishment of the Crime of Genocide (Bosnia and Herzegovina v Yugoslavia (Serbia and Montenegro), Provisional Measures* [1993] ICJ Rep 3; *Case Concerning the Arrest Warrant of 11 April 2000 (Democratic Republic of Congo v Belgium), Provisional Measures* [2000] ICJ Rep 182; *Application of the International Convention on the Elimination of All Forms of Racial Discrimination (Georgia v Russian Federation) (Provisional Measures)* [2008] ICJ Rep 113, 117. Available at: <http://www.icj-cij.org>.

[142] See Pasqualucci (n 96 above) 295–8.

[143] Although the Statute states that 'judgments' only have a legally binding effect, see Art 46(1).

[144] Rule 111 authorizes the African Commission to indicate interim measures to 'avoid irreparable damage being caused to the victim', or where 'desirable in the interest of the parties or the proper conduct of the proceedings before it', see further, GJ Naldi, 'Interim Measures of Protection in the Practice of the African Commission on Human and Peoples' Rights' (2002) 2 African Journal of Human Rights 1.

[145] *LaGrand Case (Germany v United States of America)* [2001] ICJ Rep 466, 99–103; *Application of the Convention on the Prevention and Punishment of the Crime of Genocide (Bosnia and Herzegovina v Serbia and Montenegro)* [2007] ICJ Rep 452, 468.

[146] *Constitutional Court v Peru (Provisional Measures)* [2000] (ser E) No 3. See further, Pasqualucci (n 96 above) 316–18.

[147] Communication No 869/1999, *Piandiong, Morallos and Bulan v The Philippines*, UN Doc CCPR/C/70/D/869/1999 (19 October 2000).

[148] *Mamatkulov and Abdurasulovic v Turkey*, App Nos 46827/99 and 46951/99, Judgment of 6 February 2003.

declare that a state that has failed to abide by its indication of interim measures is in breach of the principle of *pacta sunt servanda* enshrined in Article 1 of the Banjul Charter.[149]

4.5 Advisory jurisdiction

In accordance with Article 53(1) of the Statute the Court has the competence to give advisory opinions on any legal question at the request of the Assembly, the Parliament, the Executive Council, the Peace and Security Council, the Economic, Social and Cultural Council, the Financial institutions, or any AU organ authorized by the AU.[150] The authority of the Court to render advisory opinions is discretionary, as evidenced by the inclusion of the verb 'may' in the provision.[151] However, Article 53(3) of the Statute states an explicit exception in that a request must not relate to a pending application before the African Commission or the African Committee of Experts. This should ensure that the jurisdiction of these bodies is not undermined. It remains to be seen in what other circumstances the Court may choose to decline to exercise its advisory jurisdiction. The ICJ is of the view that it may do so for 'compelling reasons'.[152] The jurisprudence of the Inter-American Court of Human Rights suggests that a request for an advisory jurisdiction may be rejected in circumstances where the Court's contentious jurisdiction may be undermined, where the protective system would be impaired, or where the question is wholly academic, amongst others.[153]

The fact that so many AU organs have a right to request an opinion is noteworthy and, unlike the ACHR, there is no indication that the AU organs are restricted to their sphere of competence.[154] Nevertheless, the range of applicants authorized to request an opinion, while comparable in ambit to Article 96 UN Charter, is not as broad as that of the Protocol on the African Court on Human and Peoples' Rights which is the most extensive of the regional human rights systems.[155] Particularly worthy of mention is the fact that under Article 4(1) of

---

[149] *International Pen, Constitutional Rights Project, Interights on behalf of Ken Saro-Wiwa Jr. and Civil Liberties Organisation v Nigeria*, Communication Nos 137/94, 139/94, 154/96, and 161/97, Twelfth Annual Activity Report 1998–1999. See further, Naldi (n 144 above) 6–8.

[150] It seems to be the Full Court, rather than the Sections, that has this capacity. It should be observed that the African Commission has the power to interpret the Banjul Charter under Art 45(3) thereof, described by an eminent author as amounting to authorization 'to issue what are in effect advisory opinions', AH Robertson and JG Merrills, *Human Rights in the World* (3rd edn, Manchester: Manchester University Press, 1992), 221.   [151] Cf Art 65 ICJ Statute.

[152] *Legality of the Threat or Use of Nuclear Weapons (Advisory Opinion)* [1996] ICJ Rep 226, 235.

[153] See, eg, *'Other Treaties' Subject to the Consultative Jurisdiction of the Court (Art 64 of the American Convention on Human Rights) (Advisory Opinion)* [1982] (ser A) No 1; *Judicial Guarantees in States of Emergency (Articles 27(2), 25 and 8 of the American Convention on Human Rights) (Advisory Opinion)* [1987] (ser A) No 9. See further, Pasqualucci (n 96 above) 61–3.

[154] Cf Art 96(2) UN Charter, and see *Legality of the Use by a State of Nuclear Weapons in Armed Conflict (Advisory Opinion)* [1996] ICJ Rep 66; Pasqualucci (see n 96 above) 39–44.

[155] Cf Art 64(1) ACHR and Art 47(1) ECHR. The latter limits standing to the Committee of Ministers only. It is instructive to note that as a result of an imaginative interpretation of *locus*

the Protocol on the African Court on Human and Peoples' Rights all member states of the AU are able to request an opinion, whether or not they are parties to the Protocol.[156] The right is also extended to other African organizations, which could include ECOWAS or SADC for example. The Statute is therefore considerably narrower in this respect.

A further point worth drawing attention to concerns the wide-ranging areas subject to the Court's advisory jurisdiction.[157] It is evident that the Court will be able to consider matters relating to the Banjul Charter or other relevant human rights instruments. This conclusion arises from the scope of the term 'legal question' in Article 53(1) of the Statute, by implication from Article 53(3) of the Statute, Article 28(c) of the Statute, and the aims and objectives of the Statute as a whole.

Such a sweeping competence would suggest, if the precedent established by the Inter-American Court of Human Rights, which enjoys a similar jurisdiction, were to be followed,[158] that the Court could make creative use of the advisory procedure to strengthen human rights significantly. The Inter-American Court of Human Rights has therefore interpreted substantive and procedural provisions of the ACHR and addressed such important questions as the death penalty, reservations to treaties, the non-derogability of certain rights, the right of non-discrimination, and the freedom of thought and expression, amongst others.[159] While advisory opinions are necessarily strictly non-binding they can acquire a persuasive status that makes a substantial addition to our understanding of human rights.[160]

The Court must give its opinions in open court.[161] With respect to other procedural aspects of the advisory jurisdiction Article 56 of the Statute states that the Court will be guided by the procedure applicable in contentious cases.[162] Amongst other things, this should enable judges to deliver separate or dissenting opinions, which conforms to standard international judicial practice.[163]

---

standi requirements the Inter-American Court of Human Rights has allowed *amici curiae*, including NGOs, to participate in advisory proceedings, Pasqualucci (see n 96 above) 74–5; AA Cançado Trindade, 'The Operation of the Inter-American Court of Human Rights' in DJ Harris and S Livingstone (eds), *The Inter-American System of Human Rights* (Oxford: Oxford University Press, 1998), 133, 142.

[156] Cf Art 64(1) ACHR. See further, Pasqualucci (n 96 above) 37–9.

[157] By way of contrast, the European Court of Human Rights has a narrow jurisdiction and can interpret only the ECHR and Protocols, Art 47(1) ECHR, leading Robertson and Merrills to comment that the European Court of Human Rights 'had its advisory competence defined so restrictively that it is difficult to think of any important issue of interpretation that would have fallen within it', Merrills and Robertson (see n 14 above) 292.

[158] Pasqualucci (see n 96 above) 44–58.

[159] Ibid, 47–55; Trindade (see n 155 above) 142–5.   [160] Pasqualucci (see n 96 above) 80.

[161] Art 55 Statute.   [162] Cf Art 68 ICJ Statute.

[163] Cf Art 66(1) ACHR, Art 49 ECHR, and Rule 88(2) European Court of Human Rights. It should be observed Art 4(2) Protocol on the African Court on Human and Peoples' Rights expressly allowed judges to deliver separate or dissenting opinions.

4.6 Procedure and practice

The Court must conduct its hearings in public unless it decides, *proprio motu* or upon application by the parties, that they be held in camera.[164] No guidance is provided as to the circumstances that might lead the Court to take this step; the Rules may address this issue, but both the Inter-American Court of Human Rights and the European Court of Human Rights indicate that this should happen only in 'exceptional circumstances'.[165] However, the latter proceeds to list grounds such as the interests of morals, public order, or national security, the interests of juveniles, or protection of the private life of the parties.[166]

A state party to a case is represented by agents, with the assistance of counsel or advocates before the Court if necessary.[167] AU organs are represented by the Commission's Chairperson or representative.[168] The African Commission, the African Committee of Experts, African Intergovernmental Organizations, and African National Human Rights Institutions can be represented by a person of their choice.[169] Individuals and NGOs can similarly be represented by a person of their choice.[170] It is unfortunate that the possibility of free legal representation in the interests of justice provided for in Article 10(2) of the Protocol on the African Court on Human and Peoples' Rights has been omitted.[171]

Any person, witness, or representative of parties who appears before the Court is guaranteed such protection necessary for the proper discharge of their functions and duties before the Court.[172] Individuals and others should therefore be able to appear before the Court without fear of retribution, and this is a particularly welcome development in the context of human rights since arbitrary detention, ill-treatment, and disappearances for defying the authorities are all too common in parts of Africa. It is unclear how, if at all, individuals are to be effectively protected within the jurisdiction of a state party to the Statute but it is submitted that this guarantee could be strengthened were the Court to use creatively its competence to indicate provisional measures under Article 35 of the Statute. A state that failed to protect such people could ultimately be found to be in breach of its obligations under the Statute and the Banjul Charter.

An important power conferred upon the Court is that to 'order any appropriate measures in order to remedy the situation, including granting fair

[164] Art 39 Statute.
[165] Art 24(1) Statute of the Inter-American Court of Human Rights, Art 14(1) Inter-American Court's Rules of Procedure, and Rule 63(1) European Court of Human Rights.
[166] Rule 63(2) European Court of Human Rights.   [167] Art 36(1)–(2) Statute.
[168] Art 36(3) Statute.
[169] Art 36(4) Statute. Cf Rules 35 and 36 European Court of Human Rights.
[170] Art 36(5) Statute.
[171] Rule 92 European Court of Human Rights states that legal aid will be granted only if it is necessary for the proper conduct of the case, and the applicant has insufficient means to meet all or part of the costs.
[172] Art 36(6) Statute. Cf Art 50 Inter-American Court's Rules of Procedure in relation to witnesses and expert witnesses.

compensation' if it concludes that human rights have been violated.[173] This is a power additional to that to make reparation under Article 28(1)(h) of the Statute. It appears that according to the wording of the provision the Court is not under an obligation to make an award if a violation is established,[174] but may do so at the request of a party. This suggests that the Court cannot order appropriate measures on its own motion. However, the wording seems to give the Court a broad mandate to order suitable remedies of which fair compensation, which by definition must include awards of a pecuniary nature, or reparation are but options. Although it is unclear whether the Statute envisages restitution in kind as a remedy it could be covered by the concept of 'reparation' and implied in the general wording of the provision.[175] The Court may wish to take account of the practice of the Inter-American Court of Human Rights on reparations which provides ample examples of the extensive nature and forms that remedies can take.[176]

As may be expected, the Statute addresses a number of issues concerning the Court's judgments in contentious cases.[177] Thus, judgments must be taken by a majority,[178] must be reasoned,[179] read in open court,[180] and separate and dissenting opinions may be attached.[181] An interesting innovation is the requirement on the Court to render its judgment within 90 days of having completed its

---

[173] Art 45 Statute. Cf Art 27(1) Protocol on the African Court on Human and Peoples' Rights which included the power to order reparation. It is interesting to note that the African Commission accepts the concept of restitution as a remedy in individual communications despite the lack of any express authority either in the Banjul Charter or the African Commission's Rules of Procedure. In *Malawi African Association, Amnesty International, Ms Sarr Diop, Union Interafricaine des Droits de l'Homme and RADDHO, Collectif des Veuves et Ayant-droit, and Association Mauritanienne des Droits de l'Homme v Mauritania*, Communication Nos 54/91, 61/91, 98/93, 164/97–196/97, and 210/98, Thirteenth Annual Activity Report of the African Commission on Human and Peoples' Rights 1999–2000, the African Commission hence made detailed recommendations and proceeded to recognize the principle that compensatory damages may be payable as a form of indemnity. See further, GJ Naldi, 'Reparations in the Practice of the African Commission on Human and Peoples' Rights' (2001) 14 Leiden Journal of International Law 681–93.

[174] Cf Art 63(1) ACHR.

[175] Art 24(2) of the Cape Town Draft Protocol clearly envisaged this possibility since it read that fair compensation or reparation was 'to be paid or made to the injured party', see Naldi and Magliveras (n 21 above) 962–3.

[176] Pasqualucci (see n 96 above) 230–81. For a more critical account, see D Shelton, 'Reparations in the Inter-American System' in DJ Harris and S Livingstone (eds), *The Inter-American System of Human Rights* (Oxford: Oxford University Press, 1998), 151.

[177] Appropriately applicable by analogy to advisory cases, see Art 56 of the Statute.

[178] Art 42(1) Statute. In the event of a tie, the presiding judge has the casting vote, Art 42(2) Statute. Cf Art 23(3) Statute Inter-American Court of Human Rights and Rule 23(1) European Court of Human Rights.

[179] Art 43(2) Statute. Cf Art 66(1) ACHR, Art 55(1) Inter-American Court's Rules of Procedure, Art 45(1) ECHR, and Rule 74(1) European Court of Human Rights. The Rules are considerably more detailed.

[180] Art 43(4) Statute. See also Art 55 Statute with regard to advisory opinions. Cf Rule 77(2) European Court of Human Rights.

[181] Art 44 Statute. Cf Art 66(2) ACHR, Art 55(2) Inter-American Court's Rules of Procedure, Art 45(2) ECHR, and Rule 74(2) European Court of Human Rights.

deliberations.[182] This does not seem an unreasonable expectation in the context of the protection of human rights and is a welcome development. The Statute is silent on the publication of judgments but it is likely that in these modern times they should be made available to the public promptly.[183]

In addition, the Court's judgments, which include those of the chambers and sections,[184] are final.[185] The use of the term 'judgment' may be problematic since it is normally associated with the Court's final conclusion which it issues at specific stages of contentious proceedings, that is, jurisdiction and admissibility, merits. It seems preferable to have followed the example set by Article 29(3) of the Rules of the Inter-American Court which states that, 'Judgments *and orders* of the Court may not be contested in any way' (emphasis added). This provision has a broader scope, taking in the various rulings made by the Court, for example on interim measures, on the taking of evidence, etc. The provision in the Protocol on the African Court of Human and Peoples' Rights stipulating that judgments are additionally 'without appeal'[186] has been dropped from the Statute even though it has the advantage of legal clarity. However, the Court may be asked by a party to interpret the meaning and scope of a judgment if a dispute over it should arise.[187] The Statute does not actually set a deadline for the submission of such a request although that omission may be addressed by the Rules.[188] Furthermore, the Court has the capacity to review its judgments in the light of new facts subject to a number of mandatory and discretionary conditions.[189] First, that the application for revision is based on the discovery of a new fact which, if it had been known at the time to the Court and the party claiming revision, would have been a decisive factor, provided that such ignorance was not due to negligence, presumably on the part of the party. Secondly, that a double statute of limitations has been observed: the application was lodged no later than six months of the new fact's discovery and not later than ten years from the date of the judgment. Thirdly, that the Court first may require the party in question to comply with the judgment.

[182] Art 43(1) Statute.
[183] Cf Art 30 Inter-American Court's Rules of Procedure and Rule 78 European Court of Human Rights.   [184] Art 19(2) Statute.
[185] Art 46(2) Statute. Cf Art 67 ACHR.
[186] Art 28(2) Protocol. Cf Art 67 ACHR. Among the significant reforms introduced by Protocol No 11 ECHR is the fact that judgments given by a Chamber may be referred, in effect appealed, to the Grand Chamber whose decision is final, see Arts 42, 43, and 44 ECHR. See further, DJ Harris, M O'Boyle, and C Warbrick, *Law of the European Convention on Human Rights* (2nd edn, Oxford: Oxford University Press, 2009), 826–9.
[187] Art 47 Statute. Cf Art 61 ICJ Statute, Art 67 ACHR, and Rule 79 European Court of Human Rights. According to the Inter-American Court of Human Rights, the purpose of this procedure involves 'not only precisely defining the text of the operative parts of the judgment, but also specifying its scope, meaning and purpose, based on the considerations of the judgment', *Velasquez Rodriguez v Honduras (Interpretation of the Compensatory Damages)* [1990] (ser C) No 9, 26. See further, Pasqualucci (n 96 above) 216–18.
[188] Rule 79(1) European Court of Human Rights sets a deadline of one year but the ACHR is strict, 90 days, Art 67.   [189] Art 48 Statute. Cf Art 61 ICJ Statute.

The decisions of the Court are binding upon the parties to a case[190] which 'shall comply with the judgment ... within the time stipulated by the Court and to guarantee its execution'.[191] However, the Court itself has no power to enforce its judgments, although it must refer a failure to comply to the Assembly for a decision.[192] To ensure compliance from recalcitrant states the Assembly may impose sanctions under Article 23(2) of the Constitutive Act.[193] As a matter of policy, it is likely that such an option will be exercised only in the most egregious circumstances. A creative interpretation of the Court power to award compensation could lead it to award punitive damages in cases where the applicant establishes that a state has flouted a judgment of the Court and has failed to make reparation to a victim.

Although the Court's judgments are binding only upon those states parties to a case international practice suggests that the Court's interpretation of the law will have a persuasive effect on other states.

In the context of states seeking to petition the Court attention must be drawn to Article 49(1) of the Statute allows any member state or AU organ that has a legal interest in a case before the Court which could be affected by a decision to request the Court to intervene in the case. The decision on the request rests with the Court so that the views of the applicant or the parties to the case cannot bind the Court.[194] There is no guidance as to what the nature of the 'legal interest' might mean but the Court may choose to be guided by the practice of other tribunals.[195] The practice of the ICJ under Article 62 of its Statute demonstrates that the ICJ has applied a very strict policy in this area.[196] Moreover, the ICJ has held that a question that was not decided in the original case cannot be submitted for interpretation.[197] The use of the term 'member state' means that

---

[190] Art 46(1) Statute.

[191] Art 46(3) Statute. Cf Art 68(1) ACHR and Art 46(1) European Court of Human Rights.

[192] Art 46(4) Statute.   [193] Art 46(5) Statute.

[194] *Continental Shelf (Tunisia v Libya) (Malta Intervening)* [1981] ICJ Rep 3. The state seeking to intervene has the burden of proof, *Land, Island and Maritime Frontier Dispute (El Salvador v Honduras) (Nicaragua Intervening)* [1990] ICJ Rep 92, 117. Under Art 46(3) Statute the Court may invite any member state, AU organ, or person concerned that is not a party to the case to submit written observations or take part in the hearings in the interests of the effective administration of justice.

[195] Art 36(2) ECHR, which is limited under para 1 thereof to cases where a national of a state party is an applicant, requires the intervention to be in the interest of the proper administration of justice. See further, Harris, O'Boyle, and Warbrick (n 186 above) 853–6. It is interesting to note that Art 5(2) Protocol on the African Court on the African Court of Human and Peoples' Rights is less strict, requiring a state party simply to have an 'interest'.

[196] See C Chinkin, 'Third Party Intervention Before the International Court of Justice' (1986) 80 American Journal of International Law 495. Art 81(2)(a) ICJ's Rules of Procedure requires the intervening state to set out the interest of a legal nature that will be affected; and see *Sovereignty over Pulau Ligitan and Pulau Sipadan (Indonesia/Malaysia) (Philippines Intervening)* [2001] ICJ Rep 575, where the ICJ explained the meaning of an 'interest of a legal nature'. For the factors that will persuade the ICJ to accept a request for intervention, see *Land, Island and Maritime Frontier Dispute (El Salvador v Honduras) (Nicaragua Intervening)* [1990] ICJ Rep 92.

[197] *Request for Interpretation of the Judgment of 31 March 2004 in the Case concerning Avena and Other Mexican Nationals (Mexico v United States of America)* [2009] ICJ Rep 44, <http://www.icj-cij.org>.

the permission to intervene extends to AU member states which are not contracting parties to the Protocol. This follows from the definition of the term 'member state' provided in Article 1 of the Statute. It also corresponds with the practice of the ICJ which has established that a 'jurisdiction link' by the intervening party is not required.[198] Given the nature of the AU extending this right to its organs seems sensible. The competence of the Court to invite other member states, AU organs, or persons to participate in the case in the interest of the effective administration of justice appears an insightful step.

In a departure from comparable documents, paragraph 2 thereof states that the Court's interpretation is equally binding upon the party that was allowed to intervene. This only seems right and proper.

Article 50 of the Statute permits intervention in a case where the interpretation of the Constitutive Act arises. The wording of Article 50 gives rise to some confusion. Paragraph 1 thereof proclaims that interested 'member states' will receive notification, the definition of which, as has been established above, refers to non-contracting parties. However, paragraph 2 declares that, 'Every State Party and organ of the Union' has the right to intervene. Based on the definition of the term 'state parties' provided in Article 1 of the Statute the right to intervene appears to be limited to only those states that are parties to the Protocol. There seems to be no rational explanation as to why a distinction appears to have been drawn in this instance with Article 49(1) discussed above, particularly in view of the fact that all AU member states potentially have an interest in the interpretation of the Constitutive Act. It may simply be a drafting error.

Article 51(1) of the Statute makes provision for member states and AU organs to be notified where the interpretation of a treaty which the former have ratified is at issue. This provision potentially confers upon the Court an extremely wide competence which again raises concerns about possible divergent interpretations of international law. Under paragraph (2) thereof every state and AU organ taking advantage of this right is bound by the interpretation given by the Court. However, Article 51 of the Statute differs from the corresponding provision in the ICJ Statute, Article 63, in one important respect. Article 51(3) of the Statute specifically excludes cases of alleged violations of human and peoples' rights. The ACHR makes no mention of a right of intervention while under the ECHR intervention is limited to cases where a national of a state party is an applicant, so that the African system can be said to reflect the general stance on this issue.[199] It should be observed that Article 51(1)–(2) of the Statute repeats the 'member states'/'state party' issue discussed above in relation to Article 50.

A notable omission from the competence of the Human Rights Section Court is mention of amicable, or friendly, settlements in accordance with the Banjul

---

[198] *Land and Maritime Boundary (Cameroon v Nigeria) (Equatorial Guinea Intervening)* [1999] ICJ Rep 1029.   [199] Art 36(1) ECHR.

Charter.[200] Such a procedure can be found in the other regional human rights systems[201] but under the ACHR the role of reaching an amicable settlement is assigned to the Inter-American Commission on Human Rights.[202] In fact, the African Commission already performs this function under the Banjul Charter.[203] Again, it may be a matter addressed by the Rules.

5. Conclusion

The Protocol on the Statute of the African Court of Justice and Human Rights is a document that skilfully manages the merger of two quite distinct courts. The establishment of the sections is an ingenious solution to what was a sensitive and potentially difficult situation. Mishandling this matter could have resulted in the complete loss of faith in Africa's resolve to ensure effective protection of human rights. However, as this chapter has sought to illustrate, the Statute has to an extent resulted necessarily in the diminution of the identities of the courts it replaces. Many of the detailed provisions governing the African Court of Human and Peoples' Rights and the Court of Justice have been omitted but it may well be that the Rules will provide the desired particulars. It seems impossible to say what effect the single instrument on the courts will have on the institutional protection of human rights in Africa since the African Court of Human and Peoples' Rights has not had the opportunity to establish itself. However, there is no reason to believe that the Human Rights Section should be any the less capable.

The expectations of the Human Rights Section will be considerable and, therefore, its fundamental philosophy is of importance. Commentators will be anxious to see the position of the Human Rights Section on a number of crucial issues. Will it adopt a statist approach or will it emphasize the object and purpose approach?[204] Will it adopt a purposive or evolutive method of interpretation?[205] Will it draw inspiration from the rich jurisprudence of the Inter-American Court of Human Rights and the European Court of Human Rights? It would be surprising if the Human Rights Section did not look to these well-developed sources but then adapt them to an African setting.[206]

---

[200] Cf Art 9 Protocol on the African Court of Human and Peoples' Rights.

[201] Cf Art 38(1)(b) ECHR and Rule 62 European Court of Human Rights.

[202] Art 48(1)(f) ACHR. See further, Pasqualucci (n 96 above) 147–9.

[203] Art 52 Banjul Charter.

[204] Both the Inter-American Court of Human Rights and the European Court of Human Rights have stressed the latter, making clear that the conventions are special treaties that impose objective obligations on states parties, see Pasqualucci (n 96 above) 328; Harris, O'Boyle, and Warbrick (n 186 above) 5–6.

[205] As applied by the Inter-American Court of Human Rights and the European Court of Human Rights, see Pasqualucci (n 96 above) 328; Harris, O'Boyle, and Warbrick (n 186 above) 7–8.

[206] The case of *Zimbabwe Human Rights NGO Forum v Zimbabwe*, Communication No 245/2002, Twenty-first Annual Activity Report 2005–2006, is an especially interesting

Notwithstanding the lack of an exclusive human rights mandate, the Statute nevertheless constitutes a significant advance towards enhancing the promotion and protection of human rights in Africa. It should remedy one of the basic weaknesses of the African human rights system, the lack of an authoritative, robust, and effective supervisory and enforcement mechanism. The fact that a body now exists with the mandate to adopt binding legal decisions may be considered revolutionary when the human rights record of many African states and the complacent attitude of the OAU over many years is considered. Its import is therefore immense. But the Statute should not be assessed in a vacuum. It is but a part of Africa's design to make progress on human rights which must be viewed in the wider context of the AU's Constitutive Act, NEPAD, the human rights undertakings of the sub-regional organizations, and the domestic commitment to constitutionalism, even though the AU's stated assurances regarding the latter sometimes ring hollow. The Court cannot be expected to solve Africa's human rights problems; some of these are not amenable to judicial resolution and alternative mechanisms, for example diplomatic negotiation may, in some instances, bear better fruit. Nevertheless, if the Court plays its part constructively at the appropriate times it will contribute to this objective. The Court is therefore but one element in strengthening Africa's 'democratic security' project. It may be that the recent opposition of African states to the International Criminal Court will raise the profile of the Court as a local forum and will provide it with an opportunity to assume a decisive role in the protection of human rights in Africa.[207]

At a more particular level, the Statute is not a radical instrument. Unlike the Banjul Charter, the Statute cannot be said to have any special distinguishing features that set it apart to any discernible degree from other regional human rights systems. Rather it complements them satisfactorily on the whole. The Statute is not perfect, the wording sometimes lacks clarity, Article 8(3) of the Protocol is especially problematic, there are gaps and omissions, but these are minor criticisms that will no doubt be addressed by the Court, either in its Rules of Procedure or by its practice. If the hypothesis that the jurisdiction of the Human Rights Section to receive petitions from individuals and NGOs under Article 30(f) of the Statute is dependent upon states making a separate declaration is correct then that constitutes the Statute's weak spot, its fundamental flaw. This situation potentially undermines one of the most important protective functions of the system, rendering the avenue of individual petition almost worthless in practice. It effectively allows the worst violators of human rights to 'drive a coach and horses' right through the mandate of the Human Rights Section. Experience from other jurisdictions informs us that it is the right of

illustration because of the extensive references to international law, including the jurisprudence of the European Court of Human Rights, the Inter-American Court of Human Rights, and the International Criminal Tribunal for the Former Yugoslavia.

[207] In 2005 the UN Security Council referred the Darfur crisis in Sudan to the International Criminal Court, see UNSC Res 1593.

individual petition that has proven to be the most effective weapon in holding states to account and it is therefore a matter of regret that the African system has disregarded this lesson. The role assumed by the African Commission will therefore be all-important. As a body with direct access to the Human Rights Section its leadership will be key. Nevertheless, the Statute constitutes a welcome development which improves on the existing system. Much, of course, will depend on the stance adopted by the Human Rights Section and the Court. If it sets out to be a forceful defender of human rights and fundamental freedoms there can be little doubt that the Human Rights Section will make a contribution to the enhancement of peace and security in Africa. Commentators keenly await its first decision.[208]

[208] It is interesting to note that in December 2009 the African Court of Human and Peoples' Rights delivered its first judgment in the case of *Michelot Yogogombaye v Republic of Senegal,* App. No. 001/2008, dismissing the case for lack of jurisdiction.

13

The African Commission on Human and Peoples' Rights as a Collective Human Security Resource: Promise, Performance, and Prospects

*Obiora Chinedu Okafor**

1. Introduction

It is almost trite these days to state that the attainment and maintenance of peace and security depends, to a highly significant degree, on the enjoyment within the target population of a broad range of human rights, including economic, social, and cultural rights. The scholarly and institutional literature is now replete with evidence and arguments that justify such a conclusion.[1] Indeed, one commentator

* Professor, Osgoode Hall Law School of York University, Toronto, Canada. PhD, LLM (University of British Columbia, Vancouver, Canada); LLM, LLB (Hons) (University of Nigeria, Enugu Campus). I should like to thank Ademola Abass for his invitation to write this chapter. I should also like to thank Uche Gwam, Ikechi Mgbeoji, Ibironke Odumosu, Obinna Okere, Natalie Oman, Kofi Quashigah, and Ugochukwu Ukpabi for their knowing and unknowing contributions to the thoughts contained in this chapter. I am indebted to Chikeziri Igwe and Bernadette Maheandiran for their able research assistance. Small portions of this chapter have appeared in some of my earlier publications on the African human rights system, namely: *The African Human Rights System, Activist Forces and International Institutions* (Cambridge: Cambridge University Press, 2007); *Legitimizing Human Rights NGOs: Lessons from Nigeria* (Trenton, NJ: Africa World Press, 2006); and 'The African System on Human and Peoples' Rights, Quasi-Constructivism, and the Possibility of Peacebuilding within African States' (2004) 8 International Journal of Human Rights 413. For their kind permission to reproduce and use this material, I am also grateful to Cambridge University Press, Africa World Press, and the International Journal of Human Rights. This chapter is dedicated to Bukhari Bello, sometime executive secretary of the Nigerian National Human Rights Commission, for his humanist passion, administrative excellence, and important contributions to the human rights struggle.

[1] eg, see JS Sutterlin, *The United Nations and the Maintenance of International Security* (Westport, CT: Praeger, 2003), 81; *A More Secure World: Our Shared Responsibility*, Report of the Secretary General's High-Level Panel on Threats, Challenges and Change (New York: United Nations, 2004) (hereinafter 'A More Secure World'), viii, ix, 5, 23–56, and 88–90; and JF Jones, 'Human Security and Social Development' (2004) 33 Denver Journal of International Law and Policy 92, 95–102.

has recently gone as far as arguing that the intimate connection between peace and security, on the one hand, and respect for human rights, on the other hand, has long been recognized across civilizations that were as different as 6th Century China and the USA of the 1960s.[2]

Yet, until more recently, within the dominant literature sets and in the prevalent institutional praxis, the concept of collective security has not been traditionally linked in as close or positive a manner with the enjoyment of human rights. By contrast, as fluid and organic a concept as it has been,[3] the collective security concept has been historically captive to and mostly discussed in terms of international action to constrain the use or threat of the use of military force by one state against another: the multilateral prevention or stoppage of the inappropriate uses of military violence across state borders.[4] As Anne-Marie Slaughter has stated:

in 1945, when the founders of the U.N. talked about . . . the security council as a whole being responsible for international peace and security [that is Collective human security], they were talking about state security. They were not [for the most part] worried about what would happen if a government or [some within] one ethnic group decided to massacre hundreds of thousands of fellow citizens. They worried about what happened if one state invaded another.[5]

Leon Gordenker and Thomas G Weiss underline the deep-rooted position of this traditional conception of collective human security as well as its seemingly enduring quality when they declare that:

the central idea [of collective security] has remained the same: the governments of all states would join together to prevent any of their number from using coercion to gain advantage, especially conquering another. Thus, [within this kind of arrangement] no government could with impunity undertake forceful policies that would fundamentally disturb peace and security.[6]

However, Tom Farer has offered a characteristically insightful definition of collective security that captures its enduring commitment to the traditional overly state-centred conception of security as the avoidance of the use or threat of military force, while being flexible enough to reflect the changing conception of that expression. To Farer, a collective (human) security arrangement is 'a collective

---

[2] J Moore, 'Collective Human Security with a Human Face: An International Legal Framework for Coordinated Action to Alleviate Violence and Poverty' (2004) 33 Denver Journal of International Law and Policy 43, 44–5.

[3] I Mgbeoji, *Collective Insecurity* (Vancouver: University of British Columbia Press, 2003), 49.

[4] Ibid, 53. See also S Fukuda-Parr et al, 'Preface' in L Chen et al (eds), *Human Insecurity in a Global World* (Cambridge, MA: Asia Center of Harvard University, 2003), vii; L Gordenker and TG Weiss, 'The Collective Human Security Idea and Changing World Politics' in TG Weiss (ed), *Collective Human Security in a Changing World* (Boulder, CO: Lynne Rienner, 1993), 3, 7; and SN MacFarlane and YF Khong, *Human Security: A Critical History* (Bloomington, IN: Indiana University Press, 2006), 1.

[5] A-M Slaughter, 'A New UN for a New Century' (2006) 74 Fordham Law Review 2961, 2963.

[6] L Gordenker and TG Weiss (see n 4 above) 3.

institutionalized commitment... to gang up on any state that acts in defiance of collective judgments about permissible behavior'.[7]

Yet, as flexible as Farer's definition seems, the traditional conception of collective human security has also suffered from the very same deficiencies as the historically dominant military/state-centred conception of one of its key terms (that is, security). As a result of a long period of increasingly intense contestation over its continued accuracy, utility, and relevance,[8] the traditional security conception and framework eventually proved unable to accommodate and cope with many of the emergent security-related pressures of our time, including such challenges as environmental degradation, mass international migration, and certain mass human rights violations.[9]

Only more recently has a different conception of security gained currency in the relevant literature; one that promises to re-orient substantially the collective human security idea. This emergent concept is represented by the term 'human security'. Currently much-discussed, this concept has emerged as a result of the felt academic and institutional need to 'fashion a new and broader understanding... of what [security, and thus] Collective human security means';[10] one that would expand that concept well beyond its historically near-exclusive focus on the use of military force and on the state.[11] As MacFarlane and Khong have noted:

the discussion of security has expanded horizontally beyond military issues to take into account others, such as the economy, the environment, health, gender, and culture, in the context of an expansion of core values to include welfare and identity. It has also expanded vertically, questioning the rationale for exclusive focus on the state and suggesting that security might have other referent subjects.[12]

Thus, as Slaughter has correctly noted, from the perspective of the human security concept, it does not matter whether one dies from a bullet or from AIDS or hunger; what matters is that one dies.[13]

First popularized in the early 1990s by the United Nations Development Program (UNDP),[14] the arrival of this newer concept signals a concerted and necessary attempt to link security discourse much more closely to 'conditions of

---

    [7] T Farer, 'The Role of Regional Collective Human Security Arrangements' in ibid, 155.
    [8] SN MacFarlane and YF Khong (see n 4 above) 1.
    [9] L Pettiford and M Curley, *Changing Security Agendas and the Third World* (London: Pinter, 1999), 108.
    [10] 'A More Secure World' (see n 1 above) [Synopsis] 11. See also A-M Slaughter, 'Security, Solidarity, and Sovereignty: The Grand Themes of UN Reform' (2005) 99 American Journal of International Law 619, 620.
    [11] eg see Mgbeoji (n 3 above) 53; VP Nanda, 'Preemptive and Preventive Use of Force, Collective Human Security, and Human Security' (2004) 33 Denver Journal of International Law and Policy 7, 10; and A-M Slaughter (n 10 above) 619.
    [12] SN MacFarlane and YF Khong (see n 4 above) 1. See also JF Jones (n 1 above) 94–5.
    [13] See n 5 above, 2963.
    [14] VP Nanda, ibid, 11; and S Fukuda-Parr et al (see n 4 above) vii.

existence and immediate vulnerability'.[15] As Fukuda-Parr has argued, the broad goal of security is, and should be, to enable people to live without fears for their survival, well-being, and freedom—hence the emergence of the term 'human security'.[16] What is more, this new approach is much more in keeping with the sense in which the vast majority of the world's peoples experience and think about security.[17]

This does not mean, however, that the human security concept is susceptible to easy definition. Indeed, one commentator has been able to document approximately 25 definitions of human security.[18] Although there is really no compulsion to dwell on the question of the definition of this concept in a chapter such as this (which does not focus on the nature of human security concept per se), it is necessary nevertheless to adopt a working definition of the concept. As it is used in this chapter, and as also noted in Chapter 1 of this volume, the term 'human security' means:

> the security of people—their physical safety, their economic and social well-being, respect for their dignity and worth as human beings, and the protection of their human rights and fundamental freedoms.[19]

Focused as it is on 'the individual as the *principal* referent of security'[20] the human security idea re-conceptualizes security (and thus collective human security) no longer in terms of state security exclusively, but rather in terms of human needs.[21] For, the interests of a people are not always coterminous with the interests of the state of which they are a part. At the core of this newer vision of security is the well-being and dignity of people, rather than the protection of national borders.[22] Clearly therefore, the human security conception is also 'necessarily attentive to human rights'[23] and does devote as much attention to economic, social, and cultural rights as it does to civil and political rights.[24] Indeed, the idea of human rights seems so central to the human security conception that one commentator has even gone as far as arguing that human rights analysis forms the very foundation of human security discourse.[25] It was in fact the palpable dissonance that was caused by attempting to fit the square peg of human rights (and any other such conception of human dignity) into the round hole of the traditional equation of

---

[15] See n 9 above, 115.
[16] S Fukuda-Parr, 'New Threats to Human Security in the Era of Globalization' in L Chen (see n 4 above) 1.   [17] See n 5 above, 2963–4.
[18] S Fukuda-Parr, 'New Threats' (see n 16 above) 15.
[19] Report of the International Commission on Intervention and State Sovereignty, 'The Responsibility to Protect', 15, <http://www.iciss.ca/pdf/Commission-Report.pdf>. For some other important definitions, see Report of the Commission on Human Security, 'Human Security Now' (2003) 4, <http://www.humansecurity-chs.org/finalreport/English/FinalReport.pdf> and UNDP, *Human Development Report 1994* (New York: Oxford University Press, 1994), 23.
[20] SN MacFarlane and YF Khong (see n 4 above) 2 (emphasis added).
[21] D Newman, 'A Human Security Council? Applying a "Human Security" Agenda to Security Council Reform' (2000) 31 Ottawa Law Review 213, 215.   [22] Ibid.
[23] Ibid, 219.   [24] Ibid, 222.   [25] JF Jones (see n 1 above) 95–102.

security with state security that, in part, necessitated the discursive shift toward the human security end of the security-analysis spectrum.

If, as is suggested by the above analysis, the term 'security' in international law and relations should no longer be seen as a synonym for state security, then the expression collective 'human security' should not as well be equated with collective state security. In accordance with this approach, collective human security ought to be more properly understood in terms of collective human security. To draw from the writings of both Tom Farer and the International Commission on Intervention and State Sovereignty (ICISS), collective human security can therefore be said to refer to the institutionalized commitment to gang up against any state that acts in defiance of collective judgments about what can and cannot be done in regard to the human security of people—that is, their physical, economic, and social well being, and respect for their dignity and worth as human beings. It is in this broader sense that the concept of collective human security will be understood and utilized in the rest of this chapter.

Yet, given the state security-centrism of the dominant collective human security discourse, it is no wonder that until more recently, international human rights institutions (IHIs) such as the African Commission on Human and Peoples' Rights were not generally thought of, and treated with, as significant collective human security resources. Adherence to the human security approach (as the central basis of collective human security thinking and action) is one way of reversing this important historical deficiency in the relevant academic and institutional literature. The human security conception's core embrace of, and focus on, the enjoyment of a broad range of human rights renders most palpable the relevance—indeed centrality—of multilateral institutions such as the African Commission to our contemporary collective human security praxis.

Thus, the main argument that is developed in this chapter is that contrary to the way in which it has been generally imagined in the dominant collective human security literature, the African Commission is by design, and in terms of its institutional practice, an important collective human security resource in Africa. (By a collective human security resource is meant an institution that has contributed or can be pressed to contribute to the multilateral struggle to ensure peace and security (broadly defined) within a particular geographic context.)

In order systematically to develop the main argument that is made in it, this chapter is divided into six major sections; this introduction included. Section 2 provides a short background on the African Commission—the institution that is the focus of our analysis in this chapter. In Section 3, I discuss the normative and textual promise (largely contained within the African Charter) that the African Commission shall, through the effective discharge of its broad human rights mandate, serve as an important collective human security resource. Section 4 then systematically considers the institutional practice of the African Commission in this regard, and reaches analytical conclusions as to the quality of its performance. The extent to which the Commission has fulfilled its promise as a collective human security resource is an important question that is addressed in this section. In Section 5, I examine the African Commission's prospects as a collective human security resource, and make some recommendations as to what needs to be done to enhance its utility and significance as such a resource. Section 6 summarizes and concludes the chapter.

2. Brief background on the African Commission on Human and Peoples' Rights[26]

The African Commission on Human and Peoples' Rights (the African Commission) is established by Article 30 of the African Charter on Human and Peoples' Rights (the African Charter).[27] Although the African system has its intellectual origins in, and owes the impetus for its formation chiefly to, the human rights struggles that took place within African states in the colonial and post-independence eras,[28] it was not until 1986 that the African Charter entered into force and, thus, became legally binding.[29] The African Commission was set up approximately one year later; that is, in 1987.

The African Commission is composed of 11 members (styled 'Commissioners') who are supposed to be

chosen from among African personalities of the highest reputation, known for their high morality, integrity, impartiality and competence in matters of human and peoples' rights; particular consideration being given to persons having legal experience.[30]

Although in the exercise of much of its mandate, the African Commission tends to function like a quasi-judicial body, as with most IHIs, its decisions are formally non-binding.

[26] Very small segments of this section are reproduced from ch 3 of OC Okafor, *The African Human Rights System, Activist Forces and International Institutions* (Cambridge: Cambridge University Press, 2007).

[27] African Charter on Human and Peoples' Rights, 1981 (in force 1986), reproduced in C Heyns (ed), *Compendium of Key Human Rights Documents of the African Union* (Pretoria: Pretoria University Press, 2005), 20. For more on the nature and functioning of the African Commission, see R Murray, *Human Rights in Africa: From the OAU to the AU* (Cambridge: Cambridge University Press, 2004); R Murray, *The African Commission on Human and Peoples' Rights and International Law* (Oxford: Hart Publishing, 2000), 29; M Mutua, 'The African Human Rights System in a Comparative Perspective' (1993) 3 Review of the African Commission on Human and Peoples' Rights 5, 11; CE Welch Jr, 'The African Commission on Human and Peoples Rights: A Five Year Report and Assessment' (1992) 14 Human Rights Quarterly 43; EA Ankumah, *The African Commission on Human and Peoples' Rights* (The Hague: Martinus Nijhoff, 1996); CA Odinkalu, 'The Individual Complaints Procedure of the African Commission on Human and Peoples' Rights: A Preliminary Assessment' (1998) 8 Transnational Law and Contemporary Problems 359; and OC Okafor, 'The African System on Human and Peoples' Rights, Quasi-Constructivism, and the Possibility of Peacebuilding within African States' (2004) 8 International Journal of Human Rights 413 (hereinafter 'Peacebuilding').

[28] M Mutua, 'The Banjul Charter and the African Cultural Fingerprint: An Evaluation of the Language of Duties' (1995) 35 Virginia Journal of International Law 339, 346–64.

[29] Ibid, 339–40.

[30] African Charter on Human and Peoples' Rights (see n 27 above) Art 31.

As with the newly created African Court on Human and Peoples' Rights (the African Court),[31] with which it enjoys a supplementary, complementary, and cooperative relationship, the African Commission's primary responsibility is to encourage the implementation by African states of the norms contained in the African Charter. Although the full extent of the institutional mandate of the African Commission is articulated in various provisions of the African Charter, as well as in the Protocol on the Rights of Women in Africa (the Women's Protocol), it is in Articles 45 to 62 of the African Charter itself that the mandate is most precisely stated. While Article 45 states, in some detail, the functions of the African Commission, the Commission's mandate—as provided for in that provision—can be summarized under four heads, namely: promotional (including the collection of relevant documents, research, dissemination, and subsidiary law-making); protective (including the consideration of state reports, state communications and petitions from individuals, NGOs, and others); interpretive; and general (involving all other related tasks). To these, Article 46 adds the power to resort to any appropriate means of investigation, while Article 58 authorizes the 'in-depth study' under some circumstances of situations that may involve 'a series of serious or massive violations of human and peoples' rights'.

The substantive human rights norms which are within the promotional and protective remit of the African Commission are stipulated not only in the African Charter, but also in the Women's Protocol and in other 'soft law' instruments that have been formulated and adopted over the years by the African Commission itself.[32] The African Charter contains numerous human rights provisions ranging from economic, social, and cultural rights (such as the right to education in Article 17), through so-called solidarity or third generation rights (such as the right to self-determination in Article 20), to civil and political rights (such as the right to liberty in Article 6). The Women's Protocol adds much detail to the African Charter's specific provision in Article 18(3) for the elimination of discrimination against women and for the protection of their other human rights. For example, because of their relative novelty and greater specificity in the context of the textual provisions of African human rights treaties, Article 5 of the Women's Protocol (on the elimination of harmful practices); Article 6 (on consent and equality in marriage); Article 11 (on the protection of

---

[31] The African Court was established by the Protocol to the African Charter on Human and Peoples' Rights on the Establishment of an African Court on Human and Peoples' Rights, 1998, in force 2004, reproduced in C Heyns (ed), *Compendium of Key Human Rights Documents of the African Union* (Pretoria: Pretoria University Press, 2005), 32. As its judges have now been elected and its location chosen, the Court should be fully functional very soon.

[32] eg, see the African Commission on Peoples' Rights, Resolution on the Right of Recourse and Fair Trial, 11th Ordinary Session (2–9 March 1992), reproduced in the African Commission on Peoples' Rights, *Recommendations and Resolutions* (the African Commission on Peoples' Rights, Banjul, The Gambia, 1998), 16; Resolution on the Right to Freedom of Association, 11th Ordinary Session (2–9 March 1992) reproduced ibid, 18; Resolution on the Promotion and Respect of International Humanitarian Law and Human and Peoples' Rights, 14th Ordinary Session (1–10 December 1993) reproduced ibid, 21; and Resolution on the Military (25 October–3 November 1994) reproduced ibid, 26.

women in armed conflicts); and Article 14 (on their health and reproductive rights) add value to the attempt to provide adequate human rights protection for women in Africa.

It is fairly clear therefore that the African Commission enjoys a broad human rights promotion and protection mandate. In general, any state party to the African Charter, as well as any individuals, groups of individuals, NGOs, or other such entities may file communications, that is, petitions, at the African Commission alleging a human rights violation by a state party to the Charter.[33] In the case of petitions other than by state parties, the *locus standi* provisions that govern the filing of petitions at the Commission are remarkably generous.[34] Almost any registered NGO or other entity or person (African or foreign) can bring a petition to it without first proving that that entity is in fact the aggrieved party.[35] This is an important instance of the implementation of the concept of *actio popularis* within an IHI.

On the whole, the African Commission is, of course, part and parcel of the main African human rights system that has been established by the African Charter and its Protocols. And that human rights system is an integral part of the new African Union (AU) that has now replaced the old Organization of African Unity (OAU). Needless to say, this African human rights system was also an integral part of the now defunct OAU. It will be useful to keep this in mind as we analyse the African Commission's collective human security role.

3. On the collective human security promise of the African Commission

One does not have to scratch too far beneath the surface of a few relevant and authoritative global documents, such as the Charter of the United Nations (UN Charter), and the UN's *An Agenda for Peace* and *A More Secure World* documents, in order to observe and appreciate the intimate connections that the drafters of those documents have very convincingly made between the effective promotion and protection of a broad range of human rights and the eventual attainment of the collective human security ideal.[36] Quite tellingly, Article 55 of the UN Charter mandates that:

With a view to the creation of conditions of stability and well-being which are necessary for peaceful and friendly relations among nations based on respect for the principle of

---

[33] CA Odinkalu (see n 27 above) 369–74.   [34] Ibid, 378–9.

[35] African Charter on Human and Peoples' Rights (see n 27 above) Art 55.

[36] See Charter of the United Nations (26 June 1945) 3 Bevans 1153; Report of the UN Secretary General, 'An Agenda for Peace: Preventive Diplomacy, Peacemaking and Peacekeeping' (17 June 1992) A/47/277, 5 and S/24111, 15, <http://www.un.org/docs/SG/agpeace.html> and 'A More Secure World' (n 1 above) ix, 5, and 88–90.

equal rights and self-determination of peoples, the United Nations shall promote:

a. higher standards of living, full employment, and conditions of economic and social progress and development;

b. solutions of international economic, social, health, and related problems; and international cultural and educational cooperation; and

c. universal respect for, and observance of, human rights and fundamental freedoms for all without distinction as to race, sex, language, or religion.

Similarly, in *An Agenda for Peace*, then UN Secretary-General Boutros Boutros-Ghali felt able to note that there cannot be ultimate success in the attempt to secure collectively, the security of the globe's peoples until all or almost all of them begin to enjoy a broad range of human rights in far greater measure.[37] In the Preface to *A More Secure World*, then UN Secretary-General Kofi Annan made essentially the same point when he (impliedly, at the very least) linked what he saw as the need for urgent reform of the now defunct UN Commission on Human Rights to the search for 'a more secure world'.[38] In the main body of the same document, the high-level panel that was constituted by Kofi Annan to examine—among other issues—the collective human security challenges that face our world reached a very similar conclusion.[39]

It is also fair to say that this 'human rights violation/conflict generation connection' is now recognized in the specific institutional context of the AU.[40] In the Preamble to the Constitutive Act of the African Union, separate mention is made of the AU's determination to 'promote and protect human and peoples' rights' and of the fact that 'the scourge of conflicts in Africa' constitutes a major challenge on the continent.[41] And although no *explicit* link is made on the face of that treaty between the protection of human rights and the attainment of collective human security, given the general tenor of other key AU documents, such as the now obsolete Cairo Declaration on the Establishment within the [defunct] OAU of the Mechanism for Conflict Prevention, Management and Resolution[42] and the currently applicable Protocol Relating to the Establishment of the Peace and Security Council of the African Union (the Peace and Security

---

[37] 'An Agenda for Peace', ibid.   [38] 'A More Secure World', ibid, ix.
[39] Ibid, 88–90.   [40] R Murray, *Human Rights in Africa* (see n 27 above) 117.
[41] Constitutive Act of the African Union, 2000, in force 2001, reproduced in C Heyns (ed) (see n 31 above) 4.
[42] This mechanism was established in 1993 by the Cairo Declaration (28–30 June 1993) OAU Doc AHG/Decl.3 (XXIX), <http://www.africa-union.org/root/AU/Documents/Decisions/hog/3HoGAssembly1993.pdf#search=%22Cairo%20Declaration%20on%20the%20Establishment%20within%20the%20OAU%20of%20the%20Mechanism%20for%20Conflict%20Prevention%2C%20Management%20and%20Resolution%22>. It was initially incorporated into the new AU order by the 'Decision on the Implementation of the Sirte Summit Decision on the African Union' (11 July 2001) OAU Doc AHG/Decl.3 (XXXVII), <http://www.au2002.gov.za/docs/key_oau/sirte_au.pdf#search=%22Decision%20on%20the%20Implementation%20of%20the%20Sirte%20Summit%20Decision%20on%20the%20African%20Union%22> but has now been rendered defunct by the adoption of the Peace and Security Council Protocol.

Protocol),[43] it is logical to deduce that the AU leaders who adopted the text of this Constitutive Act were not entirely unappreciative of the linkage between violations of human rights on the African continent and the scourge of conflicts that threaten the peace and security of Africans. But it is para 14 of the Preamble of the Peace and Security Protocol that provides what is perhaps the clearest and most poignant statement in any of the above-mentioned documents of the type of linkage that we are concerned with here. That clause states that the leaders of the AU are aware:

of the fact that the development of strong democratic institutions and culture, observance of human rights and the rule of law... are essential for the promotion of collective human security, durable peace and stability, as well as the prevention of conflicts.[44]

There is, thus, clear recognition within the AU system of the now well-acknowledged positive linkage between respect for human rights and eventual success in the struggle for peace and security in any given country, region, or continent.

Logically therefore, although such a connection is not *adequately* articulated in the African Charter—the instrument that created the African Commission—it is only reasonable to argue that since the Commission possesses a broad human rights mandate, and the attainment of peace and security on the African continent is positively linked to the effective promotion and protection of human rights, then the Commission (as a collective inter-African institution) can, at the very least, be said to enjoy a type of derivative collective human security mandate. For, its performance in the present respect (as measured by its fulfilment or non-fulfilment of its human rights mandate) will invariably have a significant impact on the actual enjoyment of human rights in Africa. And when considered in the light of the established connection between the enjoyment of human rights and the attainment of human peace and security, this last fact suggests that the African Commission's performance does—for good or for bad—impact on the peace and security of those humans who inhabit the African continent.

As such, an important question that needs to be asked at this juncture is the extent to which the African Charter does, at the very least, imply this type of linkage (between the Commission's work and human security in Africa), and did design and portray the African Commission as a collective human security resource; thereby promising all who live on the African continent that the Commission will in fact function in that way. Another related question is the extent to which the Commission's status as a collective human security resource appears in the self-image of the African Commission. Has the Commission itself ever promised to act as such a resource? The point here is not, of course, that the answer to these specific questions automatically and completely disposes of the broader question concerning the exact nature of the overall collective human

---

[43] The Peace and Security Protocol, adopted in Durban, South Africa (July 2002), entered into force in December 2003; reproduced in C Heyns (ed), *Compendium* (see n 31 above) 13.

[44] Ibid.

security promise of the African Commission. However, the answers to these more specific questions will contribute significantly toward the development of an overall response to the broader question.

At the very beginning, it must be noted that, on the whole, there is little doubt that the African Commission possesses a collective human security role in Africa. As an 11-person, collective, inter-African body that serves as an organ of the AU, the African Commission can reasonably be seen as an institutionalized arrangement within the AU to gang up on any state party to the African Charter that acts in defiance of collective judgments contained in that Charter or made by the African Commission regarding permissible human rights behaviour.[45] This image of the African Commission fits quite well with Tom Farer's well-crafted definition of a collective human security arrangement which was referred to and quoted earlier in this chapter.[46] The image also reflects accurately much of what the Commission does. Among other things, the members of the African Commission metaphorically gang up on non-African Charter compliant (and therefore deviant) states. It does so principally by passing resolutions, making concluding observations on state reports, and indicating its views on petitions brought against states. These pronouncements of the African Commission rely for their authority on the provisions of the African Charter. And these provisions explicate human rights standards that provide general guidance to the Commission as to what can and cannot be done by states parties to the Charter with regard to the security of their people—that is, their physical, economic, and social well-being, alongside respect for their dignity and worth as human beings.

Regarding the first question that was raised above (on the African Charter's design and portrayal of the African Commission as a collective human security resource), it can be said with confidence at the outset that the African Charter did design the Commission to function in that way. Because of space constraints, only some of the available evidence can be discussed here. This evidence will be sourced from the text of the African Charter itself. First of all, Article 23(1) of the Charter guarantees to all peoples the right to national and international peace and security. Article 23(2)(a) enjoins those enjoying the right of asylum in one African country from engaging in 'subversive activities' against their country of origin. Article 23(2)(b) further enjoins all African states not to allow their territories to be used as bases for subversive or terrorist activities against the people of any other state party to the Charter. Logically, to charge the African Commission with monitoring the implementation of these provisions by states parties was to, in effect, promise that the Commission will, via the discharge of these functions, serve as a collective human security resource. For, when a multilateral institution, such as the African Commission gangs up on a state in order to help guarantee human security, it is clearly the case that that body is at the very least acting as

---

[45] For the definition of 'collective human security' that inspired this insight, see T Farer in TG Weiss (ed) (n 4 above) 3, 155. [46] Ibid.

a collective human security resource. Such a body will also be acting as such a resource if it functions in a way that helps guarantee to some extent that subversive or terrorist activities are not launched against any state from within the boundaries of another state.

Secondly, very similar arguments can be made in respect of the provision in Article 19 of the African Charter that 'nothing shall justify the domination of a people by another'. State fragmentation and the domination of minority groups have clearly been one major source of conflicts in Africa.[47] No wonder then that the African Charter also provides in Article 20 that 'all peoples shall have a right to existence [an articulation of the prohibition of genocide]' and that 'colonized or oppressed peoples shall have the right to free themselves from the bonds of domination by resorting to any means recognized by the international community'. Both of these guarantees are designed to ensure much deeper respect for socio-cultural difference and other minority rights against a general historical background of the existence on the African continent of far too many low-level or intense intra-state conflicts that have resulted from minority repression.[48] Such conflicts are a key source of insecurity in Africa.[49] That the African Commission is charged with the quasi-adjudication of disputes relating to the guarantees in Articles 19 and 20, disputes that often relate to the prevention or just resolution of violent conflicts, provides further evidence of the type of collective human security role that the Commission was designed to play.

Thirdly, although the provision in Article 22 of the African Charter that 'all peoples shall have the right to their economic, social and cultural development' and that 'states shall have the duty, individually and collectively, to ensure the exercise of the right to development' fits far better with the human security approach than it accords with the traditional state security paradigm, by mandating the African Commission to monitor the implementation of these provisions by African states, the African Charter in effect conferred a collective human security function on that Commission. As has been demonstrated by adherents of the human security approach, there is a positive connection between the economic, social, and cultural development of a people and their security situation.[50] As such, any effort on the part of the African Commission to encourage the greater economic, social, and cultural development of any African people is at the very same time an effort to advance the security interests of those same people. It is in this sense therefore that the inclusion of these provisions as part of the African Commission's remit provides additional evidence of its collective human security promise.

Lastly, and perhaps less importantly, para 9 of the Preamble of the African Charter does state that the states parties that adopted that Treaty in 1981 did so

---

[47] See OC Okafor, *Re-Defining Legitimate Statehood: International Law and State Fragmentation in Africa* (The Hague: Martinus Nijhoff, 2000).   [48] Ibid, 136–7.
[49] Ibid.   [50] eg, see 'The Responsibility to Protect' (n 19 above) 15.

in part because they were aware of the need to, among other things, 'dismantle aggressive foreign military bases'. The presence of such foreign bases and interventionist forces has for long been a significant source of insecurity on the African continent. As such, the adoption by African states of an African Charter which, albeit in a preamble, sought the dismantling of those foreign bases at the same time as they created an African Commission to monitor the implementation of that Charter's mandate was therefore one way of affirming the Commission's collective human security role. At the very least, this shows that collective human security was one of the issues on the minds of the creators of the African Commission.

While it is possible to offer numerous other examples of the ways in which the African Charter designed and portrayed the African Commission as a collective human security resource by charging that multilateral institution to gang up and express negative views or take other suitable action against any state that deviates from explicitly stated Charter norms about permissible behaviour, the above examples suffice to ground and illustrate this first argument.

Regarding the second question that was raised at the beginning of this section (on the presence of a collective human security role within the African Commission's self-image), it suffices in order to make the intended point to refer to, and discuss, the Commission's response to one of the most important collective human security challenges in contemporary African history, the Rwandan genocide, as well as to the African Commission's 1994 Resolution on the Situation of Human Rights in Africa.[51] As the Commission's Resolution on the Rwandan genocide will also be discussed in the next section of this chapter, its consideration here will be necessarily brief and focused on the specific point that is sought to be made. The tone and tenor of the African Commission's Resolution on Rwanda[52] clearly shows that the African Commission does, at the very least, imagine certain collective human security problems as within its remit. It also suggests that it imagines itself, at least in part, as a collective human security resource. Merely passing a Resolution on the Rwandan crisis—a quintessential collective human security problem—indicates that the African Commission surely thinks of itself as seized of some significant role in bringing about a long-term solution to that problem.

Similarly, in its Resolution on the Situation of Human Rights in Africa, the Commission expressed its deep concern with what it referred to as 'the consequences of persistent wars in several African states, on the civilian population' and called on 'all those parties engaged in war on the African continent, to abide

---

[51] African Commission, Resolution on the Situation of Human Rights in Africa, 16th Ordinary Session (25 October–3 November 1994) reproduced in the African Commission on Peoples' Rights, Recommendations and Resolutions (see n 32 above) 31.
[52] African Commission, Resolution on Rwanda, 16th Ordinary Session (25 October–3 November 1994), reproduced in the African Commission on Peoples' Rights, Recommendations and Resolutions (see n 32 above) 28.

by the provisions of International Humanitarian Law...and to undertake all efforts to restore peace'. Here again, the Commission's words and actions suggest that it imagines itself as seized of some type of collective human security function. Since the Commission is unarguably a multilateral institution, and given that that body clearly regards the issue of war and peace, and the conduct of war, as within its purview and remit, then—as a body that is supposed to express the collective will of African peoples in the human rights area—the Commission definitely possesses a collective human security role. More importantly for the specific argument being made in this section of the chapter, as has been shown here, the Commission itself has recognized that it can play and does play such a role in Africa.[53]

Having systematically made the points clear that the African Commission was from its very beginnings conferred a collective human security role, that this multilateral institution was designed and portrayed in its constitutive instrument as a collective human security resource, and that the African Commission has itself recognized this collective human security role as within its mandate, it remains to examine in some detail the extent to which the Commission has in its institutional practice performed this collective human security function and lived up to its billing in the African Charter as a collective human security resource. Following that discussion, the prospects for the enhanced utilization of the Commission as such a resource will be considered. A concluding section will follow this latter discussion.

4. Collective human security: the performance of the African Commission

To what extent has the African Commission's actual practice lent itself to the conclusion that the Commission has in fact functioned as a collective human security resource? And if the Commission has in fact functioned in this way, to what extent has its performance been adequate? In other words, what exactly has the African Commission done about what Mgbeoji has famously referred to as 'collective [human] insecurity' on the African continent?[54]

The reasonably detailed examination of the African Commission's practice that follows will be conducted under the following heads: the right to national and international peace and security; regional self-determination and minority rights; and the right to their economic, social, and cultural development (in relation to the enjoyment of economic, social, and cultural rights). This corresponds to the categories around which most of the discussion in the previous section was

---

[53] See also R Murray, *Human Rights in Africa* (n 27 above) 117.
[54] I Mgbeoji, *Collective Insecurity* (see n 4 above) (in the title thereof).

organized. Due to limitations of space, not every possible such topic has been included and considered.

4.1 The right to national and international peace and security

Regarding the African Commission's institutional practice with respect to the guarantee in the African Charter of the right to national and international peace and security, the discussion below of a number of the Commission's Resolutions serves to illustrate how that body has in practice played a collective human security role by, among other things, formulating and providing important normative resources to those who struggle for the attainment of peace and security in Africa. For example, para 5 of the African Commission's Resolution on Rwanda[55] provides a good indication as to how a significant portion of the African Commission's practice demonstrates that it has in fact functioned to an appreciable extent as a collective human security resource. In that Resolution, the Commission, among other things, urged Rwanda:

to prevent the perpetration of acts of reprisals and vengeance by the rapid establishment of a new police force and a local administration respectful of human rights and composed of members of all ethnic groups of Rwanda.[56]

In para 6 of the same Resolution, the Commission also urges Rwanda to ensure the 'strengthening of the interceding peace-keeping forces throughout Rwanda'. A fuller consideration of the text of that Resolution suggests that the African Commission passed this Resolution in order to urge the view upon Rwanda and other actors that adherence to human rights norms in the governance and reconstruction of post-genocide Rwanda was the path dictated by the African Charter and was also the better way to ensure that peace and security was maintained and sustained in that country. The African Commission was in practice trying to provide normative support for the collective African attempt to promote human security in that recently troubled country. As a multilateral institution that is designed to pressure and persuade states, rather than to coerce their compliance, the African Commission's aim here was to pile normative pressure on Rwanda to act in the way the Commission considered appropriate. It matters little in this case whether the Commission's efforts were successful in the end. For the body's role is to serve as a *resource* and not a collective human security *panacea*. It clearly served the former function.

Another example of the African Commission's institutional practice with respect to the implementation of the African Charter's guarantee of the right to peace and security is the Commission's adoption of its Resolution on Anti-Personnel Landmines.[57] The adoption of this document also provides evidence of

---

[55] See n 52 above, 28.   [56] Ibid, 5.

[57] African Commission, Resolution on Anti-Personnel Landmines, 13th Ordinary Session (13–22 March 1995) reproduced in the African Commission on Peoples' Rights, 'Recommendations and Resolutions' (see n 32 above) 37.

the African Commission's real-life institutional practice of its collective human security resource role. Needless to say, landmines are a serious source of human insecurity in much of Africa and their deployment or use is increasingly seen as contravening the rules of permissible conduct even in war time. This particular Resolution of the African Commission can therefore be seen as a 'ganging up' at the collective African level against states (or even other actors) that have contravened this rule. In this sense the Commission's anti-landmine practice, as represented in this Resolution, can be read as evidence that it has actually functioned (at least in part) as a collective human security resource.

Another example of the African Commission's practice in relation to its broad monitoring of the efforts made by states to ensure the practical implementation of the right to peace and security that is guaranteed in the African Charter is the fact that the Commission has adopted a number of Resolutions through which it has sought to intervene in some way in order to help end, and/or shape the peace agreements that ended a significant number of conflicts on the African continent. In its Resolution on the Sudan,[58] it called on

all parties to the [then raging SPLA/SSIA v Sudanese Government] armed conflict immediately [sic] to cease using military force to interfere with the delivery of humanitarian assistance to the civilian population[59]

and appealed to

the Government of the Sudan to support negotiations for a settlement to the conflict and ensure that any agreement includes strong guarantees for the protection of human rights.[60]

In the more recently adopted of the African Commission's two major Resolutions on the Darfur conflict, namely the Resolution on the Situation in Darfur,[61] the Commission began by recalling the earlier Resolution that it had adopted on the same situation, and ended up calling on:

the parties to the conflict in the Darfur to observe the terms of the Ceasefire Agreements concluded in Ndjamena, Tchad, and to resume negotiations in Abuja, Nigeria, under the auspices of the current Chairman of the African Union, President Olusegun Obasanjo of the Federal Republic of Nigeria, with a view to finalize a permanent ceasefire and a Comprehensive Peace Agreement on the conflict in the Darfur.[62]

In its *Resolution on Liberia*,[63] the African Commission noted that up to that point, the warring factions had refused to disarm,[64] endorsed 'the Abuja Peace

---

[58] African Commission, Resolution on the Sudan, 17th Ordinary Session (13–22 March 1995) reproduced in the African Commission on Peoples' Rights, 'Recommendations and Resolutions' (see n 32 above) 32.   [59] Ibid, 4.

[60] Ibid, 6.

[61] African Commission, Resolution on the Situation in the Darfur Region of the Sudan, 37th Ordinary Session (27 April–11 May 2005, Eighteenth Annual Activity Report), <http://www1. umn.edu/humanrts/africa/res-darfur37–2005.html>.   [62] Ibid, ii.

[63] African Commission, Resolution on Liberia, 19th Ordinary Session (26 March–4 April 1996) reproduced in the African Commission on Peoples' Rights, 'Recommendations and Resolutions' (see n 32 above) 41.   [64] Ibid, 4.

Accord as the best means for the cessation of hostilities and restoration of peace to Liberia',[65] and among other things, called on all 'the Warring Factions to take all necessary steps to disarm their fighters'.[66] In the Commission's Resolution on South Africa,[67] it condemned 'very strongly the cycle of violence and the massacre of innocent civilians by the different armed factions [to the conflict that attended the transition from apartheid to democracy in that country]'. And in its Resolution on Burundi,[68] the Commission, decided to 'involve itself more in efforts to resolve the crisis affecting Burundi by, among other things, sending a mission to Burundi and participating actively in the process of national reconciliation'.[69]

All the examples discussed above serve to demonstrate that the African Commission has to a significant extent done what the African Charter mandated, and in fact did promise that it would do. More specifically, these examples show that the Commission has in practice actually made efforts to encourage the implementation of the right to peace and security that is guaranteed in the African Charter; and that it did so in ways that clearly suggest that it has served as a significant collective human security resource.

4.2 Regional self-determination and minority rights

The significance of the African Commission's efforts to encourage states parties to the African Charter to implement those provisions of the Treaty that guarantee regional self-determination and other minority rights can be illustrated by the following examples. First of all, in *Katangese Peoples' Congress v Zaire* (the so-called *Katanga* case),[70] the Commission played an important normative and signalling role in the admittedly still incipient attempt at the inter-African level to construct a more conducive socio-political and legal environment for the amelioration of many of the grievances of sub-state groups on the African continent.[71] In that case, a communication, alleging the denial of Katanga's right to self-determination, including its right to independence from the country then known as Zaire (now the Democratic Republic of the Congo), was submitted on behalf of the Katangese Peoples' Congress. It requested the African Commission to, among other things, recognize the independence of Katanga; and recognize that body as a liberation movement entitled (under Article 20 of the African Charter) to support in the achievement of independence from

---

[65] Ibid, 6.   [66] Ibid, 7.

[67] African Commission, Resolution on South Africa, 15th Ordinary Session (18–27 April 1994) reproduced in the African Commission on Peoples' Rights, 'Recommendations and Resolutions' (see n 32 above) 24.

[68] African Commission, Resolution on the Sudan, 19th Ordinary Session (26 March–4 April 1996) reproduced in the African Commission on Peoples' Rights, 'Recommendations and Resolutions' (see n 32 above) 46.   [69] Ibid, 6.

[70] *Katangese Peoples' Congress v Zaire*, Communication No 75/92 (1996) 3 International Human Rights Reports 136.   [71] OC Okafor, 'Peacebuilding' (see n 27 above) 441–2.

Zaire.[72] Among other things, the African Commission held that:

In the absence of concrete evidence of violations of human rights to the point that the territorial integrity of Zaire should be called into question and in the absence of evidence that the people of Katanga are denied the right to participate in Government... the Commission holds the view that Katanga is obliged to exercise a variant of self-determination that is compatible with the sovereignty and territorial integrity of Zaire.[73]

The clear implication of this very important decision is that an oppressed sub-state group has a *conditional* (if exceptional) right to secede from its parent state if it could show that the treatment meted out to members of the group by the relevant state is so intolerable when adjudged against the human rights barometer as to justify such a radical measure.[74] Thus, no longer can an African state deal ruthlessly and highly oppressively with a sub-state group and yet demand that inter-African institutions such as the Commission ratify and support its forcible retention of such a group within its borders. Thus, the signal that was sent by this decision was that if a state wants normative or legitimizing support from the African Commission in an effort to maintain its integral existence, then it must find relatively non-oppressive ways of retaining its sub-state groups.

Lending further support to its decision in the *Katanga* case to interpret the African Charter's guarantees of certain rights to entities referred to as 'peoples' as beneficial to sub-state groups, in the subsequent *Ogoni* case,[75] the Commission accepted—by implication—that sub-state groups, including those that form minorities, qualify to be referred to as 'peoples' within the meaning of the relevant provisions of the African Charter. The complaints made on behalf of 'the Ogoni population' by the Nigeria-based Social and Economic Rights Action Center (SERAC) and the US-based Center for Economic and Social Rights was accepted and declared successful without any argument as to whether 'the Ogoni population' constituted a 'people' under the African Charter. In this way the African Commission has also helped develop the law of minority rights in Africa, thereby contributing to the strengthening of the normative resources available to such groups as they struggle for greater equity and justice within the states that en-globe them. The collective human security role played here by the Commission is evident from the fact that the intra-state conflicts that too often result from the lack of adequate equity and justice in 'state v minority group' relations are a serious problem in Africa, as the world over.

The African Commission's Resolution on Rwanda also illustrates its efforts to further the implementation in that country of the African Charter's guarantee in its Article 19 of the right of all peoples (that is, intra-state or so-called

---

[72] *Katangese Peoples' Congress v Zaire* (see n 70 above) 1.   [73] Ibid, 6.
[74] OC Okafor (see n 27 above) 442.
[75] *Social and Economic Rights Action Centre (SERAC) and another v Nigeria*, Communication No 155/96, decided in 2001). This case is also reproduced in C Heyns (ed), *Compendium* (see n 31 above) 159.

ethnic groups) to equality with, and freedom from domination by, more power-ful groups. It illustrates the Commission's attempt to further the implementation of the implied right of minority and other such groups to be fully included in all aspects of the governance of their countries. In that Resolution, the Commission urged the post-genocide government of Rwanda to ensure the 'rapid establish-ment of a new police force and a local administration...composed of members of all ethnic groups of Rwanda'.[76]

Another example of the ways in which the African Commission has in practice sought to further the implementation of, and breathe some life into, the regional self-determination and minority rights provisions in Article 20 of the African Charter (and so on) is through the activities of its Working Group on Indigenous Populations and Communities. For instance, this working group has undertaken fact-finding missions to certain African countries (such as Burundi in March/April 2005); and launched its report in Geneva at a session of the now defunct UN Commission on Human Rights (in April 2005).[77] In addition, this working group, from time to time, organizes seminars on the indigenous rights question in Africa. For instance, one such seminar was organized in Yaounde, Cameroon in September 2006.[78] This was the first in a series of regional seminars earmarked by the working group so as to foster dialogue with relevant stakeholders on the rights of indigenous peoples in Africa, and thereby help promote and protect the rights of such populations on the continent.[79]

These examples suffice to illustrate the ways in which the African Commission's actual institutional practice in the regional self-determination and minority rights area bears out the characterization of the Commission in this chapter as a significant collective human security resource. By striving to promote and pro-tect this category of rights, the Commission has at the same time helped further the search for peace and security in Africa. As a multilateral African institution that functions as an organ of the AU, the Commission's work has expressed the collective human security ambitions of the AU.

4.3 The enjoyment of economic, social, and cultural rights

As has been noted earlier in this chapter, the broader human security approach and optic appreciates and integrates within it the now well-acknowledged tru-ism that the enjoyment by a given population of the types of economic, social, and cultural rights (ESC rights) guaranteed in various provisions of the African Charter is essential to their security. As such, efforts by the African Commission

---

[76] Resolution on Rwanda (see n 52 above) 6.

[77] Eighteenth Activity Report of the African Commission on Human and Peoples' Rights, EX.CL/199 (VII) (on file with the author) 6.

[78] This was the Regional Sensitization Seminar on the Rights of Indigenous Populations/Communities in Africa, Yaounde, Cameroon (13–16 September 2006), <http://www.achpr.org/english/news/Seminar_en.htm>. [79] Ibid.

to promote and protect these ESC rights are in themselves attempts on the part of that institution to facilitate the enjoyment by the relevant populations of their human security. This is why it is important at this point to consider the Commission's performance with regard to the promotion and protection of ESC rights.

A caveat must, however, be entered at the outset. This is that the African Commission's engagement with ESC rights has occurred within, and has been shaped by, a broader social context in which ESC rights have tended not to be treated seriously in the dominant human rights approaches.[80] As importantly, 'only a modest number of socio-economic rights are explicitly included in the [African] Charter' and 'some prominent socio-economic rights [such as the rights to food, water, social security, and housing] are not mentioned by name' in that Charter.[81] What is more, the fact that only a few ESC rights cases (such as the *Ogoni*[82] and *Purohit*[83] communications) have been brought before the Commission by the relevant actors demonstrates the fact that the African Commission (and the non-state actors that have supplied it with almost all of its petitions) have, on the whole, not been as attentive to the protection of ESC rights on the continent as they could have been.[84] Compared to the Commission's engagement with civil and political rights communications, the number of ESC rights communications that it has considered so far has been 'minimal'.[85]

Nevertheless, the African Commission has, of course, engaged to some extent with the ESC rights provisions contained in the African Charter. Its efforts have resulted in the development of norms in this area. In the now famous *Ogoni* case, the Commission expressed views that have been described by Christof Heyns as 'extraordinary'.[86] In that case, the complainants alleged (on behalf of the Ogoni population of Nigeria) that the then military government of Nigeria had systematically violated the rights to health, environment, housing, and food of the Ogoni, and had also violated the right of the Ogoni to be free from the capture, spoliation, and dispossession of their natural resources.[87] In finding in favour of

---

[80] See generally, J Oloka-Onyango, 'Beyond the Rhetoric: Reinvigorating the Struggle for Economic and Social Rights in Africa' (1995) 26 California Western International Law Journal 1.

[81] C Heyns, 'The African Regional Human Rights System: The African Charter' (2004) 108 Pennsylvania State Law Review 679, 690–1.

[82] *Social and Economic Rights Action Centre (SERAC) and another v Nigeria* (see n 75 above).

[83] *Purohit and Moore v the Gambia*, Communication No 241/2001, Sixteenth Annual Activity Report 2002–2003. This case is reproduced in C Heyns (ed), *Compendium* (see n 31 above) 178 (hereinafter '*Purohit Case*'). See also C Mbazira, 'The Right to Health and the Nature of Socio-Economic Rights Obligations under the African Charter: The Purohit Case' at: <http://www.communitylawcentre.org.za/ser/esr2005/2005nov_charter.php>.

[84] OC Okafor, *The African Human Rights System, Activist Forces and International Institutions* (see n 26 above) 269.

[85] NJ Udombana, 'Social Rights are Human Rights: Actualizing the Rights to Work and Social Security in Africa' (2006) 39 Cornell International Law Journal 181, 235. See also Heyns (n 81 above) 691.   [86] Heyns, ibid, 691.

[87] *Social and Economic Rights Action Centre (SERAC) and another v Nigeria* (see n 75 above) 50, 55, 59, and 64.

the complainants on virtually all scores, the African Commission, among other things, read the rights to housing and food into the African Charter.[88] Those rights are not explicitly articulated in that Charter.[89] If it is understood that the enjoyment of the ESC rights of any people to health, environment, housing, food, and to be free from the dispossession of their natural resources are key to their enjoyment of human security, then the contribution of the African Commission's jurisprudence in this case to the search for collective human security in Africa becomes palpable. In the *Purohit* case, two mental health advocates brought a complaint against the Gambia on behalf of patients detained at 'Campana', a psychiatric unit of the Royal Victoria Hospital in that country. The complainants alleged violations by the Gambia of certain provisions of the African Charter. Their complaint centred on the character of that country's Lunatics Detention Act (LDA), the principal statute that governed mental health care there. On the whole, the LDA imposed a scheme that authorized the automatic and indefinite detention of persons labelled 'lunatics'.[90] In holding for the complainants, the African Commission wrote a decision that has helped tremendously in the development and activation of the mental health dimensions of the 'right to health' provisions of the African Charter. Among other things, the Commission expressed its awareness that a significant portion of the deprivations of the right to health that occur in Africa stem from the poverty of many African countries and, as such, it read into Article 16 of the African Charter, the obligation on the part of the states parties to the African Charter to

take concrete and targeted steps while taking full advantage of its available resources, to ensure that the right to health is fully realized in all its aspects without discrimination of any kind.[91]

It also found that the scheme of the LDA is 'lacking in terms of therapeutic objectives as well as [the] provision of matching resources and programs of treatment of persons with mental disabilities', and as such, violated Articles 16 and 18(4) of the African Charter.[92] The African Commission's development of the ESC rights provisions discussed above cannot but have enhanced the normative resources available for those who struggle to improve the ESC rights situation in Africa. And since the enjoyment of ESC rights is essential to the success of the search for peace and security, the Commission has—in this significant way—contributed to the collective struggle for security on the African continent.

What is more, the African Commission has, through other means, also sought to promote and protect the enjoyment of ESC rights in Africa. For instance, it has organized at least one major seminar on this question.[93] A significant

---

[88] Ibid, 60 and 65.   [89] Ibid.   [90] *Purohit Case* (see n 83 above) 44.
[91] Ibid, 84.   [92] Ibid, 83.
[93] Between 13–17 September 2004, the Commission (and its NGO partners, namely: Interights, the Centre for Human Rights, University of Pretoria, and the Cairo Institute for Human Rights Studies) organized a seminar on ESC rights in Pretoria, South Africa. See S Khoza, 'Promoting the

dividend yielded by this seminar was the adoption by the African Commission of a Resolution on Economic and Social Rights.[94] In that Resolution, the Commission established a Working Group on ESC Rights; urged its 'Special Rapporteurs and Working Groups to pay particular attention to economic, social and cultural rights during their missions and in the discharge of their respective mandates';[95] and adopted a very detailed and well articulated statement on ESC Rights, namely: the Pretoria Statement on Social, Economic and Cultural Rights in Africa.[96] What is more, the preamble of this Resolution reflects the depth of the African Commission's recognition and appreciation of the relationship between the deplorable ESC rights situation in Africa and the seriousness of the peace and security challenges that face all too many African countries. In its own words, it expressed its concern about 'the lack of human security in Africa due to prevailing conditions of poverty and underdevelopment and the failure of African states to address poverty through development'.[97]

Clearly, therefore, given the importance of the promotion and protection of ESC rights to the struggle for peace and security in Africa, the African Commission has (to the same extent that it has made the kinds of efforts discussed above) contributed in some measure to the struggle for collective human security on the African continent. This is, therefore, one of the important ways in which the Commission has, in practice, functioned as a collective human security resource.

5. The African Commission's prospects as a collective human security resource

In order to reach an accurate understanding of the prospects for the continued functioning of the African Commission as a significant collective human security resource, it is important first to assess and understand the extent to which institutional practice in this regard has, over time, met reasonable expectations as to its performance. The assessment of the Commission's collective human security prospects that will be undertaken here will be organized around the same three sample areas of the Commission's work in the relevant regard

---

Realisation of Economic, Social and Cultural Rights: The African Commission holds a Seminar in Pretoria' (2004) 4 African Human Rights Law Journal 334. See also NJ Udombana (n 85 above) 181.

[94] African Commission, Resolution on Economic, Social and Cultural Rights, 36th Ordinary Session (27 November–3 December 2004), Eighteenth Annual Activity Report (on file with the author) 8 and Annex 1. See also: <http://www.achpr.org/english/resolutions/resolution78_en.html>.   [95] Ibid, 3.

[96] Pretoria Statement on Social, Economic and Cultural Rights in Africa (17 September 2004), ACHPR/Res.73 (XXXVI) 04.

[97] Resolution on Economic, Social and Cultural Rights (see n 94 above) 10 (of preamble).

which have already been examined in each of the two previous sections of this chapter.

However, to be useful, such an assessment must be based on a realistic barometer; that is to say, that the standard of measure must be appropriate to the task at hand. It is thus important not to overestimate the capacity of even the most ideally functioning international institution to contribute to peace and security within specific polities.[98] It is important to keep in mind the fact that international institutions are not designed to act as *panaceas* for problems of insecurity (or any other problem for that matter). They are rather much more humbly constructed as *resources* to be mobilized by other actors (such as states, non-governmental organizations, sub-state groups, and individuals). Even the best designed and functioning international institution cannot on its own (or even in alliance with other such institutions) assure collective human security to any given people. Other forces will condition, shape, and limit such an institution's role. A keen awareness of the inevitable limitations on the capacity of international institutions such as the African Commission to contribute to collective human security (or to any other value for that matter) will allow for a much more realistic assessment of both its attainments to date and its prospects in the future. In consequence, the African Commission's actual performance as a collective human security resource will be assessed against what it could possibly have achieved, and not against what it might have achieved in an ideal world. The world in which the Commission and other such bodies operate is, of course, far from ideal.

In relation to the African Commission's work on the implementation of the general guarantee in the African Charter of the right to national and international peace and security, the Commission deserves reasonably high marks, on the whole, for discharging relatively well its possible collective human security role. Given the Commission's design as an IHI that is possessed of only hortatory powers, it could not reasonably have been expected to do much more than it has already done in this area. As discussed in Section 4, it has passed several important Resolutions on various relevant subjects and situations (for example, landmines, Rwanda, the Sudan, Liberia, South Africa, and Burundi). These Resolutions contained the appropriate normative language, and were virtually always directed to the appropriate quarters. While it is always possible for a body such as the African Commission to do more in this highly important regard, given its (inherent) character as a body that persuades and cannot compel, there was—in practice—little else that the Commission could have done.

By contrast, however, commendable as it is, the African Commission's efforts to implement the self-determination and minority rights provisions in the African Charter (and in so doing, further its role as a collective human security resource),

---

[98] eg, see D Kennedy, 'A New World Order: Yesterday, Today and Tomorrow' (1994) 4 Transnational Law and Contemporary Problems 329, 339–57 and D Kennedy, 'The Move to Institutions' (1987) 8 Cardozo Law Review 841.

do not deserve as high a grade. Certainly, the Commission's reasoning in the *Katanga* case was, to say the least, bold and commendable. This decision has undoubtedly made an important contribution to our understanding of the right to sub-state group self-determination and minority rights, not only in Africa, but also the world over. The Commission's other efforts in this area (for example, its Working Group on Indigenous Peoples/Communities, the *Ogoni* case, and its Resolution on Rwanda) are also commendable. Nevertheless, given the centrality of the denial to sub-state groups of their self-determination and minority rights to the insecurity that plagues far too many portions of the African continent,[99] the African Commission's efforts in this specific area of its collective human security mandate have not been as adequate as they could have been. For one thing, despite its efforts toward the drafting and adoption of instruments such as the recently concluded Women's Protocol (which details and deepens women's rights provisions in the African Charter)[100] and the Fair Trial Guidelines (that expand on the fair hearing provisions in the African Charter),[101] very little, if anything, has been done by the Commission toward the drafting and adoption of a detailed Protocol or Resolution that explicates in much greater detail the minority protection rights that sub-state groups in Africa are to enjoy. Given the normative/hortatory utility of such a detailed document to the work of the activists who struggle on behalf of sub-state groups in Africa, and the centrality of the ill-treatment of sub-state groups to the insecurity that exists in much of the African continent, this gap in the law-creating activities of the African Commission is, it is submitted, a major one. Secondly, although the Commission has most commendably appointed a working group on the rights of indigenous peoples in Africa, it needs to work toward the establishment (within or without it) of a specialized mechanism for the third party (that is supra-state) 'adjudication' of the rights claims made by sub-state groups against the states of which they form a part. Such a mechanism should be able to focus on *preventing* internecine conflict, even before a related case is brought before the African Commission. The Commission also needs to undertake more explicitly focused promotional work in the sub-state group self-determination and minority rights area. More therefore needs to be done by the African Commission with regard to strengthening its work in this general area if it is to discharge its Charter-mandated collective human security obligations more effectively.

Such strengthening will also be required with regard to the African Commission's work in the ESC rights area. As has been discussed above, it is

---

[99] OC Okafor, 'After Martyrdom: International Law, Sub-State Groups, and the Construction of Legitimate Statehood in Africa' (2000) 41 Harvard International Law Journal 503 (hereinafter 'Martyrdom').

[100] Protocol to the African Charter on Human and Peoples' Rights on the Rights of Women, adopted 2003, reproduced in C Heyns (ed), *Compendium* (see n 31 above) 38.

[101] African Commission, 'Principles and Guidelines on the Right to a Fair Trial and Legal Assistance in Africa', 2003, reproduced in C Heyns (ed), *Compendium* (see n 31 above) 210.

well recognized in the relevant literature that the African Commission has been *relatively* inattentive to the protection of ESC rights on the continent.[102] As such, the burden that rests on the shoulders of the African Commission to interpret the ESC rights provisions of the African Charter appropriately and develop its own ESC rights jurisprudence is quite considerable. As the *Ogoni* case indicates, 'the approach of the Commission in filling the [ESC rights] gaps in the Charter' has been 'creative and bold'.[103] Yet, while its activities in the area of ESC rights have been increasingly significant in both quantitative and qualitative terms, much more still needs to be done by the African Commission in this area if it is more effectively to discharge its collective human security role in Africa. The link between the enjoyment of ESC rights and the attainment of human security is now so clear that no further explication is required here. By contributing much more to the enjoyment of ESC rights, the African Commission will greatly enhance its role as a useful collective human security resource on the continent.

Nevertheless, it is acknowledged that the African Commission's collective human security efforts have been hampered by all the institutional and other problems (mostly beyond its control) that it has faced since inception. These problems are well documented in the relevant literature.[104] Some of the more serious and relevant of these problems include: the Commission's lack of adequate finan-

---

[102] C Heyns, 'The African Regional Human Rights System' (see n 81 above) 690–1. See also C Mbazira (n 83 above) 2.

[103] Ibid, 691.

[104] See generally, J Oloka-Onyango, 'Human Rights and Sustainable Development in Contemporary Africa: A New Dawn, or Retreating Horizons?' (2000) 6 Buffalo Human Rights Law Review 39, 70; AAR Mohamed, 'Article 58 of the African Charter on Human and Peoples' Rights—A Legal Analysis and How it Can be Put into More Practical Use' [1996] ASICL Proceedings 290; R Murray, 'Decisions of the African Commission on Individual Communications under the African Charter on Human and Peoples' Rights' (1997) 46 International and Comparative Studies Quarterly 412, 414; R Murray, 'On-Site Visits by the African Commission on Human and Peoples' Rights: A Case Study and Comparison with the Inter-American Commission on Human Rights' (1999) 11 African Journal of International and Comparative Law 460, 463–4, and 473; S Gutto, *ICJ Workshops on NGO Participation in the African Commission on Human and Peoples' Rights: A Critical Evaluation* (Geneva: International Court of Justice, 1996), 14–16, and 'Non-Governmental Organizations, Peoples' Participation, and the African Commission on Human and Peoples' Rights: Emerging Challenges to Regional Protection of Human Rights' in B Andreassen and T Swineheart (eds), *Human Rights in Developing Countries*, 1991 Yearbook (Oslo: Scandinavian University Press, 1992), 40–2; U Essien, 'The African Commission: Eleven Years After' (2000) 6 Buffalo Human Rights Law Review 93, 94, and 97–9; UO Umozurike, *The African Charter on Human and Peoples' Rights* (The Hague: Martinus Nijhoff, 1997), 67–73; FD Gaer, 'First Fruits: Reporting by States under the African Charter on Human and Peoples' Rights' (1992) 10 Netherlands Quarterly on Human Rights 29, 29–31; F Korley, 'The Role of Human Rights Institutions in the Promotion and Protection of Human Rights in Africa: A Ghanaian Appraisal' (1998) 10 ASICL Proceedings 199, 200; F Butegwa, 'Using the African Charter on Human and Peoples' Rights to Secure Women's Access to Land in Africa' in RJ Cook (ed), *Human Rights of Women: National and International Perspectives* (Philadelphia, PA: University of Pennsylvania Press, 1994), 495, 504, and 506; and W Benedek, 'The African Charter and Commission on Human and Peoples' Rights: How to Make it More Effective' (1993) 11 Netherlands Quarterly of Human Rights 25, 28–32.

cial and human resources;[105] the insufficient publicity that the Charter and the African Commission's work have received so far;[106] and a weak 'state-compliance' record.[107]

Although these problems have each contributed in some measure (but not necessarily evenly) to the inability of the Commission to fully realize its potential as an important collective human security resource, as I have argued elsewhere, the greatest promise for the more adequate realization of the humanist promise of the African Commission (and the other institutions of the African human rights system) lies not as much in the character of the Commission itself or what it does itself, but more in the ability of domestic activist forces creatively to deploy the Commission's views, decisions, resolutions, and other such resources *within their own domestic institutions* (such as their national courts and legislatures).[108]

Overall, however, Joe Oloka-Onyango has (for understandable reasons) felt able to declare that 'unfortunately, even the most positive reviews of the performance of...the African Commission...generally agree that the institution has performed at less than par'.[109] Yet, as Nsongurua Udombana has more recently concluded, 'the African Commission has come a long way since its inauguration in 1987. In its early years, the Commission was more careful than courageous... it now interprets its mandate boldly and creatively.'[110] A similar conclusion has been reached by Christof Heyns, another very knowledgeable observer of the African Commission.[111]

In view of this increasing, albeit incremental, innovativeness and boldness on the part of the African Commission, it is not unreasonable to conclude that the Commission will, as time goes on, grow in capacity, creativity, boldness (and therefore stature). As such, it is also fair to suppose that that inter-African human rights mechanism is more likely than not to become better able to discharge its functions more satisfactorily. If this turns out to be true, then the Commission is also as likely to function much better as a collective human security resource. Without such increased creativity and boldness, it will be extremely difficult for an African Commission that is in practice equipped with only hortatory power to make an appreciable impact within the high-stakes world of *realpolitik* in which a considerable portion of collective human security issues are still dealt with. Even the non-military/state security and more human rights issues that affect human security in Africa (such as questions of food security) are all too often seen as part of a high-stakes global political game of sorts. Thus, it is in part because the African Commission's developing institutional posture tends to suggest that it will get even bolder and more innovative as time goes by that a relatively optimistic reading of its prospects as a collective human security resource is offered here.

---

[105] J Oloka-Onyango, ibid, 70–1.   [106] See n 26 above, 269.

[107] EA Ankumah (see n 27 above) 40.   [108] OC Okafor (see nn 26 and 27 above).

[109] See n 80 above, 70.   [110] NJ Udombana (see n 85 above) 233.

[111] See n 81 above, 691.

6. Conclusion

The chapter began with some background and definition of the key concepts and terms which are analysed and discussed. Subsequently, the intimate and positive link between the enjoyment of a broad array of human rights and the success of the collective human security effort in our time was noted and discussed. Thereafter, a brief background discussion of the nature and character of the African Commission (the pan-African institution that was focused on in this chapter) was offered. It was shown that this linkage is now well recognized by both the United Nations and the AU. Thereafter, a detailed discussion of the extent to which the African Charter—the 'Constitution' that governs the activities of the African Commission—designed and portrayed that Commission as a collective human security resource was undertaken. It was also shown that the African Commission itself accommodates this collective human security resource role in its construction of its self-image.

The above discussions presaged a detailed examination of some of the ways in which significant aspects of the African Commission's institutional practice justify that body's characterization in this chapter as a significant collective human security resource. The chapter concludes with some thoughts on the African Commission's prospects as a collective human security resource.

14

The Role of NGOs and Civil Society in Advancing Human Security in Africa

*Rachel Murray**

1. Introduction

It is now generally accepted that it is important to involve non-governmental organizations (NGOs) and civil society at the international level[1] and the African Commission on Human and Peoples' Rights, as created by the African Charter on Human and Peoples' Rights (ACHPR),[2] has been no exception in adopting this approach. Indeed it has been generally very open and accommodating to NGOs. As will be seen below, NGOs have been very influential in the African human rights system and the way in which the sessions of the African Commission are run enables NGOs to make statements on any of the agenda items in the public sittings, with the exception of the state reporting procedure.[3]

International bodies have seen benefits in involving NGOs in their work for a number of reasons. First, there is a sense that NGOs democratize the system. By involving civil society[4] at this level of decision making, it is argued, participation in governance is assured.[5] They also offer an alternative perspective from the state

* Professor of International Human Rights Law, University of Bristol.

[1] A Clapham, 'Defining the Role of Non-Governmental Organizations with Regard to the UN Human Rights Treaty Bodies' in AF Bayefsky (ed), *The UN Human Rights Treaty System in the 21st Century* (The Hague: Kluwer Law International, 2000), 183–94, 183. Art 71 Charter of UN and ECOSOC Resolution 1296 and 1996/31; European Convention on the Recognition of the Legal Personality of International Non-Governmental Organisations, 1986 C/M of C/E; MA Olz, 'Non-Governmental Organisations in Regional Human Rights Systems' (1997) 28 Columbia Human Rights Law Review 307.   [2] Art 30 ACHPR.

[3] For which see further below.

[4] For discussion of the concept of civil society see C Monga, 'Civil Society and Democratisation in Francophone Africa' (1995) 33(3) Journal of Modern African Studies 359–79. JD Holm, PP Molutsi, and G Somolekae, 'The Development of Civil Society in a Democratic State: The Botswana Model' (1996) 39(2) African Studies Review 43–69, 43.

[5] OC Okafor, 'Reconceiving "Third World" Legitimate Governance Struggles in our Time: Emergent Imperatives for Rights Activism' (2000) 6 Buffalo Human Rights Law Review 1, 8–9. NGO participation 'has introduced a new dynamic of embryonic participatory democracy to the global community and to the shaping of international law', D Otto, 'Nongovernmental

view. However, many have called into question the extent to which NGOs can be said to be 'representative' of any particular community[6] and note that NGOs themselves are 'rarely run in open, participatory fashions'.[7] Furthermore, NGOs and governments are often portrayed as being on opposite sides of the spectrum,[8] creating an adversarial system[9] and hiding the true position of some NGOs.[10] Thus:

involvement in a local human rights organisation can become a means of political opportunism. It is common to have a revolving door between political office and human rights monitoring and activism. Criticising the human rights record of a government is perhaps the most legitimate means of criticising it, and can become a cover for smuggling in many other non-human rights criticism as well. Involvement in a human rights

Organizations in the United Nations System: The Emerging Role of International Civil Society' (1996) 18 Human Rights Quarterly 107–41, 120.

[6] 'NGOs themselves are not necessarily democratic, which raises the question of who represents what to whom....NGO leaders may push their own personal agendas rather than those of constituents', L Gordenker and TG Weiss, 'NGO Participation in the International Policy Process' (1995) 16(3) Third World Quarterly 543–55, 553.

[7] CE Welch, 'Taking Rights Seriously: Citizen Action Through NGOs' (2001) 19(2) NQHR 119–22, 121.

Nongovernmental organizations (NGOs) have a certain mystical, venerable quality to them. They are often portrayed as fighting for the poor and helpless, especially in developing countries...It is sometimes difficult to develop a clear, unbiased, and realistic understanding of what role NGOs really do play in the context of democratic transition and human rights protection. S Dicklitch, 'Action for Development in Uganda

C Welch, *NGOs and Human Rights: Promise and Performance* (Philadelphia, PA: University of Pennsylvania Press, 2000), 182, as cited in OC Okafor, 'Modest Harvests: On the Significant (But Limited) Impact of Human Rights NGOs on Legislative and Executive Behaviour in Nigeria' (2004) 48(1) Journal of African Law 23–49, 25.

[8] 'This is not the story of good NGOs confronting evil governments....This is the story of humanity assuming responsibility for its own future, through increasingly representative forms of political organization and through a full engaged civil society', ML Schweitz, 'NGO Participation in International Governance: The Question of Legitimacy' (1995) 89 American Society of International Law Proceedings 415, 417.

[9] 'They should recognise that "non-governmental" is not a synonym for "anti-governmental"', Olz (see n 1 above) 372.

In the 1990s, the adversarial stance has not changed. In dealing with governments in Africa, Asia and Latin America, principle counts more than influence, to the extent that some human rights organisations appear to be dogmatic, insisting on operating in their standard manner even when it is obviously not the best strategy for producing results. Thus, for a western human rights organisation to become engaged in helping an African government set up its legal system, or celebrating with a legal aid scheme, might be rejected on the grounds that it would compromise the 'independence' (or by implication the ethical purity) of the human rights organisation

A de Waal, 'Human Rights in Africa: Values, Institutions and Opportunities' in K Hossain et al, *Human Rights Commissions and Ombudsman Offices: National Experiences Throughout the World* (The Hague: Kluwer Law International, 2001), 759–81, 767.

[10] eg, there have been occasions when government personnel have adopted false NGO names in order to attend the NGO forum that precedes the sessions of the African Commission to try to obtain information from organizations about what other NGOs are saying.

organisation can give a politician profile and publicity as well as moral protection and an income.[11]

In addition, as has been raised elsewhere,[12] for some of the most influential NGOs that participate in the African human rights bodies, they cannot be said to be grassroots organizations.[13] One often finds operating within the African Commission those NGOs which are 'professionalized' and

> may work with issue specific or case specific organisations, but they do not aim at mobilising a mass constituency. Rather, they tend to focus on influencing a liberal and educated elite on behalf of people in faraway countries.[14]

Despite these concerns, it has been generally believed by the international and regional bodies that 'the introduction of nongovernmental concerns into international dialogue is healthy'.[15]

Secondly, international institutions have looked to involve NGOs out of a sense of pragmatism: 'New demands for UN problem-solving capacities have not been met by similarly expanding resources.'[16] NGOs can assist international organizations in fulfilling their remits and a certain element of their work can be 'delegated' to NGOs: 'both governments and UN organisations increasingly rely on NGOs to deliver services'.[17] Through involving NGOs in their work, international organizations may be able to obtain alternative sources of funding and increase the visibility of their own programmes at the national levels.[18] Indeed,

---

[11] de Waal (see n 9 above) 771.   [12] Okafor (see n 7 above) 47.

[13] 'The NGO community in Nigeria is in general both elitist and urban-centred. It is very much dominated (though not exclusively populated) by a cadre of very highly educated, legally trained and largely urbanized activists', OC Okafor (see n 7 above) 48. 'African human rights NGOs still lack legitimacy, representing an urban elite and not being sufficiently grounded in rural areas, and also being attached to their Northern sponsors', K Appiayei-Atua, 'Civil Society, Human Rights and Development in Africa: A Critical Analysis' (2002) 2 Peace, Conflict and Development 21.

[14] Most human rights organisations are now staffed by people who did not grow up during the domestic struggle for civil rights and for whom human rights is less a vocation than a profession. Their peer group is in government, academia, law and commerce and they do not have the moral reference group of protest marchers that so strongly influence their predecessors

A de Waal (see n 9 above) 765 and 766.

[15] Perhaps the best that can be hoped for may be a kind of crude balance at the local, national and international levels in which a mixture of governmental, intergovernmental and nongovernmental voices more closely reflects reality than a state-dominated framework with only a smattering of intergovernmental input

See n 6 above, 553.

[16] E Dorsey and B Pigott, 'The UN System and NGOs: New Relationships for a New Era?' in UN, *The UN System and NGOs: New Relationships for a New Era?*, *25th United Nations Issues Conference 1994* (Muscatine, IA: Stanley Foundation, 1994), 14–15. See also S Grant, 'The NGO Role: Implementation, Expanding Protection and Monitoring the Monitors' in AF Bayefsky (ed), *The UN Human Rights Treaty System in the 21st Century* (The Hague: Kluwer Law International, 2000), 209–17.   [17] See n 6 above, 554.

[18] P Uvin, 'Scaling up the Grass Roots and Scaling Down the Summit: The Relations between Third World Nongovernmental Organisations and the United Nations' (1995) 16(3) Third World Quarterly 495–512, 500.

there is a recognition that these international and regional bodies may not be able to operate without NGO involvement and support. The African Commission has consistently made reference to the need for NGOs to support it in its work to the extent that in reality much of what the Commission does involves NGO input and has been delegated to NGOs to fund and implement.

Lastly, the strength of the NGO voice now means that it is increasingly difficult for international bodies to ignore it. NGOs have become regular participants in the international arena and their influence recognized.[19] When taken with the recognition that without NGO support the African human rights system would not have been able to carry out all the initiatives that it has done, the African system has given a central voice to NGOs in its sessions and deliberations.

In turn, NGOs have seen the value of participation at the international level, not only because this may increase the 'availability of funds', but also it enhances their ability to influence the organizations' programmes as well as the state itself.[20] For example, as Okafor has written in relation to the use by Nigerian NGOs of the African Commission as a platform to highlight abuses in their country during the Abacha regime, 'in this way the African Commission has been sensitized and "recruited" by these NGOs toward the goal of positively affecting governmental action in Nigeria'.[21]

This chapter will examine, in the context of the above, the role of NGOs in the African human rights mechanism and their contribution to the development of issues relating to human security. There are some opportunities for NGOs and civil society to be involved in the African Union (AU) as an institution through, for example, the Economic, Social and Cultural Council (ECOSOCC) which has as its mandate the objective of ensuring dialogue between civil society organizations and promoting civil society participation in the AU.[22] Although it includes some human rights organizations among its membership, this body has not yet reached its full potential. Beyond ECOSOCC the few NGOs and civil society organizations that do engage and influence the AU institutions or understand how they operate are few and far between. This is in contrast to the impact NGOs have had before the African Commission on Human and Peoples' Rights. This institution has given them the greatest opportunities for interaction. In doing so NGOs have influenced the human security agenda at that level.

---

[19] P Alston (ed), *Non-State Actors and Human Rights* (Oxford: Oxford University Press, 2005); A Clapham, *Human Rights in the Private Sphere* (Oxford: Oxford University Press, 1993); RA Higgott et al (eds), *Non-State Actors and Authority in the Global System* (London: Routledge, 2000); MT Kamminga, 'The Evolving Status of NGOs under International Law: A Threat to the Inter-State System?' in P Alston, *Non-State Actors and Human Rights* (Oxford: Oxford University Press, 2005), 93–112; H Cullen and K Morrow, 'International Civil Society in International Law: The Growth of NGO Participation' (2007) 1 Non-State Actors in International Law 7; D Shelton, 'The Participation of Nongovernmental Organizations in International Judicial Proceedings' (1994) 88 AJIL 611.   [20] See n 18 above, 500.

[21] Okafor (see n 7 above) 44.

[22] Statutes of the Economic, Social and Cultural Council of the African Union, Art 2.

However, this has not been through any strategic or consistent approach to the issue, with each NGO pursuing its own agenda. Furthermore, neither has any attention to human security been the result of a proactive policy on the part of the African Commission itself, rather as a reaction to what is being asked of it by NGOs. While NGOs have provided the Commission with much needed funding and assistance, the Commission and the AU, until recently, came to rely on them as a source of finance and support. This resulted in a lack of ownership in the system and a failure to develop a proper institutional history, making the Commission vulnerable to government criticism.

This chapter will first outline how NGOs can work with the African Commission before detailing the impact of their involvement on the human security agenda.

2. Opportunities for NGOs to engage with the African Commission

Testament to the importance to which the African Commission attributes NGOs within its work is its reference to them in its documents and decision making. It is notable in this regard to refer to the Brainstorming Meeting on the African Commission organized by the AU in May 2006,[23] a meeting at which NGOs were also present. This meeting dealt with a range of factors and was an attempt at stocktaking on the African human rights mechanism as the Commission approached its twentieth year of operation. Among the matters discussed was the relationship of the Commission with other actors including NGOs. The considerable amount of space given to discussing this issue reflects the importance attributed to the matter by the Commission. Among the conclusions were that states should increase their cooperation with NGOs, for example, in the implementation of their obligations under the Charter[24] and that there was a need for the Commission to play some role in their protection.[25]

However, what this meeting also reflects is the continued difficulty the Commission has in accommodating NGOs, on the one hand, given its reliance on their support, and addressing concerns by governments, on the other, that the Commission is too influenced by its non-governmental friends. In this regard at various points in its history the Commission has wavered between openly

---

[23] Report of the Brainstorming Meeting on the African Commission, Twentieth Activity Report (2006) EX.CL/279 (IX), Annex II.

[24] 'States should cooperate with NGOs and NHRI [National Human Rights Institutions] in the preparation of their reports', ibid, 26(c). 'Certain state Parties do not accept to work with NGOs and do not facilitate the work of the NGOs', para 47.

[25] 'Certain States do not cooperate with NGOs at national or international levels: Governments do not provide them with funding or information. Human rights activists are sometimes arrested for their activism', ibid, 57.

accepting NGOs without any real apparent restrictions on their participation, to responding to government pressure and criticizing the way in which they operate. The report of the Brainstorming Meeting reflects this tension by recognizing that although the Commission was grateful for NGO cooperation,

the information supplied by NGOs on the human rights situation in African countries may, in certain cases, be inaccurate, and this affects the credibility of the work of the NGOs. Many NGOs do not comply with the principles of cooperation with the ACHPR.[26]

There is also recognition of the impact of too great an NGO involvement on the Commission itself: 'The ownership of the activities of the ACHPR was however emphasised. The meeting identified challenges experienced in relationship with partners.'[27] It then went on to recommend that

The ACHPR should enforce the existing provisions regarding its relations with NGOs and take appropriate action against those that do not comply with the said provisions. NGOs should provide accurate information in their draft resolutions and the ACHPR should set up a verification mechanism to that extent.[28]

2.1 Participation in sessions and determining the agenda

The African Charter itself makes little reference to the role of NGOs: Article 45 provides that among the promotional functions of the Commission are the requirements that it 'encourage national and local institutions concerned with human and peoples' rights' and 'cooperate with other African and international institutions concerned with the promotion and protection of human and peoples' rights'.[29] Article 46 enables the Commission to 'resort to any appropriate method of investigation; it may hear from . . . any other person capable of enlightening it'. Both these Articles are sufficiently broad to enable the Commission to develop its own direction and the Commission has elaborated on these in its Rules of Procedure. These provide that NGOs can propose items for inclusion on the Commission's agenda[30] and there is provision for them to be sent a copy of the agenda.[31] Rule 72 sets out more detail on participation in the sessions of the Commission but this is permitted without voting rights and Rules 75 to 76 provide that those granted observer status by the Commission may 'appoint authorised observers to participate in the public session of the Commission and its subsidiary bodies' and for the Commission to consult NGOs 'either directly or through one or several committees set up for this purpose', whether they are set up at the initiative of the Commission or the NGO itself. NGOs have exploited these provisions to their full extent and, as Motala notes, they have played a role from not only drafting the African Charter itself but then 'since its establishment,

---

[26] Ibid, 53.   [27] Ibid, 43.   [28] Ibid, 58(a) and (b).   [29] Art 45(1)(a) and (c).
[30] Rule 6(3)(f), provided this is sent at least ten weeks prior to the session, Rule 6(5).
[31] Rule 7(2) and (3).

a close and beneficial relationship has developed between the Commission and NGOs'.[32]

Beyond these provisions in its Rules of Procedure and general reference in the ACHPR, for many years the African Commission did not have strict rules prescribing how it would deal with NGOs, permitting them to attend the sessions as they wished and to make statements. Many of those who participated in its earlier sessions, due to the relative invisibility of the Commission on the African continent, were international organizations such as Amnesty International and the International Commission of Jurists.[33] Indeed, it was these organizations which were the first ones to be granted observer status by the Commission at its third session in 1988.[34] Since then many more NGOs, both international and African, have taken advantage of this, although for many years the procedure for doing so was not rigid and the African Commission did not see lack of observer status as a bar for participation in its sessions, still permitting those without to give oral statements and distribute material at its sessions.

In parallel with the sessions NGOs, initially under the auspices of the International Commission of Jurists, have organized pre-session workshops bringing together primarily African NGOs to discuss items of mutual interest and to introduce them to the African system.[35] Unfortunately, while an important networking forum, much of the discussion at these meetings lacks focus and many NGOs leave before the session of the African Commission actually gets under way. In addition, there has been continued controversy over the relationship between the Resolutions adopted by the NGOs at this pre-session forum and subsequently delivered to the Commission, and those adopted by the Commission itself. Whilst, on the one hand, this gives NGOs considerable power to influence the agenda and direction of the Commission's work, on the other hand, governments have highlighted on numerous occasions the close parallels between the Resolutions adopted at the NGO forum and those adopted by the Commission, believing this undermines the Commission's independence and integrity. More recently this concern, among others, prompted the delay of the publication of Resolutions in the Commission's annual report until certain governments had had a chance to include their observations on their content.[36] In many of these

---

[32] A Motala, 'Non-Governmental Organisations in the African System' in MD Evans and R Murray (eds), *The African Charter on Human and Peoples' Rights: The System in Practice, 1986–2000* (Cambridge: Cambridge University Press, 2002), 246–79, 246.   [33] Ibid, 249.

[34] For the first time the Commission heard representatives of certain NGOs with observer status within the Commission ... [they] expressed their wish to establish sound, multiform and lasting cooperation with the Commission. (7) The Commission expressed great satisfaction at this collaboration which would enable it to widen and further the scope of its action for promotion and protection. (8) Moreover the Commission accorded observer status to other NGOs.

Final Communiqué of the Fourth Ordinary Session of the African Commission on Human and Peoples' Rights; similarly Final Communiqué of the 15th Ordinary Session of the African Commission on Human and Peoples' Rights, para 14.   [35] See n 32 above, 249.

[36] Resolutions on a number of countries that the Commission adopted at its 38th Session in December 2005, made public at that stage and which were initially included in its 19th Annual

Resolutions governments referred to similar Resolutions adopted by the preceding NGO workshop.

For many years, then, NGOs enjoyed considerable freedom in their participation at the Commission's sessions, the Commission only alluding to the need for NGOs to do more and 'from time to time inform the Commission of their activities in the field of human rights to assist the Commission in its work'.[37] NGOs, from the Commission's 11th Session, therefore, were required to submit reports every two years on 'their activities which are relevant to the work of the Commission'.[38]

But it was pressure from governments that eventually forced the Commission to adopt a more rigorous procedure for dealing with applications for observer status, culminating in the Mauritanian government, having tried to stop local NGOs from attending the Commission's session, asking whether those who were not recognized by their own states could have observer status.[39] Given this context and the fact that many of those NGOs who had obtained observer status with the Commission then did not continue to have any relationship with it, it was perhaps not surprising that the Assembly of Heads of State and Government of the Organization of African Unity (OAU) asked the Commission 'for reasons for efficiency, to review its criteria for granting observer status and to suspend further granting of observer status until the adoption of new criteria'.[40]

The African Commission felt vulnerable to such criticism, recognizing that without the support of NGOs, more work would fall on its shoulders and its ability to delegate would be severely hampered. It suspended consideration of observer status applications whilst it pondered how best to proceed, deciding eventually in 1990 to adopt a Resolution on observer status which set out a little more clearly the obligations, procedure, and responsibilities of NGOs before the African Commission.[41] It then continued to process applications.

The practical effect of this Resolution has been fairly limited, although the African Commission is now much more forceful in checking whether those who wish to speak at its sessions have observer status and turning down requests from those who do not. The process for applying for observer status, however, is not stringent and the obligations on NGOs once status has been acquired are few and have never been properly upheld.[42]

Report submitted to the Assembly of the AU, were then rejected by the latter in January 2006. They were then included in the Twentieth Activity Report of the Commission adopted at the next summit in July 2006 with government comments on the Resolutions included.

[37] Fifth Annual Activity Report of the African Commission on Human and Peoples' Rights, para 20.

[38] Ibid.

[39] See n 32 above, 250. See also, R Murray, 'Report on the 1997 Sessions of the African Commission on Human and Peoples' Rights' (1988) 19 Human Rights Law Journal 169–85.

[40] AHG/Dec.126 (XXXIV), June 1998.

[41] Resolution on the Criteria for Granting and Enjoying Observer Status to Non-Governmental Organizations Working in the Field of Human Rights with the African Commission on Human and Peoples' Rights, Twelfth Activity Report 1998–1999.

[42] Other international bodies have rules managing NGO participation, Otto (see n 5 above).

The Resolution states that NGOs wishing to apply for observer status have to send in relevant documentation 'with a view to showing their willingness and [sic][43] capability work for the realisation of the objectives of the African Charter on Human and Peoples' Rights'. Thus,

All organisations applying for observer status with the African Commission shall consequently:

- Have objectives and activities in consonance with the fundamental principles and objectives enunciated in the OAU Charter and in the African Charter on Human and Peoples' Rights;
- Be organisations working in the field of human rights
- Declare their financial resources.[44]

The application should be written and contain a statement setting out the intentions of the organization, the statutes of the organization, its proof of legal existence, list of members, its organs, sources of funding, last financial statement, and statement on its activities, both past and present. The latter should include a plan of action and 'any other information that may help to determine the identity of the organisation, its purpose and objectives as well as its field of activities'.[45] It must be submitted three months prior to the session. This is then assigned to a particular Commissioner, usually according to language and geographical region, for their consideration. Further information may be sought from the applicant at this stage. The application is then considered in public at the session in a process which can take considerable time and, although it could be praised for its transparency and openness, NGOs being able to see what decisions are taken, is tedious and long-winded with no apparent sense of institutional history and no catalogue of similar decisions taken in previous sessions upon which to draw. As a result, providing the NGO has the required paperwork, little prevents it from being given status. The Commission rarely rejects an application and where applications have been deferred this is mainly due to lack of appropriate documentation rather than any objection in principle to the organization. The Commission seems more led by the fact that the NGO has shown an interest in its work and is another potential source of support, actually encouraging them to apply for observer status,[46] than whether it has commitment or may be using this for other means.

Once admitted, so far in reality there is little to test the NGO's commitment to the Commission. In principle the Resolution appears to be prescriptive, requiring NGOs to 'establish close relations of cooperation with the African Commission

---

[43] Resolution on the Criteria for Granting and Enjoying Observer Status (see n 41 above) ch 1.
[44] Ibid.   [45] Ibid.
[46] 'The Chairman issued a call to Nigerian NGOs to seek observer status with the African Commission on Human and Peoples' Rights', Intersession report of Chair 1989–1990, Annex VI, Third Activity Report of the African Commission on Human and Peoples' Rights, adopted 28 April 1990, para 4.

and to engage in regular consultations with it on all matters of common interest', to present activity reports to the Commission every two years.[47] Indeed the Commission has the power to take a number of measures against NGOs that default on their obligations, including 'non-participation in sessions; denial of documents and information; denial of the opportunity to propose items to be included in the Commission's agenda and of participating in its proceedings', and suspension and withdrawal of observer status if necessary.[48] The Commission has gone so far as to publish NGO compliance with this,[49] but this has not been at every session and in practice there has been no sanction for failure to do so, other than publicity in this document, something which is not taken too seriously.[50] Few of the 370 NGOs that have observer status attend the sessions of the Commission. Although this is clearly going to be the situation in a continent where resources for such organizations are scarce, travel expensive and difficult, and many NGOs have been prompted to apply for observer status only after the Commission has held a session in its country, it means that observer status is relatively meaningless in terms of the support provided to the Commission or their participation in its work.

It is to be welcomed, then, that the Commission's amended interim Rules of Procedure[51] are more prescriptive over the sanctions that apply for NGOs who 'are in default of their obligations', suggesting that the Commission will start to take a more rigorous approach here. The place accorded by the Commission to NGOs is apparent from the platform that it provides to them at its sessions. At the opening ceremony, after an introductory speech by the Chair of the Commission, speeches are heard by what one can see are the main actors in the African system, reflecting their order in the hierarchy: states, NHRIs, and then NGOs. On each of the agenda items at the public sessions participants can make statements in these orders. There is no restriction on the number of NGOs which can make statements on each item and while this may be democratic and open, the practical result is that discussion on some items can be lengthy and repetitive. While there have been attempts in the past, either by the Commission or NGOs, to obtain coordination of their statements and make joint submissions, this has not worked well. Many NGOs see it as essential that they are able to attend this high-level session and make an oral statement criticizing the government in public and see this as a privilege even if it produces no tangible result, giving them a platform for their grievances. As a result, while

---

[47] See n 41 above, ch 3.   [48] Ibid, ch 4.

[49] eg Status of Submission of NGOs Activity Reports to the African Commission, 39th Ordinary Session, 11–25 May 2006, Banjul, the Gambia.

[50] This is not unusual to the African Commission, however: 'the demand by local and international NGOs for the right to be represented in international forums has not been matched with an adequate effort to define concomitant responsibilities to accompany such rights' (see n 6 above) 553.

[51] Draft Rules of Procedure, in particular, Rule 73, see <http://www.achpr.org/english/other/Interim%20Rules/Interim%20Rules%20of%20Procedure.pdf>.

most of the NGO statements are not lacking in passion and commitment, out-lining the atrocities that may have occurred in their home states, few of them are strategic in their approach, asking for the Commission to carry out certain key functions and tasks and lobbying Commissioners to do so over a number of sessions. However, without this more strategic approach the Commission may be democratically permitting all NGOs to speak but their expectations are likely to be falsely raised. One statement by an NGO alone is not going to force the Commission to act or force the state to respond. Yet few NGOs have the resources, or sometimes the desire, to carry through the sustained lobbying that any results will require.

As a result, it is often a core group of a few NGOs, many of them international, that dominate the work of the Commission. With the exception of Mauritanian, Nigerian, and Zimbabwean NGOs which have been vociferous and joined together with some positive results at the Commission, many African NGOs have limited visibility and influence at the sessions of the Commission.

3. Impact of NGOs in developing the human security agenda

The concept of human security is not one that, as a single issue, has been the focus of the African Commission or any particular NGO within the African system. The definition of 'human security' has been a notoriously tricky one to identify and has pulled scholars, international institutions, governments, and NGOs in different directions.[52] As the Human Security Commission's 2003 report out-lines, human security is:

to protect the vital core of all human lives in ways that enhance human freedoms and human fulfilment. Human security means protecting fundamental freedoms—freedoms that are the essence of life. It means protecting people from critical (severe) and perva-sive (widespread) threats and situations. It means using processes that build on people's strengths and aspirations. It means creating political, social, environmental, economic, military and cultural systems that together give people the building blocks of survival, livelihood and dignity.[53]

The AU, in contrast to the African Commission, has seized upon this term and its organs have referred to it in a range of situations. Although much of the reference to 'human security' is linked closely with conflict situations, the definition pro-vided in its Common African Defence and Security Policy, one which has been

---

[52] See G Oberleitner, 'Porcupines in Love: The Intricate Convergence of Human Rights and Human Security' [2005] European Human Rights Law Review 588–606; R Paris, 'Human Security: Paradigm Shift or Hot Air?' (2001) 26 International Security 87–102; 'What is Human Security' (2004) 35 Security Dialogue 3.

[53] Commission on Human Security, *Human Security Now* (New York: Commission on Human Security, 2003), 4. See also United Nations Development Programme, *Human Development Report 1994: New Dimensions of Human Security* available at: <http://hdr.undp.org>.

used by the AU on other occasions, is broader than this:

This newer, multi-dimensional notion of security thus embraces such issues as human rights; the right to participate fully in the process of governance; the right to equal development as well as the right to have access to resources and the basic necessities of life; the right to protection against poverty; the right to conducive education and health conditions; the right to protection against marginalization on the basis of gender; protection against natural disasters, as well as ecological and environmental degradation. At the national level, the aim would be to safeguard the security of individuals, families, communities, and the state/national life, in the economic, political, and social dimensions. This applies at various regional levels also; and at the continental level, the principle would be underscored that the 'security of each African country is inseparably linked to that of other African countries and the African continent as a whole'.[54]

Whether the notion of 'human security' adds anything as a concept to the existing human rights agenda has been questioned[55] and the relationship between human rights and human security has been explored by several authors.[56] What the rest of this chapter seeks to do, therefore, is to take the definition as provided by the AU as the starting point and to examine the extent to which NGOs have developed some of these concepts within the African Charter. Although it will highlight various issues and this may be seen as a superficial selection, this chapter cannot deal with the breadth of what many consider human security as a concept to cover. It does, however, give an illustration of the range of issues where NGOs have had an impact. As will be seen below, these developments have not been the result of any drive by individuals or groups of NGOs to look at human security as an issue per se, neither has it been a concern of the African Commission itself. Any attention to this issue is the result of NGO pressure to examine particular items of interest to them. Due to their lobbying, involvement, and relationship with the African Commission, however, NGOs have prompted it to examine the issue of human security from a variety of different perspectives.

3.1 Right to participation

NGOs, before the African Commission, have used the communication procedure to argue for increased participation in government, through Article 13 of the African Charter, linking this expressly with Article 20 and the right to self-determination, the latter being 'the counterpart of the right enjoyed by individuals

---

[54] Solemn Declaration on a Common African Defence and Security Policy, 28 February 2004, para 6, available at: <http://www.africa-union.org>.

[55] C Tomuschat, *Between Idealism and Realism*, The Collected Courses of the Academy of European Law, Vol 13/1 (Oxford: Oxford University Press, 2003).

[56] Oberleitner (see n 52 above); B Ramcharan, 'Human Rights and Human Security' (2004) 1 Disarmament Forum 40; D Petrasek, 'Human Rights "Lite"? Thoughts on Human Security' (2004) 35 Security Dialogue 59–62.

under Article 13'.[57] In a number of decisions the African Commission has found that the annulment of elections, that had been held to be free and fair, violated Article 13.[58] Article 13 also includes a right to vote[59] and protection for political parties and political opponents.[60] As has the AU, the African Commission has spent some time focusing on the electoral process, stating that 'elections are the only means by which the people can elect democratically the government of their choice in conformity to the African Charter on Human and Peoples' Rights'.[61]

The right to political participation is a right reflected in various cases and documents of the African Commission, prompted by NGO influence, and has been described by the Commission as one of the 'most cherished fundamental rights'.[62] The Protocol on the Rights of Women contains provisions requiring states to 'promote participative governance and the equal participation of women in the political life of their countries through affirmative action' through ensuring women can participate in elections without discrimination, they are represented equally in the electoral process and in development programmes.[63]

3.2 Development and access to resources

Despite the African Charter being among the very few human rights documents which have a right to development among its provisions, little use has been made of Article 22. The peoples' rights provisions in Articles 19 to 24 have been exploited mainly by NGOs advocating indigenous peoples' rights[64] and by NGOs bringing cases on electoral issues using self-determination and, to a lesser extent, concerning the treatment of ethnic groups within a particular state.[65] In the seminal case against Nigeria, Communication No 155/96, brought

---

[57] Communication No 102/93, *Constitutional Rights Project and Civil Liberties Organisation v Nigeria*, Twelfth Activity Report of the African Commission on Human and Peoples' Rights, 1998–1999, Annex V.   [58] Ibid.

[59] Communication No 241/2001, *Purohit and Moore v The Gambia*, Sixteenth Activity Report of the African Commission on Human and Peoples' Rights, 2002–2003, Annex VII.

[60] Communication No 133/94, *Association pour la Défence des Droits de l'Homme et des Libertés v Djibouti*, Thirteenth Activity Report of the African Commission on Human and Peoples' Rights, 1999–2000, Annex V, paras 66 and 67; Communication No 97/93, *John K Modise v Botswana*, Fourteenth Activity Report of the African Commission on Human and Peoples' Rights, 2000–2001, Annex IV, paras 95 and 96.

[61] Resolution on the Electoral Process and Participatory Governance, ACHPR/Res.23 (XIX) 96.   [62] Communication No 97/93 (see n 60 above) 96.

[63] Protocol to the African Charter on Human and Peoples' Rights on the Rights of Women in Africa, 2003. Assembly/AU/Dec 14 (II), Art 9.

[64] See C Morel and C Baldwin, 'Group Rights' in MD Evans and R Murray (eds), *The African Charter on Human and Peoples' Rights: The System in Practice 1986–2006* (2nd edn, Cambridge: Cambridge University Press, 2008), 244–88.

[65] See eg Communication Nos 54/91, 61/91, 98/93, 164/97–196/97, and 210/98, *Malawi African Association, Amnesty International, Ms Sarr Diop, Union Interafricaine des Droits de l'Homme and RADDHO, Collectif des Veuves et Ayants-droit, Association Mauritanienne des Droits de l'Homme v Mauritania*, Thirteenth Activity Report of the African Commission on Human and Peoples' Rights, 1999–2000, Addendum.

by two NGOs—Social and Economic Rights Action Centre and the Centre for Economic and Social Rights—the African Commission was asked to consider the violation of individual and peoples' rights provisions of the African Charter in respect of the oil exploration in the area of Nigeria inhabited by the Ogoni people. Interpreting Article 21 of the Charter the African Commission held that the right to dispose of natural resources needed to be seen in its historical context:

The origin of this provision may be traced to colonialism, during which the human and material resources of Africa were largely exploited for the benefit of outside powers, creating tragedy for Africans themselves, depriving them of their birthright and alienating them from the land. The aftermath of colonial exploitation has left Africa's precious resources and people still vulnerable to foreign misappropriation. The drafters of the Charter obviously wanted to remind African governments of the continent's painful legacy and restore co-operative economic development to its traditional place at the heart of African Society.[66]

As the government had enabled oil companies to act in this region of the country and this had impacted on the livelihoods of the Ogoni people, the Commission found that

by any measure of standards, its [the Nigerian government] practice falls short of the minimum conduct expected of governments, and therefore, is in violation of Article 21 of the African Charter.[67]

Governments 'have a duty to protect their citizens, not only through appropriate legislation and effective enforcement but also by protecting them from damaging acts that may be perpetrated by private parties' which entailed only 'positive action'.[68]

3.3 Economic, social, and cultural rights

This is an area, prompted by NGOs, where the Commission has spent considerable resources in developing relevant standards. The adoption of the Pretoria Declaration on Economic, Social and Cultural Rights reflected the conclusions of a seminar held in South Africa in 2004[69] and contributes to the development of standards in this area. It includes reference to, for example, the obligation of states under the right to health in Article 16 to provide 'access to the minimum essential food which is nutritionally adequate and safe to ensure freedom from hunger to everyone and to prevent malnutrition' as well as 'access to basic shelter, housing and sanitation and adequate supply of safe and potable water'.[70]

---

[66] Communication No 155/96, *Socio Economic Rights Action Centre and Centre for Social and Economic Rights v Nigeria*, Fifteenth Annual Activity Report of the African Commission on Human and Peoples' Rights, 2001–2002, Annex V, para 56.   [67] Ibid, 58.

[68] Ibid.

[69] Pretoria Declaration on Economic, Social and Cultural Rights, as adopted by Resolution on Economic, Social and Cultural Rights in Africa, ACHPR/Res.73 (XXXVI) 04.   [70] Ibid, 7.

NGOs have also, as noted above in relation to Communication No 155/96, used the binding economic, social, and cultural rights provisions in the African Charter to bring governments to account through the communication procedure. This has resulted in the Commission pronouncing that denial of access to doctors and medical assistance to individuals in detention would violate the right to health under Article 16 of the Charter,[71] and has read into the Charter the right to housing, shelter, and to food.[72] The failure of the government to provide basic services such as clean drinking water, electricity, and even sufficient medical supplies can violate the right to health.[73] Similarly, the closure of universities and secondary schools can violate the right to education under Article 17.[74]

3.4 Gender

NGOs have succeeded in encouraging the African Commission to spend a considerable amount of time examining the rights of women. This has led to the adoption of the Protocol on the Rights of Women in Africa in 2003 and the creation of a Special Rapporteur on the issue.[75] Beginning with a seminar in 1995 organized by the Women in Development in Africa, the Commission took on board recommendations from the seminar to appoint two of its Commissioners to consider the possibility of a Protocol. In the meetings held subsequent to this, at which drafts were considered, NGOs were present.[76] The successful adoption by the AU in 2003 of the Protocol elaborating rights of women in Africa,[77] going much further in some circumstances than the rights provided in the Convention on the Elimination of Discrimination against Women, has been an important contribution to the development of these rights on the continent.[78] Through the heightened profile given to the process of adopting the Protocol, this has impacted on other aspects of the Commission's mandate. It is now the norm that questions will be asked of states during the examination of their Article 62 reports about their treatment of women and how they ensure gender parity.

---

[71] Communication Nos 105/93, 128/94, 130/94, and 152/96, *Media Rights Agenda, Constitutional Rights Project, Media Rights Agenda and Constitutional Rights Project v Nigeria*, Twelfth Activity Report of the African Commission on Human and Peoples' Rights, 1998–1999, Annex V.   [72] See n 66 above.

[73] Communication Nos 25/89, 47/90, 56/91, and 100/93, *Free Legal Assistance Group, Lawyers' Committee for Human Rights, Union Interafricaine des Droits de l'Homme, Les Temoins de Jehovah v Zaire*, Ninth Annual Activity Report of the African Commission on Human and Peoples' Rights, 1995–1996.   [74] Ibid.

[75] Ninth Annual Activity Report of the African Commission, para 19.

[76] Motala (see n 32 above) 266.   [77] See n 63 above.

[78] See F Banda, 'Protocol to the African Charter on the Rights of Women in Africa' in Evans and Murray (n 64 above); F Banda, *Women, Law and Human Rights* (Oxford: Hart Publishing, 2005); R Murray, 'Women's Rights and the Organization of African Unity and African Union: The Protocol on the Rights of Women in Africa' in D Buss and A Manji (eds), *International Law: Modern Feminist Approaches* (Oxford: Hart Publishing, 2005), 253.

3.5 Environment

As with the right to development, it is unfortunate that few NGOs have taken the opportunity to make use of the existence of Article 24 of the African Charter and its protection for a people of the right to a general satisfactory environment favourable to their development. Indeed, it is only in one case brought by two NGOs where the Commission has been forced to consider this provision. In Communication No 155/96 the Commission linked this with Article 16 and the individual's right to health 'in so far as the environment affects the quality of life and safety of the individual'. Article 24 imposed 'clear obligations upon a government':

It requires the State to take reasonable and other measures to prevent pollution and ecological degradation, to promote conservation, and to secure an ecologically sustainable development and use of natural resources. Article 12 of the International Covenant on Economic, Social and Cultural Rights (ICESCR), to which Nigeria is a party, requires governments to take necessary steps for the improvement of all aspects of environmental and industrial hygiene. The right to enjoy the best attainable state of physical and mental health enunciated in Article 16(1) of the African Charter and the right to a general satisfactory environment favourable to development (Article 16(3)) already noted obligate governments to desist from directly threatening the health and environment of their citizens. The State is under an obligation to respect the just noted rights and this entails largely non-interventionist conduct from the State for example, not from carrying out, sponsoring or tolerating any practice, policy or legal measures violating the integrity of the individual.[79]

The government should take care to protect the rights of the victims of violations and should not have engaged in contact which attacked villages and homes of the Ogoni.[80] The recommendations directed at the government in the conclusions of the communication are broad and include provision for adequate compensation to victims of violations, preparation of environmental and social impact assessments, provision of information on health and environmental risks, and existence of oversight bodies. Beyond this case, Article 24 and environmental concerns have had little mention by the Commission.[81]

---

[79] See n 66 above, 53.   [80] Ibid, 54.

[81] See, however, Art 18 of the Protocol on the Rights of Women which provides for a right of women 'to live in a healthy and sustainable environment' which requires states to take measures to:

(a) ensure greater participation of women in the planning, management and preservation of the environment and the sustainable use of natural resources at all levels;

(b) promote research and investment in new and renewable energy sources and appropriate technologies, including information technologies and facilitate women's access to, and participation in their control;

(c) protect and enable the development of women's indigenous knowledge systems;

(d) [c. sic] regulate the management, processing, storage and disposal of domestic waste;

(e) [d. sic] ensure that proper standards are followed for the storage, transportation and disposal of toxic waste.

4. Conclusion

NGOs have been central to the functioning and development of the African human rights system. Key to the drafting of the African Charter, supporting its Commission, staffing its headquarters, funding its activities, holding seminars, developing its publicity, submitting cases, and creating special rapporteurs and working groups, it is clear that the African Commission would not be in the position it is at present without their support.

NGOs in the African system have not, perhaps because of the openness of the procedures before the Commission, always worked together in as many ways as they perhaps could have done. The result is fragmentation. Similarly, there has not been a coherent and strategic approach to the issue of human security but any developments in this field have been on an ad hoc basis, dependent on the concerns of any particular NGO and the desire or willingness of the Commission to respond to them. It is not unusual for two or more NGOs to propose different and contradictory suggestions to the African Commission during its sessions which both undermines their cause and any hope for action on the part of the Commission. Various initiatives were attempted in the late 1990s to encourage NGOs to collaborate further in their statements before the Commission, albeit in response to concerns by governments that they were given too much space. It is unfortunate that further ways of developing this have not been considered. The NGO Forum held prior to each session of the Commission would, one might think, provide the ideal opportunity for such collaboration and, indeed on the face of it, this is what it does. However, the large number of issues on the agenda and numerous Resolutions that result from this Forum dilute the impact that they can make.

Up until 2008 the African Commission relied extensively on NGOs to perform its mandate effectively and efficiently, in part because of budgetary constraints. Whilst this has enabled those organizations with expertise to influence the Commission and provide it with the necessary information to carry out its work, this has been at the expense of the Commission developing its own agenda, funding base, and direction. The result is a Commission that has been largely passive in its response to activities, lacking strategic direction, and prompted to act only by pressure from states and NGOs. While the Commission has been lauded for its contribution to the development of international human rights law, its adoption of some seminal decisions in the human security field and more broadly, these advancements are due less to the dynamism of Commissioners pushing the agenda in that direction, than the determination of a certain select group of NGOs which have been able to influence the Commission to focus on certain themes or countries. Because the Commission has largely been reactive to NGO requests, it has made itself vulnerable to government criticism. It has swayed between an open-armed approach to NGOs, on the one hand, to clamping down on their involvement when governments have expressed concern, on the other hand. This hardly gives the impression of an independent institution.

When the AU dramatically increased the funding of the Commission in 2008 the African Commission for the first time was able to consider how it will develop the agendas of its special rapporteurs and working groups without requiring the financial back-up of NGOs. There is a concern that this shift will mean less involvement of NGOs. What may occur, however, is that the African Commission will be forced to develop its own strategy and direction rather than being so subject to the whim of others. The issue of human security is one which so far has not been picked up by the Commission or NGOs before it.

From an NGO perspective the African system offers an open and participatory forum in which sustained and continued involvement with the Commission can yield real results. There are a number of factors which have had an impact in terms of effectiveness of NGOs in the African system. First, the Commission itself has been open to NGO participation, albeit to bolster its own lack of resources. Even when faced with criticism from states it has reluctantly become more prescriptive of the role of NGOs in the system, yet continually stresses the need for their support. Secondly, NGOs which are willing to provide funding and/or logistical or administrative support for the projects that they propose are more likely to obtain the cooperation of the Commission. Thirdly, it is clear that it is the commitment and drive of certain individuals which has had the most influence on the Commission.[82] These individuals are highly motivated and respected by the Commission. They have a detailed knowledge of the Commission, the AU, and the political context in which they are operating and maintain a continued presence at the sessions and continued and personal contact with the Commissioners. In short, they are known and visible and it is this factor perhaps that is key to understanding the ability of certain NGOs and individuals to direct the work of the Commission.

NGOs at the African Commission can count most of the successes of the Commission as their achievements. This has not, however, been done, on the whole, through a particularly coordinated approach between them. Save for the few international NGOs that work closely with the Commission, many of the African NGOs act individually and previous attempts at coordinating statements have not been successful, it seeming that NGOs view it as important to speak and participate separately above all else. The result, however, is that the African Commission has been dominated largely by a few select international NGOs, albeit by African individuals within them, than by African-based organizations. The consequence of such has been criticisms, from government, NGOs, and other quarters, that these select NGOs act exclusively and in fact 'are the Commission'.

---

[82] Similar factors are apparent to the success of NGOs at the national level: 'unrelenting disposition, remarkable tenacity and extraordinary courage of the activists who ran these NGOs', Okafor (see n 7 above) 45.

In turn, NGOs have obtained a number of benefits from being able to participate in the African system. Besides offering them a voice before governments at an African regional gathering, the Commission itself has gone further and provided greater protection for NGOs through the appointment of its Special Rapporteur on Human Rights Defenders.

The aim of this chapter is not to undermine the significant and immensely important role of NGOs in protecting human rights on the continent. However, the African Commission is at the whim of NGOs with particular agendas. This has begun to be criticized by states and it is unlikely to gain greater respect from them if those states believe that they are in the hands of NGOs. NGOs should lobby the Commission to become increasingly self-dependent, to look to the AU rather than external partners for funding and other support, and to lobby the Commission to do more of its essential tasks in-house, rather than outside. In this sense the Commission can develop a sense of ownership over its work and plan a strategic direction in the future.

III

CONCLUSION

15

The Future of Human Security in Africa

Ademola Abass

The trouble with Africa is not that it lacks legal and policy frameworks to combat the numerous threats to human security that continue to make the continent the most underdeveloped in the world. As a matter of fact, Africa is endowed with some of the most progressive multilateral instruments, be it in the area of human rights or with regards to the responsibility to protect people from insecurity. Examples abound. The African Charter on Human and Peoples' Rights (the Banjul Charter) was the first human rights treaty to recognize economic refuge. Although this was thought to be a reflection of the African reality at the time the treaty was adopted, economic migration has today become a global reality.

The Protocol adopted by the Economic Community of West African States (ECOWAS) in 1999[1] was the first of its type by any regional organization to authorize the use of force in member states' conflicts even if the interpretation of this treaty arguably conflicts with a norm of the UN Charter prohibiting the use of force.[2] For better or for worse, that trend was perpetuated by the Constitutive Act of the African Union which, in Article 4(h), empowers the Union to intervene in conflicts within its member states if certain thresholds are crossed. Although the legality of these last two treaties has been a subject of considerable academic debate, this does not detract from the fact that as legal instruments they are bold, forward looking, and groundbreaking.

However, it is one thing to have laws in place, but it is quite another to be able to implement them in accordance with the rationale for their promulgation. In this area, most African organizations and states considerably lag behind other regions. Ineffective implementation of legal and policy frameworks is one issue that resonates within virtually all the chapters of this book. From a comprehensive review of the problem of food security in Africa through to a rigorous exposé

---

[1] The Protocol Relating to Conflict Prevention, Management, Resolution, Peacekeeping and Security adopted on 10 December 1999, Lomé, Togo. See A Abass, 'The New Collective Security Mechanism of ECOWAS: Innovations and Problems' (2000) 5(2) Journal of Conflict and Security Law 211.

[2] But see A Abass, 'Consent Precluding State Responsibility: A Critical Analysis' (2004) 53 International and Comparative Law Quarterly 211.

of corruption, we confront the devastating consequences of ineffective implementation of international obligations and domestic laws and policies.

The present and future costs of corruption are as devastating to an infected society as the lack of people-oriented developmental policies by states. History is replete with famine-induced deaths worldwide. While famine is perhaps unavoidable in countries with genuine agricultural problems, there is no excuse for famine in most places in Africa. The abundance of rainforests and generally favourable ecological factors should normally ensure that Africa's food production is among the world's most guaranteed. Unfortunately, corruption has made this dream unrealizable; the lack of people-oriented developmental policies has led to a constant struggle by African people to fight for little in the midst of plenty. The Africa environment has huge potential which could be turned into substantial resources for the benefit of the African people.

In any given society, nothing is probably worse than the abdication of socio-political responsibility by the state, for where such an occasion arises, self-help by citizens often fills the gap. The tragedy of citizens' self-help measures is not merely that they are unregulated by the state—being mostly illegal and conducted in the underworld—but also that, like a whirlwind, you can never predict how it will end. Citizens' self-help manifests itself in several forms. Surely, when hunger is not addressed, it will eventually lead to desperation whereby those affected might turn to criminality to protect themselves from perennial wants. Such a desperate move will ultimately lead to acquisition of personal weapons, usually in the form of light weapons and small arms with which most parts of Africa are currently awash. One only needs to look at the case of Ghana (and indeed many other African countries such as Nigeria and South Africa) in order fully to appreciate the threat posed by this menace.

When a state breaks down partially or totally, and unfavourable domestic living conditions (such as in the Niger Delta) are exacerbated by complicitous international plundering of its natural resources (such as the illegal, unauthorized, and unregulated fishing in the Somali waters), the resultant self-help measures by citizens of such states can be brutal and devastating. Considerable effort is currently being deployed to combat piracy on the high seas, especially off the coast of Somalia. The response by Western states to the threat of piracy, as with that of environmental threat, is particularly reassuring and, in the short term, will address the issue. Piracy is a crime that escapes the type of *ghettoization* that food security and corruption suffer since these predominantly affect the developing world. Nonetheless, while NATO and US warships can mount effective military campaigns against these ocean thieves, the truth is that the morally reprehensible act of illegal fishing in Somali waters, especially by powerful Western states, will compromise the campaign. As the maxim goes, those who come to equity must come with clean hands.

Africa requires the support of the international community in managing and ensuring that proceeds from its vast natural resources do not end, like most international financial aid to Africa, in the private pockets of kleptomaniac leaders and warlords. Currently, multiple international efforts are underway to assist Africans towards this end in the hope that through a more effective resource-management regime Africa can reclaim itself from the vicious cycle of natural resource-fuelled conflicts. However, the world needs to move away from a dog-eat-dog approach whereby looted African diamonds adorn high street shops in European capitals and with concerned Western governments feigning helplessness about reining in the nefarious activities of their companies.

The theme of a stronger regime of human rights features strongly throughout the book. Whether it is a call on states to step up their efforts in protecting their peoples' rights, or that the African Human Rights Commission, non-governmental organizations, and civil society organizations should be more proactive and vigilant in promoting human rights, there is no doubt that human rights protection is important to any civilization.

For a start, several African states have adopted legislation dealing with domestic violence, as seen in Sierra Leone, South Africa, and Zimbabwe. In June 2009, Mozambique passed its Domestic Violence Bill which not only criminalized domestic violence, but prescribed up to 24 years' imprisonment for the offence.[3] The Bill has several flaws. For instance, it only criminalizes men who beat their women, thus leading to some Mozambicans regarding the Bill as 'mulherismo'—an entirely new word in the Portuguese language, and which could roughly be translated as 'female chauvinism'.[4] Be that as it may, the Bill is a step in the right direction. With all its imperfections, it is a remarkable improvement upon the country's generic classification of domestic violence under a nineteenth-century assault law inherited from Portugal, and certainly more encouraging than Burundi and Uganda where the parliaments still regard domestic violence as a private affair.

A strengthened protection regime is as crucial to ensuring that those who are internally displaced during conflicts or those who flee their countries are well shielded from both natural and man-made disasters, as it is for those who toil on farmlands or who work as domestic helps across Africa. The International Labour Organization has liberated labour from the clutches of discriminatory legislation. But world leaders need to do much more to eradicate surreptitious slavery, such as is common in Africa, apart from condemning women to 'voluntary' labour on the home front.

It is important that the African Court of Human Rights adopts a robust approach in adjudicating cases brought before it. The sacred duty of the court in protecting the rights of all Africans cannot be overemphasized. This is of

---

[3] See 'Mozambique: Assembly Passes Amended Domestic Violence Bill', *Pambazuka News*, 30 July 2009, Issue 444, available at: <http://www.pambazuka.org/en/category/wgender/58077/print>.

[4] See allAfrica.com, 'Mozambique: Assembly Passed Amended Domestic Violence Bill', 21 July 2009, available at: <http://allafrica.com/stories/200907210957.html>.

particular importance in Africa where domestic courts are often prevented from effective functioning by governments.

African regional organizations must also show great commitment to protecting their people from all forms of insecurity. The African Union (AU) seems to be taking this responsibility very seriously at present. Its liberal interpretation of the circumstances that constitute an unconstitutional change of government and its suspension of errant states from membership are all good news. However, the AU should not remain silent in the face of tyrannical governments. Surely, if a coup d'état is undemocratic, as it definitely is, and leads to suspension, the holding of a people to ransom by their government through violent repression of their rights, the torturing of constitutions to extend *tenure ad infinitum*, the refusal to accept popular electoral victories, should merit the same treatment. Such reprehensible practices should draw sharp and strong condemnation from the AU if it is to be taken seriously. It smacks of hypocrisy for the AU to keep silent while President Tandja oppressed the people of Niger and Lansana Conte plundered Guinea for decades, only for the Union quickly to dismiss those who ousted them. The danger with such an approach is that it may put the AU on a collision course with the people's wishes, especially where the coups are popular, and they may see the AU's anti-unconstitutional principle as self-serving.

Unlike some other global concepts, human security did not arrive with its own toolkit, so that we can unpack the box and get to work immediately. Yet, we did not simply happen upon it, as with penicillin, when looking for something else. In a sense, human security has been with us from the start of humanity. The problem is that humankind's original vision of security was clouded by a collective preoccupation with nuclear security. Human security is the new way of rethinking our survival.

Selected Bibliography

Abass, A, 'Consent Precluding State Responsibility: A Critical Analysis' (2004) 53 International and Comparative Law Quarterly 211–25.

—— *Regional Organisations and the Development of Collective Security: Beyond Chapter VIII of the UN Charter* (Oxford: Hart Publishing, 2004).

——'Extraterritorial Collective Security: The European Union and Operation Artemis' in M Trybus and ND White (eds), *European Security Law* (Oxford: Oxford University Press, 2007), 134–56.

—— 'The United Nations, the African Union and the Darfur Crisis: Of Apology and Utopia' (2007) 54(3) Netherlands International Law Review 415–40.

—— 'Proving State Responsibility for Genocide: The ICJ in Bosnia v Serbia and the International Commission for Inquiry for Darfur' (2008) 31(4) Fordham International Law Journal 871.

Abraham, K, *The Missing Millions: Why and How Africa is Underdeveloped* (Trenton, NJ: Africa World Press, 1995).

Alao, A, *Natural Resources and Conflict in Africa: the Tragedy of Endowment* (Rochester: University of Rochester Press, 2007).

Alfredson, L, *Sexual Exploitation of Child Soldiers: An Exploration and Analysis of Global Dimensions and Trends* (London: Coalition to Stop the Use of Child Soldiers, 2001).

Anamela, A, 'Managing Aid Delivery, Joint Financing Arrangements as a Tool to Achieving Aid Delivery', MA thesis (East and Southern African Management Institute (ESAMI) / Maastricht School of Management (MSM), 2008).

Anaya, SJ, 'Indigenous Rights Norms in Contemporary International Law' (1991) 8 Ariz JICL 1.

—— 'International Human Rights and Indigenous Peoples: The Move Toward the Multicultural State' (2004) 21 Ariz JICL 13.

Andreassen, B and Swineheart, T (eds), *Human Rights in Developing Countries* (Oslo: 1991 Yearbook, Scandinavian University Press, 1992).

Andresen Guimaraes, F, *The Origins of the Angolan Civil War: Foreign Intervention and Domestic Political Conflict* (London: Palgrave Macmillan, 2001).

Aning, KE, Addo, P, and Sowatey, E, 'Transnational Organised Crime: The Ghana Case Study' (Vienna: UN Office for Drugs and Crime, 2004).

—— *Ghana. Conflict Vulnerability Assessment*, mimeo (2003).

—— and Sowatey, EA, 'Coping Mechanisms of Refugees at the Bujumbura Refugee Camp in Ghana', unpublished mimeo (2002).

——, Yakubu, A, Abdulai, N, and Dawarula, M, *Between Indifference and Naïveté: The Need for a National Policy Framework on Small Arms in Ghana* (New Delhi: CHRI & FOSDA, 2001).

Ankumah, EA, *The African Commission on Human and Peoples' Rights* (The Hague: Martinus Nijhoff, 1996).

Bald, SH, 'Searching for a Lost Childhood: Will the Special Court of Sierra Leone Find Justice for its Children?' (2002) 18 American University International Law Review 537–83.

Banda, F, 'Protocol to the African Charter on the Rights of Women in Africa' in MD Evans and R Murray (eds), *The African Charter on Human and Peoples' Rights: The System in Practice, 1986–2006* (2nd edn, Cambridge: Cambridge University Press, 2008), 441–74.

Barnett, J, *The Meaning of Environmental Security: Ecological Politics and Policy in the New Security Era* (London: Zed Books, 2001).

Barsh, RL 'Indigenous Peoples in the 1990s: From Object to Subject of International Law?' (1994) 7 Harv HRJ 33.

Bayefsky, AF (ed), *The UN Human Rights Treaty System in the 21st Century* (The Hague: Kluwer Law International, 2000).

Benedek, W, 'The African Charter and Commission on Human and Peoples' Rights: How to Make it More Effective' (1993) 11 Netherlands Quarterly of Human Rights 25, 28–32.

Berman, EG and Sams, KE, 'The Peacekeeping Potential of African Regional Organizations' in J Boulden (ed), *Dealing with Conflict in Africa: The United Nations and Regional Organizations* (New York: Palgrave, 2003), 35–77.

Boyden, J, 'Children's Experience of Conflict Related Emergencies: Some Implications for Relief Policy and Practice' (1994) 18 Disasters 254–67.

Brand, D, 'The Right to Food' in D Brand and C Heyns (eds), *Socio-Economic Rights in South Africa* (Pretoria: Pretoria University Law Press, 2005).

Brett, R and McCallin, M, *Children: The Invisible Soldiers* (Stockholm: Radda Barnen, 1998).

Campbell, AIL, 'Positive Obligations under the ECHR: Deprivation of Liberty by Private Actors' (2006) 10 ELR 399.

Charlesworth, H and Chinkin, C, 'The Gender of Jus Cogens' (1993) 15(1) Human Rights Quarterly 63–76.

Chen, L et al (eds), *Human Insecurity in a Global World* (Cambridge, MA: Asia Center of Harvard University, 2003).

Chigara, B, 'From Oral to Recorded Governance: Reconstructing Title to Real Property in 21st Century Zimbabwe' (2001) 30 CLWR 36.

—— *Land Reform Policy: The Challenge of Human Rights Law* (Aldershot: Ashgate, 2004).

—— 'Latecomers to the ILO and the Authorship and Ownership of the International Labour Code' (2007) 28 HRQ 706.

—— 'Social Justice: The Link Between Trade Liberalisation and Sub-Saharan Africa's Potential to Achieve the United Nations Millennium Development Goals by 2015' (2008) 26 NQHR 9.

Clover, J, 'Food Security in Sub-Saharan Africa' (2003) 12(1) African Security Review 9.

Cook, RJ (ed), *Human Rights of Women: National and International Perspectives* (Philadelphia, PA: University of Pennsylvania Press, 1994).

Cotter, AM, *Gender Injustice: An International Comparative Analysis of Equality in Employment* (Aldershot: Ashgate, 2004).

Cullen, 'Siliadin v France: Positive obligations under Article 4 of the European Convention on Human Rights' (2006) 6 HRLR 4.

Debeljak, J, 'Barriers to the Recognition of Indigenous People's Human Rights at the United Nations' (2000) 26 Mon ULR 159.

Dennis, MJ and David, PS, 'Justiciability of Economic, Social, and Cultural Rights: Should there be an International Complaints Mechanism to Adjudicate the Rights to Food, Water, Housing, and Health?' (2004) 98 AJIL 462.

Denov, MS, 'Wartime Sexual Violence: Assessing a Human Security Response to War-affected Girls in Sierra Leone' (2006) 37 Security Dialogue 319–42.

—— and Gervais, C, 'Negotiating (In)security: Agency, Resistance and Resourcefulness among Girls Formerly Associated with Sierra Leone's Revolutionary United Front' (2007) 32 Signs: Journal of Women in Culture and Society 885–910.

Essien, U, 'The African Commission: Eleven Years After' (2000) 6 Buffalo Human Rights Law Review 93.

Fairhead, J and Leach, M, *Reframing Deforestation: Global Analyses and Local Realities: Studies in West Africa* (Aldershot: Ashgate, 1998).

Faulkner, F, 'Kindergarten Killers: Morality, Murder and the Child Soldier Problem' (2001) 22 Third World Quarterly 491–504.

Fonseka, B, 'The Protection of Child Soldiers in International Law' (2001) 2 Asia-Pacific Journal on Human Rights and the Law 69–89.

Fox, M-J, 'Girl Soldiers: Human Security and Gendered Insecurity' (2004) 35 Security Dialogue 465–79.

Franck, TM, *The Power of Legitimacy Among Nations* (Oxford: Oxford University Press, 1990).

Gaer, FD, 'First Fruits: Reporting by States under the African Charter on Human and Peoples' Rights' (1992) 10 Netherlands Quarterly on Human Rights 29.

Gberie, L, *Sierra Leone: Destruction and Resurgence* (London: Hurst, 2005).

Giles, W and Hyndman, J (eds), *Sites of Violence: Gender and Conflict Zones* (Berkeley, CA: University of California Press, 2004).

Gleditsch, NP, 'Environmental Change, Security and Conflict' in CA Crocker et al (eds), *Turbulent Peace: The Challenge of Managing International Conflict* (Washington, DC: US Institute for Peace, 2001), 53.

Goodwin-Gill, G and McAdam, J, *The Refugee in International Law* (3rd edn, Oxford: Oxford University Press, 2007).

Goudal, J, 'Agricultural Development and Indigenous Labour in the French Colonies of Tropical Africa' (1939) 40 ILR 209.

Guilfoyle, D, 'Piracy off Somalia: UN Security Council Resolution 1816 and IMO Regional Counter-Piracy Efforts' (2008) 57 ICLQ 690.

Gutto, S, *ICJ Workshops on NGO Participation in the African Commission on Human and Peoples' Rights: A Critical Evaluation* (Geneva: ICJ, 1996).

Hansen, L and Olsson, L, 'Guest Editors' Introduction' (2004) 35 Security Dialogue 405–9.

Happold, M, *Child Soldiers in International Law* (Manchester: Manchester University Press, 2005).

Hathaway, JC, *The Rights of Refugees under International Law* (Cambridge: Cambridge University Press, 2005).

Heyns, C, 'The African Regional Human Rights System: The African Charter' (2004) 108 Pennsylvania State Law Review 679.

Heyns, C (ed), *Compendium of Key Human Rights Documents of the African Union* (Pretoria: Pretoria University Press, 2005).

Hoddinott, J, *Operationalizing Household Food Security in Development Projects: An Introduction* (Washington, DC: International Food Policy Research Institute, 1999).

Hodges, T, *Angola: From Afro-Stalinism to Petro-diamond Capitalism* (London: James Currey, 2001).

Holst-Roness, FT, 'Violence against Girls in Africa during Armed Conflicts and Crises', Second International Policy Conference on the African Child: Violence against Girls in Africa, International Committee of the Red Cross, Addis Ababa, 11–12 May 2006.

Hoogensen, O and Rottem, S, 'Gender Identity and the Subject of Security' (2004) 35 Security Dialogue 155–71.

Ibeanu, O, 'Aguleri-Umuleri Conflict in Anambra State' in T Imobigbe (ed), *Civil Society and Ethnic Conflict Management in Nigeria* (Ibadan: Spectrum Books, 2003).

Johnson, DH, *The Root Causes of Sudan's Civil Wars* (Bloomington, IN: Indiana University Press, 2003).

Jones, JF, 'Human Security and Social Development' (2004) 33 Denver Journal of International Law and Policy 92.

Keairns, YE, *The Voices of Girl Child Soldiers* (New York: Quaker United Nations Office, 2002).

Kennedy, D, 'The Move to Institutions' (1987) 8 Cardozo Law Review 841.

——'A New World Order: Yesterday, Today and Tomorrow' (1994) 4 Transnational Law and Contemporary Problems 329.

Kent, G, *The Political Economy of Hunger: The Silent Holocaust* (New York: Praeger, 1984).

Khoza, S, 'Promoting the Realisation of Economic, Social and Cultural Rights: The African Commission holds a Seminar in Pretoria' (2004) 4 African Human Rights Law Journal 334.

Kneebone, S (ed), *Refugees, Asylum Seekers and the Rule of Law: Comparative Perspectives* (Cambridge: Cambridge University Press, 2009).

Korley, F, 'The Role of Human Rights Institutions in the Promotion and Protection of Human Rights in Africa: A Ghanaian Appraisal' (1998) 10 ASICL Proceedings 199.

Krause, K, 'Human Security' in V Chetail (ed), *Post-Conflict Peace Building: A Lexicon* (Oxford: Oxford University Press, 2009), 47.

Legrand, J-C and Weissman, F, 'Les Enfants Soldats et Usages de la Violence au Mozambique' (1995) 18 Cultures et Conflicts 165–80.

Lind, J and Sturman, K (eds), *Scarcity and Surfeit: The Ecology of Africa's Conflicts* (Pretoria: RSA Institute for Security Studies, 2002).

McColgan, A, 'Principles of Equality and Protection from Discrimination in International Human Rights Law' (2003) 2 European Human Rights Law Review 157–75.

McDonald, M, 'Human Security and the Construction of Security' (2002) 16 Global Society 277–95.

MacFarlane, SN and Khong, YF, *Human Security: A Critical History* (Bloomington, IN: Indiana University Press, 2006).

McKay, S, 'Girls as "Weapons of Terror" in Northern Uganda and Sierra Leonean Fighting Forces' (2007) 28 Studies in Conflict and Terrorism 385–97.

—— and Mazurana, D, *Where Are the Girls? Girls in Fighting Forces in Northern Uganda, Sierra Leone and Mozambique: Their Lives during and after War* (Montreal: International Centre for Human Rights and Democratic Development, 2004).

McNeely, J, 'War and Biodiversity: An Assessment of Impacts' in J Austin and CD Bruch (eds), *The Environmental Consequences of War* (Cambridge: Cambridge University Press, 2000).

Madubuike-Ekwe, JN, 'The International Legal Standards Adopted to Stop the Participation of Children in Armed Conflicts' (2005) 11 Annual Survey of International and Comparative Law 29–48.

Magliveras, KD and Naldi, GD, *The African Union* (The Hague: Kluwer Law International, 2008).

Maul, DR, 'The ILO and the Struggle Against Forced Labour from 1919 to the Present' (2007) 48 Labor History 481.

Mazurana, D and Carlson, K, *From Combat to Community: Women and Girls in Sierra Leone* (Washington, DC: Policy Commission of Women Waging Peace, 2004).

—— and —— *The Girl Child and Armed Conflict: Recognizing and Addressing Grave Violations of Girls' Human Rights* (Florence: United Nations Division for the Advancement of Women in collaboration with UNICEF, Innocenti Research Centre, 2006).

Meek, CK, *Land Law and Custom in the Colonies* (Oxford: Oxford University Press, 1949).

Mgbeoji, I, *Collective Insecurity* (Vancouver: University of British Columbia Press, 2003).

Mischkowski, G, *Abducted, Raped, Enslaved: The Situation of Girl Soldiers in the Case of Uganda* (Cologne: Medica Mondiale, 2005).

Mitchell, AF III, 'Sierra Leone: The Road to Childhood Ruination through Forced Recruitment of Child Soldiers and the World's Failure to Act' (2003–04) 2 Regent Journal of International Law 81–114.

Mohamed, AAR, 'Article 58 of the African Charter on Human and Peoples' Rights—A Legal Analysis and How it can be put into More Practical Use' (1996) ASICL Proceedings 290.

Moore, J, 'Collective Human Security with a Human Face: An International Legal Framework for Coordinated Action to Alleviate Violence and Poverty' (2004) 33 Denver Journal of International Law and Policy 43.

Morel, C and Baldwin, C, 'Group Rights' in MD Evans and R Murray (eds), *The African Charter on Human and Peoples' Rights. The System in Practice 1986–2006* (2nd edn, Cambridge: Cambridge University Press, 2008), 244–88.

Murray, R, 'Decisions of the African Commission on Individual Communications under the African Charter on Human and Peoples' Rights' (1997) 46 International and Comparative Studies Quarterly 412.

—— 'On-site visits by the African Commission on Human and Peoples' Rights: A Case Study and Comparison with the Inter-American Commission on Human Rights' (1999) 11 African Journal of International and Comparative Law 460.

—— *The African Commission on Human and Peoples' Rights and International Law* (Oxford: Hart Publishing, 2000).

—— *Human Rights in Africa: From the OAU to the AU* (Cambridge: Cambridge University Press, 2004).

Mutua, M, 'The African Human Rights System in a Comparative Perspective' (1993) 3 Review of the African Commission on Human And Peoples' Rights 5.

Myers, N, *Ultimate Security* (New York: WW Norton, 1993).

Naldi, GJ, 'Future Trends in Human Rights in Africa: The Increased Role of the OAU?' in MD Evans and R Murray (eds), *The African Charter on Human and Peoples' Rights: The System in Practice, 1986–2000* (Cambridge: Cambridge University Press, 2002).

Nanda, VP, 'Preemptive and Preventive Use of Force, Collective Human Security, and Human Security' (2004) 33 Denver Journal of International Law and Policy 7.

Newman, D, 'A Human Security Council? Applying a "Human Security" Agenda to Security Council Reform' (2000) 31 Ottawa Law Review 213.

Newman, E and van Selm, J, *Refugees and Forced Displacement: International Security, Human Vulnerability, and the State* (Tokyo: United Nations University Press, 2003).

Nyembezi , A, 'Gaining an In-depth Understanding of the Meaning and Processes of Initiation and Male Circumcision in the Eastern Cape Province', PhD thesis (University of Maastricht, July 2008).

Odinkalu, CA, 'The Individual Complaints Procedure of the African Commission on Human and Peoples' Rights: A Preliminary Assessment' (1998) 8 Transnational Law and Contemporary Problems 359.

Okafor, OC, 'After Martyrdom: International Law, Sub-state Groups, and the Construction of Legitimate Statehood in Africa' (2000) 41 Harvard International Law Journal 503.

—— 'Reconceiving "Third World" Legitimate Governance Struggles in our Time: Emergent Imperatives for Rights Activism' (2000) 6 Buffalo Human Rights Law Review 1.

—— *Re-Defining Legitimate Statehood: International Law and State Fragmentation in Africa* (The Hague: Martinus Nijhoff, 2000).

—— 'The African System on Human and Peoples' Rights, Quasi-constructivism, and the Possibility of Peacebuilding within African States' (2004) 8 International Journal of Human Rights 413.

—— *Legitimizing Human Rights NGOs: Lessons from Nigeria* (Trenton, NJ: Africa World Press, 2006).

—— *The African Human Rights System, Activist Forces and International Institutions* (Cambridge: Cambridge University Press, 2007).

Oloka-Onyango, J, 'Beyond the Rhetoric: Reinvigorating the Struggle for Economic and Social Rights in Africa' (1995) 26 California Western International Law Journal 1.

—— 'Human Rights and Sustainable Development in Contemporary Africa: A New Dawn, or Retreating Horizons?' (2000) 6 Buffalo Human Rights Law Review 39.

Oğuzlu, TH, 'Turkey and the European Union: The Security Dimension' (2002) 3 Contemporary Security Policy 78.

Padelford, NJ, 'The OAU' (1964) 18 International Organization 521.

Papastavridis, E, 'Interception of Human Beings on the High Seas: A Contemporary Analysis under International Law' (2009) 37 Syracuse Journal of International Law and Commerce (forthcoming).

Paris, R, 'Human Security: Paradigm Shift or Hot Air?' (2001) 26 International Security 87–102.

Park, A, 'Other Inhumane Acts: Forced Marriage, Girl Soldiers and the Special Court for Sierra Leone' (2006) 15 Social and Legal Studies 315–37.

Pauwelyn, J and Bonanomi, EB, *Human Rights and International Trade* (Oxford: Oxford University Press, 2005).

Pérotin-Dumon, A, 'The Pirate and the Emperor: Power and the Law on the Seas, 1450–1850' in C Pennel (ed), *Bandits at Sea: A Pirates Reader* (New York: New York University Press, 2001), 25.

Pettiford, L and Curley, M, *Changing Security Agendas and the Third World* (London: Pinter, 1999).

Phillips, TP and Taylor, DS, 'Food Insecurity: Dynamics and Alleviation' in JI Hans Bakker (ed), *The World Food Crisis: Food Security in Comparative Perspective* (Toronto: Canadian Scholars' Press, 1990).

Piot, P, *Address to the 22nd Meeting of the UNAIDS Programme Coordinating Board* (24 April 2008).

Redress, *Victims, Perpetrators or Heroes? Child Soldiers before the International Criminal Court* (London: Redress Trust, 2006).

Richards, P, 'Rebellion in Liberia and Sierra Leone: A Crisis of Youth?' in O Furley (ed), *Conflict in Africa* (London: I B Tauris, 1995).

Rynning, S, 'Why Not NATO? Military Planning in the European Union' (2003) 26(1) Journal of Strategic Studies 64.

Saad, NM, *Announcing the Successful but Partial Defeat of SARS*, interview with Voice of America (New York, 17 June 2008).

Sage, C, 'Food Security' in EA Page and M Redclift (eds), *Human Security and the Environment: International Comparisons* (Cheltenham: Edward Elgar, 2002).

Sahn, DE, 'Economic Liberalization and Food Security in Sub-Saharan Africa' in U Kracht and M Schulz (eds), *Food Security and Nutrition: The Global Challenge* (New York: St Martin's Press, 1999), 137.

Save the Children, *Forgotten Casualties of War: Girls in Armed Conflict* (London: Save the Children, 2005).

Schoofs, 'Challenge for AIDS Fighters: Circumcising Africans Safely', *Wall Street Journal*, September 2007.

Shearer, D, *Private Armies and Military Intervention* (London: IISS Adelphi Paper, 1998).

Singer, PW, *Children at War* (New York: Pantheon Books, 2005).

Slaughter, A-M, 'Security, Solidarity, and Sovereignty: The Grand Themes of UN Reform' (2005) 99 American Journal of International Law 619, 620.

—— 'A New UN for a New Century' (2006) 74 Fordham Law Review 2961.

Somavia, J, 'A Global Alliance against Forced Labour', International Labour Conference 93rd Session, Report IB (2005).

Stefiszyn, K, 'The African Union: Challenges and Opportunities for Women' (2005) 5 African Human Rights Law Journal 358.

Steiner, HJ, Alston, P, and Goodman, R, *International Human Rights in Context: Law, Politics, Morals: Text and Materials* (3rd edn, Oxford: Oxford University Press, 2008).

Suhrke, A, 'Human Security and the Interests of States' (1999) 30 Security Dialogue 265–76.

Sutterlin, JS, *The United Nations and the Maintenance of International Security* (Westport, CT: Praeger, 2003).

Swepston, L, 'A New Step in the International Law on Indigenous and Tribal Peoples: ILO Convention No 169 of 1989' (1990) 15 Ok City ULR 677.

Temmerman De, E, *Aboke Girls: Children Abducted in Northern Uganda* (Kampala: Fountain Publisher, 2001).

Tennant, C, 'Indigenous Peoples, International Institutions, and the International Legal Literature from 1945–1993' (1994) 16 HRQ 1.

Terburgh, E, 'The Child Soldier: Psychological Trauma' in E Bennett, V Gamba, and D Van der Merwe (eds), *ACT Against Child Soldiers in Africa: A Reader* (Pretoria: Institute of Security Studies, 2000).

Tevoedjre, A, 'A Strategy for Social Progress in Africa and the ILO's Contribution' (1969) 99 ILR 61, 63.

Thomas, A, 'The International Labour Organisation: Its Origins, Development and Future' (1921) 1 ILR 1.

Tieku, EK, 'African Union Promotion of Human Security in Africa' (2007) 16 African Security Review 26–37.

Tomasevki, K, 'Has the Right to Education a Future Within the United Nations? A Behind-the-scenes Account by the Special Rapporteur on the Right to Education 1998–2004' (2005) 5(2) Human Rights Law Review 205–37.

Treves, T, 'Piracy, Law of the Sea, and Use of Force: Developments off the Coast of Somalia' (2009) 20 EJIL 399.

Turshen, M, 'The Political Economy of Rape' in CON Moser and FC Clark (eds), *Victims, Perpetrators or Actors? Gender, Armed Conflict and Political Violence* (London: Zed Books, 2001).

Twum-Danso, A, *Africa's Young Soldiers: The Co-option of Childhood*, Monograph No 82 (Pretoria: Institute of Security Studies, 2003).

Udombana, NJ, 'Social Rights are Human Rights: Actualizing the Rights to Work and Social Security in Africa' (2006) 39 Cornell International Law Journal 181.

Umozurike, UO, *The African Charter on Human and Peoples' Rights* (The Hague: Martinus Nijhoff, 1997).

United Nations Commission on Human Security, *Human Security Now: Protecting and Empowering People* (New York: United Nations Commission on Human Security, 2003).

United Nations Development Programme, *Human Development Report 1994* (New York: Oxford University Press, 1994).

US State Department, *Trafficking in Persons Report* (Washington, DC: US State Department, 2004).

Verhey, B, *Where are the Girls? Study on Girls Associated with Armed Forces and Groups in the Democratic Republic of Congo* (London: Save the Children and the NGO Group, 2004).

Viljoen, F, *International Human Rights Law in Africa* (Oxford: Oxford University Press, 2007).

Vincent-Daviss, D, 'Human Rights Law: A Research Guide to the Literature—Part III: The International Labour Organization and Human Rights' (1982–1983) NYUJIL & Pol 241.

Weiss, TG (ed), *Collective Human Security in a Changing World* (Boulder, CO: Lynne Rienner, 1993).

Weissberg, M, 'Conceptualising Human Security' (2003) 13 Swords & Ploughshares: A Journal of International Affairs 3–11.

Welch, CE Jr, 'The African Commission on Human and Peoples Rights: A Five Year Report and Assessment' (1992) 14 Human Rights Quarterly 43.

Wessells, M, *Child Soldiers: From Violence to Protection* (Cambridge, MA: Harvard University Press, 2006).

Index